REPUBLIC
OF SPIN

ALSO BY DAVID GREENBERG

Calvin Coolidge

Nixon's Shadow

REPUBLIC

OF SPIN

AN INSIDE HISTORY OF THE AMERICAN PRESIDENCY

DAVID GREENBERG

W. W. NORTON & COMPANY

INDEPENDENT PUBLISHERS SINCE 1923

NEW YORK · LONDON

For information about permission to reproduce selections from this book, write to
Permissions, W. W. Norton & Company, Inc.,
500 Fifth Avenue, New York, NY 10110

For information about special discounts for bulk purchases,
please contact W. W. Norton Special Sales at specialsales@wwnorton.com
or 800-233-4830

Manufacturing by RR Donnelley Harrisonburg
Book design by JAMdesign
Production manager: Julia Druskin

ISBN: 978-0-393-06706-4

W. W. Norton & Company, Inc.
500 Fifth Avenue, New York, N.Y. 10110
www.wwnorton.com

W. W. Norton & Company Ltd.
Castle House, 75/76 Wells Street, London W1T 3QT

1 2 3 4 5 6 7 8 9 0

TO

SUZANNE, LEO, AND LIZA

Liberalism will become an enclave conviction of a shrinking minority unless those who call themselves liberal reconnect their faith in tolerance, equality, opportunity for all with the more difficult faith in the dirty, loud-mouthed, false, lying business of politics itself. This disdain is cynicism, masking as high principle.

—MICHAEL IGNATIEFF, "Letter to a Young Liberal,"
The New Republic, Nov. 24–Dec. 8, 2014

One belief, more than any other, is responsible for the slaughter of individuals on the altars of the great historical ideals—justice or progress or the happiness of future generations, or the sacred mission or emancipation of a nation or race or class, or even liberty itself. . . . This is the belief that somewhere, in the past or in the future, in divine revelation or in the mind of an individual thinker, in the pronouncements of history or science, or in the simple heart of an uncorrupted good man, there is a final solution.

—ISAIAH BERLIN, "Two Concepts of Liberty"

CONTENTS

CAST OF CHARACTERS

Presidents

WILLIAM McKINLEY (1897–1901)
THEODORE ROOSEVELT (1901–09)
WILLIAM HOWARD TAFT (1909–13)
WOODROW WILSON (1913–21)
WARREN G. HARDING (1921–23)
CALVIN COOLIDGE (1923–29)
HERBERT HOOVER (1929–33)
FRANKLIN DELANO ROOSEVELT (1933–45)
HARRY S. TRUMAN (1945–53)
DWIGHT EISENHOWER (1953–61)
JOHN F. KENNEDY (1961–63)
LYNDON JOHNSON (1963–69)
RICHARD NIXON (1969–74)
GERALD FORD (1974–77)
JIMMY CARTER (1977–81)
RONALD REAGAN (1981–89)
GEORGE BUSH (1989–93)
BILL CLINTON (1993–2001)
GEORGE W. BUSH (2001–09)
BARACK OBAMA (2009–17)

Other Politicians

WILLIAM BENTON, senator, Connecticut; founder, Benton & Bowles advertising agency

WILLIAM JENNINGS BRYAN, congressman, Nebraska; three-time Democratic presidential nominee; secretary of state under Woodrow Wilson

SAMUEL DICKSTEIN, congressman, New York; founder, House Un-American Activities Committee; Soviet spy

EVERETT DIRKSEN, Republican Senate minority leader

BARRY GOLDWATER, senator, Arizona; 1964 Republican presidential nominee

AL GORE, senator, Tennessee; U.S. vice president; 2000 Democratic presidential nominee

CHARLIE HALLECK, Republican House minority leader

HUEY LONG, governor and senator, Louisiana

"PITCHFORK BEN" TILLMAN, senator, South Carolina

ADLAI STEVENSON, governor, Illinois; two-time Democratic presidential nominee

GEORGE WALLACE, governor of Alabama

Spin Doctors

ROGER AILES, television aide to Richard Nixon; campaign manager for George Bush; founder, Fox News Channel

GEORGE AKERSON, White House press secretary under Hoover

LEE ATWATER, campaign consultant to George Bush

DAVID AXELROD, campaign consultant and White House aide to Barack Obama

BRUCE BARTON, founder, BDO (later BBD&O) advertising; author, *The Man Nobody Knows*; adviser to Coolidge, Hoover, Eisenhower; U.S. Republican congressman from New York City

EDWARD BERNAYS, public relations counsel; occasional political adviser

JOSEPH BUCKLIN BISHOP, journalist; information officer for Panama Canal project

PATRICK CADDELL, pollster to Jimmy Carter

HADLEY CANTRIL, public opinion researcher; wartime pollster for FDR

JAMES CARVILLE, campaign consultant to Bill Clinton

GEORGE B. CORTELYOU, White House stenographer, clerk, secretary; cabinet official

GEORGE CREEL, muckraking journalist; director of the Committee on Public Information; Democratic candidate for U.S. Senate from California

ELMER DAVIS, journalist and broadcaster; director of Office of War Information under FDR

MICHAEL DEAVER, public relations aide to Ronald Reagan

MILTON EISENHOWER, brother of Dwight Eisenhower; public information officer under FDR

GEORGE GALLUP, pollster; supporter of psychological warfare

DAVID GERGEN, communications aide to Nixon, Reagan, and Clinton; pundit

JOSEPH GOEBBELS, minister of propaganda and popular enlightenment in Nazi Germany

JAMES HAGERTY, White House press secretary under Dwight Eisenhower; executive at ABC News

LOUIS HARRIS, pollster to JFK

WILL HAYS, chairman, Republican National Committee; president of the Motion Picture Producers and Distributors of America

EMIL HURJA, pollster for Democratic National Committee and FDR

WILL IRWIN, muckraking journalist; aide to Herbert Hoover

C. D. JACKSON, publisher, *Fortune* magazine; special assistant to Dwight Eisenhower for psychological warfare

GERARD LAMBERT, advertising mogul; partner of Hadley Cantril in wartime public opinion research

ALBERT LASKER, president, Lord & Thomas advertising agency; adviser, Republican National Committee and Warren Harding

IVY LEDBETTER LEE, public relations pioneer; publicist on Democratic campaigns

WILLIAM LOEB, White House secretary under TR

FRANK LUNTZ, Republican pollster

ARCHIBALD MacLEISH, poet and playwright; Librarian of Congress and director of Office of Facts and Figures under FDR

CHARLES MICHELSON, longtime journalist; Democratic National Committee publicist; speechwriter to FDR

ROBERT MONTGOMERY, Hollywood actor; television coach to Dwight Eisenhower

DICK MORRIS, pollster to Bill Clinton

BILL MOYERS, political and press aide to Lyndon Johnson

JOE NAPOLITAN, Democratic political consultant

PEGGY NOONAN, speechwriter to Ronald Reagan

ARTHUR W. PAGE, public relations aide at Department of Defense during World War II

OLIVER QUAYLE, protégé of Louis Harris; pollster to Lyndon Johnson

GERALD RAFSHOON, media consultant to Jimmy Carter

ROSSER REEVES, advertising executive; consultant to Dwight Eisenhower

LEONARD REINSCH, radio and television adviser to Harry Truman and JFK

SAMUEL ROSENMAN, speechwriter for FDR; New York state judge

KARL ROVE, campaign consultant and White House aide to George W. Bush

WILLIAM SAFIRE, public relations aide; speechwriter for Richard Nixon

PIERRE SALINGER, magazine journalist; press secretary to JFK

TONY SCHWARTZ, radio programmer; advertising consultant; Democratic political consultant

SCOTT SFORZA, television aide to George W. Bush

GEORGE STEPHANOPOULOS, campaign consultant and White House aide to Bill Clinton

ARTHUR SYLVESTER, Defense Department public relations aide under JFK and Johnson

ROBERT TEETER, Republican pollster

JOSEPH TUMULTY, White House secretary under Woodrow Wilson

GEORGE SYLVESTER VIERECK, propagandist for Germany in World Wars I and II

JUDSON WELLIVER, speechwriter for Harding and Coolidge; journalist

CLEM WHITAKER AND LEONE BAXTER, full-service California-based political consultants

WILLIAM WILSON, television adviser to Adlai Stevenson and JFK

RICHARD WIRTHLIN, pollster to Ronald Reagan

Intellectuals and Journalists

JOSEPH ALSOP, syndicated columnist

STEWART ALSOP, brother of Joseph Alsop; syndicated columnist

HANNAH ARENDT, political theorist, University of Chicago, The New School

RAY STANNARD BAKER, leading muckraker; press aide to U.S. delegation to Paris peace talks after World War I; biographer of Woodrow Wilson

DANIEL BOORSTIN, professor of history, University of Chicago; Librarian of Congress; author of *The Image*

STEPHEN COLBERT, satirist, *The Colbert Report*

CHARLES COUGHLIN, Catholic priest and radio broadcaster

HERBERT CROLY, editor of *The New Republic*; progressive theorist

OSCAR KING DAVIS, *New York Times* correspondent; press aide to TR, 1912 campaign

RICHARD HARDING DAVIS, reporter; chronicler of Spanish-American War, World War I

JOHN DEWEY, philosopher and theorist of democracy

ROBERT DREW, filmmaker; director of *Primary* and *Crisis*

JACK GOULD, *New York Times* television critic

ARTHUR KROCK, reporter, bureau chief and columnist, *New York Times*

GEORGE LAKOFF, linguist, author, *Moral Politics* and *Don't Think of an Elephant!*

WALTER LIPPMANN, founder, *The New Republic*; Wilson administration aide; author, *Public Opinion*; leading syndicated columnist

SAMUEL "S.S." McCLURE, founder and publisher, *McClure's* magazine

JOE McGINNISS, journalist; author of *The Selling of the President, 1968*

MARSHALL McLUHAN, professor of English; communications theorist

H. L. MENCKEN, critic and columnist

CLYDE MILLER, Columbia University Teachers College; founder, Institute for Propaganda Analysis

VANCE PACKARD, journalist, *American Magazine*; author, *The Hidden Persuaders*

JAMES RESTON, reporter, bureau chief and columnist, *New York Times*

JACOB RIIS, muckraking journalist

LINDSAY ROGERS, Columbia University political scientist; author, *The Pollsters*

EDWARD ROSS, University of Wisconsin sociologist; theorist of public opinion

UPTON SINCLAIR, leading muckraker; author, *The Jungle*; Democratic nominee for governor of California, 1934

FRANK STANTON, communications researcher, president of CBS

LINCOLN STEFFENS, leading muckraker

IDA TARBELL, leading muckraker

GARRY TRUDEAU, cartoonist, *Doonesbury*

THEODORE H. WHITE, journalist for *Time* magazine; author, *The Making of the President, 1960*, and sequels

WILLIAM ALLEN WHITE, editor, *Emporia Gazette*; contributor, *McClure's*; chairman, Committee to Defend America by Aiding the Allies

REPUBLIC
OF SPIN

INTRODUCTION

A WORLD OF SPIN

OUR POLITICAL WORLD is awash in spin. Over many decades now, elected officials and their aides have forged a huge arsenal of tools and techniques to shape their messages, their images, and our thinking. From the White House on down, virtually every politician of note boasts a brigade of speechwriters, press secretaries, campaign consultants, media gurus, handlers, pollsters, hucksters, flacks, hacks, and other assorted spinmeisters to ensure that each utterance and pose is rendered in the best achievable light. Sometimes our politics seem to be nothing but spin—a dizzying, cacophonous whirl of claims and counterclaims. Each side charges the other with spin while asserting for itself a purchase on the truth.

The growth of spin has given rise to a series of now familiar complaints. We hear that our politics are phony and corrupt; that our leaders are packaged and unprincipled; that their rhetoric is shallow and poll-tested; that even the most important political events—debates, conventions, speeches, interviews, press briefings—are scripted, staged, and choreographed. Worse, we hear, spin misleads or deceives us. And even if it's disbelieved or evaluated skeptically, it chokes off the honest and open discourse our democracy needs, rendering our politics vapid, artificial, or bankrupt. And because the White House dominates the channels of communication, presidential spin in particular plays into long-standing American fears of a too powerful executive.

Running for president in 2008, Barack Obama was only the latest candidate to run against spin, depicting himself as a straight shooter, true to his principles and allergic to Washington cant. With his roots in community organizing and his stand against the invasion of Iraq, Obama claimed to offer a clean break from Bill Clinton and his poll-tested centrism, and from George W. Bush and his deceptive rhetoric about the Iraq war. "Most of us are wise to the ways of admen, pollsters, speechwriters, and pundits," a pensive Obama wrote in *The Audacity of Hope*, the book that launched his campaign. "We know how high-flying words can be deployed in the service of cynical aims, and how the noblest sentiments can be subverted in the service of power, expedience, greed, or intolerance." Obama described his rude awakening upon coming to Washington, as he saw how "jokes got screened, irony became suspect, spontaneity was frowned upon, and passion was considered downright dangerous." Eventually, he confessed, "I started to wonder how long it took for a politician to internalize all this, ... before even the 'candid' moments became scripted, so that you choked up or expressed outrage only on cue. How long before you started sounding like a politician?" On *Larry King Live* in 2008, he pledged "less spin and more straight talk."[1]

Fed up, like many of us, with the Kabuki rituals of Washington politics, Obama surely did not want to sound "like a politician." But his own "high-flying words" were also, for lack of a better word, spin. After his 2008 victory, his own spin doctors gloated about their clever, even deceptive messaging. Once he took office, his White House communications team labored as mightily as any to promote his image and message. To the vast machinery that a century of presidents had built before him—press conferences, public affairs bureaus, speechwriting teams, pollsters, media coaches, advertising campaigns—Obama added twenty-first-century innovations like a White House videographer and a Twitter feed.[2]

But when Obama faced setbacks, as all presidents do, he chalked up his troubles to bad spin. "Given how much stuff was coming at us," Obama said in 2010, "we probably spent much more time trying to get the policy right than trying to get the politics right. ... And I think anybody who's occupied this office has to remember that success is determined by an intersection in policy and politics and that you can't be neglecting of marketing and P.R. and public opinion."[3]

This, too, was spin. Politicians routinely blame bad PR for their troubles. They and their supporters find it comforting to claim that they lost a political battle not on the merits, but only in the superficial, grubby, and disreputable realm of communication. Yet if spin can help sell a policy or a candidate, its powers tend to be overrated. Obama's White House communications team may not have done him any great favors, but his poll numbers sagged mainly because of the wheezing U.S. economy and chaos around the globe. "The *Titanic* had an iceberg problem," the political consultant Paul Begala quipped. "It did not have a communications problem."[4]

Whatever its merits, Obama's call for *more* White House spin flew in the face of his previous calls for *less* spin. And yet the president's acknowledgment of the need for spin was welcome. He showed that he understood that in a democracy, spin is how leaders make their case to a sovereign public. It's a way to engage, persuade, and mobilize the people in whom power ultimately resides.

In deploring spin while also desiring it, Barack Obama is like the rest of us. We denounce spin when we see it as misleading. But we embrace spin when we see it as leading.

This ambivalence has a venerable lineage. In ancient Athens, philosophers debated the value of rhetoric, the Greeks' version of spin. Plato believed it was always bad. Unlike philosophy, which used reason in the pursuit of truth, rhetoric relied on emotion and sophistry to induce in listeners *conviction*, not necessarily true belief. Rhetoric, to Plato, was a fraudulent, debased form of philosophy, likely to delude an excitable public.[5]

Plato's student Aristotle took a different view. Aristotle considered rhetoric a neutral instrument to be used for good or ill. Because he believed in the public's capacity for deliberation, he allowed a place in public debate for emotion, which he thought wards off indifference and encourages engagement. What Aristotle decried wasn't the use of rhetoric but its abuse, its employment for immoral ends.[6]

Today, like the Obama of 2008, we fancy ourselves Platonists, deploring the inauthenticity of media politics and the unholy ministrations of the spin doctors. But deep down—perhaps unwittingly—we're Aristotelians. Like the Obama of 2010, we're ready to embrace spin if it serves what we consider legitimate purposes.

*   *   *

We sometimes assume that spin is a new feature of politics, that it began with Ronald Reagan, or John F. Kennedy, or television. Joe McGinniss, in

The Selling of the President, 1968, said that Richard Nixon's campaign that year invented the idea of hawking a candidate like a pack of cigarettes. A generation later, the political reporter Joe Klein, in *Politics Lost*, traced the decline to a 1976 memo by Jimmy Carter's pollster Patrick Caddell outlining a "continuing political campaign" to maintain popular favor. But neither McGinniss, who was twenty-six when he covered Nixon, nor Caddell, who was twenty-six when he wrote that memo, noted the abundant antecedents for what they described.[7]

In fact, in the broadest sense of the term, spin has always been a part of politics. Politics involves advancing one's interests and values in the public sphere, and political leadership means winning and sustaining public support. From the orators of Plato and Aristotle's day to the European monarchs who superintended their images, leaders have always given thought to the words and images that will help them remain popular and achieve their goals.[8]

In liberal democracies, especially, leaders have to make their case to the public. Despots can compel allegiance through force; closed societies can bludgeon their people with propaganda. But democracies require politicians to appeal to the public, and that means putting some argument, some slant, some spin, on the facts. To be sure, when government bureaus furnish basic news and information—unemployment statistics, airline regulations, accounts of international events to which only they have access—we should expect uninflected accuracy. But it would be strange if a president gave an Oval Office address lobbying for a new program, or bill, or war, only to follow it with a second address arguing against the same thing. We expect presidents to lead in the direction they deem prudent and to arrange the facts to add up to a persuasive argument, albeit one that remains, we hope, within the range of defensibly truthful claims.

The president of the United States is probably even more dependent on public approval than other democratic leaders. In parliamentary systems, a prime minister leads as the head of a party; in the United States, the president derives power directly from the populace. This was true even in the nineteenth century, before the tight relationship between presidents and parties atrophied, before the advent of mass communications, and before the presidency became the driver of policy that it is today. In 1858, Abraham Lincoln deemed public opinion to be the heart of democracy. "Public sentiment is everything," he declared in his debates with Stephen Douglas. "With public sentiment nothing can fail; without it nothing can succeed." Nineteenth-century presidents also paid attention to spreading their messages and fashioning their images. They didn't have today's huge spin machine, but they did have vibrant party newspapers such as Andrew Jackson's highly partisan *Washington Globe*.[9]

Yet for most of the nineteenth century, presidents largely accepted the constitutional vision of Congress as the first branch of government and the seat of policy making, with the president an administrative officer. "The business of the president, sometimes great, is usually not much above routine," wrote Woodrow Wilson, then a political scientist, in 1885. A few powerful exceptions, such as Jackson and Lincoln, used their status as the people's tribune to augment the powers of their office. But as the litany of forgettable nineteenth-century presidents suggests, the White House simply wasn't where the action was. The Washington correspondent for a major newspaper didn't spend time at the Executive Mansion (as it was then called), which had no press office and no accommodations for reporters. But the Senate press gallery teemed with writers, who plied their trade in sumptuous digs, replete with red leather couches, mirrors framed in gold, and a standing supply of alcohol.[10]

Not until the twentieth century—with the ascent of Theodore Roosevelt and what has been called "the public presidency"—did presidents make courting public opinion central to their job. When TR assumed the White House in 1901, there existed almost none of the means that today's presidents use to shape their images and messages. But Roosevelt, unusually keen to make the office into a seat of activity, sought authority for his ambitious agenda by appealing directly to the mass public. Eight years later, he had put in place key elements of the White House spin machinery, from his use of the "bully pulpit" to informal afternoon press conferences to the hiring of press agents to promote his pet causes. Afterwards, there was no turning back.[11]

But if Progressives like TR hailed the president's public engagement as a key to activist government, presidential spin from the outset also had its detractors, who accused TR (as critics would accuse his successors) of using the press and other tools of communication for political gain or personal aggrandizement. A pattern was thus set: For the next century, presidents and their aides crafted strategies to mobilize the public on behalf of their goals, while rivals and critics—in Congress, the opposing party, the press, the intelligentsia—decried these innovations as deceptive, illegitimate, self-serving. All believed they were arguing on behalf of American democracy.

This book is a narrative history of spin and the American presidency.[12]

It contends that the emergence of a strong presidency in the twentieth century brought with it an increasing need for presidents (as well as their aforementioned rivals and critics) to master the arts of public persuasion, in order to promote their policies and themselves. To support and illustrate this contention, the book tells the story of the architects and engineers who created and refined the tools and techniques, institutions and practices, that presidents since TR have relied on to influence public opinion—for leading and for misleading. Many of these people were presidents, who strove to lead public opinion. Others were advisers—some famous, some obscure—who helped presidents and other politicians gauge the public mood, deliver speeches, deal with the press, and otherwise work the levers of the growing spin machine. Interacting with one another across administrations and generations, sharing certain basic qualities, these innovators embodied a professional type that came to dominate politics in the twentieth century: experts in information, trained in journalism, media, advertising, social science and related fields, traffickers in the words, images, and symbols that have come to define modern democratic politics.

The rise of White House spin was not uncontested. The book also argues that the steady refinement of presidential spin gave rise to a pervasive anxiety about political persuasion, expressing a fundamental concern about the future of American democracy in a time of a strong presidency, far-reaching mass communications, and sophisticated professional techniques. Hence, intertwined with the story of the presidents and their spin doctors, this book also recounts the evolving and clashing attitudes of the journalists, writers, and intellectuals who observed and dissected spin as it developed. Some were boosters who celebrated advances in spin, believing that new tools of image and message craft would help our leaders fulfill democracy's promise. Others were critics, warning that these new practices were corrupting democracy by assisting politicians in manipulating the public. Still others might be called *realists*, who accepted the new world of spin yet tried to demystify it, hoping to improve democracy by educating citizens about how political words and images and symbols work. Together, their ideas constituted a vast, rolling argument about spin and what it means for a modern democracy.

* * *

In the beginning, they didn't call it *spin*.

Though many of the practices we associate with spin are ancient, they used to go by different names. In Theodore Roosevelt's day, to promulgate a message or image was called *publicity*. Originating as a synonym for exposure, *publicity* evolved into a term for self-promotion. As it did so, it took on a whiff of salesmanship, akin to that Roaring Twenties neologism *ballyhoo*. *Public relations* similarly began as an upstanding, well-groomed scion of the seedier *press agentry*, but was soon itself exposed as a slick euphemism. *Propaganda*, which started as a Catholic Church term, kept a neutral meaning for centuries, but after World War I it came, as the political scientist Harold Lasswell wrote, "to have an ominous clang in many minds." After Hitler and Stalin, its use in the context of an open society struck most people as inapt. Scholars of propaganda like Lasswell now began to study *communication*.[13]

Other coinages arose. The Cold War brought *news management*, an ungainly shard of bureaucratese designed to capture the postwar presidents' regulation of the information flow amid superpower tensions. (On the international front, we got *psychological warfare*, which later became *public diplomacy*.) Television, with its flood of commercials, gave rise to *selling, advertising, packaging, marketing,* and *image making*. Today, with those terms tainted, a new crop of euphemisms has sprouted, each with its nuances: *messaging, branding, framing, strategic communications*. Political scientists Larry Jacobs and Robert Shapiro have proposed *crafted talk*—the "use [of] research on public opinion to pinpoint the most alluring words, symbols, and arguments in an attempt to move public opinion to support . . . desired policies")—while the philosopher Harry Frankfurt serves up *bullshit*.[14]

Yet *spin* remains the shorthand of choice—pithy, lighthearted, evocative, and, I would argue, not necessarily derogatory. To be sure, not everyone uses *spin* the same way. Like its antecedents, it can be descriptive or pejorative. For some people, *spin* has already degenerated into a synonym for damage control or glossing an unpleasant reality or even lying. But dictionary definitions retain the more neutral meaning: "a bias or slant on information, intended to create a favorable impression when it is presented to the public," "an interpretation or viewpoint," or the "deliberate shading of news perception; attempted control of political reaction." *Spin* implies a deliberate attempt to stop short of lying, while still putting the best face on one's position.[15]

Spin also gives off notes of playfulness, irony, and even postmodern self-consciousness. Just as *ballyhoo* and *news management* belong to their eras, *spin* belongs to ours, reflecting the acute public awareness of political manipulation that has developed over the last century. In contrast to *pro-*

paganda, *spin* signals that audience members aren't passive objects to be acted upon but active players in the game, participants in creating meaning. In calling something *spin*, moreover, we're indicating that we can see through it; paradoxically, *spin* implies a certain ineffectiveness. As Obama noted, most of us are wise to the ways of admen, pollsters, speechwriters, and pundits. We're creatures of the age of spin.

The self-conscious dimension of *spin* is clear from the term's history. At first *spin* was applied only to individual statements, not to any larger phenomenon. For ages people have talked about "putting a positive spin" on something. But only recently did spin become the catch-all term for a distinct *feature* of politics—the systematic use, through a range of tools and techniques, of public image and message craft. Although it cropped up in the 1970s, it was in the Reagan years that David Gergen, Lee Atwater, and other aides were regularly using the word in this new sense. The following years gave Americans the rock band the Spin Doctors, the political sitcom *Spin City*, and the delightful low-budget documentary *Spin*, which was assembled from raw satellite feeds showing politicians behind the scenes, unguarded, honing their messages for public consumption.[16]

The term *spin* achieved takeoff between 1984 and 1988, thanks to the presidential debates. Since 1976, during post-debate commentary, candidates' surrogates had been loyally lavishing praise on their man's performance whether they believed it or not. By 1988, journalists had christened the corridor where these cheerleaders congregated "Spin Alley." (It was later upgraded to "the Spin Room.") One partisan who was plumping for Democratic nominee Michael Dukakis in the UCLA Student Union that fall was a vanquished rival of his from the spring primaries, one who embraced his thankless sales job with uncommon zeal (or admirable self-awareness), even donning a white hospital coat and a name tag proclaiming himself "Senator Albert Gore, Jr.: Spin Doctor."[17]

Spin here connoted something slightly different from previous synonyms. In that its practitioners acknowledged their words to be less than fully straightforward, *spin* winked at its own stretching of the truth. It signaled to the journalists who reported the spin, and to the audiences who consumed it, that they were getting a partial, perhaps insincere, version of events.

From a Platonic viewpoint, Spin Alley and the Spin Room are absurd. "Every presidential election year," wrote the journalist Michael Kinsley, mystified, "thousands of journalists fly to strange cities to sit in the overflow room and watch on TV the presidential debates they could be watching on TV at home. They do it mainly in order to be in another large room after the debate, where spinners for the candidates recite lines written before the debate about how their clients won the debate." The very names of these holding pens dispense with any pretense that the talking heads on view are offering objective or even honest analysis. Reporters know they're getting a scripted, one-sided take yet compliantly pass on the spin for the audience to sort out.[18]

From an Aristotelian viewpoint, however, there's something refreshing about the frank admission that what we're watching is spin, a duel of interpretation. It can actually be fun to watch. Many of us enjoy (sometimes) the post-debate spin, applauding those who give voice to our own sentiments, confident that we can see through self-serving claims, curious to see how the rhetorical skirmish will play out. We realize that spin is met with counterspin; that we are not helpless in the face of clever arguments or slick ads (though we may fear our neighbors are); that our knowledge and beliefs provide ballast against being fooled. On this view, taking pleasure in spin isn't a cause for concern. It reflects our mindfulness that politics is full of competing versions of events and ways of ordering reality. Indeed, in a time of political disaffection like ours, audiences need to find ways to enjoy politics, and while objective information is indispensable for informed debate, the theatricality and combativeness of spin are more likely to draw in citizens than are antiseptic or Olympian statements that purport to tell citizens all they need to know.[19]

Spin, moreover, isn't the all-powerful force that, in our Platonic moods, we may presume it to be. Events, more than messages and images, largely determine who wins presidential campaigns or battles for public opinion. Although presidents have many forums for putting across their messages, they're almost always met by counterspin from the opposing party, Congress, or the press—especially these days, with the rise of cable news, talk radio, and the Internet. And public opinion is much more resistant to persuasion than popular depictions typically suggest.[20]

Besides, just as rhetoric was an inherent part of ancient politics, spin is a permanent part of ours. It's hardly possible to imagine politics without it. There is of course a "No-Spin Zone" on television—but it is hosted by the highly opinionated and provocative conservative pundit Bill O'Reilly. Even the ostensibly neutral "fact-checking" features that news outlets have introduced to call out politicians for misleading ads, false statements, or other microdeceptions, though useful when explaining the source or justification for a contested claim, often arrive at conclusions that are based on subjective judgments and informed by ideological predilections. Through-out history, spinners have invariably claimed to be truthtellers who were simply dispelling falsehoods, while those aiming to dispel falsehood have seldom resisted the temptation to spin. Journalists and citizens should and do call out politicians when they distort, exaggerate, or lie; we need public vigilance about spin to keep politicians honest. In an aphorism usually attributed to Daniel Patrick Moynihan (but first coined in slightly differ-ent form by Bernard Baruch), everyone is entitled to his own opinion but not to his own facts. Usually, though, determining which facts are relevant or important is part of the challenge—and the disagreement. Instead of trying somehow to banish spin from the kingdom of politics, we'd be better off, like the pragmatic critics described in the pages ahead, trying to inculcate a critical sense that helps us question and evaluate spin—and maybe, just once in a while, to know when to believe it.

In the end, a surfeit of partisan advocacy, or even a margin of dis-simulation in politics, is far less dangerous than the claim by a powerful party, especially the government, to have a monopoly on the truth. Walter Lippmann, one of the twentieth century's champions of disinterested expertise, warned against pursuing a single, monolithic truth in poli-tics because, he noted, such a posture forecloses the debate of ideas and worldviews that a free society requires. "In real life there is not, as there is in every jigsaw puzzle, one picture and one picture only, into which all the pieces will eventually fit," he wrote. "It is the totalitarian mind which thinks that there is one and only one picture."[21]

It's tempting to romanticize a politics that relies exclusively on rational persuasion. But in politics rational argument has always been commingled with emotional appeals and the partial or selective presentations of evi-dence. If we want to allow for the fullest possible extent of the former, we have to tolerate a great deal of the latter. That means the candidate or party or position we prefer will sometimes lose in the court of public opinion, or that the public will sometimes be led to make bad policy choices. But if we're engaged in a debate that presumes no final verdict, no single authori-tative answer, we can lose and live to fight another day.

PART I

THE AGE OF PUBLICITY

Since ancient times, political leaders have used words and images to win public favor and sustain their legitimacy. Yet by and large the American presidents of the nineteenth century did not devote their daily energies to mobilizing public opinion. It was Theodore Roosevelt, more than any of his predecessors, who made it his mission to enlist the citizenry behind his policy goals, turning the presidency into the engine of social reform. Touring widely, delivering speeches, convening informal press conferences, staging publicity stunts, hiring press aides, and otherwise commanding public attention, Roosevelt launched an Age of Publicity, in which presidents and other politicians championed the disclosure of their activities as a way to promote themselves and their goals. Woodrow Wilson, building on Roosevelt's foundations, articulated a belief common among progressives that broad-minded leaders could, through their leadership of public opinion, forge an enlightened citizenry and a stronger democracy. Wilson added to the White House's publicity capacities, ushering in a host of historic reforms. His project culminated in the wartime Committee on Public Information, which veered uncomfortably into propaganda, feeding a popular cynicism toward presidential efforts to guide public opinion—a cynicism with which his successors would long have to contend.

1

THEODORE ROOSEVELT
AND THE PUBLIC PRESIDENCY

WHEN PRESIDENT WILLIAM MCKINLEY led the United States to war against Spain in the spring of 1898, the nation sprang into action, and no one was keener to see battle than Theodore Roosevelt.[1] Scion of an upper-crust New York family, the brash assistant Navy secretary had, at thirty-nine, already built a reputation as a reformer as a New York state assemblyman and as Gotham's police commissioner. Lately, from his perch in the Navy Department, he had been planning, and agitating, for an all-out confrontation with the dying Spanish Empire. He drew up schemes for deploying the American fleet, which he had helped strengthen, in not only the Caribbean, where Spain ruled a restive Cuba, but also the Pacific, where it held the Philippines. After the deadly February explosion of the USS *Maine* off Cuba's shores, Roosevelt shared with journalists his firm but mistaken conviction that the Spanish were to blame. "Being a Jingo," he wrote a friend, using the slang for war hawk, "I would give anything if President McKinley would order the fleet to Havana tomorrow." Privately, he mocked his president, who was trying to negotiate a solution: "McKinley is bent on peace, I fear."[2]

In April, after some provocations, McKinley bowed to pressure and opted for war. Roosevelt resolved not to validate the sneers of his detractors that he was just playing at combat. "My power for good, whatever it may be, would be gone if I didn't try to live up to the doctrines I have tried to preach," he told a friend. Newspaper editorialists called on him to remain at the Navy Department, where they said his expertise was needed. But TR quit his desk job, secured a commission as a lieutenant colonel, and set up a training ground in San Antonio, Texas. Along with his friend Leonard Wood, the president's doctor, he readied for battle a motley regiment of Ivy League footballers and polo players, cowboys and roughnecks. Roosevelt telegrammed Brooks Brothers for an "ordinary cavalry lieutenant-colonel's uniform in blue Cravenette."[3]

As competitive as he was patriotic, Roosevelt meant for his men to vanquish the Spanish. But he also wanted them to seize their countrymen's imagination, with himself in the lead. The new mass media would provide his means.[4] Photographers and journalists swarmed the Texas camp, where a sign on the gate said, "All Civilians, Except Reporters, Prohibited from Camp." Some journalists called them "Teddy's Terrors," even though Wood was the unit's commander—testament to Roosevelt's ability to hijack the headlines. Reporter Richard Oulahan dubbed them the "Rough Riders," enhancing the group's mystique.[5]

Publicity-hungry, TR wrote to Robert Bridges, the editor of *Scribner's* magazine, offering him "first chance" to publish six installments of a (planned) first-person account of his (planned) war exploits—a preview of what would be a full-blown book and, in Roosevelt's humble assessment, a "permanent historical work." Bridges accepted. Once TR set off for Cuba, he made sure that his favorite reporters—notably, the daring, dashing Richard Harding Davis—joined him. And although the boat that left Tampa, Florida, was too small to fit all the Rough Riders comfortably, TR insisted that they make room for a passel of journalists. One account, probably apocryphal, had him ushering on board two motion picture cameramen from Thomas Edison's Vitagraph Company.[6]

Roosevelt focused on how the war was covered as much as on how it was fought. Journalists had been writing with feverish interest about the Cuban uprising since it began in 1895. Playing on, and playing up, American sympathy for the Cubans, the mass circulation newspapers and magazines, led by William Randolph Hearst's *New York Journal* and Joseph Pulitzer's *New York World*, avidly covered the rebellion. When war came, some 500 reporters, editors, illustrators, and photographers streamed to Florida. They included the novelists Stephen Crane and Frank Norris, the artist Frederic Remington, the Russian adventurer George Kennan (uncle of the future Cold War diplomat), the future Democratic

Party publicist Charles Michelson, and even the showboating Hearst himself. Many climbed aboard Navy vessels bound for Cuba and Puerto Rico. Western Union telegraph cables connecting Havana with Key West, and hence the whole of the United States, would relay battlefront news with unprecedented speed. The clash was called "The Correspondents' War."

To this journalistic flotilla, the charismatic Roosevelt was an obvious draw. When he charged into combat at the Battle of Las Guásimas, Richard Harding Davis, on assignment for the *New York Herald* and *Scribner's*, and Edward Marshall, of Hearst's *Journal*, marched alongside him; Stephen Crane, whom TR disliked, was consigned to the rear. A week later, when Roosevelt led the advance up Kettle Hill as part of the larger Battle of San Juan Hill, the embedded journalists recorded his courage for readers back home. Though Roosevelt's bravery was by all accounts genuine, the precise nature of his exploits would prove controversial: he boasted that he had initiated the Kettle Hill charge, whereas some witnesses credited Charles Taylor, a captain. No one, however, disputed that Roosevelt hurried to the front and led the way up the slope. In any case, his leadership beguiled the press. Davis's account was particularly florid. He described Roosevelt speeding into combat with "a blue polka-dot handkerchief" around his sombrero—"without doubt the most conspicuous figure in the charge. . . . Mounted high on horseback and charging the rifle-pits at a gallop and quite alone, he made you feel that you would like to cheer." Others inflated Roosevelt's heroics, crediting him with taking San Juan Hill proper rather than its smaller neighbor—a substitution TR would come to make as well. The legend endured, and grew. A few years later, the Russian painter Vasili Vereshchagin would portray TR in full glory at San Juan and exhibit his work at New York's Waldorf-Astoria Hotel.[7]

Newsreels, too, seared Roosevelt's heroism into the public mind. Although Albert E. Smith's films of the assault on San Juan Hill appear to be inauthentic, the Rough Riders' more quotidian activities did make it into cinemas. Despite the pedestrian actions on screen, audiences lapped up shorts like *Roosevelt's Rough Riders at Drill*, which captured the troops' early steps toward war. They took in as well films like *Raising Old Glory Over Morro Castle*, even though the American flag that the film depicted had been hoisted by actors on a Manhattan rooftop. Some of the anonymous, valorous grunts in the Cuban battles resented TR's publicity, but it made the young lieutenant colonel, as the *New York World* wrote, "more talked about than any man in the country."[8]

Within weeks, what Roosevelt's friend John Hay called the "splendid little war" in Cuba was over. That fall, basking in the hype, Roosevelt was elected governor of New York. Two years later, almost as predictably, he was chosen vice president of the United States. And when a gunman took McKinley's life in September 1901, the American presidency had, in this forty-two-year-old gamecock, its first full-fledged celebrity.

*   *   *

Theodore Roosevelt was born for the spotlight. "One cannot think of him except as part of the public scene, performing on the public stage," wrote the philosopher John Dewey, who was Roosevelt's junior by one year and an unlikely enthusiast. Many Americans, to be sure, found it hard to stomach Roosevelt's antics. Mark Twain saw TR as one of his own parodic creations come to life, a juvenile, showboating ham, "the Tom Sawyer of the political world of the twentieth century." H. L. Mencken similarly bridled at TR's grandiosity. "What moved him was simply a craving for facile and meaningless banzais, for the gaudy eminence and power of the leader of a band of lynchers, for the mean admiration of mean men." Woodrow Wilson, once an admirer, came to regard TR as "the monumental fakir of history."

To Dewey, all of this was carping. Roosevelt was merely succeeding on the terms of his age. "To criticize Roosevelt for love of the camera and the headline is childish," the philosopher wrote, "unless we recognize that in such criticism we are condemning the very conditions of any public success during this period." Dewey tolerated Roosevelt's grandstanding, which he considered a prerequisite for achievement in the new century. As the journalist Henry Stoddard explained, the plutocrats of the Gilded Age had come to wield so much economic and political influence that it would have been futile for TR to try to fight them with "soft stepping and whispered persuasion." Only a head-on assault would do.[9]

The endless attention Roosevelt got was not unmerited. His talents were such that he made a mark in almost every endeavor he tried, from writing history to exploring the Amazon and from politics to war. He could claim distinction as a Harvard graduate and a cowboy, soldier and athlete, hunter and biographer, journalist and conservationist, student of law and champion of science, state assemblyman and police commissioner, reformist governor and unshackled campaigner, and the youngest man to become president. His intellect was partly responsible for these achievements; the English writer H. G. Wells credited him with "the most vigorous brain in a conspicuously responsible position in all the world." But the mainspring of Roosevelt's success was his preternatural self-confidence. Seldom did he betray uncertainty about his ability to meet a task, whether finishing a manuscript, ramming a bill through Congress, or jawboning a visitor into accepting his view.

TR fancied himself above all a man of action. With typical theatricality, he proclaimed the moral superiority of "the man . . . in the arena, whose face is marred by dust and sweat and blood; who strives valiantly; who errs and comes short again and again, because there is not effort without error and shortcoming; but who does actually strive to do the deeds." He insisted on the need for political change in industrial-age America; just as vehemently, he scorned the genteel idealism of the "silk stocking" types, as he called his era's upper-class reformers, who were his natural allies. But his vigor and self-possession had their drawbacks. Impatient with the faint of heart, Roosevelt mistook ambivalence for weakness. "I don't care how honest a man is," he asserted, "if he is timid he is no good." His glee often gave way to bluster, and the moralism that served as a wellspring of reform also produced an ugly faith in the superiority of his own race, class, and sex to rule. He justified the conquest of the West and America's assumption of lands in the Pacific in nakedly racist terms.[10]

Most associates forgave these flaws, some of them capitulating to his overpowering charisma. "You go to the White House, you shake hands with Roosevelt and hear him talk," wrote the journalist Richard Washburn Child, "and then go home to wring the personality out of your clothes." Roosevelt's allure seemed to inhere in his very visage. His iconic profile would remain as vivid decades after his death as it was to his contemporaries. His stocky, muscular physique revealed a lifelong obsession with the manly virtues of strength and athleticism. His pale blue eyes, squinting behind thick-lensed pince-nez, conveyed an irrepressible drive. And his gleaming rows of teeth, flashing from below the thick, drooping mustache—"very white, and almost as big as a colt's teeth," wrote Arthur Brisbane of Pulitzer's *World*—lit up his ruddy face in a glow of joy or menace. They could frighten people when he worked his will, or amuse them when he laughed his high-pitched cackle. "Probably the thing that has saved Roosevelt is his laugh," wrote his friend and admirer William Allen White, the famed editor of the *Emporia (Kansas) Gazette*. "Time and again he has punctured the cant and sophistry of an argumentative statesman with a twinkling grin and a gurgling, 'Oh, come now, Senator!'"[11]

Then there was the sense of movement, constant movement. Roosevelt was always striding, leaning forward in his chair, pacing purposefully. He waved his arms, clenched his fists, tugged at his watch chain, bounded exuberantly. Companions stood in awe at his appetite for physical exertion—swinging chest weights in Wood's Gymnasium as a teenager, boxing with hulks as a rising politician, thundering through Washington's Rock Creek Park on horseback as president. His devotees marveled at the vitality, but detractors saw only an adolescent lustiness. Either way, it stemmed from a deep sense of purpose and ego, coiled together like the double helix of his own DNA. "He was his own limelight," wrote his friend Owen Wister, a well-known novelist, "and could not help it: a creature charged with such a voltage as his, became the central presence at once, whether he stepped on a platform or entered a room."[12]

Roosevelt exploited this luminosity. Elected to the assembly at twenty-three, he leveraged the interest in him as a personality to win attention for his work. He befriended George Spinney, the *New York Times*'s Albany correspondent, whose favorable stories served the young politician's ends. In the 1890s, as New York's police commissioner, Roosevelt collaborated with Jacob Riis, author of *How the Other Half Lives,* a soon-to-be classic exposé of the wretchedness of the urban poor, and Lincoln Steffens, then starting his own storied muckraking career. Roosevelt conscripted the reporters to guide him through the demimonde of criminals and cops. In return he buffed their reputations—he called Riis "the most useful citizen of New York"—and tried to help them publish in *The Atlantic* an investigation of police corruption that he thought would help him reform the force.

Some thought the young commissioner too eager to ingratiate himself. But TR never stopped cultivating reporters, whose company he manifestly enjoyed. His gubernatorial victory in 1898 elated friends like Riis, who had given speeches on TR's behalf, and minted new fans, including Ray Stannard Baker, who wrote a cooing profile in *McClure's* magazine. Once in the New York statehouse, Roosevelt initiated twice-daily meetings with correspondents. Plopping himself on the edge of his desk, one leg folded underneath him, he would serve up a rapid-fire stream of tidbits, judgments, and jokes, all of it off the record.[13]

By the time he became president, Roosevelt was fully at ease with the press. His outsized personality, ambitious agenda, and taste for political theater provoked endless fascination. So did his burgeoning family. Roosevelt was the first president since Lincoln to bring young children to the White House, and, though mindful of their privacy, he couldn't hide their mischief or suppress their exuberance, which may even have outrun their father's. From Alice, his daughter from his first marriage, who at seventeen burst upon the Georgetown social scene, to the three-year-old Quentin, who joined his three brothers and two sisters in hurling snowballs at Secret Service agents and springing out of linen closets during games of hide-and-seek, the first family engineered a fusion of political news and society journalism that Washington had never before seen.

Roosevelt surrendered another bastion of presidential privacy by turning family retreats to Sagamore Hill, his Oyster Bay homestead, into working vacations. When McKinley had escaped Washington's fishbowl with visits to his native Canton, Ohio, reporters seldom followed. But in 1902, after the Roosevelts began renovating the Executive Mansion and repaired to Long Island, a horde of correspondents tagged along. When the reporters filled the lulls with gossipy accounts of the first family's antics, the president protested, oblivious to his own role in having whetted the appetite for presidential news. Presidential vacations would never be the same.[14]

If TR drew notice when he didn't seek it, more often he pursued it—actively. "The spotlight of publicity followed Roosevelt all his life with curious devotion—by no means without Roosevelt's encouragement," wrote William Allen White, who provided TR with more than his share. "The master press agent of all time," declared Isaac Marcosson, another correspondent. But, again, Roosevelt's goal wasn't just to be loved; it was to be effective. "Yes—it is true that TR liked the centre of the stage—loved it in fact," wrote Henry Stoddard; "but when he sought it he always had something to say or to do that made the stage the appropriate place for him." On one occasion, he descended to the bottom of Long Island Sound in a submarine to show his support for the new ships; on another, he rode ninety-eight miles on horseback to prove the reasonableness of new Army regulations. TR's publicity stunts served a purpose.[15]

Understanding Roosevelt's quest for publicity requires reconciling two meanings of the word. In his day, *publicity* meant, primarily, not the self-aggrandizing pursuit of attention, though that usage was catching on, but a commitment to making facts public, akin to *transparency*. The word signified an objective, not a subjective, presentation of information. Progressives like Roosevelt believed that if the backroom political deals and corporate malfeasance were exposed for the public to pass judgment, the outcry would force those in power to change their ways. "Publicity is justly commended as a remedy for social and industrial diseases," the future Supreme Court justice Louis Brandeis wrote. "Sunlight is said to be the best of disinfectants." Thus, when the *New York World* wrote that TR's strategy as police commissioner was "Publicity! Publicity! Publicity!"

it wasn't to mock his love of the headlines; it meant that he was laying open his department's workings for public view. "We shall be glad to have reputable outsiders inspect and oversee everything that is done, and a complete record will be kept," TR was quoted as saying. His first presidential message to Congress in 1901 prescribed publicity to check the trusts. "The first essential in determining how to deal with the great industrial combinations," he said, "is knowledge of the facts—publicity."[16]

Within a few years, the emergence of public relations professionals would set the word's two meanings in conflict. The hired pros would become known for what we now call spinning information to put the best face on it, or promoting phony events that lacked intrinsic news value. In so doing, they transformed publicity from a synonym for full disclosure into something like an antonym, a term for selective, self-serving disclosure. But it was possible to use publicity in both ways at once, as Roosevelt did: He could climb behind the controls of a steam shovel while visiting Panama to dramatize the need for the canal, or release a government report on Chicago stockyard squalor to secure the passage of a meat inspection bill he was touting. Transparency and self-promotion alike advanced his agenda—and himself.

* * *

More than a tactic, publicity thoroughly informed Roosevelt's conception of the presidency—a conception that was as bold, novel, and purposeful as the man himself. Typically, presidents had accepted the framers' view of the executive as chiefly an administrative office, with Congress the center of governmental activity. TR, in contrast, believed the president should actively promote social change. In his *Autobiography*, he set forth what became known as his "stewardship theory":

> My view was that every executive officer . . . was a steward of the people bound actively and affirmatively to do all he could for the people and not to content himself with the negative merit of keeping his talents undamaged in a napkin. I declined to adopt the view that what was imperatively necessary for the nation could not be done by the president unless he could find some specific authorization to do it. My belief was that it was not only his right but his duty to do anything that the needs of the nation demanded, unless such action was forbidden by the Constitution or by the laws.[17]

This groundbreaking theory fused two related ideas: an activist presidency and a reformist federal government. TR's vision required not only that Washington meet the "needs of the nation" but also that the president, as opposed to Congress, take the lead in doing so. By positing a direct relationship between the president and the people, Roosevelt turned the executive into a job of public opinion leadership. It led him to try to discern the public will and the public interest; to go over the heads of Congress and other intermediaries to fashion his image and messages; and ultimately to usher in an age in which presidents would be perpetually engaged in the work of publicity and opinion management—the work of spin.

At the root of the theory was Roosevelt's conviction, shared by his fellow Progressives, that the times demanded federal activism. No institution but the national government could check the enormous power of corporate capitalism, which he (and many others) saw as the overriding problem of the age. TR envisioned a strong state that would preserve a basic equality in American economic life. He wanted to toughen antitrust laws and regulate industries like the railroads and the meatpackers, and he backed social reforms like better conditions for workers.

This program, which Roosevelt called the "Square Deal," embodied a moderate Progressivism. Many who wanted to use state power more aggressively were socialists or populists or otherwise stood to TR's left. Scorning them as irresponsible, Roosevelt held that taming capitalism's excesses required thoughtful, non-ideological governance, carried out for the benefit not of particular classes but of the nation as a whole. Herbert Croly, the great theorist of Progressivism, called Roosevelt "the first political leader of the American people to identify the national principle with an ideal of reform. . . . He was the first to realize that an American statesman could no longer really represent the national interest without becoming a reformer."[18]

In Roosevelt's view, only the president could govern in the name of the "national interest" that Croly described. Congressmen spoke for discrete and clamorous regional constituencies; the president alone could rise above particular interests to distill and promote what served the entire nation. "I acted for the public welfare," TR declared in his *Autobiography*. "I acted for the common well-being of all our people."[19]

In the early republic, ideas of virtuous leadership and the common good had been central to republican thought. But in the 1820s and 1830s, the parties became the dominant political vehicles, assembling coalitions based on appeals to the self-interest of their constituencies. For the rest of the nineteenth century, powerful machines, run by cagey bosses, corralled voters into loyally supporting their candidates at the polls. In return, the machines doled out jobs, welfare assistance, and other forms of aid that local governments failed to provide. This spoils system, however, thrived on corruption, and in the Gilded Age self-styled reformers agitated for change. Small-r republican ideas made a comeback. Reformers replaced federal patronage with a merit-based civil service and promoted independent voting through the secret ballot. Parties fell into disrepute, seen no longer as instruments of democracy but as barriers to its fulfillment. "We were ruled under the party system by an aristocracy which was financed by greed," wrote the Progressive William Allen White, "and it was the problem of democracy to break down that aristocracy."[20]

Though a proud Republican, Roosevelt exemplified the anti-party spirit. In his earliest days in politics, he joined with Harvard friends to found the City Reform Club to oust crooked politicians "irrespective of party." As governor, he prided himself on "going over the heads of the men holding public office and of the men in control of the organization and appealing directly to the people behind them." When in 1900 McKinley was casting about for a new vice president, it wasn't Roosevelt's Republican Party ties that got him noticed; it was his wild mass popularity. After McKinley's assassination, TR used his popular standing to silence talk that he was an "accidental" president, and in 1904 he became the first presidential understudy who, having acceded to the Oval Office on his predecessor's death, went on to win the presidency outright. He was elected as "a man rather than a party," Woodrow Wilson said at the time, beholden to no "local constituency." Roosevelt thus distinguished himself as the pivotal figure in the long-term shift from the party-based politics of the nineteenth century to the candidate-centered system of the media age.[21]

The president was now a statesman rather than a party man, a public tribune rather than the interests' advocate, and a driver of policy change rather than an administrator. And in this new world, publicity became not just an ego indulgence but a sine qua non of governance. Roosevelt's activist agenda meant that he had to not only monitor the public pulse but also keep the public emotionally invested in him. "His ordinary and native acts," wrote John Dewey, "gained a representative significance." Whether through private gestures such as "chopp[ing] down a tree at Oyster Bay" or in official acts like "sending a fleet around the world, he was the man in whom we saw our own ideals fulfilled or betrayed."[22]

No one, indeed, was more attuned than TR to the special place that the presidency occupied in citizens' inner lives, to the president's unique role as national symbol. After a tour of the West, Roosevelt wrote about the throngs who had come to hear him. "Most of these people habitually led rather gray lives," he wrote. "And they came in to see the president much as they would have come in to see the circus. It was something to talk over and remember and tell their children about. But I think that besides the mere curiosity there was a good feeling behind it all, a feeling that the president was their man and symbolized their government, and that they had a proprietary interest in him and wished to see him and that they hoped he embodied their aspirations and their best thought." Or as he wrote to his friend the British historian G. M. Trevelyan: "Whatever value my service may have comes . . . more from what I am than from what I do. The bulk of my countrymen . . . feel that I am in a peculiar way their president, that I represent the democracy."[23]

Roosevelt could claim to be the first president of the modern age not just because he used the power of the presidency on behalf of sweeping social reform—a feat in itself—but because he redefined the job by governing with an acute consciousness of his symbolic role. Tackling major national problems meant the president had to set the political agenda through speeches, the press, and the other emerging media of mass communication. This in turn meant commanding public attention by mastering the tools and techniques of persuasion and image craft that would, decades later, come to be known as *spin*.

WILLIAM McKINLEY AND THE PASSING OF THE OLD ORDER

IN SEIZING THE NATIONAL IMAGINATION, Theodore Roosevelt had one great advantage: his immediate predecessors were a decidedly dreary lot. In a 1934 short story called "The Four Lost Men," Thomas Wolfe wrote: "And where was Harrison? Where was Hayes? Which had the whiskers, which had the burnsides; which was which?" Yet TR's predecessors laid the foundation on which he built the modern presidency, and the most accomplished among them were far from unmindful of public opinion. "No hours of my day are better employed than those which bring me again within the direct contact . . . of the average of our whole people," wrote Abraham Lincoln of what he called his "public-opinion baths." This attention to public opinion was one reason TR idolized Lincoln. "I suppose you know Lincoln is my hero," Roosevelt wrote to John Hay, Lincoln's secretary, and later his biographer. "He was a man of the people who always felt with and for the people but who had not the slightest touch of the demagogue in him." Along with Andrew Jackson, TR said, Lincoln inspired his own view of "the executive as subject only to the people," instead of as "the servant of Congress."[1]

Still, paying attention to public opinion was one thing; actively cultivating it was another. Lincoln consciously fashioned his public image, met with journalists, and spoke to the nation; but he never hired publicists to spread his arguments, or toured the country on behalf of an agenda, or set up a White House press operation. Gradually, though, his successors developed rudimentary practices for getting their messages out. Andrew Johnson gave the first newspaper interview. Grover Cleveland took pity on the covey of White House correspondents who composed their dispatches standing up, without even so much as desk, and gave them a table inside the Executive Mansion. Most of all, though, it was a president widely seen as isolated from the public and devoid of panache—William McKinley—who devised the new methods of communication on which TR would build.

* * *

A popular Republican governor of Ohio and former congressman, McKinley was a transitional president. As the last Civil War veteran to be president, he represented the end of an old order: the last man elected in the nineteenth century and, as William Allen White wrote, the last president "to stand apart from the people, pedestaled, shielded from publicity." But McKinley also exhibited modern tendencies, including an awareness of the mass media. Just as he dipped his toe into the twentieth century, living until September 1901, so too did he nudge the presidency into the age of mass communications.[2]

The campaign of 1896 pitted the affable fifty-three-year-old McKinley, with his sedate corporate conservatism, against the rousing prairie populist William Jennings Bryan, Democrat of Nebraska. Passionate, imposing, and only thirty-six, Bryan, "the Boy Orator of the Platte," was, with his crusade for a silver-backed U.S. currency, the most economically radical candidate either major party had ever fielded. Running as the fusion candidate of the Democrats and the upstart People's Party, Bryan embodied the fiery insurgency that moderate Progressives like Roosevelt deplored. McKinley, in contrast, defended the "sound money" of the gold standard, aligning himself with banks, corporations, and the rising middle class. Polarizing Americans as no election had since the Civil War, the 1896 race remade the political landscape. The victorious Republican Party cobbled together a sturdy coalition of business, finance, the professional classes, and skilled workers that would allow it to dominate the whole country except the South until the Great Depression.[3]

The 1896 contest also changed how campaigns were run. Traditionally, candidates hadn't physically campaigned. Fashioning themselves as the "mute tribune" of their constituents, they hewed to an older belief that plunging into the hurly-burly of crowds and tours compromised the dignity of an aspirant to high office. Bryan zestfully broke this mold. With bottomless energy and a youthful indifference to bunking in run-down rooms and napping on trains, he unleashed his rhetorical gifts before audiences of farmers and miners desperate for relief. He traveled more widely than any candidate before.

McKinley, recognizing his own restrained temperament, turned himself over to Mark Hanna, a coal magnate and die-hard supporter. Hanna urged McKinley to conduct his own barnstorming tour. McKinley opted instead for a "front porch" campaign, in which he delivered hundreds of studied sermons to eager crowds imported to Canton, Ohio, his hometown. Like pilgrims at a shrine, McKinley's enthusiasts left with clods, twigs, even pieces of the porch itself.

*   *   *

McKinley's front-porch campaign constituted one gingerly step into a political culture that required charisma, self-promotion, and mass media savvy. Another step was Hanna's amassing of a multi-million-dollar war chest, much of which he spent on a mammoth advertising campaign. A "literary bureau," run by newspaperman Perry Heath, sent out millions of posters and lithographs of the candidate, as well as cartoons, stickers, and—a novelty in 1896—the celluloid pin, a cheap and durable advertising tool that could display images not possible on the metal badges of earlier times. Brandishing slogans like "A Full Dinner Pail," the trinkets stressed McKinley's commitment to prosperity. TR groused that Hanna's marketing offended good taste. "He has advertised McKinley as if he were a patent medicine," Roosevelt cried, blind to his double standards.[4]

As part of this blitz, McKinley made the first ever campaign film. In 1896, motion pictures were just escaping the vaudeville booths and amusement arcades and arriving in urban theaters. Huge numbers of Americans could now see, or think they were seeing, real-life events in full motion. McKinley's younger brother, Abner, had invested in the American Mutoscope and Biograph Company, an early motion picture firm, and helped make sure that the Republicans were the ones to exploit this new phenomenon.

On September 18, William K. L. Dickson—a colleague of Thomas Edison's who helped invent the movie camera and projector—hauled the oversized contraption that was his camera to Canton to record the first presidential campaign film. Soaking up the Ohio sunlight, which proved perfect for capturing sharp images, Dickson and Billy Bitzer, his twenty-four-year-old cameraman, recorded McKinley and his secretary strolling the grounds of the homestead, and then joined the candidate and his wife, Ida, inside for lunch.

Less than a month later, on Wednesday night, October 12, Bitzer showed up at Hammerstein's Olympia Music Hall in Manhattan, a Louis XVI–style performance palace on Broadway in the West Forties, recently built by the theater impresario Oscar Hammerstein. Ascending to the mid-balcony boxes, Bitzer positioned himself behind a projector dubbed "The American Biograph," a seven-foot-tall vertical box whose body was as ungainly as its name. After a vaudeville act finished onstage—movies alone did not yet constitute a night at the theater—Bitzer unspooled his celluloid reel. It began with footage of a parade through the Canton streets before cutting to a sequence labeled "Major McKinley at Home," in which the candidate descended the steps of his house. Accompanied by an aide, McKinley strode toward a fixed camera, stopping on the lawn to don his hat and glasses and inspect a telegram. The men exchanged words, and McKinley took off the hat, mopped his forehead, and resumed his path to the camera until he exited the frame.[5]

The short clip provoked a frenzy. To audiences unaccustomed to seeing their leaders "in the flesh," as one paper put it (using scare quotes to acknowledge the illusion), it was as if the governor had literally ambled into the theater. The crowd cheered; some called for the apparition to speak. "The whole house went wild," noted the *New York Advertiser*. Hammerstein's Olympia re-screened the film several times before Election Day, as did other theaters around the country, thrilling partisans, generating revenue, and handing the Republican National Committee a publicity coup.

Bryanites were flummoxed. Some booed when the GOP candidate appeared on their movie screens. Others scrambled to match the Republicans' gimmick. "Send me a film of W. J. Bryan before November 3rd," pleaded Robert Fischer, a Denver entrepreneur, in a letter to the Vitagraph Company. "It would not be safe for me to show McKinley's here until after election." But no film of the Democrat was forthcoming for his devotees in the mining centers and farm communities of the American West.

*   *   *

As president, McKinley continued to look for ways to reach the public. After the sensation of "Major McKinley at Home," cameramen turned out in force for his March 1897 inauguration, recording the festivities for newsreels. McKinley also improved upon Grover Cleveland's shoddy treatment of the press. Cleveland had shunned journalists ever since the 1884 presidential race, when they taunted him for fathering an illegitimate child. "Mr. Cleveland," noted his aide George Parker, "simply would not consent to see representatives of the newspapers or press associations." McKinley was more solicitous. During the campaign, he gave out copies of his speeches, and after his swearing-in he hosted an afternoon reception for journalists in the East Room at the White House. A familiar face in Washington, having served in the House for fourteen years, McKinley shook hands, welcomed correspondents by name, and mingled. "Gentlemen," he said, "I am glad to see you here, I want you all to feel that the Executive Mansion is a public office, and that you are welcome here at any time." Most newsmen had never seen such warm behavior from Cleveland and only a few recalled a much less extravagant reception thrown by Benjamin Harrison.[6]

McKinley appeared to grasp that the Washington press corps was becoming a force to be reckoned with. The last decades of the nineteenth century had been boom years for journalism. Newspaper readership was skyrocketing, reflecting America's exploding population. From 1870 to 1900, the number of daily papers more than tripled, to more than 2,000; so did the number of readers, which now encompassed perhaps 25 percent of the populace. In keeping with the anti-party zeitgeist, the newspapers' party loyalties gave way to an ethic of journalistic independence. Fact-based news supplanted opinion.

These developments capped decades of changes in newspaper history. In the early decades of the republic, papers like Samuel Harrison Smith's *National Intelligencer,* an unofficial organ of administrations from Jefferson's onward, and the *Washington Globe*, run by Andrew Jackson's cronies Amos Kendall and Francis Blair, were unabashed mouthpieces for the parties. But in the 1830s the penny press—one-cent sheets featuring crime stories, human interest articles, and gossip—had found a much wider audience, and after the Civil War, dailies like Pulitzer's *World* and Hearst's *Journal* emerged to satisfy the growing urban audiences, boasting readerships that toward the century's end reached more than a million. Partisanship persisted, but many newspapers fashioned identities independent of the parties that had once funded them. "The ambition of the director of every great political journal," said Whitelaw Reid of the *New York Tribune*, "should be to make his reports, his election returns, every article and item of *news*, so impartial and truthful that his political opponents will accept them as unquestioningly as his political friends."

The new model was epitomized by the *New York Times*, purchased in 1896 by Adolph Ochs, who proclaimed his paper independent of party or cause, devoted to reporting events "without fear or favor." Americans who followed politics now relied less on a party paper's editorials to form their judgments than on ostensibly disinterested, fact-filled news. The age of the editor gave way to the age of the reporter.

Reporters believed that digging up facts benefitted the public. "Facts," said Ray Stannard Baker, "facts piled up to the point of dry certitude, was what the American people really wanted." This cult of facts didn't dictate a posture of pristine disinterestedness or a renunciation of political commitment. On the contrary, many crusading reporters believed that the weight and power of accumulated empirical evidence would persuade readers of the political and moral lessons that their stories carried.[7]

Factual news also brought a surge in reporting from Washington. From 1868 to 1900, the number of correspondents in the nation's capital roughly tripled, from 58 to 171. They formed associations like the Gridiron Club and the National Press Club, marks of a new professionalism. Equally important, they turned their attention from Congress to the White House. In the Reconstruction years, the legislative branch had driven the news agenda. But presidential duties were accumulating, especially with America's rise to global influence. By 1900, a leading political scientist wrote that the president stood at "the front of affairs." Noted Princeton's Woodrow Wilson, "There is no trouble now getting the president's speeches printed and read, every word."[8]

*   *   *

These changes forced McKinley to work with the press corps. He lacked Roosevelt's vitality, his activism, and his obsession with publicity. He never highlighted his role in policy decisions or fed the press personal tales to buff his image. When he granted interviews, reporters gleaned little of substance; he "talked much," said journalist Isaac Marcosson, "and said little." In posing for photographs, he fussed over his appearance without conveying warmth, coming across like a stiff burgher in an oil painting. Nonetheless, the presidency was becoming a choice beat for reporters, and their interest spurred McKinley to find ways to try to exert some influence over them.[9]

He began by opening the White House door a little wider. At the start of his term, Washington correspondent David S. Barry praised the president for having "set a good example by assigning a day for meeting all the representatives of the newspapers at the capital, by attending the dinner of the Gridiron Club . . . and by letting it be known that the reporters are at liberty to call upon him and the members of his cabinet for information on public affairs." Of course, the president still enjoyed a berth of privacy. Ida Tarbell of *McClure's* called it "part of the unwritten law of the White House that the newspaper men shall never approach the President as he passes to and fro near their alcove or crosses the portico to his carriage, unless he himself stops and talks to them." Such bargains between president and press would remain a fixture of the relationship: correspondents followed ground rules, accepting restrictions as a fair price for access to presidential news.[10]

The journalists' access could be seen in the space within the Executive Mansion that McKinley afforded them. The enclave that Cleveland had begrudged them turned into a permanent home. Outside the office of John Addison Porter, McKinley's secretary, reporters huddled at a table to jot down shards of information, making note of the president's visitors, pigeonholing the officials who went by. At noon and again at 4 pm, they met with Porter for a rundown of the day's events.

McKinley called on his tiny staff to help. Much of the work fell to Porter, a former owner of the *Hartford Post*, appointed to the job of White House secretary in an act of patronage. Established in 1857, the secretary's position was an all-purpose one, combining duties later handled by a slew of White House officials, from the chief of staff down to the lowliest functionary. Under Porter, the job came to encompass the care and feeding of journalists. He furnished his charges with information orally and—apparently a new development—in printed handouts. He also gave them advance texts of McKinley's speeches. And because the relationship was, as always, a two-way street, Porter also supervised the clipping of news articles that were passed on to the president for perusal.

But the gentlemanly Porter never relished the work of press management. Aloof, and proud of his Yankee gentility, he lacked a rapport with the correspondents, who in turn ridiculed his regal manners. He seemed less interested in servicing the press corps' needs than in enjoying the social scene, if not in exploring his own future in Connecticut politics. In time, Porter began delegating most of this work to a thirty-five-year-old carryover from the Cleveland administration named George Bruce Cortelyou, who would become the model for every White House press secretary since.[11]

*   *   *

Both talent and luck played their parts in Cortelyou's improbable rise. In November 1895, on a Friday afternoon, President Cleveland mentioned to a group of advisers that he needed a stenographer. "I believe I have in mind the very man you want," volunteered Wilson Bissell, the postmaster general. "He's a handsome young fellow, as smart as lightning, as methodical as a machine, and a gentleman above everything." Cleveland asked Bissell to send this specimen over. The next day, Cortelyou—a former school-teacher and law reporter with two law degrees, then working for the fourth assistant postmaster general—was plucked from the bureaucratic ranks to begin a term of presidential service that would last thirteen years, through three administrations, and take him to the pinnacle of power.[12]

A youthful man with swarthy skin, Cortelyou had strong bone structure, a high, unwrinkled forehead, and deep black hair that began to gray while he was in his twenties. He wore a bluff pompadour, a thick push-broom mustache, and a dandyish wardrobe. As he climbed the ranks in government, he still lunched most days at a small shop opposite the Treasury Building, gulping down buttermilk, biscuits, and apple pie. Inclined to subordinate his own ego to the needs of the men he served, Cortelyou kept secrets faithfully and worked overtime without complaint. Soft-spoken, serious, and reserved—"almost as modest and unassuming as a woman," wrote the journalist O. O. Stealey—Cortelyou shunned speeches, public appearances, and Washington parties. He preferred to exert influence behind the scenes, working late at the White House, sometimes until midnight.[13]

The antithesis of the hacks who once occupied the seats near power, Cortelyou embodied the Progressive ideal of efficiency. He wore two watches, and his house featured a timepiece in each room. "He was perhaps the most competent and most thoughtful man I ever worked with, and he knew every detail of every job in the White House, from janitor to President," wrote Ira R. T. Smith in his memoir of fifty years in the White House mailroom. When Cortelyou died in 1940, his wallet was found to contain an elementary school certificate, signed by the principal, declaring the young Cortelyou to have been "punctual, regular & obedient."[14]

Cortelyou made himself indispensable. When Cleveland left the White House in 1897, he told McKinley, "Whatever changes you make in your official force, hang onto Cortelyou. If I were continuing, I would make him secretary." McKinley created the position of assistant secretary, to which he promoted the young aide. In that role Cortelyou handled correspondence, booked the schedule, and kept the president focused on vital business.

With the run-up to the Spanish-American War in 1898, that business multiplied. "We suddenly had become a world-power," Cortelyou recalled, "and international questions that were formerly unusual events in one administration became almost weekly occurrences. President McKinley was not merely absorbed; he was engulfed." The haul of mail jumped, on some days to 1,500 pieces. As the crisis deepened, Porter and Cortelyou met regularly with the president, hashing out the statements to dole out to the mobs of thirty or forty reporters massing on the White House porch, in the foyer, and on the stairs. For the first time, a president was handing out news to reporters on a daily basis.[15]

As Cortelyou soothed tempers and stroked egos, he realized that the reporters' intense coverage of White House activities gave the administration a chance to shape the news. McKinley held nightly meetings with his cabinet, and when the secretaries left the White House, even at late hours, journalists tailed them, soliciting tidbits before rushing to file their stories. Privately, Cortelyou griped that the "yellow press" recounted nonexistent meetings or fabricated intrigues. Yet he knew that the daily routine allowed the president to put his slant on the day's events. He let reporters know that the president was cool under fire, and that any intervention would have to wait until all the facts were known. Even as the jingoes howled, Cortelyou's clipping books filled up with editorials extolling the president's prudence.

After Congress declared war in April, McKinley created a White House War Room—that name was used—replete with twenty-five telegraph keys, fifteen telephones, and maps tacked to the wall. "In all the movements of the army and navy, the president's hand is seen," Cortelyou noted in his diary. Relying on the telegraph and telephone, McKinley communicated directly with military personnel in Cuba while collecting maps, charts, and data from the battle zones. He also suppressed news when necessary. Amid July peace talks with Spain, as dozens of scribes lingered at the White House for hours waiting for updates, Cortelyou provided only a terse report that the latest exchanges with Spain would remain secret.[16]

The war's end did not diminish the interest in presidential news. War-related scandals—complaints about the edibility of Army meat or conditions in military camps—brought reporters not only to the War Department but now also to the White House itself. And because the

United States had effectively assumed Spain's colony of the Philippines, hastening the nation's ascent as a world power, the wartime prerogatives that McKinley had assumed wouldn't easily devolve to Congress.

Cortelyou took the press's escalating demands in stride. He streamlined his operation, preparing copies of presidential statements, and carving out more time for reporters to see the president. His big break came in the spring of 1900, when John Addison Porter, in poor health, resigned. (He would die eight months later, at the age of forty-four, of an intestinal disease.) Cortelyou finally reached the top. The position of secretary, a mere "amanuensis" a half century earlier, according to Fatty Price, one of the first White House beat reporters, had grown into "a position of immense influence and power." The press cheered the promotion. Already their point man, Cortelyou now flowered as, in effect, the first White House press secretary, even though that title wouldn't be used until FDR's day. *Harper's* wrote that the White House under Cortelyou was "better organized than any private business—surely a striking innovation in government service."[17]

Among his projects, Cortelyou regularized the president's communications with reporters, making sure everyone got handouts at once. He organized their correspondence with frightening efficiency. To each request, Cortelyou replied with a shorthand memo, keeping a permanent record of how the request was handled and establishing a "precedent index" and a consistent set of policies. He briefed reporters, on background, giving them reliable information that the president himself was loath to disclose. And he found ways to embargo communications, as with McKinley's 1899 message to Congress, which Cortelyou distributed in advance only to those reporters who pledged confidentiality in writing, with "any violation . . . punishable by a refusal to grant similar courtesies in the future."[18]

Cortelyou also functioned as something close to a presidential speechwriter, overseeing statements by McKinley that were issued to the press. He checked the president's facts, authenticated his quotations, and edited his correspondence. Eventually he matured into a close presidential friend and confidant. He helped care for first lady Ida McKinley, an emotionally fragile and epileptic invalid, and played the piano for the first couple in the evening.[19]

Cortelyou was there, too, on September 6, 1901, in the late afternoon, when Leon Czolgosz, the twenty-eight-year-old son of Polish immigrants, a reader of radical newspapers and the recent victim of a mental breakdown, pointed a short-barreled revolver, concealed in a handkerchief, at

McKinley, who stood in a receiving line in a Buffalo auditorium. Two shots tore into the president's stomach. Cortelyou rested the president in a chair and leaned in. "My wife," moaned the president. "Be careful, Cortelyou, how you tell her—oh, be careful."

Over the next eight days, the fifty-eight-year-old McKinley fought for his life in Buffalo—doctors dared not transport him to Washington—as gangrene and infection ravaged his body. Cortelyou, the only person besides the first lady admitted to the president's sickroom, became, *Harper's* wrote, "the acting President of the United States . . . Mr. Cortelyou's name might well appear between those of President McKinley and President Roosevelt." On September 14, when McKinley died, Cortelyou was on hand in the darkening room to hear him bid Ida farewell.[20]

When Roosevelt became president, he brought with him his own aide-de-camp from Albany, William Loeb, whom he would eventually make secretary. But TR wasn't blind to Cortelyou's skills. Less than a month passed, reported the *New York Tribune*, before the president was "leaning on Mr. Cortelyou's advice, good judgment, and tact quite as much as did President McKinley before him." He rapidly became, wrote David Barry, "the most effective tool in Mr. Roosevelt's kit."[21]

3

THE RISE OF PUBLIC OPINION

THEODORE ROOSEVELT WAS able to build his public presidency on the foundations laid by McKinley and Cortelyou because he grasped how powerful public opinion had become in political life. "No president ever took the public into his confidence or made his appeal to the public through the press as does President Roosevelt," wrote the journalist William Wolff Smith in 1905. "The public appreciates the fact and it makes him more popular—the direct method is Rooseveltian." More than any predecessor, TR tried to harness the people's will behind reforms that he believed to be in the national interest. This was as significant a change as any in the development of the modern presidency.[1]

When Roosevelt took office, the meaning of *public opinion* was in flux. Historically, in democratic societies, the term referred to the views of the bourgeoisie or the well-educated—distinct from popular sentiment, or the untutored predilections of the rabble. But in the nineteenth century, the expansion of education, literacy, newspaper readership, and voting rights narrowed the gap between the bourgeoisie and the wider populace. The British scholar James Bryce wrote that whereas in Western Europe public opinion encompassed the judgment of the set that "wears black coats and lives in good houses," in the United States it was "the opinion of the whole nation, with little distinction of social classes."[2]

Views about public opinion fell upon a continuum. Conservative thinkers considered the new mass public opinion to be little different from older
notions of the "mob," which was emotional, unreasoning, and vulnerable
to demagoguery. These men favored limiting the masses' power through
immigration restriction and literacy tests for voting. At the other end of
the spectrum, socialists and populists idealized the democratic hordes as
the repository of wisdom. In the middle stood moderate Progressives like
Roosevelt, who wanted to honor the democratic imperative to heed the
popular will while ensuring that it was nurtured and guided by society's
leaders.

*　　*　　*

The man who did perhaps the most to theorize these issues for Progressives was the sociologist Edward Alsworth Ross. Ross was a casual
acquaintance of TR, having met him one summer night in 1892, when the
two men debated the merits of populism at the University of Pennsylvania. TR, at thirty-three already a nationally known figure, had little use
for the farmers' movement, which he considered demagogic. Ross, three
years his senior, harbored a lifelong faith in the virtues of agrarian life. But
while Ross's midwestern Progressivism differed in important ways from
Roosevelt's northeastern variant—and Ross's pacifism contrasted with
Roosevelt's gung-ho militarism—they agreed that government needed to
address economic injustice and that public opinion was needed to legitimize the government's reforms.[3]

Intellectuals like Ross, as much as politicians like Roosevelt, gave Progressivism its lifeblood. Born in the 1850s and 1860s, contemporaries of
TR and Wilson, scholars such as John Dewey, Charles Horton Cooley, and
Robert Park were schooled in the values of science and objectivity espoused
at the fledgling research universities of the day. They made it their project
to explain how people lived and interacted, by studying not only the state
but also institutions, customs, and mores. Along with European counterparts like Ferdinand Tonnies and Emile Durkheim, they invented the
discipline of sociology—a field whose very creation represented a response
to the mass society that they were trying to understand. Their ideas about
society, communication, and group psychology would help politicians like
TR justify and enact the strong presidency, centered on public opinion,
which would alter American political life.

Born in Iowa, Edward Ross was always a farm boy at heart. Six and a
half feet tall, with a lanky frame and a large Easter Island head, he took as

much pride in his physical prowess as his mental abilities. "I was vaunted among farmers," he reflected in his autobiography, "for the way I could slip my pitchfork under a haycock or a wheat shock and toss it onto the wagon." Ross subscribed to the pseudoscientific ideas of the day that ranked "Nordics" at the top of an imaginary racial hierarchy, and he saw his corporeal bulk as a mark of his genetic superiority. His 1936 autobiography detailed his "anthropometric data," from the length of his face to the breadth of his nose. He boasted of having coined the term *race suicide*, the notion that Anglo-Saxon Americans would vanish if immigration continued unchecked, years before TR popularized it—another (regrettable) affinity between the two men.

After college in Iowa, the bookish Ross earned his PhD at Johns Hopkins, which was creating a model for the modern research university. Among his professors were the economist Richard Ely; James Bryce, visiting from Oxford; and Woodrow Wilson. Ross also discovered the writings of Lester Frank Ward, which were overturning the reigning Social Darwinist doctrines that Ross despised for the sanction they gave to "the most odious anti-social practices of private capitalism." Ross adopted Ward as his intellectual mentor and, after he married Ward's niece, a surrogate father. He went on to jobs at Stanford (from which he was let go in a cause célèbre over academic freedom), the University of Nebraska (where he befriended William Jennings Bryan, a neighbor), and the University of Wisconsin. He wrote for *The Atlantic Monthly* and lectured widely. He corresponded with Roosevelt, whose histories Ross cited and whom he extolled as a hero. TR in turn read Ross's scholarship, invited him to a White House conference, and provided an introduction to Ross's *Sin and Society*. One year they spent New Year's Eve together in Oyster Bay.[4]

Ross's journey from the farm to the national stage paralleled the nation's evolution from a *community* to a *society*, to use the terms from Ross's first major work, *Social Control*, a seminal book in Progressive thought. Conceived in a fit of inspiration in a Stanford library alcove in the winter of 1894, and published in 1901, the book aimed to identify the mechanisms that imparted order to modern society and to show how the social concord and moral center that Ross found in the agrarian community, which he said cohered naturally with "living tissue," could be recreated within the industrial, mass society, which was "held together by rivets and screws."[5]

Presaging manifestos like Herbert Croly's *Promise of American Life* and Walter Lippmann's *Drift and Mastery*, Ross's book argued that through purposeful action people could tame the forces producing class strife and social disorganization and shape institutions for their betterment—an idea that underpinned Progressive drives to improve prisons, repair run-down neighborhoods, tutor immigrants, enrich schools, and educate voters. Drawing on a distinctively American optimism, Ross held that the right kinds of "social control" could check predatory capitalism and ease class conflict, creating "the most welfare for the least abridgement of liberty." Public opinion played a crucial role in this process, and to shape public opinion, Ross looked to those he called the "ethical elite." As "the accredited possessors of traditional learning," endowed with "instincts of sympathy and fair play," these intellectual leaders could enlighten society about the wisest values and policies.

Because of his racism, nativism, and fondness for elite leadership, Ross would sometimes in later years be classified as conservative. But most of his ideas were Progressive and egalitarian. He was a fervent Bryanite, a critic of big business, a devotee of the muckrakers, a supporter of Roosevelt and Wilson, and, in his later years, chairman of the American Civil Liberties Union. Ross described the eclipse of the corporate-dominated politics of the 1890s by TR's Progressivism as "sleet . . . giving way to sunshine"; the return of the Old Guard Republicans in the 1920s was the "next Great Ice Age." To the extent that he favored limits of pure democracy, it was "to protect ourselves against the lawlessness, the insolence, and the rapacity of overgrown private interests." The "social" in "social control" was an alternative to control by the state or by the wealthy. It meant the control of the people by the people, of individuals by the society that they constituted.[6]

To ensure the triumph of enlightened opinion, Ross championed free speech. Although he deplored the big newspapers' sensationalism and commercialism and inveighed against the way the press covered "the stock appeals of a political campaign," he argued that the tools of publicity—"press, telegraph, cheap travel, cheap books, free libraries"—could "substitute discussion of principles and policies for petty gossip, and attention to general concerns for attention to private, family, or neighborhood concerns." Rejecting "Flaubert's doctrine that the people is 'an immoral beast,'" he argued instead that "the remedy for the abuses of public opinion is not to discredit it but to instruct it." When anti-alcohol activists emulated Carry Nation by destroying saloons with pickaxes, they were acting as mobs, Ross said. It was public opinion that "quickly intervened to check the spread of the movement."

Ross elaborated these ideas in his later works. "The polling of people on a question when first it comes up brings to light much prejudice, passion, and stupidity," he wrote in *Social Psychology*. "The polling of the same persons after there has been time for free discussion and the maturing of a public opinion, reveals an intelligence and foresight far above that of the average man." Properly guided, therefore, "the decisions of a political democracy may be quite as intelligent as those of an aristocratic society, and at the same time free from the odious class selfishness of the latter."[7]

Though paternalistic, Ross's philosophy was democratic in its desire to lift up the poor and uneducated. Progressives of the day, from sociologists like Cooley and Park to public philosophers like Dewey and Lippmann, agreed that public opinion would benefit from the tutelage of leaders endowed with reason and vision. To teach the public about its own best interests entailed not the devious manipulation of the rabble but a progressive step in the cultivation of mass democracy.[8]

* * *

Progressive politicians shared these ideas. "With almost all that you write I am in full and hearty sympathy," Roosevelt told Ross. "Public opinion, if only sufficiently enlightened and aroused, is equal to the necessary regenerative task and can yet dominate the future."[9]

Just as TR drew strength from the mass public, so he aspired to govern in its interest. Ross said that Roosevelt "gave the public interest such a recognition as it had not had since Lincoln." This view was widely held. When in 1902 Roosevelt broke from presidential custom to settle a major coal strike, the *New York Times* editorialized that he succeeded because of "his perception of what public opinion would sustain and the courage and fairness with which he undertook to satisfy its demands."[10]

Emphatically, this did not mean pandering. "I do not represent public opinion," Roosevelt told Ray Baker. "I represent the public. There is a wide difference between the two, between the real interests of the public and the public's opinion of these interests." At times, TR asserted, a president "must antagonize public sentiment, even if the public sentiment is unanimous." When the public is swept up in a mania, he said, echoing Ross, "it is the duty of the persons whom they have appointed to be the guardians of [the people's] interests to withstand the temporary delusion in order to give time and opportunity for more cool and sedate reflection." To William Allen White, this quality constituted the signal difference between Roosevelt and McKinley. "McKinley went to the people. He was a great follower," White noted. "Roosevelt influences the people. They follow him. He is a leader."[11]

*　*　*

If the public was a source of legitimacy stronger and truer than any faction or party, then speaking to it—shaping it—was indispensable to leadership. This insight underpinned another important practice that TR brought to the presidency. The same nineteenth-century norms that deterred presidential aspirants from trawling for votes among the hoi polloi had also discouraged sitting presidents from making bald appeals to the people. But TR made them. He pitched his arguments "over the heads" of Congress, as it was often said, directly to the voters.[12]

"Most of us enjoy preaching," Roosevelt memorably declared, "and I've got such a bully pulpit!" No president before him made such regular and skillful use of this declamatory vehicle, which Roosevelt, by naming, fairly invented. No president had so acutely discerned or so eagerly seized the opportunity to win public attention with rousing, morally laden speeches. Roosevelt's precursors had given addresses mainly on ceremonial occasions; TR used speeches about policy and legislation to mobilize public opinion—to lead. "The presidency has given to Mr. Roosevelt a far-reaching, megaphone-like Voice," wrote the journalist William Kittle, "raucous and strident indeed, but of high purpose, like the prophets of old." Within a short time, presidents would be expected to promote or defend their programs through direct popular appeals.[13]

Roosevelt's faith in a common good depended on a strong dose of moralism not found in the pragmatic liberalism of later generations; his belief in social improvement was high-minded, hortatory, even messianic. Political problems were, for him, spiritual ones: he inveighed against greedy corporations, excoriated corruption, implored his audiences to improve their character, and championed the manly virtues he held dear. His scorn fell equally upon the "malefactors of great wealth" and the "apostles of discontent"—radicals who whipped up resentment or encouraged violence. Roosevelt damned "real and great evils," "the wicked who prosper," "wolfish greed and vulpine cunning"; he exalted "the eternal principles of right and decency." Herbert Croly compared him to "Thor wielding with power and effect a sledge-hammer in the cause of national righteousness." Audiences, if not blinded, would be "rewarded by certain unexpected gleams of insight."[14]

The stridency, certainly, could grate. "Probably some offended persons see in Roosevelt a kind of masculine shrew who merely storms and frets without purpose or direction," wrote White, who was himself more forgiving. Harsher observers noted that while TR denounced his rivals as demagogues, he often lapsed into demagogic simplifications himself. But Roosevelt, a raging moderate, framed his causes as sensible and judicious, located at a golden mean between extremes. Doing so helped him keep public opinion at his side. He prevailed, White concluded, "because he has taken the right side of a simple issue that people could understand, and always has kept the moral side of that issue before them."[15]

To reach the widest possible audiences, Roosevelt embarked on "swings around the circle," as presidential tours were called. Knowing the excitement that his travels produced, he elevated the old ritual of visiting different regions into a modern publicity device. He traveled to New England and the Midwest in 1902, the South in 1905, and even abroad—a first for any U.S. president—to Panama in 1906, to publicize his plans for a transoceanic canal. A 1903 western swing was especially ambitious: for nine weeks Roosevelt traversed 14,000 miles, delivering 265 speeches in some 150 cities and towns. Large crowds turned out. In Colorado, TR wrote of "processions, masses of school children, local Grand Army posts; sweating, bustling, self-conscious local committees; universal kindliness and friendliness; little girls dressed up as Goddesses of Liberty." Packed into local halls, audiences jumped to their feet to cheer.[16]

The turnout testified to Roosevelt's personality more than to any silver-tongued grandiloquence. "He had a style that did not lend itself to moving oratory," his friend Oscar King Davis gently remarked. Untrained in rhetoric, Roosevelt lacked the classical orotundity of Bryan or the professorial polish of Wilson. Because of his boyhood asthma, he never learned to "speak enough from the chest," as he once wrote his mother, "so my voice is not as powerful as it ought to be."[17]

He compensated with sheer vigor. He spoke quickly and confidently, in a steady, determined tempo. (Ever keen to reach the masses, TR recorded some of these speeches on wax cylinders for popular distribution.) His incongruously high-pitched voice often climbed into the upper register—reaching a comical falsetto ("Dee-lighted!") when he harpooned a point. Upton Sinclair, who never forgot his first White House meeting with TR, once explained how to mimic him: "You must recite the discourse with slow emphasis, showing your teeth, and hitting the table at a separate thump at each accented syllable: 'The most in-nate-ly and es-sen-tial-ly mal-e-vo-lent scound-rel that God Al-might-y ev-er put on earth!'" His gestures were jerky—smacking his open left palm with his right fist, thrusting out the finger of an extended arm from the rear platform of a train, or grasping the occasional prop for illustration. But this lack of inhibition gave his presence a winning charm. And he fully exploited his expressive face, running through a gamut of emotions as he narrowed and widened his eyes and bared his gleaming teeth.[18]

Roosevelt disdained the classical style not just because he lacked the skills but also because he had no interest in leading listeners through the kind of long, discursive reasoning characteristic of nineteenth-century debate. A punchier modern style fit his personality and his message. "Make your point as clear as possible," he wrote, "and thrust the steel well home." Aware of the influence of the mass circulation newspapers, TR also favored brevity so as not to be misquoted. "I try to put the whole truth in each sentence," he explained to Lincoln Steffens, noting how "one sentence quoted without context can be made to stab back and hurt me." Over the years, he contributed a stream of pithy slogans to the lexicon, from "Speak softly and carry a big stick" to "My hat's in the ring" to the name he gave to his agenda, the "Square Deal." That phrase's succinctness inspired his activist successors similarly to name their agendas, reinforcing the idea of the White House as the cockpit of national policy making.

When speaking, he fed off the crowd's energy. "If you desire an idea of the way in which Roosevelt's admirers admired him," recalled Charles Willis Thompson of the 1912 presidential campaign, "you may get it from the fact that by the time he reached Oklahoma on the way back, the single suit of clothes which he brought with him had been nearly wrecked by the frenzied crowds." A woman in Joplin, Missouri, had torn his coat from the armpit down on the right side; in Tulsa an excitable man ripped the left; other fans were soon grabbing for swatches as souvenirs. "When I get back to Oyster Bay," TR concluded, "the only thing I can do with this coat is to burn it."[19]

* * *

The chief criticism of Roosevelt's presidency was that his rhetoric was unmatched by action, that his denunciation of the trusts led to meager substantive reform. Though the charge had some merit, Roosevelt did on several notable occasions convert words into policy. His most potent use of the pulpit came in 1905 and 1906 on behalf of regulating the railroads, among the most formidable of the Gilded Age business behemoths.

For decades Americans in the Midwest and West lived at the mercy of the railroads, which, by handling long-distance shipping, effectively set crop prices and land values, and otherwise dominated the economies of rural America. Investigative journalists had exposed deceptive and corrupt practices, from favoritism to price-fixing, but courts had mostly sided with the railroads, whittling away the power of the 1887 Interstate Commerce Act to curb them. TR meant to pass a historic bill—not a government takeover of the rails, as some desired, but a means to check their power. Representative William Hepburn, an Iowa Republican, sponsored a bill that, among its many provisions, gave the Interstate Commerce Commission the power to cap railroad rates. But with pro-business forces dominating the Republican Party, TR faced a tough fight, especially in the Senate. He devised a series of stratagems to rally public opinion—one of the first cases of a president using his full arsenal of tools of persuasion and mobilization to achieve his legislative goals.[20]

One tool was the press. For more than a year, TR kept railroad regulation in the headlines by releasing reports and announcing investigations of railroad malfeasance. Between January and mid-March of 1906, he garnered eleven front-page stories on the subject in the *New York Times* alone. He marshaled support from editorialists and magazine reporters. Ray Baker, who consulted with TR throughout the railroad fight, contributed a five-part exposé to *McClure's*, which the president, reading the pre-publication galleys, said inspired "two or three thoughts for my own message." Another TR ally, Harry Beech Needham, writing for Walter Hines Page's *World's Work*, reprimanded the Old Guard Republican senators who were impeding passage of a regulatory bill. "It is not hazardous to say that the president's underlying idea has very steadily gained public favor," Needham wrote, reflecting Roosevelt's spin if not the actual state of popular sentiment; "and it is a safe prediction some bill, which shall embody this underlying idea, will become law—if not during this Congress then during some other."[21]

Roosevelt also undertook public speaking tours, beginning in January 1905 in Philadelphia, continuing through the Midwest and Southwest in April and May, and finally, in October, making his pitch across the Southeast, which held the balance in the fight. The spectacle of a northeastern Republican president touring the South made headlines—an angle TR played up with gimmicks like calling on Stonewall Jackson's widow. Judging from press reports, Dixie now adored TR as much as the North. In Raleigh, the president was made a "guest of the city," his carriage given pride of place in a parade. In Atlanta, 12,000 schoolchildren lined Peachtree Street, the main thoroughfare, tossing bouquets and trilling patriotic songs. Roosevelt hammered home his theme of regulation as an alternative to government ownership, positioning his Square Deal as the essence of moderation. "Actual experience has shown that it is not possible to have the railroads uncontrolled," he argued. Fair and just regulation, he said to bursts of applause, was in the interest of the big shipper as much as the small shipper, the railroad owner as much as the consumer. "No President—not even Jackson when he defied the power of the National Bank—has ever before initiated a struggle with powers so strong as those which President Roosevelt now summons to a trial of strength before Congress and at the bar of Public Opinion," said *The Washington Post*. Unrelenting, Roosevelt returned to the issue in his December 1905 message to Congress.[22]

The railroads struck back. Professional public relations firms were on the rise, and the railroads were quick to exploit these new hired guns. Baker, in *McClure's*, revealed an elaborate strategy—"the most sweeping campaign for reaching and changing public thought ever undertaken in this country"—that relied on a Boston-based outfit called the Publicity Bureau to thwart the intended reforms. The firms spent lavishly on newspaper ads, commissioned articles, and circulated supportive speeches.

But popular opinion was running in TR's favor, or so it seemed to those in Washington gauging the public mood. In February 1906, the House passed the Hepburn bill, 364 to 7, and eyes turned to the recalcitrant Senate. Sensing the limits of his bully pulpit, TR worked out a compromise that empowered the Interstate Commerce Commission to set maximum rates but let the courts review the commission's decisions. The revised bill sailed through the upper chamber in May, and Roosevelt signed a reconciled version the next month.[23]

Not everyone thought the bill went far enough. Roosevelt himself conceded it was imperfect. But the Hepburn Act began the taming of the railroads and furnished an important precedent for federal agencies to act in the public interest. Friends and foes agreed that it would never have passed without Roosevelt's leadership. "He believed that if he got the people," remarked Henry Stoddard, "he was certain to get the politicians."[24]

4

"THE FAIR-HAIRED"

FOR ALL HIS MORAL FERVOR, for all his bravado, Roosevelt understood that the activist presidency he desired required more than lung power. He would have to contend with not only Congress and the public but another influential group—an institution, really. Roosevelt had come to believe that mass circulation newspapers and magazines were indispensable to disseminating his message. "No other body of our countrymen," he said, "wields as extensive an influence as those who write for the daily press and for the other periodicals."[1] Having charmed reporters as police commissioner in New York, as a soldier in Cuba, and as governor in Albany, he relished the presidential task of courting the Washington press corps as well.

Roosevelt's dexterity with the press was apparent from his first day in the White House. Hours after McKinley's burial, he summoned the three leading wire service reporters to the Executive Mansion. As recounted by David Barry, who was running the *New York Sun*'s wire service, the men sat around the Cabinet Room table as Roosevelt prattled on. The president promised that he would be accessible and candid, but only if the journalists used discretion in publishing what he told them. Anyone who broke his trust would be cut off. Barry tried to protest against this high-handedness, but TR, more amused than offended, brushed past the objection. He ended the meeting with a toothy grin. "All right, gentlemen," he declared, "now we understand each other."

A mix of charm and imperiousness marked Roosevelt's dealings with reporters for the next seven and a half years. An avid reader of papers and magazines, he believed they played a vital role in shaping public opinion. But he also knew that with the advent of news reporting, the journalists' influence now stemmed more from the information they delivered, and the way their news columns framed the issues, than from the opinions they proclaimed. All this strengthened the president's hand. As newspapers lost some of their power to shape readers' opinions, politicians could do so instead. "President Roosevelt," Barry said, "knew the value and potent influence of a news paragraph written as he wanted it written."[2]

TR thus cultivated newsmen with enthusiasm and calculation. He befriended them and sought their advice. He learned details about their families; Isaac Marcosson was floored when Roosevelt told him how the teenage sons of his boss, editor Walter Hines Page, were faring in college. ("How the President learned that Walter H. Page had two boys at Harvard, and furthermore, how they were getting along, was a mystery to me," wrote Marcosson.) Some reporters got personal notes that teemed with praise or catalogued an article's mistakes. Others received letters coaxing them into writing things TR thought it impolitic to state himself.[3]

Even independent-minded newsmen succumbed. One October day Ray Baker received in the mail proofs of Roosevelt's upcoming message to Congress, along with a request for confidential comments—a bald-faced cooptation that left Baker, he confessed, with "deep joy and satisfaction." "Many a journalist of national standing," wrote Norman Hapgood, editor of *Collier's*, "was cured of amused or serious criticism by the radiance shed on him . . . by the White House."[4]

If he didn't impress reporters with his letters, Roosevelt won them over by force of personality. "I first met him in the White House," recalled Will Irwin, who wrote for the *Sun*. "As he advanced toward me, clicking his teeth so violently that I was afraid he would break them, extending his hand with a motion like that of a heavyweight wrestler grabbing for a hold, I marveled that any human frame could store and exude such energy." William Allen White's first encounter with TR bordered on the biblical: "I was afire with the splendor of the personality that I had met, and I walked up and down our little bedroom at the Normandie [Hotel] trying to impart . . . some of the marvel that I saw in this young man." Rudyard Kipling recalled sitting with the president at Washington's Cosmos Club, where he waxed orotund. "I curled up on the seat opposite," Kipling noted, "and listened and wondered until the universe seemed to be spinning around and Theodore Roosevelt was the spinner."[5]

TR developed practices to shape his message and his image, many of which became staples in the presidential bag of tricks. He discovered that releasing bad news on Friday afternoons could bury it in the little-read Saturday papers, while offering good news on languid Sundays could capture Monday's headlines. He leaked information to reporters, floating "trial balloons" by whispering possible future plans to select reporters under the protection of anonymity; the reporters then tested the fallout without the president having to declare his course publicly. TR also studied the presence, or absence, of cameras at events. He once delayed the signing of a Thanksgiving proclamation until the Associated Press photographer arrived. Without a picture, the story would be unlikely to make the front page.[6]

He could go out of his way to please reporters. On trips, Charles Willis Thompson wrote, Roosevelt "seemed to sense the immense amount of toilsome and unnecessary work the reporters have to do," and "after a speech he would round us up" and tell the press pack whether his next remarks contained any news. He made sure that the local honchos who welcomed him extended their hospitality to the reporters as well. And when Roosevelt renovated the White House in 1902, he upgraded the shabby press room, creating more space, installing telephones, and fostering an esprit de corps among the press.[7]

Most heady of all were Roosevelt's informal news conferences, the first held by a president. TR would ask five or six reporters—his "newspaper cabinet," as he called them; or "the fair-haired," as others said with derision—to join him in the afternoon in a small room next to his office. There, a Treasury Department messenger who moonlighted as the barber-in-chief groomed Roosevelt as he held forth on politics, policy, and gossip. Frequently, in mid-shave, the excitable president would spring out of his armchair, lather flying off his face, to lecture the newsmen on an issue. Walter Clark of the *Sun*, writing to a colleague of his "bully long confab with Teddy," gushed: "I wish I had time to tell you all the funny things he said; he talked a blue streak even while the barber was shaving him." Barely able to squeeze in a word, let alone a question, the journalists devised stratagems to assert themselves. Steffens would let Roosevelt ramble until the barber's razor skimmed his lower lip, forcing it shut; then the journalist fired off his queries, as the president, wriggling in his chair, would be stilled by the barber's admonition: "Steady, Mr. President." "A more skillful barber never existed," declared Louis Brownlow, a young reporter who would later work for FDR.[8]

In these "séances," as they were called, and in other meetings, Roosevelt strictly limited the ways reporters could use his words. As he had in Albany, he placed almost everything he said off the record (not to be used at all) or on background (the president would not be quoted), unless otherwise noted. Paradoxically, these rigid rules enabled TR's candor: since he felt confident that his words wouldn't come back to haunt him, he could carry on uninhibitedly, and his sessions became masterpieces in self-serving disclosure. "No man ever talked more freely to reporters," said Thompson—"not for publication."[9]

Roosevelt didn't hesitate to reward those who truckled to him or to punish those who crossed him. With equal parts humor and gravity, Roosevelt created the "Ananias Club," named for a Christian biblical figure who dropped dead after lying to the apostle Peter; TR awarded membership to reporters he felt had violated his trust. The president wasn't above barring a paper's whole staff from the White House press facilities, as he did when a *Boston Herald* reporter wrote that the mischievous Roosevelt boys had tortured a Thanksgiving turkey. (The punishment extended to the *Herald*'s meteorological reports, which were forbidden from using the federal weather bureau in Boston.) Roosevelt had his secretaries send the offenders' names to the cabinet departments, lest the reporters try to bypass the White House and get their information elsewhere. His most severe retaliation against a newspaper came in 1908, when he sued Joseph Pulitzer and his *New York World* for accusing him of lying and corruption. (Pulitzer's charges were unfounded, but the libel case was tossed out.) Roosevelt insisted that he punished only those who published falsehoods or broke their word. But sincere differences of opinion or interpretation, seen through Roosevelt's pince-nez, inevitably became matters of truth versus lies.[10]

Worse, TR had no qualms about falsely denying that he had said things that he simply wished to disavow. Once, a Parisian visitor cabled home a juicy string of presidential comments, only to have TR deny that he had ever spoken to the Frenchman. Later, the president admitted to a confidant, "Of course I said it, but I said it as Theodore Roosevelt and not as the President of the United States!" In the face of such practices, some reporters took to interviewing Roosevelt only in groups, trusting that their colleagues would vouch for their veracity—sacrificing scoops for security.[11]

As reporters established themselves as independent of party politics, and as presidents assumed a more activist role, their criteria for judging what merited publication diverged. Reporters had to consider not only the accuracy of their information but also its newsworthiness—its importance to the public, the interest it held for readers. Presidents, in contrast, had to consider whether publication would advance or retard their goals, whether in war, diplomacy, policy making, or politics. These distinct institutional perspectives inevitably produced conflicts. In the years ahead, the relationship between presidents and the press would fluctuate between conflict and cooperation, with friendly gab sessions and mutual assistance giving way to clashes over what news to present and how to present it.[12]

* * *

Assisting Roosevelt in supervising the press was the redoubtable George Cortelyou. In 1902, TR gave his aide responsibility for all executive branch communications—a leap forward in the centralization of information. This step had the added benefit of preventing cabinet secretaries and other agency heads from putting out messages at cross purposes with Roosevelt's own. Although some took Cortelyou's expanded role to signal the advent of a "White House press agent," TR saw it simply as a way "to correct," as one newspaper wrote, "misinformation about White House affairs that has given authorities there much trouble."[13]

Eventually, the policy of silencing other executive branch officials proved impossible to sustain, and Roosevelt deployed Cortelyou's talents elsewhere. He promoted him first to run the Department of Commerce and Labor, then to head the Republican National Committee and TR's 1904 presidential campaign, and finally, in the second term, to be postmaster general and then Treasury secretary. By 1908, the former stenographer to the fourth assistant postmaster was a contender for the GOP presidential nomination, though TR ultimately tapped Secretary of War William Howard Taft instead.

In the meantime, TR promoted William Loeb—"the man who has been closest to me politically"—to replace Cortelyou. A tidily dressed veteran of New York politics, with a dimpled chin and piercing eyes, Loeb had thoroughly attached himself to TR in Albany, even mimicking his boss's mustache, pince-nez, and short-cropped hair. Loeb proved a worthy successor to his efficiency-minded boss, making it his task to keep the press operations running smoothly. He expanded Cortelyou's repertoire of publicity techniques, from holding briefings and fielding questions to leaking information. Eventually, he would dress down Cortelyou, then postmaster general, for daring to speak to the press about cabinet meetings. For Cortelyou and Roosevelt alike, old habits died hard.[14]

Loeb also made permanent Cortelyou's practice of issuing daily press releases about the president's activities: bills signed, pardons issued, visitors met, speeches scheduled, positions taken. In time handouts would become routine for all government agencies and treated by reporters with raised eyebrows, if not yawns. But in these years, the novel device gave Roosevelt sway over what the reporters wrote. Because competitive reporters were hungrier than ever for news, yet unaccustomed to viewing the handouts as government spin, the press releases became the foundation of many a story. Roosevelt himself sometimes wrote in longhand what he wanted a reporter to publish and saw his own prose, or Loeb's, appear in newspapers verbatim. And because TR barred reporters from quoting from their privileged gab sessions, the handouts became the main source of presidential quotations. This development made the spontaneous, garrulous TR sound oddly practiced and scripted in print, but it gave the president considerable leverage in shaping his message.[15]

The retention of publicity aides, the hammy stunts, the bully pulpit speeches, the courtship of the fair-haired, the séances, the handouts, the stroking, the punishments—Roosevelt was endlessly resourceful in managing his press coverage. Though he believed in government transparency, his regard for it ran up against his expectation that the press portray him precisely as he wished. To outsiders, this contradiction looked like hypocrisy: Roosevelt loved to leak information but raged about unauthorized disclosures, loved to schmooze with reporters but wanted to control what they published, wallowed in publicity but used bad press as an excuse to traduce reporters' freedoms. But while the mercurial Roosevelt was unusually capable of tolerating contradiction and self-deception, these were systemic, not personal, problems; the same conflicts would return under his successors. In the modern era, the presidential desires for publicity and for control would be in constant tension. TR's personality merely magnified the strain.

5

MUCKRAKING AND ITS CRITICS

AS INSTRUMENTAL TO Roosevelt's cultivation of public opinion as the Washington correspondents was another group of political writers who during TR's presidency achieved a rare degree of celebrity and acclaim. In the mass circulation magazines, Lincoln Steffens, Ray Baker, Upton Sinclair, Ida Tarbell, Will Irwin, Charles Edward Russell, and dozens of other journalists sparked support for Progressive reforms with their vivid and often outrageous dispatches from the underbelly of American life. They came to be known by a name that TR gave them, more out of pique than affection: the muckrakers.[1]

Although the White House reporters and the muckrakers weren't wholly discrete groups, significant differences divided them. Beat correspondents like David Barry and Richard Oulahan, as Will Irwin wrote in a critique of the Washington press corps, tended to adopt the viewpoint of their high-placed sources; if not openly sycophantic, they identified with and at times defended those in power. In contrast, the muckrakers positioned themselves as outsiders, critics of the system—even though Steffens, Baker, and several others would appear on any list of TR's favorites. They allied themselves with Roosevelt not because they identified with power but because TR had seized the reins of the Progressive movement in which they believed. Mark Sullivan, who counted himself among the muckraking crowd, said that while his colleagues "kept the pages of the popular magazines glowing with support of Roosevelt's crusades," they "as frequently inspired Roosevelt as they were inspired by him."[2]

The muckrakers' journalism was at first called the "literature of exposure." At length and in detail, its practitioners laid bare the sordid realities of industrial-age life: police corruption, tenement overcrowding, child labor exploitation, crooked political machines. They expected that their charged accounts would jolt the public and the politicians into imposing new laws and regulations. The muckrakers differed among themselves, sometimes feistily, over whether they were first and foremost activists or reporters. Some, like Baker, stressed the primacy of bringing to light the facts, which they believed more or less spoke for themselves. Baker laughed when he saw himself described as a "flaming crusader," since he thought himself anything but. He favored moderation, he told TR—"evolution rather than revolution." Ida Tarbell, too, told Roosevelt, who accused her of encouraging socialism, "that we on *McClure's* were concerned only with facts, not with stirring up revolt." Later in life, she distanced herself from her activist colleagues, who she said "wanted attacks. They had little interest in balanced findings." Yet others in their set, such as Steffens, proudly trumpeted their radicalism. They fully intended for their exposés to serve the cause of remaking the state and society. Stylistically, too, the muckrakers varied. Some wrote in a dry, dispassionate style that suggested an appeal to the record would on its own suffice; others were partial to dudgeon or melodrama. What they all shared was a commitment to journalism as a tool of social change.[3]

The muckrakers' experiences bore out their faith in mass circulation journalism. They owed their large followings not only to their stark snapshots of social injustice but also to their preferred platform: the slick yet affordable magazines, now widely available owing to the advent of cheaper paper. At one third the price of sedate literary monthlies like *The Atlantic*, these ten- or fifteen-cent magazines amassed readers in the hundreds of thousands, and their profits allowed their editors to bankroll time-consuming, heavily researched investigations. On the whole, these magazines weren't uniformly earnest, or deeply analytical, or even terribly ideological. They juxtaposed the muckrakers' toothsome investigative reports, with flashy photography and celebrity puff pieces.[4]

"The outstanding and pre-eminent example of this new journalism," Baker noted, was *McClure's*. Its impresario, Samuel "S.S." McClure, was a compact, blond, mustachioed dynamo, and, according to Mark Sullivan, "the greatest magazine genius America has ever known." Launched in 1893, *McClure's* etched its name in the annals of journalism history with its January 1903 issue containing Steffens's "Shame of Minneapolis," one of the first in a series on municipal corruption; Tarbell's account of the Standard Oil Company's cruel history of exploitation; and Baker's bleak report about strikebreaking Pennsylvania coal miners, which elicited from Roosevelt an invitation to Oyster Bay. "I have wondered if there could have been a more interesting editorial office than ours, one with more of the ozone of great ideas, touch-and-go experimentation, magic success," recalled Baker. "We were all young ... scandalously young." The staff and contributors included Steffens, White, Kipling, Frank Norris, Willa Cather, Stephen Crane, Jack London, and O. Henry, to name only the most famous. Its formula inspired imitators. Soon the newsstands teemed with a half dozen high-quality periodicals, from *Collier's* to *Everybody's* to *The World's Work*, competing to publish tales that might spur readers into demanding ameliorative measures to fix local and national problems. The philosopher William James declared that the leading minds of his day were "passing away from the universities to the ten-cent magazines."[5]

Over time, the muckrakers took on a heroic glow. In their own day, however, some assessments were more restrained. "Often muckraking consists merely in dressing up a public document with rhetoric and pictures, translating a court record into journalese, or writing the complaints of a minority stockholder, a dislodged politician, or a boss gone 'soft,'" admitted Walter Lippmann, who began his journalism career working for Steffens. In truth, muckraking was never far from sensationalism. Its progenitors included the much-maligned yellow journalists of the 1890s, who similarly prided themselves on bringing scandalous secrets to light, though in a less high-minded fashion.

To be sure, the newer genre dwelled on social problems remediable by legislation, where the older form often trained its fire on politicians' sex lives, drinking habits, or other personal failings. But muckraking owed more than its practitioners cared to admit to Hearst and Pulitzer. Both styles used broadly drawn, melodramatic morality tales to grab readers' attention; both invoked the public's "right to know"—a principle enlisted to justify not just self-evidently worthy investigations of corruption but also the prurient fare, which was said to deter transgressors by exposing them to public shame. David Barry, the Washington press corps doyen, wrote that *McClure's* caused more harm than the yellow newspapers, since the public knew the latter to be unreliable, whereas the magazines enjoyed cachet among the educated. "No matter how preposterous a story, let it be given circulation in one of the popular magazines and the public will rise to it like a black bass to a gaudy fly," Barry noted, "whereas in a newspaper . . . it would be turned aside as sensational." Even as muckrakers extolled factual reportage, they delivered lurid stories with pronounced points of view—and, sometimes, egregious bias. Almost as much as the yellow journalists, they could exaggerate, slant material, and deploy loaded language.[6]

Against such sensationalism, calls for journalistic restraint had been issuing forth for more than a decade, including from such intellectuals as Henry James, Charles Dudley Warner, E. L. Godkin, and, most famously, Louis Brandeis and Samuel Warren, whose influential 1890 *Harvard Law Review* article, "The Right to Privacy," decried the ever-expanding zone into which reporters were encroaching. "Instantaneous photographs and newspaper enterprise have invaded the sacred precincts of private and domestic life," the lawyers wrote. "To satisfy a prurient taste the details of sexual relations are spread broadcast in the columns of the daily papers."[7]

Nonetheless, for all its flaws, muckraking did at least as much as Roosevelt's leadership to galvanize public opinion behind reform. By taking middle-class readers into the coalfields and the tenements, the brothels and the back rooms, the investigative journalists of the new century roused Americans from complacency. They didn't always hew to neutral language, but not because their professed regard for scientific inquiry was insincere. They understood, rather, that touching their readers required a skilled and artful presentation of the facts that they had doggedly unearthed. In its own way, muckraking was a form of spin.

*　*　*

Nothing spoke better to the popularity of muckraking than the decision, in 1905, by the king of the yellow press, the forty-two-year-old William Randolph Hearst, to buy *Cosmopolitan*. Still something of a radical, Hearst was eager to promote his causes; always the businessman, he saw profits in a more upscale market. Perhaps most important, Hearst—having been elected to Congress in 1902 as a Democrat and having flirted with a presidential run in 1904—wanted a national platform and a middle-class readership for going after Theodore Roosevelt, a personal rival.[8]

That fall Hearst and Charles Edward Russell, his editor, commissioned David Graham Phillips to write a multi-part takedown of the U.S. Senate, which was justly derided as a "millionaires' club." Before the passage of the Seventeenth Amendment, which required popular election of its members, the Congress's upper chamber happily catered to the interests of the era's plutocrats, frequently blocking Roosevelt's agenda. These Old Guard senators invited the muckrakers' wrath. Hearst's papers had been calling for the direct election of senators for years.

David Graham Phillips, like many muckrakers, wrote fiction as well as journalism, and he had just published a novel, *The Plum Tree*, that portrayed the Senate as a sewer pit of graft. He wrote essays attacking the hold of the wealthy over the political system. In carrying out Hearst's assignment, Phillips channeled his ire at the robber barons and their protectors into acidulous sketches. His first draft was so shrill that Hearst himself had to tone it down. "I had intended an exposé," the publisher told his writer after reading a version of the first installment. "We have merely an attack. Voice is not force. Windy vituperation is not convincing. . . . The facts, the proof, the documentary evidence are an important thing, and the article is deficient in them."

But Hearst wasn't asking for a judicious essay. On the contrary, he hyped Phillips's finished pieces with the garish title "The Treason of the Senate." The first installment appeared in the March 1906 issue of *Cosmopolitan*. From the opening paragraph, which offhandedly called two senators "change-pocket thieves," Phillips stuffed his legitimate critique with hyperbole, name-calling, and ill-founded accusations. He saw no need to put a single insult into a sentence where three might fit. "Depew's public front of light-hearted, superficial jester and buffoon, and his private reputation, and character, of spineless sycophant," Phillips wrote, going after New York's junior senator, "have combined to make him mentally underestimated both by others and by himself." *Cosmopolitan* also illustrated Phillips's polemic with images of Depew's opulent homes and of the senator in his car, as if basking in his own wealth—the last photograph deviously cropped and misleadingly captioned. Promoted with bombastic Hearstian advertisements and press releases, the piece wrought its desired effect: readers snapped up every copy from the newsstands, subscription requests poured into *Cosmopolitan*'s offices, and the magazine's circulation jumped 10 percent. Some later credited the series with mobilizing an outcry for the Seventeenth Amendment.

Among journalists, however, the reaction was mixed. Professional envy surely muted some colleagues' praise; the Washington regulars, fancying themselves responsible professionals, viewed Phillips as an interloper who had let fly with a poor work of reporting, however laudable the goal. David Barry wrote a rebuttal to Phillips entitled "The Loyalty of the Senate." Even some Progressives balked. "For the stark citation of documents that had given convincing force to Miss Tarbell's exposures of railroad rebates," wrote Sullivan, "Phillips substituted—sure sign, in a writer, of haste and paucity of fact—lavish exclamation-points." Despite muckraking's roots in yellow journalism, Phillips's critics wanted to maintain a bright line between their own legitimate exposés and their colleagues' Hearstian dross.[9]

Roosevelt, perpetually stymied by the Senate's naysaying, should have found reason to applaud Phillips's diatribe. "Phillips in his wildest moment never said anything against the 'Old Guard' senators more extreme than I had heard Roosevelt say with his own lips at his own luncheon-table," claimed Upton Sinclair. But the *ad hominem* and hyperbolic nature of the attack on Depew, a personal friend, angered TR. So did several other sensationalistic pieces the president had recently read; they brought out his conservative side, his esteem for stability, moderation, and order. Phillips's broadside struck him as "nothing but a mixture of hysteria and mendacity," as TR wrote, its truthful points vitiated by unjustifiable omissions and misleading implications.[10]

Journalists struggled to explain Roosevelt's unhappiness, given his long-standing support for reform journalism. Ida Tarbell surmised that the president felt the muckrakers were stealing his thunder. Roosevelt had always been both their rival and their ally. Though he believed that they shared his goals, and he was pleased to use them for his ends, he preferred to direct the course and tone of reform, and he had long complained about those he felt went too far. When Phillips's piece appeared, Roosevelt was upset about the gathering strength of the socialist movement, which he believed fed off the wild, unfocused criticism of the American system. Phillips's article was the final straw—a sign that the literature of exposure, for all its utility, needed to be reined in if it were to remain on the side of the angels.[11]

Roosevelt's first riposte came through George Cortelyou, now postmaster general. In a Lincoln's Birthday speech, Cortelyou belittled "a style of journalism" that won readers by "pandering to unholy passions, making the commonplace to appear sensational, fanning the fires of sectionalism and class hatred, invading the privacy of our firesides." But Roosevelt wasn't one to let a surrogate's comments suffice, and on March 17 he used a white-tie Gridiron Club dinner to fire off his own broadside, denouncing "the man with the muck-rake" who "in newspapers and magazines makes slanderous and mendacious attacks upon men in public life and upon men engaged in public work." Not deigning to mention Phillips or any other offenders by name, he left it unclear just how far-reaching he meant his condemnation to be.[12]

Although the Gridiron dinner was off the record, no speech to a roomful of journalists could stay secret for long. Political circles buzzed with talk of Roosevelt's shot at the press. His supporters worried about this uncharacteristic turn, and Roosevelt felt obliged to reassure his covey. Replying to a vexed letter from Baker, TR wrote: "People so persistently misunderstand what I said, that I want to have it reported in full. For instance, you misunderstand it. . . . I feel that the man who in a yellow newspaper or in a yellow magazine"—and here he singled out Hearst's publications—"makes a ferocious attack on good men or even attacks bad men with exaggeration or for things they have not done, is a potent enemy of those of us who are really striving in good faith to expose bad men and drive them from power. I disapprove of the whitewash brush quite as much as of mudslinging, and it seems to me that the disapproval of one in no shape or way implies approval of the other." He also assured Steffens and others that he wasn't displeased with their work. These assurances were at best disingenuous, however, since TR had in fact told others that Steffens and Baker needed to display more restraint.[13]

Roosevelt tried to clarify his views on April 14 at a dedication of the House Office Building on Capitol Hill. But again he only muddied the waters. While the text of his speech was balanced and moderate, full of caveats and qualifications, his irrepressible gusto blotted out any nuance and stoked the controversy. Making explicit a reference to John Bunyan's *Pilgrim's Progress*, he described the "man with the muck-rake" this time as "the man who could look no way but downward with the muck-rake in his hands; who was offered a celestial crown for his muck-rake, but would neither look up nor regard the crown he was offered, but continued to rake to himself the filth of the floor." Baker and others said that the speech made no distinction between responsible and irresponsible muckraking, but—as Jacob Riis, among others, saw more clearly—TR did take pains to state that he supported the press's "relentless exposure . . . of every evil man" and "every evil practice." Calling investigative journalism "often indispensable," he repeated his argument to Baker, that to indict indiscriminate attacks was not to damn all exposés. TR also used the speech to reassert his Progressive bona fides—calling for a progressive tax on "all fortunes" and federal "supervision over corporations engaged in interstate business." These proposals showed that his attack on muckraking hardly signaled a rightward turn in his governance.[14]

A few writers endorsed what one called the president's "impregnable position" of moderation. Sober press corps veterans who looked askance at the muckrakers, like David Barry, praised the speech. Conservatives, though hostile to TR's tax proposals, used his muckraking remarks as a cudgel against investigative journalism. The *New York Sun* gleefully predicted muckraking's demise—a prophecy abetted by the decision by Tarbell, Steffens, Baker, and others to abandon *McClure's* after a falling out with S. S. McClure.[15]

Most of the muckrakers, though, focused on the muckrake passage and took offense—though they would soon convert TR's epithet into a badge of honor. Upton Sinclair griped that the speech "gave great comfort to the reactionaries," and Baker concluded that it would alienate the conscientious journalists and abandon the field to "ranters and inciters." Baker, Steffens, and others started to sour on their hero and to seek out new idols in the years ahead, including Woodrow Wilson. Theodore Roosevelt would not be the last president to begin his tenure with the press corps in his thrall, only to end it in disillusionment and acrimony.[16]

6

IF THERE WERE any doubt in the spring of 1906 about Roosevelt's commitment to Progressive reform, it should have been assuaged by his actions. Not only did he push for progressive taxation and shepherd the Hepburn railroad regulation bill into law; he also spearheaded a historic campaign to clean up the shoddy and predatory practices in the food and drug industries. "Traffic in foodstuffs which have been debased or adulterated so as to injure health or to deceive purchasers," he declared in his December 1905 message to Congress, "should be forbidden." Determined to surmount congressional resistance by enlisting public opinion, he seized on a popular outcry triggered that spring by the reporting of a crusading twenty-seven-year-old socialist with whom, despite profound ideological disagreements, he happily locked arms.[1]

Upton Beall Sinclair wasn't a core member of the group of journalists clustered around *McClure's*, but more than any other, his name would come to epitomize muckraking. His fame derived mainly from the success of *The Jungle*, his melodramatic 1906 novel about the wretched world of Chicago meatpackers, written in the left-wing naturalist style of Jack London and Theodore Dreiser. A best-seller in its day, *The Jungle* made Sinclair rich and famous, and it would grace high school reading lists for a century.[2]

Precocious and eccentric, Sinclair discovered his passion for writing early. At thirteen he enrolled as an undergraduate in City College, at eighteen in graduate school at Columbia. Slender, bony, and pasty in complexion, with spongy lips and deep pools for eyes, the young Sinclair struck his friends as temperamental and romantic. His poems confirmed as much. "I, Upton Sinclair, would-be singer and penniless rat . . . ," began one juvenile foray. In 1902 he came under the tutelage of George Davis Herron, a well-known minister and author, who had helped found the Socialist Party of America. Herron sustained Sinclair financially as he spun out a Civil War novel, *Manassas*, which sold only 2,000 copies but caught the eye of, among others, the editor of *Appeal to Reason*, a Socialist weekly.

Like other muckrakers who wrote fiction, Sinclair did not care if his art read like agitprop. He saw his fiction as kin to his journalism, rooted in reportage and designed to spur social change. To write *The Jungle*, he spent seven weeks in the fall of 1904 in the slaughterhouses and meatpacking plants of Chicago, donning grubby clothes and carrying a lunch bucket to mix in with the immigrant workers whose stories he planned to tell. During the daytime he visited the squalid, lethally dangerous workplaces, documenting the indifference of management to the workers' hardships and the lack of government oversight. In the evenings, he knocked on the workers' doors, his pencil ready to record their accounts.

As a messianic socialist, Sinclair wanted to steer attention to the plight of the exploited Lithuanian immigrants in Packingtown, and the novel he wrote was a frankly melodramatic yarn of desperate working-class life. The passages in the book that caught the popular fancy, however—though they spanned just a few pages—told a more particular story about the meat that Americans were consuming daily. Sinclair described rats scampering across heaps of rotting flesh, leaving droppings; tubercular meat packaged and sold at market; acid corroding workers' flesh; and most shockingly, men tumbling into cooking-room vats and ignored "till all but the bones of them had gone out to the world as Durham's Pure Leaf Lard!" Those gut-churning images would long outlive any ideological message about the workers that Sinclair intended. "I aimed at the public's heart," he later wrote, "and by accident I hit it in the stomach."[3]

The Jungle ran in serial form in *Appeal to Reason*, starting in February 1905. That publication, however, carried neither the weight nor the audience of a magazine like *McClure's*, and Sinclair wanted a larger forum. But the book's socialist catechism, along with fears of a lawsuit—not to mention the implausibility of some of his tales—scared away five different publishing houses. At one point, resolving to publish it himself, Sinclair placed an ad in *Appeal to Reason*, using blurbs from David Graham Phillips and Jack London. (The work, wrote London, "depicts what our country really is, the home of oppression and injustice, a nightmare of misery, an inferno of suffering, a human hell, a jungle of wild beasts.")[4]

Sinclair's ploy brought in a thousand orders, demonstrating a market potential that enticed Walter Hines Page, the genteel editor of Doubleday, Page. But Page wanted to make sure he wasn't party to a hoax; the novel's power rested on its claim to reportorial authenticity. Defending his portrait of Packingtown, Sinclair insisted, "I have not invented the smallest detail." After sending a lawyer to Chicago to verify Sinclair's portrait, Page, "confident that *The Jungle* told the truth," published the book in February 1906—just as "The Treason of the Senate" was hitting newsstands.[5]

The timing was fortuitous. In recent months, other muckrakers, including Ray Baker and Charles Edward Russell, had also taken on the so-called Beef Trust, though they hadn't focused specifically on the bad meat, and their reports lacked Sinclair's stomach-churning vividness. Meanwhile, Mark Sullivan and Samuel Hopkins Adams had been advancing the cause of a food and drugs bill by exposing the fraudulent claims of patent medicines, whose advertisements were ubiquitous in the mass circulation press (and whose regulation TR also sought). Yet *The Jungle* was an altogether different phenomenon. Unharmed by the early doubts and poor reviews, the book became a sensation, translated into seventeen languages. "Not since Byron awoke one morning to find himself famous," wrote the *New York World*, "has there been such an example of worldwide celebrity won in a day by a book as has come to Upton Sinclair." The press hyped the tales from the meatpacking industry, causing sales of meat, industry spokesmen claimed, to fall by one half.

In publishing as in politics, publicity was the order of the day, and Sinclair began a promotional campaign. The author pumped out a round of magazine articles, including "Stockyard Secrets" in the March 24 issue of *Collier's*. In the offices of Doubleday, Page off Union Square in New York Sinclair worked with Isaac Marcosson, who had drifted into public relations work. Marcosson saw that to generate blockbuster sales, the publisher needed to promote not only a book but also its author. He issued a welter of statements and photographs on Sinclair's behalf and made the writer available for interviews. Reporters called, as did theatrical producers and filmmakers, who clamored for the rights to the breakout book.[6]

The publicity campaign also entailed mailing out copies of *The Jungle* to important people—including Roosevelt. As it happened, the president received at least four copies from various advocates of regulation. For good measure, Doubleday sent TR the advance page proofs of three articles from an issue of *The World's Work* substantiating Sinclair's claims— articles designed, Marcosson wrote, to "tell in fact the story that Sinclair thinly disguised as fiction." TR thought little of Sinclair's prose and judged the young man a "crackpot"—another muckraker run amuck. But he shared the novelist's dim view of the meat moguls, and he promised his correspondent: "I shall read it with interest." He followed up with a three-page letter that mocked the young man's "pathetic belief" in socialism while offering a critique of *The Jungle*, replete with disquisitions on the literary merits of Zola, Tolstoy, and Gorki. "The specific evils you point out shall, if their existence be proved, and if I have the power, be eradicated," Roosevelt concluded. He extended an invitation to the White House.[7]

Roosevelt also told Sinclair that he had asked the Agriculture Department to investigate conditions in Chicago. TR thought that if he could confirm even a portion of Sinclair's report, he could galvanize public opinion and force the balky Congress to move on legislation. Roosevelt's strategy worried Sinclair, who feared, as he told the president, that having the Agriculture Department examine the issue "was like asking a burglar to determine his own guilt." Instead, he urged TR to open "a secret and confidential investigation" by a disinterested party. Still, Sinclair wasn't one to decline an invitation to Washington, and on April 4 he took the train down from his home in Princeton for a meeting with the president.

Roosevelt met Sinclair in his White House study. Piles of papers, magazines, and reports lay on the coffee table. *The Jungle* rested beside the president's chair, index cards sticking out from its pages. Next to it lay a copy of "The Treason of the Senate." Roosevelt told Sinclair that he had no affection for the meatpackers, having eaten their bad meat in Cuba during the Spanish-American War. He asked Sinclair his opinion of David Graham Phillips, offered his own scathing judgment of the writer, and finally segued into a rant against the reactionaries in the Senate.

By this point, TR had come to agree that an independent body would indeed be better poised than the Agriculture Department's team to get the full story about the stockyards. Charles Neill, Roosevelt's commissioner of labor and a reliable aide with a Progressive bent, agreed to undertake a second investigation. Roosevelt asked Sinclair to promptly go see Neill and his partner, James Reynolds, who were ready, TR promised, to "do everything you suggest in terms of interviewing witnesses and gathering information."[8]

As Neill and Reynolds began their inquiry, the original investigating committee returned its verdict—rendering, as Sinclair had feared, a low opinion of the novelist's work. Their report made clear the downside of Sinclair's histrionic style. If it could arouse readers with shock and horror, it also lent itself to easy dismissal, owing to its breathless tone. Wilson's investigators did just that, judging *The Jungle* guilty of "willful and deliberate misrepresentations of fact." "In his anxiety to be as sensational and 'yellow' as possible," they said, Sinclair had "selected the worst possible condition which could be found in any establishment as typical." And though they confirmed problems with the meat inspection system, they insisted that the federal government had virtually no power, as the laws stood, to correct them.

By the following week, Sinclair was nervous about the fate of food and drug reform—and his reputation. The meatpackers now had their own publicity campaign in high gear. The *Saturday Evening Post*, whose editor, George Lorimer, had worked for the Armour Beef Company, was running ghost-written articles under the byline of the firm's president J. Ogden Armour, who was bent on quashing the reform bill. Having failed to persuade Frank Doubleday to halt his campaign for *The Jungle*, Armour was now openly attacking Sinclair and asserting that the industry's products contained "not one atom of any condemned animal carcass." Upsetting to Sinclair, too, was an article in the conservative, pro-meatpackers *Chicago Tribune* reporting the Agriculture Department team's anti-Sinclair findings. The *Tribune* added that Roosevelt—who by this point had fired his initial Gridiron dinner salvo at the muckrakers—was preparing to go after Sinclair in a forthcoming speech.[9]

Sinclair panicked. He tried to reach the president by phone; failing to do so, he sent a telegram. Too prudent to attack a key ally at such a delicate moment, Roosevelt assured Sinclair that he planned no rebuke in his forthcoming speech, although in truth he did consider Sinclair guilty of many of the journalistic sins he was assailing. "You *must* keep your head," he wrote, as if to a child. "I intend before I get through to be able to have authoritative reasons for saying 'proved' or 'unproved' . . . of each specific charge advanced against the packers."[10]

Sinclair kept up his publicity campaign. He opened an office in a New York hotel suite, "with two secretaries working overtime," as he recalled. He drafted rebuttals to Armour, which ran in *Everybody's Magazine* and

The Independent, and continued to publish articles about his findings, he wrote, "until I was dizzy."[11]

Roosevelt was equally keen not to lose the war for public opinion, which he expected would dictate the bill's fate. In March, he had personally given marching orders to Charles Neill: "I want to get at the bottom of this matter, and be absolutely certain of our facts when the investigation is through." Now he was awaiting the findings. In late May, Neill and his team provided the president with a bleak picture of putrid conditions and reckless practices in the stockyards—mostly in line with Sinclair's account. Neill described workers spitting or urinating on the floors, workroom surfaces blanketed in dirt and rotten meat, and the reheating of bad meat to be relabeled for sale. Neill couldn't substantiate *The Jungle*'s tales of human workers being processed into lard—Sinclair claimed that the Beef Trust had paid off the victimized families or shipped the widows back to the old country—but the overall verdict was supportive.

For tactical reasons, Roosevelt kept Neill's report under wraps. He wanted to use it as leverage with Congress, leaking hints of its damning details and threatening the release of more in order to pressure the meat industry's patrons. This strategy took time, frustrating the politically naive Sinclair, who wanted the document released, not least to vindicate himself.[12]

Neither man need have worried. Public support for reform was building. With TR's support, Senator Albert Beveridge of Indiana introduced an amendment to the agriculture appropriations bill that imposed stringent rules on meat inspection, including the dating of canned meat, with meatpackers forced to pay the costs. Spurred by the flurry of activity on meat inspection, the Pure Food and Drug bill—which prohibited the adulteration and mislabeling of foods, beverages, medicines and other drugs—also now started to advance, separately, toward passage.

On the defensive, the meatpacking and livestock industries joined forces. They warned that any legitimation of Sinclair's charges would dry up foreign markets for American meat; federal regulation, moreover, would shift control of the industry from the businessmen with the relevant know-how to "theorists, chemists [and] sociologists," as one spokesman warned. When it became clear that some version of the bill was likely to pass, the industrialists switched to trying to strip out the bill's most stringent provisions. The beef companies even placed newspaper ads inviting readers to visit the packinghouses and judge conditions for themselves.

While the battle raged on Capitol Hill and in the press, Sinclair gave in to his impatience. On the evening of Sunday, May 27, he walked into the office of *New York Times* editor Carr Van Anda with a briefcase containing letters, affidavits, and other materials that Neill and his team had collected. Van Anda promptly sat Sinclair down for several hours with two *Times* stenographers, and by 1 am a story was ready for Monday's paper. Roosevelt, who read it the next day, erupted at Sinclair for his "utterly reckless statements." But he proceeded to make Neill's full report public, sending it to the House with an urgent call to pass the Beveridge amendment and its meat inspection provisions.[13]

The beef industry had been routed in the court of public opinion. As the packinghouses literally whitewashed their facilities as part of a desperate cleanup job, press reports grew withering. The *New York Evening Post* captured the mood in doggerel: "Mary had a little lamb/And when she saw it sicken/She shipped it off to Packingtown/And now it's labeled chicken." Before a House committee, Neill and Reynolds rehearsed with great fanfare their gory findings, including an account of a pig carcass that fell into a urinal before getting hung, unwashed, in a cooling room.[14]

House conservatives made a defiant stand, and Roosevelt and Beveridge ultimately made some concessions. But the Indiana senator proclaimed the final bill "the most pronounced extension of federal power in every direction ever enacted." As with the Hepburn bill, its achievements outshone its deficiencies, and it established important standards and precedents. On June 30, Roosevelt, with a stroke of the pen, made meat inspection the law of the land—and with another stroke signed into law the Pure Food and Drug Act. "In the session that has just closed," he said to the press, "the Congress has done more substantive work for good than any Congress has done at any session since I became familiar with public affairs."[15]

The episode confirmed Roosevelt's support, philosophically and practically, for the journalism of exposure, despite his trumpeted disdain for its excesses. With William Allen White he shared his view of Sinclair: "I have an utter contempt for him," TR wrote. "He is hysterical, unbalanced, and untruthful. . . . Nevertheless, in this particular crisis he was of service to us."

The meat inspection episode showed the president's skill not only at discerning public opinion aroused by the press but also at using statements, leaks, and the cultivation of journalists to pass his agenda. Riding public opinion to legislative victory was becoming a Roosevelt trademark. In an article hailing "The Reign of Public Opinion," Lincoln Steffens called it "the real power behind Theodore Roosevelt." Congressmen submitted to the presidential will, Steffens said, because he was "the leader of public opinion," and they feared popular retribution if they defied him. Even Sinclair, who wanted a much stronger bill than the final compromise, praised TR: "He took the matter up with vigor and determination, and he has given it his immediate and personal attention from the very beginning."[16]

Sinclair himself received ample credit, too. "It would be difficult to overrate the influence of 'The Jungle' by Upton Sinclair," wrote a journalist in *The Arena*, in 1909. "It led to immediate investigation and legislation by the national government." With book sales booming, the young writer became a wealthy man. A few years later he would play himself in a movie version of *The Jungle*. A prosperous career flowed from the success of his socialist melodrama. Still, he could not help noting with a hint of regret that the press had turned out to be more interested in his celebrity than in the plight of the luckless Lithuanian stockyard workers.[17]

7

THE DAWN OF PUBLIC RELATIONS

BENJAMIN RYAN TILLMAN, known as "Pitchfork Ben," was a six-foot-tall Democratic senator from South Carolina who had earned his nickname by threatening to spear President Grover Cleveland with a farm implement. At fifty-eight, he was an imposing man, with short, tousled hair, pudgy cheeks, and a face marred by an empty left eye socket—the eye having been extracted when he was seventeen because of a tumor. Known for his brusque manners, populist politics, and racist demagoguery, he had nursed a hatred for Theodore Roosevelt ever since the president withdrew a White House invitation as punishment for Tillman's manhandling of a Senate colleague.

On January 17, 1906, at half past noon, Tillman strode to the Senate floor. Reporters crammed into their allotted rows, and the galleries were packed to the last seat with spectators. Not a legislator was absent. For a week, Washington had been abuzz with talk that the hotheaded senator was planning to attack the president. No one dared miss it. As one contemporary wrote, "Going up to the Senate to hear Tillman make a speech was like running to a fire."

A rousing orator of the old school, Tillman plunged into a two-and-a-half-hour tirade against the president. Interrupted only a few times by colleagues beseeching him to temper his remarks, he slammed TR for a series of alleged offenses, from his Dominican policy to the recent ejection of a visitor from the White House. He hit his stride, however, when he got to what he deemed the president's cardinal sin: his unquenchable hunger for publicity. The president, Tillman told the galleries, was a sham, a self-promoter who had exaggerated his achievements ever since the Spanish-American War. "He had press agents with the Rough Riders down at Guantánamo," Tillman sneered. He dug up the old charges about TR's inflated heroics in Cuba, charging that the "grand painting" by the Russian painter Vasili Vereshchagin showed Roosevelt "on horseback riding up San Juan Hill, when as a matter of fact he was not on San Juan Hill at that time."[1]

The audience sat spellbound. Even the reporters, one of their number noted, "became infected with the prevailing feeling of suppressed and almost hysterical excitement." Tillman roared on. "Theodore Roosevelt owes more to newspapers than any man of his time, or possibly of any other time," he thundered. He recited TR's practices for shaping his news coverage—stiffing unfriendly reporters, muzzling cabinet officials, using the White House secretary to drug the press with his talking points on Panama, railroad rates, and "everything pertaining to public affairs." TR's claim to be in tune with the public was bogus. "The newspapers are the men who have made him what he is," explained Tillman, because "he has never had the opportunity in all his journeyings and speeches to meet more than one in a thousand of his fellow-citizens, and it is through the great instrumentality represented in that press gallery that he has become puffed to such a degree."

This was more than a grudge. Tillman had watched with alarm the steady shift in power from Congress to the presidency. In the Jeffersonian tradition, he considered limited executive authority to be sacrosanct. TR's manipulation of the press, Tillman charged, enabled his arrogation of power and made him no different from "Andrew Jackson or Napoleon Bonaparte"—a monarch or a tyrant. However overwrought, Tillman's argument against presidential publicity—a critique of the way that mass media dangerously enhanced executive power at the expense of Congress or other countervailing institutions—would recur through the decades.

If the root of Tillman's frustration was the eclipse of Congress by the presidency, though, the proximate cause was one particular recent episode. Tillman referred to it in passing when he blasted TR for retaining a "trusted friend, at $10,000 a year, to misinform the public about the administration of Panama Canal affairs." The friend was Joseph Bucklin

Bishop, whom Roosevelt had named to be secretary for his Panama Canal project, making Bishop the first dedicated government public relations officer. That appointment triggered a furor over the government's use of information officers, the contours of which would reappear under virtually all of his White House successors.[2]

It started with Roosevelt's battles against the railways and corporations. Early in his second term, he had become fed up with the publicity campaigns they mounted to block the Hepburn bill and other regulations, and when he announced his plan to build a canal through Panama, the railroads, fearing a loss of business, tried to stop that project too. TR concluded he needed a countercampaign to combat the railroads' distortions. To this end he hired Bishop, a friendly journalist for the *New York Globe*. Bishop shared Roosevelt's view of his assignment as a benign charge to simply air the facts. "I give out the situation as it is," he said. But Bishop soon found himself in the predicament that would bedevil other public relations officials. What he and his patron considered a neutral provision of information—or a counterweight to partisan misinformation—struck others as self-serving and selective, if not outright dishonest.

Some of these critics were journalists, who were developing norms of objectivity and independence that made them leery of government-proffered news. Reporters accused Bishop of "withholding the truth" and "evasions and suppressions." TR's political foes also took issue with Bishop's hiring. When in December the House took up funding the canal, Congressman John Fitzgerald of New York questioned Bishop's appointment, and the Senate Appropriations Committee called him to testify. Coached by TR, Bishop defended his role as reasonable, even anodyne. For a time he seemed to disarm, or at least exhaust, what *The Washington Post* described as "sharp questioning." Two days later, however, during the floor debate, Tillman renewed the assault. The only reason Roosevelt might want to retain a public relations officer, he charged, was for "hypnotizing public opinion," by spreading "slander and abuse and misrepresentation and lying."[3]

Roosevelt feared he was losing the fight. He sent word to the Hill that if Bishop could remain as secretary to the Panama Canal Commission, the duties of handling the press could be deleted from the job description. A deal was struck. Bishop was allowed to assume his post without being called a publicist. Although wrangling continued for many months, Roosevelt's concession had been relatively painless. Bishop continued as before to provide information to the press—only without being labeled a public relations officer.

The Bishop controversy highlighted a budding backlash against TR's publicity machine. Some complaints amounted to little more than routine carping from reporters. "It is becoming more difficult to get uncolored news," Walter Clark lamented, "yet the press agency feature of the executive departments was never so active." Others came from partisans: J. J. Dickinson, a Bryan devotee, branded the press corps "cuckoos" who kowtowed before the president—allowing Roosevelt to pour "into the public mind and imagination the thoughts that seethe and sizzle in his own, so that when the time for action arrives, he has the battle more than half won." (Dickinson would display no such compunctions during the Wilson administration, when he conspired with German propagandists.) Still others voiced the privileged resentments of the business class. Corporate attorney Roswell Benedict penned a diatribe charging that TR plotted with "his cringing newspaper followers" to circumvent Congress and "deceive the public into moods favorable to his schemes."[4]

Such critiques were not surprising. TR's commitment to press management led him not only to hire Bishop, not only to set Cortelyou and Loeb to work on his behalf, but indeed to support other executive branch publicity campaigns, most controversially his friend Gifford Pinchot's aggressive salesmanship on behalf of the U.S. Forest Service's policies, which, not coincidentally, also served to remind the public of TR's passion for conservation. Precisely at this moment, too, observers were awakening to the role of public relations throughout American culture—from Mark Hanna's campaigns on McKinley's behalf to Sinclair's flogging of *The Jungle*, from big business's anti-regulatory efforts to TR's Square Deal proselytizing. Certainly, a new vocabulary was being heard. *Publicity* expanded its meaning from transparency to encompass the more aggressive concept of promotion. The phrase *public relations* appeared, with its smooth, antiseptic gloss of professionalism. Even the word *sell*, as Mark Sullivan noted, enlarged its domain so that instead of "going to" the people as Lincoln had done, or "educating" the people as Progressives prescribed, politicians would now *sell* voters on a policy. The lexicon arose to meet a need, to describe a phenomenon permeating political life.[5]

Though TR's methods were primitive next to his successors', he had created the most extensive presidential system yet for managing the press and his image. If Tillman and others exaggerated the danger that posed, they rightly warned that politics by publicity would benefit presidents far more than other governmental officials. Chief executives after TR would feel obliged to use all the tools at their disposal to win over public opinion.

All the same, it was noteworthy that critics of TR's publicity machine came mainly from the ranks of those who opposed his policies. Though they presented their criticisms as principled objections to executive publicity, they were far less likely to object to a campaign on behalf of goals they endorsed—or even to consider such promotion to be a publicity campaign at all. Only when the president led public opinion in a different direction did they discern illegitimate manipulation. Charging the president with seducing the press corps or hijacking public opinion—or being a fraud—let his critics believe that the public would side with them if only they had a fair chance to make their case. For decades to come, defeated parties in electoral or legislative battles would comfort themselves by saying that they hadn't lost on the merits, but only because they sold themselves less effectively.

In any case, Ben Tillman's complaint—that Roosevelt's sole talent was for publicity—could only go so far. As John Dewey recognized, with news traveling across telegraph wires, newspapers reaching millions, and Americans wallowing in celebrity, no politician could or should ignore the mass media. "When one has performed a resounding act," Dewey wrote, "it is stultifying not to allow it to resound." Moreover, where men like Tillman disparaged the public as dupes, Dewey maintained confidence that an engaged people could see through political posturing. "A petty deed cannot be made great by heralding," he wrote. TR could not have won over the public on theatrics alone.[6]

But how susceptible was the public to manipulation? Progressive thinkers were ambivalent. Typically, they acknowledged the limited information and weakly rooted opinions of the ordinary citizen while ultimately professing faith in his reasoning. Edward Ross could be cutting toward the public's ignorance, citing Mark Twain's quip that while 75 million Americans untrained as tailors would never dream of cutting their own suits, "they all think they can competently think out a political . . . scheme without any apprenticeship." Yet no sooner had Ross seconded Twain's dim view of the public than he insisted that "collective rumination" would lift public opinion out of its ignorance. For many Progressives, the key to that uplift lay in a group like Ross's ethical elite that could educate public opinion.[7]

This hope, however, stemmed from the era's faith in progress. In the coming years it would be challenged, as the new practitioners of public relations plunged into the business of politics.

*   *   *

Public relations was not new to the Progressive Era.[8] Since medieval times, press agents had promoted traveling fairs and performances. By the nineteenth century they worked on behalf of theater companies, circuses, and amusements, bringing fame to P. T. Barnum and Buffalo Bill. In the 1880s, hotels, steamboat lines, and athletic teams were devising tricks to get attention in the mass circulation newspapers. "Journalism has come to such a state," wrote an observer, "that any enterprise which depends to any extent upon advertising in the public press must have especial men hired solely for the purpose of 'working the press' for notices, free advertising, and the like." Political campaigns, too, had long used promotional materials; few major candidates or causes had ever lacked for public advocates. Samuel Adams was deemed the first American press agent for staging the Boston Tea Party and publicizing (and naming) the Boston Massacre. And since the 1830s, the parties had honed an arsenal of election-year publicity gimmicks, from candidate biographies to staged events, and retained literary bureaus to write articles and dispense pamphlets.[9]

What was novel in the Progressive Era were the self-consciously professional firms whose express purpose was to help clients burnish their images and spread their messages. Shaped by the Progressive values of expertise and efficiency, aimed at public opinion, these publicists distanced themselves from the old-style huckster who, as the journalist Henry Pringle wrote, "wore a checked suit, patent-leather shoes, possibly spats, a brown derby, and yellow gloves." They cultivated a disciplined, systematic style of generating coverage and molding mass opinion. Businesses that once played the inside game—working the political machines or buying off legislators—now felt compelled to court the public too.[10]

Around 1900, dedicated PR firms began to pop up. That year, George Michaelis and James Ellsworth of Boston founded the Publicity Bureau, which did work for utility companies, railroads, and universities. Washington, DC, claimed its first public relations professional in William Wolff Smith, a newspaperman who opened his own shop in 1902, soliciting work from groups with a stake in budding legislation. Notably, though, Smith disavowed the label of *publicist*. Throughout TR's administration, he continued to produce journalism and even sued *Collier's* magazine for calling him a "a press agent for the highest bidder."[11]

It fell to Ivy Ledbetter Lee to distinguish his craft from that of the older press agents. Lee embraced the label of "public relations adviser," which may be one reason he came to be remembered, inaccurately, as the first of his kind. A six-foot-tall Georgian with a trim physique and chestnut hair, Lee had the courtly manners and formal carriage of a southern gentleman. (His father was a distinguished minister, and one of his nephews would grow up to be the novelist William S. Burroughs.) His jowly face conveyed an air of satisfaction, if not condescension. He studied at Princeton, where his professors included Woodrow Wilson, with whom Lee later purported to have forged a close bond. "I remember so well those long walks which Wilson and I used to take in the beautiful country surrounding Princeton," he said, very likely plying his trade. Somewhat more evidence supports Lee's claim of having befriended Grover Cleveland, a local resident. The former president, having become something of a recluse, emerged one evening when Lee organized a group of collegiate carolers to serenade him. Lee, who wrote for *The Princetonian*, was ready with notebook in hand. Even then, he was as enterprising as he was drawn to power.[12]

After graduating, Lee passed an aimless semester at Harvard Law School before pursuing journalism in New York City. He secured an offer to work the police beat at the *New York Journal* from Charles Edward Russell, who would remain a lifelong friend. Frustrated with the low pay, however, he left journalism in 1903.

Days later, Lee was asked to recommend someone to run publicity for New York mayor Seth Low's reelection campaign. He recommended himself. His job was to handle campaign communications and prepare literature. Low lost the race, but along the way Lee met George Parker, a former Cleveland aide, who brought the younger man onto the 1904 presidential bid of Democrat Alton Parker (no relation). Parker and Lee managed the campaign's news coverage. Their main innovation seems to have been creating press releases mocked up to look like newspaper columns and distributed on galley sheets for instant use by newspapers with column inches to fill.

After the election, Lee and Parker found an office on 20 Broad Street, next to the New York Stock Exchange, and called themselves Parker & Lee. Even though the Publicity Bureau and other small firms were already engaged in similar work, Parker and Lee touted theirs as the first full-time publicity shop. Adopting the motto "Accuracy, Authenticity, Interest," they pledged to furnish information to newspapers on behalf of their clients about "topics of real interest, phrased so as to attract attention of both editors and readers—never sensational, never libelous, always accurate, always trustworthy, always readable."[13]

Parker and Lee distinguished their firm in several ways. Unlike an advertising bureau, they didn't pay newspapers to run their copy. Unlike what they called the "secret press bureau," they claimed that "all our work is done in the open." Many analysts hailed this practice of openness as a step forward in public relations, but Parker and Lee were simply capitalizing on a Progressive Era vogue for transparency. As the Gilded Age awe for the robber barons gave way to suspicion, corporations saw the wisdom in adopting publicity—as opposed to secrecy—in communicating with the news-reading public. As the most vocal advocate of this approach, Lee was a publicist for his brand of publicity.

Lee and Parker soon parted company. Parker's contribution to the development of public relations would fade into history, but Lee blossomed into a celebrity. In 1907, the Pennsylvania Railroad Company, one of Parker & Lee's clients, opened an internal public relations division, and Lee was hired as a full-time employee—the first of several in-house corporate public relations jobs.[14]

In the spring of 1914, Lee came to the attention of John D. Rockefeller, Jr., just after the so-called Ludlow Massacre. On April 20, 1914, a combined force of Colorado National Guardsmen and security guards for the Rockefeller family's Colorado Fuel & Iron Company in Ludlow had attacked a group of striking miners and their families, leading to roughly two dozen deaths, including of women and children. The deaths triggered a crisis for the Rockefellers. At least since Ida Tarbell's history of Standard Oil for *McClure's* in 1903 the seventy-five-year-old patriarch had epitomized the robber barons' slide from esteem into disrepute. Now, as news of Ludlow spread, critics reviled the mogul as the personification of heartless capitalism. Editorials fulminated about his ruthlessness, citing "the charred bodies of two dozen women and children." Upton Sinclair convened a rally outside the Rockefeller residence. The family sought help, and Arthur Brisbane of the Hearst papers recommended Lee.[15]

As Lee recalled, "Junior," as the son was called, came to him to say that "the public had, by reason of very inaccurate information, spread abroad by the United Mine Workers of America, conceived a wholly wrong impression of the facts of the Colorado strike." (Big labor practiced publicity too.) Lee urged Rockefeller toward "absolute frankness." Instead of issuing a stiff corporate line that would spur resentment, Lee said, the company should encourage the Colorado coal mine operators to tell their version of what happened. Lee put out a series of bulletins that would make the company's case. Titled simply "Facts Concerning the Strike in Colorado for Industrial Freedom," and framed as a factual reply to a skewed public record, these 5-by-11-inch leaflets, printed in black ink on a single side of high-quality vellum paper, were distributed nationally to the press every few days from June until September.[16]

Separating facts from spin turned out to be more easily said than done. Lee's publicity materials were slanted toward the railroads' perspective—so much so as to call into question the practicability, if not the sincerity, of his principles. The bulletins weren't literally false, except in one case, where Lee seems to have accidentally misstated the salaries of union organizers. But the selection and presentation of information was neither neutral nor straightforward. One bulletin quoted a woman named Helen Grenfell testifying that the women and children at Ludlow died not by gunshot, as some supposed, but by suffocation, as the result of an accidental fire. That was true, but Lee's materials neglected to mention—as the muckraker George Creel pointed out in an exposé of Lee for *Harper's Weekly*—that Grenfell, the wife of a railroad executive, hadn't witnessed the incident. Lee's other bulletins similarly omitted facts or placed truthful data in the service of misleading claims.[17]

The distortions inevitably came to light, through Creel's and other muckrakers' rebuttals. (Lee considered the muckrakers to be propagandists who twisted facts to suit their goals.) The exposés tarnished Lee's reputation, opened a new gusher of fury toward the Rockefellers, and caused their pronouncements to be viewed warily. If Lee's bulletins "converted or influenced anyone," one newspaper stated, "we have not heard of it." This resistance showed the limits that public relations gambits, even those premised on openness, would invariably face.

Over time Lee did soften the Rockefellers' image. When the federal government investigated the massacre, Lee rejected a suggestion that Junior slip into the hearing room through a back entrance. "The days of the rear door philosophy are over," he said. "Mr. Rockefeller will have to enter through the same door as everyone else." Rockefeller won praise for walking unafraid down the center aisle and shaking hands with the redoubtable labor leader Mother Jones. In the hearings, he disarmed critics with his blunt and accommodating manner. The public relations offensive continued with a two-week tour of the Colorado mining camps in September 1915, during which Junior donned denim overalls, chatted with workers, visited their homes, and danced with their wives. In later years Lee advised the elder Rockefeller to publicize his fondness for handing out dimes to poor children—a stunt that would become part of the Rockefeller mythology. Junior, meanwhile, emerged as a statesmanlike voice advocating an amicable relationship between workers and ownership, though his critics remained fierce and numerous.

Lee's handling of the Ludlow affair left more than one legacy. If he restored to the Rockefeller name a measure of respectability, he also drew undesired attention to himself as a shadowy manipulator, and to public relations as a Machiavellian trade. He was demonized by Carl Sandburg (who called him a "paid liar") and Upton Sinclair (who dubbed him "Poison Ivy"). In his *U.S.A.* trilogy, John Dos Passos used Lee as the model for his character J. Ward Moorehouse, an unctuous PR counsel who promotes industry behind a blandly malign businessspeak.[18]

By hiring Ivy Lee, Rockefeller turned the press agent into a public figure in his own right. Lee continued working to dispel notions that he or his profession were inherently dishonest, stressing their professionalism and expertise. Just as everyone deserved legal counsel regardless of guilt or innocence, he argued, so everyone needed advice on how to address the public (though lawyers, noted the critic Silas Bent, can be disbarred). Lee argued that public relations amounted to more than trying to persuade others of a point of view. It meant listening to public opinion and adjusting policy accordingly—"shaping their affairs so that when placed before the public they will be approved." The idea was never to hoodwink clients, he insisted, but to bring about confidence in the corporations he represented.

It was a good line.

*   *   *

Lee's activities made Progressives wonder whether paid manipulators might so pollute the stream of public information as to call into question the very premises of democracy. Ray Baker, George Creel, Will Irwin, and Mark Sullivan all published articles blasting the corporations' use of publicity bureaus and meditating on their effects. In 1906, Baker examined the railroads' campaign against TR's regulatory bills. While upholding their right to advance their case, Baker saw two problems with their methods. The first was their "unlimited money," put in the service of "a private interest which wishes to defeat the public will." Against such resources, average citizens had no chance to get a fair hearing. "The result is that the public gets chiefly the facts as prepared by the railroad for their own defense." The second problem was that the railroads advanced their arguments secretly, deceiving the public about their provenance. They sought, Baker wrote, "*not to inform* but to *corrupt and deceive* public opinion, and that strikes at the very root of democracy."[19]

Will Irwin wrestled with the same problem. Though critical of corporate flacks, he was loath to damn all public relations agents, since some championed worthy causes—"a tuberculosis society," or a dentists' group whose calls for cleanings and checkups "do not stretch the truth or the scientific spirit in the least." Labor unions, suffragists, and other Progressive movements were wise to seek out up-to-date publicity techniques. Like Irwin, future critics of PR would remain unsure whether to condemn the whole enterprise, to oppose only its most unsavory methods, or to take up its methods on behalf of honorable and urgent causes.[20]

The rise of publicity agents also raised questions about their work for the federal government, especially the executive branch. At first only a few bureaus used publicists, but over time every department and agency would have its own. Some critics feared that the unmatched resources of the government, like the immense wealth of private corporations, could prove impossible for ordinary Americans to combat.

A telling conflict erupted in 1913, when the Bureau of Public Roads took out a newspaper ad for a "publicity expert" who could place news items in "various periodicals and newspapers, particularly in country newspapers." The *New York Times*, which ran the ad, published an editorial objecting to the idea. Massachusetts congressman Frederick Gillett, later to become speaker of the House and eventually senator, introduced an amendment to an appropriations bill barring federal funds from compensating publicity experts. The executive departments, Gillett argued, were already perfectly capable of "finding men and means to put before the country in the press the duties and purposes of their administration." His amendment passed both chambers and went to the new president, Woodrow Wilson, for his signature.[21]

At a press conference Wilson was asked if he would veto the bill. He said no. He agreed that the departments shouldn't rely on publicity agents. "It won't affect [this] office," he added. "We'll have publicity, I can promise you that."[22]

8

WILSON SPEAKS

"I BEGIN WITH a list of the topics I want to cover, arranging them in my mind in their natural relations—that is, I fit the bones of the thing together; then I write it out in shorthand. I have always been accustomed to writing in shorthand, finding it a great saver of time. This done, I copy it on my own typewriter, changing phrases, correcting sentences, and adding material as I go along."[1]

Woodrow Wilson was explaining to Ida Tarbell, one of the many Progressive journalists who had transferred their loyalties from Roosevelt to his Democratic rival, how he wrote a speech. "Usually," he continued, "the document is not changed after it comes from the typewriter, but sent as it is to the printer. . . . I rarely consult anybody about it."[2]

Eloquent, learned, self-confident, and disciplined, Wilson was one of the finest orators of his time. Possessing neither Bryan's evangelical fire nor TR's hectoring persistence, Wilson spoke in well-wrought, logically arrayed sentences that, although didactic, could soar to inspirational heights. Even when he spoke extemporaneously, he was dazzlingly fluent. "His thoughts," said Henry Jones Ford, a colleague from Princeton days, "came with their clothes on." Good speechmaking, Wilson believed, consisted of neither bombast nor linguistic pyrotechnics but of seductive logic. "Oratory is not declamation, not swelling tones and an excited delivery," he wrote as a young man to his first wife, Ellen, when he was assiduously studying rhetoric, "but the art of persuasion, the art of putting things so as to appeal irresistibly to an audience." Apart from a soft spot for alliteration ("watchful waiting," "pitiless publicity"), Wilson forswore verbal flourishes in favor of crystalline clarity. He preferred laying out principles to piling on detail, crispness to effervescence. Instead of making broad bodily gestures, he extended an index finger; instead of bellowing, he enunciated precisely in a well-modulated tenor.[3]

Roosevelt mocked his rival's "empty elocution," but most people who beheld Wilson at the podium were impressed. Ray Baker, on hearing Wilson for the first time in 1910, thought he had found the ideal "thinking statesman." At the 1910 New Jersey state Democratic convention, when the party nominated the Princeton University president for governor, the candidate's remarks converted hardened opponents, some of whom left in tears of excitement. Even critics gave him grudging credit. TR's friend Owen Wister carped that Wilson "drugged" the public into following his course with "smooth knockout drops of rhetoric."

As a boy, Wilson used to walk in the woods and recite speeches by history's great rhetoricians. As a scholar, he wrote that the "ideal statesman" should display "an orator's soul, an orator's words, an orator's actions." He admired men like Daniel Webster who used crafted, reasoned speeches to bring their audiences around to a noble position. But Wilson also borrowed from TR, more than he admitted, in his use of the bully pulpit. The fusion of public appeals and presidential activism marked his most significant contribution to the methods of modern political leadership.

*   *   *

Scarcely a month after taking office, Wilson unveiled his rhetorical presidency. To much fanfare, and not a little consternation, the White House announced on April 6, 1913, that the president would deliver his first message to Congress not in written form, as every executive since Jefferson had done, but in person, from the well of the chamber. The gesture illustrated Wilson's belief that leadership required words as well as deeds—the belief that in their delivery words could become deeds, persuading and rallying legislators and citizens.[4]

The idea of addressing Congress orally had been percolating for a while. After Wilson's election in 1912, friendly journalists urged him to do so. But the president didn't need prodding. More than two decades earlier, as a young political scientist, he had faulted Jefferson for discontinuing the speeches to Congress that George Washington and John Adams had begun. Jefferson's retreat, Wilson noted, had made the United States the only modern government whose administrative chief took no part in the legislative proceedings. Had presidents continued to address Congress in person, Wilson wrote, there might have developed "a much more habitual and informal, and yet at the same time much more public and responsible, interchange of opinion between the Executive and Congress," as in a parliamentary system. Although Wilson discarded his preference for a British-style government, he maintained that the president should set policy like a prime minister. This meant dealing more directly with Congress.[5]

Wilson also favored oral messages because he believed in what he called, borrowing from Ralph Waldo Emerson, "pitiless publicity." He shared the Progressive faith that disseminating information could elevate public opinion and abet reform. *The New Freedom*, his 1912 campaign manifesto, included a sermon called "Let There Be Light," which argued that democratic rule required openness. Arguing against the secrecy of congressional committees and convention back rooms, he insisted that "there ought to be no place where anything can be done that everybody does not know about. . . . Secrecy means impropriety. . . . There is no air so wholesome as the air of utter publicity." And as it had for Roosevelt, *publicity* meant both transparency and promotion. Addresses to Congress would not only cleanse the lawmaking process of corrupt deals among special interests but would elevate the president's profile as a leader.[6]

Not everyone liked the idea of a congressional address. Senators, especially southerners, were jealous of their institution's constitutional prerogatives. Some warned in Jeffersonian language of executive aggrandizement. John Sharp Williams of Mississippi muttered darkly about Wilson's royal tendencies. "The speech from the throne," he called the impending address. Some cabinet members, too, wondered about the wisdom of the move.[7]

Prudently, Wilson minimized the pomp surrounding his visit. On Tuesday, April 8, when he made his way down Pennsylvania Avenue from the White House, only a single Secret Service guard joined him in his car. Wearing a black frockcoat, light trousers, and a period cravat tied in a four-in-hand knot, Wilson looked almost jaunty—as much as he ever did—and, at fifty-six, younger and more spry than photographs of his wizened mien from just a few years later suggested. Still, there was no denying the astringency in what Wilson called his "old Scotch face." The long, gaunt visage with its sallow cheeks and heavy lantern jaw, the high forehead with iron gray hair swept over it, and the slate blue almond eyes peering through his rimless pince-nez, all gave Wilson a forbidding air. And yet his schoolmaster facade was often belied by a spontaneous smile, which he liked to flash, and a twinkle in his eye, which showed the warmth, liveliness, wit, and even mischief that companions swore he displayed in small settings. Aloof, high-minded, and prone to moralism he could be, but Wilson was neither hardhearted nor humorless. "The Wilson in private life," wrote Henry Stoddard, was "genial and witty; he could tell a story magnificently, and he had a highly developed sense of humor."[8]

There was a spring in his step as Wilson arrived at Congress. The halls bustled noisily with well-appointed women and men in knee-length coats, while hundreds of would-be spectators massed outside, some besieging the doorkeepers in vain for admission. The House chamber bustled with legislators, cabinet members, and international diplomats, including Wilson's friend and old colleague James Bryce, now the British ambassador. Some congressmen looked tense and sullen, even suspicious. But when Wilson entered the room, at three minutes before 1 pm, the crowd rose in raucous applause. Wilson bowed and smiled. He lifted the narrow sheets of paper before him and, in a voice low and easy for the whole room to hear, began to read.[9]

The speech was short—as Wilson intended, in another Rooseveltian move, so that the newspapers would reprint it in full. His trip to the Hill, he told his audience, was meant as a demonstration that the president is "not a mere department of government hailing Congress from some isolated island of jealous power" but "a human being trying to cooperate with other human beings in a common service." Yet Wilson also plainly meant to set the agenda. The heart of his speech was a call for tariff reform—a perennial headache in Washington—and he summoned Congress to action. Lower rates were a first step, he said, toward rejuvenating the economy and abolishing "everything that bears even the semblance of privilege or of any kind of artificial advantage." He provided little detail; he thought it more important to offer a vision than to hash out the fine points of policy, which didn't much interest the public. With no grand conclusion, he broke off his big speech after nine minutes. Some people didn't realize he was done.[10]

Despite the abrupt ending, the speech was a hit. *Harper's Weekly*, hailing "the speech-making spirit of John Adams . . . reincarnated," was one of many publications to shroud the event in the founders' aura. Even the conservative *Chicago Tribune* praised Wilson's "dignity and impressiveness." Louis Brownlow, who had once basked in TR's press conferences, judged that the president "established himself as a result of one bold stroke as the leader not only of his party but of the nation."[11]

In the following years, Wilson spoke to Congress regularly. He did so to kick off campaigns for antitrust laws and banking reform; he did so again in 1917 to announce his decision to enter the world war and in 1918 to unveil his vision for postwar peace. His action set a precedent: presidents ceased to reserve congressional addresses for ceremonial matters and came to use them to advance policy goals as well. Wilson didn't foresee how often his successors would be called upon to pronounce on current controversies or provide policy leadership with their remarks. But he did anticipate that his oratorical coup on that April day in 1913 might help advance the ambitious agenda he meant to enact.

Wilson was uncharacteristically buoyant as he drove back to the White House with his family. Ellen, his wife, was pleased as well. It was the kind of thing, she said, that Teddy Roosevelt might have done—"if only he had thought of it." Wilson laughed. "Yes," he said, "I think I put one over on Teddy." Wilson's vanquished rival was on many minds. Clifford Berryman, the cartoonist who had sketched Roosevelt taking mercy on a wounded bear cub, giving rise to the Teddy bear craze, now drew TR leaping from his chair after reading about Wilson's speech, berating himself for not having come up with the idea.

*   *   *

Besting Roosevelt hadn't been Wilson's motive, but it provided satisfactions. Theirs was a rocky relationship. Early in TR's administration, they had been friendly and mutually supportive. Roosevelt visited Princeton, and Wilson visited Oyster Bay. They consulted each other for all manner of advice. But toward the end of TR's presidency they began sniping at each other, and by the 1912 presidential election, when they competed in a three-way race against the incumbent William Howard Taft, Wilson and Roosevelt had become enemies.[12]

The turn of events was unsurprising, perhaps inevitable, given their temperaments and styles. Wilson was shy where Roosevelt was effusive, professorial where Roosevelt was bombastic, and cerebral where Roosevelt was physical. A product of the middle class, Wilson viewed the social change sweeping America with equanimity if not optimism, while the wellborn Roosevelt, for all his commitment to reform, feared upheaval. Then there were the two men's dueling campaign trail economic programs and slogans: Roosevelt's "New Nationalism," which sought to use government power to regulate the big corporations; and Wilson's "New Freedom," which held out the ideal of breaking them up altogether.

Yet William Allen White correctly deemed the discrepancy between the two programs a "fantastic imaginary gulf," like the difference "between tweedle-dum and tweedle-dee." In the larger scheme of things, both men's plans mounted historic challenges to the domination of big business. *The New Republic*, a liberal magazine founded in 1914 by TR fans Herbert Croly, Walter Lippmann, and Walter Weyl, correctly predicted that historians "will interpret the work of President Wilson as a continuation of the work begun by ex-President Roosevelt."[13]

Indeed, their similarities were more striking than their differences: the two most intellectual and literate presidents since the founders, they wrote close to thirty books combined. Each served as president of the American Historical Association; each won a Nobel Peace prize. More important, in the battles of their own day, both sat squarely in the Progressive camp. They believed in strong government, led by an activist president, deriving his power from public opinion, addressing the iniquities of the age. Wilson had warmly praised Roosevelt during TR's presidency—for his Progressive achievements, his valuation of public opinion over partisan interest, and his performance as "an aggressive leader" of Congress. Reaching the Oval Office before Wilson, Roosevelt was first to lay claim to the "modern" presidency. But it was Wilson, the political scientist, who articulated the office's potential more expansively and carefully.

In his first book, *Congressional Government*—based on his doctoral dissertation and published in 1885 to much acclaim—Wilson had written disparagingly of the secretive congressional committees and hollow floor debate that had rendered the national legislature ineffectual. But in an age of weak executives, Wilson saw little promise in the presidency. Its work, he wrote, consisted mostly of "mere administration, mere obedience of directions from the masters of policy, the Standing Committees." By 1900, however, as the book entered its fifteenth printing, Wilson appended an introduction that acknowledged the "greatly increased power and opportunity for constructive statesmanship" that the presidency had assumed since the Spanish-American War. By 1908, he concluded that the old book would no longer do. His new treatise, *Constitutional Government*, extolled presidential leadership full-throatedly. "The nation as a whole has chosen him, and is conscious that it has no other political spokesman," he asserted, in passages that were Rooseveltian in content if not in style. "He is the representative of no constituency, but of the whole people." "Times of stress and change" had "thrust upon him the attitude of originator of policies. His is the vital place of action in the system, whether he accept it as such or not."[14]

Once in the White House, Wilson strove to abide by his own theories. He stayed attuned to public opinion, sounding out his cabinet secretaries and White House reporters for readings of the public mood. Assisting him was the thirty-three-year-old White House secretary Joe Tumulty, a jovial product of New Jersey's Irish Democratic machine, who boasted a native wit, an even temper, and an easy rapport with newsmen. "You boys are great personages in public affairs," Tumulty promised the press corps, "and in Washington I will look after the publicity of this administration myself." One magazine called Tumulty "a Washington institution with an amazing technique in handling publicity," while reporters passed around doggerel: "Who's got to listen to the bores/Who ooze through the White House doors/And hear all of the kicks and roars?/Tumulty!" Assisted by White House mailroom hand Ira R. T. Smith, Tumulty clipped newspaper articles, as his recent predecessors had, and kept Wilson apprised of reporters' views.[15]

Like Roosevelt, Wilson wasn't afraid to buck the popular will. "If what we are preparing to do is right," Secretary of War Newton Baker recalled Wilson telling his cabinet, "and public opinion is at the moment uninformed and wrong, our duty is to do what is right." Wilson's view was that the president was obliged to try to read public opinion and interpret it, to mark out a course of action for the common good. "I believe in the people: in their honesty and sincerity and sagacity; but I do not believe in them as my governors," Wilson wrote. "I believe in them, rather, as the wholesome stuff out of which the fabric of government . . . is woven." Like the "ethical elite" of his onetime student Edward Ross, Wilson's ideal leader could ascertain the "deep" public will amid the din and whirl of "momentary and whimsical" popular sentiments. His job was to articulate his reading of that will back to the public, who could then understand and endorse it.[16]

Educating the public didn't mean overwhelming audiences with information. For Wilson, persuasion depended on "simplicity and directness . . . purged of all subtlety." It meant making an argument in terms that were comprehensible but never demagogic. The high-minded Wilson would have recoiled at the suggestion that he resembled Roosevelt, who aroused public interest with dramatic stunts and moral stridency. But in his view that leadership of public opinion meant articulating broad principles, Wilson was refining Roosevelt's blunt credo that "the public cannot take in an etching. They want something along the lines of a circus poster." Both men simplified things for public consumption. But where TR dramatized, Wilson distilled.[17]

These stylistic distinctions spoke to the two men's differences, or what Wilson's ally Henry Morgenthau called the "Wilsonic method—the deliberate, watchful-waiting style"—versus "the flamboyant T.R. style." The histrionic Roosevelt belittled Wilson's "academic manner," telling Charles Willis Thompson, "He doesn't get under the skin of the people. His manner is still that of the college professor lecturing his class." Wilson scorned his predecessor's theatrics. He even looked askance at the popular use of the nickname "Teddy" (which TR also disliked) as a sign of the unfortunate return of the "old spirit of Andrew Jackson's time over again, the feeling of disrespect and desire to make everything common property." But Wilson's disparagements concealed a hint of envy. Once in 1912, when an audience member cried out, "That was a good one, Woody!" Wilson beamed. "Did you hear?" he asked a reporter. "They called me Woody!"[18]

This mix of jealousy and disdain toward TR emerged in Wilson's discussions of their styles. "I feel that Roosevelt's strength is altogether incalculable," he wrote to his friend (and suspected paramour) Mary Ellen Peck. "He appeals to their imagination; I do not. He is a real, vivid person. ... I am a vague, conjectural personality, more made up of opinions and academic prepossessions than of human traits and red corpuscles." Wilson nonetheless saw danger in appealing to the public too often, too uninhibitedly, or too directly, for it could lead the president to descend into demagoguery. Wilson thought Roosevelt's bluster had undermined his aspirations to statesmanship. Turning the tables on those who might deem him unduly aristocratic, Wilson said that it was TR's crowd-pleasing style that was in fact elitist, since it implied that the president initiated policies and then simply sold them to a star-struck, quiescent public. His own more austere style, in contrast, facilitated a democracy "from below," because he was seeking to fathom and implement the public will of an engaged citizenry.[19]

Accordingly, Wilson made speaking to Congress the hallmark of his leadership, whereas Roosevelt had gone to the people directly. Initially partial to TR, *The New Republic* came around to Wilson's approach. Roosevelt, the editors wrote, "had his eye fixed not on Congress but on the American people" and "used his messages not primarily for the purpose of informing and influencing Congress, but for the purpose of arousing public opinion." Eventually, though, TR had found himself deadlocked with the Senate. Wilson, in contrast, used speeches as "a means of persuasively and conspicuously submitting a programme to Congress"—making perhaps "a feebler impression on the American people," but ensuring that "the legislature may yield with less reluctance to executive leadership." Wilson took such votes of confidence to heart. For the rest of his presidency, he continued to place hope—at times too much hope—in the ability of his finely reasoned messages to lead Congress along his favored path.[20]

9

PITILESS PUBLICITY

SOME POLITICAL OBLIGATIONS had never come easily to Woodrow Wilson. Having entered elective politics late in life, he hated what he called the "campaign mummery" of shaking hands and sweet-talking supporters. Slick salesmanship and Rooseveltian histrionics ran contrary to his high-minded, scholastic style. He considered mass communications—movies, photography, phonograph recordings—artificial and undignified. The very mechanisms that might allow a professorial Progressive to guide the nation thus required practices of self-promotion that he abhorred. This dilemma would pose a recurring challenge for Wilson, and in time contribute to his undoing.[1]

Wilson's hesitation about new media techniques was evident in his 1912 race for president. "He is not yet fully educated up to the value of publicity," sighed Frank Stockbridge, a newspaperman who worked on the campaign. Wilson balked at posing for photographs, which he considered contrived, and thought it beneath him to milk a cow or plow a field for the cameras. He resisted the clever suggestion of Josephus Daniels, the North Carolina editor who oversaw the campaign's publicity shop, that he record his speeches on phonograph. Daniels wanted to play the recordings in sync with silent films of the candidate's speeches to excite crowds at moviehouses. Wilson protested that he disliked "canned speeches." Only

Ellen Wilson could persuade her husband to participate, and even then, Daniels recalled, "He went at it as if he were going to the stake."[2]

Motion pictures, too, elicited Wilson's scorn. After the short films pioneered by McKinley and Roosevelt, cameramen had begun filming inaugurations, conventions, and even TR's 1906 trip to Panama. Leon Franconi, who worked for the French filmmaker Charles Pathé, witnessed the arresting spectacle of Taft's inauguration amid a blinding snowstorm and hit on the idea of a weekly cinematic digest of world events. Soon newsreels found a niche in moviegoers' routines. By 1912, TR was doting on the retinue of cameramen that trailed him, delaying campaign stunts until the photographers readied their equipment. Wilson, true to form, shunned the moviemen. His high sense of dignity made him loath to pose or ham it up, rendering him "an involuntary actor in the 'photo-play,'" one magazine reported, "trailed by a squad of moving picture men, who followed him from stump to stump." The Democratic Party joined with Universal Films to make pro-Wilson films anyway.[3]

After his election Wilson continued to rebuff the filmmakers. Hollywood producers asked for footage of cabinet meetings and executive branch business, but Wilson, envisioning cameramen overrunning the White House, let them film only public events. The filmmakers protested that millions of Americans were going to the cinema, and that film was a "universal language" that reached immigrants of foreign tongues. Captive audiences, moreover, couldn't turn the page when they encountered disagreeable messages, as they could with printed material. But Wilson demurred. "It is just the simple fact that I do not know how to lend myself to plans of this sort," he said to William Brady, who led Hollywood's trade association. "The speeches will be flat and my self-consciousness in the face of the camera will make the whole thing awkward and ineffective." When he did appear in newsreels, he winced at "the extraordinary rapidity with which I walk," "the instantaneous and apparently automatic nature of my motions," and "the way in which I produce uncommon grimaces." Only in the 1916 campaign did George Creel, working in the publicity department, make headway. Creel insisted that Wilson retain the director D. W. Griffith as "consulting-architect" for the campaign's films, apparently resulting in at least one movie, *The President and His Cabinet in Action*. Advances in titling would wait until another day.[4]

The most foolish manifestation of Wilson's contempt for self-promotion was his aversion to the basic presidential duty of courting the workaday press. Early on, journalists numbered among his most committed backers.

Daniels, Walter Hines Page, George Harvey of *Harper's*, Norman Hapgood of *Collier's*, William Bayard Hale, Ray Baker, and George Creel were all boosters in the 1912 campaign, and some of them went on to join the administration. Despite his starchy exterior, Wilson managed to charm the campaign trail reporters, who had fun drinking with him, indulging his gift for mimicry and his love of limericks.

But the same traits that made Wilson leery of film and of celebrity also kept him from wooing the press more assiduously. He protested to Frank Stockbridge about having to meet with local scribes in each city he visited. "Do I have to go through that again?" he grumbled. Once he refused to reschedule a speech even though it conflicted with a World Series game. He even spurned, or adopted belatedly, such elementary practices as giving interviews and circulating advance speech drafts, which would have protected him against out-of-context quotation. "I wish I could do that," he said. "I've tried to do it over and over again, but I can't."

The new media environment demanded, however, that Wilson not only articulate his ideas but dramatize them. When journalists urged him to reveal his lighter side, he shook his head. "I have heard how excellently Colonel Roosevelt succeeds in making himself intelligible by following the very course you advise, and often I have wished that I could do it," Wilson said ruefully. "But it's not my nature."[5]

* * *

It was ironic, given this attitude toward the press, that President Wilson was the one to inaugurate biweekly conferences open to the entire White House press corps. The decision is often credited as Wilson's second breakthrough in communication, after the addresses to Congress. Roosevelt had had his séances, and even the publicity-averse Taft briefly hosted once-a-week sessions with perhaps fifteen correspondents, though his coolness left them muttering about the "good old days" under TR. Thus for Wilson to meet with reporters wasn't so much a groundbreaking step as an acknowledgment that the Washington correspondents had become an indispensable channel for reaching the public. The press conferences, like the speeches to Congress, appealed to him precisely because they allowed him to limit the time he spent with reporters while still helping him spread his message.[6]

Wilson convened his first press conference two weeks into his presidency. On Saturday, March 15, he invited reporters to what he called "a friendly chat." He expected 20 to 30; roughly 125 showed up. Crowding into his office, they formed a thick semicircle, enclosing Wilson. Gone was any hope of a free-flowing exchange, as Wilson reverted to his formal style, issuing edicts from behind his desk. "There was a pause, a cool silence, and presently some one ventured a tentative question," recalled Edward Lowry, a participant. "It was answered crisply, politely, and in the fewest possible words. A pleasant time was not had by all." The playful intellect who could revel in banter had yielded to the starchy professor.[7]

A few days later, Wilson tried again. He held a second meeting with journalists, this time in the East Room, hoping that the bigger space would provide aeration. Now 200 reporters showed up and Wilson again waxed didactic. Thinking he was extending a friendly hand, he came across as condescending, even imperious. He asked the newsmen to join him in a "partnership" not on his own behalf but "for the people of the United States." Their role was not to "tell the country what Washington is thinking, for that does not make any difference," he said. "Tell Washington what the country is thinking."[8]

The injunction reflected Wilson's Progressive conception of presidential leadership. But even the reporters who shared his politics bristled. Some resented his arrogance in assigning them a place in his grand plan; others despaired at his solemn manner. "He came into the room suspicious, reserved, a little resentful," one newsman later wrote to Ray Baker. "No thought of frankness and open door and cordiality and that sort of thing." Several walked away "almost cursing, indignant."

Yet the conferences went forward. Wilson held sixty-four of them in each of his first two years, more than one a week. On a given day, anywhere from twenty to seventy-five correspondents would gather in the lobby of the executive building next to the White House, waiting for a cue from Patrick McKenna, the doorman. Streaming into his office, they would arrange themselves in a half-moon while the president stood alone before a bay window, hands clasped behind him. Frostily polite, projecting boredom or a wish to be somewhere else, Wilson struggled to keep his eyes off his desk clock. He scarcely hid his contempt for his guests. "What you saw there," wrote Hugh Baillie, one of the flock, "was his severe manner, his long Covenanter countenance, his cold and challenging eye. And he could be brutal to anyone he didn't respect." He answered questions evasively or not at all. "Pitiless publicity," the correspondents took to joking, had given way to "Pity, less publicity."[9]

From the president's viewpoint, the reporters were to blame for wallowing in the trivial and the superficial. As early as a post-election holiday in

Bermuda, he had tangled with reporters over the stories about his teenage daughters, and the tension with the press over respecting his privacy never diminished. He also stewed over the press's focus on gossip and trivia and its appetite for political drama and conflict—standing interests of journalism. He rejected the legitimacy of the public's interest in him as a personality. Time and again he spurned advice to humanize himself by displaying his fun-loving side. To a group of journalists in 1914 he protested that no article about him had ever accurately captured his personality; he was not "a cold and removed person who has a thinking machine inside" but "a fire from a far-from-extinct volcano, and if the lava does not boil over it is because you are not high enough to see into the basin and see the cauldron boil." But he wouldn't lower himself to let them peer in.[10]

Wilson also resented the endless speculation to which reporters were prone. "His theory was that nothing was news until it was completed," wrote David Lawrence, Wilson's former student and later the founder of *U.S. News*; "only conclusions or decisions were of interest to the public." News, he believed, consisted of his decisions. The way he reached them wasn't properly a public matter.

Wilson blamed the press corps for the soured relations. "I believed that close relations with the press would be my greatest aid," he told George Creel. "I prepared for the conferences as carefully as for a Cabinet meeting, and discussed questions of the day frankly and fully. . . . But I soon discovered that the interest of the majority was in the trivial and personal. In the middle of an exposition of policy I would be asked about the sheep on the White House lawn, what we ate for dinner, and even about intimate family affairs." He carped about the papers' inaccuracies and biases, which he believed reflected their owners' politics. He sometimes said flatly that they weren't to be trusted.[11]

Wilson's press conferences were not a total failure. At times he achieved a happy banter and familiarity, if not exactly camaraderie. Some journalists, such as Walter Lippmann and Richard Oulahan, spoke warmly of their interactions with him. The positive coverage that Wilson garnered as he steered one bill after another through Congress also showed that whatever personal strain plagued the relationship didn't have to poison the reporters' copy. In an age that permitted the open expression of partisan preferences, many journalists—including Tarbell and other muckrakers—remained openly supportive of the president through the 1916 campaign.[12]

At their best, Wilson's press conferences helped reporters understand his designs. On the same day in June 1913 that Wilson went before Congress to promote banking reform, he hosted the White House correspondents for a long, technical discussion of the bill's intricacies. Amid its coverage of the president's congressional address, the *New York Times* praised the news conference as a "splendid defense of the currency bill" and laid out Wilson's case in detail. On these occasions, when reporters delved into policy—and Wilson was ready to discuss it—the president's openness could yield the kind of thoughtful, sympathetic coverage he desired.

What was more, from time to time Wilson hosted small gatherings with a markedly different feel. The same ease that reporters had glimpsed on the campaign trail reappeared when, as president, he let reporters linger after his large conferences. The ones who stuck around, said Lippmann, not a little self-servingly, were those "concerned not with the raw news of announcements and statements in the formal press conference but with explaining and interpreting the news." With this more simpatico audience, Wilson relaxed. "The President would sit back in his chair," Lippmann recalled, and "clear up or amplify this or that piece of news." On the whole, however, the sheer size of the regular sessions precluded the intimacy of Roosevelt's séances and encouraged a practiced, studied manner. To David Barry, Wilson's overstuffed meetings "were not in fact press conferences at all," but wearisome, ritualized performances.[13]

Still, Wilson's press conferences set an important precedent. In the years afterward, the press conference as a practice widened from a singularly presidential activity into a mechanism for the growing number of executive branch officials—and members of Congress and political candidates—to reach the public. In time, they would become a permanent and inescapable feature of Washington publicity.

* * *

Wilson's problems with the press stemmed not just from his circumspect nature but from structural features of the new political environment. At bottom, he failed to appreciate the transformation of news in the twentieth century. Wilson believed in publicity—in transparency—for government as well as business, deploring the closed-door sessions in which politics and lawmaking often occurred. But publicity in the sense of hype he considered alien to his character and unpresidential. As early as *Congressional Government*, Wilson had noted the rise of the mass circulation press with more alarm than excitement, lamenting that journalism was displacing the oratory of statesmen as the chief means for the discussion of public affairs. Though he later conceded that daily journalism might allow "a studied and deliberate . . . interchange of thought," he never stopped complaining that newspapers and magazines favored diverting trivia over the enrichment of political discussion.[14]

By deeming much of the press corps' output to be illegitimate, Wilson was rejecting their conception of their own job. Newsmen thought their job required reporting on the full range of items that they gathered: lighthearted matters as well as serious ones, gossip as well as policy, developments in progress as well as concluded decisions. But Wilson expected journalists, like the president, to aspire to "a minor kind of statesmanship," as he told a group of editors—to midwife his project of educating the public.[15]

Envisioning a "partnership," Wilson, like TR, thought the facts should be self-evident, and he bristled when the press presented them in ways that clashed with his understanding. He sneered at the "fictions" he found even in reputable papers like the *New York Times*. No doubt the press often distorted the news, intentionally or not; but sometimes those fictions were merely differences of interpretation—something Wilson had trouble understanding. "If the president was ever fearful of anything in his life, it was publicity," wrote Ray Baker; "he was afraid, I think, not so much of the facts themselves, but of the way they were presented. As a highly cultivated scholar, he disliked exaggeration, distrusted sensationalism. And yet he recognized the need for publicity and often seemed irritated and offended if the clear stream of news was fouled at its sources or muddied with propaganda."[16]

Reporters, however, saw their job as sifting truth from the president's selective presentation of events. To them, Wilson seemed "an excellent hair splitter when it comes to the use of words," as one reporter wrote, or a consummate "verbal strategist," in the words of another—a smooth talker who didn't lie outright but "took such an intellectual pleasure in stating a thing so as to give an opposite impression to the fact, though he kept strictly to the truth, that one had to be constantly on the alert to keep from being misled." Suffering this treatment, reporters stopped trusting Wilson's candor.[17]

That distrust wasn't unfounded. Privately, Wilson confessed to "grazing the truth" with reporters: not lying, but shading things just so. He was cagey if not obstructive in talking about the delicate discussions that went on among his counselors. He didn't regard this discretion as a violation of his commitment to publicity, because he pointedly distinguished between the corrupt secret meetings of congressional committees or convention bosses and the responsible deliberations of government, which he considered justifiably off-limits to the press. To be sure, an overdose of publicity could compromise diplomacy or hamper sound policy making. But Wilson's reticence flew in the face of his sweeping pronouncements about the virtues of publicity, undermined his call for reporters to take him at his word, and fostered a mutual suspicion. Their irreconcilable viewpoints kept the president and the press corps from achieving the harmonious partnership that Wilson had hoped for.

After a year of "these strangely unsatisfactory meetings," as the *New York Tribune* called them, the testy relationship between the reporters and Wilson was the talk of Washington. In late 1914, a dispirited Wilson pared them back to once a week. Six months later, with the war in Europe consuming more and more of his attention, he suspended them outright and turned the job of briefing the press over to Tumulty—to everyone's satisfaction. Though Wilson resumed his conferences for a spell in 1916, he was reluctant to share his thinking on matters of war and peace, especially since foreign correspondents in the room might relay sensitive information to their home governments. But the European rumblings also gave the president an excuse to escape a routine that he had never relished and that he now privately described to George Creel as "a waste of time." Publicity for the war would take a different form.[18]

THE PRESS AGENTS' WAR

IN THE SUMMER OF 1915, George Sylvester Viereck, a thirty-one-year-old German-born American writer, had been editing *The Fatherland* for nearly a year. Founded at the outbreak of the European war, the weekly newspaper declared in its first issue that it intended to combat "misstatements and prejudices" toward Germany in the American press and "to place the German side of this unhappy quarrel fairly and squarely before the American people." In short order, *The Fatherland* emerged as the chief organ of pro-German opinion in America. Viereck, known for his poetry, with Theodore Roosevelt among his fans, became a clarion voice in pleading Germany's case.[1]

On July 24, an unseasonably mild Saturday in Manhattan, Viereck walked into the offices of the Hamburg-American Steamship Company on lower Broadway. Unbeknownst to him, his advocacy had piqued the suspicion of the federal government, and he was being watched by two agents of the U.S. Secret Service. At three o'clock, Viereck resurfaced on the desolate summer streets, accompanied now by a slender, fiftyish German man with graying hair and scarred cheeks. The agents tailed the Germans to Rector Street, where they boarded an elevated train heading up Sixth Avenue.[2]

Viereck got off at 23rd Street. One agent, William Houghton, followed him, while the other, Frank Burke, stayed on the train. At 50th Street, the German looked up from his newspaper and noticed he had reached his stop. He hurried off the car, leaving behind a brown briefcase. Burke grabbed it. Realizing his mistake, the German darted back for the bag, but he was blocked by a heavyset woman talking to a transit official. Burke fled the train, accidental quarry in hand. On the sidewalk, he saw the German in pursuit and jumped onto the running board of a trolley car, telling the conductor that his pursuer was a lunatic. The motorman hit the accelerator, leaving the stranded German to wave his fist from the pavement.

Once safely out of range, Burke called William Flynn, chief of the Secret Service. Flynn picked up his agent and they drove to the Custom House back down near the Battery. In the briefcase they found sheaves of documents, some in English, many in German. The man whose bag they confiscated, it turned out, was Heinrich Albert, an attaché in the German Embassy.

Flynn and Burke hastily called Treasury Secretary William Gibbs McAdoo, who was vacationing in Maine, and then brought him the documents. In considerable detail, the papers limned a sweeping campaign of secret propaganda designed to sway American public opinion toward Germany in the world war. Alarmed, McAdoo took the cache to Cornish, New Hampshire, the summer retreat of Woodrow Wilson.[3]

For the past year, Wilson had been struggling to tamp down Americans' ethnic and national passions. Now he realized that the German mischief would complicate his diplomacy and inflame public opinion. Over time he had become convinced, he wrote to his adviser Edward House, that the country was "honeycombed with German intrigue and infested with German spies." He instructed McAdoo to consult with House and Secretary of State Robert Lansing to devise a response.

McAdoo also worried that American neutrality was being undermined. "I saw an opportunity," he recalled, "to throw a reverberating scare into the whole swarm of propagandists—British and French as well as German—and I decided that this could be done most effectively through publicity." Continuing his rounds through New England vacation spots, McAdoo won his colleagues' agreement for a plan. They would leak the documents to a trusted friend, Frank Cobb, the editor of the *New York World*, if he promised to keep his source anonymous. House told Wilson that he was worried the stratagem might lead the country into war, but concluded, "I think the publication should go ahead."[4]

In a series of front-page stories in August, the *World* revealed the most shocking of the German intrigues, traceable all the way to German chancellor Theobald von Bethmann Hollweg. Berlin was subsidizing not only Viereck's *Fatherland* but other American journalists and publications. Germany was hoping to buy a controlling interest in the *New York Evening Mail*, and it had other plans to bankroll films, lecturers, and pseudo-indigenous movements. (The kaiser's agents, for example, took control of the National German-American Alliance, organized years earlier by the beer industry to fight Prohibition, and used it to press for pro-German war policies.) The German efforts included sabotage and espionage; plans to foment strikes in American munitions factories; even a scheme to acquire the Wright Brothers Aeroplane Company and its desirable patents. Soon after these revelations came news of German plans to incite strikes in munitions plants and to blow up the Welland Canal, a vital Great Lakes waterway.[5]

The secrecy, funding, and scope of Germany's propaganda blitz outraged even anti-war journalists. The *New York Evening Post* editorialized that while Berlin had a right to "establish legitimate press bureaus and circulate news," its surreptitious actions and "offense against good taste" had crossed a line. Prominent German diplomats, including the ambassador to Washington, who was implicated, were sent home. Viereck, however, insisted that Berlin was merely countering the Allies' lies and that the *World*'s story was part of a British propaganda plot.[6]

In the short term, the German propaganda campaign aroused opinion against Berlin. In the longer term, it primed Americans to cooperate with unconscionable anti-German practices and civil liberties crackdowns that they justified as wartime exigencies. The disclosures also showed the importance of American public opinion to winning the war—"a sector of the battle-front," Mark Sullivan wrote, "rather more important to capture than Mons or Verdun."

* * *

If the Spanish-American War had been the Correspondents' War—brought home to readers by the stringers dispatched to the Caribbean—then World War I was, the *New York Times* wrote, the "Press Agents' War." One month in, the *Times* noted, the Allies and the Central Powers had set up bureaus "to disseminate reports their governments desire to have published, especially in the United States." London and Berlin courted reporters, planted stories, showcased spokesmen for interviews, and published news releases and circulars for American newspapers.[7]

What made this competition so fierce and consequential was the

American position of neutrality—a policy that Wilson proclaimed as soon as hostilities had erupted across the European continent in August 1914. At the time, the president's wife, Ellen, fifty-four, was dying, and as he returned to Washington from her burial in her native Georgia, Wilson brooded over how to frame the neutrality question for the public. On four slips of paper, he wrote an eloquent public message appealing for calm. It instructed his countrymen to remain "impartial in thought as well as action." This injunction would have taxed Americans no matter what, but the European belligerents made it their task to thwart the president. If anything would persuade Wilson to throw America's weight one way or the other, it was the public opinion that he esteemed.

The public was split. Decades of immigration had transformed the nation into a congeries of ethnic groups, many still tied to their countries of origin. German-Americans felt loyal to their homeland. Americans of British, French, and Western European descent tended to favor the Allies—except Irish-Americans, the most nationalistic of whom, loathing Britain, made common cause with the Germans. Progressive sentiment was repulsed by Germany's militarism, while southern and western Populists nursed suspicions about eastern corporations that stood to profit.

Partly because of the high stakes, "press agents," to use the *Times's* innocuous phrase, were being transmogrified into something more menacing: propagandists. Like that of *publicity*, the evolution of the word *propaganda* revealed changing attitudes. It originated with the Catholic Church, whose College of Propaganda, founded in 1622, promoted Vatican doctrine abroad; later, it came to encompass any act of propagating a doctrine—a neutral meaning it retained for centuries. But with the world war, when German actions linked the word to violent sabotage and treacherous espionage, it could no longer signify mere advocacy. To some, the newly ominous term now implied advocacy of surreptitious provenance; to others, it connoted deliberate deceit or distortion of evidence; to others still, it meant an emotional appeal designed to conjure an emotional response. All these gradations of meaning carried a whiff of the sinister and rendered mere *publicity*—press conferences, press releases, and the like—benign in comparison.[8]

* * *

In courting American opinion, advocates for the Allied Forces had some advantages. The most important was their cultural affinity with the United States. Entwined in their history, institutions, and language, the American and British people enjoyed a long-standing bond. France, too, shared with the United States a warm and venerable sense of friendship. The British, moreover, had severed the Germans' undersea cables, preventing Berlin from communicating securely with the western hemisphere, while Britain enjoyed unfettered access. The British also set up a publicity bureau, directed by the novelist and politician Gilbert Parker. It monitored American opinion, cultivated U.S. reporters based in England, and trotted out British eminences for interviews. In the States, Parker's staff rained down their literature on a mailing list of roughly 200,000 public figures, from college presidents to scientists, as well as public libraries, private clubs, universities, and YMCAs.[9]

Allied propaganda was most influential early on. In the fall of 1914, the German military rampaged through Belgium, slaughtering civilians and laying waste to public buildings. From not only Allied propaganda mills but also eyewitness reporters like Richard Harding Davis came tales of German atrocities: The kaiser's armies, it was said, chopped off babies' hands and women's breasts, or literally crucified enemy soldiers and shipped them home to be made into soap and grease. Even had these stories hewed rigorously to uncontested facts or been recounted in bloodless prose, their barbarism would have horrified the world. But embellishment and invention guaranteed the inflammation of anti-German feeling. So too did the findings the next spring of a British government inquiry led by James Bryce, which, dubiously, certified the atrocity tales as authentic. That Bryce's report appeared just when a German U-boat sank the British ocean liner *Lusitania*, killing 1,200 passengers—more than 100 from the United States—further disposing Americans to believe the tales of German cruelty.[10]

Though lacking a pipeline to the western hemisphere, the Berlin Foreign Office was also adept at spreading propaganda on U.S. shores. To newspapers, Berlin sent bulletins and capsules of the news from the German viewpoint. It placed articles, published books and pamphlets, and secretly bought periodicals to skew their editorial line. Berlin's propagandists spun their own atrocity tales, too—of Allied soldiers gouging out the eyes of prisoners of war and poisoning German wells with cholera.

The belligerents' paid publicity, of course, constituted only a fraction of the news. Over two and a half years, as the Germans, French, and British carried on a brutal war of attrition from their dugouts on the Western front, supporters and opponents of American involvement, guided by their own principles and passions, engaged in their own trench warfare in the realm of public opinion. Theodore Roosevelt led the northeastern Republicans in banging the drums for war, while William Jennings Bryan marshaled the agrarian hinterland for peace. Civic leaders of various stripes formed societies for one cause or another that made public statements, published pamphlets, placed advertisements, and held rallies. Film was politicized as never before, as directors discovered the power of moving images unspooling in a darkened theater to play upon the emotions. In 1916, D. W. Griffith, whose *Birth of a Nation* Wilson had screened at the White House, released *Intolerance*, a thinly veiled, melodramatic plea for harmony. J. Stuart Blackton of the Vitagraph Company, a friend of TR and Gilbert Parker, made *The Battle Cry of Peace* (1915), which imagined a militarily backward and unprepared country decimated by an unspecified foreign power—whose soldiers were outfitted in familiar-looking spiked helmets.[11]

Events, not spin, exerted the decisive influence. Germany's repeated sinking of ships carrying American passengers, first in 1915 and again after Wilson's reelection, made Americans willing and eager to fight. Still, the protracted struggle for public opinion made the interpretation of the war itself—questions of guilt and motive, of right and wrong—a chief prize amid the spoils.

*   *   *

The battle for the American mind played out most consequentially in the battle for the mind of Woodrow Wilson. Ever conscious of public opinion, the president endeavored, as he told Bryan, "to carry out the double wish of our people, to maintain a firm front in respect to what we demand of Germany and yet do nothing that might in any way involve us in the war." Neither a jingo nor an isolationist, Wilson sought for three years to divine a consensus within popular sentiment that would legitimize his middle way.[12]

His commitment to neutrality was sincere. Wilson knew that war would fracture the consensus behind his Progressive agenda at home, while neutrality promised the surest route toward brokering a lasting peace that would avert future conflicts—his overriding international goal. He therefore pushed for neutrality with the full weight of presidential publicity. He followed his original August 1914 proclamation with a request to Tumulty to have the statement printed and displayed in post offices nationwide. At Bryan's suggestion, he wrote a longhand call for neutrality that was copied onto film stock and shown in moviehouses.

But neither the foreign powers nor the American public deigned to respect Wilson's summons. The belligerent leaders accused each other of misrepresentations and lies, while violating or skirting neutrality laws, pressuring Wilson to respond. And if neutrality of deed proved difficult, neutrality of thought was impossible. Inevitably, American sympathies gravitated toward the British and French, for whatever the Allies' violations, they paled next to Germany's practice of torpedoing ships carrying civilians. Yet hearing reports of the sanguinary trench warfare and poison gas, the public remained leery of war. Rollin Kirby, cartoonist for the *New York World*, inked a cartoon showing Wilson poised uncomfortably between the anti-war Bryan, holding a caged dove of peace, and the bellicose Roosevelt, bedecked in cowboy regalia and firing pistols.

In the summer of 1915, however, Wilson tilted in the hawks' direction. Without renouncing neutrality, he supplemented it with a plan of military "preparedness" that he hoped would deter German aggression on the seas. What set this shift in motion was the assault on HMS *Lusitania*. On May 7, 1915, German U-boats sank the majestic British ocean liner off the shores of Ireland. Germany had torpedoed vessels before, but none of those assaults had been as lethal. American anger toward Germany boiled over, as editorials denounced the strike as wanton murder. Still, a poll of editors showed just 6 of 1,000 people nationwide wanted to go to war. Wilson responded with a protracted exchange of diplomatic letters with Germany, but Berlin showed little interest in conciliation. By summer the president concluded that only a stronger naval force and a reserve army could put teeth into his threats to hold the Central Powers accountable for any further loss of life.

A battle for public opinion was joined. Wilson thought preparedness would strengthen the chances for peace; isolationists and pacifists saw it as a prelude to war. In June, Bryan resigned from the cabinet. "I believe that I can do more on the outside to prevent war than I can do on the inside," he said. "I can work to direct public opinion so it will not exert pressure for extreme action." Speaking around the country, he attracted zealous crowds and gained encouragement from like-minded congressmen. From the other side, Republican hawks, eyeing a winning issue for the upcoming presidential race, hectored the president as pusillanimous.

In August came not only the exposure of the Albert affair but also Germany's sinking of yet another British ship, the *Arabic*, which killed more civilians. Wilson now formulated a preparedness plan, which he touted publicly in the fall, including in his annual message to Congress.

Mail to the White House suggested that he had found what the *Springfield Republican* called the "middle ground where the average man proverbially stands."

But Wilson's shift also stimulated opposition. Many Progressives turned against him, and reports came to the White House, particularly from the Midwest, that Americans were growing uneasy with the expenditures and taxes that a military buildup would require. Tumulty persuaded Wilson to make the kind of Rooseveltian swing around the circle that he had previously avoided. Only presidential leadership, he argued, could give shape to the masses' inchoate impulses. Wilson agreed. "It is my duty to explain this matter to the country and summon its support," he replied.[13]

In late January of 1916 and into February, Wilson traveled by rail through the Midwest with his new wife, Edith, Joe Tumulty, and a car of reporters. His route took him up from New York out to Wisconsin and Illinois, and down through Missouri, with stops in heavily German industrial cities such as Milwaukee and Chicago and rural isolationist redoubts in Iowa and Kansas. He spoke in armories and auditoriums and often from his train, drawing crowds as large as 18,000—some 1 million people in total. In Cleveland, some 3,000 citizens, having waited an hour in the pouring rain, sat hushed and still as Wilson laid out his tricky but compelling argument: only by preparing enough forces for combat could America increase the likelihood of peace. By the end of his address, the crowd was cheering wildly. They filed out of the building, David Lawrence reported, sobered and awed, ready to assume the burdens Wilson had placed on them.

Wilson's tour gathered momentum. From his train's back platform, he gamely traded quips with admirers, and he warmed to well-wishers at his hotels and in city streets. Parades and fanfare gave the tour the whiff of a campaign trip. "The president's political advisers privately admit that far more than the mere fate of the 'preparedness program' hinges on the trip," wrote *The Washington Post*. "It will afford opportunity to find out just how he stands with the people themselves." Yet if Wilson was thinking about his reelection, only ten months away, he asked for no votes and muted his partisanship in favor of an appeal to the national good. "I want you to go home determined that, within the whole circle of your influence, the president—not as partisan, but as representative of the national honor—shall be backed up by the whole force that is in the nation," he said.[14]

Wilson returned to Washington confident that he had public opinion behind him. "The President, journeying through districts where he was supposed to be weak, has, in fact, received more attention and been applauded more vigorously, than any previous Executive on tour," noted the *New York Times*. While some midwestern pacifists charged that Wilson was spreading panic, and a few Democrats began talking up a nomination challenge by Champ Clark, Wilson had gained a hearing from farmers and isolationists in "enemy country." Advocates of a strong, Progressive presidency, meanwhile, celebrated his initiative. "It is a wonderful example of that opportunity for aggressive leadership which the Presidency of the United States places in the hands of the bold political strategist and the effective platform speaker," editorialized *The New Republic*. To Herbert Croly, Wilson had finally "become an independent executive whose power rests on his direct influence on popular opinion."[15]

Precisely how much Wilson's tour moved public opinion remained unclear. To broker even a modest preparedness plan, Wilson had to resort to horse-trading with Congress—the kind of insider bargaining that public appeals were supposed to supersede. The final deal—too mild for Secretary of War Lindley Garrison, who resigned in frustration—doubled the Army's size and added 150 ships to the Navy. It was enough, at least, to eliminate "preparedness" as an election issue in 1916.

Wilson also made unexpected progress on the diplomatic front. After a year of intransigence, Germany pledged to limit its submarine warfare and for the rest of the year sank no ships carrying American civilians. Wilson now seemed poised to bring Germany to heel without sending GIs into combat, and as a result he basked in popular favor. By June, when the Democrats gathered in St. Louis for their convention, no one was pushing a challenge to his nomination. Bryan—denied a seat as a delegate but attending as a journalist—announced: "I agree with the American people in thanking God we have a president who has kept—who will keep—us out of war."[16]

* * *

In Bryan's off-the-cuff remarks lay the seed that would flower into Wilson's campaign slogan. Later viewed as naive or deceptive, "He Kept Us Out of War" in fact reflected pride in an achievement Wilson hoped to sustain. It grew into a household phrase, thanks to a redoubled commitment to publicity by Wilson's reelection team.

Despite the president's feelings about mass media, his 1916 campaign staff used advertising and mass communications as never before. McAdoo advised party chairman Vance McCormick to "employ three or four of the brightest young advertising experts and enthusiasts in this country.

... Snappy, pungent advertisements, consistently employed throughout the campaign, will have a tremendous effect." Publicist Robert Woolley, assisted by the muckraker George Creel, spearheaded the operation, which he billed as "widespread publicity of a kind never before attempted." Their shop circulated a 12-page brochure, given to newspapers for easy use as a magazine supplement, as well as campaign literature on every salient topic aimed at every conceivable voting bloc. They exchanged memos on how to pitch Wilson's record on crises from Mexico to the German assault on Belgium. And they plastered "He Kept Us Out of War" on billboards, trolley cars, subway stops, and electric signs, and promoted it in ads in newspapers and magazines.[17]

Wilson wasn't entirely happy with this blitz. As Creel recalled, the president showed up at party headquarters one day "white hot with indignation" after "every billboard in the land began to blaze with the battle cry." He rebuked the publicity team for "deliberately giving the impression that my policy is one of unchangeable neutrality, no matter what arises." Wilson read from speeches he had given that were nuanced in tone, and Woolley and Creel promised to desist. But the slogan was already on people's lips. Besides, Wilson wasn't above oversimplification himself. Late in the campaign, he took to arguing speciously that since the Republican nominee Charles Evans Hughes was promising to radically change Wilson's policy, and since Wilson's was a policy of peace, Hughes could only be planning for war.[18]

In November, Wilson became the first Democratic president since Andrew Jackson to win a second consecutive term. Republicans blamed advertising. TR, with typical hyperbole, credited Woolley with "the most brilliant achievement in the history of American politics," and Hughes, who had resigned from the Supreme Court to run for president, sourly ascribed his loss to the "enormous picture-posters, giving a lurid display of the carnage of war, while on the side-lines stood a mother and her children looking on." Hughes neglected to mention that his own campaign had retained the Batten advertising agency—and, thanks to corporate donations, had had more money than the Democrats to spend on publicity and ads.[19]

But if the Democrats played on emotions, Wilson's anti-war rhetoric wasn't insincere. His reversal the following spring was not the cynical fulfillment of a long-planned bait and switch but a reluctant reassessment of his neutrality policy in the face of renewed German hostility. In December 1916, he had embarked on a full-scale initiative to engineer an end to the war, and as late as January 1917 had gone before the Senate to call for a "peace without victory," a "peace between equals"—an American-led negotiation to end the carnage, not the smashing of one side. Yet Berlin was unmoved. On March 18, German U-boats sank three American ships. Meanwhile, Ambassador Walter Hines Page cabled Wilson from London to alert him that British intelligence had deciphered a telegram from the German foreign minister, Arthur Zimmermann, to the Mexican Embassy, proposing a secret alliance. Wilson decided to seek a declaration of war.[20]

Progressives signed on, endorsing Wilson's visions of a liberal postwar order, as John Dewey said, as "genuine possibilities, objects of a fair adventure." Crusades against German militarism were of a piece with the Progressives' crusades against corruption, both advancing the dream of democracy. Yet anti-war sentiment also remained robust. Voicing the deepest objections was the young writer Randolph Bourne, a disillusioned Dewey acolyte. Bourne took a dim view of the "herd," as he called the public, and questioned his compatriots' ability to resist publicity. "The minorities are either intimidated into silence," he said, "or brought slowly around by a subtle process of persuasion which may seem to them really to be converting them." To Dewey and pro-war Progressives, he asked, "If the war is too strong for you to prevent, how is it going to be weak enough for you to control and mould to your liberal purposes?"[21]

On the night of April 2, the president ascended again to Capitol Hill and recited his history of forbearance toward Germany. But now, he argued, only military action could preserve liberal values and lay the groundwork for a lasting peace. "The world," he said, "must be made safe for democracy." Senator John Sharp Williams, the Mississippian who had frowned upon Wilson's first address to Congress, started to clap, and as his colleagues and the galleries joined in, the applause cascaded into a roar. After avowing unambiguously that most Americans of German birth were "true and loyal Americans," Wilson, calling to mind incidents of German subterfuge and sabotage, warned that "if there should be disloyalty, it will be dealt with with a firm hand of stern repression"—a statement clearly aimed at spies and saboteurs, not mere dissenters.[22]

In his peroration, Wilson waxed philosophical. "It is a fearful thing to lead this great peaceful people into war," he reflected, "into the most terrible and disastrous of all wars, civilization itself seeming to be in the balance." After leaving the Hill, cheered by onetime pacifists and Republican antagonists, Wilson returned to the White House, where, according to Tumulty, he called his address "a message of death." He put his head on the cabinet table and wept.[23]

11

THE JOURNEY OF GEORGE CREEL

ON APRIL 13, 1917, days after America declared war on Germany, Woodrow Wilson's chief cabinet officers—Secretary of the Navy Josephus Daniels, Secretary of War Newton Baker, and Secretary of State Robert Lansing—sent the president a memorandum proposing a new body for handling wartime information. Together, the three men would constitute a committee overseeing all executive communications. It would ensure that relevant war news reached the public, avoiding "premature or ill-advised announcements" that might pose "a source of danger," while providing "full, frank statements concerning the conduct of the public business." To run this body they would hire a civilian director, "preferably some writer of proved courage, ability, and vision."[1]

The letter was pro forma: Wilson had already created the body. The next day he signed Executive Order 2594, establishing the Committee on Public Information, whose work he intended to be "intimately associated with the policy of the administration." Over time, it became the largest and most controversial government vehicle ever formed for influencing mass opinion and a landmark step in Wilson's expansion of presidential power.[2]

No small part of that achievement—or its controversy—stemmed from Wilson's choice of a director. Though others, notably a young Walter

Lippmann, had wanted the job, the president placed his trust in George Creel. Alas, the tenacity that had made Creel a fearsome muckraker—fighting for women's suffrage, child labor laws, and an end to police corruption—and a stalwart campaign warrior didn't equip him well for forging civic harmony. A squat former amateur boxer, Creel, forty-one, had wiry dark hair, deeply recessed brown eyes, a misshapen nose, and a pronounced churlish streak. He was tart, feisty, and prone to demonize his enemies. His one previous stint in government, as police commissioner of Denver, lasted fifteen days.[3]

Creel was first taken with Wilson in 1905, when the Princeton president came to Kansas City, Creel's hometown. Wilson dazzled the journalist with "the clarity of his thought, the beauty of his phrasing," and Creel wrote one of the first articles touting Wilson for president. During the 1912 campaign, when Wilson visited Denver, he gave Creel an hour-long interview in his railroad car. That year Creel also married Blanche Bates, a leading stage actress who went on to befriend the president's daughter Margaret. After his work on the 1916 campaign, Creel was asked by Wilson to join the administration, but he returned to journalism. One of his first pieces that winter was a fawning interview with the president for *Everybody's Magazine*.[4]

Once war came to seem likely, however, Creel lobbied Daniels and Wilson to run the planned publicity bureau. From April 1917 until the armistice of November 1918, he met with the president roughly three times a month and corresponded with him often—"almost," Creel feared, "to the point of annoyance." But Wilson wasn't annoyed; he told Congress that "the Committee on Public Information was created by me," and that "Mr. Creel is my personal representative." Even loyal Joe Tumulty was shunted aside as the press briefer. Yet Creel's tenure proved an unhappy one, as he tussled with Congress, irked colleagues, alienated the press corps, and helped saddle the president with a reputation for managing information with an insufferably heavy hand.[5]

* * *

Wilson had long been contemplating, as he wrote in a 1914 letter, "a publicity bureau which would handle the real facts as far as the government was aware of them, for all the departments." The idea had been in the air at least since Roosevelt's abortive foray to streamline executive branch communications under George Cortelyou. Despite that cautionary precedent, though, Wilson clung to his idealistic notion that newsmen should responsibly relay the government's message. He also had some basis to think that reporters might welcome the bureau, since they had come to appreciate the time-saving handouts, advance speech texts, and publicity officers that were now sprinkled throughout the government.

Many journalists liked the idea of a wartime information bureau. Advocates included Wilson's former students David Lawrence, now writing for the *New York Post*; Albert Bullard, the author of *Mobilising America*, a manifesto for boosting public morale; and the twenty-eight-year-old Lippmann, who met with the president in March 1917 after writing him about the importance of public opinion to the war effort. Weighing in with his own memo as well was the indefatigable Creel.[6]

Progressives all, these writers saw nothing nefarious in the information management regimes they proposed. On the contrary, they thought a publicity bureau would refute misinformation and foreign propaganda and educate the public about war news, without resorting to the censorship urged by jingoes like the young Army major Douglas MacArthur. When an espionage bill that Wilson sent to Congress included provisions for censorship, Creel, like the other journalists, opposed them, and they were removed. The government, Creel believed, should suppress only "information of a properly secret nature" such as advance news of troop movements. Nor should it cook up falsehoods, as the European governments were doing: no phony claims of battlefield routs, no cover-ups of embarrassing setbacks, no hyperbolic atrocity tales. Instead of suppression, Creel and Wilson's other journalistic correspondents urged expression; instead of secrecy, publicity.[7]

Government publicity also promised to forge the national unity that war demanded. Although by 1917 the public largely favored intervention, pockets of resistance persisted. Publicity, Wilson's correspondents contended, would rally the holdouts to the national mission and sustain support for controversial measures like the draft. Wrote *The New Republic*, "A nation is forced to advertise its needs in order to win recruits, just as a manufacturer is forced to advertise his promises in order to gain purchasers." Though Creel and other publicity bureau advocates thought the twin goals of informing and mobilizing the public compatible, they were bound to conflict. The former goal required the straight, dry, provision of facts; the latter prescribed the emotional and arguably partial presentation of those facts into persuasive appeals.[8]

For Creel—onetime scourge of public relations ace Ivy Lee—to have become a government propagandist has struck some historians as a betrayal of his values. But, like most advocates, Creel believed he was on the side of truth, seeking to lead, not mislead, the public. His committee, he insisted, didn't lie, and the charges that he knowingly issued false statements resulted from differences of interpretation between hawks and doves, or between the press and the administration. Of his committee's work, he wrote, "We did not call it 'propaganda,' for that word, in German hands, had come to be associated with lies and corruptions."

Nonetheless, Creel admitted that his bureau became "a vast enterprise in salesmanship," with "energy exerted to arouse ardor and enthusiasm." Although some critics, such as Lippmann, argued that this embrace of advocacy led Creel into propaganda, it too could be understood— or rationalized—as something closer to muckraking, which likewise involved disclosing facts to enlighten and move public opinion, using passionate appeals, florid writing, and even cartoonish stereotypes to add potency to one's case.[9]

In his support for government publicity, moreover, Creel was in good progressive company. Enlisting to help him were academics, journalists, and artists, as well as future public relations pioneers such as Edward Bernays, Carl Byoir, and Heber Blankenhorn. Arthur Bullard signed up as a deputy to Creel. *McClure's* veteran Will Irwin, a lifelong propaganda critic who had been reporting on the fighting from Europe, ran the Creel Committee's Foreign Section. "S.S." McClure, Charles Edward Russell, and Ida Tarbell filled athenaeums and union halls with speeches on behalf of American war aims. Even Upton Sinclair, formerly a pacifist, asked Creel to have the committee translate, serialize, and distribute abroad *Jimmie Higgins*, a novel-in-progress featuring an anti-war Socialist laborer who, on realizing he had been duped by the kaiser's Germany, gives his life for democracy on the fields of France. Creel liked the unfinished manuscript, which rehearsed a host of German atrocity stories in page-turning, *Jungle*-like prose, but decided that he lacked the manpower to handle it. Later, Sinclair turned against the war and rewrote the ending to have Higgins devote himself to the Russian Revolution.

* * *

Fueled by the commitment to defeat Germany in the name of liberal values, Creel built a mammoth enterprise, harnessing popular passions to industrial-age capacities to produce and distribute information on an unprecedented scale—"the largest and most intensive effort to carry quickly a fairly uniform set of ideas to all the people of a nation," said

Lippmann. Creel began with a small staff operating out of a library in the Navy building near the White House, and at first concerned himself with dispensing news. But his ambition and imagination quickly spawned a multitude of divisions; at its peak the committee employed 395 staffers and thousands more volunteers. Over the next year and a half, the Creel Committee continually outgrew its quarters, moving first to a town house up the street on Jackson Place, and then, after every basement corner and attic hideaway was filled, branching out into one adjacent dwelling after another.[10]

Creel and his team created and distributed all manner of words and images. Their labors yielded such memorable artifacts as James Montgomery Flagg's "I Want You" recruitment poster of Uncle Sam and the eight-reel documentary film *Pershing's Crusaders*. But those icons scarcely conveyed the volume of the committee's output. Creel's shop churned out roughly ten press releases a day—a flood of notices that yielded, by his estimate, 20,000 columns of material in American newspapers each week. It printed nearly 7 million copies of Wilson's 1917 Flag Day address calling for civic unity. A traveling "War Exposition" drew receipts of $583,000 in Chicago, $167,000 in Cleveland, $17,000 in Waco, Texas. Creel's shop produced literally millions of press releases, news bulletins, syndicated feature articles, advertisements, movies, political cartoons, classroom lesson plans, songs, museum exhibits, Chautauqua-circuit speeches, talking points, and overseas radio broadcasts (a major step in developing that medium), all designed to inform the public, explain the administration's views, and stoke popular support for the war.

The committee's prime function was to release information. Washington's wartime business was unparalleled in its scope, and the committee took charge of issuing not just casualty lists and battlefront advances but official data from the White House, the cabinet departments, wartime agencies like the War Industries Board, and other bodies. Only the State Department, whose secretary, Robert Lansing, despised Creel, refused to let the committee handle its news. The committee also issued a periodical, the *Official Bulletin*, containing every war-related federal regulation, announcement, and presidential statement.[11]

In these efforts, Creel forswore cooked-up propaganda of the German and British variety, insisting that he was just publishing the facts. Yet at other times he acknowledged that he saw the war as a "fight for the *minds* of men, for the 'conquest of their convictions,'" and a portion of his committee's output used pictures, photographs, and films—vivid, color-

ful, flamboyantly presented—to achieve emotional effects. Charles Dana
Gibson, the illustrator whose willowy "Gibson Girls" graced magazines
and popular books, assembled a Division of Pictorial Publicity that met
weekly at Keens Chophouse in Manhattan; the brigade of portraitists,
muralists, lithographers, cartoonists, and designers volunteered to draw
up posters and advertising illustrations to "appeal to the heart," as Gibson
said. In their posters, beneficent, maternal nurses promoted the Red
Cross and weary, worthy doughboys touted the YMCA. Some trafficked
in dehumanizing, anti-German imagery, such as a poster titled "Bachelor
of Atrocities" that denounced "Prussian Terrorism" and featured a menacing, mustachioed Teuton looming over a gang of soldiers pillaging the
University of Louvain. Creel claimed that he tried to prevent that controversial poster and other inflammatory fare. Still, on billboards, trolley cars,
subway stations, and the sides of barns along the roadside, these images,
though not typical of the committee's work, became its most visible face.[12]

Playing to popular passions, too, were the Four-Minute Men, another of
Creel's divisions, which enlisted citizens to deliver brief pro-war speeches
to captive audiences in public spaces such as movie theaters, during the
interval between reels. With a name chosen to evoke the Revolutionary
War, the Four-Minute Men proved wildly successful, as local volunteers
vied to participate. The division's spokesmen encompassed businessmen
and workers, whites and blacks (in separate departments), and Italian and
Yiddish speakers, and units sprang up as far away as Alaska and Guam.
Though plenty of moviegoers found these speakers insufferable, the Four-
Minute Men, as much as any Creel Committee unit, helped foster the
hyperpatriotism, conformity, and intolerance for which the world war's
home front would come to be known.[13]

*   *   *

Brahms was banned. Sauerkraut was renamed "liberty cabbage." Eugene
Debs was jailed for an anti-war speech. Rampaging Illinoisans lynched
Robert Prager, a German-American, after wrapping him in an American
flag. Violence also fastened upon the jingoes; one Four-Minute Man from
Kentucky was beaten up for speaking for seventeen minutes. Such tales of
hysteria and vigilantism—comic, tragic, barbaric—have become infamous,
frequently held out as excesses brought on by Creel's propaganda. But neat
claims of causality do not hold up. The Creel Committee operated amid a
public clamor for unity and a reasonable worry about subversion. "There was
enough obnoxious German propaganda," John Dewey said, "to create legiti-

mate fear." It was ordinary citizens, moreover, at least as much as the government, who mobilized to quash dissent, deriving their motivation not from Creel or Wilson but from their own homespun values and long traditions of civic duty. Grassroots groups like the American Protective League monitored and rooted out putatively seditious behavior. The Pittsburgh Press Club put members to work scouring Pennsylvania's newspapers for disloyal articles, while the *Literary Digest* called on readers to mail in subversive items.[14]

In the world of motion pictures, too, private citizens also outstripped the Creel Committee in fanning the wartime fervor. Like its news division, the committee's film division mostly trafficked in informational fare, distributing Army Signal Corps movies of the soldiers for use in newsreels. Some of its films had a patriotic cast, like the hour-long documentary *Pershing's Crusaders*, which framed General John J. Pershing's troops as the moral heirs to the Anglo-Saxon warriors who battled the Saracens, and which featured melodramatic title cards, written by a young Bruce Barton, describing "the young men of America" marching off "to rescue Civilization." But the footage in *Pershing's Crusaders* was mild, most of it historical in nature. In contrast, the studios' "Hate the Hun" pictures, like *The Prussian Cur* and *The Kaiser, the Beast of Berlin*, boasted messages as subtle as their titles, depicting Teutonic butchers who flung babies through open windows. Creel Committee officials actually took pains to condemn these films, and both Wilson and his wife intervened on occasion to tone down Hollywood's propaganda.[15]

Even within the government, the Creel Committee couldn't claim primacy in fomenting excess. Although Wilson declared that he never wished to "deny to the people of a free republic like our own their indisputable right to criticize their own public officials," his administration failed to uphold that ideal. Congress overwhelmingly passed the much-derided Espionage Act, and eleven months later it added a series of amendments informally called the Sedition Act. A third law, the Trading with the Enemy Act, controlled foreign communications. Designed to crack down on Americans who might be materially aiding the Central Powers, these laws were written so broadly and construed so loosely as to criminalize legitimate expression. Postmaster General Albert Burleson, a reactionary Texan whom Edward House called "the most belligerent member of the cabinet," denied use of the mails to publications like the left-wing *Masses*, usually on flimsy grounds. Around the country, meanwhile, Thomas Gregory's Justice Department prosecuted socialists, pacifists, and German-Americans for deeds—and words—deemed, in the Sedition

Act's sweeping language, "disloyal, profane, scurrilous, or abusive" toward the government. Of 1,500 arrests under the law, only 10 involved actual sabotage. To the Progressives' dismay, Oliver Wendell Holmes, the liberal icon, led a unanimous Supreme Court in upholding three Espionage Act convictions, including Eugene Debs's.

In this context, George Creel's exertions were comparatively tame. The bulk of his publicity, when not informational, encompassed legitimate calls to enlist in the Army, buy war bonds, and help the Red Cross. Inside the administration, he clashed with the fanatical Burleson and Gregory. Rejecting their prosecutorial madness, Creel told Wilson that the cabinet officers bore the blame for the Democrats' losses in the 1918 midterm elections. "All the radical or liberal friends of your anti-imperialist war policy," Creel fretted, "were either silenced or intimidated" or "besmirched." After the war, Creel complained that Gregory, "a vicious old reactionary," had tried to tar Creel and his bureau as "pacifists, pro-Germans and Bolsheviks. . . . My own dossier . . . was a foot thick and accused me of every treason."[16]

Indeed, for all the taunts Creel suffered from Progressives, he drew more fire from the right, which called him "pacifistic" and charged him with "giving comfort to the enemy." The National Security League denounced one of the committee's innocent pamphlets as "a masterpiece of Hun propaganda." Within the administration, Assistant Secretary of War Benedict Crowell berated Creel for not doing enough to boost the soldiers' morale: "May I suggest that a little savagery be added to the carefully prepared and exceedingly moderate statements of the official news?" When Creel refused to spread uncorroborated atrocity tales, Republicans attacked him for being soft on Germany. "Conservatives call me a radical," he complained as he was hauled before a hostile Congress, "and the radicals all call me a conservative."

Clearly, whatever success Creel's publicity techniques achieved in conjuring nationalistic ardor or in ostracizing dissenters, he mustered no comparable skill in stifling criticisms of his own bureau. "His enemies," observed *Everybody's Magazine*, "far exceed . . . his friends." Will Irwin believed that his sharp-tongued boss became a scapegoat for generalized dissatisfaction. Anyone with a grievance against the administration, Irwin wrote, simply "took it out on Creel."[17]

* * *

He made a ripe target. Never beloved by his colleagues, he was described as a bad choice from the start. On his hiring, the *New York Times* editorialized that he lacked the "judicial temperament" for the job, and Lippmann, who had feuded with Creel since 1915, seems to have had him in mind in warning Wilson not to hire "anyone who is not himself tolerant, nor . . . unacquainted with the long record of folly which is the history of suppression."

The first major conflict of Creel's tenure erupted three months into the war, over what became known as "The Fourth of July Hoax." (Creel denied it was a hoax.) It began when an Associated Press article contradicted a boosterish committee account of a U-boat attack on an American trans-port ship and implied that Navy Secretary Daniels had concocted the affair. The AP soon retracted its story, and Creel proved guilty of nothing worse than some extravagant "phraseology," as he defensively put it. But the episode confirmed many people's worst fears about the bureau and its director. For weeks, Wilson's Republican foes, who remembered Creel's campaign work in 1916, joyously seized on the gaffe. Blasting Creel on the Senate floor, Boies Penrose of Pennsylvania demanded an inquiry and the publication of the names, duties, and salaries of his staff. Others unfairly denounced the U-boat incident as a "fable" or a "fairy tale," and the GOP milked the fracas for weeks. For the rest of the war, accusations that Creel fabricated news kept coming, even though he was guilty of little more than a few minor mistakes and some routine hyperbole, such as uninten-tionally exaggerating the speed with which planes were being shipped to France.[18]

The legislators' attacks on Creel were, like Ben Tillman's earlier attacks on TR, partisan and institutional. Branding Creel "Wilson's press agent," some Republicans charged that he was promoting the president instead of the war. Others fretted that executive branch publicity was infringing on Congress's prerogatives. In December 1917, Frederick Gillett—the author of the 1913 anti-publicity bill and now the acting Republican leader—tried to tie the committee's funding to the release of its staffers' salaries, attest-ing to an enduring concern about executive power.

A year into the war, in April 1918, the Republicans used the debates over the Sedition Act to engage in another round of Creel-bashing. Argu-ing that the emerging bill would punish free speech, they noted wryly that some of Creel's own utterances would be subject to prosecution should the bill pass. Creel struck back in a talk in New York City when, queried about his critics, he replied: "I don't like slumming, for that reason I won't explore the heart of Congress." Demands for Creel's ouster followed. Republican Joe Cannon proposed that he be "taken by the nape of the neck and the slack of the pants and thrown into space." Apologizing, the beleaguered director agreed to accept congressional supervision, but his perfunctory contrition satisfied few. His chief patron, however, remained steadfast. "When I think of the manner in which Mr. Creel has been maligned and persecuted," the president said, "I think it a very human thing for him to have said." Unappeased, Congress halved the Creel Committee's allocation in the next appropriations bill.[19]

Besides Congress, Creel also fought with reporters—both about the allegedly manufactured news and about censorship. Creel insisted that all wartime censorship was voluntary; the administration was simply laying down terms for what Wilson called "a patriotic reticence about everything whose publication could be of injury." This was technically true. In passing the Espionage Bill, Congress rejected flat-out censorship provisions, and Creel never redacted statements in individual newspaper stories. But military censors did vet the information cabled from Europe (which fell outside Creel's purview), and Wilson did, with an executive order in October 1917, establish a board, which included Creel, that could censor external communications from specified foreign countries. Violations of Creel's voluntary guidelines, moreover, carried the implicit threat of a referral to the tender mercies of Burleson and Gregory, and even Creel chewed out editors who flouted the rules.[20]

As Congress's clashes with Creel were rooted in institutional conflicts, so were the press's. The Fourth Estate hadn't suffered large-scale control since the Civil War, and any government-imposed restrictions were bound to raise hackles. And as journalists defended their turf, Creel and Wilson often acted as if it were the height of generosity to let the press publish with as much freedom as they did.

The end came swiftly for the Creel Committee. In October 1918, a new German chancellor informed Wilson that he was ready to negotiate for peace. Although jingoes still wanted to see the kaiser's empire crushed, Wilson pursued diplomacy, based on his recently unveiled Fourteen Points—the liberal principles he formulated to undergird a new postwar order. An armistice was signed on November 11. Among the operations that wound down was the embattled Committee on Public Information, which its industrious leader somehow kept humming until June 1919, when his appropriation expired and he filed his final report to an unappreciative Congress.

*   *   *

The Committee on Public Information left a mixed legacy. Surpassing the publicity operations of McKinley and Roosevelt, it showed the potential of the federal government to spread its version of the news on a massive scale and confirmed the presidency as the cynosure of Washington. Republican gripes that Creel was serving as Wilson's personal press agent could be dismissed as partisan haymaking, but the committee's steady stream of materials did keep Wilson—however camera- and press-shy—front and center in the public eye.

Yet if world war enabled the president to ramp up his publicity apparatus, the visibility and scope of that publicity paradoxically undermined its legitimacy. Creel's feuds with Congress, his catfights with reporters, and the administration's abuses in its bid to control public debate spawned lasting bitterness and suspicion. Creel became a pariah. When he published his book *The War, the World, and Wilson*, some bookstores refused to stock it.

In the closing years of the Wilson administration, the war itself fell into disrepute. Seeking to account for their former enthusiasm for combat, observers found a convenient explanation in the widespread government-sponsored propaganda—American, German, Allied—that had played upon their emotions. Propaganda became a way for critics to make sense of the brew of groupthink, hypernationalism, and repression that they now wished to disavow. Accordingly, the war's aftermath produced a cottage industry of tracts that sowed a lasting distrust of government publicity—of all publicity—far greater than anything Ben Tillman or Frederick Gillett could have anticipated.

The denunciations of propaganda, which would continue until the eve of the next world war, had bigger targets than Creel. But the journalist and his committee were continually excoriated. Lippmann wrote a devastating review of *How We Advertised America* ("an excruciating title"), Creel's memoir of the committee. While conceding that Creel and his committee "were unjustly attacked on many occasions," Lippmann called the author "disingenuous" in claiming that he was "devoted to information alone." Worse, Creel's propaganda, in exciting popular passions, had failed to prepare the public for the sober spirit of negotiation and adjustment after the war—undermining Wilson's ultimate purposes. "The opinion created by war propaganda was almost entirely hostile to the official American view," he wrote. Creel's indiscriminate, shortsighted messaging had failed to educate the postwar public about the international burdens it was assuming and the honest-broker role it would have to play.[21]

Few criticisms of Creel in the years that followed were as sophisticated as Lippmann's. One critic said that the Creel Committee had engineered "the greatest fraud ever sold." Perhaps the cruelest attack came from a series of articles in the *Saturday Evening Post*, later collected in a volume called *Spreading Germs of Hate*, which was graced by an introduction from a penitent Edward House. The author mocked Creel as a "messianic spirit" and "chief evangelist of American propaganda." (Wilson was its "High Priest.") The book pinned blame on Wilson and Creel for whipping up American anger toward Germany and making the country so "war mad" that the president, during the peace negotiations, had to jettison his Fourteen Points. The author of this tract, a discredited writer who had been lately rehabilitated, was George Sylvester Viereck.[22]

12

DISILLUSIONMENT

IN THE FALL OF 1918, the Republicans eyed an opportunity. Riven in 1912 by Theodore Roosevelt's third-party bid, the party remained split between its Progressive and Old Guard wings. But as the world war wound down, the factions reunited in opposition to Wilson. Republicans were particularly wary of the president's plan, outlined in his Fourteen Points, to establish "a general association of nations" to keep the peace after the war.

One man determined to capitalize on the rising anti-Wilson sentiment was Albert Lasker, a high-strung, animated Chicagoan. Tall and trim, the thirty-eight-year-old Lasker had a ruddy face, deep brown eyes, and a close shave he maintained fanatically. Born in 1880 to a German-Jewish peddler who had ridden a one-eyed horse from Portsmouth, Virginia, to settle in Galveston, Texas, Albert was as a boy drawn to journalism. At sixteen he started his own news syndicate and he once scored an interview with Eugene Debs. Pressured by his father to find more lucrative work, he joined the Lord & Thomas advertising agency, which he eventually bought and built into an international powerhouse.[1]

Lasker revolutionized advertising. Under his leadership, Lord & Thomas became the first agency to have its own copywriting staff. He developed what charitably became known as "scientific" techniques, such as holding trial runs for planned campaigns. Later in his career, Lasker pioneered radio commercials, sponsored programming, and the use of direct mass mailings. His most celebrated breakthrough, forged with his first copywriter, John E. Kennedy, was "reason why" advertising. Simple in retrospect, the idea was novel at the time: not just to alert consumers to a product's existence, as admen had once thought it sufficient to do, but to offer a positive, persuasive argument for preferring the product to its rivals. In pursuit of the reason why, Lasker stripped away the literary phrasings, arch humor, and fey appeals that had been trendy, in favor of direct language.[2]

In June 1918, Lasker met Will Hays of Indiana, the Republican Party chairman, who would later become known for the censorship code he imposed on Hollywood. Hays asked the wunderkind adman to come work for the Republican National Committee. Lasker was "as interested," he recalled, "as if he had asked me to become chief ballet dancer with the Russians." But when Hays dangled the chance to meet Theodore Roosevelt, one of Lasker's heroes, a trip to Oyster Bay was scheduled. Hays and Lasker arrived to find TR, still in the news as Wilson's loudest critic, standing on his porch bedecked in khaki and boots. "They tell me you are America's greatest advertising man!" Roosevelt boomed. "Colonel," Lasker remembered replying, "no man can claim that distinction as long as you are alive!" The luncheon closed the deal. Lasker took a leave from Lord & Thomas to handle publicity for the Republicans during the 1918 midterm congressional races.

Peace was not yet at hand, but everyone was looking ahead to the postwar settlement. Lasker fervently opposed further entanglements in Europe. On behalf of the Republicans, he published and distributed at his own expense millions of copies of a pamphlet called *After the Peace, What?*, designed to shore up opposition to Wilson's plans. In late October, when Wilson called on voters to elect Democrats to Congress to help realize his war aims, Lasker and Hays charged the president with politicizing the war and impugning the Republicans' patriotism. Where Wilson had called for "peace without victory," Hays countered, Republicans wanted peace *through* victory—a "reason why" voters should vote Republican that could hardly be challenged on patriotic grounds. In November, the GOP took control of both chambers, erecting new obstacles to the implementation of Wilson's dreams.[3]

* * *

The armistice of November 1918 buoyed hopes for a more liberal world order—for the fulfillment of Wilson's vision of a lasting international comity, in which imperialist aggression would give way to self-determination and collective security.

No one cherished this goal more than Ray Stannard Baker. For some years, the muckraker and onetime TR confidant had been a steadfast Wilsonian. He had come to believe that Wilson had tendered government more "responsive to the people than ever before," and made democracy into something more than a "meaningless political slogan." Baker had worked informally for the president in 1916, causing colleagues to wonder if he had relinquished his independence. But his fealty to the president only hardened. When in 1918 Edward House asked him to gather intelligence about European radicals for the State Department in the guise of a foreign correspondent, the journalist scraped up an assignment from Herbert Croly of *The New Republic* and set to work.[4]

That work placed Baker in Europe in December 1918 when Wilson and the American delegation arrived on the USS *George Washington* to begin peace talks. Across the continent, the president was hailed as a savior, his name chanted—*Veel-son! Veel-son!*—from the sidewalks of the Champs-Elysées and the piazzas of Rome. George Creel—on hand, inauspiciously, to run publicity, while Joe Tumulty resentfully tended his Washington charges back home—claimed credit for the exuberant welcome, since his committee's Foreign Division, with its ubiquitous pamphlets and pioneering use of radio, had done much to popularize the president and his war aims. Wilson's own radio broadcasts—of the Fourteen Points in 1918 and of a peace overture to Germany that fall—made him, William Allen White noted, "the first leader to use wireless transmission for spreading his propaganda around the world." The American president was now an international celebrity.[5]

Paris was clogged with some 150 journalists, including many of the world's best—Steffens, White, Irwin, Tarbell, Sullivan, Villard, Lawrence—as well as intellectuals like W. E. B. DuBois and future stars like Arthur Krock. All needed minding. Creel urged Wilson to create a bureau for this purpose, presumably hoping to run it himself. Wilson agreed on the need. But one of Creel's staffers, Edward Bernays, released word that a large group from the much-maligned Committee on Public Information was setting up shop in Paris, resulting in a wave of bad press and more attacks on Creel. Wilson realized that his once-trusted aide was persona non grata among the press corps and sent him home to shutter his unpopular committee.[6]

For the Paris press job, Wilson instead chose Baker, describing him to House as "a man of ability, vision and ideals." Though reluctant at first to accept, Baker proceeded to devote himself to Wilson, and would even serve after his presidency as his authorized biographer. At Wilson's suggestion, Baker held daily press briefings, which regularly drew fifty reporters to the Hôtel Crillon. But Wilson's unease with reporters overtook his commitment to openness, as it had when he had curtailed his first-term press conferences. He neither attended Baker's briefings nor gave his aide enough information to make them worthwhile for the reporters.[7]

More troubling was Wilson's acquiescence to the Allied leaders' demand to deliberate in secret. Publicizing the talks, Wilson told Tumulty, "would invariably break up the whole thing." The president wasn't wrong to acknowledge the virtues of closed-door diplomacy; even the framers of the Constitution had operated in secret. But Wilson had for years sermonized in favor of transparency, and Baker foresaw trouble.

When a news embargo was announced, reporters rebelled. "After all that has been promised concerning open discussion," wrote Richard Oulahan, "steps were taken at today's session . . . to keep the people of the world in the dark." The correspondents banded together to protest what they called a "gag rule." Charged with mediating between president and press, Baker was torn. "While the President stands for 'pitiless publicity' and 'open covenants openly arrived at'—a true position if ever there was one—it is so difficult for him to practice it," he wrote in his diary. "He speaks to the masses in terms of the new diplomacy but he deals with the leaders by the methods of the old." House, whose own relations with Wilson were fraying, rebelled by leaking promiscuously. From his suite at the Crillon, and in strolls with journalists along the Seine, he blabbed about the negotiations—"the one satisfactory source of news of American activities at the conference," reported Frederick Essary of the *Baltimore Sun*.[8]

Wilson spent the balance of his time in Paris, wrote William Allen White, "almost ignoring his press relations." He was busy battling David Lloyd George and Georges Clemenceau, as well as a debilitating illness. As the Allied Powers stitched together the settlement and rumors of deal-making trickled out, Baker pushed Wilson to give reporters—and thus the public—hints of what to expect. Believing that only final decisions, not ongoing deliberations, amounted to news, the president resisted, and the two men had "a sharp argument," Baker recalled, that left him seething. Wilson and the Allied leaders had failed, Baker wrote, "the acid test of the democracy of any people": how it treats its press corps.

When Wilson unveiled the settlement on May 7, Progressives were crestfallen. "We are confronted with a peace that almost certainly cannot last," declared an unsigned *New Republic* editorial by Walter Lippmann, who had returned to his magazine after two years working for Wilson. On issues from the reparations imposed on Germany to the carving up of its colonial territories, Wilson had caved to the Allies. Though some horse-trading surely had been necessary to reach consensus, greater fidelity to Wilson's axiom of publicity might have helped liberals stomach the inevitable disappointments; at the least, it could have shown the president striving to uphold his principles. Still, governmental practices for managing the news had by now become a permanent feature of American democracy; any president, by virtue of his immense responsibilities, would have to be selective in what he shared with the press corps. But Wilson's secrecy ensured that a feeling of betrayal would seep into the American consciousness as rapidly as the ink on the parchment of the treaty signed in the Hall of Mirrors at the Palace of Versailles that June.[9]

*   *   *

Over his two terms, Wilson's fashioning of a public presidency—the press conferences, the speeches, the Creel Committee—in the service of strengthening his office had, while heartening Progressives, also offended traditionalists. To these critics, Wilson's aggressive leadership upset the proper balance among the branches of government. "In the nation's affairs," wrote Henry Campbell Black, author of the widely used *Black's Law Dictionary*, "we have witnessed the decay of representative government and the substitution for it of a presidential autocracy."[10]

This sort of discontent had posed challenges for Wilson before. But now, coupled with Progressive disillusionment over the postwar settlement, it threatened his paramount goal: winning Senate approval of the Treaty of Versailles. With the Republicans running Congress, the president needed his liberal base more than ever to inspire popular enthusiasm for ratification. But liberals were divided, with key intellectuals such as those at *The New Republic* coming down against the treaty. Meanwhile, Wilson's unprecedented months-long absence from Washington had allowed Republican majority leader Henry Cabot Lodge to unify the opposition in Congress. An array of strange bedfellows—Theodore Roosevelt Progressives, heartland isolationists, southern Democrats—joined hands to mount a publicity campaign against the treaty as vibrant as Wilson's advocacy was pallid. From Washington, a despairing Tumulty cabled Paris about the need for better publicity.

Republican opposition centered on the decision to create a League of Nations to preserve peace through international arbitration. Most troublesome was Article X of the league's covenant, which pledged league members to act against any violation of a member's sovereignty. Had he compromised, Wilson probably could have secured Lodge's support and that of the two thirds of the Senate he needed for ratification. But Wilson believed that Lodge's proposed amendments would eviscerate the commitment to collective security, and he judged the battle for the league as the last great fight of his presidency. It was a self-fulfilling prophecy.

With the stakes so high, Wilson chose again to take up another rhetorical appeal. He had reason to believe in the power of his speeches. His tour for preparedness in 1916 had energized his presidency and helped him obtain a strong bill. His stirring addresses to Congress had served him well in readying the country for war in 1917 and unveiling the Fourteen Points. Tumulty pushed for a swing around the circle that might revive the old Wilsonian magic. The president was still, after all, "truly formidable as a speaker," as former president Taft, a qualified league supporter, noted, and his stumping might well "frighten Republicans into a more reasonable frame of mind." Creel, characteristically, told Tumulty that a tour would dissipate the "partisan lies" poisoning public opinion.

On September 3, Wilson boarded a train for Columbus, Ohio, and points west. His tour followed the familiar grooves that Roosevelt had cut: a taxing journey of 8,000 miles, over twenty-six days, with thirty-seven stops, out to the Pacific coast. He hoped to unleash a surge of public support that would sweep aside defiant senators. Tumulty reserved a press car to house a score of journalists and movie cameramen, and he sent advance men to prep the local reporters at each stop. The pace was frenetic. Wilson had never before given so many speeches in such a short time. Having battled poor health since Paris, he showed the fatigue, and his early speeches fell flat.

On the fly, Tumulty drafted a series of memos outlining a strategy by which the president could lift the debate out of partisan haggling. By the time the caravan reached Wyoming and Utah, the audiences' cheers were growing louder, according to reporters, and Wilson was showing more vigor. With the correspondents he threw off his usual inhibitions, exulting in what one writer described as gabby bull sessions. As he swung down the

California coast, newspapers noted that crowds were coming away electrified. He predicted "with absolute certainty" that America's failure to join the league would guarantee "another world war."

On September 25, Wilson spoke in Pueblo, Colorado. Through the morning, when he spoke in Denver, he suffered from a pounding in his skull so intense that he could hardly see. But in the afternoon he rallied to deliver at the state fairgrounds what David Lawrence called "a masterpiece of eloquence" and Tumulty deemed the finest performance of the tour. Wilson lashed out at the campaign of "organized propaganda," which he said came "from exactly the same sources" that had "threatened this country here and there with disloyalty." Promising "to check the falsehoods that have clustered around this great subject," he coldly rebutted the arguments against the league. Then, with heartrending sincerity, he reminded his audience what was at stake. "I advised the Congress of the United States to create the situation that led to the death of their sons," he said. Now he was concerned with "the next generation," who, he vowed, "shall not be sent upon a similar errand." He ended by calling for a just and lasting accord, for "pastures of quietness and peace such as the world never dreamed of before." It left audience members in tears.[11]

On the train that night, Wilson banged on the door of Edith's compartment, complaining of an excruciating headache. His face twitched, and the pain kept him up until five in the morning. These were symptoms of a cerebral thrombosis—a stroke. Wilson wanted to forge onward, but Tumulty and Cary Grayson, the president's doctor, insisted he stop the tour. On his return to Washington, Wilson was felled by another, far more severe stroke, which the White House concealed from the press. The illness incapacitated Wilson for weeks and, despite a partial recovery, would leave him impaired for the rest of his term.

Capitol Hill, meanwhile, was a hive of counterspin. Anti-Wilson journalists worked with the Republicans to spread anti-league publicity. Some wrote speeches for league opponents. Lodge fastened amendments onto the treaty—fourteen points of his own. His judgment possibly impaired by the stroke, Wilson demanded that trusty Democrats reject the terms. Loyally but foolishly, his own party mates twice did so, ensuring the treaty's defeat. Wilson was left, as his presidency expired, with no League of Nations, and no peace pact to sign.[12]

The loss was tragic. At a moment when the presidency had seemed ascendant, its limits now reappeared: for all its transformational potential, the bully pulpit hadn't repealed the checks and balances of the Constitution; for all the firepower it gave the White House, the spotlight of press attention didn't free the president of external constraints. Publicity from the Oval Office, though it could ring loud and carry far, often fell on deaf ears. In the years ahead, presidents after Wilson would push, probe, and expand these limits on executive power, sometimes with glorious success. But the limits were real, and even the ablest leaders ignored them at their peril.

PART II

THE AGE
OF BALLYHOO

After World War I, men such as Albert Lasker, Bruce Barton, and Edward Bernays enthusiastically brought the methods of advertising and public relations into the world of politics. The arrival of radio as a communications medium—along with the spread of newsreels and splashy newspaper photography—multiplied the channels by which presidents and others could now take their ideas to the people, leading Silas Bent to christen the decade an "Age of Ballyhoo." And so, even in a time of conservative governance, the White House message machine inexorably grew: Warren Harding brought professional speechwriting into the Oval Office; Calvin Coolidge mastered the press conference and the radio speech; and Herbert Hoover promoted himself through groundbreaking campaign films and a souped-up White House press office. But amid all the hype, public distrust of government publicity still escalated, fueled by deep and continuing disillusionment with the world war. From Walter Lippmann and John Dewey to H. L. Mencken and Will Irwin, philosophers and journalists pondered and argued whether publicity could still be expected to create an enlightened, self-governing citizenry as the Progressives had not so long ago hoped.

13

AFTER THE 1918 CONGRESSIONAL RACES, Will Hays of the Republican National Committee persuaded Albert Lasker to stay on and help with the 1920 presidential campaign. With Wilson and his League of Nations in disrepute, the Republicans stood poised to reclaim the White House. But in early 1919 the GOP experienced a setback. Theodore Roosevelt—Lasker's hero and the Progressive Republicans' perennial hope—died at age sixty of an embolism resulting from an abscessed tooth. By the time the party held its convention in June 1920, no clear front-runner for the nomination had emerged to replace him.

Gathered in Chicago, the GOP delegates deadlocked. Lasker favored the stalwart league opponent Hiram Johnson of California, who had won several primaries, but Johnson lost momentum as the convention balloting wore on. Then, on the ninth ballot, the delegates broke for a dark horse candidate who had been tapped by GOP panjandrums upstairs in Suite 404 of the Blackstone Hotel: the small-town newspaper publisher and one-term Ohio senator Warren Gamaliel Harding.[1]

Regal and debonair in bearing yet undistinguished in the Senate, Harding was, in the cruel judgment of Connecticut senator Frank Brandegee, "the best of the second-raters." Lasker met him for the first time during the convention's backroom dealing, when Harding visited Johnson's hotel room to offer the Californian the vice-presidential slot, only to have John-son decline. (Instead, the convention delegates stampeded for the color-less but quietly canny Massachusetts governor Calvin Coolidge.) Lasker concluded, as he later recalled, that "the end of the world had come." He decided to return to Lord & Thomas.

But a week after the convention, Harding summoned Lasker to Marion, Ohio. The nominee said that Hays, who was staying on as party chair, wanted Lasker to remain at the RNC to run election "propaganda." (That term wasn't yet fully discredited.) After confirming that Harding opposed membership in the League of Nations, Lasker agreed. He found himself overseeing a publicity division led by journalists Scott Bone and Judson Welliver—the first time a lifelong advertising man, not a career journalist, was in charge of promoting a candidate for the White House.

For several months Harding forswore stumping to run a front-porch campaign from Marion—an homage to McKinley that included hauling the late president's flagpole across the state from Canton. Lasker's publicity team operated from the home of George Christian, Harding's longtime aide, who lived next door. To a public that scarcely knew him, Harding wanted to convey homey midwestern reliability, and the campaign's pub-licity centered on his biography. Despite its echoes of McKinley's strategy, however, Harding's campaign was a leap into modernity.

* * *

Woodrow Wilson's presidency capped a quarter century in which presi-dential campaigns had changed dramatically. During the nineteenth century, when the great parties dominated, their hierarchical machines vied to mobilize armies of loyal, lockstep voters, sometimes achieving turnout rates of 80 percent or more. But the reforms that had cleaned up machine politics also bestowed unforeseen power on the individual citi-zen. The secret ballot, which came into use in the 1880s, allowed voters to break from the party line without fear of reprisal. The direct primary, an early twentieth-century innovation, gave them greater say in picking their parties' nominees. The Seventeenth Amendment, ratified in 1913, let them elect their senators directly. As these practices and assumptions weakened the bosses, power migrated to the new class of publicists. They used the tools of mass communication to sell an individual candidate's personality to an electorate that was now prone to reject unblinking party loyalty.[2]

The trend toward the candidate-centered campaign had begun in

1896, when William Jennings Bryan took to barnstorming and McKinley experimented with cinema. It accelerated in the new century under public relations men like Ivy Lee and George Creel. With each election, journalists noted the expanding role of advertising and publicity. In 1908, Oscar King Davis of the *New York Times* revealed "The Game and Cost of Making a President," exposing the literary bureaus that were distributing hundreds of thousands of copies of a candidate's speeches or statements. In 1912, *McClure's* George Kibbe Turner exposed "The New Art of Making Presidents by Press Bureaus," showing how primaries empowered image-conscious publicists like Wilson's aide Frank Stockbridge, or Oscar King Davis, who had quit the *Times* to assist TR. Four year later, the *Times* reported on a Republican plan to have "trained publicity experts ... for the first time apply to politics the same merchandising principles that are applied to successful business enterprises." On it went.[3]

Advertising's advance from its beachhead in private commerce into the public world of elections—to say nothing of its role in sustaining support for the war—heralded the maturation of a field. In the postwar years writers flocked to the lucrative warrens of Madison Avenue, even if they often treated their stints there as a form of indentured servitude. The senior men in the field fancied themselves Wilsonian interpreters of public opinion, giving voice to popular yearnings. "The product of advertising is ... public opinion," declared a pamphlet from Barton, Durstine & Osborn, an up-and-coming firm, "and in democracy public opinion is the uncrowned king." The democratic language aimed to dispel impressions that their business was deceptive and mercenary. Yoking its aims to the spirit of Progressivism, it sought to legitimize advertising's place in the political sphere.[4]

Public relations also boomed. Journalists fretted that the end of the European conflict had uncorked a geyser of what *New York World* editor Frank Cobb, in a 1919 speech to the Women's City Club of New York, called "private propaganda"—a flood of one-sided news, worked up by the legatees of Ivy Lee, who were now laboring on behalf of every conceivable cause. Before the war, a New York newspaper survey had found some 1,200 press agents employed at different companies; now they were uncountable, serving corporations, banks, railroads, "all the organizations of business and of social and political activity," Cobb noted, "even statesmen." While conceding that "in some respects they perform a highly valuable service," he argued that the hired guns existed "not to proclaim the truth, the whole truth, and nothing but the truth," but merely to convey "the particular state of facts that will be of the greatest benefit to their client—in short, to manipulate the news."[5]

Wartime propaganda, pervasive advertising, and public relations together yielded a conflicting set of lessons for politics. Many Progressives now rethought their optimistic view of an educable populace. They inched toward a darker conception of the public—more like the long-standing European conceptions of the mob—as malleable, susceptible to emotional pitches and shrewd manipulation. In the coming decade, Silas Bent, Will Irwin, Walter Lippmann, and many others would warn readers against trusting in the hired molders of opinion and even in the daily press.

To those running political campaigns, however, the emerging idea of a manipulable public suggested a different lesson: that shaping voters' opinions required the talents not so much of a professor like Woodrow Wilson as of an adman like Albert Lasker.

* * *

In promoting Warren Harding, Lasker was operating in a visual age, a landscape of illustrations, billboards, newsreels, and photography. "Photographs have the kind of authority over imagination today," wrote Lippmann, "which the printed word had yesterday and the spoken word before that." Harding, fittingly, was the first presidential contender whose good looks were key to his popularity, and Lasker assigned photographers to get up close to the candidate. Photographs would not only publicize but humanize him; a campaign memo instructed the cameramen to capture "good intimate detail stuff" of Harding at home, such as "Mrs. Harding dictating her mail." By the end of the campaign, Lasker's shop was sending out 8,000 semiweekly photographic bulletins, landing the Hardings' faces on billboards and posters and in farm journals and mass magazines.[6]

Meanwhile, motion picture cameramen filmed the proceedings at Harding's stone porch, to which politicians arrived daily by train for guest appearances. (That site, too, became the destination for a brigade of theater and film stars led by Al Jolson, who crooned a composition, "Harding, You're the Man for Us." Eventually the homestead became so busy that the Hardings had to replace their trampled lawn and flowers with gravel.) Though the newsreel footage usually pleased the Harding campaign, there were gaffes. One clip of the senator golfing loosed a minor tempest, with Democrats jeering at the Republican indulging the rich man's sport. Lasker devised a damage-control strategy. As part owner of the Chicago Cubs, he instructed the team's president, William Veeck, Sr., to bring the ball club to Marion for an exhibition game. Harding suited up and threw a few pitches, two of which turned out to be wild, though an umpire saw fit to call the Cubs' right fielder out on strikes. Harding then gave a speech chock-a-block with tortured baseball metaphors, calling for "team play" in government—a remark that implicitly tweaked Wilson for his failure to compromise with Lodge.[7]

As the baseball speech suggested, the rise of the image did not spell the death of the word. Harding retained an all-star speechwriting team that included Richard Washburn Child, Judson Welliver, George Harvey, and the future Supreme Court justice George Sutherland. But they could only do so much with their "bloviating" candidate. H. L. Mencken, who made a hobby of mocking "Gamalielese," called Harding's rhetoric "a string of wet sponges . . . tattered washing on the line . . . stale bean soup. It is rumble and bumble. It is flap and doodle. It is balder and dash." Later, William McAdoo described a Harding speech as "an army of pompous phrases moving over the landscape in search of an idea."[8]

Concerned that attention to Harding's handlers would diminish the candidate's stature, Lasker took pains to keeping the speechwriters and image makers out of view. When Lasker devised a slogan for Harding— "Let's be done with wiggle and wobble," which he placed in a Harding speech and plastered on buses and billboards nationwide—he concealed his authorial role. "We want it to appear that when the candidate wrote this sentence in his speech it was merely a passing sentence that he injected," he explained in a memo, "but that it was so forceful that it was spontaneously picked up." Amazingly, Lasker kept his role in the campaign almost completely out of the press. He declined interviews and tried, as he recalled, to "sneak in and out so the newspaper boys couldn't see me." He claimed he liked it that way: "It is my eccentricity or fancy—or maybe egotism—to want to be behind the throne and not on it."

Lasker's low profile also allowed him to carry out a pair of delicate errands. One was to refute rumors that the dark-haired, olive-skinned Harding was of African ancestry, which Lasker countered with a lily white family tree worked up by the Wyoming Historical and Genealogical Society and a cringeworthy statement boasting of Harding's "blue-eyed stock" and "finest pioneer blood." The second was to muffle whispers about Harding's long-running affair with a local woman named Carrie Phillips, which Lasker did by sending Phillips and her husband on a round-the-world tour, sustained by a cash payment of $20,000. Public relations meant controlling not just what appeared in the press but also what didn't.[9]

Lasker's publicity feats generated good copy, but not everyone lapped them up. After the baseball stunt, the *New York Times* called on both candidates to knock off the "trivialities and follies." Few voters expected Wilsonian grandeur, the *Times* conceded, but both Harding and Democrat James M. Cox should "bear in mind the dignity of their position and to pay the people the compliment of speaking to them seriously." If journalists let Lasker's role go unreported, moreover, they weren't indifferent to the publicity he generated, which was widely derided. Reporter Richard Boeckel noted that in the absence of strong party machines, "the publicity man is this year's president maker" and "the man with the best story wins." Floundering, Cox blamed his opponent's advertising. "I do not subscribe to the idea of 'selling a candidate,'" he huffed. His running mate, the charismatic Franklin Delano Roosevelt, echoed the point, warning, "Photographs and carefully rehearsed moving picture films do not necessarily convey the truth."[10]

As Americans were learning, advertising and public relations oversimplified and distorted. Ultimately, however, when Harding and Coolidge prevailed on Election Day, it had little to do with the ministrations of Lasker, Welliver, and their team. They won because Cox and FDR were pro–League of Nations Democrats at a time when the public was turning against the league, Wilson, Democrats, internationalism, and Progressivism. People wanted, as Harding said, in a famous fusillade of purple prose, "not heroics, but healing; not nostrums, but normalcy; not revolution, but restoration; not agitation, but adjustment; not surgery, but serenity; not the dramatic, but the dispassionate; not experiment, but equipoise; not submergence in internationality, but sustainment in triumphant nationality." Headline writers went with "normalcy"—a coinage that pundits mocked but that summed up well the country's downsized appetites.

It was notable that professionals like Lasker had taken over the job of selling this relative cipher to the public. Publicity professionals might lack, as a *Times* correspondent wrote, "the detached passion for truth which is the glory of the scientific mind," but these new experts were now inside the tent, and they weren't about to leave.[11]

*　*　*

Harding's administration came to be remembered for the Teapot Dome scandal, an orgy of graft and malfeasance that implicated the president's closest aides and set a benchmark for White House wrongdoing unsurpassed until Watergate. In smaller ways, however, Harding made noteworthy contributions to the development of the presidency, not least in the field of public persuasion.

Judson Welliver, who was named White House clerk, judged his boss "a well-nigh hopeless failure in the art of publicity." But that verdict formed only after scandal sullied the administration. Earlier on, Harding was judged adept at the new methods of public persuasion. Unlike Wilson, he welcomed cameramen, who recorded him smiling with guests ranging from Boy Scout troops to Albert Einstein. He displayed what Richard Oulahan called "the nose for news" of a good newspaperman. He revived twice-weekly press conferences, which contrasted favorably with Wilson's tense affairs. Half-sitting on the edge of his flat-topped desk, Harding would chat with the correspondents freely. Harding also opened a wireless station on Long Island, from which he could do what Wilson had only barely begun to do: broadcast selected speeches and messages to a worldwide radio audience.[12]

Though politically conservative, Harding accepted that the growth of the presidency under his Progressive predecessors couldn't be reversed. "Year by year, month by month, day by day," he complained, "Congress is adding to the work of the president." But the growth of the office wasn't just Congress's doing. It was the public that had made the president an object of consuming interest. "We magnified the office of president and satisfied that primitive instinct in us which must see the public welfare and the public safety personified in a single individual," wrote the journalist Clinton Gilbert. "The president speaks and you read about him in the daily press; the president poses and you see him in the movies and feel assured." Given this burden, Harding looked for help. At one point he and Lasker toyed with appointing a "director of administrative publicity," but in the end the president simply offloaded the job of writing the growing number of speeches that a president was expected to give. Welliver assumed the duties.[13]

Before Welliver wrote speeches for Harding, other presidents, including Washington and Lincoln, had at least occasionally received help writing their remarks. George Cortelyou, William Loeb, and Joe Tumulty all worked on presidential speeches, but no one doubted that TR and Wilson—men of intellect and pride—wrote their own words. (Wilson kept a typewriter at his desk.) But Harding, despite his newspaper background, was no literary man, and his campaign experience had taught him the value of a hired pen.[14]

Welliver, a round-faced, snub-nosed man with arched eyebrows, was born in Illinois and schooled at Cornell College in Iowa. Having worked as a reporter for the *Sioux City Journal* and the *Des Moines Register*, he joined the Washington press corps during TR's administration. He made his debut at the séances in 1906 by daring to criticize the president's railroad regulation policy. While other correspondents sat dumbstruck, expecting Roosevelt to banish the impudent newcomer, the president perked up, invited Welliver to the White House the next night to chew over the issue, and then sent him to Europe to study transportation problems on the continent. Welliver entered the charmed circle. Over the next decade he compiled an impressive body of work of White House reporting, muckraking features, and war correspondence.[15]

As White House clerk (sometimes called "literary clerk"), Welliver helped Secretary George Christian perform jobs like those that Cortelyou and Tumulty had done. He represented Harding on Capitol Hill and apprised the president of public opinion as divined through the newspapers and the White House mail bag. He also continued to write for magazines, including profiles of his boss—without, it seems, any public objection.[16]

Yet for the prolix Harding, speechwriting was the main job. Roosevelt and Wilson had taught voters to expect public speeches from the president, and after his much-mocked campaign trail oratory, Harding found himself questioning his own abilities. "I really never thought much about 'style,'" he sighed, "until the critics got after my nomination for the presidency. I suppose I am too old to materially change it now."

Welliver's way with words came in handy. Even Mencken, normally parsimonious in his praise, credited the speechwriter with helping his rhetorically challenged boss: "He is a journalist of the highest skill and knows how to write simply and charmingly, but he is also a fellow with a sense of humor." Harding continued to write major speeches himself, including his inaugural address (which cemented his reputation for bombast). But on routine talks, Welliver did the heavy lifting. And Harding spoke often. Following Wilson, he delivered messages to Congress orally and undertook swings around the circle, bringing Welliver along in the secretarial car.[17]

Apart perhaps from the phrase "Founding Fathers," which Harding is sometimes credited with having coined, Welliver left no immortal words for posterity. But in holding the position of White House speechwriter—a job he continued to perform, with somewhat less urgency, during Calvin Coolidge's presidency—he confirmed the need for an augmented presidential staff. The speechwriter joined the White House secretary and the campaign publicists as a key shaper of presidential communication and spin.[18]

Americans accepted that presidents now had to delegate administrative chores. But because they now invested so much in the president as a person, they also disliked the idea that hired hands were drafting his words and fashioning his poses. In his uneventful tenure in government, Judson Welliver himself escaped controversy. But over time the existence of the White House speechwriter would feed anxieties about whether the voters were really getting the men they thought they were electing.

14

WALTER LIPPMANN AND THE
PROBLEM OF THE MAJORITY

IN THE SPRING OF 1921, Walter Lippmann was restless. After his wartime service to Wilson, the wunderkind journalist had returned to *The New Republic* as managing editor. But Wilsonian ideas were in eclipse, and the magazine's Progressivism was no longer the fashion. Lippmann had begun writing political profiles for *Vanity Fair*, a cheeky, upscale upstart, and he recruited a young editor there, Edmund Wilson, to relieve him at *The New Republic*. With his wife, Lippmann moved to a dilapidated beach house on the north shore of Long Island to begin a new book.[1]

At thirty-two, Lippmann had accomplished more than many journalists achieve in a lifetime. Born into an assimilated German-Jewish New York family, he studied philosophy at Harvard with William James, George Santayana, and the British Fabian thinker Graham Wallas. Despite his family's wealth, which had enabled boyhood trips to Europe, he remained, as a Jew, an outsider at Harvard, where he lived in a dingy dorm room with no heat or running water. But his intellect and ambition helped him thrive. With his classmate John Reed he founded an undergraduate Socialist Club—though Reed, who would go on to chronicle the Russian Revolution, always regarded Lippmann's radicalism as an affectation. Reed teasingly referred to Lippmann as "the future president of the United States."[2]

After his graduation and an apprenticeship with Lincoln Steffens—their exposé of Wall Street's financial houses led to congressional investigations that built support for the Federal Reserve Act—Lippmann worked briefly for the Socialist mayor of Schenectady. A pair of books—*A Preface to Politics* and *Drift and Mastery*—followed, establishing Lippmann's reputation, in TR's words, as "the most brilliant young man of all his age in the United States." He found himself writing memos for Roosevelt by day while by night drinking and debating with Reed, Steffens, Max Eastman, Emma Goldman, and others in Mabel Dodge's Greenwich Village salon. He also joined, at its inception in 1914, *The New Republic*, which in the wake of muckraking's demise became the most vital magazine of its day, supporting TR and then Wilson, and rallying liberal support for American entry into the world war.

That role brought Lippmann into the confidence of Wilson and of Edward House. Passed over to lead the wartime Publicity Bureau, Lippmann took a series of administration jobs, including assembling a body of intellectuals called "The Inquiry," which met at the New York Public Library to map out new postwar borders for Europe and help formulate Wilson's Fourteen Points. From there he served under public relations man Heber Blankenhorn in the Military Intelligence Branch of the War Department, where he blanketed Europe with materials articulating U.S. war aims. In this role, he ran afoul of the territorial Creel. Asked to arbitrate, Wilson, annoyed by *The New Republic*'s rebukes of his suppression of wartime speech, sided with Creel. "I am very much puzzled as to who sent Lippmann over to inquire into matters of propaganda," the president fumed to House. "I have found his judgment most unsound . . . because he, in common with the men of *The New Republic*, has ideas about the war and its purposes which are highly unorthodox from my own point of view." Lippmann carried out his mission anyway, writing copy for 5 million pieces of literature that were spread behind enemy lines by infiltrators and balloons. Then, in late 1918, House sent Lippmann to Paris to flesh out the skeletal Fourteen Points, which he did with Frank Cobb of the *New York World* in one frantic October day.[3]

Lippmann remained in Paris to socialize with Steffens, Baker, William Allen White, and the others who descended on the city after the armistice. In mid-January 1919 he returned to *The New Republic*, where his disillusionment with Wilson and the war intensified. He ran denunciatory editorials of the Versailles Treaty and excerpts of John Maynard Keynes's searing *Economic Consequences of the Peace*. This disenchantment led him to ask big questions about the role of the press in a mass democracy. With Charles Merz, a colleague from Military Intelligence, he published in *The New Republic* a critique of the *New York Times*'s coverage of the Russian Revolution that found glaring errors of fact strewn throughout the ostensibly objective articles. "The news about Russia," they wrote, "is a case of seeing not what was, but what men wished to see." Next came a series for *The Atlantic*, republished as *Liberty and the News*, in which he castigated ill-trained, irresponsible reporters for serving up opinion instead of blunt facts. He called for the professionalization of journalists so they could better play their democratic part.[4]

This critique served as a foundation for a great deal of press criticism in the decades to come—as well as for Lippmann's own disquisitions on democracy. But it also drew fire. A *New York Times* review mocked the author's ignorance of how newspapers actually worked. Lippmann, the reviewer noted, "has never been a newspaper man, and while he knows a good deal about news, most of what he knows is not true." Considering the news as a consumer, not a producer, Lippmann failed to appreciate just how difficult objective information was to come by, or how valiantly good reporters strove to obtain it. "Mr. Lippmann appears to think news is like sunshine—something which on its appearance is instantly recognized by all men," the *Times* charged. But "trained and disinterested" editors disagreed about what merited inclusion in the paper. Even the *New York Times* found Lippmann's simple faith in objectivity to be naive.[5]

* * *

In response to criticisms like these, Lippmann took to Long Island in 1921 to compose his most famous book, *Public Opinion*. A meditation on democracy, journalism, and publicity, it was written in an Olympian tone that reflected the cool objectivity that Lippmann prescribed. As became clear from the first excerpts in *The New Republic*, the book was markedly bleaker than *Liberty and the News*. In the earlier work, Lippmann claimed that "the present crisis of western democracy is a crisis in journalism." He now saw the crisis as one of epistemology. The public's confusions about public affairs, he argued, stemmed not just from shoddy reporting but from more basic and stubborn truths.[6]

First, the sheer complexity of modern life—the emergence of the vast entity that his old mentor Graham Wallas called "the Great Society"— placed the mastery of public affairs beyond the layman's grasp. On any issue, only a handful of trained experts could render informed judgments. "Man is no Aristotelian god contemplating all existence at one glance," Lippmann wrote, but a frail mortal who can apprehend only "a sufficient portion of reality to manage his survival." This was not elitism, and Lippmann didn't condemn the rabble as intellectually deficient. The limitations he discussed were common to all, since to become proficient on every public issue would overwhelm even the most assiduous student of public affairs.

A second intractable problem was the human mind. Having been among the first Progressives to reckon with Freud's insights into the unconscious, Lippmann understood that people filtered information through personal biases and frames of reference—what he called "the pictures in our heads." Drawing on Dewey and Harvard's pragmatists, Lippmann presented knowledge as shaped by emotions, habits, preconceptions, and attachments to existing values. "For the most part we do not first see and then define," he aphorized, "we define first and then see." Like the inhabitants of Plato's Cave, Lippmann's citizens lived in a "pseudo-environment," perceiving the world but darkly, oblivious to the limits of their knowledge. This epistemology carried implications for a mass democracy. In Lippmann's most radical claim, he rejected the conceit of the "omnicompetent citizen" that was implicit in democratic theory: the notion that the freestanding member of society could reliably make his own judgments about public affairs, which, together with those of his countrymen, formed the basis for decision making. What might have suited a Greek city-state or a New England village was no longer tenable in the Great Society.

Although Lippmann, now working at the *New York World*, would remain for a half century one of America's leading journalists, he no longer thought the press could solve these problems of self-governance. Despite their exalted role in democratic theory, reporters were scarcely better than average citizens at mastering the torrent of information in the modern world. Where in *Liberty and the News* Lippmann had declared that "the chief purpose of 'news' is to enable mankind to live successfully toward the future," in *Public Opinion* he compared the press to "the beam of a searchlight that moves restlessly about." Little trust was to be placed in its "descriptions of personalities, of sincerity, aspiration, motive, intention, of mass feeling, of national feeling, of public opinion, the policies of foreign governments" or anything that hinged on "data that are at best spasmodically recorded." Newspapers functioned best where clear, hard statistics existed: the box score of a ballgame, the close of the stock exchange, the election returns.

Sharing in the postwar propaganda backlash, Lippmann argued that the press was unreliable for another reason, too: because it had come to rely so much on public relations men like Ivy Lee to provide the news. Lippmann did see a need for what the publicists did—distilling and framing information—but believed it could be done better by disinterested experts with no stake in the outcome of their research. He thus proposed an array of "intelligence bureaus," housed inside the government, composed of issue experts, to supply leaders with analyses to make decisions. Ordinary citizens, instead of shouldering the mounting burdens of direct self-governance, could accept a limited role—not judging the "details in legislation," as James Bryce had put it, but setting forth "broad principles" for their leaders to follow. They would pass judgment on Election Day.[7]

Publicists also provided a positive model for Lippmann by showing how to forge popular consent. Words, images, phrases, myths, and rituals had long been "the common bond of common feelings, even though those feelings were originally attached to disparate ideas." To unite the citizenry, he pointed out, leaders had throughout history manipulated these symbols to elide ideological differences among different constituencies. But if "the creation of consent is not a new art," Lippmann wrote, it had "improved enormously in technic, because it is now based on analysis rather than rule of thumb. . . . Persuasion has become a self-conscious art and a regular organ of popular government." The manipulation of words and images to shape public opinion would remain a key part of leadership.

* * *

Public Opinion drew glowing notices from eminent scholars, including Robert Park and the political scientist Charles Merriam. Perhaps none admired the book more than John Dewey, "the foremost and most characteristic living American philosopher," as the *New York Times* called him. A generation older than Lippmann, and of similar pragmatic cast, Dewey had long served as a model for the younger man. Both wrote for *The New Republic* in its salad days; both carried the liberal banner into the world war; both believed that democracy could be improved through education, social science, and the embrace of expertise.[8]

These affinities were apparent in Dewey's review of *Public Opinion*, which he called "perhaps the most effective indictment of democracy as currently conceived ever penned." Writing in *The New Republic*, he noted that the book "shivers most of our illusions, and this particular Humpty Dumpty can never be put together again for anyone who reads these chapters with an open mind." Dewey made his agreement with Lippmann plainer five years later in his own book, *The Public and Its Problems*, which acknowledged a debt to his younger colleague. Although decades later Lippmann and Dewey would be cast as polar opposites in a debate, the elitist versus the democrat, Dewey actually endorsed Lippmann's project. He agreed that technological strides, the nation's burgeoning size, and the geographic dispersal of modern life had brought on a crisis of democracy; that these developments undermined the Enlightenment premise of an omnicompetent citizenry; and that governmental affairs had become "technically complicated matters to be conducted properly by experts."[9] Reviewers read Dewey's book not as a rebuttal to Lippmann but as a work of kindred sensibility.[10]

Dewey's quarrels with Lippmann came over his remedies. Lippmann, Dewey noted in his review, had chosen "to surrender the case for the press too readily." Dewey himself, who had once flirted with creating a sociological newspaper called *Thought News*, still hoped to develop a journalism that united "social science, access to facts, and the art of literary presentation." Quixotically, he envisioned a press that was "sensational" but "in a good sense"—one whose dispatches would trigger in readers "a thrill which no report confined to the superficial and detached incident can give." More plausibly, he also questioned Lippmann's intelligence bureaus. Though he agreed that experts should advise policy makers, he said the public needed to be included in the discussion. "The enlightenment of public opinion," Dewey contended, "still seems to me to have priority over the enlightenment of officials and directors."[11]

Ultimately, Dewey said, Lippmann believed that knowledge "originated in individuals by means of isolated contact with objects," and hoped to purify the streams of information at the source. Dewey, in contrast, denied the possibility of knowledge "uncontaminated by contact with use and service" because knowledge was "a function of association and communication," forged by a public community freely exchanging ideas. The public's ideas and questions had to inform the policy-making discussion as it was unfolding, or the experts would become "shut off from knowledge of the needs which they are supposed to serve." As he wrote, "There can be no public without full publicity in respect to all consequences which concern it."

Dewey understood the double sense of the word *publicity*. He granted that its meaning had devolved into "advertising, propaganda," gossip, feature news, and other superficialities; he lamented that America was "approaching a state of government by hired promoters of opinion called publicity agents." But he held that the publicists' exploitation of the "prejudices and emotional partisanship of the masses" mattered less than the public's own disorganization, "of which the exploiters of sentiment and opinion only take advantage." This disorganization was what had to be fixed.

Far from being in a debate, Dewey and Lippmann shared a view of the problems afflicting modern democracies and of public opinion. It was, they agreed, biased, scattered, overly self-assured, malleable, unreflective, mercurial, and confused—and, for all that, utterly necessary for democratic leaders to take into account.

15

THE LIKES AND DISLIKES OF H. L. MENCKEN

IF WALTER LIPPMANN could be said to have been locked in debate with any contemporary, it was not John Dewey but the exuberantly cranky columnist and critic Henry Louis Mencken. Mencken—of the *Baltimore Sun*, *The Smart Set*, and later *The American Mercury*—flourished amid the normalcy of the 1920s, when liberals as well as conservatives reveled in his wholesale slaughter of sacred cows. Better than anyone, the so-called Sage of Baltimore captured the decade's cynicism with his free-swinging, invective-filled diatribes. "So many young men," wrote Ernest Hemingway in *The Sun Also Rises*, "get their likes and dislikes from Mencken."[1]

Lippmann once numbered among those men. Early in his career he admired Mencken's writing, and the two carried on a lively if intermittent correspondence, peppered with references to cocktails and social outings, though privately Mencken was more disparaging. In many ways they were alike. Like Lippmann, Mencken mixed a gimlet-eyed view of Progressivism's ambitions with a disdain for the normalcy that replaced it. When writing about Harding or Coolidge, they could sound very much alike. Most important, both men dared to question the liberal romance of democracy, judging the average American—overwhelmed and distracted by modern life—out of his depth in contemplating the intricacies of public policy.[2]

Yet these similarities masked core differences. One was a matter of style: Lippmann was sober and careful, Mencken wild and heedless. Even when they worked in concert, friction was evident: once, in editing a letter by Mencken to the *New York World*, Lippmann told him to drop a mock-honorific "Dr." before Woodrow Wilson's name as well as a gratuitous reference to "cow-state John the Baptists," which Lippmann thought "inexpedient, if you care about that." Yet more than temperament divided them. Lippmann, even as he drifted toward conservatism, harbored a smoldering liberal ember that sustained a regard for American democracy. Mencken, though he thrilled liberals by debunking Rotarian clichés and evangelical delusions, was at heart an old school aristocrat, enamored of the high culture fostered by European dynasties.[3]

* * *

Born into a Victorian petit-bourgeois Baltimore family in 1880, Mencken walked into the *Baltimore Morning Herald* city room at age eighteen and asked for a job. He wrote his way onto the paper and then moved to the more illustrious *Sun*. From his perch there he rained contempt on all comers: right-wing censors and Progressive do-gooders, puritans and professors, and indeed much of the American public, whose members he belittled as "morons," "anthropoids," and "the booboisie." His iconoclasm won him a national following and a measure of celebrity. With his jug ears, slicked hair parted down the middle, and a cigar and suspenders that came across as props, the pudgy, diminutive Mencken both looked and wrote like a teenage troublemaker. Like an adolescent, too, he mistook his pedestrian cruelties and complaints for insight.

Mencken's jibes at fundamentalists and bureaucrats led some observers to classify his politics as libertarianism. In truth it was closer to a comic nihilism, equal parts Nietzsche (whose work he translated and popularized) and Groucho Marx ("Whatever it is, I'm against it"). While Mencken had his passions—proud of his German ancestry, he championed Beethoven and Brahms and defended Kaiser Wilhelm—his true talent lay in criticism, or more precisely contrarianism. In that mode he could showcase his leveling wit, his arcane vocabulary, and even his brazen bigotry. Partial to the classics, Mencken derided not just middlebrow fare but also Faulkner, Thomas Mann, and other paragons of modernism; for all his highbrow pretensions, he often showed a crude anti-intellectualism. Many eminent thinkers he dismissed with a smirk—including Lippmann, whom he once cited in an article about the most boring authors. He railed, too, against politicians of every stripe—not just the easy targets such as the Ku Klux Klan and Prohibitionists but also politicians from Bryan and Roosevelt to Harding and Coolidge, excluding not even the sainted Abraham Lincoln. "What this country really needs," he once told Edward Bernays, "is a swell euphemism for *politician*. It has always seemed to me that *skunk* and *polecat* are too harsh."[4]

Mencken handled Lippmann's *Public Opinion* roughly. When the first, admiring reviews appeared, the sage could barely wait to dissent. Most critics found the book unsparing and bleak in its view of democracy, but Mencken judged it overly optimistic, especially the conclusion, which he called "mystical gurgle," nothing more than "the old democratic answer" of "spreading enlightenment . . . democratising information . . . combating what is adjudged to be false with what is adjudged to be true." Lippmann, he charged, had flinched from the cold truth that "it is no more possible to teach [the public] what every voter should theoretically know than it is to teach a chimpanzee to play the *viola da gamba*."[5]

Mencken saw no hope for salvaging democracy. He couldn't conceive of anyone capable of educating the public as the Progressives prescribed, since, he wrote, "the inevitable tendency of pedagogy . . . is to preserve and propagate the lies that happen to be . . . salubrious to the current masters of the mob." Betraying his Germanophilia, he impishly invoked Lippmann's wartime propaganda service. How could democracy's champions expect to find any disinterested tutor of the public, he asked, if even such an upstanding, civic-minded, pensive philosopher as Lippmann could have drunk of the wartime hysteria? Mencken concluded that a need remained for a "new science" of how demagogues played on the "mental and gastric processes of the mob." But who could write it? "The practical politicians are no doubt afraid that they would be lynched if they gave the secrets of their craft away," he wrote, "and the political amateurs among the *intelligentsia*, as the book of Mr. Lippmann shows, are too academic to grapple with realities." Lacking other viable candidates, Mencken alerted his readers, "I consecrate myself to the task."[6]

After this drubbing, Lippmann could hardly resist a rebuttal, which he presented a few weeks later in *The New Republic*. Gibing that Mencken "has taught us how unnecessary it is to read a book before reviewing it," Lippmann proceeded to review his rival's unwritten manifesto. In a tone as caustic as Mencken's, he charged his reviewer with the ultimate vice for a self-described cynic: naïveté. Mencken, he wrote, had uncritically accepted "the whole current buncombe that you can do anything by publicity and advertising." Reciprocating the *ad hominem* attack, Lippmann sniffed that traffic in words had always been Mencken's "only means of action and his sole occupation." Consequently, he deluded himself that "the slogans of politics are the essence of politics." This "childlike faith in the omnipotence of words" was a superstition akin to those that Mencken lampooned—"the same stuff at bottom as Mr. Bryan's or Billy Sunday's."[7]

*   *   *

This feud continued through the decade. In 1926, Mencken delivered his promised treatise, *Notes on Democracy*, a taunt and a rejoinder to Lippmann. "Public opinion?" Mencken wrote. "Walter Lippmann, searching for it, could not find it." But Mencken thought it easy to spot. "Public opinion, in its raw state, gushes out in the immemorial form of the mob's fears," he wrote. "It is piped to central factories, and there it is flavoured and coloured, and put into cans."[8]

That fairly summed up the book's thesis. Described by Edmund Wilson as "an obverse of Whitman's *Leaves of Grass*," Mencken's *Notes* comprised a medley of variations on his low opinion of humankind. It opened with a rejection, like Lippmann's, of the democratic myth of the public's essential wisdom. But where Lippmann voiced his doubts in sorrow, Mencken announced his with glee.[9]

For Mencken, humanity was divided between a small, intelligent, civilized minority and an immense, stupid, uneducable majority. His book thrummed with an affection for aristocracy as fuzzy-minded as the paeans to democracy that he despised. He imagined the princes and dukes of old Europe as cultured, honest, public-spirited, and honorable. The majesty of old-time continental aristocracy contrasted with the "clown-show" of democracy, which yielded corruption and mediocrity. The American public, he said, craved not liberty but only "the warm, reassuring smell of the herd." The press, moreover, could never elevate the public. In language that made Lippmann seem positively Deweyan, Mencken deemed editors to be fools, devoid of "sound knowledge and genuine intelligence. . . . Thus they give their aid to the sublime democratic process of eliminating all sense and decency from public life."

At moments, Mencken seemed poised to deliver on his promise to illuminate the workings of democracy, which he said revolved around "the business of victimizing" the public. He called it "a lucrative profession, an exact science, and a delicate and lofty art." But he never went beyond the sketchy contention that democratic leaders advanced in politics through "the discovery, chase, and scotching of bugaboos." Democracy to him was little more than manipulation.

For a brief spell, *Notes on Democracy* became the rage. Kaiser Wilhelm, in exile in the Netherlands, professed particular admiration. But Lippmann wasn't impressed. In a tongue-in-cheek review, he slyly purported to praise Mencken, contending that "to discuss it as one might discuss the ideas of first-rate thinkers like Russell, Dewey, Whitehead or Santayana would be to destroy the book and miss its importance." He described the book as "sub-rational"—but, he insisted, "in the best sense of the word." Lest his facetious praise be misinterpreted, Lippmann also called it "a collection of trite and somewhat confused ideas."[10]

Lippmann did admire Mencken's style: his verve, humor, and candor, and the "cleansing and vitalizing effect" of his assaults. Mencken might sneer at politicians who played on popular prejudices, but his own skill at arousing gut-level emotion was what made him effective. Instead of persuading opponents through exposition, he would, Lippmann wrote, thrust his "violent hands upon them in the conviction, probably correct, that you accomplish results quicker by making your opponents' back teeth rattle than by laboriously addressing his reason." Less a rational argument than a sensory experience, *Notes on Democracy* was to be judged, Lippmann concluded, like "a barrage of artillery, for the general destruction rather than for the accuracy of the individual shots."

Still, Lippmann couldn't resist dismantling Mencken's claims. He pointed out that while Mencken swooned over liberty and brayed about democracy, he failed to grasp that his beloved aristocracies had restricted freedoms of speech and opinion. Extending those freedoms to the masses was exactly what had eroded traditional authority, upended values, revised cultural standards, and enshrined public opinion as the basis of government. Mencken's wish for a cultured, ordered society with complete liberty was therefore, Lippmann concluded, "as thoroughgoing a piece of utopian sentimentalism" as anything that Mencken ever mocked.[11]

* * *

Nothing illustrated the differences between Lippmann and Mencken better than their treatments of the Scopes Trial, a cause célèbre of the 1920s. In 1925, the state of Tennessee indicted John Scopes, a twenty-four-year-old high school biology teacher in the town of Dayton, for violating a law against teaching evolution. The affair, which spotlighted the role of public opinion and scientific expertise in a democracy, drew a nationwide audience, as each side recruited a famous lawyer to lead its case: William Jennings Bryan for the prosecution, Clarence Darrow for the defense.

For Mencken, the "Monkey Trial," as he labeled it, confirmed his prejudices about both religious dogmatists and starry-eyed democrats. Having helped to foment the controversy itself—he wrote to Darrow to offer his services—Mencken became its best known chronicler. True to his contrarian nature, his first piece about the trial sided with the prosecution. In *The Nation*, he claimed that John Scopes, having contracted to teach for the state, had no free speech rights at stake. Soon, however, the pleasure of provoking *Nation* readers gave way to the greater joys of lampooning the backwoods hicks of the rural South and their primitive superstitions.[12]

As the summer trial began, Mencken set out for the "ninth-rate country town" of Dayton. From the jury selection, in which a prospective juror was challenged for not attending church, to Bryan's sudden death five days after Scopes's conviction, Mencken wallowed in the "religious orgy" even as he deplored it. Bryan made a ripe target, not only as a hidebound believer in biblical literalism but also as an untiring celebrant of democracy. Mencken described the Great Commoner as "ignorant, bigoted, self-seeking, blatant and dishonest . . . a peasant come home to the dung-pile." And that was in his obituary.

Compared to such vitriol, Lippmann was utterly respectful. He credited Bryan with a lifelong principled consistency. In *Harper's*, he argued that Bryan, far from having become unmoored in his dotage, "had always argued that a majority had the right to decide. . . . To question this right of the majority would have seemed as heretical to him as to question the fundamentalist creed." What needed examination, Lippmann insisted, was the premise "that the majority is right sovereign in all things." Pushing beyond his arguments in *Public Opinion*, he said that the *Scopes* case posed problems for the hope that popular education would elevate democracy, because the majority in Tennessee had used its power to stifle education itself.

As in *Public Opinion*, however, Lippmann ultimately reaffirmed his democratic commitments. He sought to strip away the "superstition . . . attached to majority rule," he assured his readers, only because he wanted to "arm the minority for a more effective resistance in the future."[13]

16

SILAS BENT CALLED the 1920s the "Age of Ballyhoo"—a decade of flashy display and cheerful salesmanship. In Times Square, neon signs and blinking streams of bulbs hawked toothpaste, Coca-Cola, and cigarettes amid the blinding dazzle of theater marquees. Admen and public relations agents tapped out self-consciously snappy prose that moved to the syncopated rhythms of the Jazz Age. Newspapers not only teemed with advertising; they also reflected the values of promotion, as gossip-filled tabloids served up arresting photographs and glossy magazines featured beguiling illustrations. Technological invention, a humming economy, and a revolution in manners and morals chased one another in a dizzying whirl.[1]

Even American values seemed to be shifting. The old tenets of ascetic living and artisanal pride gave way to personal choice, leisure, and material comfort. Midwifing this change in values were the advertising gurus, who some credited with stimulating the prosperity. "Speeded-up mass production demands increased buying," observed John Dewey. "It is promoted by advertising on a vast scale, by installment selling, by agents skilled in breaking down sales resistance. Hence, buying becomes an economic 'duty' which is as consonant with the present epoch as thrift was with the period of individualism."[2]

No one fused the new values and the old—the salesmanship and the piety—better than Bruce Barton, magazine journalist, best-selling author, advertising executive, public relations adviser to presidents, and, later, a congressman. Six feet tall, with a sturdy build, Barton had narrow light blue eyes and reddish-brown hair that curled at the top in a thick, neat wave. Hard-charging, insomniac, and almost manic, he was forced by exhaustion to check in throughout his life at various clinics and spas; according to his brother, he nearly "ended in a sanitarium." But normally he juggled his multiple roles deftly, and his career in the 1920s proved that Albert Lasker's use of advertising techniques on Harding's behalf was but a foretaste of how the salesman's sensibility could be brought to bear on the American presidency.[3]

* * *

Barton was born in 1886, the son of a Congregationalist minister. After graduating from Amherst College—valedictorian and most likely to succeed—he shuttled between magazine journalism and advertising. During the war, he worked for the United War Work Campaign, an ad hoc group assembled by the War Department to promote the YMCA, the Jewish Welfare Board, and the Salvation Army. Afterward, he pivoted to commerce. "And they shall beat their swords into—Electroypes," he prophesied in a December 1918 article that proposed harnessing advertising's know-how to the peacetime goals of security and prosperity.

With Roy Durstine and Alex Osborn, colleagues from the United War Work Campaign, Barton founded an advertising firm called BDO (and, when it merged with the George Batten Agency in 1928, either BBDO or BBD&O). It was headquartered on 45th Street, a block and a half west of Madison Avenue, the thoroughfare whose name became shorthand for the industry. With a staff of fourteen, BDO built an august client list, including General Electric, General Motors, and General Mills—the top brass of the business world—emerging by 1923 as the fourth largest advertising firm in the country, behind Lasker's Lord & Thomas. Barton was its public face.

His timing was exquisite. In the 1920s advertising was gaining cachet. "It is a great responsibility to mold the daily lives of millions of our fellow men," declared copywriter James Wallen, "and I am persuaded that we are second only to statesmen and editors in power for good." The agencies were changing the culture; what had been luxuries, they sought to make necessities, using the latest insights. The J. Walter Thompson Agency, seizing on a vogue for psychology, hired John Watson, a founder of behaviorist psychology—a move that symbolized the profession's intention to use "science" to plumb the unconscious. A generation earlier, Lasker's plainspoken "reason why" philosophy had deemed design and clever language to be distractions from a clear message. Now those frills became the rage, as ads promised consumers transformative results from their products—physical fitness, contentment, love, sex—and darkly hinted at the risks of going without. Few doubted that these seductive advertising appeals worked. Debates about advertising centered not on its efficacy but on its morality.

Barton, for his part, considered brevity and punch to be essential. When explaining copywriting, he would cite the Lord's Prayer, the Twenty-Third Psalm, and the Gettysburg Address, each of which, he noted, comprised less than 500 simple words. "Jesus hated prosy dullness," he pronounced. In his office he hung a photograph of a summer swarm at Coney Island to remind his employees—of whom he had 2,000 by the end of his career—of the crude impulses of the masses and the dangers of undue subtlety.[4]

Optimistic by temperament, Barton avoided the "scare copy" that pricked readers' anxieties about athlete's foot or body odor. He preferred sunny puffery. (Norman Rockwell illustrated his campaign for Edison's tungsten light bulbs.) For Barton, the decade's rah-rah spirit of consumption was a ticket to both riches and moral regeneration. Long partial to a rhetoric of religious uplift, Barton sanctified the modern businessman's can-do faith in 1925 with *The Man Nobody Knows*, a portrait of Jesus Christ as a "magnetic personality" and charismatic entrepreneur. A far cry from the fundamentalism that Bryan was defending in Tennessee, Barton's consumer-friendly Protestantism refashioned Jesus as an advertising man *avant la lettre*—skilled at summoning the language to arouse and persuade his audiences. Jesus was, Barton wrote, "the founder of modern business," his parables "the most powerful advertisements of all time," the apostles "twelve men from the bottom ranks of business . . . forged . . . into an organization that conquered the world." Unlike the gentle soul of Victorian sermons, Barton's Jesus was outgoing and sociable, with an "interesting set of friends." By marrying a vibrant religious faith to an appreciation of hustle and acquisition, *The Man Nobody Knows* signaled that a life of goodness wasn't incompatible with the good life.[5]

Barton promoted his book with all his professional know-how. He urged ministers to teach it in Sunday School classes and his clients to buy it in bulk. Reviews were kind; sales were better. The director Cecil B. De Mille hired Barton as a consultant on his Christ biopic, *The King of Kings*.[6]

But not everyone was sold. Traditionalists deemed the book sacrilegious—

a reaction that Barton capitalized on with a book-burning publicity stunt. Highbrows mocked the Rotarian platitudes. Copywriter-turned-critic James Rorty charged Barton with painting a "grotesque ad-man Christ in his own image," while Mencken chortled over the idea "that John the Baptist was the first Kiwanian." The cult of salesmanship was not without its detractors.

* * *

Barton ventured into politics the same year he established his agency. In 1919, the financier Dwight Morrow introduced Barton to Calvin Coolidge, the blue-eyed, sandy-haired governor of Massachusetts whose grim demeanor and tight-lipped ways concealed a martini-dry wit and political acumen. Coolidge had gained celebrity for firing the striking members of the Boston police force—an act that, amid a nationwide panic about labor radicalism, infuriated Progressives but made the governor a folk hero and a presidential contender. Barton began advising Coolidge, while simultaneously profiling him in major magazines. "The radicals and reactionaries fill the newspapers, but the great majority of Americans are neither radicals nor reactionaries," Barton wrote in *Collier's*. "They are middle-of-the-road folks who own their own homes and work hard. . . . Coolidge belongs with that crowd." Among the evocative photographs that illustrated the paean was a shot of the governor behind a two-horse hitch at the Vermont farm where he was born and where his father still lived. Imagery as much as Barton's slick prose conveyed the rural bona fides that would define Coolidge's persona.[7]

Over the next decade, as he counseled Coolidge, Barton wrote more encomiums, portraying the politician's stony New England reserve as a hallmark of his flinty integrity. Barton also saw that Americans, growing uncomfortable with the role of publicists in politics, were questioning their leaders' authenticity. He thus presented Coolidge's simplicity as a refreshing antidote to the decade's ballyhoo. Here was authenticity contrived.[8]

In 1920, Barton helped engineer a Coolidge-for-president boomlet. When Houghton Mifflin published a book of Coolidge's speeches called *Have Faith in Massachusetts*—which included his famous declaration, "There is no right to strike against the public safety by anybody, anywhere, any time"—Barton distributed 65,000 copies to key political players, coaching the governor on inscriptions for certain recipients. Barton arranged interviews, placed ads for the book in targeted markets, and enlisted Coolidge's fans to have the *Literary Digest* include the governor among its profiles of presidential aspirants. At the convention, Barton's team, operating out of Dwight Morrow's hotel suite, distributed leather-bound copies of yet another speech collection, *Law and Order*, with each delegate's name embossed in gold. And although Coolidge, a long shot for the nomination to begin with, dropped out of the presidential balloting, he came away with the vice-presidential nomination, thanks to the delegates' enthusiasm.

As Harding's understudy, Coolidge kept a low profile. But in the summer of 1923, while vacationing at his family's Vermont cottage, he was awakened after midnight with the news that the president, on a Pacific coast tour, had suffered a fatal heart attack. In a downstairs parlor suffused with the glow of a kerosene lamp, John Coolidge, the vice president's seventy-eight-year-old father and a notary public, swore in his son as president. The atmospherics couldn't have been more Bartonesque.[9]

That Barton and Coolidge exploited the new president's style didn't mean it was phony. Coolidge's quiet exterior faithfully expressed his reticence, modesty, and simple decency. Stories abounded of the president's uncommunicativeness—most famously the one about the woman who bet that she could elicit more than two words from him one night, to be met with a wry, "You lose." Self-effacement marked Coolidge's public speech as well. "What he thinks of himself I daresay will never be known," wrote Mencken. "His self-revelations have been so few and so wary that it is even difficult to guess. No man of his august station ever talked about himself less." This reserve, together with his plain demeanor and upright bearing, conveyed rectitude—a signal political virtue as Harding's Teapot Dome scandal was coming to light. As Harding's cronies went to jail, the new president got credit for cleaning up the mess.

Politically, Coolidge espoused a conservative agenda of balanced budgets, light business regulation, and low taxes. Culturally, in a world of speakeasies and skyscrapers, he was a throwback, with his woolen suits, *McGuffey's* maxims, and disapproving grimace. "We were smack in the middle of the Roaring Twenties, with hip flasks, joy rides, and bathtub gin parties setting the social standards," wrote Edmund Starling, the president's Secret Service agent and daily walking companion. "The president was the antithesis of all this and he despised it." Yet Coolidge embraced both consumer capitalism and the latest technology, offering the public, in Walter Lippmann's analysis, a "Puritanism *de luxe*, in which it is possible to praise all the classic virtues while continuing to enjoy all the modern conveniences." By his example, Coolidge gave hope to an anxious nation that the mores of the bygone century might survive in the new one.[10]

*   *   *

In his pro-business politics and disdain for presidential activism, Coolidge rejected the Progressive ambitions of his predecessors in the White House. "Both Mr. Roosevelt and Mr. Wilson cherished visions of a better America," noted *The New Republic*. "But Mr. Coolidge has not seen the vision of an America better than the America of which he is president." Yet Coolidge followed them in believing that the president, not Congress, best spoke for the public interest. "It is because in their hours of timidity the Congress becomes subservient to the importunities of organized minorities," he wrote, "that the president comes more and more to stand as the champion of the rights of the whole country." He governed through what his aide C. Bascom Slemp called "direct reliance upon the mass of the people."[11]

Aware of his symbolic role, Coolidge was compelled by circumstances to tend his public identity. He accepted PR as part of modern politics. "In public life it is sometimes necessary," he wrote, "in order to appear really natural, to be actually artificial." While hardly Rooseveltian in his theatrics, he applied this lesson to small acts like posing for photographs. "Let's spruce up a bit," he said to a companion while sidling up to the cameras. "And let's talk. It looks more natural and makes a better picture."

Throughout Coolidge's administration, too, Bruce Barton continued to provide advice. No sooner had Harding been interred in August 1923 than the irrepressible salesman was writing more magazine profiles of the new president. A September 1923 valentine in the *American Review of Reviews* assured readers of their new president's "courage and glorified common sense." Already thinking about getting Coolidge elected president in his own right, Barton argued that the election would turn on personality, not partisanship. "This is not a party campaign in the old sense," he said. "I have not met anybody who is going to vote for the Republican Party. They are going to vote 'for Coolidge' or against him." He drafted pamphlets with biographical themes and contracted with Charles Scribner's Sons for yet another tome of speeches. "We will build up a wonderful Coolidge legend in the country," he gushed. "Emotions affect votes much more than logic. I am sure of the soundness of this plan." Charles Merz, Walter Lippmann's old collaborator, was dejected. "Columns of newspaper copy spread denials of the story that Coolidge was an iceberg," he wrote, and cast him as "just an average fellow with his neighbors, 'Cal,' not Calvin, to the cobbler in the corner store."[12]

* * *

Unopposed for the 1924 Republican nomination, Coolidge found the fall campaign almost as effortless. In July, the Democrats tore themselves apart in a nomination battle that lasted through 103 ballots, settling on the colorless corporate lawyer and diplomat John W. Davis of West Virginia. The tatters of the old Progressive Party reconstituted themselves behind Robert La Follette, but it was a hollow shell of TR's movement. In the face of the "Coolidge Prosperity" and the unassuming, upright man in the White House, neither rival stood much of a chance.

What distinguished the 1924 campaign was the arrival of radio. From its scattered audiences, wrote the pioneering communications scholar Hadley Cantril, it created "the largest grouping of people ever known." Barton saw potential for campaigning. Radio "made possible an entirely new type of campaign," he said; it "enables the president to sit by every fireside and talk in terms of that home's interest and prosperity."[13]

Since Wilson's experimental broadcasts in 1918 and 1919, radio had come a long way. The airing of the 1920 election returns on Pittsburgh's station KDKA established the medium as a carrier of breaking news, and Harding on occasion broadcast his speeches to crowds, though he always focused on the audiences in front of him. But Coolidge used radio as more than an accoutrement. With it, he could assemble audiences of unprecedented size. Theodore Roosevelt reached perhaps 13 million people with all the speeches he ever gave; Coolidge did so with a single address. In 1923, he delivered the first radio-borne State of the Union address; in 1924, the first nomination acceptance speech; the next winter, the first inaugural. Each garnered audiences of record size.[14]

Over the airwaves Coolidge exuded a surprising charm. In person, his nasal New England quack prompted endless joking, but it sounded calming over the airwaves. "The radio filtered most of the Yankee peculiarities from his accent," wrote Will Irwin, "and left the quality of a well-bred, cosmopolitan American." "Over radio," agreed William Allen White, "he went straight to the popular heart." Coolidge accepted the praise with humility. "I am very fortunate I came in with the radio," he reflected. "I can't make an engaging, rousing, or oratorical speech to a crowd . . . but I have a good radio voice and now I can get my messages across . . . without acquainting them with my lack of oratorical ability." In truth, he had won prizes in high school and college for oratory.[15]

In July 1924, a radio campaign became all the more useful to Coolidge after his teenage son, Calvin, Jr., died from an infected blister developed while playing tennis on the White House lawn. The tragedy made the naturally withdrawn president even more reticent, and radio provided an alternative to touring. "Supplemented by motion pictures showing the president in action," the *New York Times* reported, "persons identified with the campaign believe that addresses by President Coolidge, broadcast throughout the country, would prove a great attraction even to audiences that do not ordinarily go to political meetings." Coolidge stumped less than Davis or La Follette that fall, ignoring criticisms that he was too unavailable. The country, his secretary Ted Clark explained, "likes his silence, and it would be a dangerous thing to tear down the picture which they have built."[16]

Barton, meanwhile, recruited surrogates to speak, "fill[ing] the air with Republican addresses . . . during the entire month of October," as a GOP operative crowed. The night before Election Day, Coolidge spoke on a coast-to-coast hookup. Playing to exhilaration about the event's novelty, he saluted his audience, "including my father, up on the Vermont farm, listening in." Bruce Bliven of *The New Republic* marveled: "Coolidge's speeches have been heard by at least ten times as many people as have heard any other man who ever lived." This fact alone, Bliven said, provided hundreds of thousands of voters with "a link between themselves and the White House and a powerful reason to vote in his favor."[17]

Barton's image making also helped. On a trip to Plymouth Notch, Coolidge chopped trees and pitched hay in his business suit and homburg, as Henry Ford, Thomas Edison, and Harvey Firestone—longtime "camping pals," according to the press copy—joined him. The president gave Ford a sap bucket that belonged to his great-great-grandfather, John Coolidge, the first of his line to settle in Plymouth. A sixteen-minute GOP biopic played up Coolidge's rugged virtues.

Journalists winced. Opponents howled. "The American people dearly love to be fooled, to worship politicians of whom they have created portraits which bear little or no resemblance to the originals," wrote *The Nation*. "The Coolidge myth has been created by amazingly skilful propaganda." Bliven said Coolidge was sold "as though he were a new breakfast food or fountain pen," in a campaign in which "the Republican National Committee had the whole-hearted aid of the editors, film producers, etc., to an extent which was likewise without any parallel in our history." But these charges damaged Coolidge no more than they had hurt TR in his day. In November 1924, voters returned the incumbent to the White House in what Bliven called "not a Republican victory, but a Coolidge triumph."[18]

*   *   *

Though Coolidge weathered the criticism of his public relations offensives in 1924, the grumbling persisted. His friendship with Barton came in for special reproach. At the end of Coolidge's 1926 summer vacation, the Bartons joined the Coolidges in the Adirondacks and rode together back to Washington by train. On behalf of the Associated Press, Barton proposed an interview, to let Coolidge show the world a "human, friendly picture" of himself. Barton conceived it as an informal front-porch chat with the "appearance of spontaneity." Ted Clark told Barton his name "carried a conviction of sincerity which was absolutely essential."

Sincere perhaps, but hardly spontaneous. Barton gave Coolidge the interview questions beforehand, along with proposed answers, and the president drafted replies, which Barton stitched together. "It was put out ... in such a way as to be mostly Barton and little of myself," Coolidge admitted. The article showcased Coolidge professing to enjoy small chores on his Plymouth farm, where he could "repair the fence where it is breaking down, and mend the latch on the kitchen door." He spoke lovingly of his wife, urged young boys raised in comfort to work hard, and gently reaffirmed his faith. "It would be difficult for me to conceive of anyone being able to administer the duties of a great office like the presidency," he said, "without a belief in the guidance of a divine providence."[19]

The interview, though banal, was a sensation, syndicated by the Associated Press and reprinted nationwide. David Lawrence, who should have known better, claimed it was "not prearranged." Others were less naive. "T.R.B." of *The New Republic* wondered whether it was "Republican party propaganda, an example of the Associated Press's great new policy of livening up its news report, or just a shrewd bit of publicity in the interest of Bruce himself." Democrats fumed at the free publicity given to the GOP under the guise of human interest—with congressional elections underway. As it happened, though, Coolidge's popularity wasn't transferable; Republicans lost seats in the midterms.[20]

Coolidge repaid Barton by speaking to the Association of American Advertising Agencies, of which Roy Durstine was then president. Barton contributed to the address. In language that his audience of admen would have been hard-pressed to top, Coolidge rejected the criticism that advertising misled buyers. "Of all our economic life," Coolidge said, "the element on which we are inclined to place too low an estimate is advertising." If some dishonest men plied the trade, the president insisted nonetheless, "There can be no permanent basis for advertising except as a representation of the exact truth. Whenever deception, falsehood, and fraud creep in, they undermine the whole structure." Properly understood, he said, advertising was a form of "education. It informs its readers of the existence and nature of commodities by explaining the advantages to be derived from their use."

Crediting advertising with influencing public behavior, Coolidge deemed it to be a salutary force for democracy. He thanked the admen for sustaining the nation's prosperity and well-being. "Rightfully applied," he said, advertising "is the method by which the desire is created for better things." But, he cautioned, the ends that advertising in America had to pursue were more than material. They were also moral—nothing less than "the high responsibility of inspiring and ennobling the commercial world ... part of the greater work of the regeneration and redemption of mankind." Bruce Barton was surely proud.[21]

17

"SILENT CAL"

PRESIDENT COOLIDGE'S NICKNAME, "Silent Cal," may have captured his personality, but it masked a surprising conscientiousness when it came to addressing the public and the press. Though laconic in personal conversations, Coolidge used the presidential pulpit often and deliberately, expanding his reach enormously through radio. As important, he further institutionalized press conferences, meeting with reporters twice a week throughout his presidency—more regularly than any chief executive before or since. At his first session, held with 150 reporters after his return from Vermont in August 1923, Coolidge "talked at length" and "answered every question propounded and elaborately elucidated his answers," wrote the White House correspondent Fred Essary. "He was communicative almost to the point of garrulousness. And he has been ever since."[1]

Indulging the press corps was a concession to modernity that Coolidge made happily. Open exchanges with reporters kept him on the front pages. He made the press conference, wrote Charles Willis Thompson, "an engine for bringing himself almost daily into the American home." The sessions also helped him shape the news: like Harding, Coolidge made reporters submit questions to him in writing beforehand, so he wouldn't be caught off-guard, and he followed precedent, too, in speaking only on background so he could talk with relative freedom. Reporters accepted the bargain, which, Essary said, gave them "some intimate close-up of what the president is thinking, or the lines he may eventually take on a given policy."[2]

These policies helped win him respectful treatment in the newspapers, as a sizable minority of frustrated dissenters never tired of pointing out. "Contrast what Mr. Wilson went through, in the shape of press criticism of his foreign policy, with the trivial nature of the Coolidge criticism," wrote Willis Sharp in *The Atlantic Monthly*. "I venture to say that neither in the domestic nor the foreign field has any president in this generation had as little as Mr. Coolidge—few have had less since the beginning. He has now, and has had since the day he first entered the White House as President, a most amazing newspaper support."[3]

The only flaw in this claim was that its very frequency belied it. Coolidge actually had lots of critics, including prominent columnists such as Lippmann, Mencken, and White, who inveighed against his conservative policies and mocked his dour personality. Yet few aspects of his presidency elicited more diatribes than his management of the press corps. "We are witnessing an innovation unique in all history—government by publicity," blared *The New Republic*. "No predecessor of Mr. Coolidge ever did anything like it. Mr. Roosevelt was once thought to be something of an expert at such business, but we now see he was a tyro. . . . No ruler in history ever had such a magnificent propaganda machine as Mr. Coolidge's, and certainly it would be impossible for anybody to use it more assiduously."[4]

* * *

Coolidge attracted these criticisms because he governed in an era that was suspicious of publicity. That suspicion—present during TR's presidency, amplified by the world war—made popular targets of press agents even as their achievements propelled their ascent. Interest groups, professional bodies, trade associations, and ad hoc issue coalitions multiplied in the 1920s, and almost all of them embraced PR. Every species of private organization retained flacks who came to journalists bearing a self-serving mélange of facts. Determined to expose their pernicious influence, journalists tallied the stories in the daily papers that were inspired by publicists, if not reprinted whole cloth.[5]

Even more worrisome, in many eyes, were the government's own press officers—once shocking enough to inspire congressional prohibitions, now merely a routine administrative function. As Charles Merriam noted in

Recent Social Trends in the United States, a mammoth social science survey of 1933, politics had changed dramatically since the century's beginning. The older system of personal appeals and lobbying, Merriam wrote, had given way to "the employment of press agents, public relations counsels, and propagandists," conducting "organized educational campaigns on an elaborate scale." Journalists moaned. "In almost every department," wrote Essary, "there is a chief of a 'bureau of information' which is merely a title for an official press agent." Worst of all was the White House, which issued a daily stream of "speeches, messages, proclamations, pronouncements, executive orders, appointments, ... dinner and reception arrangements and tributes to deceased football coaches and foreign potentates."[6]

The anxiety surrounding the surge in publicists had several sources. Journalists saw a challenge to their autonomy, a rival group whose ways of organizing and interpreting facts threatened to eclipse their own. In 1919, the congressional correspondents even voted to bar professional public relations men from galleries at the Capitol, as if to draw bright lines between the two pursuits.[7]

More consequential were the possible implications for democracy. Propaganda critics feared that campaign publicists would sell the voters a phony image of a candidate, or that government flacks would deceive the public about vital policies. As Lippmann noted, propaganda struck at the core of the Progressive Era vision of an independent citizenry, and it was easy to see the most unassuming agency information officer or press secretary as a propagandist.

In the 1920s, therefore, Progressive intellectuals took up the attack on propaganda and publicity as eagerly as they had once joined the Creel Committee. James Bryce, whose endorsement of German atrocity tales had helped to swing American public opinion against the kaiser, now feared that the propagandists were "skillfully and sedulously supplying false or one-sided statements of fact to beguile and mislead." Even George Creel, in an *apologia pro vita sua* written five years after the war, argued that the overall "lack of trustworthy information" coming from a partisan, sensationalistic press had degraded public opinion. The panic continued for more than a decade.[8]

* * *

In this context, Calvin Coolidge's advances in White House communication came to be viewed as downright sinister. The "Coolidge myth," editorialized *The Nation*, "has been created by amazingly skilful propaganda

. . . a character has been created for the president which bears no relation to the man in the White House." Though plainly hyperbolic, alarms like these reflected a real concern about the president's power to shape his image and the news in the age of mass communications.[9]

Typical was the outcry about Coolidge's press conferences, which he intended as a convenience to the Fourth Estate—a chance for them to question him regularly and assess his thinking. Many journalists saw these sessions as a way for the president to foist his message on a captive flock. The most bothersome requirement forced reporters to attribute Coolidge's comments to an "Official Spokesman" or "White House Spokesman." These ground rules differed little from those of previous presidents, but over Coolidge's seven and a half years in office, the requirement came to feel onerous. Since the identity of this unnamed spokesman was an open secret, humor columnists, gag writers, and vaudeville comics made sport of it. The whole flap, noted the political scientist Lindsay Rogers, suggested that reporters were making a devil's bargain in letting the president hide behind his veil of anonymity, however transparent it may have been.

There was, inevitably, a partisan dimension to the criticisms. Those most unnerved by Coolidge's policy, noted David Lawrence, were Democrats, who were otherwise at pains to explain the success of their nemesis. *The Nation*'s Oswald Garrison Villard charged that the practice brought shame on president and press alike—on the president because "no public man ought to utter any words for which he is not willing to assume the authorship," and on the reporters because their complicity compromised their honor. Rogers was more dire. "This newly appointed, anonymous, extra-legal official," he warned, was a creation of "the God of Publicity" and amounted to "an extra-constitutional person who increases both presidential influence and irresponsibility." Although Coolidge at first defended the White House Spokesman device, insisting that he could never let his unfiltered comments appear in the papers, eventually he too found the fiction unsustainable and asked that the mythical creature be retired. Yet because he continued to bar reporters from quoting him directly, the rule change was largely meaningless. Reporters now simply claimed insight into what "the president thinks" or "the president feels," without giving any attribution at all.[10]

The critique of Coolidge's "government by publicity" also extended into the realm of the visual. As photography assumed an ever larger place in the newspapers, and newsreels improved in quality, Coolidge surpassed Harding in exploiting the lenses. In April 1925, two years before Al Jolson, he appeared in a talking film, shot by inventor Lee De Forest's Phonofilm, which played before a New York Friars Club dinner of some 500 guests. "The tones of his voice came clear and synchronized perfectly with the movement of his mouth," the *New York Times* reported excitedly. "Once during the speech the synchronization was so perfect that the guests gave involuntary applause." Meanwhile, among newspaper photographers—whose tripods and boxes became fixtures at the White House—Coolidge won a reputation for solicitude. "He avoided every appearance of publicity seeking, but he probably was the most photographed man who ever occupied the White House," noted one journalist. "It was a joke among the photographers that Mr. Coolidge would don any attire or assume any pose that would produce an interesting picture." As radio made Coolidge's voice and words known to more Americans than ever heard TR, the ubiquity of his image made "his face, mannerisms and gestures," wrote Charles Willis Thompson, equally "familiar to every one of the multitudes who go to the movies or look at the newspapers."[11]

Many considered all the pictures to be so much more propaganda. *The New Republic* noted peevishly that on his 1927 summer vacation in the Black Hills, Coolidge was joined by "some thirty-odd newspaper correspondents, a group of a dozen or more moving-picture men, several unofficial but effective press agents disguised as syndicate writers, a number of expert telegraph operators, camera men representing the photo syndicates . . . every last man of them devoted to the task of publicity for Mr. Coolidge." The shots that resulted included one of the president bedecked in an Indian headdress as he addressed 10,000 members of the Sioux tribe and another of him in cowboy regalia, from chaps and silver spurs to flaming red shirt and blue bandanna. Coolidge's trips to the family homestead in Vermont provided settings to catch him pitching hay, wielding a scythe, or riding a tractor—providing Rockwellian decoration to Bartonesque profiles and fodder for cinematic shorts like *Visitin' Round at Coolidge Corners*. The more audiences enjoyed these films, the more Coolidge's critics stewed. "Certainly no president has ever been willing to submit to such nauseating exhibitions in the news reels as has Coolidge," wrote journalist Sherwin Cook. "Cultured Americans wince at the thought of their president putting on a smock frock to pose while pitching hay and milking a bossy." But in their indignation, the critics forgot that Coolidge's image-making stunts often backfired, striking some audiences as phony and staged. "I doubt if the average farmer would believe it was real and not especially prepared for the occasion," said Ted Clark, warning against circulating one egregious photograph.

Coolidge's popularity wasn't the result of any grand deception, any more than TR's or Wilson's had been. Voters had taken his measure as a man restrained in temper and leadership style, and by and large they liked him. His popularity stemmed from the prosperity over which he presided and the reassurances he offered. The editorials deriding his publicity techniques spoke less to any Machiavellianism on Coolidge's part than to the wariness of publicity now permeating the political scene. Coolidge was charged with manipulation and inauthenticity because presidential politics itself was coming to be seen as a realm shot through with misleading appearances.

18

THE OVERT ACTS OF EDWARD BERNAYS

ON JANUARY 4, 1931, in the middle of the afternoon, New Yorkers fiddling with their radio dials could listen to Arturo Toscanini conducting the New York Philharmonic, or to a comedian named Charles Rothman, or to a program of *Negro Folk Songs*. Or, if they settled on WOR, they could hear a rather intellectual debate on the question, "Is Propaganda a Constructive Force in American Life Today?" Speaking in the negative was the erudite Silas Bent, who rejected the fashionably scornful view of the masses as easily manipulated. "This is a literate and highly intelligent nation," he said. "It can form its own opinions competently if it has access to the facts uncolored by interested agencies and undistorted by special pleading." But Bent worried that public relations men and others who slanted the truth on behalf of an agenda blockaded or obstructed—rather than contributed to—the flow of public information. The propagandist, Bent said, "does not want us to use our own heads. He wants to do our thinking for us, as though we were mentally unfit." Bent didn't suggest banning publicists, but he proposed "segregating propaganda in a sort of 'red light' district." Like lawyers or doctors, he believed, publicists should have to hold a license to practice, or at least should have to register, like lobbyists. Ethics violations could mean disbarment.[1]

Opposing Bent was Edward Bernays. Like Bent, Bernays spoke in the name of the people and against elites who would make decisions for them. "It might be wiser," Bernays said, to have "committees of wise men who would choose our rulers, dictate our conduct, private and public, and decide upon the best types of clothes for us to wear and the best kinds of food for us to eat. But we have chosen the opposite method— that of open competition." He granted that the tools of persuasion were sometimes "misused," but held that propaganda was still necessary in any society whose "system demands mass distribution of products and ideas." Many conscientious propagandists worked for schools, churches, theaters, charities, social services. Without their work, he said, "scores of minority groups of all factions . . . could never bring their views before the public." Since these tools of propaganda were "available to all," he concluded, "it is an insurance against autocracy in government" and a public boon.[2]

Arguments like Bernays's were a tough sell in a political culture steeped in fear of propaganda. But they weren't wholly new. A decade earlier, when Bernays was starting out, Ivy Lee was fighting the negative image of public relations with similar claims. In a slim volume called *Publicity: Some of the Things It Is and Is Not*, Lee cleverly took issue with a description of propaganda, offered by Coolidge, as a message that "seeks to present a part of the facts, to distort their relations, and to force conclusions which could not be drawn from a complete and candid survey of all the facts." To this seemingly sound and careful definition, Lee countered that *no* factual recitation of events could ever be complete and that subjective judgment *always* influenced what information was relevant and how it was presented. "All I can do," Lee said, "is to give you my interpretation of the facts." That interpretation was inevitably shaped by bias—whether natural biases, like Walter Lippmann's unconscious preconceptions, or more calculated (not to say purchased) ones, like those reflecting a client's interest. Either way, said Lee, "all of us are apt to try to think that what serves our own interests is also in the general interest."[3]

Lee's acknowledgment of subjectivity—to the exclusion, even, of any objective knowledge—contradicted the just-the-facts protestations he had made as a front man for Rockefeller and Bethlehem Steel and United Artists. But his admission that a margin of subjectivity was inescapable was hardly without merit. Critics of propaganda had always been at pains to explain from where the uncolored truth was supposed to emerge. Whose version of events could be credited as purely factual?

To some, the only practical response was to acknowledge the reality of propaganda and disassociate it from moral questions. The leading exponent of this view was the political scientist Harold Lasswell, author of one of the most rigorous and influential propaganda studies. A self-described "despondent democrat," Lasswell frankly admitted that government leaders needed propaganda to tame "the mighty rushing wind of public sentiment." It could be used for good or ill, he insisted. "Propaganda as a mere tool is no more moral or immoral than a pump handle."[4]

Like Lasswell, Bruce Bliven thought it necessary to accept publicity as a permanent part of politics. "We are only at the beginning of the Age of Propaganda," he wrote. "The daily press, the radio and the motion picture, have come to be the eyes and ears of the citizen." This meant an obligation to engage with argument: "All of us have a tendency to be more than fair to our own group and less than fair to our opponents. The harmful and dangerous thing is the suppression of all opinions save one." Defining propaganda in its neutral sense, Bliven called for a debate among all points of view—to answer propaganda, as he said, with a wink and a nod, with "more propaganda!"[5]

Whether liberal upholders of reason should aspire to use publicity—including emotion, sensationalism, and manipulation—presented yet another dilemma. The novelist John Dos Passos argued that liberals should appropriate the corporate propagandists' techniques for their purposes; they needed, he wrote, "An Ivy Lee for Liberals." In fact, progressive institutions and causes, from organized labor to public health, had been among the most farsighted in their use of publicists and modern methods of persuasion to advance their goals. But propaganda still struck most liberals as a tool that was used for ill.[6]

The problem with allowing each group its own publicist was that it threatened to lead to an untenable relativism—to a belief, close to Ivy Lee's claim, that the truth lay simply with whichever side presented it more appealingly. Walter Lippmann agreed with critics like Bent that publicity and propaganda muddied the common reservoir of information. "The old adage of our salad days about the curative effects of publicity under popular government seems rather naive in this age of publicity," he wrote in 1927. Yet he also shared Bliven's conclusion that publicists couldn't be barred or wished away. They existed, he said, because they filled a need: their influence reflected the reality that "the facts of modern life do not spontaneously take a shape in which they can be known. They must be given a shape." As he told Mencken, however, Lippmann opposed the recourse to sensationalist "Hearstian" methods. The only solution was to promote objectivity and expertise, whether through the government "intelligence bureaus" that he proposed in *Public Opinion*, or other institutions and practices that could help the public grasp the import of arcane and specialized facts.[7]

* * *

In the 1920s, as debates like these swirled, Edward Bernays displaced Ivy Lee as the leading practitioner and spokesman for public relations. Like Lee, Bernays built an impressive client list and a lucrative practice and brought his talents to bear on presidential politics. But even more than his predecessor, and with greater gusto, he thrust himself into the limelight, arguing in books and lectures, in magazines and radio debates, for the legitimacy of his profession. Bernays boasted that he taught the first university course in public relations, at New York University in 1923. He defended public relations advisers against attacks from newspapers and advertising trade journals. When Mencken wrote derisively of *public relations* as a slick euphemism in his *American Language*, Bernays convinced him to revise the entry in his next edition, which included a short essay on the subject by Bernays. These labors earned Bernays the moniker "the father of public relations," a title he deserved no more than Lee. Yet Bernays won and held onto the honorific by dint of his facile mind, his incessant braggadocio, and his sheer longevity—he lived to one hundred three.[8]

Bernays advanced his profession, too, by demanding that it be made more professional. In this stance he was aligned with his debating adversary Silas Bent. Bernays argued that public relations should be treated, like law or medicine, as a profession—afforded the commensurate respect and held to a professional code of ethics. In 1924, he tried unsuccessfully to have a law introduced in the New York state assembly for the licensing of public relations professionals. After the Public Relations Society of America was founded in 1947, he often argued that its standards were too low.

Bernays personally projected an aura of professionalism that was vital to his success. An elfin man with a receding hairline, he sported an elegant wardrobe and a trim black mustache than ran the length of his lip. He infused public relations with flair, sophistication, and even glamour. Rising quickly to the heights of his field, he consorted with celebrities and lived in high style. For years he and his wife Doris Fleischman, who was also his business partner, inhabited a penthouse in the Sherry-Netherland Hotel on Fifth Avenue.

He was born in Vienna in 1891, the nephew twice over of Sigmund Freud. (Edward's mother, Anna Freud Bernays, was the great psychoanalyst's sister; Edward's father, Ely Bernays, was the brother of Freud's wife Martha.) He celebrated his first birthday on the family's voyage from Europe to New York, where he grew up in East Harlem, then a tony neighborhood. His upbringing resembled Lippmann's: raised in comfort among Manhattan's well-to-do German-Jewish community, educated at Dr. Julius Sachs's School for Boys and at Ivy League colleges (Bernays went to Cornell), and intellectually beholden to Freud. Bernays, of course, had the closer connection to psychoanalysis, and he kept up a warm relationship with his famous uncle, visiting with him in Europe as well as on Freud's 1909 trip to the United States. Bernays played up the connection shamelessly, even though his knowledge of psychoanalysis was skimpy, having come, as he once admitted, mainly from "osmosis." But the kinship gave Bernays a mystique, as if he possessed some family secret for working magic on the unconscious. The journalist Henry Pringle, in a typical profile, called Bernays a "Mass Psychologist."[9]

Although Bernays, following Ivy Lee, presented himself as the antithesis of the old plaid-coated press agents, he had begun his career in the theater, promoting Sergei Diaghilev's Ballets Russes and the tenor Enrico Caruso on their American tours. (The press agent to Caruso, wags said, was the Caruso of press agents.) Like many of his generation, he had worked for the Creel Committee, in no small part because Creel personally wrote to Bernays's draft board. At the committee, Bernays soaked up knowledge about how to influence public opinion, including, he recalled, the insight that "what could be done for a nation at war could be done for organizations and people in a nation at peace." After the war he opened his own firm, from an office on 19 East 48th Street.[10]

In the next decade, Bernays began his proselytizing for public relations, which he claimed to be elevating into a "science" or a "profession." He took to calling himself "counsel on public relations," to don the respectability and stature of the legal profession. He even tried to differentiate his work from Lee's, calling his own craft a science where Lee's was merely an art. But Bernays never made clear what was supposedly scientific about his method. He touted his use of market surveys, but that invention was already common in advertising. Above all, intuition and cleverness guided his work. Terms like *science, professional*, and *counsel* were elements of his salesmanship, tossed about to give his practice an air of methodical efficacy.

All the same, Bernays perfected a handful of clever, reliable tricks. More than anyone since P. T. Barnum, he devised promotional methods that rested on ingenious indirection, creating an allure for his product or client while masking the commercial or self-interested purpose. To sell Ivory soap, he held a soap sculpture competition for children—an irresistible topic for light feature stories in the papers. To boost book sales, he enlisted architects and contractors to make built-in bookshelves in homes and apartments—which occupants then felt obliged to fill. A multitude of similar stories filled the magazine profiles with which he happily cooperated. The free attention was better than paid advertising, he grasped, because readers wouldn't automatically regard the news stories with the skepticism they typically brought to advertisements.

Bernays was partial to what he dubbed the "overt act," or what was more mundanely called a publicity stunt. The most famous of these (no small thanks to Bernays) was his "Torches of Freedom" campaign, undertaken on behalf of the American Tobacco Company. Young women in the 1920s were challenging social mores—bobbing their hair, raising their hemlines—and Bernays touted smoking as an emblem of liberation. Covertly, his secretary recruited a group of young feminists to march down Fifth Avenue on Easter Sunday, proudly puffing away; Bernays predicted that the news stories would "take care of themselves, as legitimate news, if the staging is rightly done." Sure enough, the parade earned write-ups everywhere and inspired copy-cat marches, whose participants were blind to American Tobacco's original sponsorship. Though Bernays exaggerated the campaign's importance (smoking had become popular with women some years before), the creative cunning was undeniable. Bernays hadn't just interpreted reality. He had shaped it.

In 1924, Bernays dreamed up his first political overt act, on behalf of Coolidge. Coolidge had been receiving advice from Bruce Barton, but Bernays's style was different. Where the midwestern minister's son reassured audiences with the comforts of the ordinary, the Jewish émigré excited them with the power of the extraordinary. Bernays argued that the "Silent Cal" persona that Barton had fashioned for the president made him seem too aloof. So Bernays organized a troupe of Broadway actors to visit Coolidge, under the theory that "stage people symbolized warmth, extroversion and Bohemian camaraderie." In late October Bernays's party of forty, which included Al Jolson and Ed Wynn, took a night train from New York to Washington, arriving at the White House for what Bernays recalled as a breakfast of "good, strong, steaming coffee with cream, . . .

hot griddlecakes and Deerfoot sausages doused with Vermont maple syrup." After the meal, Jolson, continuing the political crooning he had done for Harding, led the assembled in a corny song: "Keep Coolidge!" The next day, the *New York Times*'s headline marveled: "Actors Eat Cakes with Coolidge . . . President Nearly Laughs." Crediting Coolidge as "politically keenly aware," Bernays later reflected, "The country felt that a man in the White House who could laugh with Al Jolson and the Dolly sisters was not frigid and unsympathetic."[11]

Besides the overt act, Bernays's other favorite device was the expert testimonial. In what may have been his most important public relations insight, Bernays concluded that people deferred to the judgment of ostensibly disinterested experts, or what he called "group leaders." To promote his causes, he would find—or invent—these experts. He enlisted doctors to tout hearty breakfasts on behalf of the bacon industry. Or he would create an "institute" or "committee"—say, on sanitary food and drink, which would call for the use of paper cups. For Coolidge, Bernays established a "Coolidge Non-Partisan League" to attest to the president's bona fides outside die-hard Republican circles. Though its impact appears to have been negligible, he resorted to the device throughout his career. In 1986, for example, he assembled a "Committee of Ninety-Five" leading dignitaries to celebrate the ninety-fifth birthday of Edward Bernays.[12]

In his quest to promote his clients, his trade, and himself, Bernays, inspired by Lippmann's *Public Opinion*, wrote prolifically on the nature of publicity work. The most important of these writings, *Crystallizing Public Opinion* and *Propaganda*, aimed to distinguish public relations work not just from the tacky salesmanship of press agents but also from mere "publicity." The nature of public relations, Bernays claimed, went far beyond the production and distribution of "handouts." But in defending his craft, Bernays confronted a paradox: To dispel fears of its malignancy, he had to minimize its power—but to minimize its power was to call into question its utility. Bernays walked this fine line in *Crystallizing Public Opinion* by offering a more modest role for the public relations counselor than Lippmann had. Bernays arrived at the key word *crystallizing* after much reflection. He wanted to suggest that the public relations man neither imposed ideas on the public nor simply discovered public opinion, but found existing points of alignment between his client and the public. Successful public relations, he stressed, depended on policies and practices that would give people what they wanted, and did not require distortion or deception.[13]

Settling into his role as a pop theorist, Bernays next wrote *Propaganda*, hoping, like Harold Lasswell and other realists, to salvage the once neutral term. Like Lippmann, Bernays gradually became comfortable in the 1920s prescribing a leadership role for a select group. Power in a modern democracy, he now argued, resided with "the relatively small number of persons who . . . understand the mental processes and social patterns of the masses" and "who pull the wires which control the public mind." His tone in this second book turned darker, more Machiavellian. He now used words like *manipulation* as much as *crystallization*; he invested public relations men with substantially more power than he had previously allowed. "The conscious and intelligent manipulation of the organized habits and opinions of the masses is an important element in democratic society," he wrote. "Those who manipulate this unseen mechanism of society constitute an invisible government which is the true ruling power of our country."[14]

Bernays would come to regret this language, which carried overtones of the Nietzschean *Ubermensch*. But he continued to push for a key role for public relations professionals in democratic life. That conviction drew him into politics, whose practitioners he regarded as hapless amateurs. "Politics has failed to learn very much from business methods in mass distribution of ideas and products," he wrote. Campaign managers should focus less on "bombast, glitter, and speeches" and more on studying public opinion in a scientific manner. They needed to conduct survey research and make sure that their emotional appeals "coincide in every way with the broad basic plans of the campaign and all its minor details." Noting the tendency of voters to disaffiliate from the two parties, he proposed targeting the "overlapping groups" that made up the voting public—"economic, social, religious, educational, cultural, racial, collegiate, local, sports, and hundreds of others." This "segmented" approach to public opinion—later popularized by the communications theorist Paul Lazarsfeld—soon became a staple of public persuasion, offering an alternative to the blunt force of appeals to the entire public through mass media.[15]

Among Bernays's many suggestions for overhauling American politics was the idea that the executive branch include a cabinet-rank secretary of public relations. This official—much like the minister of information Woodrow Wilson once envisioned—could keep citizens regularly apprised of all the government's activities. *Time* magazine ridiculed the idea as "bizarre." But it was merely ahead of its time, and not by much.

That same year, 1928, the nation would elect the first president to appoint a de facto press secretary; the following year, the minority party would hire its own full-time publicist to counter the administration's messages. Bernays's idea of a secretary of public relations was nothing worse than a poor name—a bad public relations job—for a task that was already becoming indispensable.

MASTER OF EMERGENCIES

HERBERT HOOVER, elected president by a decisive margin over Al Smith in 1928, was a genius at publicity, and everyone in Washington knew it. "Mr. Hoover's ascent to the presidency was planned with great care and assisted throughout by a high-powered propaganda of the latest model," observed Walter Lippmann in 1930. Drew Pearson, embarking on his long career as a Washington gadfly, called Hoover "one of the great super-promoters of the age, a man who had been able by a consummate sense of publicity to create the illusion of heroism and greatness and to attain world acclaim." Hoover's "extraordinary feat," echoed the columnist Heywood Broun, was "selling himself."[1]

The first president born west of the Mississippi, the Stanford-educated Hoover was a brilliant geologist and mining engineer who made himself a millionaire by age forty. Stiff in bearing, with cherubic cheeks and a plump torso, he spoke plainly, reflecting a Quaker upbringing, and dressed simply, wearing an old-fashioned detachable Berwick collar with his three-piece suits. He also lacked all talent for retail politics. Wilsonian in his self-regard, he refused to kiss babies, toss back boilermakers, or chitchat about his personal life. He rose to fame through his achievement in unelected, technocratic posts. He belonged to a small club of presidents never voted into any political office but the nation's highest.

Hoover earned his reputation during the world war. When the Germans overran Belgium in 1914, he heroically arranged the delivery of food to starving victims. Wilson named him to oversee food rationing at home after the United States joined the fighting. Following the armistice, Hoover again fed a ravaged Europe. Wilson saluted him as a "great international figure," one of few men who "stir me deeply and make me in love with duty." The world marveled. Hoover became the "Great Humanitarian."[2]

This wartime work taught Hoover how to reach mass audiences. As food czar, he devised catchy slogans and newsy stunts—issuing pledge cards for women to sign as a way to conserve groceries, establishing "meatless" and "wheatless" days to help ration needed foodstuffs—and he assembled a corps of journalists, admen, and illustrators to spread his gospel. A regular at Gridiron dinners and a fount of insider gossip, Hoover counted among his admirers such journalistic heavyweights as William Allen White, Mark Sullivan, and Ray Stannard Baker. Detractors pegged him a "creation of press agents."[3]

As commerce secretary under Harding and Coolidge, Hoover was a whirlwind. He arrogated to his department every project he could grab, from negotiating a coal miners' strike to implementing rules for radio regulation. Coolidge made fun of Hoover's restlessness, branding him "Wonder Boy." But he used Hoover's talents, sending him to tackle the 1927 Mississippi flood, the worst natural disaster in American history until Hurricane Katrina in 2005. Hoover set up headquarters in Memphis, traveling the river valley for three months in an unprecedented rescue, relief, and reconstruction operation. His frenetic pace and solicitude toward reporters kept him in the press and the newsreels. The *New York Times Magazine* hailed his "genius"; *National Geographic* ran a 47-page spread, decorated with 53 photographs of Hoover diligently tending to the dispossessed. He designed his radio speeches so audiences could hear the river roaring behind him. But the hype couldn't persuade everyone. Mencken's *American Mercury* snarled that George Akerson—a *Minneapolis Tribune* reporter who had attached himself to Hoover—had simply "organized a survey trip through the flooded area, and accompanied by a large corps of photographers and reporters, he and the Chief floated down the river amid a fanfare of publicity."[4]

In August 1927, Calvin Coolidge forswore another term, and speculation about his successor commenced. Hoover, who was fly-fishing with Akerson at the Bohemian Grove Club in Northern California, turned to his aide. "I'm sorry, George," he said, "but it looks as if we'll have to go back to Palo Alto and get to work." Within an hour, scores of newsmen were swarming the campground. Hoover was the odds-on favorite to be the next president.

* * *

Of all Hoover's admirers in the press, none was more loyal than Will Irwin—veteran of *McClure's* golden age, acclaimed war correspondent, senior Creel Committee official. Irwin was also, ever since his 1911 series on public relations men for *Collier's*, an authoritative student of propaganda. When propaganda criticism became a cottage industry in the 1920s, Irwin returned to the topic, describing how the press agents' "mimeographed 'mail stuff' filled the editorial wastebaskets of our great metropolitan dailies." Lippmann-like, he asked whether journalists could handle "a trained liar or a subtle exponent of half truths guarding the gates of information." But Irwin clung to his Progressive optimism. Nature, he said, "has endowed the human mind with a curious sixth sense for truth."[5]

In 1927, when the Mississippi flooded, Irwin, fifty-three, put aside a biography of the movie mogul Adolph Zukor to report on Hoover's swashbuckling for *The World's Work*. Hoover was an old friend from Stanford, and covering him was an irresistible opportunity. Irwin traversed the disaster zone from a prime seat in the commerce secretary's railroad car. "The valley escaped with slight loss of life," he noted, "owing mainly to swift and certain work on the part of that master-organizer, Herbert Hoover."[6]

If the flood turned Irwin into an unwitting propagandist for Hoover, the secretary's entrance into the presidential race made him a witting one. Nominally a Democrat, Irwin had worked for Cox in 1920 and voted for Davis in 1924. But he considered his friend a statesman and a superb administrator and joined Hoover's campaign as a publicist of the sort he had long deplored. His first task was a campaign biography. Starting in the fall of 1927, writing every day for three months, he banged out a chronicle of his friend's life, allowing Hoover to edit the chapter drafts. *Herbert Hoover: A Reminiscent Biography* appeared in bookstores in March 1928, serialized in the *New York Herald Tribune* and other papers. Hoover's staff sent copies to delegates to the upcoming Republican Convention.[7]

Irwin then took an unpaid position with the campaign in New York. In the morning he would ply his journalism from home; in the afternoon he would play the flack. His own celebrity landed him high-profile work. In September, he delivered an address about Hoover's life over a nationwide radio hookup; in October, he publicly debated Norman Hapgood, an Al Smith supporter. He also wrote and arranged the titles for an hour-long campaign film, *Master of Emergencies*, one of two silent movies Hoover's team put out that summer. A high-quality, professional production, *Master of Emergencies* reviewed Hoover's career as savior of the dispossessed, from Belgium to Biloxi. The footage included aerial shots of submerged river towns, profiles of a purposeful Hoover surveying the scene, and close-ups of grateful children, black and white, fed by Hoover's teams. Even horses and pigs were saved from certain doom. The film pulled so blatantly at the heartstrings that Hoover cringed, telling Irwin that "it would get votes only from the morons." In September, however, it premiered to positive notices, and Irwin claimed vindication. "By the end they were sobbing all over the house," he told Hoover. "And when they cry, you've got 'em. Those tears mean votes. At least three fourths of the voters are moronic enough to be persuaded by their eyes and their emotions."[8]

In lending Hoover his support and his labor, Irwin was following a common journalistic practice—from Joseph Bishop to George Creel and Ray Baker to Judson Welliver—of writing about presidents one day and working for them the next. Irwin felt at least a frisson of uncertainty about his plunge into partisan politics. When he joined for the campaign, Irwin asked Hoover to make one promise.

"What is that?" Hoover asked.

"That you never offer me a political job!"

*   *   *

After Hoover's election, pundits expected he would pay at least as much attention to his image as Coolidge had. "A strong Bruce Bartonish . . . flavor" was in store, warned "T.R.B." Hoover hired a squadron of press aides, including French Strother as speechwriter and George Akerson as, in effect, the first full-time White House press secretary. Akerson briefed reporters twice daily; the president himself also faced the pack twice a week. Hoover refurbished the press room, installing plush yellow carpeting, a stately vestibule, a room for the cameramen, and mahogany desks and typewriters. Signs pointed to a beautiful relationship.[9]

Seven months later came the Great Crash. Everything changed. Hoover proved helpless to master his newest emergency. Wedded to the nineteenth-century laissez-faire ideology he had espoused in 1922 in his *American Individualism*, Hoover never mustered the vision to stimulate the economy or provide relief commensurate with the unprecedented challenge of the Depression. His public statements fell with a thud. "The fundamental business of the country . . . is on a sound and prosperous basis," he declared. With homelessness rampant and hunger worsening, he shrugged that nobody actually starved. Hospitals and morgues told a different story. Akerson, a heavy drinker and mediocre flack to begin with, quit to work for Zukor at Paramount. His replacement, Theodore Joslin of the *Boston Transcript*, was reviled as pompous and overweening. Press relations deteriorated.[10]

Hoover's technocratic polish now appeared as a contemptuous aloofness. Failing to heed Coolidge's example, he excluded reporters from his weekend escapes, retreating in relative isolation to a cottage by Virginia's Rapidan River. That he occasionally invited favorites like Irwin or Mark Sullivan only exacerbated the snub. He grew tight-lipped at press conferences and took to canceling them on short notice. His highly selective availability prompted the National Press Club to excoriate his "evasion, misrepresentation, and downright lying" and to assert "the rights of the newspapers and of the public to know in detail what their government is doing."[11]

Hoover realized he had oversold himself. "My friends have made the American people think of me as a sort of a superman, able to cope successfully with the most difficult and complicated problems," he told the journalist Willis Abbot. "They expect the impossible of me." Having advertised himself as a problem solver, he left Americans disappointed and angry when he failed to reverse the worst economic downturn the country had known. It was the lost jobs and vaporized savings accounts that did the most damage to Hoover's reputation, not his press relations. Still, his inability to cheer or comfort the public didn't help. He lacked, wrote Lippmann, the skills of the public presidency—"the capacity of a Roosevelt and a Wilson to fight fire with fire, passion with passion, slogans with slogans."[12]

But if Hoover failed in his public relations, he did not fail to try. "To strengthen the White House publicity machine, Mr. Hoover has outdone all his predecessors," wrote Fred Essary, noting the "great battery of government press agents" scattered across bureaus and departments, together forming "the greatest propaganda establishment in the world." From the White House in particular, Essary wrote, "we receive daily presidential speeches, messages, proclamations, pronouncements, executive orders, appointments, Rapidan guest lists, dinner and reception arrangements (not forgetting the flowers on the table), and tributes to deceased football coaches and foreign potentates." Democrats, indeed, attacked the president for politicizing the provision of information.[13]

Hoover's boldest move was to set up a semi-official newspaper, reminiscent of the Creel Committee's *Official Bulletin*: a 12-page weekly tabloid called *Washington: A Journal of Information and Opinion Concerning the Operation of Our National Government*. Conceived by the White House and the Republican National Committee in 1930 with an eye toward the midterm elections, it was, its publisher straightfacedly claimed, "an effort to print . . . what is going on in the administration, not politically, but in a governmental way." In the debut issue William Allen White, in a rare lapse of judgment, profiled Hoover as a "seer of visions" and "blood-brother to the great idealists of this generation—Roosevelt and Wilson," and Irwin deferentially interviewed Ray Lyman Wilbur, Hoover's interior secretary. Americans weren't impressed. Democrats romped in the midterms, and *Washington* folded after three issues.[14]

Hoover had other tricks. His empirical, data-driven mind was drawn to public polling as a way of getting right with public sentiment. The opinion surveys of the early 1930s lacked the sophisticated methods that would soon enhance their legitimacy, but Hoover gamely tried them. He consulted straw polls—surveys that didn't even try to faithfully reflect the makeup of the electorate—and established the first systematic White House mechanism for measuring public opinion. He assiduously perused editorials, setting up an "elaborate clipping bureau," as Joslin called it, more methodical in design than even his news-conscious predecessors had attempted. He read seven papers a day and assigned two clerks to analyze commentaries from scores of others. Categorizing every item by its stance toward the administration, these aides devised a complex cryptographic alphabet to signify key variables in order to help the president drill down into public opinion. But just how the administration was supposed to exploit this information-rich databank remained unclear.[15]

When Hoover wasn't monitoring public opinion, he tried to shape it. Few experts failed to receive a phone call soliciting advice. Among the chosen was Albert Lasker, whom Hoover invited to Rapidan, only to be told, "You haven't a dog's chance of getting elected." Lasker's bluntness ended their relationship. Hoover also enlisted Bruce Barton, who had quietly advised the 1928 campaign, urging the candidate to soften his image with "some fishing or tree-chopping, something that shows him [to be] a human being" and to play up his "orphan farm boy" roots. Now Barton began to visit the White House, and when Akerson quit as press secretary, his name was floated as a replacement. He never did join the administration, but he wrote speeches, supplied ideas, and assessed public opinion. Yet Barton's instincts, so well suited to Coolidge's quiet rectitude during the fat years, misfired amid the economic crisis. Sharing Hoover's devotion to laissez-faire, Barton failed to appreciate the need for bolder White House action. He advised the president to do "as much fishing as possible for a while," on the theory that "the best news that ever comes from Washington is 'all's quiet on the Potomac.'" He was equally wrong about Hoover's possible 1932 opponents. Roosevelt's nomination, he counseled, "would be the best luck the President could have," calling FDR nothing more than "a name and a crutch."

Leaving no public relations guru untapped, Hoover also sought out Edward Bernays. They had met at the Golden Jubilee of Light, a gala that the publicist staged in 1929 for General Electric on the light bulb's fiftieth birthday. Eight days later, the stock market tanked. Hoover summoned Bernays to the White House, where he offered Bernays a cigar but spoke measuredly. Afterward, Sullivan reported back to Bernays that the president had been impressed. "How do you know?" Bernays asked. "He didn't say a word."

In October 1930, Hoover set up an Emergency Committee for Employment led by Arthur Woods, an old trusty, who brought Bernays on board. The committee was supposed to help the unemployed, but it was accompanied by neither a jobs program nor any spending stimulus. Bernays advised Woods to avoid "the purely inspirational and exhortative appeal" in his press releases and statements and to provide facts about the administration's accomplishments in boosting employment. But the board lacked the legal force to compel companies to hire anyone. "It was," Bernays said, despairingly, "really a public relations committee."[16]

Still, Bernays, from his New York office, did what he could, enlisting radio and film, trade journals, and mail-order catalogues, and appealing to business leaders to ramp up their hiring. Will Hays, now working for the movie studios, oversaw the injection of upbeat messages into newsreels. William Paley, the head of CBS, aired talks by corporate bosses who had followed the committee's voluntary hiring guidelines. Woods gave speeches rife with Hooverian nostrums: "Let us all spruce up our homes—make the repairs that are needed—do that little job of painting." But when the committee made concrete recommendations, such as urging Hoover to spend hundreds of millions of dollars on highway construction and public works, the president demurred, and without any policy to back them up, the public relations ploys were, even Bernays had to admit, "all ineffective."[17]

Hoover's cosmetic approach had been futile. "Relief by Publicity," scoffed *The Nation*, which declared that "real stabilization and relief are to be accomplished only by deliberate and scientific planning with a view to permanent results." Bruce Bliven was also leery. After enduring months of boosterish appeals, he queried Bernays about "what the Arthur Woods Committee has accomplished to date." Bernays, it appears, did not write back.[18]

The lessons were lost on Hoover. As the 1932 campaign drew near, he called Bernays to the White House again to try to salvage his reelection. Bernays produced a strategy paper spinning out his usual tricks, including testimonials from disinterested experts and symbolic appeals, but Hoover was beyond rescue.

Bernays was correct that public relations without sound policy could do little. Hoover was undone by devastating realities immune to even the most skillful salesmanship. After years of public hand-wringing over their insidious power, the hired manipulators of public opinion were suddenly exposed, and mocked, as useless.

*   *   *

Propaganda still had its critics, but now they were mainly found among Hoover partisans. When Will Irwin wrote a new study called *Propaganda and the News, or What Makes You Think So?* he worked himself into a lather over the "smearing" of Hoover by publicists, which Irwin said had brought down the president in 1932. The book was taken as partisan pleading; the *New York Times* called it "propaganda against propaganda." Irwin despaired. "Practically all the reviewers leaped upon my frame for being too partial to you," he told Hoover.[19]

A leading villain of Irwin's book—and of Hoover partisans everywhere—was Charles Michelson. Diminutive and stoop-shouldered, with gray hair and a wattled neck, Michelson was a longtime newspaperman who in June 1929 went to work handling publicity for the Democratic National Committee. Trained at Hearst's papers, Michelson had a knack for the catchy phrase and a flair for the dramatic, as well as a raffish charm. At a salary of more than $20,000 a year, twice what any party publicist had ever earned, he spent his days attacking the president.[20]

With this assault, Democrats believed they were just belatedly embracing tools that their rivals had been using for years. The defeat of Al Smith in 1928—its third consecutive presidential loss—had given rise to anguish about the party's future. Since 1896, only Wilson had carried the Democratic banner to the White House, and he had done so in 1912 against a divided Republican Party. Deciding that the party of the people needed more money, Democratic sachems chose as chairman John Raskob, a General Motors executive who wooed big business and committed a quarter million dollars to the party. Raskob leased a suite of offices at the National Press Building in Washington, creating conference rooms, bringing in overstuffed furniture, and retaining a flock of secretaries, stenographers, clerks, and messengers. He also hired Charles Michelson.

Michelson, sixty, came from a highly accomplished German-Jewish family. His sister was a best-selling novelist, and his brother, Albert, won a Nobel Prize in Physics for measuring the velocity of light. Charlie was a lifelong reporter. He had spent time in a Cuban prison while working for Hearst and served for a dozen years as Washington bureau chief for the *New York World*, then became a columnist there. At the Democratic National Committee, running what was arguably the first permanent, ongoing opposition publicity shop, he used Raskob's millions to hammer the Hoover administration. The line between campaigning and governing was blurring.

Absorbing the lessons of men like Lasker, Michelson harnessed his gift for sloganeering to an ability to coordinate his messages. One observer noted that his genius lay in "applying the chain store method to the production of editorials and editorial ideas." Each day, after combing through streams of White House publicity for nuggets to exploit, he made the rounds on Capitol Hill. Armed with a memorandum about how to spin the piece of news—whether on the Smoot-Hawley Tariff, farm relief, fiscal policy, unemployment, or taxes—he would persuade a senator or congressman to put his name to the attack. Then, via messenger boys, he presented the statement as the congressman's own to the Washington correspondents scattered around the press club building. Down Pennsylvania Avenue, surrogates read Michelson's scripts into the *Congressional Record*, pressuring Republican newspapers to cover their remarks. Over 22 months, by one count, Michelson issued 504 statements under 76 different officials' names.[21]

Frustrated by Michelson's success, Hoover partisans inflated his skills into godlike powers. "The awe in which Michelson is held by Republicans is almost comic," wrote the journalist Alva Johnston. "The fame of Michelson is partly based on the superstition that press-agentry is the chief motive force in the world." Frank Kent—once a Democrat, increasingly a Hoover partisan—had recently published a book in which he calmly declared the political press agent a necessary fact of modern life. But in August 1930, in an exposé of Michelson's operation, he charged in a scandalized tone that the publicist's daily daubings served "to paint a picture of Hoover as an inept, bewildered, weak, and unworthy man, without a sense of direction, backbone, or power of decision." The GOP distributed a million copies of Kent's article, as party chairman Will Wood decried a "plot" by Raskob "to bring about a systematic and malicious misrepresentation of the President of the United States." The Republican National Committee then hired its own publicist, James West, much to the amusement of the press, which could now exult in the dueling propaganda. "Political War Rages on Typewriter Front," read the headlines. "Charges Fly Thick in Ballyhoo Fight."[22]

As significant as Michelson's achievement was, his legend was greater still. Years later, he was said to have coined the term *Hooverville*, for the tar-paper shantytowns that sprang up to house the homeless. He also got credit for the "Hoover blanket" (a newspaper), "Hoover carts" (mule-drawn cars whose drivers couldn't afford gas), and the "Hoover flag" (an empty pants pocket turned inside out). FDR particularly liked that one, and proposed a political cartoon asking, "Are you carrying the Hoover banner?" showing the empty pockets. But if Michelson invented those phrases, he kept his hand concealed. He is not linked to them in the contemporary record.[23]

There was, however, one such phrase that he did try to propagate. He called the economic collapse the "Hoover Panic." The label was meant to evoke the obverse of the "Coolidge Prosperity." That neologism, alas, failed to catch on. On the other hand, the phrase that everyone ended up using—"the Great Depression"—was originally put forward to mute the fear-inducing connotations of *panic*. Its most enthusiastic exponent, who used it with unrelenting discipline, was Herbert Hoover.

PART III

THE AGE OF COMMUNICATION

The twin crises of the 1930s and 1940s—depression and world war—softened the public suspicion of government publicity. Pulling together the nation, Franklin Roosevelt proved the equal to his late cousin in the arts of modern communication, using "Fireside Chats" to rally Americans to a common purpose and using opinion polls to gauge the public mood. Partisan critics of the New Deal and isolationist foes of intervention sounded alarms about FDR's methods. But many more Americans saw his reassuring messages as a bulwark against radio demagogues; looking fearfully at the propaganda emerging in Nazi Germany, they came to regard their own government's communications as comparatively benign. A new generation of communication scholars debunked the overheated propaganda studies of the 1920s, assuaging fears of all-powerful government media and an impressionable populace. Archibald MacLeish, the poet and playwright Roosevelt appointed to run the wartime Office of Facts and Figures, spoke for a new view that criticized the preceding era's reflexive wariness of publicity, maintaining that rallying the nation against its enemies could be consistent with telling the truth.

TUNED TO ROOSEVELT

"MY FRIENDS, I want to talk for a few minutes with the people of the United States about banking." The mellow voice wafted through radio receivers in millions of American homes, as Franklin Delano Roosevelt—president for all of nine days—began his first Fireside Chat. Roosevelt's conversational diction and rocking cadences gave no hint of the dire state of the nation's financial condition. For four months, since FDR routed Hoover in the 1932 election, the economy had done the impossible: It had gotten worse. Joblessness and hunger persisted, and now banks were folding at an alarming rate, vaporizing the life savings of millions of families. To tackle the problem, two days into his presidency FDR declared a "bank holiday"—a coy euphemism for a temporary shutdown—and six days later won authority from Congress to oversee the banks completely. These moves stanched the hemorrhaging.[1]

Still, treating the crisis of confidence required stronger medicine. FDR thought radio might be it. In 1933, although 62 percent of households had radios, it was still possible to find listeners who asked the machine to repeat a sentence, or who thought little men lived inside the wooden box. But this new political tool could now reach millions, and Roosevelt, having taken to the ether as governor of New York, resolved to avail himself of it as president as well. "The president," said his press aide Stephen

Early, "likes to think of the audience as being a few people around his fireside." Inspired by that statement, CBS executive Harry Butcher pinned the name "Fireside Chats" on the special addresses that FDR inaugurated on Sunday, March 12, 1933.

For White House aides, as for the nation, Roosevelt's performance would become a familiar ritual. Typically he would rehearse his talk several times, learning it almost by heart. As airtime neared, an aide swabbed the president's nostrils for tonal clarity, and FDR put a dental bridge in his mouth to keep the microphone from catching a whistle caused by a gap in his teeth. At ten minutes before start time—usually 9:50 or 10:20 pm eastern time—he was wheeled into a makeshift studio, normally in the White House Diplomatic Reception Room.[2]

A small audience of advisers and family members would usually be waiting on folding chairs. Roosevelt sat at a specially constructed broadcast desk cluttered with microphones, a lamp, a water pitcher, and his reading glasses. He would say his hellos, snuff out his cigarette, organize his papers, and take a sip of water. On a cue from the chief engineer, the crowd hushed and Roosevelt would speak.[3]

To those watching, said Labor Secretary Frances Perkins, it seemed as if the president mentally replaced the audience in the room with an American family somewhere in the hinterland. "As he talked his head would nod and his hands would move in simple, natural, comfortable gestures," she recalled. "His face would smile and light up as though he were actually sitting on the front porch or in the parlor with them." Listeners found the talks deeply personal, even though Roosevelt had ramped up the White House speechwriting operation, and his words thus represented a literary collaboration. "Many persons contributed suggestions and provided material," recalled George Creel, who did some work for him, "but when the first draft was placed in his hands, their connection ceased. It was common for him to go over a 'fireside chat' six or seven times; and although he was no Woodrow Wilson, he had a nice feeling for words and a very exact appreciation of shadings." Archibald MacLeish, another occasional speechwriter, noted wryly that "usually when you worked for him your 'input' was 'inputted' into the furnace."[4]

For this first banking talk, Charles Michelson had worked up a draft. But FDR tossed the document aside, he recalled, "lay on a couch, and dictated his own speech." His eyes fixed on a blank wall, Roosevelt imagined ordinary people from his native Dutchess County whom he thought of as "representative of the overwhelming majority." He pictured "a mason, at work on a new building, a girl behind a counter and a farmer in his field"—all worried about their money supposedly safe at the local Poughkeepsie bank.[5]

The Sunday-night speech was billed as "an intimate talk with the people of the United States on banking." It aimed to defuse the popular panic that was leading depositors to drain the banks. What FDR had to fix was a collective action problem: persuading individuals to act against their own narrow, short-term self-interest to achieve a goal that benefitted everyone. Like a friendly teacher, he began his speech by spelling out how banks work. "When you deposit money in a bank, the bank does not put the money in a safe-deposit vault. It invests your money in many different forms of credit." He calmly explained what had happened to the system, why he intervened, what he planned to do. Counseling patience, he concluded with a stiffening call for national unity. When the broadcast ended, Roosevelt waited quietly until an engineer indicated that the sound was off. "Was I all right?" he asked.[6]

He certainly was. "Our president took such a dry subject as banking," said the humorist Will Rogers, and "made everybody understand it, even the bankers." Americans responded with a flood of mail—a half million letters in March 1933 alone, requiring the White House to hire a whole mailroom staff. Most of it expressed gratitude, support, or an affection bordering on idolatry. "The President of this greatest Nation on earth honored every home with a personal visit last night," wrote a couple from Dubuque. "He came into our living-room in a kindly, neighborly way and in simple words explained the great things he had done." Mabel Morrissey of Brooklyn, forty-three, told FDR that "the past week is the first time that I have felt that I am an active part of the U.S.A.—your humane leadership has brought out all my latent patriotism."

The next day, when banks reopened, depositors held firm. The nation, wrote Walter Lippmann, by now the country's leading columnist, had "regained confidence in itself." By April 12, 13,000 once-destitute banks were operating again.[7]

More than words had healed the banking system. Roosevelt's emergency steps on taking office had worked, and in June he shored up the system with the Glass-Steagall Banking Act, which insured small depositors' money and regulated speculative investing. But the words had mattered. Grasping the psychological nature of the crisis, FDR directed his rhetoric toward fortifying the public's morale. Confronting a vortex of panic, he replaced it with an upward spiral of hope.

* * *

"The time may easily come—and soon—when the president of the United States in the White House can sit at his own desk," Bruce Barton had predicted in 1922, and "be heard in every household in the nation where there is a radio set." Probably since Woodrow Wilson conveyed his Fourteen Points to Europe via "wireless," and certainly since Coolidge broadcast his major speeches, radio had been changing American politics—by enormously expanding the reach of the president's spoken word, and by nationalizing politics, as it turned many audiences into one. But radio also changed the nature of speech. It killed off the orotund oratory of men like William Jennings Bryan and ushered in a conversational style. It imposed brevity, since speakers had to confine their remarks to a fixed time slot or risk losing their audience, or their live feed.[8]

In 1928, both parties had scrambled to make the most of radio's influence. They advertised on the airwaves, producing thirty-minute programs and five-minute "spots." The Democrats rescheduled their convention speeches to gain listeners. The Republicans, at theirs, softened the hard rap of the chairman's gavel. In a reference to Creel's wartime volunteers, the GOP also deployed "National Hoover Minute Men" to reach local markets with coordinated messages. Once Hoover was elected, William Paley of CBS advised the president to give "exclusive radio talks to the whole nation . . . from your study in the White House"—a tactic that Paley, touting "radio's intimate relationship to the home," said would "bring out your personality." Although Hoover wasn't too proud to hire a personal speaking coach—he later retained Richard Borden of New York University—he ignored Paley's prescient recommendation. It fell to FDR to exploit the medium to its fullest.[9]

Like his revered cousin Teddy, Franklin Roosevelt had always been media-conscious. Early in his career he relied on the reporter Louis McHenry Howe for public relations advice; later, Marvin McIntyre, a *Washington Post* and Creel Committee veteran, and Steve Early, a former newsreel man who also had worked under Creel, joined his team in the first ever White House Press Office. As president, FDR held the loosest and funniest press conferences since TR's, attracting flocks of more than 100 at a time, with correspondents jockeying to gain admission. In his twelve years as president, he hosted these sessions twice a week, nearly 1,000 in all. And though he suffered plenty of criticism from columnists and publishers, especially on the right, his cultivation of journalists created, said the columnist Raymond Clapper, a "feeling of complete ease, free-dom, just like a group around at any newspaper man's house." Favorites—Creel, Joseph Alsop and Robert Kintner, Anne O'Hare McCormick—were romanced, usually with the desired results.[10]

FDR's New Deal also brought forth an explosion in government pub-licity officers. When covering mammoth operations like the National Recovery Administration, correspondents relied on handouts as never before. "Newspaper bureaus in Washington," judged Arthur Krock of the *New York Times*, "could not . . . have covered the multifarious open activi-ties of the NRA code authorities without using the NRA press depart-ment as an auxiliary." As the left had been scandalized in the 1920s by Coolidge's publicity, now the conservative press hysterically denounced what *The American Mercury* called "Dr. Roosevelt's Propaganda Trust." In contrast, Roosevelt's supporters revived the Progressive rationale for publicity, deeming it necessary to inform and guide the public. "In these restless days," Harvard law professor Felix Frankfurter wrote the presi-dent, "in which foolishness and fanaticism and self-interest are exploited by professional poisoners of the public mind, by the Ivy Lees and Ber-nays, it becomes even more important than it was in the days of T.R. and Woodrow Wilson for the president to do what you are able to do with such extraordinary effectiveness, namely, to give guidance to the public in order to rally them to the general national interest."[11]

The most powerful publicity tool in FDR's arsenal was what his aide Rex Tugwell called his "mastery of radio." As far back as 1924, when most politicians still thought they should yell into the microphone in order to reach Pittsburgh or St. Louis, FDR had shown, the *New York Times* wrote, a "knack at making things sound personal and informal." As presi-dent, Roosevelt spoke often, but he reserved the signature Fireside Chats for special occasions. He gave thirty-one of them in his twelve years as president: on behalf of his Social Security program; his ill-fated plan to restructure the Supreme Court; and the "Lend-Lease" policy of arming the Allies in the early months of World War II. Supporters wanted more, but FDR feared overexposure. Not all these speeches went over as well as the 1933 talks. "Your latest piece of glorified propaganda—miscalled fireside chats—was disheartening and sickening," wrote Raymond Click of Pros-pect, Ohio, in April 1935. On some occasions, as with the Court-packing, the chats demonstrably failed to help FDR pass his legislation. But overall they gave FDR an incomparable advantage over his congressional rivals and election-year challengers. Opponents clamored about the unfairness and received airtime for rebuttals, but their speeches never stirred the nation as Roosevelt's did.[12]

Roosevelt's radio addresses worked because they forged a bond with his listeners. They instilled loyalty and a sense of community, a willingness to follow the president as he battled for relief and recovery, and later against the Axis Powers. The spell he cast could be uncanny. Walking along Chicago's Midway during one Fireside Chat, a college student saw a line of parked cars, their windows open, their radios tuned to "the same voice, its odd Eastern accent, which in anyone else would have irritated Midwesterners." The student—the novelist Saul Bellow—recalled: "You could follow without missing a single word as you strolled by. You felt joined to these unknown drivers, men and women smoking their cigarettes in silence, not so much considering the President's words as affirming the rightness of his tone and taking assurance from it. You had some sense of the weight of troubles that made them so attentive, and of the ponderable fact, the one common element (Roosevelt), on which so many unknowns could agree."[13]

Under TR and Wilson, newsreels and photographs had helped Americans know their presidents by their faces and expressions. FDR came even more fully alive to his constituents when his voice, a well-modulated tenor, suffused their living rooms. "Until last night, to me, the president of the United States was merely a legend. A picture to look at," wrote Mildred Goldstein of Joliet, Illinois, after the first Fireside Chat. "But you are real. I know your voice, what you are trying to do." Eleanor Roosevelt called her husband's voice "a natural gift, for in his whole life he never had a lesson in diction or public speaking." Its lucidity itself was a balm. Expertly paced with elongated vowels and pregnant silences, his speaking evoked sincerity and goodwill, tenderness and a fighting spirit.[14]

The familiarity and warmth of Roosevelt's voice also bade audiences to visualize him, much as he envisioned them when he drafted or spoke his words. Hearing him, many said in their letters, conjured up his mischievous grin (perhaps with his cigarette holder clenched within) or his agreeably nodding chin. He was, after all, a handsome man. His face, with the high forehead, fair hair, and blue eyes, had a comforting quality, and his strong upper body and broad shoulders on the six foot two, 190-pound frame conveyed vitality. Before polio paralyzed Roosevelt's lower half in 1921, Walter Camp, the founder of modern football, had called him "a beautifully built man, with the long muscles of an athlete." And after illness struck, Roosevelt—only thirty-nine—built up his arms and torso to carry himself. Although he and his aides would take pains to avoid photographs and films that showed his disability, the polio was no secret. Contrary to later suppositions, newspapers and magazines reported explicitly on FDR's physical limitations—in 1932, *Time* described his legs as "quite dead"— and the public knew about them. In 1924, Roosevelt's return to politics at the Democratic Convention met with wild applause as he agonizingly hauled himself across the stage with his crutches. Starting in 1938, he led (and announced by radio) his March of Dimes campaign to fight polio. Far from signaling weakness, his triumph over polio provided the Depression-wracked nation with a model of how to prevail over hardship.[15]

FDR's buoyancy helped him face challenges more severe than any since the Civil War. His jaunty spirit sustained his popularity even as his experiments to revive the economy yielded mixed results. FDR was a liberal but no ideologue, preferring creative pragmatism to doctrinal consistency. Here he tried a quasi-statist solution like the National Recovery Administration, with its voluntary production codes for business; there he devised a social safety net through programs like unemployment insurance; later he turned to deficit spending to stimulate the economy. Uniting these sometimes conflicting strategies was a desire to govern in the interest of the democratic masses. Inevitably, this meant expanding the power of the government, and in particular the White House.

Much of this power was symbolic and psychological. The national, mass-mediated politics of the twentieth century caused many Americans to feel adrift, estranged from their government. FDR's speeches restored a connection between the people and the president and the activities of an impersonal Washington. "Amid many developments of civilization which lead away from direct government by the people," Roosevelt said, "radio is one which tends to restore direct contact between the masses and their chosen leaders." Eleanor said that the radio "unquestionably helped him to make the people of the country feel that they were an intelligent and understanding part of every government undertaking."[16]

Letters written in response to his speeches revealed, in their content as well as their sheer volume, a glimpse of that connection. Roosevelt considered these letters a political weapon he could use against his congressional opponents; their testimony tangibly illustrated the wisdom of his course. But FDR also saw the correspondence as part of a democratic exchange, a way for the fragmented modern public to register its views with the one official who represented them all. Sometimes in his speeches he directly asked listeners to respond; even when he didn't, the invitation was implicit. "The human appeal" in Roosevelt's voice, one correspondent said, had compelled him to write in. Another described his letter to FDR as "a fireside chat from one of the common citizens of this nation." Some replied directly to questions that Roosevelt posed.

Americans told Roosevelt they valued his speeches for giving them what they considered the vital information that a democratic citizenry needed. Unhappy with their newspapers, which they considered biased—many were controlled by right-wing barons hostile to the New Deal—Roosevelt's correspondents desired direct access to the president's own presentations of his ideas. "I believe if you knew how little real information we get in this part of the country," wrote W. Hamilton Lee of Avondale Estate, Georgia, "you would deem it advisable to talk more frequently over the radio." Roosevelt agreed that the newspapers wouldn't give him a fair shake, and radio let him reach the public without the interference of opinion, analysis, or biased reporting. (Seeking to address the problem, Commerce Secretary Daniel Roper proposed a weekly government-produced news report—a peacetime *Official Bulletin* like the one Hoover tried—but the initiative sputtered.)

Information wasn't the only benefit. Americans told FDR that they felt for the first time that their president cared about them and took them into consideration, or that they were finally clued in to what Washington was doing, or that their opinions at last counted. They linked the communication between president and people to their democratic ideals. "Dictators dictate, Mr. President, Democrats discuss," James Dunn of Chicago wrote to Roosevelt, rejecting talk of the president as a Fascist. "Truly, Mr. Roosevelt you revived the modes and manners of the primitive forums of democracy. The old town meeting is now a nation's meeting."

Roosevelt agreed. "Five years of fierce discussion and debate, five years of information through the radio and the moving picture," he said in an October 1937 Fireside Chat, "have taken the whole nation to school in the nation's business." Even his detractors, Roosevelt charitably said, contributed to a collective deliberation that produced a deeper understanding of the issues. "Out of that process, we have learned to think as a nation. And out of that process we have learned to feel ourselves a nation."[17]

* * *

The Progressive tradition had long regarded new communication tools as a boon to popular self-government. Even before radio was invented, Charles Horton Cooley prophesied that technological advances would render public opinion more sophisticated and intelligent. Each innovation, Cooley said—the post office, the railroads, the telegraph, telephones— would help "society to be organized more and more on the higher faculties of man." This would usher in "an era of moral progress."[18]

When radio arrived, optimists in the spirit of Cooley hailed it as a unifying force in society, a leveler of class distinctions, even "a possible means for the salvation of democracy." Citizens could now hear politicians without interference from journalists or party operatives, wrote Eunice Fuller Barnard in *The New Republic*. Listeners didn't have to be educated or even literate. They could be far-flung geographically. Radio, argued Barnard, managed to "reproduce to some degree, for the first time in the United States, the conditions of the Athenian democracy where every voter, for himself, could hear and judge the candidates." By the time of FDR's Fireside Chats, citizens were energetically sharing their opinions with elected officials of all ranks. "That the American people is speaking its mind with a fluency and a freedom unknown in any other period," reported the *New York Times*, "is evident in the sheer weight of letters and wires that reach Washington."[19]

John Dewey was among those who, owing to his incurable democratic disposition, placed great hope in radio. In *The Public and Its Problems*, Dewey had written that "democracy will come into its own" when "free social inquiry is indissolubly wedded to the art of full and moving communication." He amplified this idea in a 1934 radio lecture titled "The University of the Air." "The radio is the most powerful instrument of social education the world has ever seen," the seventy-five-year-old philosopher declared. An unprecedented "means for exchange of knowledge and ideas," it provided a historic opportunity to foster "the formation of that enlightened and fair-minded public opinion and sentiment." Although radio could be hijacked by special interests, he conceded, and could distort and mislead, the radio town halls and forums and debates of the 1930s and '40s held immense promise for public education.[20]

Other intellectuals developed these ideas. Archibald MacLeish, for one, took up the new form of the radio drama as a vehicle for mass democratic expression. For art "to become again the thing it has been at its greatest reach," he wrote, it needed to speak to the mass public. His acclaimed radio play *The Fall of the City* (1937), about the passivity of a citizenry in facing a Fascist conqueror, fused form and content, medium and message, in dramatizing the need for the public to be knowledgeable, engaged, and courageous in defending its society's foundational ideas. The play helped establish radio as a serious artistic medium that could meet the demands of both high and popular art. Later, when he became Librarian of Congress, MacLeish created a radio program that broadcast historical dramas, and he shared with FDR his excitement over how "a network of wires" could magically create "an audience" of almost the entire nation.[21]

As influential as MacLeish in championing radio were public opinion researchers Hadley Cantril and Gordon Allport. Cantril had studied under Allport, at Dartmouth and then Harvard, and in 1935 the two men published their seminal study *The Psychology of Radio*. Although they too voiced reservations about the exploitation of radio by demagogues, on the whole they deemed it to be "inherently . . . a foe of Fascism," not to mention "the greatest single democratizing agent since the invention of printing." The airwaves, they noted, crackled with speeches and debates that presented both sides of topical issues, a serving of "balance in partisan communications" superior to what newspapers provided. Radio's continental reach, moreover, created a "sense of membership in the national family," and the numerous programs about public affairs trained voters' attention on matters of national import. "In principle," the authors concluded, "the use of the radio should increase public enlightenment, encourage responsible citizenship, and enhance interest, intelligence, and tolerance among voters." Polls even found that people trusted radio more than newspaper.

On top of this, radio promoted social equality. "Distinctions between rural and urban communities, men and women, age and youth, social classes, creeds, states and nations are abolished," they wrote. "As if by magic the barriers of social stratification disappear and in their place comes a consciousness of equality and of a community of interest." This leveling had a downside; it encouraged broadcasters to seek out the "common denominator" and "avoid subtlety and sophistication." But radio listeners, being less suggestible than members of a physical crowd, could be counted on to use reason. "Emotional appeals of the barnstorming type have less effect upon him," they noted. "The politician speaking over the radio is forced to be more direct, more analytic, and more concrete than on the rostrum." A calming authority on the air could put rumor and misinformation to rest. "Through the use of the radio in March 1933," they added, "President Roosevelt unquestionably diminished the force of the financial panic."[22]

Despite the enticing possibilities, however, it was also possible to foresee problems with radio. For one thing, not all masters of the new medium would be as benevolent as Franklin Roosevelt.

21

NAZISM AND PROPAGANDA

ON MARCH 13, 1933, the day after Franklin Roosevelt's first Fireside Chat, Adolf Hitler, newly installed as chancellor of Germany, named the thirty-five-year-old Paul Joseph Goebbels to be his "minister of propaganda and popular enlightenment." A racist ideologue who had fashioned Hitler's image as a quasi-religious savior, Goebbels had earned Hitler's confidence editing the Nazi Party's Berlin-based newspaper *Der Angriff* (*The Attack*). Within two months of assuming his new post, he was provoking horror throughout the civilized world by convening mobs to torch books whose ideas contravened Nazi doctrine. Over the next decade Goebbels would refine a sweeping propaganda campaign that pandered to hatreds, nationalism, and ethnic solidarity, fused in a core message of anti-Semitism. He would emerge as one of the key figures in the Nazi domination of Europe and the murder of one half of its Jews.[1]

Born in an industrial Rhineland town, Goebbels had been rejected for military service during the war because of a deformed foot, which made him walk with a limp. Instead of fighting, he pursued his studies, earning a PhD in Romantic literature from Heidelberg University in 1921. He wrote an unsuccessful novel and two unproduced plays before seeking work as a newspaper reporter, again without success. Then, in Munich in 1922, he heard Hitler speak. Transfixed, Goebbels abandoned the Catholicism of his youth for Nazism. He confided to his diary about his leader's "large blue eyes! like stars," and about the "wit, irony, humor, sarcasm, earnestness, passion, white heat" of Hitler's speeches. As he attached himself to Hitler, his own reputation grew. Some American reporters, searching for an analogue, credited him with "the skilful craftsmanship," as the *New York World-Telegram* wrote, "of an Ivy Lee or an Edward L. Bernays." The underestimation was vast.[2]

Goebbels went down in history as a maestro of evil propaganda. But it was Hitler who put propaganda at the center of the Nazi quest for supremacy. Scholars of *Mein Kampf*, Hitler's memoir and menifesto, judged the chapter on propaganda to be the book's sole intellectual contribution of note. Hitler claimed to have formed his ideas on the subject from examining not Germany's wartime publicity, which he believed to have been shoddy, but the Allies' more adroit practices. He argued that persuasion had to target the emotions, not the intellect, and speak to the "less educated masses," not the intelligentsia. "The receptive ability of the masses is very limited, their intelligence is small, their forgetfulness enormous," Hitler wrote. Simplicity and repetition were paramount. "All propaganda has to limit itself only to a very few points and to use them like slogans until even the very last man is able to imagine what is intended. As soon as one . . . tries to become versatile, the effect will fritter away."[3]

Mein Kampf introduced the idea of the "Big Lie," which would be seen as the Nazis' signal contribution to mass persuasion. Most people, Hitler wrote, "will more easily fall victims to a great lie than to a small one," since "some part of the most impudent lie will remain and stick—a fact which all great lying artists and societies of this world know only too well and therefore also villainously employ." It is often forgotten that Hitler described the Big Lie technique in *Mein Kampf* not to explain his own methods but, he claimed, those of "the Jews," whom he accused of saddling Germany's wartime General Erich Ludendorff with the blame for his army's defeat. "Those who know best this truth about . . . the application of untruth and defamation," Hitler wrote, "were at all times the Jews." In contrast, he claimed that he himself was offering the people only the suppressed truth. Goebbels likewise disavowed deceit. "Good propaganda . . . must not lie," he wrote, echoing the words of American public relations men, because lies "cannot have success in the long run." While the Nazis certainly did lie, they believed the ideology behind their anti-Semitic rants. More typical of their program than conscious falsehood was the filtering of facts and events through a twisted and paranoid worldview. What was wicked about the Nazis was less their lying than the ideas that they believed to be true.[4]

Hitler believed that propaganda worked best in person. At speeches and rallies and torchlight parades, individuals would surrender their reason to the emotions of the mass. Goebbels took pride in coordinating these events. But the Nazis exploited modern media too. Cinemas featured crude anti-Semitic fare such as *Jud Suss* and reverential depictions of Nazi rituals, such as Leni Riefenstahl's 1935 chronicle of the Nuremberg Rallies, *Triumph of the Will*. Radio speakers, mounted on street corners, blared government speeches and news. Newspapers—their freethinking personnel purged, their operations strictly controlled—became a state monopoly, giving the official Nazi version of events. A tabloid-style wall newspaper, *Word of the Week*, posted in public spaces from bus stops to hospitals, spread Nazi ideas through words, photographs, and arresting graphic design.

Scholars would later reject the idea that Hitler's propaganda exerted a quasi-magical force. Hitler, after all, was playing to a receptive German public battered by economic and political turmoil and steeped in anti-Semitism. And fear, as much as persuasion, enhanced his power: storm troopers and secret police went a long way toward silencing dissent. Yet to liberal observers in Germany, as well as to freedom-loving peoples across the Atlantic, Hitler's propaganda seemed brutally effective, and nothing short of terrifying.[5]

* * *

Hitler's rise stimulated fears in the United States about propaganda. The Nazi ideology repelled most Americans, and the rapid slide of a putatively civilized democracy into barbarism aroused panic. Theoretically, the inhospitality of American soil to Hitlerism should have eased fears about Nazi advocacy at home. But something closer to the reverse came to pass: A worry took hold, nurtured by memories of the world war, that German propagandists would again wreak havoc on American shores.[6]

The most outspoken scourge of Nazi propaganda was Congressman Samuel Dickstein of New York, chairman of the House Committee on Immigration. A Lithuanian Jew who came to America at age two and represented the immigrant-rich Lower East Side, Dickstein was one of several congressmen alarmed by the activities of the Friends of the New Germany (later the German-American Bund) and other right-wing groups with Nazi ties. With John McCormack of Massachusetts as chairman, Dickstein formed a House subcommittee to investigate what he termed "malicious and unwarranted alien propaganda of German policies within the limits of the United States." Called the Committee on Un-American Activities, it would evolve, in the postwar era, into the primary seat of government-led anti-Communist demagoguery, much to Dickstein's horror.[7]

Like those of its successor, the McCormack-Dickstein committee's inquiries carried a whiff of the witch hunt. But their purpose was understandable in light of the propaganda anxiety that had rippled through the country since the last war. Fears of Nazi agents and sympathizers had real foundations. Although overtly pro-Hitler groups were confined to the lunatic fringe, grassroots populists with Fascist tendencies such as the "radio priest" Charles Coughlin and the Louisiana politician Huey Long commanded huge followings. Fear spiked too after disturbing events like an alleged 1933 plot to recruit General Smedley Butler to lead a veterans' army in a right-wing coup against FDR. Between 1933 and 1941, 120 anti-Semitic organizations were founded in the United States, not including ethnic Fascist groups. Many relied on Germany's support. Though small and marginal, they made Nazi propaganda in the United States a palpable reality.[8]

One friend of the Nazis ensnared by Congress's investigations was George Sylvester Viereck. Just a few years earlier, in *Spreading Germs of Hate*, Viereck had piously denounced U.S. government propaganda, to the plaudits of the intelligentsia. Lately, however, Viereck himself had resumed the practice of propaganda on behalf of Hitler's regime. The Nazis brought him to Germany for interviews with Hitler, Goebbels, and Hermann Goering. Among his assignments was to edit a volume of self-justifying essays by Nazi leaders. Viereck likely ghost-wrote, and at least translated, Hitler's contribution.[9]

In May 1934, Viereck headlined a rally of some 20,000 Nazi sympathizers in Madison Square Garden. The arena was converted, Nuremberg-style, into an ideological hothouse, with swastika-laden bunting, the German eagle, and other Nazi iconography hanging from the rafters. Eight hundred men, dressed in high boots, military trousers, and Nazi armbands, stood erect in the aisles, policing the crowd. On stage, Viereck sang the praises of the Reich and attacked Jews and Communists, even as he claimed to renounce anti-Semitism.

Hauled before the House committee, Viereck confessed to working with Carl Byoir, a leading American public relations man and onetime deputy to George Creel, to promote German interests in the United States. Viereck further admitted that the Nazis had paid them generously. (He was paid in cash, he explained, "to avoid spies among the professional Jews and Bolsheviks.") His self-defense was the same as it had been in 1915. The Nazis, he insisted, had no nefarious intent. Their propaganda constituted merely "a proper defensive measure against a flood of billingsgate."[10]

As the surveillance of Viereck in 1915 had unraveled the Heinrich Albert affair, so his activities in 1934 led the McCormack-Dickstein committee to probe the publicity work of others—including Ivy Lee. Since 1929, Lee had been advising the American subsidiary of I. G. Farben, the German chemical giant, which collaborated with the Nazis. Traveling to Germany, Lee met with Farben officials as well as with Hitler and Goebbels. He then undertook to soften the Führer's image. He urged the Germans to proclaim their peaceful intentions and temper the regime's belligerent rhetoric, including the anti-Semitic rants. By 1934 Lee was qualifying his support for the regime, but tepidly. Those "who have tried to believe in National Socialism," he now wrote, "are beginning to realize that discrepancies exist." The mealy-mouthed self-criticism hardly assuaged American audiences.

From this ignominy, no public relations campaign could rescue Lee. Before the House committee, he protested that he had never advised the German government, only Farben—a distinction without a difference. Few people accepted his rationalizations, and news accounts witheringly painted him as doing for Hitler what he had once done for Rockefeller. For years, Lee and other boosters of public relations had maintained that every client, like every legal defendant, deserved representation. To such apologias, critics had asked whether any clients were beyond the pale. It was now clear that, at least for Lee, his principle didn't preclude working even for the darkest forces in humanity.[11]

Soon after the hearings, Lee fell ill with a brain tumor; he died in November 1934. Not only his reputation had been discredited. As a result of his Nazi dalliances, his philosophy of public relations as a purely neutral science, his posture of simply advising clients on improving their images without regard to their business or beliefs, would never be the same again.

* * *

For years Edward Bernays had defended public relations with arguments similar to Lee's. But he viewed the rise of Nazism very differently from his gentile colleague. Hitler's seizure of power in Germany led Bernays to reevaluate the amoral principles that underpinned his rhetoric of professionalism. In the 1920s, Bernays had justified the use of the term *propaganda* for his craft. But the Nazis' embrace of the term—and the practice—destroyed its benign meaning. In the new climate, Bernays felt that publicists needed to distinguish their liberal technocratic visions from the dark, autocratic philosophies of Europe's dictatorships. The Byoir and Lee scandals cemented a fear that public relations could be a hand-maiden of totalitarianism. In Sinclair Lewis's novel *It Can't Happen Here*, a dystopian fantasy of a Fascist coup, a Huey Long–style demagogue seizes the White House, helped by a public relations agent named Lee Sarason, modeled on Bernays, who then takes power himself. This was precisely the sort of association Bernays did not need.

Bernays was a Jew, and the writings of his legendary uncle—who would flee Vienna for London—smoldered in Goebbels's bonfires. In 1933, Karl von Weigand, a foreign correspondent for the Hearst papers, informed Bernays over a Sunday lunch that he had seen a copy of *Crystallizing Public Opinion* in Goebbels's library. Bernays was mortified. As Europe's plight worsened, he threw in his lot with a growing chorus of liberals who regarded Hitler as a threat not just to his own country but to the world.

Bernays also revised his arguments for public relations. Having once described his work with words like *manipulate*, he now abjured such Nietzschean language, deeming his earlier usage to be a product of "the brashness of youth," spoken "before Hitler and Mussolini gave the words bad overtones." In 1940 he published *Speak Up for Democracy*, a citizen's handbook for defending the "American Way of Life" against totalitari-anism. *Speak Up* clothed Bernays's publicity methods in all-American garb, postulating a link between public relations and toleration, open-mindedness, and deliberation. Once ominously technocratic, publicity was now presented as part of a fundamentally democratic project.[12]

Bernays also now preached a Wilsonian regard for the wisdom of the citizenry. "Leadership in the American sense is a strictly democratic func-tion," he wrote. "The leader in Democracy does not force his will or his ideas on others; he acts as a channel for the will of the group, draws it out, encourages it, gives it direction and force to make it effective." No longer did he endow the members of his profession with extraordinary powers. Publicity, which he had once depicted as requiring esoteric knowledge, was now something every citizen could—and should—do. "The barber talking to the man in his chair molds public opinion," wrote Bernays. "So does the traveler talking in the smoking-room of the Pullman car."

Speak Up was also a how-to manual. In question-and-answer format Bernays laid out rebuttals to gripes about democracy: its inefficiency, its corruption, its fractiousness. He walked readers through a PR campaign, explaining how to plan a demonstration, organize a group, get word of an event to a local paper. He even offered practical tips "for the person who can devote only a few minutes a day to furthering democracy," as Theodore Roosevelt, Jr., said in a press release from the Citizenship Educational Service, a Bernaysian dummy group of notables the author created to promote his book.

The book's significance lay in the contrast Bernays drew between his democratic methods and the illiberal nature of totalitarian propaganda. "In Nazi Germany," he wrote, the newspaper is "a government-controlled publication. It is censored, offers no real news, no real contact with the world—plenty of propaganda for war." The radio is subject to "government regimentation. And no listening to foreign short-wave under threat of death." Such methods, inimical to American values, had to be guarded against in the United States, where "saboteurs of democracy . . . attack at the instigation of enemies of Democracy." He warned: "Many keep under cover entirely. Some work behind screens or through 'stooges.' . . . The threats come not necessarily from organizations easy to spot, such as the Bund [or] the Ku Klux Klan. . . . The innocent-sounding Fellowship Forum, with good American names on its letterhead, has been exposed as an outlet for the Nazis." Calls for Americans to "mind our own business" were frequently "smoke screens, or fronts, for Communist, Nazi, Fascist and other anti-democratic forces"; they demanded watchfulness. "Do not," Bernays warned, "be taken in by appeasers."

22

THE DARK SIDE OF RADIO

IN THE 1930S, FDR demonstrated the democratic possibilities of radio, forging a community from the expanse of the nation. But the 1930s were also, in W. H. Auden's phrase, "a low, dishonest decade," and the emergence of two charismatic Americans on the airwaves showed that radio, too, had a dark side. Their ascent raised questions as to whether radio was truly an instrument of democratic fulfillment or, to the contrary, might benefit most those forces that preyed on popular prejudices.[1]

Father Charles Coughlin was a fiery Michigan-based Catholic priest, obsessed with currency schemes and, later, anti-Semitic conspiracies, who built a huge following with weekly broadcasts from his National Shrine of the Little Flower church. Huey Long was a flamboyant Louisiana populist—first governor, then senator—whose radio speeches advocating extreme wealth redistribution while excoriating communism attracted a fan base far outside his home state. Though unalike in background and profile, the mesmerizing priest and the brash Louisiana strongman shared a lot. Both promoted radical panaceas that were as emotionally satisfying to followers as they were economically impractical. Both trained their worst fire on Franklin Roosevelt after having backed him for president in 1932. Both thrived on flamboyant gestures and overheated rhetoric, which each man delivered, in his own inimitable style, to millions of loyal listeners over the radio—the medium that turned both men into national figures.[2]

The vehemence of Coughlin and Long won each man not only passionate devotees but also, from columnists and critics, a common descriptor: *demagogue.* Denoting a magnetic but cynical rhetorician who manipulated the rabble, the term dated to the time of Cleon of Athens, in the fifth century BC. In the 1930s, it was routinely pinned on both men. No word better captured the angry, galvanizing, and menacing preachments of the two enemies who caused FDR more trouble in his first term than any elected official in the dismal post-Hoover Republican Party.[3]

The rise of Coughlin and Long also challenged sunny judgments about radio's virtues. "The experiments of local demagogues on small fly-by-night stations [showed] the way to new arts of persuasion," wrote Will Irwin. "Within five years after broadcasting began its full development, Huey Long and Father Coughlin, both of whom understood the technique, were broadcasting effective fairytales to millions of wishful thinkers. So much for the part of the radio in crystallizing the news into active political and social thought." Wesleyan University political scientist Sigmund Neumann, a refugee from Germany, saw the radio as the catalyst for the new age of rabble-rousing, and perhaps the onset of fascism in America, because radio couldn't be questioned and challenged as easily as print. "It dramatizes news. It kills every criticism. It reaches everyone, even and especially the illiterate."[4]

The criticism had its mirror image across the ideological divide. Where liberals dreaded right-wing demagoguery, conservatives regarded FDR's frequent use of the airwaves as itself an anti-democratic abuse of power. Republican leaders like Everett Dirksen, representative of Illinois, and Arthur Vandenberg, senator from Michigan, assailed the administration's informational broadcasting as rank propaganda, while the far right charged that FDR's Fireside Chats were helping to make him a despot akin to Hitler, Stalin, and Mussolini. When the American Newspaper Publishers Association, a redoubt of the Roosevelt-hating press barons, warned that the exploitation of radio would lead to dictatorship, it wasn't Charles Coughlin and Huey Long they had in mind.[5]

* * *

Fears of a credulous public falling under radio's spell surged in 1938 after Orson Welles aired a radio version of *The War of the Worlds.* On the night before Halloween, at eight o'clock, the twenty-three-year-old actor and impresario and his Mercury Theatre troupe staged an hour-long dramatic rendering of H. G. Wells's 1898 science fiction novel about a Martian invasion—of New Jersey, in Orson Welles's version—done in the style of a fake news report. Roughly 6 million listeners heard bulletins of alien intruders vaporizing Americans with heat rays, vanquishing the Army with poison gas, and conquering New York City. Perhaps 1 million of these listeners, many of whom tuned in late, thought the broadcast was real. People panicked. Phone lines were jammed, city streets clogged. Some listeners fled in cars; others huddled in prayer. A sixty-year-old Baltimore man suffered a fatal heart attack. The police forced Welles to insert a reminder, at 8:42 pm, that the show was a work of fiction. By then it was too late.[6]

Front-page news the next day, the mass derangement confirmed critics' qualms about radio's powers and the public's credulity. Columnist Dorothy Thompson, one of the first journalists to sound the alarm about Hitler, said Welles's broadcast showed "the appalling dangers and enormous effectiveness of popular and theatrical demagoguery . . . [and] the failure of popular education." It shed more light on "Hitlerism, Mussolinism, Stalinism [and] anti-Semitism . . . than all the words about them that have been written by reasonable men." Newspaper editorials, columns, and letters fretted about the public's gullibility and the insidious influence of the broadcast medium. Even Hitler took notice. He used the event to proclaim the superiority of the German people who, he declared from Munich, "shall not succumb to a fear of bombs falling . . . from either Mars or the moon."[7]

Amid the hysteria, a handful of scholars remained wary of impressionistic conclusions like Thompson's. The first generation of radio researchers—Hadley Cantril, Herta Herzog, Paul Lazarsfeld, Frank Stanton—saw in the *War of the Worlds* broadcast a chance to ask how radio messages affected thought and behavior. Cantril wondered if he hadn't previously overestimated the medium's democratic nature. Having just assumed the presidency of the Institute for Propaganda Analysis, a body of social scientists devoted to demystifying political messages, he called for an academic study of the broadcast. "Our thesis is that the free-floating anxiety on the part of many individuals is a very real danger to the continuance of democracy," he wrote. "We point to the release of comparable anxieties in the German people—to their ready acceptance of the Nazi Party program." Though he had previously worried about radio's sinister side, as shown by the success of Coughlin and Long, the mass suggestibility exhibited in the Martian scare showed that radio's power to sow panic warranted closer study.[8]

With help from Herta Herzog and Hazel Gaudet, Cantril interviewed 135 New Jerseyans who heard the October broadcast. Their book, *The Invasion from Mars: A Study in the Psychology of Panic*, a landmark in communications research, avoided pat generalizations like Thompson's. It set a range of listener responses against a matrix of variables, from individual psychology and preexisting beliefs to the manner in which the program was heard. But for all his nuance Cantril's central finding was not surprising: better-educated listeners showed a greater "critical ability" than the uneducated to see through the fake news report. Cantril thus concluded on a point very much in line with Dorothy Thompson's and with his original hypothesis: Only education could inoculate the public against large-scale manipulation and protect American democracy.

A more original and perceptive analysis of the incident came from Heywood Broun, who pointed out that the show had aired at a unique historical moment. Gross generalizations about the public were problematic, because the hysterical New Jerseyans weren't listening to their radios in a vacuum. On the contrary, their responses were shaped by the escalating international hostilities of late 1938. *The War of the Worlds* aired just weeks after the Munich crisis, at which world leaders acquiesced in Hitler's annexation of the Czech *Sudetenland*—one of the first events that Americans followed in real time on the radio. They were thus already caught up in a vexed debate about their own preparedness to meet a foreign threat, not from outer space but from the Axis powers. The *War of the Worlds* incident showed that "preparedness" now entailed, as much as a supply of soldiers and armaments, the public's intellectual readiness. The debate about Americans' ability to handle bogus news reports was, in essence, a proxy for the debate about their ability to resist Hitler's propaganda.

*   *   *

The need to improve critical thinking was a tenet shared by many intellectuals of the 1930s. None stated it more plainly than John Dewey, who struggled to balance his excitement about radio's potential with his suspicion of those who would use it for manipulation. "Democracy will be a farce," the philosopher warned, "unless individuals are trained to think for themselves, to judge independently, to be critical, to be able to detect subtle propaganda and the motives which inspire it."

While Dewey popularized these ideas with his writings, Edward Filene tried to do so with his riches. A Boston department store magnate and New Deal supporter, Filene was worried about the public's ability to resist the allure of extremist ideas, especially from the right. One March evening in 1937, he convened a group of professors, psychoanalysts, and media experts in a stuffy room in Boston's University Club. Propaganda, he told the group, was battering the public's judgment, and he offered to bankroll an endeavor to tackle the problem. But when Filene asked his guests for ideas, the replies were lackluster. As one expert after another volunteered suggestions, recalled Edward Bernays, the air grew "smoke-laden and heavy." Filene's head "began to nod in little snatches of sleep." The evening ended in incoherence.

Undeterred, Filene held a second meeting several months later in New York, at the Columbia University Club. That gathering, too, degenerated into competing visions of what to do. Finally, Filene turned to Clyde Miller, a professor at Columbia's Teachers College, and offered him $10,000. "I don't care how you spend the money," Filene said. "The American people must be taught to think."

Miller set up a body called the Institute for Propaganda Analysis. He made himself treasurer and named Cantril president. Board members included the historian Charles Beard, the economist and future senator Paul Douglas, and the sociologist Robert Lynd. Later, the sociologist Alfred McClung Lee and the journalist I. F. Stone would join the staff.[9]

Though only a few thousand subscribers received the institute's bulletins, its ideas found wide circulation. It partnered with the YMCA and the National Conference of Christians and Jews, and Miller produced textbooks and lesson plans that reportedly reached a million students. A speakers' bureau offered lectures on a range of relevant topics. Articles in *Propaganda Analysis*, a monthly journal, dissected the movies, commercial radio, opinion polling, and the tricks of corporate publicity men like Byoir and Lee. The group's leaders seemed to harbor a special dislike, as Cantril wrote to Miller, for "our pal Bernays": one article in *Propaganda Analysis* disparaged Bernays, without apparent irony, for promoting the use of bogus "institutes" to invest chosen causes with the aura of authority and knowledge. Bernays shrugged that no one should hold out "any public hope for important accomplishment" by Miller's group.[10]

Miller's rivalry with Bernays seems to have been rooted in a fundamental difference of opinion about propaganda. In facing global emergency, Bernays had chosen sides, gamely enlisting his public relations know-how on behalf of America and democratic values. The Institute for Propaganda

Analysis, in contrast, sought neutral ground in the debate over intervention, pledging itself to "objective and scientific scrutiny." It promised to forego advocacy and "discover truth and fact." It aspired, Filene said, to figure out "*how* to make Americans think, not *what* to make Americans think."[11]

To maintain this analytic detachment, the institute first focused on identifying and exposing the very methods of propaganda. In an early issue of *Propaganda Analysis*, it devised a simple list of seven deadly public relations techniques that citizens could learn to recognize. These included "name-calling" (the loose use of terms like *fascist*); "glittering generalities" (the invocation of virtuous buzzwords like *truth* and *freedom*); and "plain folks" (the courtship of ordinary citizens by elites posing as ordinary citizens). Appealing in its how-to simplicity, the list caught the popular fancy. Requests piled up for reprints, as educators, ministers, and journalists found use for its pithy, easy-to-follow instructions, and the list survived in textbooks for decades to come.[12]

The focus on technique, however, proved problematic. As board member F. E. Johnson wrote to Miller, recalling the debates of the 1920s, certain propaganda techniques—such as appeals to emotion—were surely legitimate if used in the service of worthy ends. "Are we prepared to say that an effort to win sympathy for the cause of organized labor or the Jews in Germany or unpopular radical agitators must be strictly rational in order to be valid—that is, must appeal to intelligence exclusively and never to an emotional set or a habitual attitude?"

A related problem was that the group's underlying concern with right-wing demagoguery eventually became apparent. The totalitarian or anti-democratic ideologies that *Propaganda Analysis* examined were mostly on the right: a January 1939 report, "The Attack on Democracy," about Fascist and anti-Semitic groups; an exposé of Father Coughlin's descent into baldly Fascist and anti-Semitic rhetoric. This ill-concealed focus on the right in turn exposed the institute to charges of promulgating an agenda of its own.[13]

Although Cantril and Miller had run some pieces about Communist propaganda, they recognized that, given their aspirations to neutrality (and their tax-exempt status), they needed to run more critiques of left-wing or liberal publicity. Yet nothing they did was ever going to appease their right-wing critics. Over time the conservative voices reviling the institute as a radical outfit—the Hearst papers, the National Association of Manufacturers, Martin Dies of the House Un-American Activities Committee—grew louder. Even friendly outsiders, such as the pollster

George Gallup, warned of the imbalance in their coverage. Dies threatened an investigation.[14]

Some liberals, too, questioned the sincerity of the institute's claims to neutrality. In disavowing any viewpoint of its own, these critics said, the organization was denying the politics implicit in its own analyses, the value-laden premises behind its scientific veneer. "The Institute's analysis moves on a simple fulcrum," wrote the literary critic Bernard DeVoto, dissecting a *Propaganda Analysis* piece about Hollywood movies. "If the movies are not educative and liberalizing and socially enlightening, then they are propaganda." That analysis, he said, not only was fallacious but amounted to a form of propaganda itself.[15]

On the other hand, if the institute really were ideologically neutral, without any animating commitments beyond educating the populace, that raised worries that its work was fostering a debilitating disbelief in all argument. Conservatives said that the textbooks and lesson plans undermined national pride. At the same time, anti-Fascist liberals questioned the failure to promote a positive, unifying vision amid the global crisis. The institute's professedly disinterested exposure of "competing propagandas" created a "universal skepticism" that "leaves us in the end prey to the real propaganda and the real Fifth Columnism of Hitler's agents," the liberal journalist Max Lerner argued. "A mind without beliefs is incapable of criticism, heroism, or tragedy."[16]

In the face of world war, the very obsession with propaganda struck some liberals as beside the point. Lerner mocked the picture of "a nation of amateur detectives looking for concealed propaganda in every effort to awaken Americans to the real nature of Nazi world strategy." The Columbia historian Allan Nevins dismissed "these warnings to guileless Americans to look under the bed every night for propagandists." After decades of "propagandistic" appeals to the public by "the Abolitionists, the Prohibitionists, the Suffragists, the Populists, the Protectionists, and the innumerable other 'ists' who strew our history," he observed, the public had developed "the most constant practice in detecting and resisting it." In academia, the propaganda scholarship that had been booming since the 1920s now faced challenge from researchers such as Paul Lazarsfeld and Robert Merton who rejected the "widespread and somewhat hysterical notion that propaganda is omnipotent"—a neurosis they labeled "propaganditis." The critic Lewis Mumford also deplored what he termed a "pathological resistance to rational persuasion [that] characterized a great part of the civilized world." "Analysts of propaganda," he later noted, "exposing the rhetorical devices of persuasion, themselves put over one of the biggest propaganda frauds of our time: namely, the conviction that the important part about a statement is not its truth or falsity, but the question whether someone wishes you to believe it."[17]

The dread of propaganda was rooted in the experience of World War I, which now led well-intentioned liberals to misread the coming one. The tremulous alarm about mass persuasion arose, Lerner wrote, "because we have felt cheated and disenchanted by our role in the last war, and are determined never again to be tricked." That self-imposed vigilance, however, was clouding judgments, blurring distinctions, and diverting attention from the danger Hitler posed.[18]

As the institute came under fire from isolationists and interventionists alike, its efforts increasingly seemed doomed to failure. In early 1941 several liberal board members, including Paul Douglas, resigned, and in May, Cantril—who had stepped down as president by 1939 to conduct secret research for the president—followed suit. "Although my general aim is the academic search for truth," Cantril wrote privately to Roosevelt, "I am at present more interested in using the facilities to see that we may continue to search for truth in the next few decades." Clyde Miller, concluding that the political environment no longer permitted the "dispassionate analysis" that his work required, and fearing that its reports might be misused by America's enemies, joined with the remaining board members in early 1942 to close the institute's doors. For many Americans, the advance of the Nazi war machine across Europe brought home the reality that, frightening though Goebbels might be, propaganda should be the least of their worries.[19]

23

CAMPAIGNS, INC.

IN EARLY SEPTEMBER 1934, a young Sacramento couple, Clem Whitaker and Leone Baxter, holed up for three days with little to occupy them besides the complete writings of Upton Sinclair. Whitaker and Baxter weren't leftists, or even admirers of the romantic muckraker, who was now, at fifty-six, almost thirty years on in his career. Rather, from Sinclair's voluminous polemical tracts they set out to find the most inflammatory passages—of which there were many. Sinclair had likened marriage to prostitution and compared organized religion to graft. He had written witheringly of the Boy Scouts and the American Legion. He had given himself over to fads from vegetarianism to telepathy. (For a while he ate a spoonful of sand a day to improve his digestion.) With the help of a cartoonist, Whitaker and Baxter turned fragments of Sinclair's ideas into a series of illustrations to disseminate to California's newspapers. A typical sketch showed a fiendish monster labeled "Communism" hovering behind Sinclair as he preached to a demure personification of California. Some 3,000 of these editorial cartoons appeared in print that fall.[1]

Whitaker and Baxter, partners in the first ever political consulting firm, called simply Campaigns, Inc., had broken into the business the previous year, when they helped pass a statewide ballot referendum authorizing a massive water project for California's Central Valley. During that fight

Clem Whitaker, thirty-five, a lanky, chain-smoking ex-newspaperman and publicist, had met the sprightly Leone Baxter, then twenty-six and working for the Redding Chamber of Commerce. He brought her on board as a business partner; in 1938, they married. Unlike Bruce Barton or Edward Bernays, who worked mainly for business and only dabbled in politics, Whitaker and Baxter devoted their careers to politics and ran campaigns from start to finish. They handled not just speechwriting, public relations, and advertising but also strategy, organization, financial arrangements, and the general direction of the campaign.

In 1934, the pair was working for the Republican candidate for lieutenant governor of California, George Hatfield. But the Democrats' choice for that office, Sheridan Downey, was a friend of Whitaker's, and they had no wish to blacken his name. That was why they instead targeted the Democrats' more famous and controversial gubernatorial nominee, Upton Sinclair.

* * *

Sinclair, who had moved to Pasadena in 1915 when it was a vaguely bohemian outpost, had previously run for office as a Socialist, never seriously expecting to win. But in the depths of the Depression, he applied his amateur economics to a paradox that puzzled and pained Americans: countless farms lay fallow and factories idle even as millions lacked for work. California's unemployment rate was 29 percent. Sinclair came up with a political platform that he called End Poverty in California, or EPIC. It included planks ranging from the commonsensical, such as monthly pensions for the old and disabled, to the crackpot. Unfortunately, the latter group included the plan's *pièce de résistance*: an elaborate scheme, modeled on Soviet collectivist farms, under which the state would seize dormant farmland and factories in order to employ millions of out-of-work Californians. In a barterlike system that he called "production for use," the state would allocate the food and goods that its population produced. Encouraged by admirers, Sinclair agreed to run for governor on this platform, not as a Socialist this time but as a Democrat.[2]

EPIC became a sensation. Sinclair published a 64-page booklet in the style of the nineteenth-century utopian writer Edward Bellamy, prophesying a future society free of poverty. More than 2,000 EPIC clubs sprang up around California. Sinclair launched the *EPIC News* to spread his message. From a downtown Los Angeles headquarters, his shoestring team built a massive media operation, replete with women's clubs, youth clubs, and a speakers bureau. They staged radio broadcasts, plays, even a rodeo, at which Sinclair drove his car around a dusty arena, waving, before sitting through feats of steer roping and horsemanship.

Power brokers in the California Democratic Party were aghast. National party chairman James Farley and former Treasury secretary William McAdoo (elected senator the year before) desperately searched for an alternative. The man they found was as unlikely a prospect for governor as Sinclair: George Creel.

After his postwar ostracism, Creel had renewed his relationship with Franklin Roosevelt, whom he had known in Wilson administration days. Creel would write favorable magazine stories about FDR, often letting him edit or add material before publication. The ingratiation paid off with an appointment to run the west coast operations of the new National Recovery Administration. A few months later, cajoled by McAdoo, Creel—despite no experience in electoral politics and a Wilsonian aversion to "back-slapping and handshaking"—entered the Democratic primary.[3]

Creel and Sinclair had once written jokes and bits together for the *New York Evening Journal*. But the veneer of amicability between them masked a deep-seated acrimony. In the 1934 primary race, according to Sinclair's unsubstantiated account, Creel used dirty tricks, including circulating flyers touting Sinclair's alleged endorsement by a fictional "Young People's Communist League of Los Angeles." Whatever his tactics, Creel failed to derail the EPIC juggernaut. Though he showed strength in his home turf of Northern California, the Southland teemed with left-wing, utopian, and spiritualist currents, whose adherents, Creel recalled, "did everything but lynch me." On August 28, Sinclair won the primary by a wide margin. In the general election he would face the incumbent governor Frank Merriam, who had recently inherited the office upon his predecessor's untimely death.

The primary victory marked the apex of Sinclair's fortunes. The first sign of trouble that fall was his inability to secure Franklin Roosevelt's blessing. The White House worried that endorsing Sinclair would expose the Democratic Party to charges of harboring socialist tendencies, endangering other Democratic candidates. But neither did the president wish to repudiate his party's nominee. So he straddled. On September 4, Sinclair visited the president at Hyde Park, where, before a crackling fire in the library, the two men drank iced tea and bantered. FDR buttered up Sinclair, telling him that when he was a boy his mother had read him *The Jungle* over breakfast. Sinclair was perhaps too starstruck to realize that in 1906 FDR had been twenty-four years old. Sinclair recalled in turn his White House meeting with TR that year. "I don't know which of you is more indiscreet," Sinclair purred. As the sun set, the two discussed Sinclair's "production for use" plan. Sinclair left with the impression that FDR might even endorse it publicly in a Fireside Chat. In reality, the president was just leaving yet another visitor with the feeling that he agreed with him.[4]

In the ensuing weeks, Sinclair gained few endorsements of note. He won some warm words from Father Coughlin (not yet a confirmed Fascist), and from a passel of intellectuals, including Archibald MacLeish and Clarence Darrow. But the party operatives whose backing really counted remained aloof. As the fall wore on, sustaining the loyalty of liberals proved difficult. Raymond Haight, a progressive Republican, entered the gubernatorial race as a third-party candidate, threatening to siphon liberal votes from Sinclair. By the late fall, Haight was vying outright with Sinclair for FDR's endorsement, each candidate urging the other to withdraw. (Neither did.) Eventually FDR had to clarify that he had never promised to endorse EPIC. Creel, meanwhile, who had endorsed Sinclair, withdrew his support after Sinclair allegedly reneged on a pledge to tone down parts of the EPIC plan.[5]

While Sinclair was treading water, his opponents were strapping weights to his ankles. Leading businessmen, including the movie studio heads, threw their resources behind Merriam. One Sinclair foe, Charles "C.C." Teague, the head of Sunkist and a major player in California agribusiness, assembled a group of moguls to fund an anti-Sinclair blitz. Teague turned to Albert Lasker, now back at Lord & Thomas. Lasker instructed Teague to take to the radio with scripted dramas driving home the dangers of EPIC. By October, Teague's group had hired four writers and thirty-five actors to produce a quartet of radio shows, some airing daily, some three times a week. One, called *The Bennetts*, featured a middle-class family despairing over its preposterously bleak future under EPIC: the sister worried she couldn't finish college, the father that he would lose his job. Another series featured unemployed vagrants trudging across the plains to grab the subsidized bounty on offer in Sinclair's Golden State. "The novelty of the presentation is sure-fire," raved *Variety*, "and a check of the listening audience shows that a tremendous wedge is being driven in spots where other agencies of promotion have failed to make more than a superficial dent."[6]

Led by Will Hays, now running Hollywood's trade association, and MGM's Louis B. Mayer, serving as the head of California's Republican

Party, the studios amassed their own war chest to fight Sinclair. They funded cinematic advertisements called *California Election News*, produced by Irving Thalberg and designed to look like informational newsreels. One ad pioneered the "man in the street" interview, as an ostensibly objective newsman asked a motley array of California voters about their electoral preferences. "Remember," he told the audience, "they're not actors. They're nervous. I don't rehearse them. I'm impartial." One snippet featured a rumpled, furtive-looking man with a thick Eastern European accent. "I have always been a socialist," he said, "and I believe Sinclair will do best for working people." Another film "reported" on hoboes supposedly flooding California in anticipation of living large on the dole.

Joining the assault on Sinclair were the state's biggest newspapers, including Harry Chandler's right-wing *Los Angeles Times*, William Randolph Hearst's *San Francisco Examiner*, and even the relatively progressive *San Francisco Chronicle*. The loopy statements that Whitaker and Baxter discovered in Sinclair's copious writings—and the sheer radicalism of EPIC's planks—made it easy to ridicule the writer. The *Los Angeles Times* highlighted damning quotations in front-page boxes ("Sinclair on the Soviet Union," "Sinclair on Christ"), apparently gleaned from the pamphlets with which Whitaker and Baxter blanketed the state.

One trick that Clem Whitaker devised was to use Campaigns, Inc. in tandem with a Sacramento-based advertising firm he also owned. Having advertised generously in weekly papers up and down the state, he found these papers receptive when he sent along materials about his candidates. One typical packet included a news item on the expected invasion of job seekers, an editorial about Sinclair's onetime enthusiasm for free love, and a column by H. L. Mencken, who impishly said he welcomed a Sinclair victory because "It is always amusing to see a utopian in office, and this one is far bolder, vainer, and more credulous than the general."

Inexperienced in politics, Sinclair indignantly described his opponents' misleading ads and publicity as lies—although most of it, while often overdrawn, sometimes out of context, and arguably misleading, came straight from his own words. He issued a pamphlet titled *The Lie Factory Starts*, to rebut various charges, including the allegation that he lived in swanky Beverly Hills, not unpretentious Pasadena. (He owned houses in both places, having purchased the Beverly Hills residence in a foreclosure sale.) He also dug himself deeper by validating his opponents' scare scenarios. Asked about the consequences of EPIC, he replied that he had told Harry Hopkins, "If I am elected, half the unemployed of the United States will come to California, and he will have to make plans to take care of them." Thereafter, he struggled to explain his explanations.

Sheridan Downey, Sinclair's ticket mate, also objected. Downey wrote to his old friend Whitaker, griping that newspapers were running Campaigns, Inc.'s publicity materials as their own editorials, cartoons, and news articles. "Quite frankly," Whitaker shot back, "I have been envying you your nation-wide broadcast, your ability to publish your own weekly newspaper and give it state-wide circulation, your tremendous force of personal workers, etc. And now I find that you are apparently envying me my little ads in the newspapers."

Even with the proceeds from their candidate's rapidly selling manifesto, EPIC's hordes of volunteers were no match for the businessmen's hired professionals. But Whitaker was right on this much: no evidence suggested that Californians had mindlessly swallowed Hollywood propaganda. Sinclair's own counterpublicity was broadly disseminated, and the press punctured the Merriam campaign's publicity materials as happily as Sinclair's. Reporters had a field day when they learned that a series of widely reprinted photographs of the hoboes who were purportedly massing to overrun California were found to be stills from the recent Depression film *Wild Boys of the Road*.

In his memoir, Sinclair made no mention of Lasker or of Whitaker and Baxter. He knew that his own radicalism had done him in. Though given some allure by the misery of the Depression, anti-capitalist platforms had rarely prevailed in American electoral politics, and Sinclair wasn't the man to break the trend. In the nationwide radio address kicking off his fall campaign he called for a new system to replace capitalism. Even in the depths of the Depression, that was a tough sell.[7]

* * *

If Upton Sinclair had hanged himself with his own rope, Clem Whitaker and Leone Baxter had helped erect the scaffolding. Laying fair claim to having invented the field of political consulting, they soared to prominence in California and nationally. Over the next twenty-five years, they developed a daily routine: conferring over a two-hour breakfast, swapping ideas, updating each other on developments, planning strategy for their lengthening roster of clients. By their own account, they ran up a record of seventy-four victories to six defeats. They were true partners. Each year they swapped the title of president of Campaigns, Inc., and both preferred the pronoun "we" to "I."

They dominated California for years. Some years the pair might manage six different campaigns, expanding their regular staff of twelve or fifteen to as many as eighty employees. They managed referenda on behalf of the railroads, the utility and oil companies, and the shipping industry; they beat back old-age pensions and the so-called Single Tax (replacing all taxes with a single assessment on property). On occasion they fought for liberal causes such as raising teachers' pay and ending capital punishment. After helping to elect Earl Warren governor in 1942, they proceeded to defeat his plan for compulsory health insurance in 1945—and then, at the behest of the American Medical Association, worked to torpedo Harry Truman's national health insurance plan in 1948. That elaborate campaign, legendary in the annals of consulting, operated on many levels, including having senators and congressmen lobbied by their personal physicians.[8]

Journalists, political scientists, and competitors tried to divine the secrets of Whitaker and Baxter's success. Some cast it in dark tones. "The sad fact is that their manufacture of slogans and wielding of ladles has led to a grievous debasement of political debate," declared one critic. "Whitaker and Baxter's peculiar contribution, however, has been to make a precise art of oversimplification, to systematize emotional appeals, to merchandise the images they create through a relentless exploitation of every means of mass communication. Compared to these virtuosos, the old-time politician seems like an amateur." Others alleged that the pair had perfected a "push-button technique," in the parlance of the day, for winning elections—a formula of such precision that it simply couldn't fail.

Such talk testified to the pair's public relations prowess. It was Whitaker who boasted that managing campaigns was "no longer a hit-or-miss business." But the notion of Whitaker and Baxter as all-powerful really reflected Americans' fears about the professionalization of politics. Not many realized that the team owed its high winning percentage to its refusal to take on likely losers. And few acknowledged that their methods lay squarely in the centuries-old tradition of public persuasion—courting public opinion through the artful presentation of words and images. Whitaker and Baxter may have boasted a list of fifty time-tested rules that Baxter described as "the foundation of all our campaigns," but these rules were hardly the stuff of genius. Some were hoary precepts of public relations. Whitaker and Baxter recommended using emotion as well as logic; drumming home a simple message; assembling ad hoc committees and expert testimonials to create the aura of independent authority. Other techniques, though not yet routine, would soon become so: drafting a dummy opposition campaign plan the better to anticipate lines of attack; compiling dossiers of material to use against a rival, as they had done against Sinclair; or cultivating a down-home, unpretentious style. Finally, some prescriptions were mere commonsense—like flooding the mass media with your message.[9]

Even the supposed hallmark of a Whitaker and Baxter campaign—their readiness to go negative—was an ancient electioneering technique. The two simply embraced it with uncommon gusto and cleverness. When charged in 1946 with blocking the recall of San Francisco mayor Roger Lapham, who had no opponent to smear, Whitaker and Baxter invented a nefarious rival, "The Faceless Man," depicted on billboards and in advertisements throughout the Bay Area, intimating that Lapham's ouster would result in a sinister new mayor of shadowy provenance. The recall was thwarted.

If Whitaker and Baxter possessed any special insight, it was that the growing number of independent voters, or those affiliated only loosely with their parties, now could decide elections. This meant that a candidate's message had to resonate across the ideological spectrum, not just with his partisan base—making mass appeal more critical than ever. The decline of party loyalty, already underway by the 1930s, accelerated as consulting firms emphasized the public image of their candidates rather than their partisan identity.

The team's methods might have deserved less reverence than they received, but their impact was significant. They helped render the referendum and the ballot initiative, which had been created to help voters combat big business, vehicles for businesses to circumvent the legislative process. They also spawned a host of imitators, at first in California—Herbert Baus and William Ross, Murray Chotiner (who would rise to fame with his client Richard Nixon), Stuart Spencer and Bill Roberts (who would manage Ronald Reagan)—and later nationwide. And as a result of their success, running for office came to require the hiring of dedicated professionals, whose accumulated knowledge about the intricacies of campaigning was deemed a sine qua non of any successful bid. Activities once entrusted to machine politicians and party leaders now fell to the independent pros.

Most important, Whitaker and Baxter established a mystique about agencies like their own. Unsure of their own judgment in the dizzying world of media politics, or keen to pursue every avenue that might possibly bring them success, candidates for office readily placed their trust and their war chests in the hands of those with a proven record of electoral success. Whitaker and Baxter, and their legions of successors, reaped the benefits.

24

THE WIZARD OF WASHINGTON

IN THE SPRING OF 1935, Franklin Roosevelt was worried. Charles Coughlin and Huey Long, onetime supporters, had turned on him. Roosevelt's aides were quietly trying to undermine the two firebrands—Long in particular—by steering patronage jobs to Long's enemies and suspending federal projects in Louisiana. But it didn't seem to matter. When FDR's aide Hugh Johnson publicly flayed Long and Coughlin in March, the Kingfish responded with a radio address in which he took the high road, coolly presenting his Share Our Wealth scheme of radical wealth redistribution as a paragon of reasonableness. It won him his largest audience ever. Roosevelt and Johnson, concluded Turner Catledge of the *New York Times*, "probably transformed Huey Long from a clown into a real menace." Long and Coughlin even spoke about a third-party presidential run in 1936.[1]

Nervousness about the populist brushfire sweeping the nation led Democratic Party chairman James Farley to commission a secret poll gauging Long's prospects. Following a dinner with FDR, Harry Hopkins, Felix Frankfurter, Joseph Kennedy, and Will Hays, Farley and the pollster reviewed the survey results alongside a "greatly interested" president. The numbers were surprising. In a three-way presidential race, FDR still won easily, but Long took 11 percent of the vote, faring especially well among the economically distressed. Farley noted that Long's popularity was far-reaching, confined neither to the South nor to rural areas. He polled strongly in western states (32 percent in Washington) and respectably in midwestern industrial cities (16 percent in Cleveland). Long, he concluded, could "have the balance of power in the 1936 election." Worse still, the poll showed FDR to be weaker than at any time since his inauguration. After discussing the numbers, they turned to likely Republican nominees, with everyone agreeing, Farley recorded, that "Hoover would undoubtedly be nominated by the Republican party."[2]

Farley kept the poll's results from the press, offering spin instead. He told the Associated Press that he expected "no third-party [bid] of 'serious proportions.'" Privately he was less assured, and his doubts leaked. Mark Sullivan reported that FDR was planning to "go so far to the left that there will be no reason for anybody on the extreme left to have a third ticket under Senator Huey Long or anybody else." The tax hikes on the rich and corporations that Roosevelt signed into law that summer were only the clearest example of a leftward tack designed to steal Long's thunder.[3]

The man who conducted Farley's poll, under the anodyne moniker "National Inquirer," was Emil Hurja, a jowly, somber-looking forty-three-year-old employee of the Democratic National Committee—the first man to poll for an American president. An autodidact who taught himself statistics, Hurja was dubbed "Weegee" (a phonetic spelling of Ouija) by Louis Howe for his seemingly prophetic powers. Farley called him "the Wizard of Washington"; FDR's enemies called him "Farley's stooge." As much as his more famous contemporaries George Gallup and Elmo Roper, whose name-brand polling firms would exert influence for decades, Hurja brought statistical methods into the business of public opinion polling. And more than Gallup or Roper ever did, Hurja had the president's ear.[4]

Roosevelt loved to read up on what the public was thinking. He was, said Hadley Cantril, "the most alert responsible official I have ever known to be concerned about public opinion systematically." Hurja's numbers were but one set of indicators among many that the president followed. There was the mail: spurred by the Fireside Chats, Americans sent the president some 8,000 letters daily, and more than twice that at Christmastime. A beefed-up White House mailroom staff sorted through it, with each letter (apart from organized "pressure mail") getting a personal reply and several dozen pieces passed on to the president each day. The mailroom also tallied letters for and against the administration's position on any number of issues, with FDR reading the summaries. Hurja helped streamline the White House's monitoring of newspapers and radio opinion, while Charles

Michelson assembled a daily précis of the major papers' editorial views. Michelson also kept feelers out for rumblings across the country, harvesting comments, one reporter wrote, from "the filling-station attendant in Secaucus" and "the proprietor of the general store in Shakerag, Ky."[5]

All of these practices helped FDR keep his finger on the public pulse. Almost all of them built on the work of predecessors. It was in his use of public opinion polling that Franklin Roosevelt, with the critical help of Emil Hurja, broke historic ground.

*   *   *

One of twelve children born to Finnish immigrants in Michigan's Upper Peninsula, Hurja worked a series of odd jobs as a young man, roaming from Butte to Yakima to Alaska. In the 1920s, he settled in Breckenridge, Texas, an oil town, and published a newspaper, *The American*. Knowledgeable about mining from his western peregrinations, Hurja became, by covering the oil-drilling business, an expert on extractive industries. He soon received an invitation to work on Wall Street, and in 1927 moved with his wife, Gudrun, to Manhattan's Riverside Drive.

Hurja had always been interested in politics. After reading Woodrow Wilson's 1912 nomination acceptance speech, he became a Democrat. A history buff, he developed a special love for Andrew Jackson and his vision of an expansive democracy. Hurja's office walls would boast a dozen portraits of Old Hickory, and FDR would number among the friends to whom Hurja sent Jackson books and paraphernalia.[6] After he moved to New York, Hurja began applying his statistical knowledge to politics, and one day in 1928 he walked into the waiting room of Democratic Party chairman John Raskob, volunteering to apply his number-crunching talents to voting trends and demographics. Raskob judged Hurja a crank.

In 1932, Hurja tried again. This time he showed the Democratic officials how Raskob had wasted funds in 1928 in states such as Pennsylvania that Hurja could have predicted would go Republican. He wrote the DNC a long memo explaining how he would employ "a definite method of statistical control and analysis of political sentiment during the coming campaign." First, a staff would gather and aggregate all manner of data on voter sentiment. This material would range from the national straw polls conducted by the *Literary Digest* and the Hearst newspapers to state and precinct surveys carried out by party operatives. Then he would analyze it, noting how opinions changed from one election to the next. Finally, he would map out a longitudinal "picture of sentiment" that could pinpoint which battleground states and counties could be won with the proper resources. The party leaders hired him, although, they informed Hurja, they wouldn't be able to pay him.[7]

Polling was still primitive in 1932. Most of the work consisted of party-run canvasses of specific precincts or voting groups, as well as so-called straw polls, which merely tallied the votes of whoever responded. (Straw polls dated back to the early nineteenth century; Hurja discovered, through his immersion in Jacksoniana, an 1824 newspaper survey that would be cited as the first of its kind.) Politicians measured public opinion mainly by monitoring the press.

But around the turn of the century, advertisers and marketers developed questionnaires for researching consumer preferences, and in 1932 psychologist Henry Link created the first modern poll, called the "Psychological Barometer," to test attitudes toward soaps, coffees, and other goods. Soon, professional pollsters—notably Gallup, Roper, and Archibald Crossley—were applying market research methods to politics and public affairs.[8]

Hurja ran no commercial firm, but his statistical rigor rivaled that of his better-known peers. "You apply the same test to public opinion that you do to ore," he explained. "In mining you take several samples from the face of the ore, pulverize them, and find out what the average pay per ton will be. In politics you take sections of voters, check new trends against past performances, establish percentage shift among different voting strata, supplement this information from competent observers in the field, and you can accurately predict an election result." Hurja also understood, before most, other principles that would underpin modern polling, such as the need for random sampling (to ensure that the group surveyed wasn't skewed toward a biased subset) and the need for weighting (correcting for over- or underrepresentation of demographic groups). He saw the value, too, in focusing on likely voters, which he determined by looking at turnout in previous elections.

In the fall campaign, Hurja applied his methods on Roosevelt's behalf. He set up a color-coded map of the United States in his office, with individual counties shaded in dark blue (strong Roosevelt), light blue (leaning Roosevelt), dark red (strong Hoover), and light red (leaning Hoover). To color each state, Hurja drew on his array of polls—from the Hearst paper surveys to the door-to-door canvasses carried out by bookies—correcting for bias as best he could. Each day he reported to Farley, who had taken the party reins from Raskob.

Farley was spellbound. Hurja's confident updates made a Roosevelt victory seem inevitable. By late September the chairman was letting his number cruncher write press releases prophesying victory, even predicting state and electoral vote totals. Roosevelt, too, grew enamored of Hurja's ability to mine his information banks. Before starting a campaign swing in October, FDR summoned Hurja to Albany, where, having perused the pollster's state-by-state briefings, he peppered him with questions. He was especially interested in Hurja's "trend analysis"—the changing responses to the same questions over time. Before Hurja left they shared a few laughs at Herbert Hoover's expense.[9]

More important than these forecasts were Hurja's analytical reports. He worked with DNC staff members to target key constituencies, especially women, who his numbers said were breaking for Hoover. "The women's department calls up every day for 'dope,'" Hurja told a friend, about a bureau that aimed to improve the party's standing with female voters. Hurja also devised strategies to shore up the votes of loyalists to Al Smith, whom FDR had beaten in a brutal fight for the Democratic nomination.

As the campaign progressed, Hurja's reports to Farley turned exuberant. Roosevelt would carry all but 41 of the largest 1,000 cities, he predicted. "We have tabbed 387 different polls taken by newspapers, magazines, volunteers on radio, trains, ships, airplanes, for 1,921,000 votes and show Roosevelt winning an overwhelming vote," he crowed. "A single straw ballot doesn't mean a thing but a million straws in the air tell which way the wind is blowing . . . a whirlwind for Roosevelt." On the Friday before Election Day, Hurja forecast "a revolution at the ballot box" that would leave the GOP weaker than at any point since the Civil War.[10]

Roosevelt's triumph made Hurja a hero. Although the pollster hoped to be awarded the ambassadorship to Finland, Farley needed his talents at home. He placed Hurja in a series of posts where he could handle patronage for the administration. Hurja infused the old haphazard spoils system with his data-driven methods, his looseleaf binders recording information about every state and congressional district. His index card file kept track of the sixty to seventy closest congressional races. He used these factors to determine the relative worthiness of job seekers. Republicans complained that Hurja was using his data to distribute "dams, dog pounds, wading pools and canals where they produce the most votes for the New Deal," as one journalist reported. Some smelled scandal, but Hurja was just carrying on an age-old practice with modern efficiency.

By 1934, with the midterm elections looming, Roosevelt approved the pollster's return to the DNC, as executive director. With his maps and binders, Hurja channeled resources to the key races. Again, he bested his peers: where most seers expected the party in the White House, in keeping with historical patterns, to lose congressional seats, Hurja predicted Democratic gains. "The Republicans haven't a chance," he declared in August. On Election Day Hurja was again vindicated, guessing wrong in only a handful of contests. For the first time since 1902, the president's party picked up seats in the midterms.[11]

Washington wise men were floored. "I'll never question another election prediction of Emil Hurja's!" vowed Raymond Clapper, a columnist for *The Washington Post*. The president told Farley that Hurja's spot-on forecast was the "most remarkable thing" he had ever seen in politics. Hurja made the cover of *Time* and was profiled in other magazines. He and Gudrun took to the social life of the capital, entertaining diplomats, Supreme Court justices, and congressmen at their yellow brick Georgetown manse. They sailed to Europe on the *Queen Mary* for the coronation of George VI. Reporters dropped by Hurja's backroom office at Democratic headquarters, describing for their readers a gallimaufry of binders, maps, charts, newspaper clippings, almanacs, legislative reports, slide rules, adding machines, books of logarithms, colored crayons, and index cards analyzing political behavior in every state, country, and city in America. "He would strew maps on the floor and look at them all day," said one visitor. "Then he would play with the calculating machines and with a pencil and pad. Finally, he would come up with the information that it was necessary to concentrate speakers and propaganda in certain counties of a state in order to win." The press painted him as no more partisan or irrational than a machine. "His method," wrote *Time*, "is simply to avoid opinion, stick to statistical facts."[12]

For two more years Hurja polled for Roosevelt. He not only gauged Huey Long's strength as a presidential candidate but compared FDR to other potential rivals. He tested reactions to Roosevelt's programs, speeches, and tours, as well as to Republican counterthrusts. In the 1936 campaign, he developed a strategy of focusing money and time on the large states where Roosevelt's numbers rested close to the 50 percent mark, "carrying the largest possible Electoral Vote at the least possible cost."

By now, not only the president and his team were watching. "The excitement centered around public opinion polls has reached a new high in the current campaign," declared Hadley Cantril, dispatched to write about the polling wars for the *New York Times*. "Millions of people are watching the tabulations." Gallup, Roper, and Crossley were now using sophisticated weighted techniques to gauge voter opinion. Yet many Americans still trusted in the straw poll run by *Literary Digest*, which had called the last four elections correctly. Newspaper stories speculated about which pollster would get it right.[13]

Late in the summer, the *Digest* sent out 10 million ballots across the country, a quarter of which were returned completed. But despite the large sample the *Digest* didn't get a true cross section of the populace, and it predicted that Republican Alf Landon would clear 55 percent of the vote. On Election Day, FDR romped once again, taking 61 percent of the vote and losing only the combined eight electoral votes of Maine and Vermont. The *Digest* became a laughingstock, as the wisdom of "scientific" polling was seemingly confirmed. A jubilant Hurja sent the White House his black leatherette binder about the presidential polls.[14]

Afterward, however, Hurja receded from public view. He had hoped again for a diplomatic assignment to Finland in Roosevelt's second term, or perhaps the governorship of the territory of Alaska. Neither offer came. He also developed qualms about the president's leadership, bothered by FDR's ill-advised plan to pack the Supreme Court. And Hurja fell out with Farley, who resented his aide's Svengali mystique and adoring press. In 1937, Hurja abruptly quit the administration. He had left a mark, augmenting the president's leverage over public opinion by equipping him with sophisticated tools that rivals couldn't hope to match.[15]

Hurja returned to his roaming ways. He conducted public relations for Walgreens, took over a moribund newsweekly called *Pathfinder*, lobbied for Alaskan statehood, and ran unsuccessfully for Congress from his old Michigan district. He also continued to conduct polls, sometimes for private clients, sometimes for *Pathfinder*. But the Wizard of Washington had lost his magic. Although his forecasts still came close to the mark, no method of divining the future could ever be truly scientific. On November 2, 1940, three days before the presidential election, the man who had humiliated the *Literary Digest* for predicting a Landon presidency himself underestimated Franklin Roosevelt. Hurja failed to predict FDR's take of 55 percent of the popular vote en route to a historic third term. Worse, he called the race for Wendell Willkie.

THE ROAD TO WAR

THE GATHERING WORLD CRISIS of the late 1930s provoked what on American shores came to be called "the Great Debate"—a contentious and often bitter public argument about American intervention. For Franklin Roosevelt, the stakes of this debate meant that despite Emil Hurja's departure, minding public opinion remained imperative. The swirl of disagreement put Roosevelt in a bind. On one hand, he became increasingly sure that the United States had to do something to halt the march of fascism: the 1938 Munich Agreement, granting Hitler the Czech *Sudetenland*, had failed to appease the Führer, and by March 1939 the swastika was flying over Prague. But a powerful bloc of congressional isolationists, who had pushed through stringent neutrality laws, resisted further action. Roosevelt struggled against their clout.[1]

In September 1939, Germany invaded Poland, bringing Britain and France into the war and giving the question of American involvement new urgency. As with World War I, interventionists believed America to be inescapably bound up in Europe's affairs, and isolationists warned that the continent's troubles were not America's. In the battle for public opinion, both sides spoke about combating alien propaganda, though the arguments pervading the press and the airwaves were mostly home-brewed. Prominent Americans led august-sounding committees. Aviator Charles

Lindbergh spoke for the isolationist America First, whose members ranged from Charles Coughlin, by now an unapologetic reactionary, to the liberal advertising executive Chester Bowles. The venerable Progressive William Allen White, now seventy-one, headed the equally star-studded Committee to Defend America by Aiding the Allies. Each held rallies and circulated statements—volleying words and images back and forth in a spirited, rancorous exchange.

The president's plight, too, recalled the last war. Like Wilson after 1914, FDR had to walk a narrow path. He wanted to prepare the nation for war while keeping GIs out of combat. He joked that he had to please the 70 percent of Americans who wanted to avoid war and the 70 percent who wanted to crush Hitler. Unlike Wilson, however, FDR never pretended to a false impartiality. "I cannot ask that every American remain neutral in thought," he declared in a September 1939 Fireside Chat after the Nazi conquest of Poland. "Even a neutral has a right to take account of facts. Even a neutral cannot be asked to close his mind or his conscience."

Roosevelt himself was anything but neutral. Without illusions about Hitler's ambitions or imperial Japan's designs, he urgently wanted to loosen the neutrality straitjacket that constrained him from assisting the Allies. He took his case to the public, arguing in press conferences and public remarks, through spokesmen and surrogates, using radio and newsreels, that only active preparation would protect American freedom, and that passivity would only endanger it. In Washington, he worked the Congress, and by November 1939 secured a "cash and carry" bill. While short of full neutrality repeal, it allowed him to send materiel to the Allies if they paid for it up front and transported it on their own ships.

In trying to move public opinion, Roosevelt had access to two tools that Wilson had lacked. One was radio, which FDR used to bypass the largely isolationist newspapers. The second was polling.[2] As Emil Hurja had seen, Roosevelt loved reviewing the numbers. But now, instead of Hurja's data, he was relying on the private research of George Gallup and Elmo Roper, who gave him advance copies of their survey results, as well as on polls clipped from newspapers. The president learned to use these numbers strategically, as when he arranged to include poll numbers that attested to his popularity in the *Congressional Record*—the better to cow his adversaries.[3]

Roosevelt, however, didn't fully trust Gallup, a Republican who had advised FDR's rivals in the past (and would again in the future). The president even suspected the Princeton pollster of rigging his findings to create the appearance of GOP strength. As the 1940 election loomed, Roosevelt decided he needed a pollster of his own. Though coy about his intentions, he was considering running for an unprecedented third term—a decision that would please his millions of admirers but also fan fears that he had dictatorial ambitions. As much as ever, Roosevelt had to monitor the popular mood regarding both intervention and his own standing.[4]

* * *

Sometime in early 1940, Roosevelt encountered the work of public opinion researcher Hadley Cantril, who had become fascinated by opinion surveys while reporting on the polling wars for the *New York Times* in 1936. A tall, handsome man, with a commanding presence, Cantril was known for his radio studies, his work with the Institute for Propaganda Analysis, and his editorship of *Public Opinion Quarterly*. Having formed a friendship with George Gallup in 1936, he joined the Princeton psychology department in part to collaborate with the pollster, who worked nearby. In 1940, Cantril opened his own Office of Opinion Research at Princeton, focusing on, among other questions, attitudes toward the war.[5]

Early in 1940, Roosevelt's aide Anna Rosenberg told the president about Cantril's research. Roosevelt asked her to see if Cantril would share his data. A short while later, as the Nazi war machine swept across Western Europe and set its sights on Britain, FDR asked Cantril to survey American opinion about helping Britain. Piggybacking on the surveys that Gallup routinely sent out, Cantril found a strong public preference for avoiding war. This led to more requests, including for Cantril to repeat certain questions over time to note changes. "Nothing interested him more than trend charts," Cantril said.

As Germany pressed on—conquering France in June, blitzing Britain in the summer and fall—the charts showed growing support for intervention. "By and large, public opinion does not anticipate emergencies; it only reacts to them," Cantril explained. It was fluid, open to persuasion as events unfolded. The European crisis led pundits to propose suspending party politics; some urged FDR to choose Wendell Willkie, a leading Republican presidential contender and an interventionist, as his 1940 running mate. Emboldened, Roosevelt escalated his rhetoric, warning of the "delusion" that the United States could insulate itself from the conflict. To the Allies, he promised material help, resolving to work around congressional restrictions. By July 1940, Cantril found sympathy for aiding the

Allies climbing—though he cautioned that opinion on war-related questions still "shows enormous flux." In the summer he met with Roosevelt, who showed a ravenous interest in Cantril's newest numbers.[6]

The German offensive in Western Europe boosted FDR's reelection prospects and convinced Republicans to nominate Willkie. By the fall campaign, however, Willkie was foundering. To revive his chances, he went after the president's foreign policy. Muddying his own interventionist position, Willkie suddenly attacked the president for dragging the country into combat. He faulted Roosevelt for instituting a draft ("defensive preparation," FDR protested), and for giving World War I–era destroyers to Britain—clever evasions of the neutrality restrictions—even though Willkie himself had backed the same policies. The reversal alienated Willkie boosters like Walter Lippmann, who had wanted the Republican to play the role of an American Churchill. Yet Willkie gained ground. By late October, the president's lead in Gallup's surveys had dwindled to four points.[7]

Amplifying Willkie's criticism were congressional Republicans, who hollered that Roosevelt was planning to sacrifice American lives in a foreign war. Among the most vocal critics was a prominent publicity master who had grown close to Willkie: Bruce Barton. After winning election to Congress in 1937 to represent New York's Upper East Side, Barton had become a notable and quotable Republican spokesman, challenging FDR's neutrality law revisions and eliciting requests to run for the White House himself. Barton chose instead to seek a Senate seat in 1940, and that fall he stridently warned that a third Roosevelt term would spell the end of American democracy.

As Willkie and the Republicans closed in, Roosevelt counterpunched. When an aide found Barton's name alongside those of Joe Martin and Hamilton Fish on a list of FDR critics, the president glimpsed an irresistible opportunity. Speaking to a packed Madison Square Garden on October 28, he gleefully lit into the troika of "Martin, Barton, and Fish," delighting his audience with the rhythmic repetition of their names. Days later in Boston, as FDR planned to repeat his litany, an enthusiastic crowd began chanting the names before the president even had the chance. At the same time, FDR made some concessions to the anti-war side. "Your boys are not going to be sent into any foreign wars," he promised his Boston audience. His speechwriter Sam Rosenman had wanted him to add—as he normally did—the phrase "except in case of attack." But FDR smiled. "If we're attacked," he puckishly explained, "it's no longer a foreign war."

Roosevelt's rhetorical triumph presaged an electoral one. Barton lost his Senate bid, and the president beat Willkie handily. Now the management of public opinion could be aligned with the goal of bringing ruin to the Axis powers.[8]

* * *

The 1940 victory also gave Roosevelt some freedom from fear. Unburdened by the pressures of reelection, he could full-throatedly endorse what he called "Lend-Lease," his plan to let Britain "borrow" ships and munitions on the flimsy pretext that they would be returned or repaid in kind after the war. For help in passing this newest revision of the neutrality laws, he again turned to Cantril.

For months, Cantril had been feeding the president information on the public's views about the neutrality laws, finding growing though still not overwhelming support for more revisions. It was enough to encourage FDR. At a December 17 press conference, the president unveiled his Lend-Lease idea. Comparing America's situation to that of a man whose neighbor's house was burning down, so he must borrow a garden hose, Roosevelt said that the United States should lend Britain the goods it needed to put out its fire, asking only for their return afterward.[9]

The next step was a Fireside Chat, which the president drafted a few days before Christmas with Rosenman and Robert Sherwood, his favorite speechwriters, and his close aide Harry Hopkins. FDR was upbeat, Sherwood recalled, because at last he felt free to dispense with "namby-pamby euphemisms," to "lash out against the apostles of appeasement," and to make clear "the disastrous folly of any attempt at a negotiated peace." More formal than his other addresses, this one was expected to draw 80 million listeners. In the evening, wearing a bow tie and pince-nez, FDR repaired to the Diplomatic Reception Room where the audience included cabinet members, the president's mother, and Clark Gable and Carole Lombard. "Never before since Jamestown and Plymouth Rock has our American civilization been in such danger as now," Roosevelt declared when the microphone went live. Resisting aggression was necessary to safeguard peace. "There is a far less chance of the United States getting into war if we do all we can now to support the nations defending themselves against attack by the Axis," he argued, "than if we acquiesce in their defeat, submit tamely to an Axis victory, and wait our turn to be the object of attack in another war later on." Calling the United States "the great arsenal of democracy," he summoned a "spirit of patriotism and sacrifice" from the nation.[10]

The speech loosed an outpouring of interventionist sentiment. More than 90 percent of the letters and telegrams to the White House backed the president. Opinion polls showed eight out of ten Americans in support. After Democratic leaders drew up a Lend-Lease bill in early January 1941, the White House campaigned to keep support strong, securing endorsements from useful allies like Willkie and Winston Churchill. By February, Cantril was informing Roosevelt that public support, though diminished during the debate, remained robust. Steve Early arranged with Hollywood executives to film the bill's signing for the newsreels, and Lend-Lease became law in March.

In sharing his final set of numbers on Lend-Lease, Cantril lobbied Roosevelt to expand his services. "I shall be glad to make the facilities available to you at any time," he wrote. "We can get confidential information on questions you suggest, follow up any hunch you may care to see tested regarding the determinants of opinion, and provide you with the answers to any questions ever asked by the Gallup or Fortune polls." The president welcomed the offer. By the fall of 1941, Cantril was sending the president easy-to-read weekly trend analyses, with notes highlighting rising favor for Roosevelt's activist stance.

* * *

When Japanese warplanes bombarded Pearl Harbor on December 7, 1941, the Great Debate ended. Cantril, around this time, got a call from a Princeton neighbor, Gerard Lambert, himself something of an expert in public opinion. The son of the inventor of Listerine mouthwash, Lambert had retired in his thirties, having masterminded the ad campaign warning women not to wind up "always a bridesmaid, never a bride." Known as the "Father of Halitosis," he worked briefly for New York district attorney Thomas Dewey on his failed bid for the 1940 Republican presidential nomination, though the mouthwash millionaire considered himself "as liberal as any Democrat" in Washington. After Pearl Harbor, he resolved to help the administration. Having heard about Cantril's work, he invited his neighbor to join him one Sunday morning for a conversation that ended up continuing through dinner and resulting in a fateful partnership. As Samuel Rosenman, a frequent White House liaison, cheekily summarized, "Cantril does the work and Lambert pays the bills."[11]

Taking a leave from Princeton, Cantril relocated to Washington, where his wealthy partner had purchased a four-story mansion at 78 Kalorama Circle, in a secluded nook overlooking Rock Creek Park. From this spacious, fully staffed house—Cantril's "second home for most of the war years"—they ran their operation under the bland name of the Research Council, Inc. They used tabulating machines on loan from IBM for their calculations and met with White House emissaries, taking pains to hide their work. Partly, Cantril wanted to "preserve the informality of our relationships," as he told Anna Rosenberg. He also didn't want to damage his arrangement with George Gallup, who was sending out Cantril's questions along with his own surveys. "If certain Senators knew about this," Cantril feared, "they would raise hell with Gallup, and his faith in me would be shaken."[12]

Knowing that his client was "one of the busiest men in the world," Cantril stripped out the verbiage, jargon, and extraneous material, trimming the reports to two or three pages. He marked them with red pencil, highlighting findings, occasionally doodling a happy face next to good news or a scowl beside the bad. Roosevelt read the write-ups avidly, sometimes dashing off replies to his pulse-takers that praised their work as "very instructive" or "a fine public service." He also paid attention to the results. Cantril said, perhaps with overstatement, that Roosevelt never altered his policies simply because public sentiment opposed him. "Rather," Cantril wrote, "he utilized such information to try to bring the public around more quickly or more effectively to the course of action he felt was best for the country."

Like Hurja before them, Cantril and Lambert found it hard to confine themselves to providing data. The unique value of their polling and their ability to interpret it allowed them to worm their way into a general advisory role. In March 1942, when FDR ordered General Douglas MacArthur, under an intense Japanese assault, to withdraw from the Philippines to Australia, their polling confirmed the unpopularity of the move. Concluding that Roosevelt needed to frame the decision as the only sound choice available, Lambert drafted a statement, which FDR read out verbatim at his March 17 press conference: "I am sure that every American, if faced individually with the question as to where General MacArthur could best serve his country, could come to only one answer." Within months Cantril was dispensing advice on the midterm elections, wartime information policy, and overall public relations.[13]

As yet another election neared and FDR showed no signs of vacating the White House, the team's polling came to encompass electoral politics. Starting in 1943, Cantril found that Roosevelt's prospects of winning a fourth term surged when people expected the nation still to be at war;

people judged the president's international leadership to be essential, but not his domestic policies. The White House thus took steps to remind Americans that the war's end was far from view. In the *American Magazine*, Harry Hopkins wrote that the fighting would certainly last until 1945.[14]

Eventually, wartime decisions themselves were subjected to Cantril's public opinion tests. One morning in March 1944, White House aide David Niles called the Kalorama mansion wanting to know how Catholics would react if the Allies had to bomb Rome, home to the Vatican and other sacred sites. Cantril mobilized his interviewers and came up with an answer within twenty-four hours. More than two thirds of Catholics, he reported, would back the decision, provided that military leaders considered it essential to the war effort. Two days later, bombs began raining down on the Holy City.[15]

THE FACTS AND FIGURES OF ARCHIBALD MacLEISH

ARCHIBALD MACLEISH, appointed Librarian of Congress by Franklin Roosevelt in 1939, was an unusual choice for the job. But then MacLeish was an unusual man. A graduate of the Hotchkiss prep school and Yale University, an editor of the *Harvard Law Review*, a protégé of Felix Frankfurter, MacLeish had given up a partnership with a prestigious Boston law firm to write poetry in Paris in the 1920s. On his return, he established himself as one of America's leading men of letters—a poet, a playwright, an innovator in radio drama, an intellectual who always had something to say. By his mid-forties his stature was such that FDR came up with the grand idea of naming him to a post long held by professional librarians.

Ruggedly handsome, with a long, sharp-boned face, a strong chin, and a high forehead beneath graying hair, MacLeish dressed in a dapper WASP uniform of mild formality—sporty tweeds and soft-collared shirts. He was known as a liberal unafraid to question liberal orthodoxies. In the late 1930s he ran afoul of his fellow writers on the left, chiding them for their complacency in the face of the Fascist threat. MacLeish was forever haunted by the wartime death of his brother, Kenneth, a pilot, in a firefight with German Fokkers. That loss also took its toll on MacLeish's verse. Where his early poetry had included paeans to Wilson's vision of a war to end all wars, his writing in the 1920s followed the apolitical turn of Ernest

Hemingway's *A Farewell to Arms* and the alienated requiems of the Paris expatriates. "A poem should not mean/But be," he wrote in *Ars Poetica*.

MacLeish's ability to separate art from politics prepared him well for his intellectual battles in the 1920s and 1930s with the Communists, whose dogmatism taxed his patience. (MacLeish and Carl Sandburg were once kicked out of a Communist Party convention for laughing.) In poems such as "Frescoes for Mr. Rockefeller's City" and essays like "The Poetry of Karl Marx," MacLeish mocked and critiqued the Communists' perversion of art for ideological ends.

In time, however, MacLeish revised his view of the poet's job. The rise of Hitler and Stalin posed a threat to art and free thought and to the values that underpinned them, he believed, and artists and writers had a duty to defend them. As he told Sandburg, "We must now become pamphleteers, propagandists."

To promote a democratic message, MacLeish wrote radio plays. His anti-Fascist *Fall of the City* (1937), a critical and popular success, was followed by *Air Raid* (1938), inspired by the Germans' destruction of the Basque city of Guernica during the Spanish Civil War, which warned of bourgeois flaccidity in the face of a hostile invader. It was broadcast four days before another invasion drama, *The War of the Worlds*. These and other contemporaneous works dwelled on the themes of preparedness, appeasement, and the failure of nerve, and aimed at redrawing the contours of public debate. "The crucial battleground of this war," MacLeish would later declare, "is American opinion."[1]

MacLeish did not see his call for intellectuals to rally behind democracy as a repudiation of his art-for-art's-sake philosophy. It was, rather, a response to evolving circumstances, rooted in the same liberal principles he had always held. The Nazis' book burnings and contempt for "degenerate" art—to say nothing of their sheer barbarism—demanded that totalitarianism's critics forcefully uphold their own liberal values.

In advocating for his political ideas, MacLeish seemed to take a mischievous pleasure in hectoring his fellow writers. His fellow poet Karl Shapiro wrote that MacLeish made himself into "a poet of bitter enemies." Edmund Wilson, a longtime nemesis, cruelly parodied MacLeish's earnest sentiments, while William Butler Yeats insisted that the true artist could not so easily set aside the personal in favor of the topical.[2]

When MacLeish became Librarian of Congress, he wasted no time using his perch to propound his politics. Though personally reserved, he exuded charisma, and his appetite for intellectual combat kept him in the news. He continued to fault writers and journalists for shunning controversial stands and abdicating any role in the crises of the day. "It is current-day fancy to consider a journalist objective if he hands out slaps and compliments with evenhanded impartiality on both sides of the question," he said. "Such an idea is, of course, infantile. Objectivity consists in keeping your eye on the object [and] describing the object as it is." Above all, the Great Debate over intervention consumed him, as he sparred with Charles Lindbergh and joined William Allen White's Committee to Defend America by Aiding the Allies.[3]

In May 1940, *The Nation* published a speech MacLeish had recently given entitled "The Irresponsibles" that criticized the retreat of scholars from moral and political commitments in favor of bloodless scientific values of "objectivity—detachment—dispassion." He faulted writers for trying to see the world "as a god sees it—without morality, without care, without judgment." With Fascist ideas threatening the life of the mind, these forms of aloof spectatorship left civilization without its best-placed defenders. Days later, MacLeish expanded this critique in a second talk, this one published in *The New Republic*, in which he faulted anti-war novelists, including his friends Hemingway and Dos Passos, for unintentionally fostering among the youth a debilitating disbelief in "all statements of principle and conviction, all declarations of moral purpose." Nothing did more, MacLeish said, than World War I cynicism to "disarm democracy in the face of fascism" a generation later.[4]

These sallies brought forth a hail of denunciations, from Edmund Wilson, James T. Farrell, Dwight Macdonald, and others. Several critics heard in a reference MacLeish made to "dangerous books" echoes of Hitler and Goebbels. Others carped that MacLeish, known for his ambition, was simply currying favor with Roosevelt. The critic Burton Rascoe sneered that he was inclined "to jump onto band wagons." If that was the case, MacLeish knew well what he was doing.[5]

*   *   *

By the late summer of 1941, Roosevelt concluded he needed an agency to manage war-related information. Through "cash and carry" and Lend-Lease, America was becoming entwined in the global conflict. Direct military involvement seemed increasingly likely.[6]

At first the president had balked at creating a new information bureau. A Wilson administration veteran, he remembered well the excesses of the Creel Committee. He knew that his own alphabet soup administration already had plenty of press shops—including, as of July 1941, a Bureau of

Facts and Figures, housed within Fiorello LaGuardia's Office of Civilian Defense. But information management wasn't LaGuardia's focus or forte, and FDR wanted someone to deal aggressively with isolationist sentiment and flagging morale. At one point he sighed that the nation "could stand a little flag wrapping" and suggested offhandedly to his aide Harold Ickes that they hire Creel. Though mortified at the thought of Creel's return, Ickes shared the concerns about morale. So did a growing roster of intellectuals and public opinion experts; Gordon Allport, Ruth Benedict, Hadley Cantril, Erik Erikson, Erich Fromm, George Gallup, and Margaret Mead all publicly petitioned for a stronger effort. Touring the country to promote *Speak Up for Democracy*, Edward Bernays, too, urged FDR to "call in the experts—psychologists, scientists—to lend their powers of persuasion to the administration's courses."[7]

Arguments like these convinced Roosevelt, in consultation with MacLeish, in October 1941 to issue an executive order (which MacLeish may even have drafted), spinning off LaGuardia's small information bureau into the new Office of Facts and Figures. But from the start FDR's conception of the office was muddled. Raising morale was important, but as MacLeish recalled, he also wanted to avoid a debacle like the Creel Committee. The president thus sought to frame the new office as simply "a central check-out point where you could find out whether things were right or wrong"—as the organization's antiseptic name (which FDR chose) tried to convey. Yet, as always, the line between furnishing information and making a partisan case was not so easily drawn. "If OFF pipes out the undiluted, uncolored facts," cracked the *New York Times's* Arthur Krock, "it will be the first government information bureau to do that."[8]

Roosevelt had hardly hidden his interventionism since his reelection. After unveiling Lend-Lease in December 1940, he had used his 1941 inaugural address to deliver a ringing affirmation of democracy. To a crowd massed under bright skies on the Capitol lawn, he said that democracy, alone among forms of government, had "constructed an unlimited civilization capable of infinite progress in the improvement of human life." But he warned against a flagging faith in democracy. "The preservation of the spirit and faith of the nation does, and will, furnish the highest justification for every sacrifice that we may make in the cause of national defense."[9]

The ghostwriter of that address was MacLeish, whom FDR had come to call upon when he needed high-flown, inspirational fare. Since naming him to run the Library of Congress, Roosevelt had taken a strong liking to MacLeish, who more than reciprocated. "He was just the most attractive human being who ever lived," the poet later reminisced. MacLeish began joining FDR on trips to the country or aboard his Coast Guard cutter. He also carried out presidential errands, like compiling lists of mystery and detective novels for the president's diversion, and otherwise providing what one reporter called "mental stimulus." Unsurprisingly, FDR turned to MacLeish to lead the new Office of Facts and Figures.[10]

MacLeish took the job with ambivalence. Despite his fervent interventionism, and his desire to "unite and inform and hearten American opinion that the American determination to win will survive," he shared FDR's aversion to inflammatory rhetoric and his belief that the new office must simply promulgate the facts. Like Creel before him, MacLeish avoided the term *propaganda*. "I wonder . . . whether our enemies haven't so slimed that word," he said to Harold Lasswell in a radio debate, ". . . . that it is no longer possible to consider it as having any affirmative contents." Lasswell still hoped that the term could be used neutrally, to refer "to skill . . . from a purely specialist point of view."[11]

But it wasn't just the term *propaganda* that MacLeish rejected. He wanted his office to disseminate clean facts, presented without hype. "A democratic government," MacLeish announced, "is more concerned with the provision of information to the people than it is with the communication of dreams and aspirations. . . . The duty of government is to provide a basis for judgment; and when it goes beyond that, it goes beyond the prime scope of its duty." Some presidential advisers, such as LaGuardia, said the new information office should serve up "sugar-coated, colored, ornamented matter, otherwise known as 'bunk.'" Others said FDR needed an American Goebbels. But MacLeish, notwithstanding his own incorrigible stridency, argued that unadorned information would be sufficient to enlighten and awaken the public. Goebbels would be a negative example. He called for a "strategy of truth."

MacLeish imagined that solid information, of its own persuasive force, would vanquish isolationist tendencies, which were being propounded in the right-wing press, and which he believed were rooted in misunderstandings and lies. "The strategy of truth," he explained, is "the strategy which opposes to the frauds and deceits by which our enemies have confused and conquered other people the simple and clarifying truths by which a nation such as ours must guide itself." MacLeish thus became the latest of the many government publicists who, while putting out the government line, convinced themselves that they were merely countering the opposition's lies with truth.[12]

PROPAGANDA AND THE "GOOD WAR"

THE OFFICE OF FACTS AND FIGURES joined a crowded field of New Deal agencies that were already flooding channels of public communication with war-related information. Given a meager budget, MacLeish had originally planned to hire a staff of "a half dozen men." Soon, however, his office swelled to 350 full- and part-time employees, including journalists Henry Pringle, Malcolm Cowley, and E. B. White—to name just three of the better-known—as well as McGeorge Bundy and Arthur Schlesinger, Jr., twenty-something sons of MacLeish's Harvard friends. For the committed intellectual, OFF was the place to work during the war.[1]

For a while, MacLeish had the president's ear. In early December 1941, FDR asked him to prepare a comprehensive report on the progress of the defense effort. MacLeish did so in a few weeks, noting proudly that he had "purposely restrained our writers [by] requiring them to use the neutral and objective language of a government report rather than . . . hortatory and more exciting language." MacLeish also drafted a "Victory Program," outlining the ideas that the administration should present to the public to mobilize the country.[2]

Inexorably, though, as OFF grew, information bled into exhortation. MacLeish added a publications division, a poster division, a radio division. When FDR's 1942 State of the Union address unveiled his "Four Freedoms"—the principles for which America was fighting—MacLeish ordered up a pamphlet with essays on each of the four, from Reinhold Niebuhr (freedom of religion), Max Lerner (freedom from fear), Malcolm Cowley (freedom from want), and E. B. White (freedom of speech). In a similar spirit, MacLeish proposed a series of "old-fashioned town meetings," held in small towns and replete with fanfare and military ceremony, at which citizens could hear the latest government information. These undertakings combined information provision with popular mobilization.[3]

More and more, MacLeish strayed into emotionally laden territory. Most controversially, his radio division aired a series of plays called *This Is War!* that crudely dramatized the global conflict. Supervised by Norman Corwin of CBS and produced by an advertising executive from N. W. Ayer, the portentous programs aired on Saturday nights on the national radio networks. Featuring celebrities such as the actor Robert Montgomery and the poet Stephen Vincent Benét, they painted a demonic picture of the Nazis and a shining image of the president. Excitedly, MacLeish told FDR that by exploiting the existing radio networks, the government could reach "some fifty-seven million sets in 30,300,000 homes, or approximately ninety percent of the entire population—an audience which the radio industry has built up" at its own enormous expense. Private polling informed MacLeish that *This Is War!* was drawing 20 million listeners per episode.[4]

MacLeish also branched out into monitoring public opinion, creating his own Bureau of Intelligence to supplement Hadley Cantril's secret polling. Of special concern to him was the influence of Nazi propaganda on American opinion. A staunch civil libertarian, MacLeish held that "free trade in propaganda is a cornerstone of our political philosophy" and refused to censor it. But neither did he wish to let pro-Axis arguments go uncontested. One of his reports warned that if Nazi propaganda fell on receptive ears—perhaps through German-American newspapers—it would pose "definite dangers," including in the form of violence and work stoppages. MacLeish also worried that "innocent repetition by loyal Americans" of phrases favored by the Nazis might inculcate pernicious habits of mind. (Sometimes this worry was excessive, as when he cautioned that the phrase "Latin America" was intended to divide the western hemisphere.) He proposed an office of counterpropaganda to identify and resist enemy persuasion.[5]

Extensive though its activities were, the Office of Facts and Figures was hardly a happy hive of committed workers. On the contrary, for the ten months he led the office, MacLeish said, "life just really was not worth living." Problems arose from every corner. At the most basic level, MacLeish struggled to satisfy his main constituency, the press, whose members retained an inveterate hostility toward government publicity shops. Whenever the government withheld data, reporters bridled, even if the subject was something like industrial production or military plans, whose public disclosure might plausibly benefit the Axis. MacLeish also angered the correspondents when he was sent out to answer journalists' questions after Pearl Harbor without having been fully briefed, left to report only what he had heard on the radio.[6]

Soon MacLeish was experiencing widespread vilification and ridicule, much like George Creel had, and he indulged in self-pity. "I was just a natural-born target for abuse," he recalled, "and it began early." Like Creel, too, he lashed out, with a pair of speeches to journalists in the spring of 1942. While granting "that the distinction between democratic criticism and defeatist propaganda is difficult to draw," he hotheadedly accused "minority elements of the American press"—meaning the right-wing newspaper publishers—of working to engineer an American defeat. These scurrilous accusations of aiding the enemy only isolated MacLeish further.[7]

Congress also went after him. Republicans charged OFF with churning out pro-FDR propaganda under the guise of war information. The irrepressible Martin Dies of HUAC attacked MacLeish for hiring Malcolm Cowley, who had formerly been involved in radical politics. Just as aggressive was a Senate investigative committee led by Harry Truman of Missouri, who, according to MacLeish, "accused us of everything under the sun. . . . We were accused of lying, and faking the books." (Three and a half years later, as president, Truman would praise OFF's successor body for its "outstanding contribution to victory.")[8]

Still other problems arose because the Office of Facts and Figures lacked the authority it needed. The War, Navy, and State departments operated outside MacLeish's reach, and at the Treasury Department, Secretary Henry Morgenthau led a publicity campaign to sell war bonds, which, as he quipped, was really a campaign to sell the war—to boost morale by getting citizens to take some tangible action. A half-dozen other information shops within the administration also carried out work that overlapped with MacLeish's. Early in 1942, MacLeish convened a weekly interagency group called the Committee on War Information to coordinate these efforts, but it had no real power. The upshot, as MacLeish told Roosevelt, was a "Tower of Babel"—agencies working independently, redundantly, and at cross purposes. FDR declined to give MacLeish the overarching authority he had expected.[9]

Indeed, no one contributed to the problem more than the often mercurial Roosevelt himself. At the beginning, MacLeish had warned that the office wouldn't succeed unless he had direct access to the president and control over the information channels. But Roosevelt continued to rely mainly on the White House Press Office, run by Steve Early, who had served FDR faithfully since 1933. The president also cavalierly freelanced as his own press agent. He liked to pepper MacLeish and other officials with his publicity ideas, urging them to gin up attention for admiring editorials by the likes of William Allen White and Walter Lippmann (now a supporter). But when he was supposed to follow MacLeish's advice, he failed to do so. MacLeish drafted themes for the president to use in his speeches, but they were often ignored. The public, MacLeish told FDR, remained "badly informed."[10]

The office's fatal flaw was the same one that had long afflicted government propagandists: American traditions and values demanded that officials pledge to deliver only uninflected news, but the reality of wartime (to say nothing of the human tendency to regard one's own perspective as objective) made such a promise impossible to fulfill. When MacLeish's office doled out bland prose and plain data, hard-core anti-Fascists grumbled that the dull fare would never mobilize the public. Harold Lasswell, who was conducting his own propaganda research for the government, criticized the "strategy of truth," insisting that propaganda had to have "a large element of fake in it." But when OFF's posture deviated from bloodless neutrality, MacLeish was accused of distortion, emotionalism, and partisan shilling. Particularly vulnerable were OFF's radio shows. To MacLeish's irritation, one of Norman Corwin's writers had publicly called for "hate on the air," prompting angry listeners to write in. At the same time, FDR's Republican opponents took aim at a radio biography lionizing the president as a latter-day Lincoln. Neither journalists nor citizens had lost their ability to identify, resist, and quarrel with propaganda, or their tendency to filter government messages through their preexisting views.[11]

In February 1942, Roosevelt asked Milton Eisenhower, General Dwight Eisenhower's youngest brother and a longtime government publicity officer, to fix the unwieldy information apparatus. Eisenhower's report, calling for better coordination among the agencies, persuaded FDR that big changes were needed. The "difficulties the American people must face in following and understanding this war have been constantly on my mind," FDR fretted to MacLeish on February 12. Days later the president again gently chided MacLeish, who conceded the point. "So far as I am concerned," he wrote to budget director Harold Smith, "you have my resignation as Director of the Office of Facts and Figures in your hands herewith."[12]

By springtime, MacLeish was all but embracing the traffic in dreams and aspirations that he had once forsworn—envisioning a mammoth educational drive to foster "a balanced awareness of the war's significance as a whole." But MacLeish no longer wished to lead such an enterprise. His fondness for persuasion, advocacy, and even polemics had ill suited him for the job of press officer. Under fire from all sides, he asked FDR to scrap the Office of Facts and Figures altogether. In June 1942, the president did just that.

Roosevelt established the Office of War Information. One propaganda bureau was dead; a new one would live on.[13]

*   *   *

Headed by the radio newscaster Elmer Davis, the Office of War Information consolidated several of Roosevelt's information agencies, aimed at both foreign and domestic audiences. Davis couldn't claim MacLeish's closeness with FDR, but the new body rested on a stronger executive order than OFF's. It also developed more extensive programs, including in film and radio. (Its overseas broadcasts would become known as the Voice of America.) MacLeish assumed a job within the OWI, reporting to Davis.

The old problems quickly returned. Maintaining a consistent line across multiple government agencies proved as difficult as ever. The War, Navy, and State departments still did as they pleased. Davis got bogged down as he battled them over the withholding or concealment of information. During the trial of eight Nazi saboteurs apprehended off the coast of Long Island in 1942, Davis sided with the newspapers, who were clamoring for greater access. But the War Department wouldn't hear of it, and Roosevelt ruled against the OWI.

Tensions between furnishing neutral information and rallying the public resurfaced. By now MacLeish was openly calling for advocacy, clashing with Milton Eisenhower, among others. MacLeish's old bromidic hopes—that facts alone were powerful enough to boost morale and clarify the issues—were never fulfilled. As Davis noted, in what some took as a dig at MacLeish, "you cannot do much with people who are convinced that they are the sole authorized custodians of Truth and that whoever differs from them is ipso facto wrong."

MacLeish left OWI in 1943. "I hated information work," he said. "In war you were always on the verge of propaganda." Weary, he returned to his duties as Librarian of Congress, a post he had retained all the while. Toward war's end he would move to the State Department as assistant secretary for cultural and public affairs to direct that department's information policies. Milton Eisenhower, too, left for other governmental roles.

Both men's OWI jobs were folded into a new position. Appointed to the post was Gardner Cowles, an Iowa newspaper publisher, founder of the photojournalism magazine *Look*, and Wendell Willkie confidant. Cowles hired a team of advertising men, whose ballyhoo—like the radio slogan "a truth a day keeps Hitler away"—made MacLeish's Four Freedoms pamphlets look downright educative. Malcolm Cowley, who had also by now left the government, griped that Cowles's men relied not on the persuasive rhetoric that MacLeish had favored but on simple-minded, insipid, condescending ad copy. Their "promotional technique," Cowley wrote, "could be used to sell anything, good, bad, or indifferent," whether it be "the old-time religion or Newbro's Herpicide." But, he added witheringly, the "one thing it cannot sell is democracy, which is based on trust in the ability and good will of the people at large." A revolt at the OWI followed, as Pringle, Schlesinger, Philip Hamburger, and a dozen other writers quit in a mass exodus. "No one denies that promotional techniques have a proper and powerful function in telling the story of the war," they declared. "But as we see it, the activities of OWI on the home front are now dominated by high-pressure promoters who prefer slick salesmanship to honest information." The artist Ben Shahn designed a poster mocking the admen's ideas. In a parody of Norman Rockwell's *Saturday Evening Post* covers depicting the Four Freedoms, Shahn's poster showed the Statue of Liberty holding up four ice-cold Coca-Cola bottles, with the slogan: "The War That Refreshes: The Four Delicious Freedoms!"[14]

Through it all, the right sniped. An alliance of Republicans and southern Democrats in Congress regarded the OWI, as they had the OFF, as a promotional vehicle for FDR and the New Deal. Emboldened by their gains in the 1942 elections, and upset by pamphlets such as *Negroes and the War*, which praised New Deal jobs programs for helping African Americans, they slashed OWI's budget and forced it to close a dozen regional offices, its motion picture bureau, and its publications shop. They also targeted the government's other publicity agencies, long a source of contention.[15]

But if the right's barbs were in some measure partisan in nature, they suggested too that suspicion of government publicity was partly a byproduct of suspicion of Washington itself. The growth of executive power since TR had elevated the demand for government information and thus the need for public relations bureaus. FDR did as much as any of his predecessors to expand the functions of government and the presidency. From his mastery of radio to his innovations in polling, from his crowd-pleasing press conferences to his wartime information programs, he also did as much as anyone to let the American people know what he was up to. To his admirers, that publicity was a welcome dose of transparency. To his detractors, it was a decidedly unwelcome form of propaganda.

PART IV

THE AGE OF NEWS MANAGEMENT

The Cold War, setting in almost as soon as World War II ended, gave presidents new reason to monitor the flow of news and information with a vigilance normally reserved for wartime. Both Harry Truman and Dwight Eisenhower, though often misremembered as innocents in crafting their words and appearances, relied heavily on television coaches, public relations aides, pollsters, and press secretaries, in order to fashion their public identities and to sustain support for their policies as tensions with the Soviet Union spiked. A new regime of what the columnist James Reston called "news management"—including heightened secrecy around nuclear weapons, intelligence, diplomacy, and other Cold War concerns—limited the information available to reporters and the public. At the same time, presidents and politicians were learning to exploit television to present themselves directly to the public. The broadcasting of speeches, campaign spots, press conferences, and interviews—all crafted with professional expertise—fed a resurgent anxiety about newly refined methods of persuasion, voiced by social critics such as Vance Packard, who worried about the public's manipulation by self-interested elites.

28

THE UNDERESTIMATION OF
HARRY TRUMAN

ON AUGUST 6, 1945, Harry S. Truman was aboard the USS *Augusta*, returning from the Allies' Potsdam Conference on the postwar disposition of Germany. The new president was lunching with Secretary of State James Byrnes and members of the ship's crew when a captain rushed in. He carried a map of Japan and a message from Secretary of War Henry Stimson. "Results clear-cut successful in all respects," it read. "Visible effects greater than in any test." Truman, known for his spontaneity and lack of artifice, couldn't conceal his joy. "This is the greatest thing in history," he declared. He huddled with Byrnes, then tapped his glass with a fork. "We have just dropped a new bomb on Japan," he announced. "It has been an overwhelming success."[1]

In Washington, acting press secretary Eben Ayers summoned a dozen news correspondents to the White House. "There," as broadcaster Don Goddard informed radio listeners across America, "they were read a special announcement written by President Truman" about "a new bomb, so powerful that only the imagination of a trained scientist could dream of its existence. Without qualification, the president said that Allied scientists have now harnessed the basic power of the universe." Goddard's statement contained more than one exaggeration. Scientists might quarrel with his schoolbook characterization of atomic power. But Goddard also incorrectly described the president as having "written" his remarks. The author of the statement telling the world about the bomb was Arthur W. Page, a public relations executive.[2]

Page was the son of Walter Hines Page, the editor and publicist who had served Woodrow Wilson. Arthur, after taking over the editorship of *The World's Work* from his father, had for years run public relations for AT&T. At the start of World War II he joined—and eventually chaired—an Army-Navy morale committee, advising the military on how to sustain positive attitudes among service members through radio broadcasts. As chairman, his tasks encompassed a range of publicity operations, from publication of the military newspaper *Stars and Stripes* to the production of Frank Capra's *Why We Fight* film series. Before the Normandy invasion, Page traveled to England to prepare materials to help steel the soldiers for their historic mission. More generally, he worked as a wartime publicity factotum, advising Bill Donovan's foreign propaganda office and the Treasury Department's war bond drive.

In late March 1945, just before Roosevelt's death made Truman president, Stimson asked Page to assume full-time duty in the War Department's Bureau of Public Relations. Several weeks later, Stimson revealed the reason for the stepped-up commitment: he wanted Page's advice on the development of the bomb. As Page recalled, "He had a great conscience about whether he ought to use this doggoned thing or not, and if so, how. What he wanted to do was to have somebody he could talk it over with." Joining the so-called Interim Committee, which Stimson convened to advise Truman on the new weapon, Page endorsed the consensus behind dropping it on Japan without hesitation.[3]

The public knew nothing of the Manhattan Project. By midsummer it was clear that Truman would have to explain the atomic bomb to a confused nation. He needed a speech that was both somber and reassuring. William Laurance of the *New York Times*, the only reporter who had visited the atomic test site in Los Alamos, wrote a first draft. But Harvard president James Conant, who oversaw the Manhattan Project and served on the Interim Committee, rejected it as too verbose and asked Page to write a new one. Page's were the words that Truman issued in his August statement.

"Sixteen hours ago," it noted, "an American airplane dropped one bomb on Hiroshima, an important Japanese Army base. That bomb had more power than 20,000 tons of T.N.T." The statement reviewed the race between the Allies and the Axis to harness atomic energy, and praised "the greatest achievement of organized science in history." Truman said that Japan had been warned to surrender before the bomb was dropped, and he threatened "to obliterate . . . every productive enterprise the Japanese have above ground in any city," to "completely destroy Japan's power to make war." But the new president's message also offered a vision of reconciliation. He would see to it that "atomic power can become a powerful and forceful influence towards the maintenance of world peace."[4]

*   *   *

Even before historical revisionism cast its golden glow on Harry Truman, the plainspoken Missourian struck voters as refreshingly unaffected. Born to a farming family of modest means, given to homespun locutions, Truman made a virtue of his lack of pretension. He apologized neither for his breakfast bourbon shot, his Missouri poker buddies, nor his workaday, workhorse résumé—farmer, soldier, haberdasher, public official. As a senator and president, he often shot from the hip. Once, following a cruel review of his daughter's recital in *The Washington Post*, he dashed off an angry letter to the paper's music critic, threatening to sock him in the nose.

Truman did much to promote this image, but it was not a complete picture. Despite his commonsense judgments and salty speech, he was, as the reporter William Shannon observed, a "closet intellectual," well read in the classics and fond of history. Once, when minding his early-rising grandsons, ages two and four, he sat them down and read from Thucydides. His tendency to deliberate over decisions belied his public reputation for impulsiveness. And notwithstanding his blunt style, he was far from insensitive to the need, in the age of mass media, to project the proper image.[5]

Like his recent predecessors, Truman put thought and care into coordinating his administration's messages, and he had a large network of press bureaus to help him. By the time he became president, the apparatus for crafting and coordinating government messages was highly developed. In an article titled "How U.S. Tries to Influence You," *U.S. News & World Report* noted that the government spent more than $100 million a year on publicity and that "enough government handouts to fill 15 pages of newsprint daily are dumped into the hands of newspapermen." An adjacent graphic took the reader through ten steps of governmental message coordination—from the administration's creation of an official "line" to its dissemination through the media. Presidential publicity was now a well-oiled machine, and no president would think to shut it down.[6]

Truman's attention to the demands of the public presidency was most evident in his preparations for his weekly press conferences. During his tenure, these sessions evolved from bantering off-the-record gabfests into a studied public ritual. Truman usually opened by reading a written statement, setting an agenda and a formal tone. In 1946, after Commerce Secretary Henry Wallace caused a stir by publicly bashing Truman's foreign policy, the president took to meeting with aides beforehand to anticipate questions. Led by press secretary Charlie Ross, the staff would brief the president and frame possible replies. Eventually, Roger Tubby, the last of Truman's press secretaries, implemented a rigorous system under which staffers devised as many as forty possible queries, divvied them up to be researched, and assembled them into a briefing book for Truman to peruse the night before he faced the reporters. A half hour before the event, aides would review the material with the president at his desk. These steps stripped much of the spontaneity from the conferences, as did Truman's often curt style. Eroding the intimacy, too, was the growth of the White House press corps itself; Ross groused that at times "more than two hundred reporters" were "stacked like hard macaroni" in the Oval Office. Keyed up, the correspondents "made a practice of baiting the president," *The Washington Post* noted, "and Mr. Truman has too frequently responded with more heat than caution."[7]

That the public was replacing the White House gaggle as Truman's main audience became still more apparent in April 1950, when Ross moved the gatherings from the Oval Office to the high-ceilinged, gilt-and-marble Indian Treaty Room of the Executive Office Building. The larger baroque space featured bronze cherubim, frosted light globes, and a balcony that looked, in the words of James Reston, as if it had "not been dusted since Charles Evans Hughes was Secretary of State." The room's size further muted the levity and encouraged formality. It also necessitated the use of microphones, which allowed Truman's comments to be taped—which in turn brought pressure on the president to let reporters use his words verbatim. He eventually agreed to put selected segments on the record. Once a way to build personal relationships with reporters, the press conference had become a public forum.[8]

Truman also put more care into his radio speeches than he let on. His first broadcasts as a vice-presidential candidate in 1944 were disastrous. Reviewers complained about his grating voice, his Missouri twang, and his rapid delivery. In September, Leonard Reinsch, a radio executive working with the Democrats, met with Truman in his hometown of Independence,

Missouri, and told the candidate that his acceptance speech at the Demo-crats' convention was "unintelligible" because he had raced through it. "I didn't think it was very interesting," Truman replied, "and I wanted to get it over with." Reinsch took Truman to a local studio, where they practiced speaking through a microphone. Reinsch taught Truman to slow down, pause for dramatic effect, and modulate his voice to create a range of tones and expressions. As the campaign resumed, he stayed on to help Truman, inserting pages into his speeches that instructed him to "take it easy" or "remember the living room"—an admonition to visualize his audience as an average family, as FDR had been known to do.[9]

Reinsch continued to coach Truman after he became president. He even served as press secretary for two weeks, and might have stayed on, but the newspapermen wouldn't tolerate a radioman in the job. Reinsch also inserted himself into Truman's speechwriting chain, editing drafts to add rhythm and delete unwieldy clusters of consonants. As the 1948 election approached, radio assumed an even larger role in the campaign. Reinsch steered Truman back into the studio for more practice.[10]

*   *   *

Radio's dominance of presidential campaigns was short-lived. From the instant that FDR delivered a televised message at the 1939 World's Fair, the newer medium threatened to dethrone radio. The war delayed TV's development, but in 1947 Truman allowed cameras to record his State of the Union address, and that fall the White House produced its own televi-sion broadcast: the launch of a food drive for war-torn Europe. Alas, the president's team had no clue what it was doing. Little thought went into the visual tableau; poorly placed cameras captured only the bottom third of a portrait hanging on the back wall. Truman peered down into his type-script, scarcely bothering to conceal his turning of pages.

That would change. Sales of TV sets were climbing. By 1948, urban landlords were installing rooftop antennas. The average viewer now sat for three hours a day. CBS premiered a nightly fifteen-minute news report, and, during the election campaign, debuted a program called *Presidential Timber* that examined candidates' backgrounds. The parties scheduled their conventions in Philadelphia to get the footage aired in eastern cities without delay. Manufacturers enticed buyers with the prospect of wit-nessing the historic, heretofore "behind the scenes" proceedings unfold in real time. Some boosters predicted television would revitalize Ameri-can democracy by doing away with the backroom deals. Journalists were soon excitedly comparing the televised conventions to New England town meetings.[11]

TV also changed candidates' behavior. At the Republican Convention in 1948, Dewey ordered his managers not to be filmed cutting deals with competitors. The Democrats shortened the gaps between speeches and curtailed floor demonstrations. They instructed delegates how to act before the cameras: no yawning; "Take the toothpick out of your mouth"; "Don't take off your shoes." Speakers on the dais wore makeup; a few used visual props, like party official India Edwards, who waved a slab of steak and a carton of milk before the camera to illustrate the costs of inflation. Reliably grumpy, H. L. Mencken, covering his last convention in seersucker and a straw boater, was horrified by the klieg lights, whose power he considered "very little less than an atom bomb." This was more confirmation that democracy was but a clown show.[12]

Truman accommodated. He worked to improve his appearance, reading his lines off oversized cue cards, which allowed him to look straight into the camera. (In 1952 aides brought teleprompters into the White House, though accounts differ over whether Truman used them.) Reinsch, fighting the perception that the former vice president wasn't quite a legitimate president, made sure that every rostrum at which Truman spoke carried the presidential seal.

The key change in Truman's style came when he learned to speak extemporaneously, in early 1948. The looser style showed off his charming folksy regionalisms, his skill as a raconteur, and his humor. "I am stuck for 'off-the-cuff' radio speeches," he wrote in his diary. "It means lots of new work." At the Democratic Convention, he put the new style to use, firing up the crowd with a stemwinder that blasted the congressional Republicans' obstructionism. In a headline-making gambit, he vowed to call the Congress back into session to pass some legislation. Convention planners had let the schedule get away from them, and Truman took the rostrum at 2 am. But despite the hour, he looked fresh and unperturbed in a double-breasted white linen suit and black tie. "He was relaxed and supremely confident, swaying on the balls of his feet with almost a methodical rhythm," wrote Jack Gould, the *New York Times* television critic. "His 'semi ad-lib' format, using a minimum of written notes and relying mostly on extemporaneous remarks, enabled him to endow his address with both spontaneity and change of pace." The speech energized and united Democrats, including many on the left wing of the party, such as Upton Sinclair, who had been flirting with Henry Wallace's candidacy.

Though hailed for its artlessness and utter spontaneity, the speech was, like so much that Truman did in public, the product of considerable forethought. Aides Charles Murphy and Sam Rosenman, a Roosevelt holdover, had each prepared drafts of the speech and then blended their versions into a detailed reading outline. Though Truman didn't rigidly hew to the outline, he kept it in front of him for the whole speech, and it provided the basis for about 40 percent of his words. Truman was impulsive, unpretentious, and unafraid to speak his mind. But he was nobody's fool.[13]

GEORGE GALLUP'S DEMOCRACY

GEORGE GALLUP WAS THE KING of the pollsters. In May 1948, his face graced the cover of *Time* magazine, which called him "the Babe Ruth of the polling profession." A burly man, with slate-blue eyes, a glossy pate, hunched shoulders, and a bright smile, he had for two decades labored to compile as accurate a picture of the American mind as his legions of interviewers, statisticians, and punch-card computers could provide. Gallup wasn't alone in capitalizing on the new fad for opinion data. But he was better known than Emil Hurja or Hadley Cantril, or even than his fellow commercial pollsters, Elmo Roper and Archibald Crossley. By 1948, his name had become synonymous with polling itself.

Fame came to Gallup in good part because he sought it. He cultivated relationships with editors and publishers, whom he showered with press releases. More than 100 papers carried Gallup's column, "America Speaks!," reaching some 8 million readers. Once established, his firm also forged beyond politics, developing methods for measuring the star power of radio personalities and predicting the box office take of Hollywood films. Within the polling profession, too, Gallup was a leader, helping to found the American Association for Public Opinion Research in 1947.[1]

Born in Jefferson, Iowa, in 1901, the son of a farmer, "Ted" Gallup had grown up a fan of William Jennings Bryan and his radical democracy. At the University of Iowa, Gallup earned a PhD in journalism, researching how newspapers might measure their readers' interests. The Iowa publishing mogul Gardner Cowles, later of the Office of War Information, heard about Gallup's doctoral work and underwrote it. After getting his degree, Gallup taught journalism briefly and then joined the Young & Rubicam advertising firm as director of research, rising to vice president. In late 1935, with a loan from Sigurd Larmon, his mentor at Y&R, he founded the American Institute of Public Opinion, in Princeton, New Jersey, with offices on Nassau Street, above a Woolworth's, overlooking the university gates.

In 1936, Gallup confidently declared that the *Literary Digest*, which was forecasting FDR's defeat in the fall election, would be wrong. He wasn't alone in this claim; three years before, Robert Brooks, a political scientist at Swarthmore College, had spelled out the *Digest*'s methodological confusions in detail, and other pollsters also challenged the magazine's forecast. But Gallup gained notice by predicting what the *Digest* poll would end up saying. "We've been through many poll battles," Wilfred Funk, the magazine's editor, huffed. "But never before has anyone foretold what our poll was going to show before it was even started." On Election Day, Funk's humiliation was complete. Gallup actually underestimated Roosevelt's margin of victory by seven points, but in the expectations game, he emerged a winner. Gallup uncorked a bottle of champagne with his wife in a Sarasota hotel room, where she had demanded they repair to amid the madness of the fall's "polling wars."[2]

Gallup's explanation was that the *Digest* had based its predictions on ballots mailed in by voters whose names were culled from telephone books and lists of automobile owners. These lists contained few of the low-income voters—many of them phoneless and carless—who were loyal to the New Deal. Gallup's polls, in contrast, used sampling and probability to find reliable cross sections of the country. He made sure to include the right proportion of urban and rural voters, of men and women, of voters from different income strata. Ironically, Gallup's analysis of the *Digest*'s error may not have been quite correct. More likely, the *Digest* erred simply by relying on voluntary respondents. Still, Gallup had dethroned the *Digest*.[3]

After this coup, Gallup burnished his reputation and built his business. He expanded the range of his questionnaires' topics and the frequency with which he took them. Aspiring to scientific status, Gallup tried to address flaws in his system, claiming he could lower his margin of error to 4 percent. When he realized that a question's phrasing might influence the answer, he would instruct half his survey-takers pose a question one way and half pose it a different way, then note the differences. Gallup also concluded after 1936 that face-to-face interviews worked better than mailed ballots. He hired field workers to knock on doors or approach people on the street—or in laundromats, bookstores, or parks—with pencils and clipboards. Paul Sheatsley, later a noted public opinion scholar himself, started out as a hoofer for Gallup. "I remember in those days the way I would fill my relief quotas was to walk around town until I saw a WPA construction gang and I would get them on their lunch hour, three or four men sitting around eating their sandwiches and drinking their beer," he recalled. "I'd pull out my questionnaire and say, 'Do you approve or disapprove of a treaty with Germany?' I got four interviews very quickly that way." Eventually, Gallup moved beyond these informal methods, too.[4]

Gallup promoted his business by writing books and articles and giving talks in all kinds of forums. His ideas found their fullest elaboration in *The Pulse of Democracy*, a treatise he wrote with a Canadian protégé, Saul Forbes Rae, in 1940. The book presented surveys as the best means ever devised to gauge the public's desires—and thus to serve democracy. Like James Bryce, whom Gallup loved to quote, the authors foresaw a time when "the will of the majority were to become ascertainable at all times, and without the need of its passing through a body of representatives, possibly even without the need of voting machinery at all." Scientific polling, they suggested, made Bryce's vision a reality.[5]

Science was the key word. Public opinion professionals such as Bernays had invoked the word in touting their authority, but for them it meant researched and tested knowledge. Gallup placed himself in the company of chemists and physicists, men in white coats. "Measuring public opinion calls for a certain 'laboratory' attitude of mind," he wrote. "It needs people trained in the scientific method." He boasted of his rarefied knowledge of statistics—his book cited the probability theories of the seventeenth-century mathematician Jacob Bernoulli—that placed his work beyond the ken of lay citizens. Embracing the era's esteem for objectivity, he insisted his method was purely a matter of number crunching, devoid of interpretative coloration. And where his techniques were faulty, he claimed, they would be improved through experiment and research. He bridled at naysayers who put quotation marks around "scientific" when it modified "polling." "If our work is not scientific," he wrote, "then no one in the field of social science, and few of those in the natural sciences, have a right to use that word."[6]

Gallup made an even grander boast about polling's ability to foster democracy. "Throughout the history of politics," Gallup and Rae wrote, "this central problem has remained: shall the common people be free to express their basic needs and purposes, or shall they be dominated by a small ruling clique?" Gallup knew how to write a loaded question. Aligning himself with the mass public, fashioning himself the people's voice, he said that public opinion should hold sway on all major issues. "The political wisdom of the common people," he insisted, would unfailingly produce good policy. According to his polls, the people had been ready before Congress to build up the military, support a draft, and implement equitable taxation. Buoyantly, he talked of a New England meeting writ large—the American people assembling in a giant metaphorical town hall created by his surveys. Whereas interest groups crowded out ordinary Americans' opinions in the mass media's assessments of public opinion, Gallup suggested, his own dispassionately administered soundings constituted a "swift and efficient method" to gain "a more reliable measure of the pulse of democracy."

* * *

George Gallup, in all his wisdom, did not give Truman much chance to hold onto the presidency in 1948. Despite the president's electrifying convention speech, the Democratic Party remained split, with southerners flocking to Strom Thurmond's segregationist Dixiecrats and the far left rallying to Henry Wallace's Progressives. Truman still paled next to Roosevelt, whose charisma and wartime leadership could never be transferred. And the Republicans, having taken both houses of Congress in 1946, were on a roll. Gallup's polls—and those of his colleagues—predicted a cakewalk by New York governor Thomas Dewey.

Like most politicians, Truman professed to put no stock in polls. "I never paid any attention to the polls myself because in my judgment they did not represent a true cross section of American opinion," he said, adding that a leader swayed by polls might be "afraid to make decisions which may make him unpopular." He stuck to this line his whole life. In 1954, he wrote: "I wonder how far Moses would have gone if he'd taken a poll in Egypt? What would Jesus Christ have preached if he'd taken a poll in Israel? Where would the Reformation have gone if Martin Luther had taken a poll? It isn't polls or public opinion of the moment that counts. It is right and wrong, and leadership—men with fortitude, honesty and a belief in the right that makes epochs in the history of the world."[7]

But, as with his use of other media, Truman wasn't as innocent as he pretended. He didn't lap up polling data as FDR had, and he had no Hadley Cantril or Emil Hurja. The politically risky stands he took—calling for civil rights for African Americans, recognizing the state of Israel—showed him to be a man of conviction. Yet he and his aides did look at polls, including during the 1948 election.

For much of Truman's presidency, Charlie Ross, Eben Ayers, and other aides passed surveys to the president. They sent thank-you notes to the professional pollsters and others who shared their data. They even did a small amount of polling themselves. When Truman's adviser Clark Clifford set down his thoughts about the 1948 presidential race, he recommended that Truman make surreptitious use of "the private Princeton poll" by piggybacking questions onto Gallup's surveys, as FDR had done. Clifford also urged regularly testing "the attitude toward President Truman of the Negroes in Harlem or the farmers in Iowa, or the Italians in Detroit." Only after poll-testing the "do-nothing Congress" line of attack did Truman decide to use it throughout the fall.[8]

*　*　*

On September 17, 1948, Truman set out on what would become a legendary campaign tour, traversing 22,000 miles of rail aboard the armor-plated, air-conditioned Pullman green *Ferdinand Magellan*. His aides had seen surveys about the most effective lines of attack against Dewey; they had seen data about Wallace's candidacy and Gallup's polls. After the campaign was over, Ross would breezily maintain that "there were no deep-hid schemes, no devious plans, nothing that could be called, in the language of political analysts, 'high strategy.'" But in fact Clifford and Washington attorney Jim Rowe had prepared for Truman a detailed blueprint: Truman had to carry the West and the farm vote, turn out the labor vote, and rally liberals and blacks. His tour would help achieve these goals. Nor was it a lack of sophistication that led Truman to bring along Ross to handle the press, Clifford for political consultation, and four speechwriters. "I'm going to give 'em hell," Truman promised his running mate, Senator Alben Barkley of Kentucky, as he left Washington's Union Station.

For the next month, speaking from his train's rear platform and in parks and auditoriums, Truman gave voice to his scrappiest instincts. He damned the Republican Party as hostile to farmers, workingmen, and ordinary Americans. "The Democratic Party puts human rights and human welfare first," he said in Missouri. "These Republican gluttons of privilege are cold men . . . cunning men. . . . They want a return of the Wall Street economic dictatorship." Out to California and back, he hammered his rivals for their indifference to the common man. Late in the campaign, he all but called Dewey a Fascist. Pundits frowned, but audiences cheered. "Give 'em hell, Harry!" became the rallying cry.

The cross-country swing brought Truman into direct contact with voters and showcased his straight talk. But, more important, Truman also exploited modern media, spreading his message to voters in their homes. At one sparsely attended event in Omaha, he declared: "I don't give a damn whether there's nobody there but you and me. I am making a speech on the radio to the farmers." He had been practicing his semi-extemporaneous speaking style, which played well over the airwaves. Ken Fry, the Democrats' radio director, reminded him to use "facts, names, dates, and places, in hard-nosed, direct fashion, and hammer, hammer, hammer on these points" for the sake of his remote audiences. He also urged Truman to keep his remarks to fifteen minutes. More than seventy of Truman's speeches were broadcast live on the radio, twenty nationally. Others served as centerpieces for locally aired programs. Some were shown on TV; an October speech from Jersey City was the first ever paid television appearance by a presidential candidate. The Democratic National Committee produced a biopic for cinemagoers. "During the last six days of the campaign," said Jack Redding, the party's publicity director, "no one could go to the movies anywhere in the United States without seeing the story of the president." Unlike the audiences at Truman's whistle-stop speeches, who had their minds made up, the millions listening to his broadcast speeches or watching in the cinemas included the all-important undecided voters.[9]

Pundits discounted Truman's fighting spirit. Lippmann scoffed at the president striving to "talk his way to victory." *Newsweek* asked fifty political writers who would win; all said Dewey. The pollsters agreed. Roper's final survey for *Fortune*, in October, forecast that Dewey would take 44 percent of the vote, Truman 31 percent. "So decisive are the figures given here this month," the editors wrote, "that *Fortune*, and Mr. Roper, plan no further detailed reports on the change of opinion in the forthcoming presidential campaign." Gallup found Truman gaining—six points behind with two weeks to go. But he never placed Truman within less than five points of his rival.[10]

Truman soldiered on. A poll in his campaign team's possession, apparently commissioned by the Democratic National Committee earlier in the season, disputed the other prognosticators. Based on a survey of 1,287

Americans, it suggested that the electorate was open to persuasion. Independent voters hadn't given up on Truman, and party loyalties were fluid. It's unclear if Truman knew about this survey, but the spirit of the large crowds he was drawing gave him the confidence to blast the experts from his train. Dewey, he said, "is going to get a shock on the second of November. He is going to get the results of the one big poll that counts—that is the voice of the American people speaking at the ballot box." Gallup, never beloved by Democratic insiders, came in for attack. Voters "are going to throw the Galluping polls right in the ashcan—you watch 'em," Truman said at a late October rally. "There are going to be more red-faced pollsters on November the 3rd than there were in 1936."

Truman defeated Dewey. Newspaper editors, and not only at the *Chicago Tribune*, were red-faced. The *New York Times* had predicted a Dewey win with 345 electoral votes. *Life* already had Dewey on its next cover. The pollsters came in for particular abuse. H. L. Mencken, no friend of the Democrats, cheered because the outcome "shook the bones of all . . . [the] smarties." Eben Ayers, Truman's press aide, voiced a common feeling that the pollsters' flameout represented a triumph for democracy, an affirmation of voters' free will. In *The New Republic*, Richard Strout, writing as T.R.B., described "a glowing and wonderful sense that the American people couldn't be ticketed by polls [and] knew its own mind."[11]

Gallup had no explanation. Neither did Roper. "I couldn't have been more wrong," he said. "Why, I don't know."

Truman's victory wasn't so hard to explain. Precisely as his strategists had planned, he turned out the old New Deal coalition, including Catholics, blacks, and the working class, while bringing into the Democratic fold ethnic Germans (no longer alienated by FDR's foreign policy) and—something of a surprise—farmers, who warmed to Truman's attacks on the GOP as the party of privilege. Why the pollsters misfired was a harder question; clearly, their methods were less than scientific. Academic pollsters such as Rensis Likert noted that for all their high-flown claims, the commercial pollsters weren't actually using the best sampling methods, which relied on randomness rather than on filling quota categories when selecting interviewees. Intensive interviewing and open-ended questioning, he added, would also have allowed the survey-takers to probe beyond superficial answers.[12]

The crucial error, though, was the polls' failure to capture the snowballing shift toward Truman. Many respondents, including a large portion of lower-income voters, told Gallup they were undecided. He allocated these voters in the same percentages as committed voters, but they broke for Truman. Taken together, these errors meant that in 1948, Gallup had committed a blunder much like that of the *Literary Digest* in 1936: He had underestimated the ballots of the working people.

* * *

The 1948 debacle brought new scrutiny to polling.[13] For years, politicians, journalists, and academics had argued about its merits. As Gallup extolled its democratic promise, pessimists warned that polling would corrupt democracy. Even Edward Bernays, who had used surveys in his own research, fulminated that polls were being used to dictate not only political strategies but also policy goals. "We are no longer led by men," he complained. "We are led around by polls." For two decades, senators and congressmen introduced bills to curb the pollsters' activities and held hearings to investigate their practices—with Republicans assailing polling in times of Democratic success and vice versa. The 1948 fiasco amplified these voices.[14]

No one relished the pollsters' comeuppance more than Lindsay Rogers, a political scientist who had been thundering for years about the flaws in polling. In an exquisite bit of timing, Rogers published a tract in 1949 entitled *The Pollsters*—the word evoked *hucksters*—a rebuttal, in effect, to Gallup's *Pulse of Democracy*. Rogers was well qualified to make the critique. A PhD from Johns Hopkins, the holder of a named chair at Columbia University, and a former journalist, he commanded authority among academics and the literate public. A courtly man with Old World airs, he ranged widely in his work and relished controversy. In November 1941, he had written a long article for *Harper's* trashing Gallup and deflating "the exaggerated claims that are made as to what the data mean."[15]

The Pollsters assembled seemingly every charge that had been leveled at the profession. It was not always internally consistent. Sometimes Rogers conceded modest virtues to polling; at other times he damned the whole enterprise. But his arguments added up to a bracing polemic, mocking the hope of pinning down the public mind as a misguided, grandiose, and vain aspiration.[16]

His complaints centered on the profound difficulties involved in obtaining truly objective information. By now it was well known that the wording of questions, the kinds of answers that respondents were allowed to offer, and the methods of tabulating them were all susceptible to error.[17] But Rogers's critique wasn't just methodological. At a philosophical level, he argued that since the United States was a republic—a representative and not a plebiscitary democracy—elected officials weren't supposed to snap to when the masses called. They were meant to apply their judgment to policy choices. Citing Walter Lippmann, Rogers dismissed the mystical celebration of majority rule. (Lippmann also questioned the value of Gallup's polls.) As if to taunt Gallup, Rogers also quoted the pollster's hero, James Bryce. "The duty therefore of a patriotic statesman in a country where public opinion rules," Bryce wrote, "would seem to be rather to resist and correct than to encourage the dominant sentiment." To counter Gallup's Bryanite faith in the people's voice, Rogers offered a Wilsonian view of leadership that listened to public opinion but also sought to educate it.[18]

As for Gallup's linkage of polling to the pure democracy of a town meeting, Rogers noted important differences. "In the New England town meetings that Dr. Gallup views with nostalgia," he wrote, "there could be argument for and against a proposition *at the same time* in the presence of all who were to vote, and the proposition under debate could be reframed to meet objections that the discussion had brought out." And the town meeting didn't occur in a vacuum. "The questions that were to come before the meeting had been well thrashed out," Rogers noted. "Those who made the decisions acted after knowing how some, whom they regarded as leaders in the community, were going to vote." Polls, by contrast, provided simple choices and no possibility of nuance. While Gallup conceived of polls as a camera that took a snapshot of opinion at a given moment, Rogers argued that public opinion was fluid and changing, no more easily captured than quicksilver.

Rogers believed that polling was doomed to fail because it pretended to quantify the unquantifiable. Public opinion was too inchoate to lend itself to precise measurement, even when fine-tuned with open-ended questions, scales of intensity, and other methodological tweaks. Public opinion wasn't like distance or mass or other scientifically measurable phenomena; it had no freestanding existence apart from the operation of measuring it. Like others in the increasingly data-driven social sciences, Rogers charged, the public opinion analysts were following false gods of methodology. Properly understanding the public required not pseudoscientific methods but human insight.

For all his intellectual range and panache, Rogers eventually faded into relative obscurity, a forgotten prophet. Yet his concerns about polls weren't easily left behind. Politicians continued to rely on them and journalists came to treat opinion surveys as major news. But deep misgivings

Theodore Roosevelt took to the bully pulpit (a term he coined) to mobilize public opinion behind his reform agenda. In so doing, he transformed the American presidency.

In managing the press, TR drew upon the expertise and efficiency of George Cortelyou, one of the unsung behind-the-scenes architects of what has been called the "public presidency."

PIONEERS OF SPIN

Upton Sinclair, author of *The Jungle*, joined forces with Roosevelt to wage a campaign in the press for historic meat-packing regulations. Decades later, he himself was battered by corporate publicity in his failed bid for California governor.

A consultant to Democrats, Ivy Ledbetter Lee made his name as a publicist for John D. Rockefeller—and for publicity itself.

Muckraker George Creel exposed the distortions of Ivy Lee and other corporate publicists. He went on to run the first war-time government propaganda agency under Woodrow Wilson.

During World War I, Creel's committee spread government messages through press releases, movies, posters, and local "Four-Minute Men," who recited brief public speeches in public venues to boost morale.

Naturally introverted, Woodrow Wilson struggled to win the affection of reporters, but he succeeded in implementing his ideas about public opinion leadership and fulfilling TR's vision of an activist presidency.

With the help of Albert Lasker, a pioneering advertising executive from Lord & Thomas, Warren Harding vaulted from obscurity to the White House.

As early as the 1920s, the White House had become the object and obsessive focus of journalists and photographers, forcing even unambitious presidents to pay attention to their public image.

Walter Lippmann, the century's leading political columnist, formulated many of the key questions about public opinion and mass democracy that would occupy intellectuals and politicians for decades to come.

Although historians sometimes talk about a debate between Lippmann and the philosopher John Dewey, both Dewey and Lippmann believed in a "pruned and temperate democracy." Lippmann's real debate was with the curmudgeonly conservative H. L. Mencken, who believed that democracy was a hopeless project in the age of mass media.

Calvin Coolidge shunned the activist presidency of TR and Wilson, but he did experiment with new uses of media, gaining a reputation as perpetually game for the cameras.

The energetic advertising executive Bruce Barton helped craft the image of "Silent Cal." He went on to counsel other presidents—and win a seat in the U.S. Congress himself.

Edward Bernays, Sigmund Freud's nephew, devised soap sculpture contests to sell Ivory soap and "torches of freedom" parades to make cigarettes sexy. Politicians from Coolidge to Adlai Stevenson sought his expertise.

During the Depression, Charlie Michelson became the Democrats' full-time publicist, hectoring President Herbert Hoover daily for his callousness and incompetence. Contrary to legend, though, he did not invent the term "Hooverville"—the name of the run-down encampments for the homeless and hungry that did the president in.

FDR's first pollster was the self-taught Emil Hurja, whose statistical wizardry and red-and-blue election maps inspired confidence among Democratic insiders.

In his "Fireside Chats," Franklin Roosevelt used the power of radio to convey reassurance and hope to a troubled nation. People pasted photographs of FDR over their living-room radios.

The husband-and-wife team of Clem Whitaker and Leone Baxter formed the first full-service political consultancy, running all aspects of a candidate's campaign—including the spin.

Librarian of Congress Archibald MacLeish became "a poet of bitter enemies" for his insistence that writers face up to the threat that fascism posed to the life of the mind. Roosevelt appointed him to run the wartime Office of Facts and Figures.

Nazi propaganda on American shores in the 1930s inspired fear, especially when jackboots and swastikas filled Madison Square Garden.

After dethroning the *Literary Digest* in 1936, George Gallup won a reputation for the accuracy of his so-called scientific polls—except, as in 1948, when he was woefully wrong.

Harry Truman's salt-of-the-earth image was in fact the product of careful preparation, as the president crafted his public statements with the help of press aides, speechwriters, poll crunchers, and even a speaking coach.

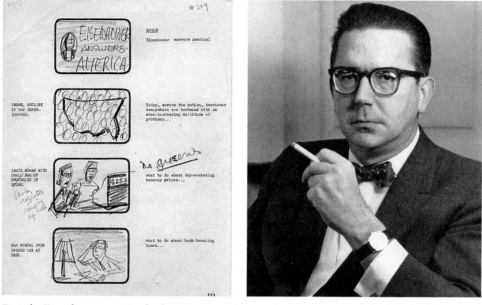

Dwight Eisenhower retained advertising wiz Rosser Reeves, master of the "hard sell," to create the first-ever televised campaign "spots." Though pedestrian by later standards, they caused Democratic nominee Adlai Stevenson to charge that democracy was being degraded.

As president, Ike brought the first full-time television coach, the actor Robert Montgomery, into the White House, and placed almost unbounded trust in his press secretary, James Hagerty. Both aides fussed over his Oval Office addresses.

DECONSTRUCTING SPIN

Vance Packard's best-seller, *The Hidden Persuaders* (1957), exposed the ways advertising played on the unconscious. Its success revealed the era's anxiety about television and high-tech methods of shaping people's opinions.

The veteran reporter Teddy White found fame with his own hit book, *The Making of the President, 1960*, which demystified the drama of the presidential race even as it romanticized the glamorous young John F. Kennedy.

Marshall McLuhan, who won a cult following for his esoteric koans about the new media environment (and for an unforgettable cameo in Woody Allen's *Annie Hall*), was studied by campaign consultants for Richard Nixon and Jimmy Carter.

Few presidents mastered television as effortlessly as John F. Kennedy, who used his live news conferences to defuse crises.

Pierre Salinger was one of many press aides whose relations with reporters often grew contentious, belying the popular myth that journalists gave JFK a free pass.

Lyndon Johnson and his press aide Bill Moyers together devised all manner of political spin. The 1964 "Daisy" campaign ad never mentioned LBJ's rival for the presidency—Barry Goldwater—but simply by evoking nuclear weapons, it revived fears about Goldwater's recklessness.

By the early 1970s, attacks on prefabricated politicians and the consultants who crafted them were ubiquitous. None was more influential than the Robert Redford film *The Candidate*, about a blow-dried cipher who rises to power.

Richard Nixon professed to disdain television, but he leaped to national attention in 1952 with his Checkers speech. Early in his 1968 campaign, he hired the TV genius Roger Ailes, later the founder of the Fox News Channel.

Before Jimmy Carter was a failed president, he was saluted as a media genius. His wunderkind pollster Pat Caddell convinced Carter to wage a permanent campaign, arguing that constant image-making took precedence over the mastery of substantive policy.

Public relations expert Michael Deaver—deemed "the real executive producer of the television network news"—made sure that Ronald Reagan was rarely left to depart from his scripts for long.

Reagan's speeches resonated because they drew from a wellspring of archetypes, cultural memories, and national myths—and were often set against visually arresting backdrops.

Bill Clinton assumed the White House in an age of unending spin. His young aide George Stephanopoulos manned a campaign "war room" (so dubbed by Hillary Clinton) that previewed the kind of "rapid response" to attacks and scandalmongering that would characterize his presidency.

When American troops toppled the Iraqi dictator Saddam Hussein, George W. Bush staged a celebration on board USS *Abraham Lincoln*, declaring: MISSION ACCOMPLISHED. Months later, as the Iraq effort faltered, Bush's once-winning image came to symbolize the administration's hubris.

In 2008, Barack Obama presented himself as the candidate of no spin, a man true to his principles and allergic to Washington cant. But he and his chief adviser, David Axelrod, spun as energetically as any politician, using twenty-first-century innovations like a White House videographer and a Twitter feed.

remained, rooted in Rogers's critiques, about whether Gallup-style surveys truly captured the mind of the electorate. Many Americans learned to read polls with a critical eye. Even Gallup conceded that "the widespread discussion of the polls has created an alert and critical attitude toward them." While people wanted their leaders to know and weigh the majority's opinion when making decisions, they also wanted them to consider other factors as well. Or so said one poll about the polls.[19]

Never again after 1948 would elections be free of stories about which candidate was ahead or behind. But neither would they be free of scoffers rising to point out overstatements and errors in the pronunciamentos of pollsters and pundits. After Truman's victory, Lindsay Rogers's hopes for a political science based on insight rather than method went into eclipse. But so did George Gallup's utopian dream that scientific polling would be the handmaiden to a new and better stage of democratic life.[20]

30

PSYCHOLOGICAL WARFARE

HARRY TRUMAN DESCRIBED the Cold War as "a struggle, above all else, for the minds of men." It would be lost, he told the American Society of Newspaper Editors in 1950, "unless we get the real story across to people in other countries." Although Truman was eager to fold up the beleaguered Office of War Information when World War II ended, he kept alive its international propaganda programs, moving them to the State Department to give them a permanent home. There, Archibald MacLeish was stepping down as assistant secretary for public affairs and cultural relations, and William Benton, co-founder of the Benton & Bowles ad agency, was taking over.[1]

Not everyone wanted to see the international propaganda efforts continue. Walter Lippmann—who had been offered, and rejected, MacLeish's job—believed that government-sponsored news outfits like the Voice of America compromised journalistic independence and democratic ideals. Improving America's image abroad, Lippmann wrote in declining the job, wasn't simply a "kind of advertising which can be farmed out to specialists in the art of managing public opinion." It was "inseparable from leadership," best carried out by statesmen, not flacks.[2]

Lippmann lost the argument. As tensions with the Soviet Union rose and Europe fell into disarray, the administration pressed forward. Truman approved a National Security Council white paper, known as NSC-4, calling for stronger and better-coordinated information programs. Benton pushed Congress to give explicit authorization for the programs, promoting a bill to start new international information activities, from shortwave broadcasts and a news service to artistic exchanges and overseas libraries. At first congressional suspicion of the State Department, especially among conservatives, kept the legislation bottled up. But as communism made inroads in Europe, sentiment coalesced around the need for a well-funded effort to counter Soviet propaganda. "Europe today has become a vast battlefield of ideologies in which words have to large extent replaced armaments as the active elements of attack and defense," stated a congressional report by Senator Alexander Smith of New Jersey and Representative Karl Mundt of South Dakota. The two men sponsored Benton's bill, which became law in January 1948.[3]

The law established the first explicit overseas propaganda campaign during peacetime. Benton, like his predecessors in government information work, professed only to be disseminating factual information, and avoided the word *propaganda*. The term he and other proponents of the new programs now favored was *psychological warfare* or *psy war*—phrases General Dwight Eisenhower and his aides had used to describe the military campaigns to win foreign hearts and minds during the war. With its overtones of hard-nosed action, psychological warfare was also an easier sell to Congress.[4]

Still, Congress, leery of executive branch publicity, barred the government from propagandizing to domestic audiences. Like past prohibitions on propaganda, this ban was unenforceable, owing to the slippery definition of the term and to the blurry line between international and domestic messaging. So long as the government was burning up resources to proclaim communism's evils and America's virtues, domestic audiences were bound to inhale some of the vapors. Indeed, notwithstanding the ban, the administration helped produce a number of TV shows promoting its Cold War policies. From 1949 to 1951, the Defense Department produced *The Armed Forces Hour*, trumpeting the strength of the military services, which aired on NBC and the DuMont network. From 1950 to 1953, State produced *The Marshall Plan in Action*, which touted the plan's success in fortifying European and Asian nations against Communist subversion. The White House also assisted in making NBC's *Battle Report—Washington*, which opened with John Steelman, Truman's chief of staff, introducing "a firsthand account of what the federal government is doing in the worldwide fight against Communism." The hearts and minds being targeted were not only to be found abroad.[5]

* * *

If these TV shows danced up to the line of domestic propaganda, even more problematic were Radio Free Europe and Radio Liberation (later renamed Radio Liberty), purportedly private overseas broadcasters that were actually funded in part by the CIA. The pivotal figure in these operations was Charles Douglas ("C.D.") Jackson, a veteran of Eisenhower's wartime psy-war unit, who took over Radio Free Europe in 1951. Forty-nine years old, Jackson was resolutely unassuming in his appearance, with a soft face, alert eyes, and brown swept-back hair that had long since receded from its original hairline—all but impossible to pick out of a crowd in a midtown Automat.[6]

But Jackson's plain demeanor concealed a cowboy personality and a taste for wild ideas. Labeled a "balloonatic" for his 1951 "Winds of Freedom" plan to send millions of propaganda-bearing balloons into Poland and Czechoslovakia, Jackson was known to preach the virtues of "fanaticism." He spoke derisively of "the hammer and sickle boys"— "fuzzy-headed, self-styled Liberals fascinated by this Russian mystery," as he described them, "totally oblivious of the fact that they will be the first ones stood up against a wall and shot if Communism were ever to take over in this country." Another Jackson plan, floated during the trial of the atomic spies Julius and Ethel Rosenberg, involved "making one more crack" at extracting information from the tight-lipped defendants by getting "some really skillful Jewish psychiatrist . . . to insinuate himself into their confidence."[7]

Jackson was no screwball. Raised in a well-to-do New York household, he had in his youth traveled widely, learned multiple languages, attended Princeton University, and climbed the establishment ladder. Colleagues called him a "renaissance man" and "great idea man." Several years after college, he joined his friend Henry Luce's Time, Inc., which, despite his forays into government service, would long remain his home base.

Jackson became a devotee of psy war. A vocal interventionist before World War II, he logged stints for the State Department and the OWI. As the chief of the Army's Psychological Warfare Division, he impressed Eisenhower with his creativity and energy. (He also impressed Beatrice Eden, wife of British foreign secretary Anthony Eden, with whom he had an affair.) Even when Jackson returned to the Time empire, as publisher of *Fortune*, he stayed close to Ike. The two men became "great friends," in the view of Abbot Washburn, a longtime colleague, and Eisenhower developed "enormous confidence in C. D. Jackson in the field of opinion-molding and propaganda and international actions and reactions."

At Radio Free Europe, Jackson falsely represented these networks as purely private organizations. Doing so, he believed, would heighten their effectiveness. News emanating from the U.S. government had to be completely straight and factual or it would lose credibility. But at Radio Free Europe, he noted, "we can play tricks, we can denounce, we can take chances, we can act fast, all things that an official Government propaganda agency cannot do." That ability rested on a presumed separation from the U.S. government. The CIA's support would remain concealed.[8]

Though Radio Free Europe was meant for overseas audiences, Americans were exposed to its messages. In 1950, the National Committee for a Free Europe, its parent group, undertook what it grandly billed as a "Crusade for Freedom" to fund its operations. Arthur Page led a gargantuan advertising and PR campaign involving theatrical films, TV shows, newspaper ads, parades, radio appeals, subway and bus posters, and a traveling 10-ton "Freedom Bell." The crusade used ballyhoo worthy of George Creel to play up the American commitment to freedom and democracy for the oppressed minions of Eastern Europe—or, as one brochure called them, the "80 million sturdy people living between Germany and Russia . . . still in bondage." Jackson enlisted Eastern European émigrés as researchers and prominent Americans such as Eisenhower and Luce as figureheads. By 1950 the public roundly supported an anti-Soviet foreign policy, so the Crusade for Freedom couldn't be said to have swayed American opinion. But it did reinforce Manichaean interpretations of the conflict and confirmed the importance of freeing Eastern Europeans from Soviet domination. In so doing, it also showed the permeability of any imagined boundaries between domestic and international messages.[9]

*   *   *

By the end of Truman's presidency, many people both inside and outside the administration concluded that its propaganda efforts weren't working well enough. The Soviet acquisition of the atomic bomb, the triumph of the Communists in China's civil war, and the outbreak of the Korean War all fed fears of communism's worldwide ascent. William Benton, now a senator from Connecticut, offered better psy war as the solution. It was, as C. D. Jackson liked to put it, a way "to win World War III without having to fight it." Backed by a diverse swath of Senate colleagues, Benton called for "a Marshall Plan in the field of ideas."[10]

The Truman administration joined the charge in 1950, launching what it called a "Campaign of Truth" that would combine robust advocacy with undistorted information. In his 1950 speech to the American Society of Newspaper Editors, Truman called for a bigger and better program. Senate hearings to consider a larger budgetary appropriation, which took place as the Korean War was escalating, featured testimony from Eisenhower, George Marshall, and John Foster Dulles. The next year Truman established a Psychological Strategy Board, based in the White House, to coordinate the government's psy-war efforts. The administration revamped its messaging, having concluded that its strident anti-Communist rhetoric was alienating the foreign citizens it hoped to court, and adopted a softer tone.

None of these refinements brought noticeable improvement, however, and critics went after Truman. George Gallup, whose scientific pretensions had never fully masked his Republican leanings, began inveighing against the public "ignorance" that he feared could "lead the American people to decisions which they will regret." The problem wasn't a shortage of anti-Communist resolve—which the public amply possessed—but a "lack of appreciation of ideological warfare." Gallup noted, for example, that Americans resented the readiness of a famine-struck India to accept grain donations from Russia—a public relations coup for the Soviets. Understanding the Soviet offer as a ploy in a global battle for hearts and minds, Gallup argued, would encourage Americans to support their own government's efforts to similarly cultivate the loyalties of non-aligned peoples.[11]

As the 1952 election neared, Gallup continued his attacks. He mocked Truman's psy war as "so feeble as to constitute little more than a gesture," comparing it to an army of "a hundred men equipped with squirrel rifles." The Russians, he noted, were propaganda heavyweights, publishing 100 party-line newspapers in Western Europe alone. Facing such a huge enterprise with a rinky-dink force was like having put "a spindly two-year-old child into the ring with the world's champion." Gallup called for the creation of a new cabinet department, a Department of Ideological Warfare. Having once endorsed the unerring good sense of public opinion, he now warned against the delusion that "only the gullible could be fooled by such tactics." When the Senate empaneled a committee to consider the Truman psy-war programs, Gallup appeared as a star witness.[12]

The most important convert to psy war was Dwight Eisenhower, on whom Republicans were pinning their hopes of reclaiming the White House in 1952. In May 1952, C. D. Jackson, Abbott Washburn, and Arthur Page held a conference at Princeton of academic experts and government officials to explore Cold War psychological warfare. Its report declared that "political (psychological) warfare, properly employed, can win World War III for us without recourse to arms," and called for a "more dynamic and positive policy" to gain an edge over the Soviets. Jackson took the report to Ike, who praised it as "extremely interesting" and "of the utmost significance." That fall, after winning the Republican nomination, Eisenhower placed Jackson in his speechwriting shop, where he earned a reputation for what chief speechwriter Emmet John Hughes called his "quickness of mind and patience of temper."

Among the speeches Jackson wrote was a manifesto for psychological warfare, which Eisenhower delivered on October 8 in San Francisco. "Don't be afraid of that term just because it's a five-dollar, five-syllable word," Eisenhower said. "Psychological warfare is the struggle for the minds and wills of men." Taking aim at Truman for neglecting this dimension of Cold War strategy, Ike pledged to make it central to his own.[13]

31

EISENHOWER ANSWERS AMERICA

AS THE HERO OF WORLD WAR II, Eisenhower struck many Republicans as the
perfect presidential candidate for 1952. Having avoided elective politics,
and lacking a divisive record, he seemed uniquely capable of unifying a
fractious GOP. His internationalist foreign policy would please the party's
northeastern wing, while his provincial heartland streak promised to pla-
cate Main Street conservatives—as did his newly sharp rhetoric slamming
the Yalta Accords and the "loss" of China to Mao Zedong's Communist
forces. Polls ranked him as the most popular man alive.[1]

But Ike also had liabilities. Born in 1890 and raised in rural Kansas, he
was a plain man, without charisma or sex appeal. Unpracticed in modern
media, he spoke in notoriously garbled syntax. Moreover, since 1948, TV
had become a presence in American living rooms and a political force.
It was altering presidential politics, making sudden contenders of men
like Tennessee's Estes Kefauver, who had small-screen appeal. L. Richard
("Lou") Guylay, one of Ike's public relations gurus, noted a shift. "In the
days of Charlie Michelson," he said, image management involved "publicity and speechwriting and nothing else," but "with the advent of nationwide network radio and television, new technical skills were required."
Thus far, Ike had shown little proficiency with television.[2]

To kick off his campaign, Ike's handlers scheduled a televised speech at a local ballpark at his childhood home of Abilene, Kansas, on June 4, 1952. Just before start time, the skies burst open in a downpour. Ike plodded through his script, barely able to read through fogged-up glasses. Pallid in a plastic raincoat and gray suit instead of his smart khaki uniform, his wispy hair mussed by a wayward breeze, he looked on TV, wrote the columnist Marquis Childs, "like an old man." Henry Cabot Lodge, the Massachusetts senator who led the campaign to draft Eisenhower, groaned that people on the grandstand were traipsing back and forth "as though nothing important was happening." Robert Montgomery, an actor and Ike supporter, made what he remembered as a "frantic long-distance phone call" to the campaign advising urgent repairs.[3]

Nearly sixty when TV entered American life, Eisenhower seemed unlikely to adapt. When CBS reporter David Schoenbrun told him that his bald head reflected the glare of the television lights and recommended a dab of makeup, Ike growled, "Why don't you just get an actor?" But his media advisers pushed him. Sig Larmon of Young & Rubicam, his friend and confidant, told Eisenhower that "television, plus radio, should be the keystone of your public communications plan. They must not be considered as supplementary media, but as the heart of your program to 'win friends and influence people.'" Ike realized that his aversion to TV was a generational blind spot, not an instinct to trust.[4]

Suggestions also came from Bruce Barton, who urged Ike to emulate Truman and speak from notes, to appear as if he were "talking to people as one frank, unassuming American to his fellow Americans." Following this advice, and similar suggestions from Larmon and his TV advisers, Eisenhower dramatically announced in mid-June that he was jettisoning his speechwriters. "All my prepared remarks are thrown out the window," he declared before a Detroit audience. "If I make blunders, I know my friends will excuse it. I hope the others will realize at least that I'm sincere." Journalists applauded. "We are going through the process of meeting a man of courage and conviction, and we are meeting him without the intermediaries of speech-preparers," wrote the *New York Times*, which endorsed his candidacy. With one bold public relations stunt, Eisenhower thus demonstrated his authenticity.[5]

The speechwriters soon went back to work.[6]

* * *

Eisenhower's greatest political asset had always been his air of decency and statesmanship. Americans of all stripes—including Harry Truman—

beseeched him to seek the presidency. But Eisenhower forswore any interest in elective office, serving instead an uninspired stint as president of Columbia University and then as supreme commander of NATO in Europe.

As Ike temporized about a presidential run, friends conspired to engineer his nomination. In December 1951 Henry Cabot Lodge gathered a band of supporters, including advertising and broadcasting professionals, at New York's Commodore Hotel to develop a television strategy. To create the appearance of a grassroots draft, they kept their activities secret even from BBD&O, their advertising firm, and from their employers (which for some was NBC). Soon Lodge and others were appearing on shows like *Arthur Godfrey's Talent Scouts* and *The Kate Smith Evening Hour*, instructing audiences to mail "I Like Ike" postcards to NATO headquarters in Europe. They also arranged a series of "Draft Eisenhower" TV events, including a Madison Square Garden extravaganza featuring Ethel Merman, Humphrey Bogart, and Lauren Bacall, staged by public relations impresarios Tex McCrary and Jinx Falkenburg. "We especially bought time on a Boston station," recalled McCrary's assistant, William Safire, "because the station's signal reaches New Hampshire," whose March 11 primary Ike had to win. Lodge's team delivered a film of the show to Ike in Europe. Viewing the footage, Eisenhower became teary. "Go back and tell them I'll do it," he said.[7]

Lodge had Ike's name entered in the New Hampshire primary, where the general bested Ohio senator Robert Taft, the conservatives' favorite— the first in a string of victories. By April 1952, whether he admitted it or not, Eisenhower was the front-runner. When he braved the Abilene downpour in June, he was only making official what everyone already knew.

* * *

For the 1952 race, the Republicans signed up an all-star cast of public relations professionals. The Kudner Agency oversaw print advertising. Clem Whitaker and Leone Baxter ran a "Professional Committee for Eisenhower and Nixon," which organized white-collar groups on behalf of the GOP ticket. BBD&O supervised the TV campaign. And Rosser Reeves, an up-and-coming executive at the Ted Bates Agency, was charged with drafting a series of short, punchy television spots—the first in presidential politics.[8]

Dubbed the "high priest of hard-sell," Reeves was a Virginian who had become a Madison Avenue phenom. Known as a playful spirit, he was an enthusiast of recreational flying, yachting, backgammon, and chess, and would later in life insinuate himself in Bobby Fischer's entourage. His contribution to advertising lay in reviving and refining Albert Lasker's hard-sell techniques. Reeves coined the acronym *USP*—an ungainly phrase for an adman—to refer to the "unique selling proposition," the differentiating pitch that he believed should underpin every product's campaign. Subtlety wasn't Reeves's strong suit. One of his ads, for Anacin, showed cartoon hammers pounding at the inside of a man's head. Viewers claimed to find these spots insufferable, but Reeves insisted they worked. The Anacin spot, he boasted, "made more money in seven years than *Gone with the Wind* did for David O. Selznick and MGM in a quarter of a century. . . . Not bad for something written between cocktails at lunch."[9]

Reeves thought political ads needed a unique selling proposition. He disliked long political programs, like Eisenhower's Madison Square Garden spectacular, which bored viewers and even induced hostile feelings by preempting people's favorite shows. In contrast, short spots were cost-effective; they were likelier to be seen by undecided voters; they could be targeted to specific markets; they could hold an audience's interest. They were also memorable: In a test of viewers, Reeves found that while 2 percent of his sample remembered the gist of long speeches they had watched, 91 percent retained the point of his spots.[10]

In 1948, Reeves had tried unsuccessfully to get Tom Dewey to use spots. By 1952, however, Republicans were warming to the idea. The party's publicity director, Robert Humphreys, called spots "a must for stimulating the voters to go to the polls and vote for the candidates." Reeves's assistant Michael Levin wrote a 25-page memo entitled "How to Insure an Eisenhower Victory in November" that put them at the center of what he grandly billed as "a new way of campaigning." Struck by the effectiveness of spots during recent state campaigns, and influenced by Samuel Lubell's voting analysis in *The Future of American Politics*, Levin pinpointed sixty-two counties in twelve states to be blanketed with the ads. At New York's 21 Club, Reeves showed his storyboards to the leaders of Citizens for Eisenhower-Nixon—the successor to the Draft Eisenhower group—and closed the deal.[11]

To fashion a USP, Reeves asked Gallup to identify an issue for the general to run on. Gallup offered three: the petty corruption in the Truman administration; pocketbook issues; and the Korean War. These issues weren't easily merged, but Reeves arrived at the phrase "Eisenhower, Man of Peace," to conjure the image of a war hero entering politics to restore domestic and international tranquility—a non-ideological trope with broad appeal. (Later in the campaign, Eisenhower would reinforce the theme by vowing, at C. D. Jackson's suggestion, to "go to Korea" and end the war—a vague pledge, decried by liberals as emotionally manipulative, that would do at least as much to shore up Ike's victory as Reeves's ads.)[12]

Reeves hunkered down at New York's St. Regis Hotel to write. The ads all followed the same formula. First an announcer would declare: "Eisenhower Answers America." Then an "ordinary citizen," plucked off the street, would ask about one of Gallup's issues. Finally, Eisenhower would offer a brief, self-assured reply. One questioner, for example, began, "General, the Democrats are telling me I've never had it so good," to which Ike replied, "Can that be true when America is billions in debt, when prices have doubled, when taxes break our backs, and we are still fighting in Korea? It's tragic, and it's time for a change." Whatever the answer, Ike's sympathy for the questioners and confidence in tackling the issue was expected to convey compassion and competence.[13]

On September 11, Reeves and two associates showed up at the Transfilm studio on West 43rd Street with a portable typewriter. Eisenhower was still ambivalent. As his speechwriter Emmet John Hughes explained, "His greatest aversion was the calculated rhetorical device. . . . All oratorical flourishes made the man uneasy, as if he feared the chance that some hearer might catch him *trying* to be persuasive." For the spots, Eisenhower agreed to devote only one day to filming. Reeves, who had drafted only twenty-two of roughly fifty planned ads, began frantically banging out scripts, passing them to Milton Eisenhower for vetting. Reeves pushed Ike for more polished presentations as the general sweated under the hot lights. Then Reeves asked Eisenhower to take his glasses off, for aesthetic reasons, but he couldn't read the words and a Ted Bates employee had to print them in big letters on cue cards. Trying to stifle his irritation, Eisenhower blurted out, "To think that an old soldier should come to this." But his groans concealed an underlying complaisance. Reeves claimed that the general wrote one spot himself, which the adman declared "the best of the lot."[14]

In the following days, three women from Reeves's team recruited people off the street near Radio City Music Hall. Reeves wanted to find "real people in their own clothes, with wonderful native accents," to deliver his lines. Approaching pedestrians "who by their appearance and manner impressed us (call it feminine intuition) as likely to be sympathetic toward the Eisenhower cause," the recruiters found seventy-seven volunteers.

Cutting the ads was easy. BBD&O bought the airtime for the spots, in forty states, at a cost of roughly $1.5 million.[15]

* * *

By this point in the fall, the Democrats had chosen their own standard-bearer: Adlai Stevenson, the former governor of Illinois. At fifty-two, Stevenson had served in the State and Navy departments, cleaned up corruption in Illinois, and earned a reputation as a reformer and New Deal liberal. Balding and bug-eyed, with a chicken neck, Stevenson was scarcely more telegenic than Ike. But he had an infectious appeal that stemmed in part from his regal disdain for politics. His manner was professorial, his dress shabby-genteel; once, after a photograph showed a hole in the sole of his shoe, he played up the gaffe as proof of his unpretentiousness. He spoke in well-turned sentences and a clipped, upper-crust accent, and his wit became legendary. "If the Republicans will stop telling lies about us," he promised, "we will stop telling the truth about them." Unlike FDR and Truman, however, Stevenson abhorred the hurly-burly of politics. As the journalist Theodore H. White later wrote, "Public affairs and politics are as linked as love and sex. Stevenson's attitude toward politics . . . seemed that of a man who believes that love is the most ennobling of human emotions while the mechanics of sex are dirty and squalid."[16]

At a Cold War moment when national unity seemed paramount, Stevenson's rhetoric suggested a capacity to bind up the nation, and his probity offered a welcome contrast to the nakedly political Truman administration. Yet Stevenson's style had its limits. FDR had crammed into the Democratic tent workers and professionals, blacks and southerners, Jews and Catholics, the poor and the working class. Stevenson never reached so many constituencies, partly because he resisted gestures designed to do so—believing, according to the historian Arthur Schlesinger, Jr., one of his speechwriters, that "the kinds of things he was asked to do were false."

Stevenson's strongest supporters were upscale liberals—dubbed "egg-heads" by columnist Stewart Alsop—who thrilled to his finely crafted phrases. Although Stevenson stood to Truman's right on many issues—his record, judged the *New York Times*, was "that of a moderate reformer, a person of social conscience who is basically conservative in outlook"—he struck the high-minded liberals as one of their own. "Here was this remarkable man from Illinois," the critic Irving Howe wrote, "so charming and cultivated, so witty and so . . . well, *somewhat* weary . . . come to represent and speak for them." Sharing the Wilsonian belief that he could persuade the public with sensible arguments, Stevenson attracted voters with his idealized picture of America as a place of reason and virtue.[17]

Stevenson was even less inclined than Eisenhower to embrace mass media politics. At a time when politicians were celebrating admen for their imputed genius, Stevenson held fast to the view that advertising was a menace to a rational society. "The idea that you can merchandise candidates for high office like breakfast cereal," he said, "is the ultimate indignity to the democratic process."[18]

This outlook didn't keep Stevenson from seeking help from Edward Bernays. By August 1952, Bernays was dispensing public relations advice to Porter McKeever of the Stevenson team, apparently free of charge. In a 16-page "Master Plan"—a seemingly halfhearted document much inferior to Michael Levin's—Bernays laid out methods by which Volunteers for Stevenson, the counterpart to Citizens for Eisenhower-Nixon, might spread the candidate's gospel. The suggestions were mundane and commonsensical—for example, that educators be reminded of Stevenson's positions on education, unions of his stand on labor conditions. The tactics came from Bernays's standard playbook: recruit support from independents and Republicans; target voters according to their racial, ethnic, or professional affiliations; find trusted group leaders to vouch for Stevenson. The section headed "Research" included such bold ideas as consulting the *World Almanac* "and other similar books." The document made fleeting mention of TV and radio.[19]

Then again, if Bernays had focused on television, Stevenson probably wouldn't have listened. Although the campaign hired Leonard Reinsch, Lou Cowan, and other TV experts, the candidate largely ignored them. His hostility to TV was "pathological," said producer Charles Guggenheim, who made ads for Democrats. Stevenson didn't even own a TV set. (Eisenhower did, and would watch an RCA 21-inch color set in the White House.) This rejection of television extended into the 1956 campaign as well, when Stevenson again faced off against Ike. When aides booked Stevenson that year as the "mystery guest" on the game show *What's My Line?*, the candidate canceled on the day of the program. Nothing summed up his view of his media advisers better than the time during the 1956 convention when his hotel room TV went on the blink and he called in Bill Wilson, his television adviser, to fix it—he was, after all, the TV guy.[20]

Stevenson's resistance to the new rules of the game revealed an admirable and rare set of qualities: a faith that the electorate could handle sophisticated arguments, a contempt for the inanity of popular culture, a desire to preserve a distinction between commercial advertising and political persuasion. He believed in his slogan of "talking sense to the American people." But he also allowed these sentiments to trump political good sense. He failed to see the wisdom of making the most of the available methods.

* * *

At first, the Republicans' plan to air TV commercials drew little comment. But when a Democratic National Committee official obtained copies of the Republicans' scripts and memos, they struck Stevensonians and his aides as political gold—proof of the Republicans' deviousness. Lou Cowan argued for countering with a commensurate ad buy, which would supplement the TV time the Democrats had purchased to air some of Stevenson's speeches. But the campaign lacked the funds, and the candidate lacked the inclination. Though the campaign eventually cut some spots, it spent hardly any money on them—"a feeble effort to compete on their own ground," recalled George Ball, the campaign director for Volunteers for Stevenson. The ads, moreover, were stupendously banal. One featured an attractive blonde singing a jingle ("I'd rather have a man with a hole in his shoe / Than a hole in everything he says"). Another played "Old McDonald" while raising fears of farm foreclosures under a Republican administration.[21]

Stevenson's strategy was to cry foul. At an October 1 press conference, George Ball hyperbolically blasted Eisenhower for enlisting the "high-powered hucksters of Madison Avenue" to "sell an inadequate ticket to the American people in precisely the way they sell soap, ammoniated toothpaste, hair tonic, or bubble gum." Ball spun out the metaphor at excruciating length. "From morning to night, during interludes normally throbbing with the merits of some new Follicle shampoo, or some new, improved detergent that takes the drudgery out of your laundromat, the air waves and the TV screens will be filled by the omnipresent General Eisenhower every hour on the hour," he said. As for Stevenson's ads, Ball said that while his candidate refused to engage in crass commercialism, he would find it necessary to "counter sham with truth." Other Democrats also tried to make an issue of Ike's spots. Senator Edwin Johnson, a Colorado Democrat, warned of a bid "to monopolize the airwaves for GOP propaganda during the closing days of the 1952 campaign" that would "conflict with the spirit if not the letter of the law," and the campaign filed a complaint with the Federal Communications Commission. These efforts went nowhere.[22]

Eisenhower's blitz ran as scheduled. It commenced on Tuesday, October 21, "with a thunderous roar," as Reeves's aide Al Taranton boasted. The GOP saturated the airwaves in eleven big states; overall, thirty-one spots ran in forty states. Stevenson, high-minded to the last, refused to watch them.[23]

The Democrats spent 95 percent of their television budget on half-hour slots to broadcast speeches. These talks highlighted Stevenson's rhetorical skills, and he actually fared better among voters who watched TV than among those who didn't (probably because his appeal was strongest among upscale voters). Still, Stevenson's programs, which aired at a discounted 10:30 pm time slot on Tuesday and Thursday nights, drew few viewers. Even a decision to buy time one evening on all three networks backfired. "You either had to watch Adlai Stevenson or turn off your set that night," said Lou Guylay, "and this created a tremendous amount of unhappiness."[24]

Stylistically, too, Stevenson bombed. He shunned the teleprompter, on which, his aide Willard Wirtz said, he thought "the devil him- or herself had a personal copyright." And he agonized over the writing of his speeches; Ball told Stevenson he "would rather write than be president." Last-minute scribbles made it hard for Stevenson to read his own words, and all the revising ate into rehearsal time. On the air, he would speak too slowly, then race to finish, only to overrun his allotted time, leading the networks to fade out before the end. The campaign tried to make his unpolished style into a mark of his authenticity, like his battered shoes, but few bought it. As Jack Gould wrote mournfully, "There was an aloofness, one might say almost a loneliness, that came between him and the viewer."[25]

Ike's ads proved historic, not because they helped him win—he surely would have prevailed without them—but because they furnished presidential candidates for generations with what could indeed be called "a new way of campaigning." They mattered, too, because of the reaction they provoked—a revival of the old fears of a malleable public succumbing to sophisticated techniques of manipulation.[26]

The nub of these fears was hard to grasp. A common complaint was that the Republicans' coffers allowed them to buy more ads than the Democrats could, but the GOP advantage in wealth didn't explain the insidious power imputed to the spots. Another criticism centered on the ads' commercialism, but both parties had used advertising for eons. The claim that the spots oversimplified issues came closer to the mark, but, again, campaigns had always thrived on slogans, jingles, and snappy rhetoric, as Reeves noted. "Politicians from time immemorial have been using spots, whether they know it or not," he told a correspondent. "Winston Churchill's 'Blood, sweat, and tears' statement was such a condensation."[27]

The new ingredient in the mix was television, which was fast becoming a repository for anxieties about the technological future. Once, the radio success of Father Coughlin and Huey Long had bred nightmares of demagoguery. Now TV seemed "the thought controller's dream," as *The American Mercury* wrote. "A nation of TV gazers is set up for a new-style demagogue who has mastered television's unique art of folksy, sincerity-loaded talk." Hollywood would capture these dark visions with films like Budd Schulberg's *A Face in the Crowd*, in which a skilled television manipulator, oozing contempt for the public, propels himself to the brink of the presidency. Eisenhower's commercials evoked fears like these because they employed the slick techniques of professionals and reached into every living room. They augured a future of fabricated candidates, constructed to win elections, popular because of the images they projected. Coming at a moment in the Cold War when the culture seemed smothered by conformity and when questions of individual identity seemed up for grabs, the prospect of a soulless, manufactured leader cut to the core of what American democracy was supposed to be.[28]

32

SALESMANSHIP AND SECRECY

ON SEPTEMBER 23, 1952, at NBC's El Capitan Theatre in Los Angeles, one block from Hollywood and Vine, the television guru Ted Rogers was choreographing a squad of cameramen, control-room operators, lighting men, and technicians in an all-day rehearsal of an important speech. The set was dressed up to resemble a middle-class suburban den. Draperies and a bookcase barely disguised the soundstage. Only the speaker was absent: twenty minutes away at the Ambassador Hotel with his legal pads, tinkering with his draft, was California's junior senator and Eisenhower's running mate, thirty-nine-year-old Richard M. Nixon. As a stand-in, Rogers hired a salesman of Nixon's height and coloring to go through the paces in preparation for a speech that would reach the largest audience that any politician had ever enjoyed.

Days earlier, Nixon had convinced Eisenhower to let him deliver the talk in hopes of snuffing out a financial scandal. The *New York Post* had exposed a private bank account containing $18,000, which Nixon used to pay for travel between Washington and California and other costs not covered by his Senate expense account—a technically legal arrangement that nonetheless smacked of favor trading. Controversy engulfed the campaign. Leading Republicans, including some of Eisenhower's aides, wanted Nixon off the ticket.[1]

For six years, Nixon had been a rising star. Hailing from conservative Southern California, he had won election to Congress in 1946 as part of a GOP sweep, in a campaign that played on resentment of big government and the promise of free enterprise. Distinguishing himself by his hard work, Nixon put his name to key legislation, and as a member of the House Un-American Activities Committee helped expose former State Department official Alger Hiss as a Soviet spy. His 1950 Senate campaign against Congresswoman Helen Gahagan Douglas, in which Nixon insinuated that the former actress was a Communist shill—"pink right down to her underwear"—marked a nadir of dirty campaigning and earned him lasting enmity from liberals. Yet in 1952 Nixon—popular with the McCarthyite right wing of the GOP, but also admired by eastern establishment types like Dewey—seemed the perfect vice-presidential choice. Eisenhower, getting on in years, needed a youthful companion and an attack dog who could manhandle the Democrats while letting the general play the statesman.

Still, "Tricky Dick," as he was known after the 1950 campaign, had lots of enemies, who found him viscerally offputting. "He had," said Speaker of the House Sam Rayburn, "the meanest face I've ever seen." His coarse black hair and ineradicable five-o'clock shadow enshrouded him in a cloak of gloom. His hyperbolic charges and imputations of bad faith—a cavalier disregard for the norms of political behavior—cast him as liberals' most despised political villain. "All the time I've been in politics," said Harry Truman, "there's only two people I hate, and he's one." The fund's exposure gave the Nixon haters hope that their nemesis might get his comeuppance.[2]

When Nixon arrived at the El Capitan, he practiced posing in a variety of stances before taking his seat behind the desk. Donning an earnest demeanor, he looked into the camera as the red light blinked on. He opened by explaining the fund's relatively innocuous purpose and noting (as had been reported the day before) that Adlai Stevenson kept a similar account—a tidbit that kept the Democrat from making more of the issue. Nixon went on to paint himself as a quintessential American Everyman. Drizzling his self-portrait with syrupy touches, Nixon spoke melodramatically about his trying childhood and the struggles he and his wife faced, "like so many of the young couples who may be listening to us." In a jab at the Truman scandals in which officials took furs as bribes, Nixon added: "I should say this, that Pat doesn't have a mink coat. But she does have a respectable Republican cloth coat. And I always tell her that she'd look good in anything." As a crowning touch, he invoked a gift to his daughters, "a little cocker spaniel dog . . . black-and-white spotted. And our little girl, Tricia, the six-year-old, named it Checkers. And the kids love the dog and . . . regardless of what they say about it, we're gonna keep it." Nixon ended by enjoining his audience to telegram the Republican National Committee to say whether he should stay on the ticket.

Most people wanted Nixon to stay. "The telephone switchboard is lit up like a Christmas tree," crowed Rogers. Millions of letters and telegrams poured in, heavily pro-Nixon, praising him for baring his soul and his finances. "We were overwhelmed by the sincerity of your speech last night," wrote Jeanne Wells of Artesia, California, who mailed her letter because of hour-long queues at the telegraph offices. "Your honesty and sincerity are unquestionable," wrote the animator Bill Hanna of Metro-Goldwyn-Mayer Productions, on Tom-and-Jerry stationery. "Count my Democratic vote for 'Ike and Dick.'"[3]

The key judgment, of course, would be Eisenhower's. Bruce Barton had urged that Ike's reaction be "expertly stage managed." "He and Mrs. Eisenhower—no advisers, no managers, just the two of them"—should be shown watching the speech alone. But Ike chose to view the address with a group of advisers, who gathered in a manager's office at the Cleveland auditorium where the general was to speak. The general's reaction echoed the general reaction. "Your presentation was magnificent!" Ike wired Nixon, before telling the Ohio crowd that he would rather have "one courageous, honest man" at his flank than "a whole boxcar full of pussyfooters."[4]

The notion that Americans might see Nixon as an authentic tribune of the middle class confounded and enraged Stevenson supporters. "On the level of political soap opera, there can be no question of the effectiveness of the Nixon performance," wrote Max Lerner, now a columnist for the *New York Post*. "The pretty and adoring wife, the mortgages on the houses, the saga of a poor boy who became senator—these were sure-fire stuff." Lerner insisted that he expected voters would be able to "strip away the phony from the real," but when it became clear that most people did not think Nixon a phony, liberals blamed the high-tech staging, the power of television, and, as the *New York Times* wrote, "the genius of American advertising agencies." Lerner, who had once tried to put the intelligentsia's fear of propaganda in sober perspective, now fell prey to similar fears. "Ask yourself whether you are fool enough to fall for one of the slickest and sleaziest fake emotion routines that ever gulled a sentimental people," he challenged his readers. "The lesson of the Nixon case now is how a cynical group of men, using money and the new communication arts and the tried and true techniques of the propaganda masters, can stand an issue of morality on its head and make the faker appear the martyr."[5]

As primitive as the set of the Checkers speech was, as amateurish as the camerawork appeared, Lerner wasn't alone in deeming it all to be dangerously deceptive. Walter Lippmann, an Eisenhower supporter, called the speech a "disturbing experience" that was, "with all the magnification of modern electronics, simply mob law." Memories of the German populace rallying to Nazism remained vivid; with Joe McCarthy riding high, the public's responsiveness to right-wing demagoguery was palpable. Nixon, many feared, was a television-age successor to Long and Coughlin.[6]

The notion that the masses were being fooled carried uncomfortable implications. Stewart and Joe Alsop, who wrote a syndicated column together, reported that some of their readers claimed to see past the speech's melodrama even as they believed "the common people" couldn't. Likewise, the *New York Post* editorialized, "On many occasions during the last few days we have heard the same remark from a lot of journalists, scholars, and gentlemen: 'I know the Nixon speech was strictly soap opera, but you can't expect the ordinary guy to see through it.'" Wishfully, however, the *Post*'s editors affirmed that "most of the people know the difference between a slick press agent's mind and a responsive human heart."[7]

History remembered Nixon's performance as the "Checkers speech," the name mocking Nixon's maudlin touches and strained performance. But if liberals were justified in distrusting Nixon's resort to public relations, their reaction to the speech, like Stevenson's response to Eisenhower's ads, showed the enduring power of the old fears of propaganda. Instead of grappling with the appeal of Eisenhower and Nixon's message, liberals found solace in ascribing the defection of Democratic voters to the insidious powers of broadcasting and Madison Avenue and the deceptions of its most odious practitioners.

* * *

Stevenson had wryly warned that Ike's election would mean the eclipse of the New Dealers by the Car Dealers, and, as predicted, the businessmen with whom Eisenhower stocked his cabinet showed a distinct comfort with the ethos of salesmanship. "Politics these days is like a business," explained Republican National Committee chairman Len Hall. "First you set up a real business shop. . . . Then you sell your candidates and your programs the way a business sells its products." Governing, as much as campaigning, was now suffused with the language and techniques of marketing.[8]

"We all suddenly realized we were busy manufacturing a product down here, but nobody was selling it," an administration aide told the *Wall Street Journal* a few months into Ike's presidency. So the White House created an office to do just that. Heading it was a Seattle mortgage banker named Walter Williams, dubbed by Ike "the greatest salesman in the world." Williams had led Citizens for Eisenhower and served briefly in the Commerce Department. Though it would take two decades before Nixon, as president, created the White House Office of Communications, Williams's shop was a prototype and precedent. When administration officials went on TV or radio, his small staff would furnish talking points—simply "the facts," administration sources insisted—so that they wouldn't "get tied in knots" on the air. The new unit also aggressively promoted Eisenhower's accomplishments to reporters: its aid to drought-stricken farmers, its improvement of public housing, its "hard money" economic policies.[9]

Besides Williams, Eisenhower also employed a who's who of experts who would, Lou Guylay said, "rely on scientific methods [rather] than on instinct alone" in selling his policies. Ike's younger brother, Milton, who had schooled the general in his Army days on wooing reporters, remained a trusted adviser. Sig Larmon of Young & Rubicam declined the president's requests to join the White House staff but served on ad hoc committees and offered regular counsel. Arthur Page, who had helped spin Hiroshima, joined "Operation Solarium," Ike's project to draft a defense strategy. Edward Bernays was brought in to help when Joe McCarthy attacked the new United States Information Agency. Bruce Barton, though rebuffed in his modest offer to reorganize "the whole public relations and propaganda machinery of government," built a relationship with Nixon through private Manhattan dinner briefings. BBD&O furnished a poll-hungry Eisenhower with weekly survey research, while Gallup and other pollsters also shared data. The heavy reliance on public relations men was noted with dismay by the press. "There's too much BBD&O," groused *New York Times* correspondent Bill Lawrence.[10]

Of all Ike's information managers, the most visible was his press secretary, James C. Hagerty, forty-two, formerly a newspaperman and aide to Tom Dewey. The son of a *New York Times* reporter, who never forgot his boyhood meeting with Teddy Roosevelt at Sagamore Hill, Hagerty grew up steeped in politics and adopted a *Front Page* demeanor. "A long and slightly drooping upper lip gave him a passing resemblance to Humphrey

Bogart," reporter James Deakin recalled; "his accent was *Sidewalks of New York*." A hard drinker, Hagerty was also a hard worker who reportedly declined to tell Eisenhower about his son's upcoming wedding because, he said, "I knew he'd make me go." For eight years, Hagerty manned the front lines of Ike's press relations, serving as the government's face and chief information provider. This held true even during crises, such as when news broke that the Soviet Union had launched its Sputnik satellite and Eisenhower had already decamped to his Gettysburg farm. When Ike had a heart attack in 1955, he instructed his physician, "Tell Jim to take over."[11]

Hagerty briefed the press twice a day, and, judging by the volume of phone calls he received—perhaps 500 daily—his workload outstripped that of his predecessors. Through his pale green office passed an unending stream of columnists, newsreel men, visiting editors, and other journalists, from whom he might be summoned away at any moment by a buzzer under his desk when the president called. Hagerty coordinated publicity with the departments and agencies and briefed cabinet members who were going before the press. Above all, he managed the president's roughly biweekly press conferences in the Indian Treaty Room. Though diminished in frequency since FDR's day, to reporters' irritation, these sessions were still the president's main forum for interacting with the newsmen.[12]

Hagerty followed Truman-era practices, spending considerable time in the days before a press conference anticipating questions, drafting answers, and reviewing them with the president. His chief modification—the introduction of television cameras—wouldn't come until 1954, but even before that he made small changes that gave the sessions extra formality. For one thing, Eisenhower often opened with his own scripted policy statements, which tightened his control over the sessions. They set the agenda for the questioning that followed, and, owing to the president's meandering speech, they chewed up the reporters' question time. The conferences evolved into a showcase for the president rather than a true opportunity to probe his thinking. Hagerty also planted questions (which other press secretaries had done as well) to make Ike's disclosures seem spontaneous. Most important, Hagerty put the press conferences on the record. Though the gesture was meant to foster greater openness, the effect was to make everyone—especially the president—more circumspect. The old, intimate give-and-take thus continued to devolve into a formal public ritual.[13]

Although Hagerty got on well with the correspondents, who liked his wiseguy persona, and although his practices weren't much different from those of Steve Early or Charlie Ross, reporters came to resent his practice of withholding, slanting, and inflecting the news. Hyperbolically, they charged Hagerty with harming democracy through his treatment of them. "The discourse between government and the people by means of the news communications system," the reporter Joseph Kraft hyperventilated, "has been grievously impaired."[14]

One reason the press reporters felt constantly managed was the administration's remorseless salesmanship. As the executive branch under Eisenhower inexorably grew, so did the channels for executive publicity, and there were no obvious boundaries between the government's legitimate provision of information and its promotion of propagandistic fare. As congressional Republicans a decade earlier had investigated charges that the New Deal information bureaus were serving up partisan propaganda, Eisenhower's publicity officers raised alarms on the left. Laments of the sort that Stevenson had voiced in 1952 continued throughout Ike's presidency, as journalists stitched together Reeves's spots, Nixon's "Checkers speech," Whitaker and Baxter's consulting gospel, and Walter Williams's new White House office into an ominous portrait of an administration full of hucksters and manipulators.

But the growth of government publicity wasn't the sole reason—or even the main reason—for the press's unhappiness. The new discontent owed at least as much to the administration's fetish for secrecy, which was itself a bequest not of Eisenhower's businessman friends but of his response to the gusty winds of the Cold War.

* * *

The Cold War intensified the government's resolve to control the flow of information. In the Truman years, the president and senior government officials had urged the media to voluntarily refrain from publishing information that might compromise national security. Eisenhower did the same. He believed that the dire global challenges he faced—the Korean War, the hydrogen bomb, the question of whether foreign nations would choose communism or democracy—demanded a level of secrecy that otherwise obtained only in wartime. This urgency led him and Hagerty to shut journalists out of the usual channels of information. Reporters learned little about America's atomic program, less still about the foreign coups that the CIA aided or fomented. Often these episodes were concealed by bogus cover stories.

Ike's secrecy took many forms. He expanded the doctrine of executive privilege to justify withholding information from Congress and the public. Like most of his predecessors (and successors), he fumed over leaks; on occasion, he used the FBI to investigate how sensitive information had appeared in the press. Most infamously, he deliberately misled the press when a CIA pilot on a covert reconnaissance mission, Frances Gary Powers, was shot down over the Soviet Union in 1960. Ike said that the U-2 was a weather plane. Only after Moscow produced the pilot did he own up to the deception, which he later regretted. Asked in 1962 about his greatest error as president, he said: "The lie we told about the U-2."[15]

The management of information colored domestic life as well, in more subtle ways. As described by social critics such as David Riesman and William S. Whyte, society in the Eisenhower years came to be dominated by large, hierarchical institutions that encouraged a deference to authority. Ike's rhetoric reflected the corporate ethos. Unlike FDR's chattiness or Truman's earthiness, Eisenhower's bureaucratic verbiage—far from being a clever ruse designed to throw reporters off his trail—revealed an impersonal, institutional habit of mind. Like his standoffish policies toward reporters, his corporate diction reflected his faith in his administration's managers while relegating the press and the public to a spectatorial role. His personal remoteness diminished their sense of belonging to a common project.[16]

It was in this context—expanded and professionalized salesmanship, Cold War secrecy, technocratic management—that reporters concluded that Eisenhower, Hagerty, and the administration were "managing the news," as James Reston put it in testimony before Congress. Reston's phrase became the reigning Cold War synonym for publicity. Created at a time when global exigencies afforded government officials an uncommon degree of deference from the press corps, *news management* suggested something more ominous than the mere media exposure gained by Wilson's speeches to Congress, more stealthy than the image craft refined by Coolidge's publicity men, more purposeful than the massaging of public opinion by FDR. It implied an insidious restriction of the flow of news more appropriate to wartime than to what was nominally peace. It wasn't, in the end, any personal villainy on Hagerty's part that gave the news under Eisenhower its managed flavor. It was the Cold War itself.[17]

33

THE TV PRESIDENT

DWIGHT EISENHOWER WASN'T known for crazy ideas, but his administration was responsible for one of the loopier experiments in the annals of presidential spin. Urged to make himself into what Henry Cabot Lodge called "the 'T.V.' President"—a leader who visited American living rooms regularly, winning the public's trust, regard, and affection—Ike decided to have network cameras broadcast his cabinet meetings. Like FDR, who had conjured intimacy by seeming to speak to each of his radio listeners individually, Ike would win people's trust by using what the TV people called the "keyhole technique"—letting viewers peer in on supposedly high-level deliberations. In the spring of 1953, a BBD&O staffer came to Washington to stage a televised session between Ike and his cabinet secretaries, ensconced in comfortable leather chairs, as they plodded through an agenda of topical issues. Working off a 44-page BBD&O script, produced by Bill Wood of CBS, the program was a dud, as the stilted dialogue failed to impress. Viewers felt not like flies on the wall of an insiders' meeting but witnesses to what the *New York Times* called "the newest television panel show with a homey, chatty approach." Undermining the effect further was the spate of news stories that detailed the artifice involved, replete with accounts of technicians and admen who "scurried through the lobby in a bustle of preparations," as the *New York Post* wrote, noting the "cue cards

... set up out of camera range." A second effort the next year, in which the cabinet secretaries tried to affect greater informality, also fizzled.[1]

The use of TV for public appeals was part of a plan. At the start of Ike's first term, C. D. Jackson called the move into presidential television "a must." Hagerty saw it as a way to circumvent the newspapermen. "To hell with slanted reporters," he wrote in his diary, "we'll go directly to the people who can hear exactly what Pres said without reading warped and slanted stories." Eisenhower's gut at first told him no. "I can think of nothing more boring for the American public than to have to sit in their living rooms for a whole half hour and look at my face on their television screens," he said. But he again trusted the experts. So it had been during the campaign; so it would be for the next eight years.[2]

The world of TV was uncharted terrain, and White House aides groped about in trying to exploit the medium. One superficially appealing idea was to have Eisenhower give televised "Fireside Chats," and several of his broadcasts were so labeled. But Ike failed to recapture FDR's magic using that fabled phrase, though he would not be the last president to try.[3]

But if the televised Fireside Chats and cabinet meetings flopped, some administration officials did develop a facility with the medium. Hagerty pushed senior aides to learn the official talking points and use the popular Sunday-morning panel shows—*Meet the Press*, *Face the Nation*, and others, newly transplanted from radio—to garner Monday-morning headlines. Secretary of State John Foster Dulles was especially skilled at getting his speeches aired, whether he was addressing the United Nations or a 4-H Club. When Dulles traveled, as he often did, he toted around a collapsible lectern to hold forth from any tarmac. What he achieved in quantity, though, he squandered in quality, coming across as colorless and drab. ("Dull, duller, Dulles," ran a popular quip.) Eisenhower himself, though hardly a scintillating presence, complained to his friend William Robinson, publisher of the *Herald Tribune*, about Dulles's dreary small-screen appearances. Still, the president indulged Dulles's preening, even joining his secretary on occasion in a televised sit-down after Dulles's trips, as if to leave the impression that the secretary were being debriefed in real time for all to see. These sessions, too, yielded mixed results. An appearance in 1955 in which Dulles spoke to Ike and a handful of other officials—notable mainly as the first time viewers saw the inside of the Oval Office—was judged by *The New Republic* "in technical terms . . . a brilliant half hour" that gave Eisenhower a "place near Franklin Roosevelt as an innovator in the art of political communication." But in a program featuring just

Eisenhower and Dulles, the secretary of state prattled on for twenty minutes about a recent NATO meeting, which the cameras framed in a two-
shot. In full view of the TV audience, Ike, who had heard it all before, sat
passively, playing with his eyeglasses, tugging on his suit, and scanning
the room as if uninterested in following his secretary's blather. When Ike
spoke, Dulles was caught looking at his watch.[4]

Most successful were the presidential press conferences. Under
Truman, reporters had begun quoting the president directly, and under
Ike, Hagerty had already brought in a stenographer, released transcripts,
and in one instance authorized the radio broadcast of a White House–
made recording. The television networks, which were gaining viewers and
power, pushed to be included. Hagerty at first blanched, arguing that the
room would have to be lit up "like a Hollywood premiere," destroying
what little was left of the atmosphere. But with the development of faster
film, he reconsidered. In 1954, he readied for the shift, staging a mock
press conference at which he played the part of the president. He screened
the results with chief of staff Sherman Adams and Ike in the White House
basement. They concluded the risk was worth taking.[5]

On January 19, 1955, Eisenhower held the first filmed presidential press
conference. With six lights beaming down on the president and Leroy
Anderson of NBC manning a single camera, 218 reporters—many wearing
"television blue" shirts that were supposed to show up well on black-and-
white screens—shuffled into the Indian Treaty Room, some consigned to
the balcony. Amid the splendor of marble and gold leaf, utilitarian gray
folding chairs were incongruously set in close ranks as Eisenhower stood
behind bulbous microphones resting on a serviceable businessman's desk.
"We are trying a new experiment," he announced, proceeding to speak
and field questions for a half hour. Before the footage aired, Hagerty, ever
the news manager, oversaw its editing—a condition he had imposed on the
broadcasts. All four networks showed it that night.[6]

The decision to televise the parleys provoked endless commentary,
much of it focused on the implications for democracy. Jack Gould of the
New York Times, who had been touting the idea for years, rhapsodized
that the televised conferences could be pumped into schoolhouses to
awaken a civic spirit in children. He declared the experiment "an example
of democracy at work." While acknowledging the president's abundant
preparations, Gould nonetheless marveled, "The press conference proved,
if further proof were needed, that in television no staged program can
compare with actuality itself."[7]

Others feared that yoking television to presidential power would diminish the public's role in political life. One worry was that turning the once-cozy gathering into a spectacle—with the president now standing behind a podium instead of his desk, with lights, cameras, and a keen awareness of the audience—would further discourage both the reporters and the president from offering candid remarks. Another was that television would augment the White House's power to set the agenda and frame the news at the expense of Congress, the opposition party, the press, or the public. Print journalists agonized about power shifting to the broadcasters, whom they considered not kindred members of the Fourth Estate but slick professionals, part of a new image culture. "The newcomers are smart, able, alert, more self-possessed in televised questioning than newsmen and generally better paid, but their job is largely pictorial and representational," wrote T.R.B. of *The New Republic*. "They want a nice color story or a good photographic image; radio and TV men do not dig out contradictions from politicians; they rarely crusade." Most troublesome of all was the unholy alliance between the networks and the White House— a collaboration underscored by Hagerty's unilateral editing of the press conferences. "Censorship from the White House," said James Wechsler of the *New York Post*, was being "supinely accepted"—news management in its rawest form. As the novelty and thrill faded, though, so did the complaints. Most networks stopped airing the press conferences with much regularity. Instead, the networks themselves began choosing excerpts to broadcast on the evening news, reclaiming a measure of control.[8]

Although Eisenhower voiced the common presidential complaint that the press emphasized the trivial and downplayed the significant, overall he considered the "information reaching the public from my press conferences" to be "accurate and well 'played.'" White House aides also claimed that newspapermen now strove harder for accuracy because the cameras were rolling. Hagerty, confiding in his diary, saw a simpler result: The televised conferences, he said, were a "very potent way of getting the President's personality and viewpoints across . . . almost the same thing as the start of Roosevelt's Fireside Chats."[9]

* * *

As television assumed a central place in presidential communications, it placed a new premium on the president's physical appearance, even more than photography had. Eisenhower turned to a new guru. The fiftyish actor-producer Robert Montgomery became, wrote Jack Gould, "the first man in professional show business to have a permanent office in the White House." Youthful-looking, dark-haired, and always turned out in the latest style—he bummed cigarettes because carrying his own packs ruined the cut of his suits—Montgomery, though once nominated for an Oscar, was something of a journeyman. He had a long-standing taste for politics, acting in Norman Corwin's radio plays for the Office of Facts and Figures during World War II, serving as president of the Screen Actors Guild, and hosting his own radio show, *A Citizen Views the News*, on which he denounced the Communist infiltration of labor unions. Enchanted by the promise of television, Montgomery—like another actor then reaching the limits of his box office potential, Ronald Reagan—became the host of a weekly program, *Robert Montgomery Presents*, which ran from 1950 to 1957 and extended the actor's career. (It also featured the debut of the host's bewitching daughter Elizabeth.)[10]

Montgomery advised and actively supported Eisenhower in 1952, speaking to Republican Party dinner audiences about the need to counter the Democrats' "beguiling propaganda of something-for-nothing." At some point during the next year, Hagerty noted, "we suddenly realized that nobody on the press staff knew much about telecasting," and in December 1953, the White House public relations team invited Montgomery in for a visit. A breakfast meeting with the president followed, and soon Montgomery was working as an unpaid producer and coach. (His Hollywood income rendered a paycheck unnecessary.) Montgomery worked closely with Ike on a variety of on-air formats. These ranged from the Christmas Eve "Fireside Chat" of 1953 to Ike's 1956 convention speech to the State of the Union addresses to Congress, which had already evolved into an elaborately planned, cast-of-thousands production involving speechwriters, policy wonks, and assorted communication experts.[11]

Over time, Montgomery tweaked Ike's new look down to the last detail: clothing, cosmetics, gestures, stance, lighting, camera angles, delivery. Fussing over Ike's wardrobe, he traded dark gray suits for light ones and striped shirts for blues; banishing Eisenhower's black horn-rimmed glasses, he instructed the president to either read his cue cards without them, or use Lucite replacements. Softer lights and liberally applied makeup eliminated what one critic called "that washed-out look," and a three-inch base under the president's lectern kept him from bending his neck while reading—a gesture that had shown too much of his always problematic pate. Montgomery pulled the president out from behind his White House desk, urged him to flash his bright smile, and experimented with the teleprompter and cue cards. When he caught Eisenhower delivering his remarks into the wrong camera, he signaled the president to shift his gaze.[12]

Montgomery taught Eisenhower to use television for a variety of purposes. Adapted for film and video, the photo opportunities that Harding and Coolidge developed multiplied, with Ike taking to the airwaves for such momentous events as the unveiling of an eight-cent stamp, the activation of a hydroelectric generator in South Dakota, and (a nod to Bernays) the 75th Jubilee of the electric light bulb.

Most important, Ike made the televised Oval Office address a staple of presidential communication. With FDR's Fireside Chats still in mind, Eisenhower took to the airwaves at moments of national crisis: in September 1957, to assure the nation that federal troops would ensure the orderly integration of Central High School in Little Rock, Arkansas; or again that November to address the Soviets' Sputnik launch. These speeches not only gave Ike a platform for framing the issues and mobilizing the public; they also let him avoid reporters' pesky questions at delicate moments of national or international tension, especially since he had no compunctions about scrapping his press conferences if he thought them inopportune.[13]

Montgomery's ministrations won good marks. One year in, the United Press deemed the president's television manner "as relaxed as a neighbor leaning on his lawnmower." Merriman Smith, dean of the Washington press corps, proclaimed the president, for all his clotted syntax, a maestro of the medium—whose success was "his own doing, and not the result of Madison Avenue coaching or the lyric typewriters of literary ghosts." But if some reporters blithely relayed the White House's picture of a newly telegenic Ike, others jeered at Montgomery and his work. Detractors highlighted the staging, mocking the sudden surplus of presidential smiles that seemed neither natural nor sincere—as if, one critic wrote, a director were holding up a card saying "NOW." In letters to local papers, citizens complained that Montgomery was ill serving his client, making him seem undignified, as one *Washington Post* reader wrote, by having him "sit on the edge of a desk and make gestures with his arms akimbo."[14]

Going further, some journalists questioned whether the "contrived spontaneity" that Montgomery and Eisenhower tried to achieve held more dangers than benefits. "No man can be comfortable in a small room, speaking to an inanimate camera, and still preserve the illusion that he is ad libbing indefinitely," wrote Jack Gould. "Everyone can tell easily whether he is reading or not and, if he is, the deception only creates an irritant for speaker and viewer alike." Instructing Eisenhower and other politicians to "forget about technique" and just speak naturally, Gould wanted a world of political television less attentive to show business methods than to "the art of government." Viewers would respond to the real, he said, not the manufactured.

The advice was at odds with Gould's own long-standing TV booster-ism. It was also naive, and more than a bit glib. Gould himself had declared that under Montgomery's tutelage Ike had turned in a more relaxed and winning performance—precisely the "contrived spontaneity" that he now deemed a chimera. Intellectually, viewers might be wise to the artifice. Emotionally, they could still succumb to the Hollywood magic.[15]

The controversy about Montgomery's coaching showed that in an age of images, the ideal of a "natural" performance exerted a strong pull. Playing into fears of a manipulative executive, stories about Montgomery implied something illegitimate about his work, as if he were foisting a phony picture of Ike on the public. The use of a television adviser—or an advertising firm or pollster or press secretary—was broadly seen as an exercise in deception. Montgomery vehemently denied that he was a "coach" or that his work amounted to trickery. His function was simply to make sure that "nothing hinders President Eisenhower from express-ing himself as he wants to express himself. Certainly, it is not my job to artificialize nor to coach him in any way." Like information managers since TR's day, he believed his job was to correct distortions, not introduce them. "What I did attempt to do was, in a sense, to educate him about the uses of television, a medium unfamiliar to him except as a casual viewer when he entered the White House."[16]

In Washington, Hollywood image craft was suspect, to be down-played as modest technical assistance. But in the Los Angeles studios where Montgomery learned his craft, the president's mastery of TV was proudly toasted. In September 1955, the actor and dancer George Murphy—director of publicity at Metro-Goldwyn-Mayer, organizer of entertainment for Eisenhower's inaugural fête, boyhood friend of Montgomery, and future senator from California—told Hagerty that the Academy of Television Arts and Sciences had awarded Ike an honorary Emmy. On hearing the news, the president professed satisfaction. "It is especially gratifying," he wrote in a thank-you letter, "to be called a 'pro-fessional' by members of your distinguished association." If he wasn't sincere, he was at least a good actor.[17]

34

"ATOMS FOR PEACE"

EISENHOWER'S HEART LAY in foreign policy, and here, as much as in domestic affairs, he was eager to apply new techniques of persuasion. His "New Look" foreign policy emphasized cheaper alternatives to military force, such as nuclear deterrence, covert CIA operations, and, not least, psychological warfare to win the hearts and minds around the world. Pushed by C. D. Jackson, his special assistant for Cold War planning, psy war became integral to Ike's foreign policy vision.

At the start of Eisenhower's first term, Jackson joined an ad hoc executive committee tasked with rethinking geopolitical strategy. Chaired by William Jackson (no relation), formerly of the CIA, the body was called the Jackson Committee, but it was clear which Jackson provided the intellectual firepower. Over six months, the committee conducted more than 250 interviews and combed through reams of confidential documents. Its final report, delivered to the president in June 1953, held that the Soviet threat lay not so much in its military prowess as in its proficiency with propaganda and subversion. The United States, it said, had to raise its game. It urged Eisenhower to take control and replace Truman's old, ineffectual Psychological Strategy Board with a new "Operations Coordinating Board," closely tied to the National Security Council, that would integrate psychological approaches into the planning of international strategy. Psy war could not be treated as an afterthought.[1]

The prominence that Ike gave to psychological warfare brought it under closer inspection. Liberals, especially, wondered whether it was anything more than a buzzword and a gimmick. Walter Lippmann lambasted Eisenhower and Dulles for suggesting that psychological warfare was a true alternative to war. "The real alternative to war," he chided, "is diplomacy." Arthur Schlesinger, Jr., also argued that the administration was overvaluing psy war, as if it were "uniquely powerful by itself." Besides, Schlesinger noted, while totalitarian states might use psychological warfare effectively, open societies could not; psy war required constricting debate about foreign policy at home, since off-message comments from officials could undermine the thrust of a psy-war campaign. Psy war also had undemocratic implications for the press, imposing undue pressure on reporters not to contradict the official government line, lest they "risk wrecking the plans of the Secretary of State."[2]

C.D. Jackson put little stock in arguments like these. Contrary to Schlesinger's accusations, Jackson didn't think psy war was "uniquely powerful by itself." On the contrary, the Jackson Committee said, "The cold war cannot be won by words alone. What we do will continue to be vastly more important than what we say." America shouldn't try to persuade foreign peoples of things they didn't believe, the committee argued; it should aim to show them "that what we are, and what we stand for in the world, *is consistent with their own aspirations.*"

An appreciation of propaganda's limits also informed the committee's preference for straightforward, low-key, informational messages over drumbeating anti-Communist propaganda. For the Voice of America and similar outlets to be effective, the Jackson Committee argued, they needed to remain credible in the eyes of their foreign audiences, exhibiting "restraint and dignity." Hard-hitting propaganda might work, but only if it came from seemingly non-official sources like Radio Free Europe or front groups. "As a general rule," it said, "propaganda or information should be attributed to the United States only when such attribution is an asset."

Eisenhower supported the Jackson Committee's recommendations. But Dulles, eager to keep control of foreign policy, shared his department's suspicion of the propaganda peddlers, whom career foreign service types considered ill informed about global affairs. Seeking a compromise, Ike agreed to move the cluster of information programs that had resided at State since 1945—the Voice of America, the libraries, the news services—

to a new, independent entity to be called the United States Information Agency. But the USIA, though technically independent, would follow Dulles's policies. With this ungainly solution, Ike ensured that information and propaganda would remain a focus of struggle during his presidency.

*   *   *

An opportunity to recast American foreign policy came early in Eisenhower's first term. On March 5, 1953, Soviet premier Joseph Stalin died. Early the next morning, Dulles, Cutler, Jackson, and Hagerty met with the president in the Oval Office to figure out a response. Together, they crafted a cautious statement that would neither gloat nor provoke. Jackson, as usual, saw an opportunity for a grander gambit—the rollout of a brand-new Russia policy. "Out of such a program," he told Cutler, "might come further opportunities which, skillfully exploited, might advance the real disintegration of the Soviet Empire." Though less excited than Jackson, Eisenhower too was hopeful, especially after Georgy Malenkov, Stalin's successor, said that Russia could resolve any dispute with the United States or other countries by peaceful means. "What are we ready to do to improve the chances of peace?" the president asked Emmet Hughes.[3]

On April 16, Eisenhower delivered a major speech called "A Chance for Peace" that laid out the costs of the arms race. "Every gun that is made, every warship launched, every rocket fired," the president said, "signifies, in the final sense, a theft from those who hunger and are not fed, those who are cold and are not clothed." But Ike's plans were framed in terms so favorable to American objectives that the Soviets didn't take his speech seriously. It seemed calculated not to promote a thaw in superpower relations but to score a public relations victory in the eyes of the world.

The Soviet rejection forced Eisenhower to seek new ways to reassure the world of his peaceful designs. At the same time, he wished to impress on the American public the dangers of the newly developed hydrogen bomb. One possible solution emerged from a Truman-appointed panel led by the nuclear scientist J. Robert Oppenheimer. Echoing George Gallup's concerns about public complacency about nukes, the Oppenheimer proposal urged Ike to educate the public about nuclear dangers and advocate disarmament and coexistence with the Soviets. Ike's psy-war team agreed with the approach, arguing that, as the Jackson Committee stated, the public still didn't "grasp the import of the president's recent words that we live in an *age*, not an instant, of peril." It called for "a greater degree of candor toward the American people" about nukes.[4]

The new effort—dubbed "Operation Candor"—was to include a full-blown public relations effort, developed by White House staffers in consultation with Gallup, to be centered on a TV and radio series called *The Age of Peril*. Believing that Ike's personal authority was essential to success, Jackson drew up plans for a major presidential speech. The talk, Jackson wrote in a memo, should "convey to the American people the enormity of the threat that confronts them" and create "a climate of public opinion better adjusted to the fact of an enduring condition of national emergency." But Jackson's early drafts were so vivid about the impact of nuclear war—White House aides called them the "Bang! Bang!" papers—that Eisenhower rejected several versions as too bleak. "This leaves everybody dead on both sides, with no hope anywhere," he said. "Can't we find some hope?"[5]

* * *

On August 8, Malenkov announced that the Soviet Union had tested a hydrogen bomb. The news triggered a new round of stories about the prospect of nuclear annihilation. In the face of such apocalypticism, a peace initiative was freshly attractive. After scientists at the first international conference on atomic energy met in Oslo to promote its peaceful use, Eisenhower fastened on the idea of a U.S.-Soviet effort, under the auspices of the United Nations, to use fissionable material for purposes besides weaponry.[6]

By summer's end, Jackson was lamenting that "the Candor speech is slowly dying from a severe attack of Committee-itis." One draft after another failed to strike the right balance between hope and fear. Word was leaking out to the press. Stewart Alsop wrote a series of columns warning that even a candid presidential speech about nuclear dangers wouldn't be enough. The administration, he said, needed to offer a comprehensive plan for protecting the nation and managing the new weapons, whether through air defenses, negotiations with the Soviet Union, or both.[7]

Under these pressures, Operation Candor evolved. The TV programs were scrapped in favor of a focus on the peaceful uses of atomic energy, which soon became known as "Atoms for Peace." Dispensing with his "Bang! Bang!" drafts, Jackson now crafted a more calming, hopeful message, aiming to underscore America's dedication to comity and expose Soviet inflexibility. Jackson fleshed out the new strategy with Lewis Strauss, who ran the Atomic Energy Commission, over a series of breakfasts at Washington's Metropolitan Club. Operation Candor got yet another new name, "Wheaties," in honor of the meals at which it was planned. With the international audience now in view, it was agreed that Ike would deliver the key speech before the UN General Assembly, which was gathering in New York in December.[8]

Writing the speech remained a challenge. Dulles, wary that any peace proposals would weaken America's diplomatic position, regularly undermined Jackson. "Either they seem to give away too much of our case," Dulles complained to the president, "or else they seem to be primarily propaganda, which would be likely to provoke only a propaganda response." On November 25, Jackson attended what he described as a "big meeting in Foster Dulles' office," at which "red lights started blinking all over the place. Joint Chiefs and Defense have laid their ears back." Two days later, Jackson concluded that the "real problem" went "beyond any disagreements on wording or technical details. Real problem is basic philosophy—are we or are we not prepared to embark on a course which may in fact lead to atomic disarmament?" Jackson and Strauss thought it was worth a shot, but the hawkish Dulles was standing in the way.

Jackson kept tinkering with his drafts. When the president and his national security team departed for a conclave in Bermuda with British and French leaders on December 4, four days before the speech, there was still no final version. Rewriting continued as the Bermuda group met, and even Winston Churchill, enjoying his second run as prime minister, contributed thoughts. But when the president's entourage boarded his silver, four-propellered Lockheed Constellation, the *Columbine*, to return home, the speech was still unfinished.

Aloft, in the president's compartment, Jackson sat with Eisenhower, Dulles, and Strauss on swivel chairs, line-editing the draft, passing each page to a succession of secretaries. One copied it on a special typewriter that produced extra large lettering for the president to read, just hours later, from the podium. Another secretary set the text onto mimeograph stencils, which were in turn handed to an Army sergeant cranking out hundreds of copies by hand. So frantic were the last-minute preparations that the *Columbine* had to circle over New York for an extra fifteen minutes as aides finished collating. Even the dour Dulles was set to work stapling, with Ike calling, "Hurry up, Foster! Pick up some more copies!" The president hastily underlined words on his reading copy. As the aides clambered into the presidential limousine to drive to Turtle Bay behind a motorcycle escort, the scent of wet ink was still pungent on the mimeographed sheets.[9]

* * *

Once inside the modernist blue, gold, and green assembly hall, surrounded by dramatically sloping paneled walls and sinuous Fernand Léger murals, Eisenhower walked to the weighty green marble podium. The crowd sat rapt. Delegates listened through headphones to translations in Arabic, Chinese, French, Russian, and Spanish.

The president began with his original theme of candor, citing the destructiveness of thermonuclear weapons and cautioning against complacency. "Even a vast superiority in numbers of weapons, and a consequent capability of devastating retaliation," he said, "is no preventive, of itself, against the fearful material damage and toll of human lives that would be inflicted by surprise aggression." But he insisted that the United States wanted "to help us move out of the dark chamber of horrors into the light," and as his speech built to its finish, he laid out his "Atoms for Peace" proposal: All nuclear states should contribute to an international, United Nations–run fund of atomic material "to serve the peaceful pursuits of mankind," among them agriculture, medicine, and "electrical energy in the power-starved areas of the world." At the end, Eisenhower's eyes were moist, and the delegates leapt to their feet. Even the Russians applauded. The speech had been bold, but also a clever piece of psychological warfare: If Malenkov followed Eisenhower's lead, the United States came off as heroic; if he didn't, the Soviets seemed like spoilers.

Press reaction was overwhelmingly positive, as was the buzz on Capitol Hill. But Jackson wasn't taking chances. He immediately set up a working group at the new Operations Coordinating Board to promote "Atoms for Peace" abroad, through the U.S. Information Agency and other channels. Already, the Voice of America had aired the speech live, and the USIA distributed the text, translations of it, and a film; still to come were a TV series called *The Magic of the Atom* and a public relations kit featuring photographs and display material. Over the next two years, the administration pushed the theme of "Atoms for Peace" globally, developing a small library of films and a traveling exhibition that toured Western Europe, India, and Pakistan.[10]

Domestic propaganda remained formally prohibited by the 1948 Smith-Mundt Act, but no legislation could be expected to keep an administration from touting a presidential message. The State Department produced reams of material publicizing "Atoms for Peace." Though they took pains not to mimic the USIA materials too closely, the echo was inescapable. Other executive branch departments joined in; the Post Office issued an Atoms for Peace stamp, showing two earths, western and eastern hemispheres leaning toward each other, ringed by electronlike orbital paths. For all the concerns about the White House propagandizing to its citizens, the leader of the free world couldn't be denied his bully pulpit, from which his words were bound to resound across America.

Woodrow Wilson's critics had feared that the Creel Committee was meant to burnish the image of Woodrow Wilson; FDR's enemies worried that the Office of War Information was functioning as another New Deal propaganda agency. In like fashion, Eisenhower's promotion of his Cold War policies, even after the Soviet Union rejected the idea, was seen as redounding to his personal benefit. "Soviet Rebuffs Atomic Plan; Ike's Prestige Jumps in U.S.," read a headline from the *Christian Science Monitor.* Here was the old general, speaking before the delegates of the nations of the world, calling for a shift away from nuclear escalation and toward harnessing the promise of science. Rosser Reeves couldn't have put it better: Eisenhower, Man of Peace.[11]

35

VANCE PACKARD AND
THE ANXIETY OF PERSUASION

AS DWIGHT EISENHOWER prepared to move into the White House in 1953, his new life there was previewed in the glossy *American Magazine*. The author of the piece wrote frequently on family and consumer issues, churning out how-to articles like "Don't Let Your Plumbing Problems Get You Down" and "How I Lost 15 Pounds in One Month." His portrait of Ike's new home betrayed the naive fascination of an upwardly mobile member of the postwar middle class. Voyeuristically describing "this fabulous $40,000,000 mansion with its 107 rooms, including servants' quarters, offices, and storage rooms," the piece waxed giddy about the sumptuous perks available to presidents. "Their furniture is dusted three times a day. They have at their beck not only butlers, valets, chambermaids, and ushers, but even carpenters, plumbers and painters." The writer went on for pages in this vein, marveling at the "two dozen sleek limousines, a private super airliner, a private railroad car, and one of the world's most luxurious yachts"—and, of course, the view.[1]

The author of this fluff was Vance Packard, thirty-eight, a straitlaced and highly fluent feature writer. A man of five feet nine inches who showed the girth of middle age, Packard had an unassuming Mayberry smile, a doughy face, and a high forehead and vanishing hairline that gave him an ever-so-slight resemblance to Eisenhower. Like Ike, Packard was from the farm, in his case central Pennsylvania, and he affected a hayseed style in his writing as well as his appearance. Also like Ike, his years at Columbia—Packard earned a master's degree in journalism there—failed to instill in him the sardonic stance of a New Yorker. One of Packard's sons said that he could never recall his father telling a joke.[2]

Later in 1953, an editor at *Reader's Digest* read an article in *The Reporter* about a new craze on Madison Avenue called "motivational research"—described as "quite different from ordinary market research as done by poll takers such as Gallup or Roper" because of its use of psychoanalytic insights. The editor asked Packard to write a freelance article on the topic. Packard accepted the assignment and conducted his research, but *Reader's Digest* killed the piece because it had just begun accepting advertising and feared offending its new sponsors. Packard had begun his study of advertising's unseen influence precisely as the shadowy power of advertising was limiting his own journalistic horizons.[3]

Fortuitously, a former colleague of Packard's had recently joined the David McKay publishing house, and Packard passed along his rejected *Reader's Digest* piece. Soon he had a book contract in hand. The resulting book, an exposé of the advertising industry and its use of motivation research, came out just in time, at least for Packard's sake: in August 1956 *American Magazine* folded, and a sister publication, *Collier's*—a rival to *McClure's* back in the muckraking era—followed suit. Both were victims of television, which was siphoning off readers and advertisers. Briefly, Packard was heard to worry about losing his house. Soon, though, he had no more need for corporate employment. His new book, *The Hidden Persuaders*, was selling fast and would become one of the most widely read works of the twentieth century.

* * *

Many issues fed anxieties about political manipulation in the 1950s—from Joseph McCarthy's demagoguery to the rise of television—but at the root of it was the era's abiding fixation with "mass society." In the postwar years it became common to debate whether individuals were losing their autonomy amid the country's prosperity and technological bounty. As they had in the 1920s, citizens experienced a free-floating psychological disquiet about politics, wondering whether the tools of mass media and the ethos of consumer capitalism were altering their democracy beyond recognition.

Concerns about mass society surfaced throughout popular and intellectual literature. A string of much-discussed works of social criticism focused on the eclipse of the individual: David Riesman's *Lonely Crowd*, C. Wright Mills's *Power Elite*, William H. Whyte's *Organization Man*, John Keats's *Crack in the Picture Window*, John Kenneth Galbraith's *Affluent Society*, Betty Friedan's *Feminine Mystique*. Each, in its way, suggested that deeper needs of the soul were being sacrificed on the altar of conformity and materialism in Eisenhower's America.

Along with these sociological tracts came many books with a more targeted—and alarmist—set of themes. These books looked specifically at psychological innovations that they said were being used to influence people's minds. The sensational topic of "brainwashing" was by decade's end the subject of more than 200 magazine articles. Popularized by the journalist and sometime intelligence agent Edward Hunter, brainwashing had affinities with the idea of totalitarianism, developed by Hannah Arendt and others, which classified Nazism and communism as kindred systems that sought to pulverize the self-directed individual and instill the state's ideology within the citizen's consciousness. Brainwashing emerged as a bugaboo with the Korean War, when the Chinese and Korean Communists were alleged to have subjected American prisoners to brutal ideological reprogramming. (An equivalent Chinese term had been used to describe practices used by the Maoists on their Chinese opponents.) Like mesmerism and hypnosis—manias of a half century earlier—brainwashing was said to allow malevolent powers to remake, almost magically, the minds of individuals. By mid-decade, intellectuals could be counted on to know books like Hunter's *Brainwashing: The Story of Men Who Defied It*, Joost Meerloo's *Rape of the Mind: The Psychology of Thought Control, Menticide, and Brainwashing*, and William Sargant's *Battle for the Mind: A Physiology of Conversion and Brain-Washing*. Most widely read of all was Richard Condon's 1959 novel *The Manchurian Candidate*, which linked McCarthyite demagoguery to Communist mind control in a tale of a returning Korean War veteran programmed to assassinate a presidential candidate. Fiction, non-fiction, or something in between, these books offered a congenial explanation for the otherwise baffling question of why a POW might seem to willingly choose Soviet communism over Western democracy. Notably, many of these authors saw milder forms of brainwashing at work in the United States as well.[4]

Yet another spate of books, in a similar key, focused on advertising's dark power. In 1951 Marshall McLuhan, an obscure Canadian literature professor, published *The Mechanical Bride*, a close reading of magazine ads that sought to parse their manipulative but latent messages. More commercially successful was Martin Mayer's *Madison Avenue, U.S.A.*, a behind-the-scenes glimpse of the advertising and PR trades and their use of "emotional slogans presenting simplified and one-sided views of the complicated affairs of state." In *Brave New World Revisited*, the British novelist Aldous Huxley synthesized the arguments of all of the leading social critics into a grand critique of democratic decay. "Today, in the world's most powerful democracy," Huxley brooded, "the politicians and their propagandists prefer to make nonsense of democratic procedures by appealing almost exclusively to the ignorance and irrationality of the electors." He concluded, "The methods now being used to merchandise the political candidate as though he were a deodorant positively guarantee the electorate against ever hearing the truth about anything."[5]

Postwar fiction, finally, also betrayed fears of lost or stolen autonomy. In the spirit of *A Face in the Crowd*, political potboilers offered variations on the theme of unscrupulous manipulators subverting democracy. Eugene Burdick, a Rhodes Scholar and political theorist at the University of California at Berkeley who would be remembered for his novels *The Ugly American* and *Fail-Safe*, first made the best-seller lists in 1955 with *The Ninth Wave*, a crude dystopian thriller. Burdick's protagonist, apparently modeled on Murray Chotiner, used his talent for discerning and exploiting voters' fears to elect as governor an unqualified, populistic, alcoholic rabble-rouser. More humorously, John Schneider's *Golden Kazoo* portrayed the 1960 presidential election devolving into a race to the bottom between two slick advertising firms.[6]

In the face of this anxiety, dissenting voices tried to offer reassurance. Psychologists debunked the idea of brainwashing, exposing it as merely the refinement of old interrogation techniques like deprivation and isolation. Communication scholars like Cantril and Lazarsfeld refined the theory of "limited effects"—demonstrating just how resistant most people were to propaganda that contradicted their existing beliefs. A study by Cantril of a rough college football game showed that fans allocated blame for the violence according to their home-team loyalties, affirming Lippmann's dictum from *Public Opinion* that "we do not first see and then define, we define first and then see." On the best-seller list, Eric Hoffer's *The True Believer*—a popular study of mass movements—also injected a dose of realism into the debate. "Propaganda on its own cannot force its way into unwilling minds," he wrote; "neither can it inculcate something wholly new; nor can it keep people persuaded once they have ceased to believe.

Where opinion is not coerced, people can be made to believe only in what they already 'know.'"[7]

*   *   *

Despite such reminders, the books about mind control struck a nerve—and none more forcefully than Packard's, which appeared in 1957. Though *The Hidden Persuaders* merely partook of a widespread apprehension, and though it borrowed heavily from the *Reporter* article and other sources, it became the decade's classic statement of manipulation anxiety. It topped the best-seller lists for months, selling more than 100,000 copies in its first year, and eventually several million. More than any other work, it directed attention to what Packard called "the large-scale efforts being made, often with impressive success, to channel our unthinking habits, our purchasing decisions, and our thought processes by the uses of insights gleaned from psychiatry and the social sciences."[8]

Packard focused on the use of social science techniques by advertising marketers, unvaryingly in a critical tenor. Particularly disquieting was the multi-million-dollar business surrounding "motivational research" (sometimes glibly called "MR"). Applying psychological and psychoanalytic methods—including Rorschach tests, word association, focus groups, and in-depth interviews—motivational research sought to affect consumers' behavior at an unconscious level. With anecdotes and insider perspectives supplied by trade magazines and professional conferences, Packard detailed one clever application of the approach after another, thrilling his readers with the revelation of both the tricks and the secrets behind them. Such research, Packard warned, carried "antihumanistic implications" and promised "regress rather than progress for man in his long struggle to become a rational and self-guiding being."

Like much psychology since Freud, motivational research rejected as a fallacy the notion of *Homo economicus*, the rationally self-interested human being. Where Rosser Reeves's methods had rejected the psychological cleverness of 1920s advertisers to revive the hard sell, now the "MR boys" were returning to Freud to activate unconscious desires that stimulated consumers to purchase Golden Fluffo shortening or Hathaway shirts. In one of many colorful examples, Packard explained that housewives were found to dislike the new "just add water" cake mixes, doubting their cakes would turn out tasty or nutritious; Swansdown White Cake Mix thus changed its formula to require that they add "fresh eggs" as well. Appeals like these, Packard suggested, which were based on research concealed from the consumer, represented an especially menacing form of manipulation.[9]

While the bulk of *Hidden Persuaders* dealt with consumerism, Packard devoted a chapter to politics, arguing, as David Riesman had, that "Americans, in their growing absorption with consumption, have even become consumers of politics." According to Packard, the "symbol manipulators" unmasked in his book were also infiltrating the political arena, seeking "to engineer our consent to their projects or to engineer our enthusiasm for their candidates." Already, he warned, they had "made spectacular strides in changing the traditional characteristics of American political life."

Instead of thoughtful candidates with nuanced, substantive stances on issues, Packard said, voters were "giving the nod to the best performer" and placing undue weight on "sincerity" or the appearance thereof. But Packard's theory was weak on history. Though he made passing references to Machiavelli and Napoleon and their ideas about public opinion, he showed no familiarity with the concerns voiced since the 1920s, if not TR's day, about the tendency to "humanize" candidates by focusing on personalities. Almost arbitrarily, he claimed that these masters of persuasion "did not turn their attention to politics in a serious way until the nineteen-fifties," citing Rosser Reeves's 1952 ads for Eisenhower as the pivotal moment. He went on to review James Hagerty's influence in the Eisenhower administration, Robert Montgomery's sprucing up of Ike's image, Whitaker and Baxter's California consulting, and Murray Chotiner's role in having "groomed Richard Nixon for national stardom." Noting that the Republican Party had hired Chotiner to educate state chairmen in the art of the "smear" and "the technique of winning people's hearts with carefully simulated candor," he described Nixon, Chotiner's most famous pupil, as "the man who has benefited from many, if not all these techniques"—nothing less than "a new breed of American politician."

The politicians' investment in cynical persuasion culminated, in Packard's telling, in the 1956 race for the White House. In that contest, Packard said, Eisenhower's team advertised heavily after popular comedy shows, because their audiences included "millions of people in a will-less, helpless state, unable to resist any suggestion offered"—or so he quoted John Steinbeck, a well-known Stevenson supporter but not known as a particular authority on human psychology. Packard's severe view of the Republicans' methods may have had something to do with his own politics, which were close to Stevenson's. Indeed, he closed his chapter on politics with a quote from Adlai: "The idea that you can merchandise candidates for high office like breakfast cereal . . . is the ultimate indignity to the democratic process."

Packard's critique of politics and consumerism belonged to the era's larger examination of mass society. A half century earlier, sociologists like Edward Ross had tried to keep alive a moral code rooted in America's farms and small-town communities, even as they excitedly faced the onset of modernity. Now modernity had arrived, making Packard's Ross-like fondness for the social patterns of his youth seem nostalgic. Packard, who remembered well his father's difficulties as an independent dairy farmer competing against agribusinesses, retained elements of the old sensibility. A direct line connected the strict Methodism of his youth with his righteous prose. The historian Loren Baritz noted caustically that "when he begins to suffocate in the chrome-plated world of our time, he seeks out some New England village in which he may recreate his spirit." *The Hidden Persuaders* was, for all its dazzle, a cri de coeur against modern life.[10]

* * *

With his fierce moralism, Packard hoped to awaken the public to the menace of motivational research and perhaps mute its effects. "We cannot be too seriously manipulated if we know what is going on," he reassured his readers. "It is my hope that this book may contribute to the general awareness." That it did. His book's title entered the cultural lexicon; its themes became the subject of debate. Catapulted to literary stardom, Packard followed with a string of sequels built on the same formula of business reportage mixed with social criticism: *The Status Seekers*, *The Waste Makers*, *The Pyramid Climbers*. He provided inspiration to both the New Left (the Port Huron Statement deplored the menace of "market research") and the New Frontier (his books helped convince President John F. Kennedy to create a consumer council in 1962).

But *The Hidden Persuaders* had unintended consequences, too. Though a cause for worry, advertising was also chic—seductively stylish, as it had been during the consumerist 1920s. The menace of admen was mingling with a worldly-wise admiration for their creativity. Many people who read Packard's book were not appalled but enchanted. Deaf to his critical tone, they beseeched him to share his secrets for influencing others, promoting real estate schemes, or exporting his marketing tricks to Mexico. Ernest Dichter, a Viennese psychologist featured prominently in the book, thanked Packard for the many job applicants suddenly coming his way.

That Packard may have fed the beast he was hoping to slay was also clear from the craze for "subliminal" advertising that he set off. *The Hidden Persuaders* had quoted an unsubstantiated London newspaper report about a New Jersey cinema flashing split-second ice cream ads on the movie screen—"too short for people in the audience to recognize them consciously but still long enough to be absorbed unconsciously." This trick allegedly led, Packard said, to "a clear and otherwise unaccountable boost in ice-cream sales." Whether or not this stunt had occurred, Packard's mention of it encouraged James Vicary, a consultant to Benton & Bowles and BBD&O, to use "subliminals" for popcorn and soda in movie theaters, just as Packard had described. A backlash ensued. *Newsday* called subliminal ads "the most alarming invention since the atom bomb," and the National Association of Broadcasters barred them from the airwaves. Yet the hocus-pocus lore about these little-used gimmicks would remain potent for decades.[11]

Moreover, *The Hidden Persuaders* was unreliable in many of its core claims. Packard typically failed to say whether the strategies he documented actually worked; Dichter's explanation of why men didn't use cigarette holders failed to mention that his much-touted techniques never did persuade men to use cigarette holders. One sociology journal bluntly stated that Packard "has not convinced many professionals that he knows what he is talking about." The main problem with *The Hidden Persuaders*, it seemed, was that it was unpersuasive.[12]

While some faulted Packard's lack of rigor, others mocked his scandalized tone. The notion that audiences might actually detect and appreciate the cleverness of ads seemed not to have occurred to him. His account of the well-known Maidenform Bra ad campaign—which showed a young woman, wearing a brassiere above the waist but otherwise fully clothed, wandering out in public as if in a dream—was illustrative. Packard, the critic Irving Kristol noted, deemed the ad's Freudian appeals to be "unfair," "dangerous," and "diabolical." But, Kristol pointed out, the Maidenform ad was "the first brassiere advertisement that has ever given me pleasure," adding, "His apocalyptic vision of a society morally and politically controlled by advertising is so much day-dreaming (and self-advertising?) in its own right."[13]

Most critical of all were the admen themselves, who insisted that Packard misrepresented their work. Advertising didn't manipulate so much as inform, they said; empowering the consumer was profoundly democratic. Raymond Bauer, a public opinion researcher with industry ties, protested

that Packard didn't grasp the limits of persuasion. In Packard's imagination, "the consumer is powerless to resist these techniques, and he just
buys and buys without knowing why." In fact, consumers' motives weren't
so far below the surface. Adman David Ogilvy wrote in *Confessions of
an Advertising Man* that the Hathaway shirt ads featuring a man with an
eyepatch that Packard deemed so clever were nothing but "a moderately
good idea for a wet Tuesday morning"; motivational research had nothing
to do with their inspiration. Rosser Reeves also struck back, defending his
hard-sell methods in his own book, *Reality in Advertising*. Psychoanalytic
concepts, Reeves said, played "no part, or at most a tiny part, in reality
in advertising." Far from a "mysterious new tool" or "secret weapon," he
wrote, "motivational research is no more than a series of research techniques . . . based on what psychologists have known for years—that if you
ask a man a direct question, you may not get a direct and truthful answer,
because the man may be concealing the truth from himself."[14]

Like the advertisements Packard described, *The Hidden Persuaders*
played upon a fear deep within the collective psyche. In Packard's case—
and those of Joost Meerloo, Eugene Burdick, Aldous Huxley, and the
others—it was a fear, particularly potent in a culture that romanticized
individualism, of being surreptitiously influenced by invisible powers.
The book was a comment not only on advertising but also on attitudes
toward the loss of freedom in an age of television, bureaucracies, and mass
politics—"our primitive anxiety over manipulation," as Bauer said. What
separated Packard from other authors bearing similar warnings was the
expert way he boiled down his research for popular consumption. By 1960,
when Packard published *The Waste Makers*, the third volume in his string
of liberal middlebrow muckraking books, readers knew the formula.
They could reliably count on Packard to offer them a smoothly written,
anecdote-heavy exposé of the consumer economy's unseen subversion of
their autonomy. As the 1950s closed, it seemed that the quintessential consumer product of Eisenhower's America might well be a Vance Packard
best-seller.[15]

PART V

THE AGE OF
IMAGE MAKING

By the early 1960s, many Americans came to see their politics as scripted and staged, regarding the era of television as an Age of Image Making. Journalists and citizens, as the historian Daniel Boorstin noted, craved a deeper and fuller account of national politics, and men like the political reporter Theodore H. White and the documentary filmmaker Robert Drew attempted to provide at least a glimpse behind the familiar images and stories. John F. Kennedy, with his telegenic looks and cool public persona, did much to assuage popular anxieties about TV, as Franklin Roosevelt had with radio, by showcasing its potential for democratic communication. But JFK, too, managed Cold War information carefully, and by the end of the decade Lyndon Johnson's deeply misleading rhetoric about the war in Vietnam led to the so-called credibility gap—a distrust of presidential images and messages as pervasive as any in American history. The explosion of political consultants in the late 1960s and early 1970s further reinforced the notion that what Americans consumed through the media bore only an attenuated connection to the truth about America's leaders and its public policies.

THE UNMAKING OF PRESIDENTIAL MYSTIQUE

WHEN GLOSSY MAGAZINES began folding in the 1950s, Vance Packard wasn't the only victim. Another casualty was Theodore H. White, the forty-one-year-old national political correspondent for *Collier's*. Stocky, barrel-chested, and just over five feet tall, with big front teeth and brown eyes that peered out through thick, round lenses, White was known for the eagerness he brought to his reporting and the easy cadences of his prose. He had made his name in his twenties, covering the Communist takeover of China for *Time*, and after a falling-out with Henry Luce, he had gone to *The New Republic* and then *The Reporter*. In 1955, he joined *Collier's*—circulation 4.3 million—where he worked alongside such rising stars as Robert Massie, Peter Maas, and Pierre Salinger.[1]

In 1956, White decided to write a sweeping account of the presidential election. With primary campaigns still a small, largely neglected part of the nomination process, White found himself following Estes Kefauver around the snows of New Hampshire, often with only an Associated Press reporter joining them in the car. He amassed large files on the race and even came up with a title: "The Making of the President—1956." But at the end of 1956 *Collier's* folded. "It was a classic case of coitus interruptus," recalled White, who spoke in the raunchy language of his native Boston neighborhood. "There I was, stiff cock, ready to go for the massive summary of the 1956 campaign, and here I am out of a job and no place to write it."[2]

White was one of four children of Mary and David White, Russian Jewish immigrants who met at a Socialist clubhouse. David White, a lawyer who served indigent clients, died when Teddy was sixteen. When the bookish son got into Harvard, despite its quotas on Jews, he paid his way by winning a scholarship and teaching Hebrew school at night. His classmates included Arthur Schlesinger, Jr., whom he knew slightly, and Joseph P. Kennedy, Jr., whom he did not. His most formative influence was the China scholar John King Fairbank, who took White on as a protégé. After graduating summa cum laude, in 1938, White traveled to China, where John Hersey discovered him and brought him to *Time*.

Now, nearly two decades later, White again needed a job. He turned down offers from Edward R. Murrow to join CBS News and from Henry Luce to return to *Time*. He toyed with writing a newspaper column but Walter Lippmann told him he couldn't make a living at it. So White tried fiction. A reporter to his bones, he wrote about his own experiences and things he had seen up close—"*les choses vues*," he called them—rendering them in the dramatic style of contemporaries like James Michener and Herman Wouk. (He considered Wouk "one of the great storytellers of all time.") White's first novel, *The Mountain Road*, was rooted in his years in China during its civil war; his second, *The View from the Fortieth Floor*, was a roman à clef about the dying *Collier's*. Both enjoyed popular success, though White remained dissatisfied—he called *The View* "one of the worst novels ever written"—and longed to return to reporting.[3]

On October 15, 1959, he got his chance. At an event at the Century Club in midtown Manhattan, White was summoned to the telephone for a call from the Hollywood agent Irving "Swifty" Lazar. Lazar said that the movie star Gary Cooper wanted to buy the film rights to *The View* for $80,000 (roughly $650,000 in 2016 dollars). White accepted. "Hollywood money," he told Tillman Durdin, a reporter friend, allowed him "to resume the only profession I was ever really proud of."

White returned to his unrealized project on the 1956 campaign, now refocused on the upcoming 1960 race. "The idea was to follow the campaign from beginning to end," he explained. "It would be written as a novel is written, with anticipated surprises as, one by one, early candidates vanish in the primaries until only two final jousters struggle for the prize in November. Moreover, it should be written as a story of a man in trouble, of the leader under the pressures of circumstances."

White's ambitions were civic as well as literary. He wanted to show readers how their political world really worked. Campaign reporting at the time rarely delved beyond the candidates' public events and statements. But journalists and citizens alike were coming to see their politics as constructed, fabricated, a carefully crafted spectacle. An iceberg of planning and decision making lay beneath the surfaces that voters saw in the morning papers or on the nightly news. Americans were looking at their politics, as David Riesman had written in *The Lonely Crowd*, from the stance of an "inside dopester," and White believed his book could satisfy their hunger for this specialized knowledge. It would combine White's trademark reportage with history, sociology, and political science to create a grand civics lesson—delivered in the quaffable prose of a Michener or Wouk novel.[4]

He again had a title: *The Making of the President, 1960*.

* * *

White had a charismatic and varied cast of characters to work with. On the Democratic side, the aspirants were likely to include John F. Kennedy of Massachusetts, Averell Harriman of New York, Stuart Symington of Missouri, Lyndon Johnson of Texas, Hubert Humphrey of Minnesota, and, again, Adlai Stevenson of Illinois. The Republicans included New York governor Nelson Rockefeller and Vice President Nixon.

Nixon, having loyally served Eisenhower, was now the heir apparent, but he remained the object of scorn and even hatred from the liberal intelligentsia—and many others. As the *Saturday Evening Post*'s Stewart Alsop wrote, "He has, probably, more enemies than any other American." White harbored pity, not hatred, for the vice president, yet he felt compelled to "cast Nixon as the villain, as in a novel." His wife warned him that if Nixon won the election, the book would be "a dog."[5]

Though White favored Stevenson, the hero of his tale would turn out to be Kennedy. Early on, as White was starting his reporting, Stevenson was taking stock of the Kennedy team's fearsome organizational strength and called White to talk. "Tell me, Teddy, am I in trouble?" he asked. "Is there anything I can do to stop this?" White said the Kennedy juggernaut seemed unstoppable. "I think it's 99 percent buttoned down." Stevenson seemed despondent. His rival's staff was even circulating rumors that he was going to endorse JFK. White described the Kennedy operation as "so streamlined, so efficient, so ruthless." Stevenson seized on the word *ruthless*, muttering it to himself.

As time went on, White came to see virtues in Kennedy that were concealed by the playboy image. Like other Stevenson admirers—among them Schlesinger and the economist John Kenneth Galbraith, both of whom had been part of Stevenson's brains trust—he found himself transferring his affections to the younger man. Kennedy lacked Stevenson's stately airs. But as a onetime reporter, an author, an avid reader, a man comfortable among intellectuals if not quite an intellectual himself, Kennedy offered his fellow Harvard men much to admire.

*   *   *

Born in 1917, John F. Kennedy was just forty-three when he ran for president. Over several decades, his father, Joseph P. Kennedy, who served as ambassador to Great Britain during World War II, had made the family into society-page regulars, and John, the second of nine exceptionally handsome children, was often in the limelight. At twenty-three, he turned his Harvard undergraduate thesis, *Why England Slept*—a partial rebuke to his father's notorious isolationism—into a best-seller. Three years later, as a sailor in the Pacific, he saved a crewmember when a Japanese torpedo destroyed their PT-boat. When Kennedy was elected to Congress in 1946 from Boston's eleventh district, word resounded across the country.

Over the next fourteen years, reporters covered Kennedy avidly. There was something magnetic about this Irish Catholic who had perfected the casual affect of the WASP, including a Boston accent that sounded more like a Brahmin lilt than the honk of a Charlestown dockworker. Despite a meager legislative record, Kennedy's wit and joie de vivre won him admirers in the press, even as his insouciance irked colleagues. Many were drawn, too, to Kennedy's wry smile, twinkling blue eyes, and thick mop of sandy brown hair. "Personality led on to style," White wrote, starstruck himself, "and this was where the image, radiating out through his circle of admiring staffmen and entranced newsmen, became the public persona—the dashing, impeccably tailored Boston Irishman with the Harvard gloss."

By the time of his presidential bid, Kennedy's gaunt frame and face had filled out, likely owing to cortisone steroid shots he secretly took for a kidney disorder. Writing about JFK for *Esquire* at the 1960 convention in Los Angeles, the novelist Norman Mailer, also goggle-eyed, captured the Kennedy cool. "He would seem at one moment older than his age, forty-eight or fifty, a tall, slim, sunburned professor with a pleasant weathered face, not even particularly handsome," Mailer wrote. "Five minutes later, talking to a press conference on his lawn, three microphones before him, a television camera turning, his appearance would have gone through a metamorphosis, he would look again like a movie star, his coloring vivid, his manner rich, his gestures strong and quick, alive with that concentration of vitality a successful actor always seems to radiate." Mailer grasped that JFK's appeal resided not just in his looks but in his style—the self-possession that imbued him with an air of conviction and authority and made him appear, unlike so many back-slapping politicians, confidently indifferent to approval.[6]

Teddy White fell for Kennedy as hard as anyone. To White, the draw was Kennedy's sense of history—not a schoolbook knowledge of the American past, but a fundamental appreciation of what was demanded of an occupant of the White House. He saw this quality in Kennedy one night while traveling on his private plane from Helena, Montana, to Massachusetts, with just one other reporter, Blair Clark of CBS. With White and Clark drinking liquor and Kennedy enjoying tomato soup ("into which he stirred huge gobbets of sour cream"), the three men talked at length, ranging over history and the presidency, Lincoln and Theodore Roosevelt and Winston Churchill. "He was not now trying to impress Clark or me," White inferred, perhaps naively, "but obviously his knowledge of history went far back beyond the roots of today's politics, and his reading had a range far beyond the needs of the gamesman." His command of the American ethnic mosaic also impressed White, as he held forth on the voting preferences of Jews and Irish, and even on the differences between American and Israeli Jews.

Later in the conversation, White upbraided Kennedy for having joined, years before, a chorus of criticism of White's mentor, John King Fairbank, for being too soft on the Chinese Communists. Kennedy shook his head apologetically. "I was wrong," he said. "I didn't know anything then." For his part, he challenged White to offer a solution to the crisis in Berlin, from which the Soviet leader Nikita Khrushchev was belligerently demanding that the Western nations withdraw their troops. JFK remarked that it was easy for outsiders to second-guess politicians' decisions because they wouldn't suffer the consequences of decisions about war and peace. Here White saw Kennedy's readiness to use power—something Stevenson manifestly lacked—which to him bespoke political maturity. "It was then I began to realize," White said, "that he has a sense of the presidency."

* * *

Though credulous toward Kennedy and starry-eyed about the American political pageant, White resolved to make his book a different kind of political story. He tailed the candidates for a year, from the primaries of Wisconsin and West Virginia, where Kennedy duked it out with Hubert Humphrey to show that a Catholic could win Protestant votes, to the hotel rooms of Manhattan, where Nixon made steep concessions over the Republican platform to the liberal Nelson Rockefeller, enraging the party's conservatives.

White's research, he said, was "overkill." "I have to interview 150, 200, or 300 people during the campaign in order to get the proper stuff," he explained. A compulsive newspaper clipper who filled his cellar with files, White would scour local papers when he traveled to grasp the issues at stake in each primary. He coaxed a friend at *Time* to share the magazine's proprietary dossiers on the candidates. Unlike previous campaign chronicles, his book let readers meet the candidates and their aides up close and witness their strategy sessions. Most Americans probably thought that Kennedy's campaign had begun with his January 1960 press conference at the Senate Office Building; White chronicled a three-hour strategy session at Hyannis three months before, during which the following year's developments were mapped out by sixteen staffers and Kennedy family members. He was inside the tent, too, on election night, at the Kennedy compound in Hyannis, recording for his readers how pollster Lou Harris had converted the pink-and-white children's bedroom of Bobby Kennedy's house into a data analysis center, its long table spilling over with reams of voting statistics.[7]

White's treatment of the journalists covering the race was also revelatory. He described a press corps seduced by Kennedy and alienated by Nixon—who, still smarting from his roughing up in 1952, shut himself off. JFK gave frequent interviews, bantered with reporters, and timed his news releases to meet their deadlines. Above all, he had fun with them. "When presented with, say, a box of apples," White reported, "he might fling one of them in an underarm pitch to a correspondent, to test whether the man was on his toes. He would borrow combs and pencils from the press—or accept chocolate bars." With Nixon, it was completely different. On the list of traveling journalists, White wrote, "down at the very bottom, . . . like a Pakistani woman set off by the wall of purdah, was my name set off from the rest by a wall of asterisks." White was not charmed. "You're on a campaign plane with ten or twelve guys," he explained, "and Kennedy walks back and says, 'Hey, Teddy, come on up and have a nightcap with me.' And even though you've spent eighteen hours with him that day, you're eager to talk about the day's events.

But when Nixon walked through the plane, every reporter was looking fixedly out the window." By the campaign's end, reporters were openly rooting for JFK, singing snide songs about Nixon, and all but locking arms with Kennedy's genial staff.[8]

When *The Making of the President, 1960* was published in 1961, readers—including White's fellow reporters—found it stunning. Read sympathetically, it amounted to a grand exercise in civic education, a tableau of scenes and stories that didn't make it into the newspapers. Journalists—and readers—could no longer ignore the ways that politicians and their staffs planned their strategies, handled the press, framed the opposition, shaped their images, and otherwise engineered their campaigns. White turned his book into a quadrennial franchise (though the subsequent books declined in quality), and it launched a fleet of imitators. Newspaper editors told their reporters that they didn't want to wait for the next Teddy White book to learn what happened on the campaign trail.[9]

But if White's reportage demystified, his high-flown style glamorized the campaign anew, offering an incurably romantic view of great leaders. *The Making of the President* portrayed the race for the White House as an epic drama, recounted with suspense and majesty. Its admiring, almost reverential tone resulted in part from White's choice of sources, who tended to come from within the campaigns. As a result, he missed the underside. Well-kept secrets like Nixon's "dirty tricks" and Kennedy's ailments would surface only years later. His imitators, meanwhile, in seeking to match his close-up reporting without the fan-boy posture, ended up resorting to a superficial hash of personalities, process, strategy, and insider cynicism.

White looked upon his legacy with ambivalence. At times he showed pride in participating in what he called "the American literature of reality. It proliferated with my generation . . . John Hersey on Hiroshima . . . John Gunther's *Inside the U.S.A.* I think I fit into that stream and I'm proud of it." But he also lamented that political reporting subsequently became focused on the inside story, neglecting the other elements that had made White's books distinctive and valuable: the fine-grained analyses of regions, constituencies, and traditions; the sensitivity to the ways that race, religion, and immigration shaped the contours of the body politic; the history that had produced the particular moment at which America stood in a given year. Most reporting focused on the here and now, the gamesmanship, the positioning. The journalists assigned to the candidates had little time for reflection. They massed in huge throngs, hovering over aides and "taking notes like mad," as White later put it, "getting all the little details." Though he had midwifed that style of reporting and writing, he said, "I sincerely regret it. Who gives a fuck if the guy had milk and Total for breakfast?"[10]

37

THE GREAT DEBATES

ON THE NIGHT OF MONDAY, September 26, 1960, the studio of WBBM-TV, a CBS affiliate in Chicago, was a hive of some 800 people—politicians, staff, network personnel, Secret Service agents, local police, assorted VIPs, and, by one count, 380 journalists. They had gathered for the first televised debate between John F. Kennedy and Richard Nixon. Expectations were high—for Kennedy, for Nixon, and for everyone who saw promise in television as a medium of political communication.[1]

Nixon arrived first. At 7:30 pm he pulled up at the loading dock in a shiny Oldsmobile. As he stepped out of the car, he crunched his knee against the door. The same knee had recently been badly infected, requiring an eleven-day hospital stay. Fifteen minutes later Kennedy arrived, gaining a psychological edge with a show of nonchalant tardiness. Walking onto the studio set, Kennedy found Nixon sitting under a boom microphone testing sound levels. As he jumped up to greet Kennedy, the vice president knocked his head against the mike with a reverberating thud. "It sounded like somebody dropped a watermelon," recalled CBS president Frank Stanton. Recovering, Nixon tried to make small talk, taking note of Kennedy's bronze glow. "You get that tan the way I do?" he asked. "Riding around in open cars?" Kennedy later told his press aide Pierre Salinger that Nixon looked horrible.[2]

So began the Great Debates, as NBC board chairman Robert Sarnoff dubbed the historic face-offs. For all the buildup, these weren't technically the first presidential debates—but they were the first in a general election. Since the emergence of radio, encounters like these had been eagerly awaited, as optimists predicted that the broadcast media would elevate the nation's political discourse and bring enlightened discussions into every home. As early as 1948 Tom Dewey and Harold Stassen, vying for the Republican presidential nod, had dueled before tens of millions of listeners. In 1952, NBC televised an all-star forum of candidates from both parties; in 1956, Stevenson and Kefauver debated on ABC; and in the 1960 primaries, Kennedy had debated Hubert Humphrey on Charleston's WCHS-TV, helping JFK carry the West Virginia primary that May. All along, the networks were maneuvering for the big prize: a fall contest between the two party standard-bearers. Those debates, they hoped, would enrich their business, their reputations, and—if their rhetoric was to be believed—democracy itself.[3]

Both candidates had reason to participate in 1960. Nixon, a champion high school debater, had won his first congressional race in 1946 by besting incumbent Jerry Voorhis in a string of face-offs. The 1952 Checkers speech—and eight years of commentary hailing him as the master of the new media politics—gave him confidence that he could use television effectively, as did his televised 1959 showdown with Nikita Khrushchev in an exhibition kitchen in Moscow. And if he refused, he feared, he would look like a coward.

But for all Nixon's reputed television prowess, the public was growing wise to TV's ways, and he wasn't keeping pace. Through the 1950s, the contrivance that liberals detected in the Checkers speech became increasingly apparent, and journalists now routinely described Nixon as a phony. Douglass Cater of *The Reporter* grasped the candidate's dilemma: "Nixon's arrival in the vice-presidency coincided with the full flowering of television and he has applied many of TV's techniques to develop the potential of his office," he wrote—learning to "manipulate the fade-in and the fade-out, the filters and the cropping devices familiar to the cinematographer." But, Cater added, "In this age of fast and fleeting publicity, the merchants of modern mass communications are ready to discard the old and faded figure for someone who is fresh and interesting." Nixon's test: "He must achieve the highest form of art—the art that appears artless."[4]

Kennedy saw an opening. No stranger to television, he appeared early in his career on NBC's *Meet the Press* and, with his young wife, Jackie, on Edward R. Murrow's interview show for CBS, *Person to Person*. Running for the Senate in 1952, he debated incumbent Henry Cabot Lodge on TV, and at the 1956 convention he narrated a film about the Democratic Party's history. JFK turned the charge that he was a creature of the television age into a virtue. In 1959 he wrote an article in *TV Guide* that, while conceding the dangers of "manipulation, exploitation, and gimmicks" by "demagogues" and "public relations experts," insisted that TV could yield insight into political leaders. "Honesty, vigor, compassion, intelligence—the presence or lack of these and other qualities make up what is called the candidate's 'image,'" Kennedy noted. "While some intellectuals and politicians may scoff at these images . . . my own conviction is that these images or impressions are likely to be uncannily correct."[5]

Kennedy had another reason to debate as well. He knew that many voters considered him callow or unserious. Appearing credible next to the vice president would endow him with gravitas. "Every time we get those two fellows on the screen," predicted Leonard Reinsch, who handled JFK's broadcast media, "we're going to gain and he's going to lose."

*   *   *

Armed with a foot locker stuffed with research materials, including a "Nixonpedia" detailing Nixon's positions (its name a less felicitous pun than the "Ikelopedia" of 1952), Kennedy and his aides came to Chicago on Sunday, September 25. Ted Sorensen, the speechwriter and policy hand often called JFK's alter ego, led a brains trust that had created piles of "fact cards" of data and talking points about policy issues from unemployment to steel production. On Monday, Kennedy reviewed the cards all morning and—after lunch and a midday speech to a carpenters' union—again in the late afternoon. Lying on his hotel bed in a white V-necked shirt and Army pants, the senator would gaze at an index card, try to memorize it, then send it spinning onto the floor.

While Sorensen led the cram session, Kennedy received coaching of a different sort from Reinsch and Bill Wilson. The TV gurus reminded him that whenever Nixon was speaking, Kennedy should watch him, so that reaction shots would show Kennedy respectfully engaged. They suggested, too, that Kennedy direct his remarks not to Nixon but to the camera, the better to draw in the viewer. And they assured him he didn't have to answer the question that was asked. He could, Reinsch said, "use each question as a springboard to another topic."[6]

Nixon was less well composed. Underweight from his hospital stay, his collar loose around his neck, he had contracted a 100-degree fever. On Monday morning he too had addressed the carpenters' union—a hostile audience for a Republican—and then retreated to his room at the Pick-Congress Hotel. For most of the day, he remained in isolation—his preferred state. Ted Rogers, who had coached Nixon through the Checkers speech, tended to details at the WBBM studio. The backdrop had been painted with a pattern of gray squares and draped by a gauze scrim. Frank Stanton of CBS called for modern wooden chairs by the Danish designer Hans Wegner, meant to provide support for JFK's chronically bad back. Rogers, however, wanted last-minute changes. He asked for tiny spotlights, to remove shadows from Nixon's face; he called for a desk to be placed in front of the moderator's spot; he asked that the backdrop be painted a darker gray to contrast with Nixon's light suit. As he tinkered with the set, Rogers had almost no contact with Nixon.

The fussing continued that night. Don Hewitt of CBS, the program's producer, remarked that JFK's white shirt gave off a glare, and the senator sent an aide to fetch a blue one from his hotel. Stanton told Reinsch that Kennedy's socks were too short. Reinsch had an aide give his own over-the-calf socks to the candidate. Hewitt offered the candidates the services of CBS's makeup people, but both declined. Nixon's aides, noting his pallor, urged him to reconsider. Nixon, who weeks earlier had told CBS news anchor Walter Cronkite that even shaving right before airtime could never eliminate his five o'clock shadow, agreed to let one of his own men apply some Lazy Shave beard stick. Meanwhile, Bill Wilson told Kennedy that he would benefit from a light dusting. "Do you know what you're doing?" Kennedy asked. Wilson said he did and applied some Max Factor Creme Puff powder from a nearby drugstore.[7]

At eight thirty, the hour-long debate began. The moderator, Howard K. Smith of CBS, sat between the candidates and introduced them. Each delivered an eight-minute opening statement, after which a panel of four TV journalists asked ten questions. Most covered policy: schools, farms, taxes, wages, health care for the aged. A few dealt with qualifications: the candidates' youth, their habits of decision making. Kennedy answered crisply, if densely. Facts spilled forth, sometimes tumbling over one another, but his command of policy dispelled preconceptions of a lightweight. As important, he returned repeatedly to his campaign theme that under Eisenhower and Nixon the United States had stagnated—in economics, in defense, in civil rights. He stressed the need for new ideas and new leadership to get the country, as he had taken to saying, "moving again."

Nixon spoke in his unerringly logical way. But in trying to score debating points, he failed to develop a theme, or to distinguish his own views from Kennedy's, except on predictable partisan issues (he opposed a hike in the minimum wage). He repeatedly said that he agreed with what Kennedy had just said, or that he disagreed with Kennedy only about means, not about ends, making Kennedy seem like the one with the good ideas. At one point, Nixon waived his allotted time after Kennedy's remarks—an unforced error he would never commit again.

If Kennedy's arguments were superior, so was his appearance. Poised and tan in his dark suit, he projected composure. The fidgeting that colleagues had grown used to in private moments—and that Sorensen had seen in the car ride to the studio—gave way to purposeful gestures. Meanwhile, Nixon looked pasty and pale. His gray suit blended in with the drab studio walls. Sweat streaked his Lazy Shave. One reaction shot caught him mopping his brow.

In the control room, the candidates' TV aides, Ted Rogers and Bill Wilson, argued with Don Hewitt of CBS. Before the debate, Rogers had asked Hewitt not to show any reaction shots, but Hewitt had insisted on his editorial freedom. Now, as Wilson saw how badly Nixon came across on the monitor, he joked that the producer owed him more shots of Nixon. Rogers, seeing the same pictures, barked out, "No, no"—Nixon had been shown enough. Hewitt told both men to pipe down so he could do his job.

After the contest, the candidates' comments were few. No campaign spokesmen were trotted out to explain how their man had won, and the next day's newspapers quoted them sparingly—although Kennedy's aides, speaking on background so as not to be seen as gloating, made clear they thought they had won. That judgment was widespread. The journalist Ben Bradlee, covering the debates for *Newsweek*, thought Nixon looked like "an awkward cadaver." Eisenhower, who had urged Nixon to consult his own TV coach, later grumbled, "Montgomery would never have let him look as he did in that first television debate." Henry Cabot Lodge, Nixon's running mate, was livid. "That son of a bitch just cost us the election," he fumed.[8]

* * *

Though at first some columnists such as Joe Alsop and James Reston called it a draw—afraid, in Ben Bradlee's judgment, to be tagged as pro-Kennedy if they did otherwise—soon the press and public alike were proclaiming a Kennedy victory. So were opinion polls. The key indicator was the effect on the race. Before Chicago, the candidates were neck-and-neck. Kennedy's pollster Lou Harris, a protégé of Elmo Roper who had joined JFK's campaign team in 1957, had long argued that mass communication was vital in an age of weakening party loyalties and strong interest in personalities, and he now reported that JFK had opened up a 48 to 43 percent lead over Nixon. The turn, he said, marked "the first time that either candidate has been able to show the other open water," concluding confidently, "This is almost wholly the result of the Monday night debate." Surging crowds at Kennedy's campaign rallies confirmed the data. "The next day we hit Cleveland," press secretary Pierre Salinger recalled. "The people were coming out of the walls."[9]

Almost everyone attributed Kennedy's achievement to the visuals. A reporter for the *Chicago Daily News* quoted a makeup artist claiming that no professional could have done such a bad job on the vice president, leading to the headline: "Was Nixon Sabotaged by Make-Up Artists?" *MAD* magazine ran a parody advertisement that depicted Nixon reinventing himself with help from a Gillette razor and a copy of *The Hidden Persuaders*. Nixon agreed. "I had concentrated too much on substance and not enough on appearance," he wrote in *Six Crises*, an early memoir, framing his deficiencies in the most flattering way. For the remaining debates, he wore dark suits and hired his own makeup man. On one occasion Ted Rogers surreptitiously lowered the thermostat. "It felt like a meat locker," Reinsch recalled. In retaliation, Bill Wilson slipped into the basement to jack up the temperature as high as it would go.[10]

Kennedy, too, believed TV had helped him. Riding high, his team recycled the opening remarks from the first debate into a campaign ad. (The first version of it had included a cut-away shot to a shifty-eyed Nixon— a moment spliced in from later in the evening—triggering cries of foul.) "Television gives people a chance to look at their candidate close up and close to the bone," JFK told the journalist Rowland Evans after his election victory. "For the first time since the Greek city-states . . . it brings us within reach of that ideal where every voter has a chance to measure the candidate."[11]

The conclusion that television decided the outcome was widely shared. "If Jack Kennedy had not been so much more photogenic on television than Nixon," judged Arthur Krock of the *New York Times*, a longtime Kennedy family friend, "he would have been defeated." Two intellectuals in particular helped certify this idea in the public mind. The first was Teddy White, who depicted the debates as "a revolution in American Presidential politics." White declared in *The Making of the President* that "those who heard the debates on radio, according to sample surveys believed that the two candidates came off almost equal. Yet every survey of those who watched the debates on television. . . . It was the picture image that had done it." Afterward, no politician could afford to give television anything less than his utmost attention.[12]

If Teddy White framed popular understandings of the campaign, Marshall McLuhan legitimized the conceit of television's unique, even magical, power. A literature professor at the University of Toronto, McLuhan had been gaining renown in Canada for his writings about communications, and after the Kennedy-Nixon debate, a Toronto newspaper columnist shared the professor's debate analysis. Viewers, McLuhan explained, understood Nixon and Kennedy as archetypes familiar to them from the small screen. Nixon looked like a "railway lawyer who signs leases that are not in the best interests on the folks in the little town." Kennedy came across as "the shy young sheriff."[13]

A few years later, in his book *Understanding Media*, McLuhan elaborated on his ideas. The book contained his famous theory that "hot" media like radio were conducive to sharply defined presentation styles (like Nixon's), while "cool" media like TV were friendlier to softer images (like Kennedy's). Even as McLuhan took some gratuitous swipes at Teddy White, his own analysis rested heavily on a factoid he gleaned from the reporter. "In the Kennedy-Nixon debates, those who heard them on radio received an overwhelming idea of Nixon's superiority," McLuhan wrote, grossly distorting White's assertion. "It was Nixon's fate to provide a sharp, high-definition image and action for the cool TV medium that translated that sharp image into the impression of a phony."[14]

The debates had clearly helped Kennedy win the presidency. But the idea that he triumphed because of his looks alone, or because of television as a medium—as opposed to his overall performance in those contests—was never substantiated. The claim that Nixon outperformed Kennedy among radio listeners was often cited, with the implication that television's pictures misled while the unadulterated radio voice conveyed only logic. But only one survey, of a mere 282 radio listeners, found a Nixon edge, and its sample wasn't representative. Nor was it apparent that television conveyed less meaningful information than radio. Kennedy may well have been right in arguing in *TV Guide* that the visual medium could reveal "honesty, vigor, compassion." Kennedy "won" on the night of September 26, 1960, not just because he looked good, but because through the entirety of his performance he convinced voters that he would be a better president.[15]

38

THE POLITICS OF IMAGE

THE GREAT DEBATES captured the public fancy because they offered an unprecedented opportunity for voters to judge their presidential candidates side by side. But did they enrich American democracy, as their sponsors insisted, providing voters with the information to make an informed judgment as never before? Or were they just political theater, a political version of *The $64,000 Question*? For years after 1960, these questions would generate a great debate of another kind.

No one used more utopian rhetoric than the network executives. Reprising the boosterism surrounding TV's coverage of the party conventions, they touted the Nixon-Kennedy face-offs as a boon to the political process. Frank Stanton gave the argument its theoretical ballast. The holder of a PhD in psychology, he had pioneered the study of radio audiences in the 1930s, working closely with Paul Lazarsfeld of Columbia University before climbing the ladder at CBS, where he was known as the brains of the network. In a speech to journalists in 1960, he argued that the debates held the key to restoring thoughtful democratic participation in an impersonal mass society. By way of contrast, Stanton recalled the riotous, out-of-doors politics of the nineteenth century, when large throngs turned out at torchlight parades and rallies and—with alcohol, music, and colorful costumes—fed off one another's partisan passions. Those old-style jamborees were calculated, Stanton said, "not to inform, or to create an atmosphere conducive to the appraisal of information, but to whip up attitudes capable of overcoming any temptation to judiciousness." In the modern era, he said, America needed a higher form of political participation, and the televised debates would treat voters as independent of mind, and help them weigh the issues with care. Democracy demanded no less.[1]

After watching the Kennedy-Nixon contests, many observers agreed. Jack Gould of the *New York Times* said the debates showed "the civic usefulness of the broadcasting media," and launched an edifying public conversation about the candidates' merits. "Overnight," wrote Gould, "there was born a new interest in the campaign that had earlier been productive of coast-to-coast somnolence." Walter Lippmann, still a shaper of public opinion at seventy-one, also found much to praise. Though earlier in the year Lippmann—who detested television and rarely watched it—had spurned an offer to appear on CBS, he pronounced the Kennedy-Nixon debates an antidote to packaged politics. "The whole effect is the candidate himself," he said, "and not his ghost writers and public relations men." Nixon showed himself to be "an indecisive man who lacks that inner conviction and self-confidence," while Kennedy emerged as "a natural leader, organizer, and ruler of men."[2]

* * *

Like all great debates, this one had an opposing side. A host of intellectuals, from the historian Henry Steele Commager to *Saturday Review* editor Norman Cousins, concluded that far from enriching democracy, the debates degraded and trivialized it. "The very fact of arousing the interest of the millions," argued Max Ascoli, editor of *The Reporter*, "further lowers the level of campaign oratory that is usually not too high." Cousins wrote an article entitled "Presidents Don't Have to Be Quiz Champions."[3]

The most enduring critique came from Daniel Boorstin, a forty-six-year-old history professor at the University of Chicago. Bespectacled, bow-tied, and tweedy, Boorstin, despite his professional affiliation, identified proudly as an "amateur" historian, having never taken a U.S. history course in his life. Born in Atlanta, raised in Oklahoma, he was educated at Harvard, Oxford, and Yale Law School, coming to history through his study of law. Fleetingly a Communist Party member in the 1930s, he was branded a conservative after he cooperatively testified before the House Committee on Un-American Activities, citing a new book of his, *The Genius of American Politics*, about the pragmatic character of American liberalism, to show that his scholarship promoted anti-communism. Five years later Boorstin published *The Americans: The Colonial Experience*, the first volume of a sweeping trilogy, which won him the Bancroft Prize, his adopted discipline's highest honor.[4]

In the 1950s, Boorstin began studying how changes in mass communication were affecting politics. In a 1955 article for *Commentary*, "Selling the President to the People," he sketched a rough history of the new mass-mediated presidential politics, from Andrew Jackson and Amos Kendall to Walter Lippmann and Edward Bernays to Eisenhower's "frequent (and on the whole successful) use" of TV. Sharing in the wariness of hidden persuasion, Boorstin portrayed a White House that had become at once more finely attuned to public opinion and more manipulative in its image craft. "Never again," Boorstin predicted, "would any man attain the presidency or discharge its duties satisfactorily without entering into an intimate and conscious relation with the whole public."[5]

Among those who read the piece was Edward Bernays, who, always pleased to happen upon a reference to himself, wrote to Boorstin. The letter launched a correspondence that would last three decades. They traded thoughts about Bernays's memoir, then in progress, and Boorstin incorporated Bernays's comments into his thinking about presidential image, which he continued to develop into 1960. Giving talks that fall around Chicago and the Midwest—a conference on mass culture at Ohio State University; the ladies' auxiliary of the Anshe Emet Synagogue—Boorstin discussed the spread of contrived news stunts that Bernays had dubbed "overt acts." Boorstin called these acts "pseudo-events"—showing the influence of Lippmann's *Public Opinion*—defining them as occurrences staged expressly with the aim of producing news, and said that they had multiplied thanks to "the rise of centralized newsgathering and the rise of the Washington press corps." The main beneficiary was the president. While other government officials could also whip up fake news—Boorstin cited Joe McCarthy—he noted that "the president has an ever more ready, more frequent, and more centralized access to the world of pseudo-events."[6]

As Boorstin refined his thoughts, he was also clipping newspaper articles. He took special note of the Kennedy-Nixon debates, which he called "a clinical example of the pseudo-event . . . and of its consequences for democracy in America." The media, he recorded in his notes, "want to create 'news,' i.e., make conflicts"—a tendency shown by frivolous questions from the debate panelists about whether Harry Truman was right to tell the Republicans to "go to hell" or why Eisenhower, when asked, couldn't cite a single instance when Nixon had helped him make a decision. Unlike Lippmann, Boorstin did not think that the candidates' debate performances reflected their aptitude for the presidency. "The ability of a person under klieg lights (without notes) to answer in 2½ minutes a question that has been kept in the vault of the Manufacturer's [sic] Trust Company has a dubious relevance to his real qualifications to make deliberate presidential decisions on long-standing public questions after being instructed by a corps of advisers," he wrote. Nor could he accept Jack Gould's suggestion that the debates stimulated engagement with public policy. What captured people's fancy was, on the contrary, "the pseudo-event itself: the lighting, the make-up, the ground-rules, whether notes will be allowed, etc. . . . Even the question of whether there should be a 5th debate seemed for a while to be a lively issue. . . . The drama of the situation was mostly specious."[7]

* * *

This caustic analysis would form the basis of a book. *The Image, Or What Happened to the American Dream*, as it was originally titled, described how the rise of mass media, advertising, and public relations had fashioned a looking-glass world in which celebrities replaced heroes, traveling degenerated into tourism, credibility superseded truth, invention supplanted discovery, and personality trumped character. American democracy had always depended on the public's capacity to separate truth from falsehood, he argued, but Jefferson and Lincoln hadn't reckoned with the manufactured illusions of mass culture. Echoing Lippmann's misgivings about the wisdom of the majority, Boorstin questioned the public's ability to resist the seductions of contrived news, televised spectacles, and staged political events.[8]

The Image would influence a range of thinkers, from the conservative columnist George Will, who warmed to its portrait of a lobotomized electorate, to the French postmodern theorists Jean Baudrillard and Guy Debord, who ran with its idea of an alternate sham reality. Boorstin's terminology would provide reference points in a growing public and academic exploration of the nature of reality—and the pervasiveness of contrived reality—in the modern age. But detractors faulted Boorstin for joining in what the unflagging Bruce Bliven called a "fashionable handwringing" over "what mass communication is doing to American society." Marshall McLuhan compared Boorstin to Vance Packard: both men made it their purpose "to provide entertainment with moral disapproval as a highbrow trademark." The historian Kenneth Lynn charged Boorstin with failing to apply to the past the tart intelligence he brought to the present—an oversight that permitted him to mock Walt Disney's *Davy Crockett* TV series while taking at face value the original antebellum cult of Crockett, which was actually "the canned product of a group of Whig propagandists." Lynn, too, likened Boorstin's book, with its generalizations and its narrative of decline, to *The Hidden Persuaders*—but deemed it worse because, unlike Packard, Boorstin dressed up his popular argument in the trappings of scholarship. "By his own definition," Lynn concluded, "Boorstin has written a pseudo-book."[9]

Boorstin certainly overgeneralized. But on several subjects *The Image* went deeper than the usual complaints about political manipulation. He understood that the phenomenon had broader bases and deeper roots than the self-serving desires of politicians. "The creation and multiplication of pseudo-events is not the result of conspiracy or of evil purpose, by politicians, newspapermen, or anyone else," he wrote in an early iteration of his ideas. Rather, it "comes from the whole machinery of our culture. It is the inevitable result of the daily work of men of good will going about their jobs in honest and workmanlike fashion." As John Dewey had said of Theodore Roosevelt, the image makers were simply trying to succeed on the terms of their age. Boorstin also noted that individuals were becoming shrewder about the image culture. In his *Commentary* article he had written about "the decline of naivety," an idea that in his 1960 notes he revised into the "New Sophistication." By this, he meant that the public now realized that an "increasing proportion of events are pseudo-events" and was trying to adapt. But the New Sophistication also justified the fashionable attitude "that there is no underlying reality . . . that the reality is created by the image or is identical to it"—a cynical stance that passed itself off as the height of savvy, but was in fact a delusion, even a "New Naïveté." Boorstin himself held firmly to a traditional distinction between image and reality, holding out hope that at least some citizens would be able to "penetrate the unknown jungle of images in which we live our daily lives." Demystifying the image culture might serve as a first step toward achieving a more educated populace and a stronger democracy.

In this project, Boorstin was joined to his contemporary Teddy White. White glorified the Great Debates while Boorstin trashed them, and White adored the political scene while Boorstin viewed it with despair. But White, as much as anyone of his generation, carried out Boorstin's injunction to expose "the thicket of unreality" that constituted contemporary presidential politics. It was White who brought the hidden work of aides and private interactions with journalists into public view, who recorded for posterity Kennedy in his T-shirt flipping through Ted Sorensen's fact cards, who exposed the intense preparation behind JFK's seemingly relaxed demeanor. Boorstin, for his part, spelled out the paradox by which White's book could at once enrich the public storehouse of political knowledge and inspire an ever more frantic search for inside dope. "The stage machinery, the processes of fabricating and projecting the image, fascinate us," Boorstin wrote. "We are all interested in watching a skillful feat of magic; we are still more interested in looking behind the scenes and seeing precisely how it was made to seem that the lady was sawed in half. . . . Even after we have been taken behind the scenes, we can still enjoy the pleasures of deception."

The Kennedy-Nixon debates that Boorstin hailed as the ultimate pseudo-event captivated Americans, and the frenetic coverage of them underscored the hunger for behind-the-scenes reporting from a public growing wise to presidential image craft. White thought that informing his readers about the veiled workings of politics could make them better citizens, more knowledgeable participants in the democratic project. Boorstin believed equally in the need for demystification, but in his mournful reflections on the human taste for illusion, he displayed a deep uncertainty about whether that demystification could be had without tumbling into a cynicism that was, in its way, a treacherous new form of naïveté.

39

THE KENNEDY MOMENT

SHORTLY AFTER KENNEDY'S ELECTION, his press secretary, Pierre Salinger, flew to Palm Beach, where the Kennedy clan's sprawling white stucco estate was serving as transition headquarters. Salinger had an idea. Since TV had been key to the senator's victory, he argued, JFK should take a dramatic step: open his presidential press conferences to live coverage. "The reaction," he recalled, "was swift and violent." Several top aides, including Ted Sorensen and national security adviser–designate McGeorge Bundy, objected. Some feared overexposure; others worried that Kennedy might make a gaffe. The State Department fretted that a stray comment might trigger an international incident or even nuclear war. But the loudest objections came from the newspapermen, who, already nervous about their eclipse by their rivals in television, erupted in what Salinger called "a near riot."[1]

Yet Kennedy agreed to it. He was confident in his ability to think on his feet, calculate quickly the ramifications of his statements, and tiptoe around any topic he didn't want to address. He also believed, at least in the abstract, in the purpose of the press conference, which was, as he said to reporters some months later, "to have the president in the bull's-eye, which I think is revealing." And television, he knew, had been good to him.[2]

Two days after Christmas, Salinger met with network representatives, who agreed to periodically preempt their regular shows to air the press conferences. Salinger then had to face the print correspondents, many of whom were enjoying a working vacation covering the president-elect in Florida, desultorily carrying out their assignments in swim trunks or Bermuda shorts.[3]

Meeting at the Palm Beach Towers Hotel, the reporters fired endless questions at Salinger, who tried to assuage their anxieties. When someone asked if the White House would need to make changes to the Indian Treaty Room, Salinger went off the record to explain that he might move the parleys to another auditorium. This prospect stirred up new worries. One participant—putting his own question off the record—blurted out, "If you are going to throw in that big video tape machine for each network, there is not going to be any room for any of us little old reporters to do our work." Like Woodrow Wilson opening his press conferences to all comers, or Truman moving his out of the Oval Office, Salinger's changes threatened to extinguish any remnants of fellowship and informality. Publicly, journalistic opinion ranged from dubious to dismissive. Richard Strout, *The New Republic*'s T.R.B., offered a curmudgeonly thumbs-down. "If Kennedy wants to revive FDR's fireside chats—fine, but he shouldn't use the press conference as a vehicle. . . . The best press conference is the one where reporters remain anonymous, where they can ask unself-conscious questions without being unpaid radio or TV actors. . . . Eisenhower brought TV into the affair and formalized the press conference; we always thought it a mistake."[4]

As the torch passed from Eisenhower's salesmen to Kennedy's New Frontiersmen, members of the news media were not entirely enthusiastic. Personally, they found the new president a breath of fresh air after the aloof Ike, who, the columnist Mary McGrory wrote, had "regarded reporters as visitors from another planet." Kennedy, in contrast, "tends to think of them as fellow lodge members." Arthur Krock of the *New York Times* put it more cynically. "Such were Kennedy's wit, grace and youthful good looks that some representatives of the press, radio and television succumbed to it," he snarled. "Objectivity and even fairness . . . went out the window." Many leading journalists were also friends of the president, including Joe and Stewart Alsop, *Newsweek*'s Ben Bradlee (soon to join *The Washington Post* as executive editor), and the columnist Charlie Bartlett, who could claim the distinction of having introduced Jack to Jackie. Joe Kraft was devoted enough to do advance work for the Kennedy campaign before returning to the pundits' ranks.[5]

But if the relationship between Kennedy and reporters was a romance, it was a tempestuous one. Journalists still felt stifled by the Cold War secrecy that Kennedy, every bit as much as Ike, tried to enforce. They had also grown alert, through many administrations, to the extent of presidential image making, which now with television seemed to take on a limitless new power.[6]

* * *

To produce the live press conferences—which had become, after all, a television show—Salinger turned to Bill Wilson. The venue they selected to stage the programs was the State Department auditorium, an 800-seat hall described by *Time* magazine's Hugh Sidey as "a vast chamber with thick beige carpeting and gaudy orange-and-black padded seats." Attentive to the visuals, Wilson tinkered with the furnishings. He set up a special platform to hold two television cameras, six newsreel cameras, and a gaggle of photographers. Two more cameras would sit in the corners at the front of the room. Wilson hung a curtain to make the place feel a bit cozier, and he ordered a custom-built presidential lectern, with a 15-inch presidential seal on the front and two panes of lit glass to illuminate the president from below. (Janet Travell, Kennedy's physician, later asked Salinger to raise the lectern, so the president wouldn't have to strain his delicate back.) Wilson also suggested that the president enter the room thirty seconds after the telecast went live, giving the announcers time to introduce him and adding a frisson of anticipation.[7]

With some 60 million Americans watching, the first broadcast aired on January 25, 1961, just after 6 pm. Viewers saw a close-up of the presidential seal on the front of the lectern and heard the voice of ABC's Lewis Shollenberger: "From the new State Department auditorium in Washington, D.C., we are about to bring you the first of President John F. Kennedy's news conferences. This is being presented *live* for the first time." The camera cut to a wide shot of the auditorium, then slowly panned the reporters.[8]

The live transmission, the new, modern space, and the young president's facility with TV combined to make the event altogether more theatrical than Eisenhower's sessions. Ike, resting wearily against a desk, had been at floor level with the correspondents, who sat in makeshift rows of chairs. JFK, standing tall on a six-foot platform, loomed above them. Eisenhower's conferences, despite Hagerty's innovations, still put the print reporters first. Kennedy's were made for TV, and if the print reporters weren't quite an afterthought, neither were they the main audience. Just as

Kennedy during the fall debates had spoken to the camera, not to Nixon, so during the press conferences he remembered that most of his viewers were outside the room.[9]

Treating the press conference as a television spectacular, news reports likened Kennedy to a Hollywood leading man. The *New York Times*'s Russell Baker pronounced JFK "a new star with tremendous national appeal and the skill of a consummate showman." Gould, Krock, and other commentators revived talk of television's potential as an instrument of democracy. "He is acting to widen the sense of public participation in government," raved syndicated columnist Roscoe Drummond. "He is creating a new intimacy between the president and the people."[10]

Yet discontent lingered. The lack of intimacy, the meager amount of information disclosed, the power that the new format bestowed on the president—all occasioned grumbling. Inverting the praise, detractors were put off by what the British commentator Alistair Cooke called "the disturbing hint of Hollywood" suffusing the event. After Salinger forbade reporters from identifying themselves—to curtail the grandstanding that occurred under Ike—Peter Lisagor of the *Chicago Daily News* scoffed that "reporters became spear carriers in a great televised opera." Boorstin noted that the audience's role was diminished too, with viewers reduced to taking in the press conference "as a dramatic performance. . . . more interested to hear competing interpretations by skilled commentators" of how the president did than to actually learn anything about the issues he discussed.[11]

Resentful, Republicans charged that Kennedy was illegitimately augmenting his presidential power. Senate minority leader Everett Dirksen of Illinois claimed never to have seen an administration "so organized in the propaganda field," and he and House minority leader Charlie Halleck began holding their own weekly televised briefings, dubbed "the Ev and Charlie Show." But their counterprogramming only highlighted Kennedy's youth and energy and underscored the presidency's preeminence. The senescent Republicans, untrained in modern media, came across as burned-out vaudevillians, drawn by *The Washington Post*'s Herblock shuffling across a stage in plaid coats, striped pants, bowlers, and canes. Russell Baker noted that the day after Kennedy drew a crowd of almost 400—a typical turnout—the Republicans prepared the Capitol press gallery for a mere 75. Seventeen showed up.[12]

In time, the novelty of Kennedy's conferences wore off. Tiring of them himself, the president scaled back. Contrary to his promises, he ultimately gave them less frequently than had Eisenhower. But he used them often enough to stay in the public eye, and they allowed him to showcase his laconic wit and unflappable style. He had a rare knack, too, for sparring with the press pack in ways that seemed more playful than petulant. "In his press conference technique," *Time* said, "Kennedy has never had an equal."[13]

Weeks after the first news conference, pollster Lou Harris returned an early verdict. Although the public still lacked a grasp of Kennedy's legislative program, the press conferences were nonetheless "feats of incredible personal accomplishment . . . and fearlessness in calling a spade a spade." They had left "a truly phenomenal public imprint for only 60 days" into the new president's term.[14]

* * *

In April 1961, Kennedy endorsed plans, hatched under Eisenhower, to topple the Communist regime of Fidel Castro, who had seized power in Cuba two years before. Anti-Castro Cuban exiles would mount an invasion, with covert CIA support, in hopes of inspiring an uprising. Like Ike, Kennedy tried to keep the mission secret, but hints made their way into the news. *The Nation* even mentioned the CIA's role, and the *New York Times*, while withholding that key detail, ran a front-page story about the planned invasion on April 7. "It was about as secret," James Reston said, "as opening day in Yankee Stadium." At one point Kennedy met alone with Chalmers Roberts, of *The Washington Post*, sitting in a rocking chair "smoking one of his thin cigars, in a totally relaxed manner," and admitting to the CIA's involvement, though Roberts too chose not to publicize that fact.[15]

The bombing raids began on April 15. But at Bahia de Cochinos, or the Bay of Pigs, on Cuba's southern shore, the rebel forces found themselves outmatched. The CIA asked for air cover, but Kennedy balked, wanting to be able to deny that the invasion was an American military operation. Castro's forces routed the exiles in a bloodbath. Suddenly, Kennedy faced the greatest crisis of his three-month-old presidency.

Weeks before, the president had scheduled a talk to the American Society of Newspaper Editors for April 20, at the Statler-Hilton, near the White House. The day arrived just as the last Cuban rebels were captured. In a hastily written speech, the product of a Ted Sorensen all-nighter, Kennedy fudged the question of American involvement. He called the failed operation "a struggle of Cuban patriots against a Cuban dictator"—technically accurate, but less than truthful. Disclosing little about the U.S. role in the debacle, he focused on the future, pledging not to abandon Cuba even as he vowed to wind down the Cold War and ensure that it "reached its climax in the late 1950s and the early 1960s."[16]

But Kennedy, while loath to reveal operational details, couldn't keep hedging. He arrived at his press conference the next morning at ten o'clock in a quandary. Entering the State Department auditorium, in a blue pinstripe suit and muted red tie, and walking "at a brisk athletic pace," according to Richard Strout, he was "courteous, reserved, and controlled." When the first question about Cuba came, Kennedy declined to elaborate on his previous statements. "I think that the facts of the matter involving Cuba will come out in due time," he said tersely. "As for me, I am confining myself to my statement for good reason."[17]

The press corps wouldn't relent. The normally friendly Sander Vanocur of NBC pressed JFK on why administration sources had been "clamming up" since the invasion. "Well," the president began, "I think, in answer to your question that we have to make a judgment as to how much we can usefully say that would aid the interest of the United States. One of the problems of a free society . . . is this problem of information." He then referred obliquely to James Reston's column in the *Times* that day, in which Secretary of State Dean Rusk and Under Secretary Chester Bowles, rushing to escape blame, had leaked word that they had opposed the operation. Taking a veiled shot at his aides, Kennedy said that in the days ahead many officials would be offering self-serving accounts. "There's an old saying," he said, "that victory has 100 fathers and defeat is an orphan." But his own silence, Kennedy continued, shouldn't be read as a way to avoid blame. His desire and need to withhold "further statement, detailed discussions," he explained, "are not to conceal responsibility, because I'm the responsible officer of the government—and that is quite obvious—but merely because I do not believe that such a discussion would benefit us during the present difficult situation."[18]

Kennedy gave the correspondents what they had been waiting to hear. If he couldn't be candid about all the details of his operation, he was candid about his lack of candor. His "old saying" was the lead in Chalmers Roberts's story in *The Washington Post* the next day and the kicker in the *New York Times*. It showed the new president to be a mature leader willing to own up to his administration's failures.[19]

Yet Kennedy also dissimulated. Though he promised that the full story about Cuba would emerge "in due time," he was that same day ensuring that his own version of events would make the papers. ("Few presidents," Sorensen said, were "so skillful in evading or even misleading the press whenever secrecy required.") He quietly invited Roberts and Murrey Marder of *The Washington Post* to his office for a deep background conversation, where he filled them in on the advice he received from the CIA and the Joint Chiefs of Staff to proceed with the long-planned invasion despite his reservations. The *Post*'s story, attributed to "informed sources," tracked JFK's account closely. The *New York Herald Tribune*'s Marguerite Higgins, given similar treatment, dutifully reported that Rusk had backed the operation. Arthur Krock, too, received a personal briefing from the president, lubricated by bourbon (Krock) and "very light and small" daiquiris (JFK), in which Kennedy told the columnist that the Joint Chiefs had promised that Cuba was as sure a bet as the successful Guatemala operation of 1954. In other media outlets, Bobby Kennedy, Schlesinger, and other aides also seeded a pro-JFK storyline.[20]

Kennedy was not out of the woods. Reston, though sympathetic, devoted a column on May 10 to two of JFK's biggest deceptions: first, the administration had exaggerated the size of the landing force, hoping to inspire a Cuban uprising; later, it lowballed the figure, aiming to downplay the defeat. But the Cubans and Russians had intelligence sources that gave them a true picture of the invasions, Reston said, so that "the American people were the only ones to be fooled." Reston added that while he could abide the occasional request not to publish military secrets, he resented the attempt "to encourage the press to publish information known by the government to be false."[21]

Still, Reston had to admit that Kennedy, through his public remarks at his press conference, had satisfied most Americans. In Gallup's next poll, his approval rating shot up to 83 percent. "In the midst of one of the worst presidential blunders in recent history, over Cuba," wrote Reston, "he stands higher in the esteem of his colleagues in Washington than ever before."[22]

Kennedy agreed, albeit with puzzlement. "It's just like Eisenhower," he said. "The worse I do, the more popular I get."[23]

NEWS MANAGEMENT IN CAMELOT

THE GOOD PRESS that John F. Kennedy enjoyed in his early months was the payoff of years of cultivation, as dogged and deft as any president's since Theodore Roosevelt.

It started at the top of the journalistic pecking order. Immediately after his election victory, Kennedy showered Walter Lippmann with more attention than the columnist had received since the Wilson administration. JFK called on Lippmann at his Woodley Road home in Washington to ask advice on choosing a secretary of state. A few weeks later Ted Sorensen dropped by with a sneak preview of the inaugural address, asking for edits. (After suggesting a few, Lippmann went on to praise the speech in his column.) Soon Washington wags were joking that if Lippmann's furnace exploded during Sunday brunch, Kennedy would need to hire a new senior staff. Lippmann's rival Arthur Krock was also kept close. An old friend of Joseph P. Kennedy, Krock had helped transform *Why England Slept* into a publishable book in 1940, and in 1957 lobbied behind the scenes for *Profiles in Courage* to win a Pulitzer Prize. Dining with JFK the night of his inauguration, Krock told the president that his speech, which he too had seen in advance, surpassed any since Wilson's. The Alsops as well were back in favor—and the Executive Mansion—for the first time since FDR's presidency, securing invitations to a white-tie White House gala. And James

Reston, Lippmann's heir apparent as Washington's alpha pundit, despite having "never talked to a president" before—on the logic that "once you become sympathetic, it becomes increasingly difficult to employ the critical faculties"—nonetheless succumbed to Kennedy's entreaties.[1]

Kennedy's outreach extended to the press corps' lower tiers as well. State dinners included the editors of publications from *The Reporter* to *La Prensa*. Small-circulation newspaper editors were given luncheons, and White House staff and cabinet members were released to talk (somewhat) freely to correspondents. Kennedy spent "such a considerable portion of his attention to leaking news, planting rumors, and playing off one reporter against another," wrote William Shannon of the *New York Post*, "that it sometimes seems his dream job is not being chief executive of the nation but managing editor of a hypothetical newspaper."[2]

Images were given special scrutiny. The White House disseminated attractive pictures of the president and his family—televised footage of Jackie leading a White House tour, photographs of the Kennedy children playing under their father's desk—while the president, sensitive about his appearance to the point of vanity, tried to avoid unflattering ones. He studiously avoided headwear, and when he made the cover of *Gentleman's Quarterly*, known to insiders for its gay following, he groused, "I'll be the laughingstock of the country." To Ben Bradlee he complained about a magazine photo of the two of them sailing, shirtless, that showed what Kennedy called "the Fitzgerald breasts."[3]

As they had complained about the press conferences, reporters and Republicans objected to these wide-ranging efforts to influence how Kennedy was portrayed. An article in *U.S. News & World Report,* sensationally titled "The Kennedy 'Image'—How It's Built," asked the secret of JFK's popularity and gave a two-word answer: "public relations." The conservative writer Fletcher Knebel, writing in *Look*, offered an even more conclusory judgment. "Kennedy officialdom," he asserted, "is more concerned with its 'image,' than any Washington regime in modern times."[4]

* * *

For all his chumminess with reporters, Kennedy knew that, as he told Sorensen, "their interest and ours ultimately conflict." Speaking to the press, he put it more diplomatically. "I think that they are doing their task, as a critical branch, the Fourth Estate," he said. "And I am attempting to do mine. And we are going to live together for a period and then go our separate ways."[5]

Although Kennedy tried to play the good sport, insisting that he didn't complain about his coverage, that wasn't always the case. "He had," Sorensen admitted, "an inexhaustible capacity to take displeasure from what he read." As Knebel detailed, JFK and his staff chewed out the authors of stories they disliked and sometimes threatened lawsuits or froze out offending publications. The dispatches of the *New York Times*'s young Saigon correspondent, David Halberstam, so angered the president that he asked *Times* publisher Arthur Sulzberger to reassign him. Scribes, of course, could recall similar stories about JFK's predecessors, but these punitive steps belied Kennedy's professed cool.[6]

Like his predecessors, JFK got angriest when journalists published information that he thought should be kept secret. On a few occasions, he authorized FBI surveillance of journalists who divulged sensitive information: *Newsweek*'s Lloyd Norman, who exposed classified U.S. plans in case the Soviets moved on West Berlin; the *New York Times*'s Hanson Baldwin, who revealed the sizes of the U.S. and Soviet missile arsenals, also classified; and columnists Robert S. Allen and Paul Scott, who had disclosed information about the nation's stock of missiles. Writing about these incidents in *The Atlantic Monthly*, Baldwin described federal agents visiting reporters' homes, tapping their phones, shadowing them in Pentagon corridors, probing their friendships and associations, and pressuring them to reveal their sources. Although he granted that Eisenhower (and perhaps other presidents) had done similar things, he maintained that the surveillance served no legitimate purpose and that the stories in question in fact "nearly always dealt with subjects and facts fully known to the Russians."[7]

Kennedy set forth his view of the press's Cold War responsibilities in a second speech that he gave in the wake of the Bay of Pigs disaster. His first speech, which he had given on April 20 to newspaper editors in Washington, had merely reaffirmed his desire to see a liberated Cuba. But this next address, delivered a week later to the American Newspaper Publishers Association in New York, directly tackled the media's obligations in a time of global crisis.

When writing speeches, Sorensen often sought input from trusted journalists such as Lippmann and Krock, and in preparing the publishers' speech he drew on a memo from Lester Markel, Sunday editor of the *New York Times*. Markel urged JFK to reiterate his support for a free and critical press. But he also wanted the president to prod his listeners to consider national security when publishing sensitive information. "For this is war," Markel wrote, "even though it is undeclared, and I believe profoundly that the same attitudes as in actual combat should and must guide us." Though Sorensen softened the language, he retained the idea that the precarious international situation should inform journalistic decisions. "If the press is awaiting a declaration of war before it imposes the self-discipline of combat conditions, then I can only say that no war ever posed a greater threat to our security," Kennedy said in his speech. "If you are awaiting a finding of 'clear and present danger,' then I can only say that the danger has never been more clear and its presence has never been more imminent." He promised not to impose blanket restrictions on publication, or seek "to stifle dissent, to cover up our mistakes, or to withhold from the press and the public the facts they deserve to know." But he asked the newspapers' representatives to ask themselves, with respect to every story, not only "Is it news?" but also "Is it in the interest of national security?" This was what they could do for their country.[8]

The remarks were consistent with what government officials had been saying throughout the Cold War and with Kennedy's own previous position. But the speech still sparked a firestorm. Like Theodore Roosevelt delivering his "Man with the Muckrake" speech, Kennedy thought he had issued a balanced statement, but the press heard only fighting words. The problem arose in part because rumors had been circulating that JFK thought that advance reports about the Bay of Pigs had contributed to the operation's failure. Primed to receive criticism, journalists thus heard the speech as an effort to blame them—all the more galling from the man who had just manfully assumed responsibility for the fiasco.[9]

Journalists denounced Kennedy for prescribing censorship, or at least self-censorship. The former charge was inaccurate, as Krock noted. The latter was not incorrect, but so long as journalists could choose what they published, "self-censorship" was little different from the discretion that they had always exercised. (Under Eisenhower, many editors had happily honored government requests to hold back national security information.) The real problem, Krock noted, wasn't the call for the press to show restraint. It was the divergent judgments between the press and government about what information should be withheld and when.[10]

Apparently realizing he had blundered, Kennedy reversed course. At a peacemaking meeting with editors and publishers in May, he explained that he intended no change to his existing practice of allowing "free access to the news." Then, as the meeting was ending, he turned to Turner Catledge of the *New York Times* and, reflecting on the Bay of Pigs, mused, "If you had printed more about the operation, you would have saved us from a colossal mistake." (The next year he made a similar comment to *Times* publisher Orvil Dryfoos.) Greater disclosure probably wouldn't have stopped the invasions, but the comments pleased the journalists and reassured them that the president believed in a free and open press after all. For the moment, it signaled a truce.[11]

* * *

Cuba was about to pose an even greater danger. During the Cuban Missile Crisis of October 1962—two weeks in which Kennedy engaged in high-stakes brinksmanship to get the Soviet Union to withdraw nuclear missiles from the island—the administration quarantined not only Cuba and the Soviet nuclear explosives there but also any potentially explosive information. News management went into high gear.

At points during the crisis the administration deliberately put out relatively benign misinformation: saying that Kennedy was returning prematurely to Washington because of a cold, and that naval maneuvers in the Caribbean were being canceled because of a hurricane. At other points it clamped down on the dissemination of news: Kennedy persuaded Dryfoos of the *Times* to delay a story about the U.S. Navy's quarantine before it took effect, and broadcast media were barred from the scene of the blockade. The White House also issued a memo listing categories of information whose publication would be "contrary to the public interest." And while most newsmen found their usual information spigots shut off, the administration kept the pipelines open to a few favorites—Lippmann, Reston, Joe Alsop, Henry Luce, Philip Graham, Charlie Bartlett—to win favorable coverage.[12]

Resolving the standoff with Khrushchev relied on a ploy that wasn't revealed until decades later. The Soviet premier agreed to withdraw his missiles from Cuba if Kennedy would pull American Jupiter missiles from Turkey, but the quid pro quo was kept from the public. With or without the withdrawal from Turkey, the diplomatic resolution was a coup for Kennedy, who resisted pressure from his military advisers to bomb Cuba while forcing Khrushchev to relent. But the story of staring down the Soviet behemoth made better copy than a clean swap—even a swap that saved the planet. To secure his self-serving account in the news media, JFK and his aides recounted their version of events to Charlie Bartlett and Stewart Alsop, whose jointly authored account of the crisis Kennedy personally edited before it ran in the *Saturday Evening Post*. Effective spinning by Sorensen and others kept the legend alive for decades afterward.[13]

For all the deference that Kennedy enjoyed at this hour of maximum danger, some writers were still ready to assail both his actions and their colleagues' compliance. Perhaps the sharpest critic was Arthur Krock, who over the past two years had turned fiercely against the man whose career he had once avidly promoted. An ideological conservative in his seventies, Krock could no longer abide JFK's liberalism, and as his affection for Kennedy waned, so did his tolerance for the administration's press techniques.

On October 22, when Kennedy gave a televised speech disclosing the presence of missiles in Cuba, Krock took aim at the tight control that Kennedy had been exercising over crisis-related information. In the past Krock had happily touted Kennedy's line ("In my piece yesterday," he wrote to JFK in 1960, "I attempted to carry out your request to state your positions in the matters on which distorted reports . . . had greatly upset some very influential Southern Democrats"). But now Krock mocked the media's acceptance of the patently bogus cover story that JFK had returned to Washington suddenly because of a head cold, and he endorsed petty Republican charges that JFK was using the crisis to engineer "a marvelous public relations job" timed to help Democrats in the November elections. Peeved, Kennedy asked CIA director John McCone to disabuse Krock—and congressional Republicans—of any conspiratorial interpretations. But Krock persisted, dashing off yet another column on "the hazards incurred by the decision of a government of this democracy to manage the news as an instrument of national security policy." Alsop and Bartlett came in for abuse, as Krock trotted out his own anonymous sources to rebut the pair's hagiographic account.[14]

After tensions with the Soviets subsided, voices like Krock's multiplied. The House Subcommittee on Government Information investigated the practice of news management, and a group of newspaper representatives compiled a list of offenses committed during the missile crisis. "We are concerned lest government go beyond the legitimate suppression of strictly military information," the newsmen wrote, "and look upon news of what the government is doing not as an honest report of what has happened, but as a means to some desired end." Most alarmist was Louis Lyons of the Nieman Foundation for Journalism at Harvard, who descried "the philosophy of totalitarianism" at work in Kennedy's methods.[15]

Making matters worse, a Pentagon flack named Arthur Sylvester, assistant secretary of defense for public affairs, tried in December 1962 to explain the recent high-level deceptions. "It's an inherent government right, if necessary, to lie to save itself when it's going up into a nuclear war," Sylvester said. "This seems to me basic." In public discussions about the statement, his all-important qualifier about nuclear war was usually dropped, and many heard just a bald assertion of a governmental "right . . . to lie." This rebarbative notion provoked another round of denunciations, including comparisons of Sylvester to Goebbels.[16]

Sylvester had his defenders—of a sort. Within the administration, Salinger regarded him as "one of the most valuable men the government ever had," as he told Teddy White. But many veteran reporters also recognized that at least since Wilson's struggles in the Paris peace talks of 1919, the demands of diplomacy often collided with the goals of publicity. When dealing with genuine matters of security, or delicate negotiations, executive branch officials had always withheld and dissembled. Yet a polite fiction had allowed journalists to pretend that they were extracting the unvarnished truth from the government. Sylvester's blunt statement stripped away this cherished myth. "As long as the officials merely didn't tell the whole truth, very few of us complained," wrote Reston. "But as Sylvester told the truth, the editors fell on him like a fumble." At the Gridiron dinner, Sylvester and Salinger were serenaded with the jazz standard "Little White Lies."[17]

Again, Krock led the attack. Government publicity had been a preoccupation of his dating at least to FDR's presidency, when he condemned as "intolerable inner censorship" a plan to centralize executive communications under one roof. He resorted to hyperbole again in describing Kennedy's practices as the most sweeping and cynical Washington had ever seen. His summa of Kennedy-bashing came in a March 1963 article for *Fortune,* "Mr. Kennedy's Management of News"—commissioned at 3,000 words but, owing to Krock's zeal, submitted at nearly twice the length. Having once backed JFK's request that journalists be mindful of national security, Krock now bitterly reeled off the administration's worst offenses. Problematically, though, he defined news management as "attempts by any official unit or individual in an area of authority to influence the presentation of news"—a definition so broad as to encompass virtually any communication between press and government. Thus, his omnibus complaint included both Kennedy's press conference spectacles (because they undercut persistent questioning) and his meetings with individual reporters (because he was playing favorites). The president's socializing with newsmen came under fire, as did his refusal to talk with them enough. At one point, Kennedy, tiring of Krock's charges of news management, visited the columnist to explain himself. As Krock saw it, this too was news management.[18]

A few veterans fought to put Krock's screed in perspective. "Almost every president I have known, with the exception of Harry Truman, tried to influence the news," countered Drew Pearson (making an undeserved allowance for the quietly canny Truman). "Mr. Kennedy is no different. He is less managerial than Eisenhower and Hoover, more so than Roosevelt and Truman." A poll of White House correspondents that spring of 1963 showed that they judged Ike to be stingier with information than JFK. Krock's key variable, Pearson proposed, wasn't the behavior of the incumbent but the state of his relationship with Krock. "The president isn't dining at the Krocks' anymore," he wrote. But "failure to dine with the president, or even having the president sore at you, does not mean that the news is managed."[19]

News management remained a thorn in Kennedy's side, but one he was able to manage. At a February 21 press conference, as journalists were jousting over the issue in their columns, Mae Craig raised the issue. A gutsy newspaperwoman known for her flowered hats and offbeat questions, Craig often elicited smirks from the heavily male press corps. But her question was on many minds.

"Mr. President, the practice of managed news is attributed to your administration. Mr. Salinger says he has never had it defined. Would you give us your definition and tell us why you find it necessary to practice it?"

"That . . ." Kennedy paused for a ripple of laughter to crest. "That— You are charging us with something, Mrs. Craig, and then you are asking me to define what it is you're charging me with. I think *you* might . . ." He stopped and tried again. "Let me just say that we've had very limited success in managing the news, if that's what we've been trying to do. And—The—Perhaps you would tell us what it is that you object to in our treatment of the news."

"Are you asking me, sir?"

"Yes."

"Well," she affirmed, "I don't believe in managed news at all. I thought we ought to get everything we want." More laughter.

"Well," Kennedy said, timing his riposte. "I think that you should too, Mrs. Craig. I am for that." The room erupted in peals of laughter. Even the president began to chuckle.[20]

41

CRISIS

SHORTLY BEFORE KENNEDY took office, an executive from ABC invited Robert Drew, a documentary filmmaker, to a meeting with Bell & Howell, the camera company, which sponsored a series on ABC called *Close Up!* When Drew arrived, he realized he was competing with another producer for work. After the other producer pitched a project about sewage treatment plants, eyes turned to Drew. "Bob," he was asked, "what have you got?"

"Well," Drew replied, "I would like to make a film about the inauguration and I already have an arrangement to be with the Kennedys in the White House."

He was hired.[1]

In the mid-1950s, Drew was a photo editor at *Life* magazine. On a Nieman Fellowship at Harvard he studied documentaries and concluded that their heavy narration was stifling the creative possibilities of the genre. Television journalism needed something like the candid photographs that *Life* showcased; it needed to pierce the ever more elaborately constructed facades that, as Daniel Boorstin argued, cloaked contemporary politics in unreality. Drew thought that wireless microphones and lightweight, mobile cameras and recorders might afford a closer and truer glimpse of politics in action. In 1960, he convinced the leadership at Time,

Inc. to let him cover the upcoming Wisconsin Democratic primary as an experiment.[2]

Before starting work, Drew and his collaborator, Richard Leacock, visited Kennedy in his Georgetown home. The candidate was in his pajamas, suffering from a cold. A two-year-old Caroline scampered about. "Look, I want to be with you alone," Leacock said. "No interview, no questions, no lights—just me and my camera want to be in your suite in Wisconsin when you listen to the election results."

"That's a very personal situation," Kennedy said. "You could make me look very silly."

"Essentially, you have to trust me or you don't trust me," Leacock replied. "That's it."

Kennedy eventually agreed. So did Hubert Humphrey, his opponent. Drew and Leacock hired two more young documentarians, Albert Maysles and D. A. Pennebaker, and over five days they shot *Primary*. Though the film aired on only four local stations, it earned a place in cinematic history. Like *The Making of the President*, it aimed to expose the campaign behind the campaign. Though *Primary* lacked the rich social and political context of White's book, it provided unguarded images that surprised even the filmmakers. "At night, we'd all be like a bunch of thieves, telling each other what we had stolen that day," Leacock recalled. "Bunch of pickpockets!"

With no narration or external soundtrack, handheld cameras recorded Kennedy and Humphrey standing on Wisconsin street corners, napping in car rides, hustling for the votes of passersby, and going about their campaigning in situations that later, more media-wise politicians would never dream of allowing on camera. One shot, of Jacqueline Kennedy watching her husband give a speech, showed her elegantly gloved hands fiddling tensely behind her. Through the alchemy of cinema verité, the boring routines of the trail became compelling, the mundane minutiae eye-opening. And by portraying the dowdy Humphrey handing out business cards and the magnetic Kennedy beset by bobby-soxers, the film proved prescient about which man was likely to thrive in the television age.[3]

After the election, Pierre Salinger invited Drew to Palm Beach to screen *Primary* for the president-elect. Drew and Kennedy talked afterward. "Think of what it would be like," Kennedy marveled, "if I could see what happened in the White House twenty-four hours before Roosevelt declared war on Japan." Drew proposed a White House documentary. "If I can actually lose consciousness of the camera and it doesn't intrude," JFK said, "we might be able to do something." Agreeing to let the White House review his footage before it aired, Drew got the go-ahead.

The film Drew made was *Adventures in Reporting: Adventures on the New Frontier*, which ran in March 1961. ABC hyped it as a behind-the-scenes peek into JFK's decision making, but it struck most viewers as much less revelatory than *Primary*. "He stood around, sat around, walked around, stared out the window, and carried on a series of meaningless conversations," said one critic, in *The New Republic*. "Clearly, with the cameras and the eyes of the world on him, the president is not going to say anything that has any real relationship to his job." The techniques that in *Primary* had seemed an antidote to staged political theater came across, when showcased in prime time and with White House collaboration, as part of the Kennedy spin machine.[4]

Drew concluded that to create a successful White House documentary, he needed to show the president making decisions under pressure. He needed a crisis.

* * *

Though supportive of racial equality, JFK was reluctant to tackle civil rights for much of his presidency, afraid to run afoul of the southern Democrats whose congressional support, and votes in the next election, he needed. He limited his early actions to a few unilateral executive gestures.

But media pressure prompted JFK to act. Civil rights activists had been using the mass media at least since 1955, when Mamie Till Mobley allowed *Jet* magazine to photograph the beaten corpse of her slain son, Emmett, hoping the pictures would generate sympathy for the cause of racial equality. Martin Luther King, Jr., was strategic in his use of the media, noting that the movement had to "arouse the conscience of the nation through radio, TV, newspapers." When he and Fred Shuttlesworth organized their protests in the segregationist stronghold of Birmingham, Alabama, in 1963, they knew full well that the searing images of Bull Connor's policemen brutalizing peaceful protesters would be a public relations bonanza. Wyatt Walker of King's Southern Christian Leadership Conference jumped up and down when he saw the coverage, knowing how the awful visuals would play. "There never was any more skillful manipulation of the news media than there was at Birmingham," Wyatt judged.[5]

JFK, too, was repulsed by the footage from Birmingham. The violence spurred him to abandon gradualism and put the federal government's weight squarely behind racial equality. When a mid-May agreement to begin desegregating Birmingham unraveled, Kennedy put U.S. Army divisions on alert and prepared to federalize the Alabama National Guard, which was otherwise under the control of the state's racist governor, George C. Wallace. Before TV cameras, JFK warned Wallace and Birmingham officials not to break the deal.[6]

Weeks later, Kennedy introduced his long-awaited civil rights bill. Privately he called it "Bull Connor's bill" for all that the Birmingham police chief's excesses had done to build support for it.[7]

* * *

As the Birmingham crisis played out on TV, Greg Shuker, a member of Robert Drew's documentary team, read about two black students, James Hood and Vivian Malone, who planned to integrate the University of Alabama, in Tuscaloosa. George Wallace, unrepentant after Birmingham, announced that he would literally stand in the schoolhouse door to keep the university all-white. On Sunday, June 2, as White House press aides were putting out word of Kennedy's new civil rights bill, Wallace appeared on NBC's *Meet the Press*, preening in his defiance.[8]

Shuker had his crisis. He spoke to Don Wilson, a former *Life* correspondent now at the USIA, asking to film the president during the upcoming Alabama showdown. Wilson said that Attorney General Robert Kennedy and his deputy, Nicholas Katzenbach, had to ensure Hood and Malone's safety at Tuscaloosa, and that Shuker should pitch RFK.

The attorney general was leery. The year before, James Meredith's integration of the University of Mississippi had triggered a deadly riot that took 500 federal marshals and additional U.S. Army troops to quell. RFK feared a reprise. But the documentarians got him to watch some of Drew's work, which he liked, and he consented. Hood and Malone also signed on.

Only Wallace remained unwilling. Suspicious of the "northern" media, the governor told an aide, "They'll have Bobby Kennedy looking like an eloquent statesman, and they'll have me picking my nose." As the students' enrollment drew closer, Jim Lipscomb, another Drew associate, sat outside the governor's office for three days without getting in to see him. Finally, Lipscomb passed a note to Wallace's secretary saying that the Kennedys were on board and hinting that if Wallace wanted his side of the story told, he should cooperate too. Wallace could be as cunning about media as Kennedy or King—he could be ingratiating with reporters, skillful in staging publicity stunts, and canny about what made good copy. Concluding that the film would allow him to show Alabamians his resistance to desegregation, he agreed to participate.[9]

The film, titled *Crisis: Behind a Presidential Commitment*, covered the events of June 10, when the parties prepared for the confrontation, and June 11, when Hood and Malone tried to register. Unlike *Primary*, it used narration to help viewers follow the events, as well as some background music in the opening montage: for the Alabama scenes, "Dixie"; and for the scenes in Washington, "The Battle Hymn of the Republic." No one would miss the moral dimensions of the story.

Drew stuck to his cinema verité method. Still, this was cinema verité of a peculiar sort. The drama that he recorded contained no shortage of staged performance. Hood and Malone had already managed to enroll as students, so passing through the front door of Foster Auditorium, where they would choose their classes, was purely ceremonial. Wallace was acutely aware of the show business involved. His schoolhouse-door stand was a chance to showboat, to build up his segregationist bona fides for white southerners. Still, how the episode played out mattered. The administration not only had to protect Hood and Malone; it also had to deny Wallace his symbolic victory—to render him, as RFK said to Katzenbach in the film, "a second-rate figure," on the wrong side of history.

The participants were noticeably mindful of the filmmakers. Wallace mugged waggishly. "I'd rather live a short life of standing for principle than live a long life of compromise," he declared, before turning to the camera to add, with a practiced snarl, "Of course that may not mean much to you folks." Others showed their sensitivity to the cameras through conspicuous silence. At times during a key Oval Office meeting, JFK seemed ready to shut down the shooting altogether, but when D.A. Pennebaker saw the president glance his way, he would stop filming. Pennebaker reasoned that if JFK *ordered* him to stop, he'd have to wait for a presidential okay to start again; if he stopped voluntarily, he could resume whenever he wished.

In the Oval Office, JFK sat in a white padded rocking chair, mulling whether to deliver a prime-time speech on civil rights. The day before, he had given another major address—his "peace" speech calling for a nuclear test ban treaty—and he worried about overusing the bully pulpit. On the other hand, that morning the *New York Times* had quoted King warning Kennedy to back his bill with the "total weight of the president and his prestige." Timidity, too, carried costs.[10]

As Drew's cameras rolled, RFK urged his brother to act. The Wallace standoff, he argued, provided the perfect opportunity. Leaving the bill up to Congress would jeopardize its prospects, and for the public to hear from the president would "alleviate a lot of problems." But apart from RFK's aide Burke Marshall, other staffers—Ted Sorensen, Larry O'Brien, Kenny O'Donnell of the White House, Ramsey Clark of the Justice Department—were afraid to jeopardize the bill's chances on the Hill. The meeting ended with JFK leaning toward his brother's position. He began to map out what he would say.

The next day, Robert Kennedy spoke to Katzenbach, who was in Alabama. Katzenbach proposed skipping the schoolhouse-door showdown altogether and having the students simply go to class. This would "take the stage production out of it" and catch Wallace short. But no one knew how far Wallace would go to stop Hood and Malone from attending class, or whether violence might erupt. Instead, RFK and Katzenbach agreed that the deputy attorney general would, at the door of Foster Auditorium, call on Wallace to yield. If he refused, JFK would then federalize the Alabama National Guard—a move Wallace had hinted would force him to relent while allowing him to save some face.[11]

The climax of *Crisis* came when Katzenbach and Wallace squared off. The blazing sun had raised the temperature into the mid-90s. Holding his camera, Lipscomb climbed onto a window sill, tying himself to the window bars with his belt to get a two-shot of the antagonists. White lines on the ground demarcated where everyone was to stand. Katzenbach, arriving late, was met by a huge mob. He hadn't slept in thirty-six hours and was wilting.[12]

At six feet two inches, Katzenbach towered over the bantam Wallace. But the crafty governor, perched in the shade before the colonnaded New Deal–era auditorium, held the high ground. Katzenbach started reading a statement from the president. Wallace interrupted. "Now you make your statement," he provoked, "but we don't need a speech." Katzenbach angrily retorted that he was doing just that, and then permitted Wallace a response—which the governor proceeded to disgorge for seven long minutes. With beads of sweat dripping from his bald head, Katzenbach finally cut to the issue. "I'm not interested in this show," he said, waving at the throng of cameras and reporters. "From the outset, Governor, all of us have known that the final chapter of this history will be the admission of these students," he said. "These students will remain on this campus. They will register today. They will go to school tomorrow."

JFK then federalized the National Guard. As the players firmed up their endgames, mostly off camera, Wallace sent word that if he were permitted one last speech, he would step aside when asked. By this point JFK was in the White House Cabinet Room (also unfilmed), meeting with the Republican congressional leadership to secure their help in passing his bill. In mid-meeting, he was called away for an update from his brother, outlining the deal with Wallace.

After lunch, Wallace returned to his spot outside Foster Auditorium. "Alabama is winning this fight against federal interference because we are awakening the people to the trend toward military dictatorship in this country," he said, putting his best face on a losing outcome. "I am returning to Montgomery to continue working for constitutional government to benefit all Alabamians—black and white." His National Guard commander, feigning regret, ordered him to move.

In Washington, RFK watched in his office as a dozen Justice Department staffers stood or paced. Smiles broke out as the newscaster's voice announced that Wallace had backed down. At the White House, JFK wrapped up his meeting and, turning to Sorensen, said, "We better give that civil rights speech tonight." JFK went to the White House pool for a swim and then a nap. Sorensen got to work.

An hour before airtime, the president poked his head into the room where Sorensen was writing, but the speech still consisted of just a few typed pages and scattered fragments. JFK dictated his own thoughts to Evelyn Lincoln, his secretary, adding notes of moral passion. Sorensen dictated his version to his own secretary. Aides were aghast that the president was going on air without a finished speech.

At 7:40 pm, JFK withdrew into the Oval Office with his brother. On an envelope he sketched an outline. With fifteen seconds to airtime, he jotted down a final reminder and combed his hair with his hand.[13]

Kennedy spoke at eight o'clock. Reviewing the events in Alabama, he called on Americans to examine their consciences. "This nation was founded by men of many nations and backgrounds," he said. "It was founded on the principle that all men are created equal, and that the rights of every man are diminished when the rights of one man are threatened." The latter argument was one that King often made. Kennedy spoke of the "worldwide struggle to promote and protect the rights of all who wish to be free"—a struggle being undermined by discrimination at home. The time had come, he said, to guarantee racial equality in public accommodations and at the ballot box—key planks of his legislation.

Jumping between his written text and extemporaneous remarks, Kennedy called attention to racial disparities in health, education, and economic opportunity. "The Negro baby born in America today," he said, was far less likely than a white baby to complete high school or college, gain a job in the professions, earn a middle-class income, or live a full life. In the speech's most memorable sentences, he declared: "We are confronted primarily with a moral issue. It is as old as the scriptures and is as clear as the American Constitution." Saying that the nation faced "a moral crisis as a country and as a people," he urged Congress to pass his bill.[14]

The next day, the Wallace standoff and Kennedy's speech dueled for prominence on the nation's front pages. "Alabama Admits Negro Students; Wallace Bows to Federal Force; Kennedy Sees 'Moral Crisis' in U.S.," read a *New York Times* headline above an account of the speech and a dispatch from Tuscaloosa. Many accounts derided Wallace for posturing for the cameras. "It was a six-hour theatrical show for states' rights," noted *The Washington Post*. Meanwhile, King told Kennedy that his was "one of the most eloquent, profound, and unequivocal pleas for justice and freedom of all men ever made by a president." They had won the battle for public opinion.[15]

* * *

As for Robert Drew, no one seemed to take notice of him for many weeks. Then, in late July, word of his project made the papers. An anonymous source called the twenty-six hours of unedited footage "good inside stuff" that, in a reporter's paraphrase, "will not win the president any votes in Alabama." Two days later, the *New York Times* editorial page ran an uncharacteristically vehement denunciation. "Under the circumstances in which this film was taken, the use of cameras could only denigrate the office of the president," the three-paragraph squib pronounced. "The process of decision-making is not the occasion for creation of an 'image.'" Strangely, the editorial disparaged Drew's film as propaganda while praising Jackie Kennedy's 1962 televised tour of the White House, a piece of transparent political marketing, and other White House pseudo-events.[16]

Crisis aired on ABC on October 21. Reviews were mixed. John Horn of the *New York Herald Tribune*, who had written about the film in September when it premiered at Lincoln Center, called it a "milestone in film journalism."[17] But a pair of caustic attacks came from Jack Gould of the *New York Times*, who deemed *Crisis* a crass exercise in White House image making, akin to Eisenhower's hokey televised cabinet meetings. In the past Gould had celebrated television as a democratic force, but he found *Crisis* intolerably artificial. "A viewer could see for himself that the participants were conscious of the lens, which automatically raised the question of what was being done solely for the benefit of the cameras," he noted. "In a moment of governmental crisis, just such a concern should not be present."

Gould's remarks reflected the journalistic anxiety about news management. "Eyebrows are bound to be raised," he wrote, "when it happens that a program totally dependent on the cooperation of the Justice Department dutifully portrays its operatives in a most flattering light." Yet overall the critic's concerns centered less on the dissemination of propaganda than on the indignity to the office of the president. Bringing cameras into high-level discussions made for "a melodramatic peep show," Gould fretted. It was "demeaning," and served "to detract from the essential honor" of the administration's work.

If the *Times*'s treatment of *Crisis* was uncharitable, Gould was right to note the ways that the small screen could undermine presidential power as well as augment it. The encroachment of cameras and microphones, as they became more lightweight and mobile, into the once-private chambers of government leaders served to diminish the president's majesty. So did the increasingly informal cadences of public speech and the long-gestating emphasis on personality in politics. In time these developments would come to strip away much of the mystique from which presidential power flowed.[18]

42

"LET US CONTINUE"

FROM THE MOMENT JOHN F. KENNEDY was killed on November 22, 1963, Lyndon Johnson showed a sure grasp of the subtleties of presidential image making. Amid the chaos in Dallas, LBJ had the presence of mind to insist that he be sworn in as president before leaving the city and that Jackie Kennedy stand beside him on Air Force One—with a photographer present—when he took the oath. On the plane, as aides debated when to administer the oath, Johnson was heard to say, "We've got the press here, so we can go ahead." The visuals of the swearing-in, moreover, represented only one of the dozens of issues the new president subjected to rapid but careful analysis, as he worked to convey a balance of authority in his new office, respect for the fallen Kennedy, and reassurance to a shaken nation.[1]

If JFK's relations with the press were retrospectively romanticized, LBJ's media talents were, in hindsight, forgotten. In his later years as president, his deceptions about the Vietnam War so eroded his credibility that his inability to rally public support was seen as a cause, rather than a symptom, of his troubles. But, like Herbert Hoover before the stock market crash, Johnson was hailed as a master of public relations when he was riding high.

LBJ's leadership has often been attributed to his skill in handling Congress, but in the dark days of November 1963, his public rhetoric was just as exemplary. "Everything I had ever learned in the history books taught me that martyrs have to die for causes," he said. "John Kennedy had died. . . . I had to take the dead man's program and turn it into a martyr's cause. That way Kennedy would live on forever, and so would I." The centerpiece of his effort was a November 27 speech to a joint session of Congress, which Johnson knew would be crucial to his success. He built the speech around a phrase Kennedy had used in his inaugural. "All this will not be finished in the first one hundred days," JFK had said of his agenda. "Nor will it be finished in the first one thousand days; nor in the life of this administration; nor even perhaps in our lifetime on this planet. But let us begin." What Kennedy had begun, Johnson would continue. The new president asked Ted Sorensen to write the speech; Johnson's own man, Horace Busby, would quietly offer input, including the key phrase "Let us continue." Those words would give the speech the name by which history remembered it.

Johnson was worried about his delivery. As a public speaker, he had a reputation for being monotonous and hackneyed. He was also, in McLuhan's terms, a hot personality, given to an old-style oratory better suited for county fairs than TV. Aides worried he would shout or rush his words or wave his arms. But Johnson disciplined himself. When he got Sorensen's draft, he not only edited the text—removing some self-abasing remarks about being unable to fill Kennedy's shoes—but had it retyped into one-sentence paragraphs, to force himself to read more slowly. For good measure, he hand-wrote the word *pause* at the end of his paragraphs.

The speech was a unifying summons and a liberal manifesto. It fused a call not to linger over Kennedy's murder with an injunction to press forward with his unfinished agenda. Sensing that public opinion was building against segregation, Johnson decided, as he later wrote, "to shove in all my stack" on the issue of racial justice, making a stark plea to pass JFK's civil rights bill. More than thirty times in the course of his twenty-five-minute talk the audience erupted in sustained applause, with the endorsement of the civil rights legislation triggering the loudest and most prolonged outburst of all. Extolled in newspaper accounts the next day—*The Washington Post* pointedly complimented Johnson's "slow, solemn, measured" delivery—the speech established LBJ's prowess with the venerable presidential tool of the bully pulpit.[2]

Johnson also showed an equally unpredicted proficiency with a newer tool of presidential communication: television. In March 1964, he sat for an hour-long interview with reporters from the three networks. "The president has no reason now to worry about himself as a performer on TV," declared Walter Lippmann. "In his interview on Sunday night he was never at a loss for words or facts, or for grammar or syntax, and was immediately and shrewdly aware not only of the meaning of the questions put to him but of how his answers would be taken by the great audience." Professing faith in the president's leadership, Lippmann deemed the public fortunate to have "a president whom they trust completely."[3]

* * *

Raised in the Hill Country of south-central Texas, Johnson always harbored an intense desire to help those who struggled with want. "Some men want power simply to strut around the world and to hear the tune of 'Hail to the Chief,'" he said. "I wanted power to give things to people—all sorts of things to all sorts of people, especially the poor and the blacks."[4] Though LBJ loved the strutting and fanfare, too, the reams of liberal laws that he signed into law in the following months—the Civil Rights Act, Medicare, Medicaid, Food Stamps, Head Start, and dozens of others—signaled a rare depth of commitment and an uncommon humanity.

But Johnson was, as Russell Baker wrote, "a storm of warring human instincts: sinner and saint, buffoon and statesman, cynic and sentimentalist, a man torn between hungers for immortality and self-destruction." Tall and ungainly, with a homely hound-dog face, he was a character out of Rabelais: rough-hewn, manic, overbearing, desperately insecure, yet also magnetic. He never abandoned the provincial habits, vulgar and charming, that compelled others' fascination. He would hoist a beagle by the ears, show the press the scar from his gallbladder operation, and, in private, turn to a bystander in the men's room to show off a body part he nicknamed "Jumbo."[5]

Diagnosed by armchair psychologists as a narcissist, Johnson labored under an excruciating sense of inadequacy. His attainment of power—reaching the halls of Congress during the New Deal, the post of Senate majority leader under Eisenhower, the vice presidency under Kennedy—did nothing to balm the pain of his shortcomings. To have been leapfrogged by the younger, handsomer, and better-educated JFK rankled; to be surrounded by Kennedy's smug Ivy League loyalists burned. Johnson compensated with self-pity and grandiosity. He could manipulate others self-servingly, treat colleagues with gross cruelty, or dissemble beyond even what politics normally entails.

In the spring of 1964, Johnson's darker tendencies were not apparent to all. When he did manipulate, prod, and work his will, it was toward sweeping goals of national improvement that made his methods seem, if anything, admirable.

His ambitions caught the popular fancy. When, in his March 15 interview with the TV correspondents, Eric Sevareid of CBS asked the president if he had a slogan like the New Deal or the New Frontier, LBJ confessed that he didn't—though privately he had been badgering Richard Goodwin, a Kennedy holdover, to come up with one. Princeton professor Eric Goldman, who had assumed Arthur Schlesinger's role of court historian, proposed a title from one of Lippmann's books, *The Good Society*, itself based on Graham Wallas's *The Great Society* of 1914. Goodwin chose the bolder phrase and folded it into some remarks, which were forwarded to Jack Valenti, a Houston advertising man who had become LBJ's special assistant. Valenti hoped to construct a major address around it. So did Johnson.

The occasion they chose was a May 22 commencement speech at the University of Michigan. Before 80,000 students, faculty, and guests in the university's football stadium, Johnson declared that for the first time in history, the American people had within their reach not only prosperity but fulfillment. "The Great Society rests on abundance and liberty for all," he declared. "It demands an end to poverty and racial injustice . . . but that is just the beginning." He outlined a world of educational opportunity, a clean environment, and thriving communities. Members of the crowd, sensing that they were present at a historic speech, cheered wildly. Heading back to Washington on Air Force One, a euphoric Johnson overflowed with talk and manic energy. Though he normally didn't drink on such occasions, he poured himself a scotch highball and sauntered to the rear of the aircraft to chat with reporters. He reread passages of the speech aloud, trying to make sure the coverage reflected his sense of triumph.

Some critics greeted LBJ's capacious view of government with disapproval or alarm, and those voices would grow louder. But for now praise flowed in from the likes of Reston, Lippmann, and Luce. Luce had never endorsed a Democrat for president but told LBJ that the Great Society speech had won him over. Talking with Richard Goodwin, the president read a passage from *U.S. News & World Report* comparing him to Andrew Jackson and Theodore Roosevelt. "We'll sweep every part of the country, even New York," he predicted of the 1964 election.

In his short time as president, Johnson had brilliantly advanced Kennedy's domestic agenda—probably more effectively than Kennedy could have done. But his accomplishment had required subordinating himself to the Kennedy legacy, portraying himself as Joshua to Kennedy's Moses. Only election in his own right would quell the doubts—his own as well as others'—that he was merely an executor of Kennedy's will. He thus resolved, as his aide Bill Moyers recalled, "to roll up the biggest damned plurality ever, and he felt that anything that could help . . . was worth the price."

* * *

In 1964, liberalism was at high tide. Most Americans favored doing more for blacks, the poor, the elderly, consumers, the environment, the cities, the schools. LBJ never looked so attractive. Qualities later scorned as shortcomings seemed like assets: the drive to accomplish, the energy, the heedlessness of limits. Even his coarse Hill Country idiosyncrasies came off as winningly authentic.

Opposing Johnson was the right-wing Arizona senator Barry Goldwater—a rugged hero to an intense band of followers but to most Americans a zealot of the so-called lunatic fringe, doctrinaire on the issues, intemperate in disposition. Goldwater's ideological extremism and gunslinger persona made him prone to explosive remarks. "Let's lob one into the men's room of the Kremlin," he said early in the campaign; another time, he proposed using nuclear weapons in Vietnam as a defoliant. Goldwater further marginalized himself by voting against the Civil Rights Act and talking about making Social Security voluntary, which would effectively have ended it. Once, in venting his spleen toward northeastern liberals, he griped, "Sometimes I think this country would be better off if we could just saw off the Eastern Seaboard and let it float out to sea."[6]

Goldwater's immoderate positions on the control, testing, and use of nuclear weapons were especially damaging after the Cuban Missile Crisis and Kennedy's test ban treaty, ratified in September 1963. Goldwater's radicalism cut against a new public mood. During the GOP primaries, New York governor Nelson Rockefeller attacked him with mailings that asked, "Who Do You Want in the Room with the H Bomb Button?" and Goldwater's unreliability became a recurring theme in the media. But the senator was unrepentant. "Extremism in the defense of liberty is no vice," he said at the Republican Convention. His followers adopted the slogan: "In your heart, you know he's right." Democrats offered a riposte: "In your guts, you know he's nuts."[7]

Though Goldwater was self-destructing, Johnson took no chances. His aides, in their daily campaign strategy meetings, devised a strategy that called for opening the fall with a "rip Goldwater" phase, to highlight his extremism, then shifting to a statesmanlike phase that would paint Johnson as a strong, responsible leader. "Barry's already got a rope around him, and he's knotted it pretty firm," LBJ told his team in August. "All you have to do is give a little tug. And while he's fighting to keep standing, I'll just sit right here and run the country." The way to do it, Johnson aide George Reedy said, was "to play that atom theme as heavy as we can."

Bill Moyers turned to Doyle Dane Bernbach, the advertising firm that JFK had also been planning to use. By 1964, TV spots were deemed vital to any campaign, their power held in awe. "There are those who say that ad men know so much about how to manipulate mass emotions that they endanger democratic processes," wrote Peter Bart of the *New York Times*. DDB had impressed Kennedy, an aide recalled, with its winsome ads for Volkswagen ("Think small"), which in their playful originality rebuked the hectoring hard-sell doctrines of Rosser Reeves. Besides, as DDB partner Bill Bernbach wrote to Moyers, "We are ardent Democrats who are deadly afraid of Goldwater." Though negative campaign attacks were as old as the republic, Johnson, Moyers, and DDB would help make them a central feature of presidential candidates' all-important television campaigns.[8]

* * *

During the summer, TV producer Aaron Ehrlich, part of DDB's forty-member campaign team, placed a phone call to an idiosyncratic New York sound engineer named Tony Schwartz. An intense man, with combed-back brown hair and puffy cheeks, Schwartz, forty, was anointed by McLuhan a "guru of the electronic age." More mundanely, he was a collector of sounds. As a young radio host at WNYC in the 1940s, he would walk around Manhattan with a 16-pound portable tape recorder he designed himself, documenting the noises of daily life in Hell's Kitchen—ethnic music, children playing, street vendors—which he released on long-playing records. He developed a cult following, including, eventually, on Madison Avenue, whose executives began seeking his advice. One of his innovations was to use young children's voices in commercials, and he won acclaim for ads like one for Bosco syrup featuring the *glug-glug-glug* of a child chugging down his chocolate milk.[9]

Schwartz formulated a set of theories about television and advertising, focused on the importance of sound, which he later laid out in a book called *The Responsive Chord*. He wrote the book after befriending McLuhan, who spent a year in the late 1960s in New York, teaching at Fordham University. The two men appeared together at public events, and the scholar visited Schwartz's home studio for rambling discussions, which Schwartz recorded, and classes in "auditory perception," in which students carried out experiments in sound. McLuhan helped Schwartz crystallize his ideas about media. "I was playing the same ball game—commercials— as other people," Schwartz recalled. But, he added, they "were playing in a print-oriented ball field and I was playing in an auditory-structured ball field. After reading McLuhan's book, I understood that. It was almost as if it had been a rainy, cloudy day and my discovering this in his book just made it the clearest blue-sky day you could ever have."[10]

Reflecting McLuhan's influence, *The Responsive Chord* was a mix of insight and mumbo-jumbo. It argued that TV programming and commercials, unlike print, should be understood as sensory experiences, not linear messages. "No one ever asked of a Steichen photograph, 'Is it true or false?'" Schwartz noted. The "USP" that Rosser Reeves had touted on behalf of Eisenhower (and various consumer products) was a dead-end, Schwartz argued, because it led advertisers "to make claims for a product that are unreal," producing resistance and backlash. It was better to create messages that echoed viewers' preexisting experiences and thoughts. By "resonating"—a sonic metaphor—Schwartz meant that ads shouldn't try to convince buyers to want something new; they should convey that the advertised product embodies what they already want. In politics, analogously, the media adviser's job wasn't to package the candidate for the voter, but to "tie up the voter and deliver him to the candidate," Schwartz said. "It is really the voter who is packaged by media, not the candidate."[11]

Familiar with Schwartz's theories, DDB's Aaron Ehrlich—who had worked with him on an American Airlines campaign—asked the consultant to help with LBJ's campaign. Along with his other quirks, Schwartz was an agoraphobic, who hated to leave his apartment, so Ehrlich and his DDB colleagues trekked over to Hell's Kitchen. Their discussion turned to how they might capitalize on Goldwater's loose talk about nukes. Schwartz had recently made an ad for the United Nations featuring his young nephew's voice counting, followed by an adult voice counting backward from ten to zero, and then an atomic explosion. "Young and old," the narrator said. "Another world war means death to us all. Support the United Nations." It isn't clear whether Schwartz shared the ad with the DDB group, but he did play a tape of a different commercial using his nephew's voice, for a Polaroid instant camera, which also featured the boy counting off numbers.

After the consultation, DDB developed a script for a commercial, which the White House quickly approved. Filming took place in a park by the Harlem River in Upper Manhattan. Monique Corzilius, a freckled three-year-old child model from Pine Beach, New Jersey, stood in the untamed grasses and wildflowers of Highbridge Park. The wind had blown her auburn hair into a tangle, and the summer sun played upon her fair skin. She counted to ten as she plucked the petals from a flower—a ritual she repeated for the cameras some twenty times. Within days, DDB put the spot together.[12]

The final cut began quietly, with the girl counting the petals. As she reached nine, her voice was drowned out by a harsh, loud mission-control countdown, courtesy of Schwartz's audio library. The camera froze and zoomed in on the girl's eye—a device borrowed from the famous freeze-frame of a young boy that ended François Truffaut's *400 Blows*. In the ad, the close-up of the child's static eye dissolved into a mushroom cloud as Lyndon Johnson's voice was heard, excerpted from a speech he had given in April: "These are the stakes, to make a world in which all of God's children can live, or to go into the dark. We must either love each other or we must die" (a variation of a line from Auden's "September 1, 1939"). An even-keeled narrator concluded: "Vote President Johnson on November 3rd. The stakes are too high to stay at home."

On August 20, Bill Bernbach brought a cut to the White House for a screening. Johnson was there, as were Moyers, Valenti, and Goodwin. When the lights went up, Bernbach looked to the clients for a judgment. Everyone was silent. Moyers finally piped up. "It's wonderful," he said. "But it's going to get us in a lot of trouble."

The spot aired once, on Monday, September 7, on NBC, shortly before 10 pm. The outcry came immediately. In New Jersey, Monique Corzilius's parents were inundated with phone calls—as surprised themselves as anyone, since they had never known the identity of the client. Many more callers phoned the White House, most of them angrily accusing the president of having crossed the lines of fair play. Johnson, who was hosting a small dinner with friends, summoned Moyers in. "What the hell do you mean putting on that ad that just ran?" he asked his aide, feigning ignorance for his guests. Moyers thought he heard a faint chuckle behind the alleged reproach.

Talk of the so-called Daisy ad consumed political circles the next day.

The networks aired it on their nightly broadcasts. *Time* put the girl on its cover. Despite the implicit criticism, the exposure gave the Johnson campaign millions of new viewers, at no extra cost. When journalists criticized the spot, moreover, campaign aides agreed to pull it to avoid even the semblance of unfairness, knowing the damage was done. Besides, Johnson's aides could note that the ad never mentioned Goldwater. In keeping with Schwartz's theories, it only evoked the fears about Goldwater's bellicosity that had been in the air for months. "It was comparable to a person going to a psychiatrist and seeing dirty pictures in a Rorschach pattern," Schwartz said. "This mistrust was not in the *Daisy* spot. It was in the people who viewed the commercial." (Meanwhile, to keep the "atom theme" alive without rerunning the "Daisy" ad, Moyers persuaded the producers of the movie *Fail-Safe*, made from Eugene Burdick's novel about a nuclear crisis, to release it before the election.)[13]

Goldwater's team reacted as Adlai Stevenson's had to Ike's spots in 1952, complaining that the ads were illegitimate. Republican National Committee chairman Dean Burch filed a complaint with the Fair Campaign Practices Committee, a private body that promoted a code of campaign ethics. On Capitol Hill, the GOP leadership team of Ev and Charlie also took up the cudgels: Dirksen urged the National Association of Broadcasters to condemn the commercial, while Halleck railed on the House floor against "this kind of play on emotions, this appeal to fear." Goldwater denounced the ad at a rally in Indianapolis: "The homes of America are horrified and the intelligence of Americans is insulted by weird television advertising by which this administration threatens the end of the world unless all-wise Lyndon is given the nation for his very own."

But by pressing the issue, Goldwater's men kept their candidate's nuclear record in the headlines. One poll now showed that a majority believed that "Barry Goldwater would get America into a war." Johnson's team continued to hammer away at Goldwater's extremism: a new ad quoted Goldwater's liberal-bashing line about cutting off the eastern seaboard; another showed a pair of hands ripping up a Social Security card; a third, in the spirit of "Daisy," featured a girl licking an ice cream cone as a narrator spoke of Goldwater's support for atmospheric nuclear testing.

On Election Day, Goldwater carried only his home state of Arizona and five states of the Deep South. Voters gave LBJ the largest majorities in Congress since FDR's heyday—a clear path for passing his Great Society agenda. Jack Valenti started to develop "carefully prepared programs of public imagery," as he told the president, "to establish the real and enduring Lyndon Johnson."

Most Americans were pleased. Eager to fulfill Johnson's vision of a Great Society, they had reason to believe that they had avoided electing a headstrong, rigid anti-Communist who would embroil them in a deadly and distracting war.

43

THE CREDIBILITY GAP

IN THE SUMMER OF 1965, a lanky American marine stood beside a hut in the Vietnamese village of Cam Ne, reached up with his cigarette lighter, and set fire to the thatched roof. A CBS News camera was rolling. Days later, on the night of August 3, the footage appeared as part of a report by Morley Safer on the CBS Evening News. The segment featured Safer roaming the village, watching distraught peasants and blasé marines. About 150 dwellings were torched, Safer said, as punishment for what one marine described as a modest amount of Viet Cong sniper fire. But, Safer noted, "if there were Viet Cong in the hamlets, they were long gone" when the American troops arrived. Three women were wounded and a baby was killed. "This," said Safer, "is what the war in Vietnam is all about."[1]

The next morning, CBS president Frank Stanton received a phone call. "Frank, are you trying to fuck me?"

"Who is this?" he asked.

"Frank, this is your president, and yesterday your boys shat on the American flag," said Lyndon Johnson. An enraged LBJ tore into Stanton, a friend of many years.

Livid, Johnson had Safer's past investigated to see if he had any Communist ties. When told that Safer wasn't a Communist, merely a Canadian, LBJ replied, "Well, I knew he wasn't an American." Speaking to the press,

Pentagon flack Arthur Sylvester—still known for asserting a governmental right to lie during nuclear crises—suggested that Safer might have put the marines up to it. Later, after another hard-hitting Safer report, Sylvester pressed CBS to reassign the correspondent.[2]

Episodes like these became commonplace after Johnson's dramatic escalation of American involvement in the Vietnam War. Eisenhower had first sent troops to repel North Vietnamese Communist forces from South Vietnam, and Kennedy had boosted that commitment. But only in 1965, under LBJ, did the number of American soldiers climb to six figures—more than 125,000 by year's end. Vietnam became a consuming news story, and Johnson was consumed by how it was covered.

LBJ knew early on that as a military matter, the war was unwinnable. Yet he was determined not to "lose" Vietnam to the Communists, for reasons of politics, personality, and principle. He therefore felt he couldn't disclose the bleak prospects to the public. So, as the fighting dragged on, the Johnson administration—from the president and the White House to the Pentagon brass and officials in the field—misled the press and the public about what was happening. As a result, the word of the government and the president became subject to as much public mistrust as at any point in American history.

* * *

Since at least McKinley's day, if not the nation's founding, war had always led presidents to oversee the news with extra vigilance. Truman, Eisenhower, and Kennedy had withheld information about atomic weaponry, U-2 reconnaissance flights, foreign coups, and other Cold War machinations. But now, with a hot war raging in Indochina, presidential secrecy ran head-on into mounting demands from the press for a full and frank accounting of the battlefield progress and the goals of American policy.

Secrecy in Vietnam had been a problem since the Kennedy administration. JFK had declined to impose formal censorship, but the State and Defense departments issued restrictive guidelines for journalists in the field. "The United States information policy on Vietnam has not been marked by candor," Homer Bigart reported baldly in the *New York Times*. "Official secrecy has curbed reporting." Military ground rules discouraged any implication of "all-out US involvement" in the war and stressed that stories about civilian casualties were "clearly inimical to national interest." Reporters were barred from American-piloted helicopter assault missions and other operations from which "undesirable dispatches would be highly probable." Correspondents had to depend on obfuscatory briefings from the U.S. military command that became so unrevealing that the reporters dubbed them the "Five O'Clock Follies."[3]

Initially, most of the American reporters in Vietnam—David Halberstam, Neil Sheehan, Peter Arnett, Malcolm Browne—were young and unknown. To their surprise, they found that the U.S. government's claims often contradicted what they were witnessing. So far as they could tell, the South Vietnamese army was a feeble fighting force, and the Pacification program, despite assurances, wasn't working. They protested, to little avail. Once, at a late-night session with Sylvester, who was visiting South Vietnam, the flack chewed the reporters out. "Look," he said, "if you think any American official is going to tell you the truth, you're stupid."

In their Saigon dispatches, the correspondents intimated their dissent from the government line, irritating Kennedy and other officials. In contrast, senior Washington journalists who relied on high-level sources at the State Department, the Pentagon, and the White House tended to be optimistic about a victory. This clash of viewpoints led to intergenerational warfare, sometimes in print. In 1963, pundits including Marguerite Higgins and Joe Alsop, squired around Vietnam by U.S. officials on quick visits, returned to write columns denouncing the younger correspondents in the field. Higgins charged that their negative reports were undermining morale and hurting the war effort, while Alsop likened them to the naive journalist in China who had fallen starry-eyed for Mao.[4]

During the 1964 presidential campaign, LBJ had signaled his reluctance to increase the American presence in Indochina, but, at Bill Moyers's urging, mostly dodged the issue. Moyers told Johnson to use the words, "We seek no wider war"—a statement that was technically true but stopped short of pledging to end American involvement. Johnson and his aides would make the comment often, even after commencing full-scale bombing raids and raising the number of combat troops to 20,000.[5]

LBJ managed to avoid close scrutiny of his policy even while persuading Congress to pass the August 1964 Gulf of Tonkin Resolution, which authorized the use of force in the region and cleared the way for the massive escalation of the mid-1960s.[6] The resolution, which passed overwhelmingly, was, Johnson said, "like grandma's nightshirt—it covered everything." It grew out of two incidents in the Tonkin Gulf, which abuts Vietnam's coast, in which American naval commanders reported attacks by North Vietnamese boats—the first on a destroyer, the *Maddox*, which was conducting electronic eavesdropping in the area, and the second on the *C. Turner Joy*, which was sent to support the *Maddox* after the initial firefight. But the second incident, it was later determined, probably never occurred. It was likely imagined by crew members, who may have been responding to faulty sonar, flocks of seabirds, or freak weather. After firing on what they took to be an enemy, the seamen reported the incident up the chain of command, conveying in some dispatches apposite doubt about what precisely had happened. In public, however, Johnson and his aides suppressed their uncertainty. Speaking on TV on August 4, the president described the incident as "open aggression on the high seas against the United States of America"; the next day at Syracuse University he denounced the North Vietnamese's "deliberate, willful, and systematic aggression." Nor, in justifying the request for a military carte blanche, did officials let on that the *Maddox*'s presence in the gulf was not entirely innocent. This selective and manipulative presentation of the facts gave the war's critics grounds for complaint once the conflict became a quagmire. It also set the tone for how LBJ would handle war-related information thereafter.[7]

* * *

Even before Johnson became president, the Washington press corps had swollen to become, as *The Reporter*'s Douglass Cater wrote, "a de facto, quasiofficial fourth branch of government," with its own institutional interests, prerogatives, and dynamics. Among its roughly 1,200 members was David Wise, the soft-spoken, hardworking Washington bureau chief for the *New York Herald Tribune*. Wise was hired fresh out of Columbia University in 1951 and joined the Washington bureau late in the Eisenhower years. Seeing Eisenhower participate in a grand deception surrounding the capture of Francis Gary Powers's U-2 spy plane spurred Wise to investigate the impact of secrecy on American democracy. Wise agreed that the government needed to conceal certain facts from the public; but, as he later said, he became "troubled about a system based on the consent of the governed when the governed didn't know to what they had consented."[8]

With a colleague, Thomas Ross of the *Chicago Sun-Times*, Wise wrote a book about the U-2 affair. In the process, the journalists realized they were dealing with only one small piece of an immense new intelligence apparatus—which, still new, hadn't been subject to close examination. Ross and Wise followed up with a second book, *The Invisible Government*, an exposé of the CIA's activities, including the coups that overthrew regimes in Iran in 1953 and Guatemala in 1954. CIA director John McCone, having obtained galleys of the book from Random House, was horrified that they named agents and disclosed sensitive information. He invited the authors to lunch and, with a spymaster's genteel graciousness— he was "a wonderfully polite man," Wise recalled—demanded redactions. The authors refused; Random House stood by them; and the controversy propelled the book onto the best-seller lists, cresting at No. 2 on the *New York Times* chart.[9]

Wise exemplified the suspicion of government characteristic of the younger journalists now coming to Washington. In one article from 1965, about LBJ's decision to send marines to the Dominican Republic, Wise highlighted the shifting rationales that the president had given for intervention. "For the past two days the Johnson administration has been grappling with what might best be described as a credibility problem of its own making," Wise wrote. "The administration is discovering . . . that when the gap between a government's actions and its words becomes discernible, it is in trouble." The *Herald Tribune*'s headline writer compressed the passage into a two-word phrase: "Dilemma in 'Credibility Gap.'"[10]

The felicitous phrase entered the Washington lexicon. Reporters loved using it to challenge or mock authority. Johnson's press secretary George Reedy, who took over from Pierre Salinger in 1964, was mortified when he saw Doug Kiker, another *Herald Tribune* reporter, greet a fellow journalist with a jolly "Welcome to the Credibility Gap." Soon an enterprising board game manufacturer brought out its own Credibility Gap, in which contestants had to fight their way into the Truth Vault.[11]

The phrase provided a nifty shorthand for the chasm that reporters saw between Johnson's words and his actions, especially in the case of Vietnam. It also captured a broader reluctance to believe official statements once taken at face value. Above all, it reflected the public's declining trust in government, which polling data showed had begun with LBJ and Vietnam. Eventually, the credibility gap became a problem unto itself. "The most serious problem in America today is that there is widespread doubt in the public mind about its major leaders and institutions," declared James Reston in 1966. "There is more troubled questioning of the veracity of statements out of the White House today than at any time in recent memory." Increasingly, journalists like Wise injected skeptical notes into their reportage and commentary, conveying that they weren't taking presidential statements at face value.[12]

LBJ gave them plenty to work with. A ready dissembler, he could be, his aide Joseph Califano said, "bluntly honest and calculatingly devious—all within the same few minutes." Sometimes his drive and demons led him to rationalize his deceptions. Yet at other times Johnson's untruths were simply the embellishments endemic to political life, especially in places like the hammy Texas milieu from which Johnson hailed. In the new contentious climate, though, statements that might once have been forgiven as routine fibbing, exaggeration, or human inconsistency were subjected to unsparing perusal. When Johnson bragged to an audience in Seoul that his great-great-grandfather had died at the Alamo, reporters checked his story and found it wanting—one more exhibit in the case for LBJ's dishonesty.[13]

Johnson's relations with the press deteriorated. He had always been unhealthily attentive to press reports: he was known to clutch a transistor radio to his ear as he paced the White House grounds or at his Texas ranch and had a three-screen TV console installed in the Oval Office. Next to them were wire tickers, rattling off breaking news—"friends tapping at my door for attention," as Johnson called them. "I could stand beside the tickers for hours on end and never get lonely." LBJ's hypersensitivity to media reports also made him hard to work with. Where Ike had kept Hagerty for eight years, and JFK had kept Salinger for his thousand days, LBJ cycled through one press secretary after another, exhausting the loyalty of Salinger, George Reedy, Bill Moyers, and George Christian. Christian, the most withholding of all, was promptly dubbed "Old Blabbermouth" by a jaded and sardonic press corps.[14]

Johnson, too, withdrew. When forced to interact with journalists, he grew nasty and punitive. In 1964, he had lavished affection on Walter Lippmann, awarding him the Presidential Medal of Freedom and visiting his home on his seventy-fifth birthday, bearing birthday presents and smiles. Now, after Lippmann turned against the war, Johnson turned against him, trashing the columnist to all who would listen. The persistent attacks, along with Lippmann's advancing age and declining health, convinced America's most respected newspaperman to end his long-running column and move to Maine.[15]

*   *   *

By the summer of 1967, Johnson's support was falling and anti-war activism was spreading. More than 450,000 soldiers were now in Indochina, 100 of them dying each week. According to a Gallup poll, nearly 70 percent of Americans thought the administration had deceived the public about the war; a Harris poll found that the public's chief complaint with Johnson was that "he was not honest about sending troops to Vietnam." White House poll cruncher Fred Panzer reported to LBJ that Vietnam was the "number one obstacle" to both "higher popularity" and "re-election." White House officials concluded that they needed better public relations. In August, they embarked upon the "Progress Campaign," a media blitz designed to prove that the United States was on the verge of achieving its objectives.[16]

That LBJ had failed to make his case for the war aggressively enough was not a commonly held view. His administration coordinated the messages of its public information officers as closely as any. For two years, moreover, it had been using the full range of White House communication strategies to disseminate its rosy story. The State Department dispatched officials to Pittsburgh, Dallas, and Portland to host briefings that could reach local and regional audiences. When universities began holding anti-war teach-ins, the White House sent what it called "truth teams" to represent its viewpoint. The administration also pursued the Bernaysian strategies of enlisting independent authorities to speak on its behalf or surreptitiously supporting phony grassroots groups (later dubbed "Astro-turf" campaigns). Moyers worked behind the scenes with the Young Democrats to fund students who supported LBJ's policies, ensuring "no traceable identification" of the links, as the Young Democrats' director wrote. The White House gave money and resources to the American Friends of Vietnam, an ostensibly independent body run by Arthur Dean, a respected establishment lawyer and diplomat. Most of all, the president himself thundered away. "Lyndon has been hammering away this month on TV, in press conferences, with individual columnists, . . . trying to put Vietnam in true perspective," Lady Bird Johnson noted in her diary—in April 1965.[17]

Nonetheless, in mid-1967 the White House decided, as Johnson told his aides, "We have got to sell our product to the American people." Harold "Kappy" Kaplan, a State Department public relations officer, assembled a new weekly messaging group called the Vietnam Information Group. (Two previous "efforts of this kind," Kaplan noted, had managed to "peter out and disperse.") The new Vietnam group was labeled a "miniature Office of War Information" in the press, but it was much smaller than the OWI or the Creel Committee. A closer analog was the kind of ad hoc task forces that subsequent presidents would convene to coordinate large-scale publicity campaigns across multiple offices.[18]

Kaplan's shop monitored press coverage of the war. It developed arguments for promoting the administration's policies and provided briefing materials to officials and outsiders. For sympathetic congressmen, it wrote speeches; for friendly newsmen, it prepared white papers. It touted developments like intelligence reports of lowered North Vietnamese morale. It organized the Citizens Committee for Peace with Freedom in Vietnam, an Astroturf roster of notables headed by former Illinois senator Paul Douglas, with Presidents Truman and Eisenhower as honorary co-chairmen, which sought to counter the now vocal anti-war movement with a centrist pro-war message. In the field, General William Westmoreland, the commander of military operations in Vietnam, brought journalists such as Theodore White along on his daily excursions.[19]

With his popularity plummeting, the president threw himself into the Progress Campaign. He gave rounds of interviews to prominent journalists and in early August invited a half-dozen well-known reporters to an off-the-record session of drinks and hors d'oeuvres at the White House. From the Truman Balcony, CBS's Dan Rather marveled at a "fiery orange" sunset that seemed straight out of a Monet landscape. Rather recalled Johnson ranging freely over developments in Vietnam—discussing upcoming elections in the South; reading from classified reports from Westmoreland attesting to battlefield gains; citing his own reluctance, as he gestured to the Washington Monument, to bomb close to Ho Chi Minh's house. But even as Johnson assured the newsmen of progress, his body language told a different story. "His hands remained clasphed [sic] between his legs," Rather wrote in his notes. "As he talked about the bombing, . . . his forearms tightened. The interwoven fingers pressed harder and harder against each other . . . [and] went white."[20]

The Progress Campaign also had Johnson taking to the skies. In November, he flew around the country on a 5,100-mile tour of military bases. Speaking on Veterans Day at Fort Benning, Georgia, he denounced naysayers at academic campuses, "cocktail parties, office arguments," and "the comfort of some distant sidelines." In contrast, he said of the soldiers, "Talk does not come cheap for them. The cost of duty is too cruel. The price of patriotism comes too high." He appealed for national unity to expedite a resolution.[21]

Johnson returned to TV as well. In the previous two years, he had failed to replicate the garrulous, affecting performances of his first months in office. Instead, he typically lumbered through his remarks, his face unexpressive, coming across as stilted, pious, and inauthentic. Robert Kintner, the former FDR aide and NBC president who joined the administration in 1966 to help with image problems and Vietnam messaging, said that LBJ treated television "like an old-time Southern orator, rather than Jack Kennedy's conversational treatment." But for a November 17 East Room news conference, aides convinced the president to try something different. With a little lavaliere microphone clipped to his lapel, Johnson was urged to talk freely.[22]

Several minutes into the press conference, Johnson removed his eyeglasses, moved away from the podium, and began to stride around. An aide remotely activated the mike under his jacket. The president's demeanor changed; the funny, spontaneous Johnson reporters knew in private emerged. "He waved his arms, chopped the air, . . . scowled, laughed, and ran his voice through a range of sound from high-volume anger to quiet, self-deprecating gentleness," reported the *New York Times*. Facing a string of questions about Vietnam, he touted the positive assessments of Ambassador Ellsworth Bunker and General Westmoreland, who had flown in from Saigon. But he also tried not to oversell the war. "There are a good many days when we get a C-minus instead of an A-plus. But overall, we are making progress." To the correspondents' delight, Johnson broke from his talking points. He spoke about history, offered biblical quotations, made jokes at his own expense. Addressing a question about protesters, he defended the right to dissent. "If I have done a good job of anything since I've been president," he added, "it's to insure that there are plenty of dissenters." He even calmly defended his treatment of the press corps. "What I am trying to do," he said, "is to preserve my right to give the other side."[23]

For the first time in eons, the press raved. *Time* hailed the reemergence of "the real Johnson," who was "combative, spontaneous, self-assured." Bill Monroe of NBC said he had "never seen the president so effective on television." Looking ahead to the next year's election, William Gavin, a young aide to Richard Nixon, declared, "Johnson's new television personality makes this a whole new ball game." White House aides for their part were euphoric, hopeful that the president might reverse his two-year-long slide. Kintner, deeming the performance a "masterpiece," urged Johnson to do it more often.[24]

"Goddammit," Johnson replied with a growl, "I'm not in show business." He refused to wear the lavaliere mike again, calling it unpresidential.

Still, the Progress Campaign continued. Vice President Hubert Humphrey, a liberal stalwart reduced to a presidential prop, was trotted out to repeat key talking points on *Meet the Press*. LBJ's top advisers in Saigon returned to Washington for speeches and interviews. Inauspiciously echoing the language of Henri Navarre, the general who led France's doomed defense of Dien Bien Phu in 1954, Westmoreland promised he could see "the light at the end of the tunnel." Eisenhower and General Omar Bradley sat for an interview with Harry Reasoner of CBS, in which Ike mocked the "kooks and hippies" urging capitulation. Both urged the public to trust Westmoreland.

By the end of 1967, the Progress Campaign seemed to be making a modest impact. Johnson saw an uptick in his numbers. The press gave him some credit, with the hard-nosed Hanson Baldwin of the *New York Times* reporting "clear signs of progress." Anti-war sentiment softened slightly. But a chorus of journalists argued that the gains the administration was touting were evanescent. Some decried the public relations campaign as a way to suppress dissent. Others challenged the administration's grounds for claiming progress, which rested on battlefield numbers rather than on an assessment of the loyalties and morale of the Vietnamese people.[25]

Then, on January 31, 1968, on the holiday of the lunar new year, or Tet, North Vietnamese and Viet Cong troops launched a series of assaults on key locations around South Vietnam, including Saigon. The attacks wrought enormous devastation on the allied forces. Although the Viet Cong suffered greater losses and their gains proved short-lived, the suddenness and breadth of the Tet Offensive came as a shock. The hopes of progress that the administration had so painstakingly cultivated were dashed. "What the hell is going on?" wondered CBS anchorman Walter Cronkite, who would soon share his view of the war as a stalemate on the air. "I thought we were winning the war!"

The Progress Campaign was no substitute for progress.

THE NEW POLITICS

SIX WEEKS AFTER the Tet Offensive, the Johnson White House was in a panic. On March 12, 1968, anti-war candidate Eugene McCarthy, senator from Minnesota, had won 42 percent of the vote in New Hampshire's Democratic presidential primary—almost as much as LBJ's 49 percent. Advance numbers from Johnson's private pollster, Oliver Quayle, had given no inkling of the near upset, and certainly no sense that the president's renomination might be in danger. But now Quayle's figures painted a different picture.

Wisconsin was the next state where McCarthy was challenging LBJ. Quayle's mid-March survey of likely voters there showed the president's lead falling to five points. The pollster foresaw an "uphill struggle," with "the odds . . . very much against" Johnson. Fred Panzer, the White House's official poll cruncher, reported that LBJ's ratings—overall and specifically on Vietnam—had "declined to a new low." Worst of all, Robert F. Kennedy, now a senator from New York, joined the presidential race on March 16, offering anti-war voters a more plausible alternative than the shambling, mercurial McCarthy. Kennedy vaulted to a ten-point lead in national surveys.[1]

Three decades after FDR first pored over Emil Hurja's charts, Lyndon Johnson's reverence for poll numbers demonstrated just how important they had become. Deemed an "inveterate poll addict" by Joe Alsop, LBJ made polls a staple of the presidential diet. While JFK had elevated the pollster's role by bringing Lou Harris into his inner circle in 1960, Johnson was the first president to retain a private agency—that of Harris's protégé, Oliver Quayle—for a steady fix of survey results throughout his term. Unlike Kennedy, moreover, who used Harris's data chiefly for campaigning, LBJ commissioned polls for governing, constantly monitoring all sorts of issues. And where Kennedy shared Harris's figures only with Bobby, LBJ assigned White House aides such as Panzer and Albert "Tad" Cantril (Hadley's son) to interpret Quayle's numbers. Nothing testified to the new importance of polls better than the hefty black looseleaf binders of data that sat on these men's desks, from which they generated reports for LBJ's nightly reading.[2]

Quayle was a clean-cut Dartmouth graduate whose father had served at the Democratic National Committee under Jim Farley. He had taken over the White House portfolio from Lou Harris in March 1963 and soon had the president carrying his polls around in his pocket, like a lucky charm. "That boy seems to know what he's doin'," Johnson was heard to say.[3] At first the president openly shared his fixation with Quayle's data. At a 1966 press conference at his ranch, he rattled off a string of numbers to show how popular he was with the public. But after a *New York Times Magazine* article about Quayle depicted LBJ as suffering from something akin to "poll fever," critics attacked his poll-watching as unstatesmanlike and Johnson put Quayle in the doghouse. Johnson wasn't without his fix, however; the White House also relied on polls and data analysis from Lou Harris, George Gallup, Joe Napolitan, Paul Lazarsfeld, and others.[4]

Quayle, who soon returned to favor, polled on many issues, but none mattered more to LBJ than Vietnam. Early reports had shown the public to be supportive. "They do not believe we can walk away from South Vietnam," Harris told the White House, summarizing a secret poll he conducted in February 1965, when LBJ was first ramping up American involvement. But over the next three years, Quayle's numbers traced a downward arc. Johnson refused to change course. Like FDR and other presidents, he was interested in the polls not so he could pander to popular opinion but so he could build support for his policies through a firmer grasp of the public's thinking. When it came to Vietnam, he and his aides extracted positive news from Quayle's data and leaked it to reporters. They talked up those issues that were found to enjoy greater popular support than Vietnam. Sometimes, a dismal Quayle report simply led the White House to commission a new poll with different questions—or with a different pollster.[5]

By early 1968, these strategies were failing. Quayle was polling in New Hampshire and other primary states, assuming the role of campaign strategist. His numbers showed that TV spots featuring General Westmoreland would help the president in New Hampshire; he found that labeling McCarthy "the appeasement candidate" would hurt the challenger. Suggestions like these fed Johnson's hopes that he could win another term—until New Hampshire.

For some time, LBJ had been considering foregoing a second term. Now Tet had dashed American morale; LBJ's outside team of foreign policy "wise men" was counseling disengagement; and the president's health was poor. His reelection prospects looked dim. In late March, the White House announced that Johnson would speak on TV on the night of the 31st. What he would say remained a mystery even to insiders. Different speech drafts circulated; Johnson chose the spine of one written by Harry McPherson, which called for deescalation and negotiations with North Vietnam. Secretly, however, LBJ had Horace Busby write a special ending. "You and I are the only two people who will ever believe that I won't know whether I'm going to do this or not until I get to the last line of my speech," he told Busby the day he was to deliver it. Even senior figures in the administration were shocked to hear Johnson—after pledging immediate, unilateral steps toward ending the war—reveal that he would not seek reelection.

* * *

Oliver Quayle's polling not only helped convince Johnson to end his presidency; it also signaled the rising influence of consultants like himself. In the 1960s, professional consultants found a burgeoning market for their expertise in using television, advertising, polling, databases, computer technology, direct mail—or all of the above. By 1968, they had moved from the periphery to the center of presidential campaigns.

Previously, Madison Avenue agencies had run the campaigns' TV operations. Increasingly, though, candidates for office were turning to men like Joe Napolitan, David Garth, and Stuart Spencer, who—like Whitaker and Baxter a generation before—worked in politics full time. These consultants typically began with expertise in one area of campaigning: Charles Guggenheim was a filmmaker; Richard Viguerie worked in direct mail; Edward Nichols and Vincent Barabba employed high-speed computers to process data. The most ambitious outfits, like Spencer's and Napolitan's, gathered many experts under their roofs. By mid-decade, news articles charted the expanding role of this "new type" of professional manager.[6]

No consultant was hotter in 1968 than Joe Napolitan. A native of Springfield, Massachusetts, Napolitan was a longtime friend of Larry O'Brien—a member of Kennedy's Irish Mafia who stayed on through Johnson's presidency. In the 1950s, Napolitan was covering the Boston Red Sox for the *Springfield Union*, when he became bored with journalism. A friend recruited him to help run a local mayoral race, which he won. Napolitan began teaching himself the art of politics, even cold-calling Edward Bernays, now living in Cambridge, for advice. (Bernays, well past his prime, tossed out some uninspired suggestions.) Napolitan did some low-level work for JFK in 1960, branched out into polling, then took his practice national. His break came in 1966, when he ran a long-shot primary campaign for Pennsylvania gubernatorial candidate Milton Shapp and upset Robert P. Casey, the establishment candidate. Though Shapp lost that fall to the incumbent lieutenant governor, amid Republican gains nationally, Napolitan came out with his reputation enhanced.[7]

In the summer of 1968, after the roller-coaster presidential primaries, Hubert Humphrey emerged as the Democrats' nominee. The gloom surrounding the humorless, visionless Humphrey was deepened by the Democrats' disastrous August convention, when ugly infighting turned Chicago's International Amphitheatre into a shambles and the police bloodied anti-war protesters in the streets. July polls had shown Humphrey beating Richard Nixon, the likely Republican nominee, in a head-to-head race. By late August, Humphrey was losing.[8]

Seeking a fix, O'Brien brought Napolitan on board. At the convention, they scrambled to devise a fall strategy. At one point, Teddy White, nosing around the hotel suites, came into Napolitan's room to find him typing madly. "What are you doing?" White asked. "Writing a speech?"

"No, I'm writing a campaign plan," Napolitan said.

White was flabbergasted. "You mean this hasn't been done yet?"

O'Brien asked Napolitan to supervise the media operation. For TV ads, the Democrats had gone back to Doyle Dane Bernbach, hoping to recreate the "Daisy" magic. But Napolitan thought the slick DDB spots "lacked warmth, conviction, and emotional appeal." One spot, he recalled, featured "an elegantly coiffed, beautifully gowned woman wearing a string of pearls. . . . I swear to God, she spoke with at least a hint of an English accent." He also disliked the DDB team's message, which focused on Great Society programs, even though his polling showed a budding backlash against "handouts"—the beginning, it would turn out, of a decades-long revolt against welfare state liberalism. Napolitan got O'Brien to fire DDB, give him control of advertising and TV, and hire Charles Guggenheim and Tony Schwartz for support.[9]

The new team was indisputably talented. But so long as Humphrey refused to break with LBJ's Vietnam policy, he remained stuck. Like many others, Napolitan urged the vice president to switch to a robustly anti-war position, "an independent Vietnam policy that will win back votes that should be Humphrey's but which are now wavering." This was sound advice, though it hardly required the sort of expertise for which Napolitan and his team were hired. Yet Humphrey, afraid to cross LBJ, resisted. Only at the end of September did he change course, giving a dramatic televised speech in Salt Lake City promising a cease-fire. He started to gain on Nixon.

* * *

Vietnam haunted the 1968 campaign. The paramount issue for voters, it also catalyzed questions of trust in American leadership. In a television address that fall, Nixon felt compelled to promise, if elected, to "avoid the credibility gap" by being candid with the public. But amid the cynicism, he struggled to assuage doubts about his honesty and sincerity. Voters remembered his strained earnestness in the Checkers speech and the 1960 debates, as well as a petulant outburst at the press after losing the 1962 race for governor of California.[10]

Nixon's solution was to portray himself as newly mature and statesmanlike, to highlight his mastery of international issues. Television would be critical. As Bruce Barton had once counseled Calvin Coolidge about radio's unprecedented reach, so H. R. Haldeman, Nixon's top aide, now stressed television's power. "The reach of the individual campaigner doesn't add up to diddly-squat," Haldeman told Teddy White. As he wrote in a memo, "The time has come for political campaigning—its techniques and strategies—to move out of the dark ages and into the brave new world of the omnipresent eye."[11]

Persuaded of TV's importance, Nixon assembled a team of top-drawer media consultants. He hired Harry Treleaven of the J. Walter Thompson agency—the advertising firm that had produced Haldeman, Dwight Chapin, and Ron Zeigler; Frank Shakespeare, an eighteen-year veteran of CBS; the filmmaker Gene Jones; and, after Nixon's 1967 appearance on *The Mike Douglas Show*, a young producer from the program named

Roger Ailes. William Gavin, thirty-one, an English teacher who was hired after sending Nixon an unsolicited memo on how to showcase his "real" self, translated McLuhan's ideas about "hot" and "cool" media into semi-comprehensible prose. "It's got to appear non-calculated, incomplete—*incomplete*, that's it, the circle never squared," Gavin wrote. McLuhan thought Nixon had a chance this time. After panning his debate performance in 1960, the media theorist had praised Nixon's "doggedly creative and modest" 1963 appearance on *The Jack Paar Show*.

Of the media aides, Ailes was the most important. Blunt, impatient, given to hilarious and profane rants, Ailes at twenty-eight exhibited all the swagger that would catapult him to fame as a consultant and, later, the majordomo of the Fox News Channel. Nixon once told Ailes that he didn't like television "gimmicks"; Ailes retorted, "Television is not a gimmick." Like Tony Schwartz, he argued that TV had to be approached differently from print, with attention paid to the emotions it aroused. This could work for Nixon. Ailes freely admitted that Nixon was, as he told the writer Joe McGinniss, "a bore, a pain in the ass . . . the kind of kid who always carried a bookbag," but he maintained that Nixon could sometimes be likable. His job was to remind voters of Nixon's positive qualities—intelligence, experience, moderation—that would resonate amid the turbulence of 1968.

To this end, Ailes and the media team staged question-and-answer sessions where Nixon could come across as reasonable, practical, and spontaneous. The sessions debuted in New Hampshire during the primary season and proceeded into the fall, airing in regional markets. They featured a handpicked panel of citizens, sometimes before a live audience, who quizzed Nixon on the issues—the Kennedy debates without Kennedy. In this propitious environment, even tough queries played well. So long as Nixon responded thoughtfully, he would show himself to be unfazed by criticism or challenges. The panels, unlike debates against an opponent, allowed Nixon to control which facets of his persona he wished to showcase. He could also control the air conditioning, which the campaign pumped at full blast.

A second part of Nixon's media strategy involved cordoning himself off from cross-examination. Nixon gave few interviews; he turned down an invitation to talk with the *New York Times* editorial board and shunned the Sunday shows until the last weeks of the campaign. When he did sit with reporters, it was often as his campaign plane was descending—a "three-bump" interview, as the press corps called it. At the staged forums, no newspapermen were admitted; Ailes knew that when they saw an aide prompting the audience to applaud, reporters would write about nothing else. Network cameramen were given limited access, usually to just a single speech per day, to better influence which images appeared on the nightly news.[12]

The burden of these efforts was to offer voters a "New Nixon"—"a maturer, mellower man who is no longer clawing his way to the top," as Lippmann put it, likely influenced by his falling-out with LBJ. Of course, the "New Nixon"—an idea that had been in circulation since 1953—wasn't embraced by everyone. *Washington Post* humorist Art Buchwald imagined a debate between the two Nixons, in which the Old Nixon churlishly charged that the New Nixon was after his job. In the end just enough Americans were ready to take a gamble that Nixon had changed. He defeated Humphrey in November by the slimmest of margins.[13]

* * *

One year after Nixon's election, Joe McGinniss, a twenty-six-year-old columnist for the *Philadelphia Inquirer*, published an exposé of the campaign's image making called *The Selling of the President, 1968*. Posing as a graduate student writing a thesis, McGinniss had followed Nixon's media men into sessions from which other reporters were barred, joining them in casual chats, cafeteria planning sessions, and meals at Sardi's. He scribbled down their cynical banter about remaking Nixon's image, including salty language and snide remarks about their candidate from the reliably free-swinging Ailes. McGinniss's book owed a clear debt to Teddy White's, but his was less a sequel than a rebuttal. Mocking White's insiderly authority and noble view of politics, McGinniss assailed in cheeky, countercultural accents what he called the "con game" of politics. For McGinniss, all that mattered was the cynicism of Ailes and Treleaven. Unlike White, he made no mention of the great issues of the campaign—crime, urban unrest, student dissent, Vietnam—except as they entered the thinking of the image meisters.[14]

The Selling of the President had a lasting impact. Though its arguments would seem old hat a generation later, this perception was itself partly due to the changes it wrought. "All of a sudden everybody said, 'Oh I get it. They're trying to sell candidates the way they sell soap,'" recalled Ted Koppel, then a campaign reporter for ABC. "From that moment on, we had emerged from the Garden of Eden. We were never able to see candidates or campaigns quite the same way again."[15]

If McGinniss's reporting was revelatory, his analysis was not. Echoing critiques of political salesmanship dating back to TR's day, he quoted liberally and uncritically from Boorstin and McLuhan (notwithstanding their differences with each other). The book jacket, featuring Nixon's mug on a pack of cigarettes, brought to mind Stevenson's complaint that Eisenhower was selling himself like breakfast cereal, or TR's jibe that Mark Hanna had sold McKinley like patent medicine. McGinniss also misled readers in suggesting that Treleaven and company invented the New Nixon from whole cloth when they were simply drawing out their candidate's best traits. Perhaps most important, Nixon's media team wasn't nearly as effective as the book implied. Once Humphrey embraced an anti-war stance on September 30, Nixon's lead shrank, the media team's labors notwithstanding. Nixon's slender victory hardly proved that the electorate had been conned.[16]

Nonetheless, as the Nixon administration dawned, *The Selling of the President*, together with the attention being lavished on the consultants, raised anew the old questions of what this state-of-the-art image making meant for democracy. Some analysts warned that "new politics," as it was being called, augured a world of computer-designed schedules, unceasing polling, subliminal spot ads, and issue positions fashioned to target key constituencies with precision—threatening to overwhelm any lone citizen's rational judgment. The consultants behind these devastating techniques, moreover, were said to be mercenaries, happy to traffic in scurrilous attacks or deceptive claims to win.[17]

Amid countless books and articles, the period's archetypal critique of the consultant-driven politics was a Hollywood movie, *The Candidate*. Written by Jeremy Larner, a journalist, novelist, and former Eugene McCarthy speechwriter, the 1972 film starred Robert Redford as a governor's son recruited by a consultant to run what is expected to be a doomed campaign. As he gets caught up in the race, he makes a series of progressively more opportunistic compromises—from styling his hair to ducking questions about dicey issues like abortion. Finally, in an eleventh-hour debate, he erupts in a spontaneous burst of honesty and scores a major upset. Only at the film's end does Redford's character realize he had no ambitions for office, turning to his handler in the last scene to ask, "What do we do now?" In *It Can't Happen Here*, Sinclair Lewis's 1930s dystopia, the packaging of candidates had threatened to bring to power would-be dictators; in 1950s scenarios like Eugene Burdick's *Ninth Wave*, it was McCarthyite demagogues. Now the danger was a telegenic cipher unready to lead a troubled nation.

The new consultants were ready to defend themselves. "I am a political consultant," Joe Napolitan wrote in *The Election Game and How to Win It*. "My business is helping elect candidates to high public office. I don't see anything particularly sinister about that, but some people do." Echoing Bernays a half century earlier, Napolitan reasoned that just as no one would erect a building without an architect or an engineer, no prudent candidate would seek office without expert advice. He granted that there were "some whores in our business," and that regulating campaign ethics wasn't easy. But he insisted, "More than any other field I know of, the work we do is subject to scrutiny by the public and the press." Voters who cared could elect virtuous candidates and punish the sleazy ones.[18]

On occasion, the public did just that. The negativity and deceptiveness of campaigns itself became a common campaign issue, and deliberate and sustained deceit from politicians—as LBJ could attest—was sometimes punished. More often, though, mudslinging, scare tactics, and slippery political claims were tolerated—at least by one's own side—as an age-old part of politics. Observing the politics of the 1960s, the political theorist Hannah Arendt scoffed at the moralizers who would impose strict codes of truthtelling on politics. "No one has ever doubted," she noted, "that truth and politics are on rather bad terms with each other."[19]

*   *   *

Arendt had turned to the subject of truth and politics in her late middle age. A German-Jewish émigrée who fled the Nazi regime, Arendt had been a precocious student and sometime lover of Martin Heidegger, the German phenomenologist whose reputation was destroyed by his Nazi allegiances. In the United States, Arendt made her name with penetrating (if sometimes impenetrable) writings on totalitarianism, which brought out the common historical roots and ideological features of Nazism and communism. Arendt also fell in with the prolific, intellectually versatile New York intellectuals linked to *Partisan Review*, *Commentary*, and *Dissent*, and in the 1950s she began writing for a wider audience. Her 1963 report for *The New Yorker* about the trial of the Nazi leader Adolf Eichmann, published later that year as *Eichmann in Jerusalem: A Report on the Banality of Evil*, gave rise to friendship-shattering controversy within her New York circle. Arendt judged the criticisms of her book to be daft misreadings or (in fits of authorial vanity) deliberate lies, and she eventually refused to discuss the book with anyone who hadn't read it in full. She saw herself as having been slandered for bearing politically unpalatable truths.[20]

Like many intellectuals in the mid-1960s, Arendt turned against the

Vietnam War. As early as 1965, she considered Johnson's escalation fruitless and destructive, and she bemoaned the dishonesty she saw in his administration and in public discourse generally. In this climate, and with the Eichmann controversy still raw, she wrote "Truth and Politics," which *The New Yorker* published in 1967. Informed by her idea of totalitarianism and its claims to have a monopoly on truth, the essay took up the churning questions about governmental deception and sophisticated publicity that, she argued, infused not just closed societies but also now "the free world"—the places "where the government has not monopolized the power to decide and tell what factually is or is not."[21]

A work of philosophy, not history, "Truth and Politics" was light on names and details. But it described the political world built up over the decades by the new managers of symbols and information, from Cortelyou and Creel to Ailes and Quayle. "National propaganda on the government level has learned more than a few tricks from business practices and Madison Avenue methods," Arendt wrote. She was not particularly worried that falsehood would triumph; firmly anti-relativist, she considered facts "stubborn" and resilient. Her fear, rather, was that society would succumb to "a peculiar kind of cynicism—an absolute refusal to believe in the truth of anything."

"Truth and Politics" wasn't another *bien pensant* jeremiad about the decline of factual truth in the face of high-tech propaganda or hidden persuasion. On the contrary, Arendt argued that to insist moralistically on admitting truth alone into politics risked curtailing or preempting democratic debate. "Seen from the viewpoint of politics, truth has a despotic character," Arendt said starkly. "Factual truth"—or what philosophers call empirical or contingent truth—"peremptorily claims to be acknowledged and precludes debate, and debate constitutes the very essence of political life." While truth demands that we accept its finality, politics keeps open the possibility of future persuasion and continued debate. In the realm of politics, therefore, assertions about clear-cut truth had to be regarded warily.

Going further, Arendt suggested that untruth in politics had a certain value, because effecting political change requires envisioning the world as other than as it is—negating the existing reality—which, as she saw it, was akin to lying. "Our ability to lie," she wrote, "belongs among the few obvious, demonstrable data that confirm human freedom." In making room for alternative visions of the world, politics had to tolerate a degree of lying, and in so doing, it tended to "implicitly condone the lying denial, or distortion of facts."

Arendt didn't wish to purge politics of untruth. Her solution was to preserve those individuals and institutions that were divorced from politics and could incubate the unpoliticized search for truth—what she called *truth-telling*. "Outstanding among the existential modes of truth-telling," she wrote, "are the solicitude of the philosopher, the isolation of the scientist and the artist, the impartiality of the historian and the judge, and the independence of the fact-finder, the witness, and the reporter." When "carefully protected against social and political power," institutions such as the judiciary and the university had shown themselves able to deliver "very unwelcome truths" to politicians.

Arendt stressed the extrapolitical nature of truthtellers. Sounding a bit like Lippmann, she said that their authority as impartial arbiters depended on *not* having a stake in the political action. There were thus good reasons, she wrote, to preserve a bright line—or at least a line—between the political and non-political realms, and to uphold different expectations of truthfulness in the two. One was to keep academics, judges, and reporters from being tainted with imputations of political interest; another was to keep politics from being overly constrained. If we approach politics expecting complete truthfulness, Arendt wrote, "we remain unaware of the actual content of political life—of the joy and the gratification that arise out of being in company with our peers, out of acting together and appearing in public, out of inserting ourselves into the world by word and deed."

Arendt considered the relationship between politics and truth to be fraught with dangers and benefits. Large-scale deception, perpetrated without countervailing arguments, could erode the standards by which we establish truth and falsehood and undermine democracy. But politics would be sterile if it didn't allow a wide berth for claims that were partial, rhetorical, aligned with particular visions and interests, or less than fully truthful by philosophical standards. A forum where multiple opinions and viewpoints continually jousted, where citizens argued and joined together to imagine better realities, required subtler standards about truth. Politics had to remain a lively, contentious political sphere in order to figure out, for the purposes of self-government, what the truth is and what it should be.

PART VI

THE AGE OF SPIN

With Richard Nixon's presidency, the machinery of government publicity roared into high gear. Contrary to appearances, the presidents and politicians of the twentieth century's last decades were less innovative than their forbears, relying primarily on practices that had been built up since Theodore Roosevelt's time. But if the tools and techniques of late twentieth-century spin weren't new, the intensity and single-mindedness with which they were employed were—and so were the time and resources they consumed. As the spin machine grew, so did the news media and the number of channels for showcasing its lengthening roster of pundits. Determined not to serve as compliant conduits for government publicity, journalists increasingly questioned and contextualized politicians' crafted statements and burnished images, compounding spin with more spin. By Ronald Reagan's presidency, America had entered an "Age of Spin," with even casual observers of politics wise to their leaders' political motives and communication strategies. As the new century opened, a climate of heightened partisanship in Washington and a fragmented media landscape made spin seem at once more pervasive and less effective. Barack Obama's election in 2008—premised on a rejection of crafted talk but availing itself of the most up-to-date communication tools and techniques—and his uneven fortunes as president illustrated both the cynicism and the inspiration that spin could produce.

45

THE PERMANENT CAMPAIGN ARRIVES

WHITE HOUSE IMAGE MAKING and message control—and concerns about it—reached full flower during the presidency of Richard Nixon. Ambitious, insecure, vengeful, and ruthless, Nixon, said his close aide Bob Haldeman, "was a man obsessed with maintaining what he perceived to be a correct public image." At least since the Checkers speech, Nixon had viscerally despised the press, and to combat what he considered the media's unfair treatment of him he redoubled his public relations efforts as no president before him had. Throughout his administration, that hatred of the press flowed forth, in reams of memos and hours of taped conversations, spreading a miasma of hostility through the White House. Even the largely sympathetic news coverage that Nixon enjoyed during the 1968 campaign, which carried over into his presidency, didn't lessen his enmity. If anything, it confirmed his conviction that only an unremitting publicity blitz could prevent his journalistic enemies from distorting his record. "In the modern presidency," he wrote in his memoirs, "concern for image must rank with concern for substance."[1]

Nixon's relentless PR efforts served to strengthen his reputation for deviousness and insincerity. To counter that image, he spun even more furiously, striking a pose of authenticity and protesting that he paid image

making no mind at all. "When presidents begin to worry about images
... do you know what happens?" he said on NBC's *Today Show* in March
1971. "They become like the athletes, the football teams and the rest, who
become so concerned about what is written that they don't play the game
well. ... I don't worry about images. ... I never have." Just before that
appearance, he had instructed Haldeman to find a "full-time PR man to
really convey the true image of a president to the nation." He once even
asked Haldeman to procure professional coaching on "how I should stand,
where the cameras will be," and "whether I should [hold] the phone with
my right hand or my left hand." Pointing to "the millions of dollars that
go into one lousy thirty-second spot advertising deodorant," he deemed it
"unbelievable" that his own appearance received no such care. Of course,
Nixon did have a dedicated television aide, a producer named Mark
Goode, and overall he hired more media and image consultants than any
of his predecessors.[2]

When Nixon's image making didn't go as he liked, which was often, he
blamed the media. The claim that the press was out to get him contained
some truth but more projection. Obsessively, even fanatically, Nixon
and his staff compiled lists of journalists, divvied up into the friendly (a
few) and the unfriendly ("75% of these guys hate my guts," Nixon said).
Unfriendly ones landed on an official "Enemies List" or were simply punished. Wiretapped phones, FBI investigations, audited tax returns, threats
from the Justice Department's antitrust division, public rebukes, curtailed
access to sources, exclusion from historic trips, lousy seats at White House
dinners—Nixon's arsenal of weapons to intimidate and retaliate ranged
from the petty to the painful to, ultimately, the impeachable. But if revenge
provided a motive for these attacks, so did self-promotion. Getting a fair
hearing from the public, Nixon believed, required discrediting the media.[3]

* * *

Nixon's obsession with the media went beyond the way he was personally portrayed or judged. He "seemed to believe," said his close aide John
Ehrlichman, "that there was no national issue that was not susceptible to
public-relations treatment." As president, he put in place a host of institutions and practices that allowed him and his successors to spin practically
any policy. This enormous investment of presidential energy in shaping the
news constituted Nixon's most lasting contribution to White House spin.[4]

One formal innovation was the White House Office of Communications, a new unit devoted to overseeing all executive branch messaging.

The hope of centralizing communications in the White House had enticed presidents since TR, and in recent years Eisenhower and LBJ had made strides in message coordination across their administrations. But it was Nixon who saw that presidential news management had outgrown the humble FDR-era Press Office and created a larger outfit to run it. He put his longtime press aide Herb Klein in charge, assigning the younger, more combative Haldeman protégé Ron Ziegler to grapple daily with the beat reporters as White House spokesman. Klein's charge encompassed the jumble of activities that now supported policy promotion: synchronizing messages across multiple channels; nurturing ties with local journalists; handling press access for executive branch officials and prominent media surrogates. Radio journalists were furnished with recorded speech excerpts ("actualities") to incorporate into broadcasts. Television shows got access to cabinet officials: Attorney General John Mitchell went on *The Dick Cavett Show*, Vice President Spiro Agnew on *The Tonight Show*.

Klein's shop also played a role in another Nixon administration innovation: the development of elaborate media strategies to sell policies, nominations, and other initiatives to the public. In this effort, however, the soft-spoken, crinkly-eyed Klein, regarded within the Nixon White House as a patsy, was quickly sidelined ("The walking dead," Ehrlichman called him). The driving energy came instead from the media-conscious Haldeman, said to have coined the term *news cycle*. Haldeman led a working group that met daily to craft publicity strategies, with the president deeply involved. Sometimes called the Five O'Clock Group, but going under different names at other points in Nixon's tenure, the committee drafted voluminous, no-stone-unturned "game plans," some exceeding 100 pages, to promote major presidential undertakings. At a separate morning staff meeting, many of the same White House aides would craft a "line of the day" that they hoped would lead the nightly news broadcasts. For this daily rigor and coordination, Nixon's successors would be in his debt.[5]

Besides message control, Nixon also made polling central to governance. Nixon used survey data to talk up his policies' popularity, to refine his publicity strategies, to rebut damaging claims in the media, even at times to guide policy decisions. He held long weekly discussions about polls with Haldeman and other top aides. He spent unprecedented sums on private pollsters, commissioning 75 percent more surveys than LBJ, 150 percent more than JFK. At first, David Derge, who polled for Nixon in 1968, ran the White House operation; but by 1972, he yielded to the more technically advanced Bob Teeter, who pioneered focus groups and dial meters that tested audience's fluctuating reactions to presidential state-ments in real time. As was revealed years later, White House aides also prevailed on Gallup and Harris to engineer and publicize survey results tailored to serve Nixon's political objectives—an ethical lapse that seemed to validate old critiques like Lindsay Rogers's about the less than objective nature of polling data.[6]

The doctoring of polling data found an echo of sorts in a series of White House campaigns, also reminiscent of Johnson's, to surreptitiously drum up popular support for the president's policies. The White House relied extensively on Astroturf efforts, using the Republican National Committee or friendly interest groups like the American Legion or Chamber of Commerce to generate pro-Nixon mail, telegrams, and phone calls to elected officials, news organizations, or the White House itself. The campaigns might be launched to respond to a single magazine article—speechwriter Pat Buchanan once boasted to Haldeman that "six of the seven letters in one *Look* issue were our team's"—or to inundate the media in general with pro-Nixon messages after a big speech. Public opinion, Nixon understood, could be not only ascertained but crafted.[7]

* * *

Craving positive news coverage was nothing new. But Nixon was unique in allowing that desire to spill over into rampant illegality. When the press and the Senate began digging into the Watergate scandal, they unearthed numerous aggressions against the Fourth Estate. (The story of Watergate properly begins in 1969, when Nixon and his national security adviser, Henry Kissinger, tapped the phones of Joe Kraft, the *New York Times*'s William Beecher, and other journalists, to trace the source of leaks.) Further, Nixon sought to control the news at a time when journalists were trying ever harder not to be controlled. Partaking of an iconoclasm that pervaded American culture in the late 1960s and early 1970s, reporters assumed an adversarial posture toward authority, including the presidency. This questioning spirit intensified their conflicts with Nixon and brought concerns about manipulation of the presidential message and image to the fore.

Mistaking the press's professional skepticism for personal animosity, Nixon disliked most journalists and avoided contact with them. He cut back dramatically on press conferences in favor of prime-time addresses, with which he could seize the big three television networks to promote his policies directly. But the network news divisions, now wary of being seen as conduits for the presidential line, had started bringing talking heads onto their sets to analyze politicians' claims. After Nixon spoke about Vietnam on November 3, 1969, in a bid to circumvent what he expected would be a hostile press reception, the networks subjected his remarks to real-time on-air critiques. The president was enraged. He dispatched Agnew to decry, in a pair of frothing speeches, "instant analysis and querulous criticism" from the networks and a corrosive media bias. Thereafter, Nixon and much of the press corps went after each other regularly, and both sides labored assiduously to counter the other's purported distortions.[8]

The media's efforts to unspin Nixon's claims contributed to a change in journalism. Reporters and broadcasters now made it their mission to signal to audiences that they weren't being taken in by official accounts. At its best, this distrust of authorized pronouncements sparked a surge in investigative reporting and informed some of the century's finest journalism, including Bob Woodward and Carl Bernstein's historic work for *The Washington Post* in helping to expose the Watergate scandal. At its worst, however, the adversarialism could degenerate into a snide and captious tone, even in ostensibly neutral news reports.

Seeking to demystify presidential spin, many journalists took to writing in-depth, analytical, and explanatory pieces. They called attention to the president's political strategies and the role of the White House news operation and the ascendant consultants. They even covered how they covered the news. Journalism reviews, ombudsmen, and media columnists sprouted up. The break-out book about the 1972 campaign was not Teddy White's latest but Timothy Crouse's *Boys on the Bus*, which focused neither on political strategy nor media strategy but on the reporters themselves. Over time, the journalists' self-conscious analysis and seen-it-all sophistication would seep into the general consciousness, engendering a world-weary view of presidential politics as merely a competition of images and messages. Although this disposition could trace its roots back to World War I, it had been fortified by the searing experience of presidential deception over Vietnam. Under Nixon, it would grow stronger still, as Watergate made cynicism the default position of informed political observers.[9]

* * *

At the root of Watergate—the multitude of "White House Horrors," as Attorney General John Mitchell called them—was Nixon's lack of a moral compass. Because Nixon couldn't grasp the gravity of his crimes, he tended to view problems of morality as problems of image craft or public relations. When the president learned that his White House and election committee aides had been caught breaking into Democratic Party head-quarters on June 17, 1972, his first concern was to figure out "what our counterattack is, our PR offensive," as Haldeman recorded in his diary that day. Nixon didn't dispute this account. "I felt sure that it was just a public relations problem," he admitted in his memoirs, "that only needed a public relations solution."[10]

When Watergate broke, Nixon was waging his reelection campaign, and after his extravagantly staged trips to China and the Soviet Union, he was enjoying a bout of exceptionally good press. But whitewashing the Watergate burglary—and the other crimes in danger of exposure—required more than atmospherics. At first, Nixon and his aides imagined they could bury the scandal by crafting cover stories for the press, mis-leadingly stressing burglar Howard Hunt's ties to the 1961 Bay of Pigs operation and falsely disavowing any White House role. "My God, the committee isn't worth bugging," Nixon told Haldeman on June 20. "That's my public line." But that diversionary spin only got them so far, and by September, Haldeman noted, the president was still "mainly concerned about the Watergate, wanting to know . . . what our thorough game plan is, our PR plan on how to handle the whole thing, the need to take the offensive, develop a line, and so forth."[11]

Ultimately, no public relations offensive could suppress the irrefutable evidence of Nixon's involvement in Watergate, confirmed by the secret tapes he made of his private conversations. When he resigned in August 1974, all but his most die-hard loyalists were convinced of his duplicity. The two years of denial and misinformation had compromised not only Nixon's authority but that of the White House. After his resignation, Americans remained dubious about official claims; the press persisted in trying to contextualize those claims; and presidents—though none was as unscrupulous as Nixon—continued to use the tools and techniques of media management that he had helped to make features of the modern presidency.

* * *

Although Watergate did not banish image craft from the presidential agenda, it did place a premium on a new kind of image: the president as a simple, unpretentious, honest man. Nixon's unelected successor stressed his humble midwestern origins, calling himself "a Ford, not a Lincoln." But in the competition to fashion an aura of authenticity, Gerald Ford was an amateur compared to a newcomer then blazing across the political scene—a fifty-four-year-old former governor of Georgia who rode to the White House on his finely honed image as a peanut farmer, born-again Christian, and truthteller: James Earl Carter.[12]

If Jimmy Carter hadn't presided over one of the most unsuccessful presidencies since Hoover's, he might well have been remembered as a world-class image maker. Like Hoover and Johnson, his once-heralded public relations skills were forgotten as his policy failures mounted. When Carter, little known in 1976 outside his home state, told his mother of his plan to run for president, she asked: "President of what?" But he turned his obscurity into a virtue and his outsider status into an asset in the post–Watergate era of voter alienation. Eschewing the trappings of privilege, he slept on citizens' couches while traversing the country on the campaign trail. Slick TV ads showed him sifting peanuts with his hands, as if he supported himself by manual labor. "I'll never tell a lie, I'll never make a misleading statement, I'll never avoid a controversial issue," he vowed. Riding the anti-establishment currents sweeping the political scene, Carter joined this image of rugged simplicity to an anti-Washington populism that championed the people's goodness and rebuked corrupt insiders. His victory in the late January Iowa caucuses uncorked a gusher of media coverage—including effusive treatment on the network broadcasts, which were now the public's main source of political news—and catapulted him to the Democratic nomination.

Carter promptly ran into the headwinds of skeptical journalism. Before long, critics were deriding him as a "media candidate" and "media phenomenon." The writer Steven Brill laid out a devastating catalogue of Carter's distortions, deceptions, and misrepresentations in *Harper's*, cutting to the heart of the governor's reputation for candor. Brill called Carter's campaign "the most sincerely insincere, politically antipolitical, and slickly unslick campaign of the year." (Carter's peanut farming, to name but one exaggeration, was a lucrative agribusiness that warehoused and shelled other farmers' nuts.) Reporters now focused on Carter's own high-gloss team of consultants, including the brash young pollster Pat Caddell, the bluff Atlanta advertising man Gerald Rafshoon, and the reclusive admaker Tony Schwartz.[13]

Caddell, twenty-six, was hailed as the oracle of the baby boom generation. He had formed his own polling business while an undergraduate at Harvard and burst on the scene helping George McGovern engineer his own surprise capture of the Democratic nomination in 1972. On the campaign trail that year Caddell had captivated reporters with his energy and brilliance. When, still without his bachelor's degree, he learned that Harvard was withholding his diploma until he passed his swimming test—an anachronistic requirement then expected by many universities—he arranged to take the test in a California hotel pool, overseen by the gonzo journalist Hunter S. Thompson of *Rolling Stone*, while Theodore White, a member of Harvard's Board of Overseers, phoned in the results. A guru to outsiders, Caddell had become an insider in record time.[14]

Caddell championed the idea that "alienation" defined the politics of the 1970s. Disillusioned by Vietnam and Watergate, squeezed by inflation, unemployment, and the energy crisis, voters had become hostile to the parties, to Washington, and to politics itself. They were searching for trust and straightforwardness. In the 1976 election, Caddell urged Carter to center his campaign on thematics rather than issue-based coalition politics. Carter's down-home honesty, his ostensible rectitude, would cure the nation of its malaise. Although Carter's large lead over Ford narrowed as November approached, his ultimate victory made Caddell a bicoastal celebrity. He squired Lauren Bacall to Carter's inaugural ball and counseled Francis Ford Coppola on the marketing of *Apocalypse Now*.[15] Carter told Caddell he was "a member of our official family."

After the election, Caddell drafted a 10,000-word memo for Carter entitled "Initial Working Paper on Political Strategy" that refined his ideas about alienation. The weakening of party loyalties and the deep-dyed revulsion toward politics, he argued, meant that any officeholder had to undertake a permanent operation to sustain popular support. "Essentially, it is my thesis," wrote Caddell, "that governing with public approval requires a continuing political campaign." Caddell seemed unaware of the intensive efforts at cultivating public opinion waged by presidents since TR, and he scanted the publicity endeavors of recent White House occupants. Yet the conviction that an unmoored electorate needed constant Oval Office tending was one that Carter carried into his presidency—and one to which his successors would unfailingly pay heed.

Among the arguments that Caddell urged on Carter was the notion that "the old cliché about mistaking style for substance usually works in reverse." Politicians failed, the pollster argued (on dubious grounds), not because of bad policies but because "they forgot to give the public the kind of visible signals that it needs to understand what is happening." He persuaded Carter to play up his homespun, accessible style by "cutting back on 'imperial' frills and perks," holding "fireside chats" to foster "personal intimacy with the people" (at which the president wore a tan cardigan sweater, Mr. Rogers–style), and hosting "town meetings" in communities around the country. Stunts like these helped sustain Carter's approval ratings for months. But the press, wise to the manipulation, offered a counternarrative that emphasized the contrived nature of Carter's unpretentious persona. A May 1977 cover of the *New York Times Magazine* showed a cartoon of Carter operating a television studio console featuring multiple images of himself. That spring ABC News also got ahold of Caddell's manifesto, prompting more stories of Carter's image-consciousness.[16]

Television was, inevitably, a central focus. Armed with smaller and more portable cameras and sound equipment, correspondents trailed the president constantly. "No administration in the television age has studied the methods of the medium more religiously than this one," Curtis Wilkie of the *Boston Globe* noted. "And none designed its actions more accordingly." Barry Jagoda, a broadcast veteran hired by Carter, questioned Caddell's emphasis on town halls and fireside chats—tightly planned events might play well once or twice but would soon lose their appeal. Carter needed to make news daily, as Theodore Roosevelt had, even if that meant taking the risks associated with spontaneity. By 1978, however, Carter was struggling in vain to tame high unemployment, inflation, and energy costs, and Jagoda—blamed by first lady Rosalynn Carter for the president's dismal ratings—was demoted.

In search of a quick fix, Carter turned to Gerald Rafshoon, Caddell's Georgetown housemate and business partner. A member of Carter's "Georgia Mafia" since the mid-1960s, the Brooklyn-born Rafshoon had been a key player on the campaign. He had spent the administration's first year working mainly with corporate clients, Hollywood studios, and the occasional political candidate—notably New York's Mario Cuomo, whose failed 1977 mayoral bid Rafshoon advised, by all accounts disastrously— but now he was given charge of the Office of Communications. Insisting that "all politics is marketing," Rafshoon declared that "the presidency has become an ongoing series for television."[17]

His task was daunting, not least because many of the choice gimmicks that he and Caddell had earlier prescribed—the end of "Hail to the Chief," the cardigans—were now faulted for depriving Carter of gravitas. As his press secretary Jody Powell noted, "A president might look good in blue jeans if it is going well, and not so good if things are bad." Rafshoon did what he could. In the spate of stories touting his return to power, he was said to have convened a series of intimate dinners for news executives, increased Carter's availability for interviews, and persuaded the president to take camera-friendly trips to Civil War battlefields and to the Salmon River in Idaho. The media-savvy press corps imputed Rasputin-like influence to Rafshoon. One newspaper editorial, about Carter's veto of a weapons procurement bill, was headlined "The Rafshoon Veto," as if it had been a stunt to prove Carter's resolve. But soon the awe decayed into ridicule. *Rafshoon* became a verb, meaning to market, or dress up in PR trappings ("Can Rafshooning Save the President?"). The noun was *Rafshoonery*, as in buffoonery.[18]

* * *

All sorts of journalists and pundits blasted Carter and his team for their egregious image management—"President McLuhan," *The Nation* jeered—but the cultural critic who captured the Zeitgeist best was a cartoonist, Garry Trudeau. The brainy, Yale-educated thirty-year-old had already won a Pulitzer Prize for his satirical comic strip *Doonesbury*, in which he combined an understated wit with an eye for his trend-conscious generation's indulgences and anxieties. Delving into politics more skillfully even than Pogo's Walt Kelly in the 1950s, Trudeau targeted politicians and the news media with equal precision. In the Carter years, he concocted a parallel universe in which a desperate president hires a "Secretary of Symbolism" named Duane Delacourt—"the man behind the cardigan, the chat, the stroll, and the public education of Amy!"—to solve his problems. In one of his first moves, a newscaster recounts in one strip, Delacourt "announced that a major symbolic gesture will take place tonight at 9 pm Eastern Standard Time. NBC News will of course be providing live coverage of the gesture." Delacourt became a sensation, "interviewed" by Trudeau in the pages of *The New Republic*.[19]

Delacourt couldn't save Jimmy Carter in the panels of *Doonesbury*, and Caddell and Rafshoon could not salvage his presidency in real life. Symbolism, fittingly, played a role in Carter's downfall. By 1979, with Carter struggling to deal with severe problems in both foreign and economic affairs, Caddell urged the president to speak about the national "malaise," in an effort to tap into the popular alienation and despair. Carter did so, but despite an initially positive public response, his focus on the public's moral shortcomings ended up backfiring—especially when he fired several cabinet officers, creating a picture of a White House in chaos and extinguishing the last embers of confidence in his presidency. Compounding Carter's struggles with the economy was the seizure of American Embassy staff in Tehran by Islamic revolutionaries. For more than a year, the television news shows covered the crisis like a soap opera, while late-night specials—notably, Ted Koppel's *America Held Hostage* (which after the saga morphed into *Nightline*)—reinforced a picture of impotence. The burst of patriotism that buoyed Carter at the start of the hostage crisis faded in the face of the president's failure to free the hostages.

The negative press over Iran and the economy exacerbated image problems that had been afflicting Carter for months. His underlying weaknesses of policy and leadership were too severe for any amount of Rafshoonery to fix.

46

THE REAGAN APOTHEOSIS

RONALD REAGAN WAS the first president to spend his pre-political career working in the mass media—in radio, as a baseball announcer in the 1930s; in film, as a leading man for Warner Bros. in the 1940s; and in television, as the host of *General Electric Theater* in the 1950s. Because of his background, he was often hailed as a pivotal figure in the rise of White House image craft. "The Reagan White House, more than any before it, established the presidency as theatre," wrote *The New Yorker*'s Elizabeth Drew. But Reagan's dedication to spin wasn't markedly greater than Carter's, or Nixon's, and while he possessed superior talents as a performer, the practices that he followed had by the 1980s been part of the White House armamentarium for years. Wrongly described as a pioneer in what Washington insiders were now calling *spin*, Reagan is better seen as a master of methods that a long string of forbears had incrementally developed. He was less an innovator than an apotheosis.[1]

With the consulting business booming, Reagan, on taking office in 1981, was able to draw from a large pool of professionals trained in the traffic of political words and images. Over the course of his presidency, his image meister Mike Deaver and speechwriters such as Peggy Noonan would become media celebrities. But Reagan's most influential adviser was probably the pollster Richard Wirthlin, chief strategist of his 1980 campaign. An economist with a PhD from the University of California at Berkeley, Wirthlin developed the idea that voters' *values*, or their general principles about work, family, country, and the like, mattered more than their *opinions*, or their stances on transient policy issues—an approach that guided the Reagan White House's messaging from the beginning. During the post-election transition period, Wirthlin and his deputy Richard Beal drafted an "Initial Actions Project" that prescribed how the incoming president could push through his controversial budget of lower taxes, domestic spending cuts, and military spending increases. David Gergen—the Nixon communications office veteran who had urged Reagan to end his fall debate with Carter by asking, "Are you better off now than you were four years ago?"—translated the project into a thick Nixon-style game plan called "The First Hundred Days."[2]

The plan called for the White House to concentrate its PR efforts on passing its economic program: "Reaganomics." At first liberals, considering Reaganomics a boondoggle for the rich, fought the White House hard. But in March 1981 John Hinckley, a deranged gunman, critically wounded the president outside the Washington Hilton, generating a flood of sympathy. Reagan's approval ratings soared. The next day, Treasury Secretary Donald Regan went on TV where, borrowing a famous Reagan movie line, he urged Congress to "win one for the Gipper" by passing the economic plan. At a subsequent Blair House strategy meeting, Gergen proposed that Regan stage his triumphant return from the hospital by pressing for the economics bill before a joint session of Congress. Reagan did just that, delivering a speech that caused even Democrats to marvel and brought much of the opposition around. Against the holdouts, the White House then waged an all-out media campaign, which included strategically releasing photographs of a convalescing Reagan. The radical tax-cutting measure, once deemed a long shot, passed into law.[3]

In winning the bill's passage, Reagan and his aides employed tight discipline in their messaging, the heavy repetition of key talking points, careful management of the presidential image, and the strategic use of the bully pulpit. For the rest of Reagan's two terms, these elements of spin were often taken to be the keys to the president's popularity and success. But the story was more complicated. For one thing, Reagan didn't enjoy exceptional popularity for most of his presidency. Like all presidents since the 1960s, he experienced great fluctuations in his fortunes, and for long stretches—during the 1982–83 recession and after the Iran-contra scandal broke in 1986—he was widely disliked. Yet his high moments came when he needed them: not just in passing the 1981 Reaganomics bill but again during his 1984 reelection campaign against Walter Mondale, and once more in 1988 after he and Soviet leader Mikhail Gorbachev forged the warmest superpower relations since World War II. Nor was Reagan's news coverage unswervingly favorable, notwithstanding gripes from the left that the once-feral press corps had gone soft. Reporters did at times succumb to White House spin, as they did under other presidents, but on many other occasions they pounced on Reagan's blunders, stringently critiqued his policies, and openly questioned his competence. All the while, they advanced an analysis of his administration as unduly devoted to the politics of image.[4]

*   *   *

Having latched onto the idea of Reagan's presidency as a triumph of stagecraft, journalists endlessly detailed the White House's communications practices and methods. Americans learned, for example, that the Reagan team's morning began with a public relations meeting where aides, following Nixon, crafted a "line of the day"—a story or angle to lead the coming day's news stories. Officials faithfully mouthed the key arguments, pumping them through Washington's proliferating arteries of communication. With television news quoting politicians in diminishingly small snippets—*sound bites*—aides learned to chisel out clever phrases and quips that would make the news. Conference calls and a high-tech computer system eased coordination; Reagan's team even created a White House News Service, which, using a data distribution system from International Telephone & Telegraph, electronically circulated the administration's PR materials to subscribers. Polling, meanwhile, gauged the sound bites' effectiveness. In all of this, Reagan participated gamely. He stuck to his talking points in the face of journalistic hectoring, sometimes smiling at his own manipulative intent. "If I answer that question," he once said cheerfully to an unwelcome, off-topic inquiry, "none of you will say anything about what we're here for today. I'm not going to give you a different lead."[5]

Photo opportunities—now called *photo ops*—displaced the moribund routine of the presidential press conference. Instead of hosting weekly or semiregular confabs, Reagan would field a smattering of queries after a Rose Garden statement or an event with a visiting dignitary. Frequently these moments came as the president dashed for his helicopter, its whirring blades conveniently drowning out the shouted queries, as Reagan cupped hand to ear and smiled.

Like Nixon and Carter, Reagan gave TV special attention. "American politics today are videotropic," mused Theodore White, midway through Reagan's two terms. "Every candidate turns or pitches his entire campaign to the sun of television." Reagan's aides gave the network correspondents priority seating at news conferences, pushed administration officials as guests on the Sunday talk shows, and above all provided toothsome visuals for the nightly news broadcasts. Mark Goode, Nixon's TV supervisor, returned to the White House to help, but the imputed wizard of the video operation was Reagan's longtime aide from his days as California governor, Michael Deaver—"the real executive producer of the television network news," in one CBS official's assessment. A sandy-haired stick of a man with a comb-over and wide circular glasses, Deaver, forty-five, had shuttled for years between politics and PR. In the White House, he oversaw Reagan's public appearances down to the last detail, including the choice of setting, the placement of the audience, the lighting, the camera position, and sometimes even the color of the walls. He gloried when the nightly news led with footage of Reagan strutting manfully in a flak jacket and field glasses at the Korean demilitarized zone, or chatting amiably with his ostensible adversary "Tip" O'Neill, or kissing his wife Nancy before boarding his chopper. "Television needs Deaver to make sure they get something out of the White House today," his colleague Lyn Nofziger explained. "Deaver needs television to make sure the president is presented in a good light." The press tirelessly exposed and decried Deaver's image making, but White House officials shrugged that even critical stories about their stage management wound up showcasing the alluring visuals anew. "You don't tell us how to stage the news and we won't tell you how to cover it," Larry Speakes, the aptly named White House spokesman, chirped to reporters. He inscribed the quip on a sign on his desk.[6]

This knack for getting his desired message and image across was one reason Reagan became known as "the Great Communicator." But one reason Reagan's aides deployed their scripts and visuals so diligently was that without them Reagan wasn't a very good communicator at all. Never much concerned with details or factual subtleties, he was seen by even his closest colleagues as incurious and disengaged. Some were convinced he mentally inhabited a fantasy world, as when he talked about banding with the Russians to fight off an alien invasion, or when he confused his long-ago movie roles with actual life experiences. When speaking off the cuff, he often rambled, contradicted himself, and botched facts. These verbal gaffes ranged from the innocuous (calling his dog by the wrong name) to the factually misleading (insisting that Leonid Brezhnev had first proposed the nuclear freeze) to the politically damaging (claiming that trees caused more pollution than cars and chimneys). Beloved anecdotes resurfaced in his remarks even after being rebutted. Gergen came to see these embellished or fictional stories as "parables," which, like biblical tales, were understood by their audiences to be metaphorical and instructive, not literal. The press corps wasn't sold.[7]

Reporters started to talk about *factoids*—another Nixon-era word that entered wide usage in the 1980s thanks to Reagan—and pointed out regularly that the president either stretched the truth or was ignorant of it. Reflecting a common view, *The Washington Post*'s Lou Cannon wrote that Reagan was "embarrassingly unaware or misinformed as to the content of some of his basic policy decisions." Others took to "truth-squadding" or "fact checking" his remarks, though these sporadic efforts didn't become a staple of news coverage until years later. It was hardly shocking in 1988 when Speakes, having left the White House, admitted that he had invented statements and on his own authority attributed them to the president. In *Doonesbury*, Garry Trudeau's White House correspondent, Roland Hedley, went "in search of Reagan's brain."[8]

Because of Reagan's propensity for gaffes, Speakes, Deaver, and other aides steered him to written scripts. There, the old Hollywood star excelled. Even in meetings, he used cue cards—half sheets of heavy bond paper with words in oversized type to compensate for his nearsightedness. The White House also introduced weekly radio addresses to exploit Reagan's effectiveness when reading from a text—and to go over reporters' heads. Though ignored inside Washington, the radio addresses became a regular and important feature of White House messaging.[9]

What drew the most acclaim were Reagan's televised speeches. In the 1980s, the president could still reliably commandeer the three main networks for an address, and Reagan was able to make full use of his Hollywood experience. Usually, he worked in one of two registers. As the macho John Wayne cowboy, he would talk tough about the Soviets or namby-pamby liberals, mobilizing the resentment of the frustrated Americans who were his base. Lest he come across as bellicose or heartless, however, he could also strike the pose of a genial Jimmy Stewart, proffering idyllic visions of a wholesome America and a treacly optimism about its future. In a husky, radio-trained voice that focus groups loved, the president tapped into veins of nostalgia for a Norman Rockwell world of small-town neighborhoods, frontier individualism, and God-fearing, patriotic values. As Wirthlin argued, even when Reagan's policy positions on specific issues lacked majority support, he won popular affection with his sunny vision of America.[10]

Well-planned visuals elevated Reagan's sentimental speeches into evocative tableaus. In his 1981 inaugural address, Reagan lovingly described his majestic surroundings: "the monument to a monumental man, George Washington . . . the stately memorial to Thomas Jefferson . . . the sloping hills of Arlington National Cemetery, with its row upon row of simple white markers bearing crosses or Stars of David." Network producers, working off advance texts, switched as if on cue to the requisite scenery, producing what James Reston of the *New York Times* deemed "a theatrical triumph." Thereafter, presidential speeches were drafted with the camera in mind. In his 1982 State of the Union address, the president singled out the courage of Lenny Skutnik, who had recently rescued a woman from the icy Potomac River after a plane crash—cuing cameras to show Skutnik sitting with Nancy Reagan in the spectators' gallery. The device of singling out everyday heroes, a populistic celebration of individualism, would return in Reagan's subsequent State of the Union speeches, as well as his successors'. In 1984, commemorating the D-Day invasion, Reagan's team used shots of the breathtaking bluffs of Normandy and the assembled veterans, now stooped and gray, to great emotional effect. ("I was thinking cinematically," explained speechwriter Peggy Noonan.) And three years later, Reagan exploited the background of Berlin's Brandenburg Gate with his blustery demand that Gorbachev prove his commitment to reform and "tear down" the Berlin Wall.[11]

The *pièce de résistance* of Reagan's image making came during his 1984 reelection campaign. Skilled as they were at mounting televised spectacles, the White House specialists nonetheless sought help from Madison Avenue. Volunteers from J. Walter Thompson, BBD&O, and other ad firms formed the "Tuesday Team," so named with Election Day in mind. Reagan poked his head into an early meeting to declare, "Since you're the ones who are selling the soap, I thought you'd like to see the bar." The admen promoted not Reagan's policies so much as good feelings about the United States. They abjured the Rosser Reeves hard sell in favor of sumptuous atmospherics, honey-toned lighting, and a dulcet sound track. Emotion was larded in. Phil Dusenberry, the brains behind the era's "Pepsi Generation" ads, produced an eighteen-minute convention film featuring snippets from Reagan's D-Day speech, which made the president weep. The crown jewel was "Morning Again in America," a star-spangled montage of Americana, from a tractor tilling a field to the sun glistening off San Francisco Bay. This feel-good vision was an easy sell amid a rebounding economy and a romp by U.S. athletes at the Summer Olympics in Los Angeles, which the Soviet Union boycotted. When ABC News's Peter Jennings interviewed Reagan at the Olympics, he was forced to "play right into the center of the president's campaign," he admitted, by affording Reagan free airtime to articulate his patriotic platitudes.[12]

Morning in America also had a dark side. As aide Richard Darman wrote in a memo, the idea was to "paint RR as the personification of all that is right with, or heroized by, America. Leave Mondale in a position where an attack on Reagan is tantamount to an attack on America's idealized image of itself—where a vote against Reagan is, in some subliminal sense, a vote against a mythic 'AMERICA.'" On one balmy September afternoon in Northern California, Darman even felt a frisson of guilt as he watched Reagan finish an open-air speech to the strains of the Lee Greenwood hit "God Bless the USA" and skydivers descended with red, white, and blue parachutes: Mondale, he felt, was in the position of running against America.[13]

With Reagan's 1984 landslide, critics and analysts in the press struggled to explain his success. A common argument held that his career in entertainment had uniquely equipped him for a job that had become largely a matter of theatrics. He was, as book titles had it, an *Acting President*, playing *The Role of a Lifetime*. Some claimed that Reagan was an intellectual lightweight who sustained his popularity only by submitting himself to his handlers, mouthing his lines, and striking poses.

The movies did inform Reagan's thinking. He fired off old lines lodged in his memory bank as if they were spontaneous quips, and he drew upon Hollywood films in imagining how his proposal for a protective missile defense system would function. Secretary of State George Shultz confessed to instructing Reagan on how to act his "scenes" with Gorbachev and other counterparts. But the idea that Reagan and his team used their media proficiency to fool the public into buying a conservative agenda belonged to the tradition of frustrated protests of antagonists unwilling to credit a rival's successes. By and large Americans knew what they were getting with Reagan—his bungled facts, spurious anecdotes, and oversimplified homilies notwithstanding. His appeals resonated because he drew from a wellspring of archetypes, cultural memories, and deeply embedded national myths. Doing so required—as politics always required—skill in presentation.

This Reagan readily admitted. A month before leaving office, he was asked by ABC's David Brinkley whether show business had taught him anything of use in politics. "There have been times in this office," Reagan said with a grin, "when I've wondered how you could do the job if you hadn't been an actor."[14]

SPINNING OUT OF CONTROL

BY THE 1988 PRESIDENTIAL RACE, between Vice President George Bush and Massachusetts governor Michael Dukakis, the presence of consultants had become so pervasive that *Time* magazine proclaimed it the "Year of the Handlers." Professional consultants had been reshaping politics since Whitaker and Baxter in the 1930s, and had even formed their own trade group in 1969. But where men like Robert Montgomery and Frank Shakespeare once solemnly denied any role in coaching Eisenhower or Nixon, now marquee operatives like Roger Ailes, Bob Shrum, and Bob Squier boasted about their role in crafting messages and ads and even candidates. Journalists noticed their handiwork in the barrage of negative ads and in the homogenized, vapid tone of many campaigns. "Every four years brings the modern campaign closer to mechanical perfection as techniques like focus groups and overnight tracking polls wring the last gasp of spontaneity out of the process," wrote Walter Shapiro in *Time*, with "every movement, gesture, word and response dictated by political handlers and chaperones."[1]

In the 1988 presidential race, both sides fastidiously staged their events and scripted their remarks. The writer Joan Didion recorded the banality of Dukakis doggedly tossing a baseball with an aide for forty minutes on a Phoenix tarmac in order to burnish his ordinary guy credentials. As Didion looked on, she chatted with a producer from CNN, the upstart twenty-four-hour cable news network, who told her that the Dukakis campaign had recently staged an identical ball toss in Ohio, near a bowling alley, but that only one network had filmed it—so the stunt was now being replayed. Nonetheless, Didion noted, leading political reporters such as Joe Klein and David Broder reported the Phoenix game of catch as if untroubled by its contrived nature.[2]

Despite small victories like this for the Dukakis squad, the Bush team proved far more proficient at spin. James Baker, Bush's longtime fixer, presided over a seasoned crew that included Lee Atwater and Roger Ailes, both known for their Nixonian mercilessness. Equally important, Bush's pollster Robert Teeter, another Nixon veteran, was a pioneer in using focus groups, a newly popular means of testing ads, arguments, issues, and even words and phrases by intensively questioning small bunches of likely voters. In 1988, these focus groups found that to win over the so-called Reagan Democrats, the blue-collar voters who had carried Reagan and other Republicans to victory in the 1980s, Bush should emphasize specific issues that played to fears of American weakness abroad and lawlessness at home. In particular, noted Teeter's colleague Fred Steeper, the issues of patriotism and crime "signaled the wrong moral values on Dukakis. They helped with the women (very important) as well as the men."[3]

From this discovery two lines of attack followed. The first had the blue-blooded Bush pummeling his Greek-American rival for vetoing mandatory pledge-of-allegiance recitals in Massachusetts (which were in fact unconstitutional), in a bid to tap a vein of Reaganite chauvinism. The second had Bush flay his rival for supporting a statewide prison furlough program under which a black inmate named William Horton, while on release, had raped a Maryland woman and assaulted her fiancé. One Bush commercial about the furloughs showed prisoners ominously passing through a revolving gate. Another, made by Ailes's protégé Larry McCarthy and aired by a group that was technically distinct from the campaign, featured a glowering mug shot of the African-American Horton. Through these racially charged ads—and the free exposure their controversy earned them—Bush saddled Dukakis with a reputation for lenience on violent crime.[4]

But if Bush ran a brazenly negative campaign, it played out in a newly charged environment that subjected his allegations to cold-eyed scrutiny. Twenty years after Joe McGinniss, reporters were reflexively analyzing and contesting the candidates' claims as never before. "Everyone wants to be a pundit," said NBC anchor Tom Brokaw of the new journalistic culture.

"Everyone wants to put a little spin in there." If Dukakis's game of catch was reported uncritically, in many other instances broadcasters pointedly highlighted the made-for-TV nature of the stunts they were covering. "In the war of the Labor Day visuals," began one evening news piece by Bob Schieffer of CBS, "George Bush pulled out the heavy artillery: a Disneyland backdrop and lots of pictures with the Disney gang." Determined not to mindlessly pass on misinformation, reporters boldly questioned the legitimacy of Bush's attacks, claiming that his team had plumbed new depths of negativity, distortion, and triviality. On *Face the Nation*, Lesley Stahl of CBS schooled James Baker with an explanation of why his campaign's statements about Dukakis were dishonest. "Ad watch" segments, in print and on TV, examined the veracity of negative spots, taking a freeze-frame of an offending ad to underscore its misleading statements.[5]

Dukakis was at pains to respond. Twenty years before, he had cringed at McGinniss's portrait of politics in *Selling of the President, 1968*, and he chose to hit back at Bush by assailing his tactics, not his ideas. Called "The Packaging of George Bush," Dukakis's response ad depicted the vice president as a creature of his handlers, cynically contriving smears because he had no substance to run on. The ad was a clever critique of spin but not an affirmative case for Dukakis's candidacy. Even in the Year of the Handlers, issues like mudslinging and misleading spin weren't going to decide an election.[6]

* * *

Different people drew different lessons from the 1988 campaign. Many political observers resolved to challenge the spin even more directly than before; Kathleen Hall Jamieson, a leading communications scholar at the University of Pennsylvania, devised clever methods by which TV journalists could parse a negative ad's claims without reinforcing its message. The Bush White House, in contrast, highlighted the success of Teeter's focus groups, which quickly became a favorite tool in sussing out the best way to sell the new administration's policies. After Iraq invaded Kuwait in 1990, Bush gave a radio address to prepare the public for a military operation to expel Saddam Hussein's forces; Ailes convened a focus group to listen to the speech and spelled out for Bush which arguments had resonated, helping the president refine his case for war.

The response of the Democrats to 1988 was different still. They concluded that Dukakis's error had been to let Bush's scurrilous charges sit unanswered. Their solution was "rapid response."[7]

Four years later, when Arkansas governor Bill Clinton captured the Democratic presidential nomination, his campaign set up what his wife, Hillary, christened the "War Room"—a high-tech central command in Little Rock where top aides, including the bug-eyed senior consultant James Carville and the young, mop-topped George Stephanopoulos, could fire back quickly at the inevitable attacks. In the face of what everyone now took to be an accelerated "twenty-four-hour news cycle," the squad met twice daily, at 7 am and 7 pm, to review Stanley Greenberg's overnight polls, Frank Greer's ads, the latest Bush attacks, and any potentially troublesome news. Rapid response teams on the ground in every state relayed the Little Rock team's crafted message to supporters and news outlets for dissemination. On the night of Bush's nomination acceptance speech, they sent out a detailed "reality versus rhetoric" fact-checking sheet so quickly that one TV pundit was seen waving a faxed copy of it on the air.[8]

Clinton's War Room developed a mystique. Among those enticed were the filmmakers D. A. Pennebaker, sixty-seven, a veteran of Robert Drew's documentaries, and Chris Hegedus, thirty-nine, his directing partner and third wife. "The majority of broadcasters were content to aim their cameras at candidates walking in and out of hotels and airplanes for nightly news coverage," Hegedus noted, but "audiences were curious to see the people who had engineered this incredible campaign." For decades Hollywood had rendered consultants, in the manner of *The Candidate*, as amoral technocrats bent on victory at any cost. Taking the camera into the Little Rock inner sanctum might offer a more complex view, demystifying their much-hyped and much-maligned role in modern campaigns.[9]

The Clinton team, battered earlier in the year by controversies over their candidate's extramarital affairs and not having served in the Vietnam War, balked at granting entrée to Pennebaker and Hegedus. But in June Clinton's fortunes shifted, and suddenly, at five thirty on the Friday before the Democratic National Convention, Stephanopoulos gave the filmmakers the go-ahead. For the next four months, they followed Clinton and his aides from the convention to the campaign bus through the debates and Election Day, with frequent stints in Little Rock. Coming and going into the top-secret War Room itself, they would identify themselves as "guests" and, Hegedus recalled, "never step outside (if we could help it) for fear of not getting back in." By the end they had shot roughly thirty-three hours of film, to be pared down to ninety minutes.[10]

Ten months into Clinton's presidency, *The War Room* premiered at the New York Film Festival. Critics hailed its "glimpse of behind-the-scenes maneuvers" and "moments of remarkable candor"; one called it "one of the most illuminating pieces ever recorded about the machinations of the American ... political process." The film entranced audiences with scenes that the mainstream media had failed to capture: Carville shamelessly trying to pump up a mini-scandal about Bush; unguarded romantic moments between Carville and his girlfriend, Mary Matalin, a Bush campaign operative; staffers testing different neckties for their "sincerity" before a debate; Stephanopoulos bullying a caller into keeping mum about an alleged Clinton indiscretion. But if the filmmakers came away with choice footage, it was unclear whether they had unspun the campaign or whether the campaign had spun them. At times Clinton's aides shut down the filming or banished the crew when discussions grew delicate. Other scenes caught Carville and Stephanopoulos performing or even mugging for the camera. Yet the audiences who flocked to the film seemed not to care, treating the two men as heroes—and it was hard not to surmise that the filmmakers felt similarly. "They had the feeling they were winners and knew what they were doing and were very idealistic," Pennebaker said, likening the Clintonites to Kennedy's New Frontiersmen. Despite themselves, Pennebaker and Hegedus had bestowed upon spin and the spin doctors something that few would have thought possible: romance.[11]

* * *

The War Room notwithstanding, Bill Clinton's media coverage oscillated wildly in the 1992 campaign. One month he was the Democrats' savior and the herald of a practical politics that could break the Washington gridlock; the next, he was Slick Willie, whose marital infidelities betrayed an ideological promiscuity and a nonchalance toward the truth. For the next eight years, journalists would subject Clinton's statements and actions to withering interrogation. At their worst, they inflated stumbles (like the routine firing of White House travel office personnel) and middling transgressions (like his campaign finance violations in 1996) into an endless parade of scandal stories. Fed by an eager Republican opposition, these "pseudo-scandals," as they came to be known, kept the White House in a near-permanent state of siege.[12]

Clinton contributed to his own woes. An incorrigible spinner, he liked to defend himself with casuistic phrasings that were technically true yet aimed to mislead or dodge: "I didn't inhale" (about his youthful marijuana use); "That depends on what the meaning of 'is' is" (about an extramarital affair). But the formulations that he imagined would satisfy a feeding frenzy often served only to prolong it. More broadly, Clinton's stance toward the media was needlessly suspicious and hostile and thus counterproductive; the press wrote critically about his ambitious plan to reform the health care system in part because the administration had hatched it in secrecy. But Clinton's embattlement stemmed from something more than either the personal dislike of Washington journalists or his own poor press management. Any president serving in the 1990s would have had to contend with three big changes in the media culture: the faster speed of news; the deepening of political partisanship; and the steep spike in the kind of gossipy, insider commentary that went by the name of *punditry*.[13]

The label *pundit*, as a name for an informed Washington wise man, had been in circulation since the 1920s, when it was affixed to opinion-shaping newspaper columnists like Walter Lippmann, David Lawrence, and Frank Kent. Punditry made the leap to television in 1960, when Lippmann sat for a chin-stroking interview with Howard K. Smith of CBS. After the Nixon years, the "instant analysis" that Vice President Spiro Agnew decried spread across the tube—on the long-running Sunday talk shows, on ABC's *Nightline*, and on a growing roster of roundtable shows like *Washington Week in Review* and *Agronsky & Company*. But by the 1980s these pundit shows were veering away from sober analysis informed by expertise, favoring instead cursory judgments about political performances. The same sort of idle chatter and spin that had pervaded post-presidential debate coverage now infected everyday news.[14]

As punditry became more speculative and hollow, it also grew more partisan and contentious—reflecting a parallel polarization within the political class. Former campaign and government officials, lacking journalistic experience but accustomed to spinning without remorse, joined the pundits' ranks in droves: Carter speechwriter Chris Matthews, Nixon-Ford-Reagan communications counselor David Gergen, Bush chief of staff John Sununu, and scores of others. By the 1980s the hot shows were, in the McLuhanite sense, hot. On the syndicated *McLaughlin Group*, former Nixon press aide John McLaughlin presided over a gaggle of shouting columnists, gaining such popularity that Ronald Reagan came to its birthday party one year. On CNN's *Crossfire*, another Nixon aide, Pat Buchanan (in time succeeded by Robert Novak), and the liberal columnist Tom Braden (succeeded by Michael Kinsley) would, in Kinsley's words, "snarl and scream inhospitably at bewildered 'guests' and each other for half an hour." Even the sedate discussion shows degenerated. NBC's *Meet the Press*, once hosted by cerebral newsmen like Roger Mudd, Marvin Kalb, and Garrick Utley, devolved under Tim Russert, another former political operative, into a forum for theatrical antagonism and "gotcha" interrogations. The esteem in which Russert's colleagues held him suggested the scope of the problem.[15]

Right-wing radio also fed the partisanship. Though for decades conservative broadcasters like Paul Harvey had sustained robust followings, their opinions had scarcely registered in Washington. In 1988, however, Rush Limbaugh, a former rock deejay and sports broadcaster, launched a nationally syndicated show on ABC radio and quickly became a Republican kingmaker. In 1992, Roger Ailes, having returned to television production, put Limbaugh on TV (the show ran until 1996) and introduced him to President Bush, who hosted the two men for a night in the White House. (Bush carried Limbaugh's bags upstairs.) Extreme in their politics, aggrieved in their tone, inflammatory in their language, and deeply beloved by their listeners, Limbaugh and a raft of imitators pushed the Republicans to adopt maximalist positions while forcing establishment journalists to admit arguments from the far right into mainstream political debates.[16]

Though its full impact wouldn't be felt for several years, the most crucial addition to the array of right-wing media outlets was the Fox News Channel, founded in 1996. Owned by the Australian media mogul Rupert Murdoch, and run by Roger Ailes, Fox billed itself as "Fair & Balanced." Such pretensions to objectivity were hard to square with Ailes's long service to the GOP—or the network's unabashedly conservative content. But Ailes, like many conservatives, believed that mainstream news sources were irredeemably biased and in need of correction. His programming echoed these claims—notably the channel's hit show, *The O'Reilly Factor*, which featured a "No-Spin Zone" purporting to deliver pure, untainted news. Although Fox began with a small fraction of CNN's cable subscribers and remained a relatively minor player for some years to come, it steadily built a hard-core audience throughout Clinton's second term, in part by hyping the assorted scandals to its conservative viewers.[17]

Fox's significance lay not just in providing a national platform for conservative spin but in contributing to a news environment of almost incessant argument and chatter. Thanks to Fox, CNN, MSNBC, and CNBC (which covered politics before turning mainly to business news), as well as to the late-1990s boom in Internet usage, partisan punditry by the end of Clinton's presidency had more outlets than ever. A typical weekday on Washington cable TV in 1998 featured 146 hours of "news," most of it pure talk. The Internet also provided infinitely more sources of news and information, many of them highly partisan or ideological or amateurish, often tended without the professional scruples expected of established journalists. This eclipse of the traditional gatekeepers, along with the faster speed of news, meant that rumors, misinformation, and conspiracy theories could now make their way more easily into general discourse.[18]

*   *   *

In 1998, these trends converged for what David Halberstam judged "the worst year for American journalism" in at least half a century. The occasion for this stern verdict was the year-long drive to impeach Clinton, a nakedly partisan struggle for control of the presidency waged between two parties representing deeply divergent sets of values, carried out in the courts, in Congress, and, not least, the news media. The tortuous saga had begun the year before when Kenneth Starr, an independent counsel named to investigate Whitewater—a questionable real estate investment Clinton made in his gubernatorial days—tried to revive his faltering probe by digging into a separate scandal, centered on the president's purported sexual harassment of an Arkansas woman named Paula Jones. Months of back-channel communications ensued among Starr's aides, Jones's lawyers, conservative activists, and scandalmongering journalists. Then, in January 1998, *The Drudge Report*, an amateur right-wing website, published rumors of an affair between the president and Monica Lewinsky, a former White House intern. The next day, conservative pundit Bill Kristol aired the *Drudge* story on ABC's Sunday-morning roundtable show, and by Tuesday *The Washington Post* confirmed that Starr was looking into the Lewinsky affair and whether laws were broken in covering it up.[19]

What followed was a year of spin. With the precise details of the Clinton-Lewinsky affair known only to a few people, the ratio of conjecture to reporting in the media skyrocketed. The scandal vaulted a new crop of pundits to prominence, some destined to remain famous (such as Ann Coulter, who worked with Paula Jones's legal team), others fated to return to obscurity (Jonathan Turley, a law professor at George Washington University). Daily shows devoted to "all Monica, all the time" began running on Fox, MSNBC, and CNBC. The coverage was indicative of what the *New York Times* columnist Frank Rich called a *mediathon*, a new, cable TV–driven "hybrid of media circus, soap opera, and tabloid journalism." Although mediathons could yield ratings bonanzas for the cable networks, they also alienated much of the public, and during the Lewinsky saga, unhappiness with the news media boomed.[20]

Though Clinton felt besieged, he had many tools with which to fight back. Even as cable and the Internet created new forums for scandalmongering and adversarial punditry, they also shattered the dominance of the old media titans, allowing Clinton to select the most hospitable venues for delivering his own spin. For five years, in the face of the often hostile press corps regulars, Clinton had deftly used niche forums such as local TV, urban radio, *Larry King Live*, and even weather forecasters (to promote action on climate change) to reach his desired audiences. He also built his own highly proficient spin team. In 1994 he had hired David Gergen, the consummate White House communications maven, to stabilize his administration after a rocky start, and since then he employed a series of scandal sharpshooters, such as Mark Fabiani and Lanny Davis—lawyers skilled at heading off the onslaught of negative stories. By 1998 he had found in Mike McCurry a tremendously effective press secretary, genial in disposition but steely in his resolve; postponing plans to step down, McCurry stayed on board through the worst of the Lewinsky crisis. Not least, Clinton's string of pollsters—Stan Greenberg, Dick Morris, Doug Schoen, Mark Penn—had over the years tested possible responses to every imaginable issue, helping him to choose priorities, craft rhetoric, and launch policy initiatives with media blitzes and presidential tours.[21]

When the Lewinsky story broke, Clinton sought out Dick Morris. Starting in 1995, Morris had become close to Clinton. The previous year, Georgia congressman Newt Gingrich had collaborated with the eccentric young pollster Frank Luntz to consciously change the words that Republicans used—*tax cuts* became *tax relief*, the *estate tax* became the *death tax*—and, riding a wave of discontent, helped the GOP take control of the House of Representatives for the first time in forty years. In the wake of that setback, Clinton had turned to Morris, who helped Clinton rebound. Among his achievements were campaign-style TV ads designed to promote the president's policies and to counter the sort of attack ads that had helped sink Clinton's health care plan the year before. In the middle of the 1996 reelection campaign, however, Morris resigned when news broke that he was frequenting prostitutes. He hadn't spoken to the president since.

In January 1998, Morris was riding the subway when he saw the president's number appear on his pager. At first he wondered if the gadget was busted, but he realized that Clinton must have been phoning about the breaking scandal and hurried to a private phone to return the call. "I just screwed up with this girl," Clinton said. "I didn't do what they said, but I did do something. And I think I may have done so much that I can't prove my innocence." Morris took a poll on how the public would react if Clinton confirmed the rumors—and if he denied them. The results persuaded him that the president would need, in Morris's words, to "gradually sensitize the public to the truth."

Clinton heeded the advice. His initial statements were ones he could defend as literally true but implied behavior much milder than the months-long intimate relationship that he and Lewinsky had actually had. "There is not a sexual relationship," he told newscaster Jim Lehrer, suggesting that there perhaps had been an affair but it was now over. When that statement failed to satisfy anyone, Clinton declared, "I did not have sexual relations with that woman, Miss Lewinsky"; this formulation, too, was technically true, if by "sexual relations" he meant sexual intercourse. To aides and friends, Clinton lied more unambiguously, relying on them to spread his disinformation around Washington. Soon, however, he stopped talking about the scandal at all, leaving statements to his lawyers and flacks. The strategy of silence made sense. In neither his 1998 State of the Union address, delivered just as the Lewinsky story was breaking, nor his 1999 address, given amid his Senate impeachment trial, did Clinton mention the scandal, and both speeches were resounding successes. And while Clinton kept mum, aides reinforced the White House line that the president, supremely capable of compartmentalizing his tasks, was diligently tending to the people's business—as indeed he was.

Clinton's stonewalling worked—sort of. A few weeks after the initial turmoil, the public acclimated itself to the likelihood that the president had carried on some kind of affair in the White House with a woman barely out of college. As this reality settled in, Clinton's approval ratings rebounded, eventually topping 70 percent. Yet Starr's investigation proceeded full throttle, the Republicans kept hyping the story, and pundits filled the airtime with argument and salacious speculation. Starr and his aides kept the affair in the news with leaks about grand jury testimony—despite reprimands from Judge Norma Holloway Johnson, who oversaw the case—framing the unfolding narrative in ways favorable to the prosecution.[22]

By the time Clinton went before Starr's grand jury, in August 1998, most Americans wanted to be done with the whole business. After testifying, the president spoke to the nation, admitting at last to a relationship with Lewinsky that was "not appropriate" and apologizing for misleading the public. He also righteously called on Starr to terminate his investigation. Again, the public applauded, the pundits frowned, and the Republicans pressed ahead. Three days later, when Clinton ordered air strikes against the Islamist terrorist group al-Qaeda for its deadly bombings of two U.S. embassies in Africa, some critics charged that it was a ploy to win public support—an echo of the recent Hollywood film, *Wag the Dog*, about a political consultant who engineers a war for election-year purposes. Only recently liberals had bemoaned the people's susceptibility to spin, whether by Reagan's stage managers or Bush's admakers. Now, it was conservatives such as Bill Kristol and William Bennett who deemed the masses deluded, duped by Clinton's rhetoric.[23]

The hoopla around Lewinsky spiked again in September when Starr issued his report. Published in thick mass-market quickie books, downloaded from the Internet until computers crashed, it humiliated Clinton with its graphic sexual detail. But it failed to persuade many people to support the president's removal from office. Nonetheless, Starr and the Republicans barreled ahead, even after the electorate surprised prognosticators in November by trimming the GOP's House majority by five seats—a historically rare victory for the president's party during off-year elections. For the next three months, as impeachment proceeded, both sides rehashed the same arguments they had been making for a year, until finally a divided Senate acquitted the president in February 1999. The fusillade of arguments on both sides had changed barely a single mind.

One clear conclusion of the saga was that Washington pundits had fallen out of step with public opinion. Regarded during Watergate as indispensable watchdogs, trusted experts who could see past cynical White House messaging, members of the news media were now by and large looked upon as out-of-touch bloviators. If anything, their attacks on Clinton had backfired, boosting his popularity and hurting their own standing, along with that of Starr and the Republicans. Despite "ten months of the incessant sensation-mongering of the Monica Lewinsky scandal," observed the political scientist Samuel Popkin, the public showed that it could in fact "decline to be spun."[24]

IN OCTOBER 2005, just after the start of George W. Bush's second presidential term, the comedian Stephen Colbert premiered a new show on the Comedy Central cable channel. Playing the part of a conservative talk show windbag—a not-so-thinly disguised Bill O'Reilly of Fox—Colbert unveiled a segment called "The Word," in which he taught his viewers a coinage of his own devising: *truthiness*. In the faux-conservative persona that he would inhabit for the next decade, Colbert praised Bush's oft-stated proclivity for making instinctive decisions without regard for countervailing facts. It was more important, Colbert insisted in mock support of Bush, for something to *feel* true than for it to *be* true. "Truthiness" was the quality of feeling true in the gut.[1]

The Colbert Report quickly became a cult hit, its eight-week run immediately extended to a year, and *truthiness* became a sensation. The American Dialect Society crowned it the Word of the Year. As the *New York Times* columnist Frank Rich—formerly the paper's drama critic—wrote the following January, "Colbert's slinging of the word 'truthiness' caught on instantaneously last year precisely because we live in the age of truthiness." Rich pointed to events—from the exposure of James Frey's partially fabricated memoir to the burnishing of Supreme Court nominee Samuel Alito before his confirmation hearings—that were blurring the line between empirically discerned conclusions and gut impressions.[2]

Colbert's barbs at Bush exerted special bite in the fall of 2005 because his presidency, previously known for its effective messaging and Reaganesque mastery of visuals, was just then unraveling: The administration's response to Hurricane Katrina had proven woefully inadequate; his Supreme Court nomination of White House counsel Harriet Miers foundered (Alito was tapped instead); and above all his team could not bring peace and stability to Iraq, where, two years after U.S. troops deposed Saddam Hussein, the chaos and carnage were only worsening. Bush's anti-intellectual, gut-player persona still went over well with steadfast Republicans, but overall his popularity was falling and his rationalizations for his errors were faltering. Colbert brilliantly captured the president's blithe indifference to disagreeable evidence, his dogged determination to spin the situation his way, whatever the consequences.

* * *

Bush's ability to stick by his story regardless of criticism or credibility was evident as early as the constitutional crisis in which his presidency was born. On Election Day, 2000, he and Vice President Al Gore battled to a statistical tie in the state of Florida—so close that the law mandated an automatic recount—and without the state's 25 electoral votes, neither man could claim the presidency. For the next thirty-six days, the two campaigns engaged in a brute struggle for control of the presidency—a preview, it turned out, of the rigid partisanship that would define the coming era. Ultimately, a bitterly divided Supreme Court would halt the unfinished recount and award the presidency to Bush, who was leading by 154 votes at the time.

The fight between Bush and Gore was never just a legal one. With twenty-four-hour news channels and Internet sites covering the story incessantly, both sides hired consultants, deployed armies of surrogates, and encouraged friendly pundits to bombard the public with campaign-approved spin. Public support, they believed, would give them room to maneuver and maybe even influence the judges who, like deejays in a game of musical chairs, were abruptly stopping and starting the herky-jerky recounts proceeding in counties across Florida.[3]

The opportunism behind the spin in Florida was unusually pure and blatant because the questions at stake—whether a partly punched ballot signaled an intended vote, or whether a statutory deadline could be legally extended—had no intrinsic ideological content. Both sides' spin was completely self-serving, aimed at securing an election victory. Because Bush stood only to lose from any recount, his team tried to foster the impression that he had already won, that Gore was trying to rob him of his victory, and that the process should end. The Friday after the election, Bush staged a photo op in Austin, Texas, with his top aides, somberly planning their transition to power. For the next five weeks, his rhetoric sought to discredit the legitimacy of any recount. Gore, in contrast, argued that only a careful manual recount of the disputed ballots would determine the rightful winner. His team emphasized the importance of a fair process, however time-consuming, and aimed to lessen the urgency. His Friday photo op showed his family playing touch football, Kennedy-style.

Gore's spin had the virtue of consistency—count all the votes—but it forced him to assume a detached, statesmanlike posture unsuited for a political donnybrook. He forswore passionate appeals to mobilize his supporters (never his strong suit, given his stiff demeanor). He snuffed out a protest led by Jesse Jackson, fearing it would be seen as interfering with an orderly recount. In contrast, Bush and his aides fought tenaciously, galvanizing the righteous anger roiling his base. They encouraged the so-called Brooks Brothers riot, a pre-Thanksgiving Republican rally, organized with help from GOP officials and consultants, that physically shut down a crucial recount in Miami—an episode that typified Bush's anything goes approach. Bush's problem was the inverse of Gore's: to summon passion, he sacrificed consistency. In the legal fight, his team brazenly rotated through a series of starkly contradictory arguments. Early on, his lawyers demanded that Florida's secretary of state certify his meager lead, suggesting that Gore could always statutorily contest the official certification afterwards. But immediately after the certification, they pivoted and said that for Gore to now contest a certified vote would needlessly prolong the election. The barefaced reversal caused little trouble for Bush amid the fast-moving, spin-drenched media coverage.

Republicans had the hardest time countering what seemed to be the most unobjectionable request by Gore: that the counties in question simply obtain the most accurate vote count possible. As a result, some Republicans found themselves arguing that obtaining *any* reliable tally was impossible. As the journalist Ron Rosenbaum wrote, this belief in "the futility of the search for 'facts,'" this radical "distrust of knowledge, of evidence," was essentially a postmodern stance, and a highly unusual position for conservatives, who normally deplored relativism of all kinds. Going further than Walter Lippmann or subsequent thinkers who had grappled with the elusiveness of objectivity, the Bush team, like the radical postmodern theorists of a half century later, implied that in the present case all assertions of truth were simply masks for claims to power. Following suit, many in the news media portrayed Bush and Gore as engaged in mirror-image power grabs. "Bush will be our first truly postmodern president," concluded the political scientist Alan Wolfe, sardonically, "the first of whom it can be said that when asked how he came to be the winner, he can respond that it all depends on the perspective one brings to the question."[4]

* * *

Bush and his aides never proclaimed themselves postmodernists, but once in the White House, they showed the same tendency to portray well-established facts as partisan claims. On issues from birth control to global warming to human evolution, the administration rejected input from scientific or academic authorities as simply "the spin of experts," as the journalist Joshua Marshall wrote, "blinded by their own unacknowledged biases." An anonymous White House official mocked those who believed in what he deemed the passé concept of empirical facts, calling them "the reality-based community." As he told the journalist Ron Suskind, "We're an empire now, and when we act, we create our own reality."[5]

Bush officials felt confident flouting informed policy advice because of a long-standing project, dating to the Nixon years, to construct a right-wing counter-establishment of think tanks, research centers, and associated specialists. By Bush's presidency, these institutions had matured. During policy debates, their claims reverberated through the conservative news outlets, which the Bush White House aggressively courted (periodically hosting, for example, "Radio Days" in tents on the North Lawn for right-wing talkers). Mainstream journalists, meanwhile, recoiled from explicitly taking sides in debates over complex technical and scientific matters, even when the preponderance of experts supported one position. This non-judgmentalism infuriated the president's critics. "If President Bush said that the Earth was flat," wrote the economist Paul Krugman in his *New York Times* column, pointing up the absurdity, "the headlines of news articles would read, 'Opinions Differ on Shape of the Earth.'"[6]

As Bush's presidency wore on, journalists catalogued incidents of politicized expertise. His top Medicare official threatened to fire the program's chief actuary if he shared with Congress his dispassionately calculated cost projections of the administration's planned prescription drug benefit. A twenty-four-year-old NASA appointee ordered an agency web designer to place the word *theory* after every mention of the Big Bang, to make it sound like a matter of speculation. Richard Carmona, Bush's surgeon general, revealed that the White House had gagged him from speaking out on issues like the merits of sex education and the dangers of secondhand smoke. Most controversial of all was the administration's neglect of the rising temperatures that an overwhelming consensus of scientists held were dangerously altering the earth's climate. Enlisting a few experts who shared the fringe view that denied any human role in global warming, the administration disingenuously claimed scientific support for its own stance, and journalists often misleadingly framed the debate as one between two legitimate camps. Scientists protested. On Capitol Hill, frustrated Democrats held hearings, issued reports, and introduced bills to rein in the administration. Critics took to punning grimly about "political science." Administration officials were unmoved.[7]

Bush contributed to the profusion of spin in other ways as well. His administration developed a reputation for exceptionally tight message coordination, a penchant for secrecy, and disdain toward the press (Bush held hardly any news conferences). This discipline thwarted journalists trying to report on behind-the-scenes developments. "You go through the effort of getting Karl Rove on the phone," noted *The Washington Post*'s Dana Milbank, of Bush's top political adviser, "and he'll say exactly the same thing as Scott McClellan," the White House press secretary. Bush's nearly invisible but highly influential pollster, Jan van Lohuizen, and his focus group maven, Fred Steeper, revived the old Gingrich-Luntz strategy from the 1990s of poll-testing buzzwords and "power phrases" and repeating them, as GOP operative Haley Barbour self-deprecatingly admitted, "until you vomit."[8]

More troubling were the administration's surreptitious payments to conservative pundits to promote Bush's policies. The journalist Armstrong Williams was paid to tout Bush's education policies, the journalist Maggie Gallagher to plug his efforts to encourage marriage among poor couples. Some executive branch departments also blurred the line between news and propaganda by promoting their policies with video news releases— fake segments designed to resemble local TV news reports, with sound bites from officials and the "correspondent" signing off: "In Washington, I'm Karen Ryan, reporting." Like the press releases a century earlier that had mimicked the form of newspaper stories and were sometimes reprinted verbatim in the press, the videos fooled some local station managers into airing them whole, without noting their provenance.

At times during the Bush administration it seemed that there existed nothing but spin—or truthiness—as each side offered up not just its own opinions but also its own facts. The explosion of media outlets, the polarized environment, and the brigades of pundits and well-prepped officials ready to toe the party line all conspired to leave the average citizen unsure how to obtain reliable, non-partisan news and analysis. Of course, the ubiquity of spin hadn't actually made it possible to invent political reality, as Ron Suskind's source had teasingly suggested. But especially on matters where information was technical, recondite, or limited by government secrecy, it did make it hard to confidently gainsay official pronouncements. The consequences would become evident not only in ongoing conflicts over science and medicine but also in the debate that raged in the news media in 2002 and 2003 about whether the United States should invade Iraq.

* * *

By the end of the Clinton administration, Saddam Hussein remained a regional menace. Forced after his defeat in the 1991 Gulf War to dismantle his nuclear program, Saddam had in 1998 evicted the UN inspectors tasked with ensuring that he wouldn't restart it. Assuming office in 2001, Bush and Vice President Dick Cheney—who had been defense secretary during the Gulf War—considered Saddam's prolonged defiance of international law "unfinished business" and put Iraq high on their foreign policy agenda. Some administration officials believed that plans existed from the outset to remove its troublesome despot.[9]

For nine months, Bush said little publicly about Saddam. But al-Qaeda's calamitous attacks on New York's World Trade Center and the Pentagon on September 11, 2001, killing nearly 3,000 Americans, changed the calculus. At first Bush and other officials suspected—wrongly—that Saddam had abetted the terrorist attacks. But even after that theory was discredited, 9/11 still strengthened the case in Bush's eyes for moving against Saddam. In exposing America's vulnerability to catastrophic terrorism, the al-Qaeda assault made the prospect of letting *any* hostile power gain nuclear weapons infinitely less acceptable to those charged with protecting American security. As expressed in an unofficial "One-Percent Doctrine," the United States now had to act decisively against a range of threats that were previously deemed minor or uncertain.[10]

Newly worried about American security, and convinced of Saddam's malevolent designs, Bush and his aides proceeded to filter ill-founded or ambiguous intelligence about his weapons programs and supposed links to al-Qaeda through their preconceptions. These preconceptions also led them to put their trust in questionable human sources, such as an Iraqi defector known by the code name "Curveball," who claimed to have worked at Iraqi biological weapons labs. At the same time, administration officials downplayed countervailing evidence, even when offered by senior intelligence analysts, regarding it as bureaucratic nitpicking or knee jerk anti-interventionism. "Self-deception," and not "intentional fraud," wrote the political journalist Jacob Weisberg, thus lay behind the administration's case for war—a case whose public presentation nonetheless "fell short of any standard of intellectual honesty."[11]

While Bush and his aides likely felt confident in their judgments about Saddam, they still deemed it necessary to mount their case for war with an aggressive spin campaign. The first intimations of the possibility of an American attack on Baghdad came in late 2001, when Bush publicly warned Saddam not to develop weapons of mass destruction. Soon after, head White House speechwriter Michael Gerson asked his colleague David Frum to "sum up in a sentence or two our best case for going after Iraq"—leading to the president's declaration in his January 2002 State of the Union address that Iraq was part of an "axis of evil," bent on gaining doomsday arms. Over the next few months, pro-war administration officials, particularly Cheney, escalated the rhetoric about the danger Saddam posed. In a speech at West Point in June, Bush himself made clear that he was considering a preventive attack.[12]

In August 2002, the effort to mobilize public opinion cohered as White House chief of staff Andy Card convened the White House Iraq Group, an internal working group much like LBJ's Vietnam Information Group and other ad hoc messaging bodies over the years. Gathering each week in the Situation Room, WHIG included both senior policy hands such as National Security Adviser Condoleezza Rice and communications specialists such as Michael Gerson, Karl Rove, Karen Hughes, and Mary Matalin. A "strategic communications" task force drafted white papers and hashed out themes and talking points for the fall, when the public advocacy would commence in earnest. With the midterm elections looming and the post-9/11 public in a vengeful temper, a focus on military intervention would pressure Democrats to support the administration's plans. The public campaign would begin after Labor Day. "From a marketing point of view," Card crassly explained, "you don't introduce new products in August."[13]

To inaugurate the effort, Bush delivered a televised speech on the first anniversary of the 9/11 attacks. A team of former TV producers who regularly staged Bush's speeches chose Ellis Island as the site so they could bathe the Statue of Liberty in the bright glow of three barges of Musco lights, normally used to illuminate sports arenas. The visual effect was spectacular. "They've taken it to an art form," effused Michael Deaver, who consulted for many months with Rove about how best to convey images and messages. In the speech, Bush referred to Iraq only obliquely. "We will not allow any terrorist or tyrant to threaten civilization with weapons of mass murder," he vowed. The next day, at the United Nations, he elaborated, demanding an international effort to force Saddam to comply at long last with nuclear inspections.[14]

Bush's rollout speeches were joined to a media blitz stressing the "gathering" danger of the Iraqi despot. Three days before the Ellis Island address, Cheney, Rice, Secretary of Defense Donald Rumsfeld, and Secretary of State Colin Powell fanned out to the Sunday roundtable TV shows to argue for action against Iraq, with Rice declaring—using a WHIG-hatched line from Gerson—that the United States couldn't wait for a "smoking gun" that turned out to be a "mushroom cloud." (Bush would echo the line later that fall.) In the following weeks, linguistic legerdemain was everywhere: The administration said that Saddam funded terrorists, which was true—but Palestinian terrorists. Officials claimed that Bill Clinton had also supported "regime change" in Iraq, which was true—but only because the term originally meant encouraging indigenous forces to oust Saddam, not launching an invasion. Saddam was said to have used "weapons of mass destruction" against his people, which was true as well—but elided that he had used chemical, not nuclear, arms. Equally important, the White House's descriptions of its intelligence findings routinely omitted the dissenting views of career government intelligence analysts, who were better trained than political officials like Bush, Cheney, and Rumsfeld to assess it.[15]

Administration officials also worked the press. While tightly holding the intelligence supporting the case for war, Bush's aides shared with reporters bits and pieces that would garner headlines. Especially pliable was Judith Miller of the *New York Times*, a Pulitzer Prize–winning national security reporter with a reputation for both big scoops and a reliance on high-placed sources. During the run-up to war, her stories often highlighted the hawks' view that Saddam was reconstituting his nuclear program. An influential September 2002 front-pager, co-written with

Michael Gordon, alleged that Iraq had procured aluminum tubes to enrich uranium—a dubious factoid that would become central to the administration's talking points. Other Washington reporters, too, accepted these and similar assertions too readily.

Still, an energetic debate took place in the media about the wisdom of going to war. Prominent liberals challenged Bush's spin, while many reporters, in print and on the air, highlighted flaws with the claims about the state of Saddam's weapons programs and his links to terrorists. Weapons experts challenged the notion that the aluminum tubes were meant for uranium enrichment. In October, the *New York Times* revealed that Cheney, Rumsfeld, and others were systematically second-guessing intelligence reports that undermined the case for war—a disclosure that triggered charges of "cherry picking" intelligence. And when Cheney and other hawks maintained that one of the 9/11 hijackers had met with Iraqi officials in Prague, news outlets roundly reported that intelligence analysts, including CIA chief George Tenet, considered the theory baseless. The administration was spinning, but the public was hit by a tsunami of counterspin as well.[16]

As always, the problem was sorting it out. Just as reporters had trouble assessing climate science or medical research, so they were hard-pressed to evaluate the intelligence that officials touted in advocating for war. Most troublingly, the administration's refusal to make most of its information public rendered independent judgments all but impossible. Secrecy, more than spin, gave the administration the upper hand in the battle for public opinion.

* * *

Controversy continued to surround the administration's arguments for war, but after Congress voted in October to give Bush a free hand, he brushed aside the remaining objections and, on March 19, 2003, began bombing Iraq. Deposing Saddam and his Baathist regime took just three weeks. To much of the world, the war seemed like a rout. On May 1, Bush celebrated Saddam's ouster with what the *New York Times* called "one of the most audacious moments of presidential theater in American history." Scott Sforza, who had staged the 2002 Statue of Liberty speech and whose hiring communications director Karen Hughes called "perhaps the best decision" she made in the White House, crafted the spectacle: It featured Bush landing a fighter plane on the deck of the aircraft carrier USS *Abraham Lincoln*, posing for pictures in his flight jacket with jubilant sailors, and then, having changed into a blue suit during a three-hour interval, striding to a podium before a cheering throng to declare the end of "major combat operations." Behind him, a Sforza-designed banner proclaimed: MISSION ACCOMPLISHED. Delivered at prime time in the East, his speech took place in the so-called magic hour of late afternoon, when the sun coated the Southern California vista in a soft, radiant warmth. "If you looked at the TV picture, you saw there was flattering light on his left cheek and slight shadowing on his right," said Joshua King, who had produced events for Clinton.[17]

Bush basked not just in the Pacific sun but also in the plaudits of pundits. On MSNBC, Chris Matthews gushed about the president's "amazing display of leadership," adding, "I think we like having a hero as our president." On CNN, the conservative talking head Laura Ingraham called Bush "a real man." Some predicted that the *Lincoln* footage would make for Reaganesque campaign ads. Democrats objected, crying that Bush was wasting taxpayer dollars on self-promotional stunts and playing politics with war. Anti-war senator Robert Byrd of West Virginia, echoing a century of complaints about presidential spin, lambasted Bush's "flamboyant showmanship." But conservatives, recalling Deaver's maxims, welcomed the complaints, insisting that whenever the controversy flared, the visuals would redound to Bush's glory.[18]

Saddam's ouster turned out to be the beginning, not the end, of military operations in Iraq. Within six months, euphoria curdled into concern about the war's mounting duration, cost, and toll. Bush's set piece took on new meaning, as Americans now wondered if the president was a heroic liberator or a callow poseur. On its October 6 cover, *Time* magazine showed the president in his flight gear, with the headline: "MISSION NOT ACCOMPLISHED." When Bush wrongly stated that the sign was "suggested by those on the ship," General Wesley Clark, gearing up for a presidential run, countered: "I guess the next thing we're going to hear is that the sailors told him to wear the flight suit and prance around on the aircraft carrier."[19]

Public opinion again turned out to be harder to mold than it appeared.

49

BARACK OBAMA AND THE SPIN OF NO SPIN

GEORGE W. BUSH'S REELECTION in 2004 over Massachusetts senator John Kerry plunged Democrats into despair. Kerry had fallen victim, in part, to a smear campaign reminiscent of the elder Bush's attacks on Michael Dukakis in 1988—a tarnishing of his Vietnam War service that undermined Kerry's reputation for battle-tested steeliness. To those who took a long view, the years since 1968 were suddenly looking like an era of resurgent conservative ideology, with Bill Clinton's two terms an aberration. In previous moments of similar gloom, Democrats had rethought their policies, as groups like the Coalition for a Democratic Majority, formed after Nixon's 1972 landslide, and the Democratic Leadership Council, formed after Reagan's 1984 romp, tried to revise the party's unpopular positions on crime and defense. In 2004, however, the prevailing wisdom among Democrats was that they were losing not on the issues but on spin.

Democrats disagreed about what to do. Some, like 2004 presidential candidate Howard Dean and Joe Trippi, his chief consultant, preached the powers of the new social media websites like Meetup.com and blogs run by left-liberal "netroots" activists like the *Daily Kos*. Others poured money into the Air America radio network, to counter Rush Limbaugh and his brigades, or the Center for American Progress, a quasi–think tank designed to emulate the conservative Heritage Foundation, focused not on scholarly policy research but on shaping debates inside Washington. In the waning years of Bush's presidency, the cable news channel MSNBC reinvented itself as an attempted counterweight to Fox News, featuring commentators like Keith Olbermann and Rachel Maddow who were unrestrained in their left-wing advocacy.[1]

Among the gurus most celebrated for their answers was George Lakoff of the University of California, Berkeley, a plump-cheeked, bespectacled sixty-three-year-old linguistics professor with a graying beard and unprepossessing manner. Even before Kerry's loss, Lakoff's ideas had been finding converts in Washington. An aide to Senator Byron Dorgan, the head of the Senate's Democratic Policy Committee, brought the linguist to address the Democratic senators at their annual retreat on Maryland's Eastern Shore, where he laid out why values mattered more than issue positions and explained how voters process political information. Hillary Clinton, now a senator from New York, invited Lakoff to dinner. Tom Daschle, the Democratic leader, began patching the professor into his weekly 9 am message meeting.

Once a student of Noam Chomsky's, Lakoff earned a stellar reputation in his field over many years while remaining anonymous outside academia. Reading about the testing of words and phrases by Newt Gingrich and Frank Luntz in the 1990s, Lakoff took to studying the relation of language to politics, with an eye toward changing things. If the Republicans could combine *Roget's Thesaurus* with focus groups to spin their way to victory, why couldn't the Democrats?

In 1996, Lakoff published *Moral Politics*, which applied to politics the idea, derived from cognitive psychology, of "framing"—the notion that once we start to think about issues through a given mental structure, that structure shapes how we assimilate new information. Updating insights from Reagan's pollster Richard Wirthlin, Lakoff argued that while Democrats might hold more popular stands on many issues, Republicans had mastered the art of forming messages that tapped into deeper values. The values Republicans preached were associated with what Lakoff called the "strict father": security, discipline, a clear sense of right and wrong. Democrats in turn had to summon up values that played to their more maternal image—what Lakoff called the "nurturant parent"—and evoked qualities like compassion and decency.[2]

Though *Moral Politics* sold just 6,000 copies its first year, it slowly built a following, raising Lakoff's profile in activist circles. He met with funders. He started a think tank. He hit the lecture circuit. By 2004, he could draw a crowd of more than 1,000 to a church in Berkeley. His cult following and his mounting frustration with Kerry's uninspiring candidacy—"I went to bed angry every night" during the campaign, Lakoff said—convinced him to produce a distilled version of his ideas that summer. He called it *Don't Think of an Elephant!*, based on the cognitive psychology parlor trick that, by simply uttering the command, gets people to do the reverse. Published by an obscure progressive outfit in Vermont called Chelsea Green, the book—fueled by raves on liberal blogs and websites—ran through multiple printings and sold hundreds of thousands of copies. Congressman George Miller of San Francisco gave one to every Democrat in the House. The writer-activist Arianna Huffington, a former Gingrich devotee, now talked up Lakoff. Howard Dean, elected Democratic Party chairman, vowed to "make George Lakoff the Democrats' Frank Luntz." When a badly worded exit poll after the 2004 presidential election left the widespread impression that voters ranked "moral values" as the race's most pressing issue, Lakoff's stock climbed higher still.[3]

But as Lakoff metamorphosed from professor into guru and would-be savior, he found that people were ignoring the core of his argument: that political language had to be tied to underlying ideas and values. People seemed to expect him to provide a panacea for liberalism's woes. "They all just want to know the magic words," he said after speaking at a dinner in Hollywood. "I say: 'You don't understand, there aren't any magic words. It's about ideas.' But all everyone wants to know is: 'What three words can we use? How do we win the next election?' They don't get it." Meanwhile, fellow liberals were picking apart his work, arguing that while he might understand language, his recommendations ignored history and political context—or, more pointedly, that he imagined his own left-wing politics to mirror those of mainstream America. Lakoff took to defending himself in overlong e-mails to journalists, while continuing to advise all manner of activists and politicians. The linguist who had been moved to venture forth from the ivory tower out of aggravation with the political consultants' debasement of language had, by 2005, become barely distinguishable from a political consultant himself.

By 2008, Lakoff was old news. His book had done little to change the way Democrats talked. Instead, liberals everywhere were reading Emory psychologist Drew Westen's hot tome about neuroscience and political preferences, *The Political Brain*.

*   *   *

Exasperation with spin revived calls for an authentic politician who would ignore the polls, speechwriters, and consultants, and speak his mind. The fantasy of the uncorrupted, truthtelling politician had always carried a strong appeal: a half century earlier, Truman had disclaimed any interest in polls and Eisenhower had pretended to fire his speechwriters. The illusion of authenticity had helped elect Jimmy Carter in 1976; had given life to the third-party candidacy of the oddball Texas billionaire Ross Perot in 1992; and had served as the premise of numerous Hollywood fantasies like the NBC TV show *The West Wing*, featuring Martin Sheen as a progressive, morally grounded president, or the film *Bulworth*, in which Warren Beatty played a liberal senator whose popularity surges when he begins to speak his mind.

In 2008, much of the electorate was angry at Bush for misrepresenting the case for invading Iraq, and many people remained down on Clinton for his poll-driven triangulation. Both major parties' presidential nominees in 2008 built their campaigns around their professed authenticity. On the Republican side, Senator John McCain of Arizona, whose five years as a prisoner of war in Vietnam had invested him with a certain moral authority, had won a reputation as an appealingly gruff "maverick" given to "straight talk." "Any man who spent five years in a box is entitled to speak his mind," said his Senate colleague Bob Dole. Prominent writers such as the journalist Michael Lewis and the novelist David Foster Wallace hailed McCain as a different kind of politician—"the anti-candidate," in Wallace's phrase. Like other politicians who shot from the hip, from Barry Goldwater to Perot, McCain sometimes got into trouble, as his ill-considered remarks reminded everyone why politicians hired consultants in the first place. (Preparing for his 2008 race, McCain backpedaled from his earlier description of evangelical preachers like Jerry Falwell as "agents of intolerance," placating some Christian conservatives but alienating those who had cherished his bluntness.) When burned, McCain could retreat to the pabulum and hedging common to every other politician.[4]

On the Democratic side, the perception of previous standard-bearers Al Gore and John Kerry as uptight and lacking in spontaneity made the desire for a truthtelling candidate even more intense. Though Hillary Clinton was initially the front-runner, her own tightly guarded public persona, along with the public's sense that she shared her husband's ideological mutability, made her seem hopelessly inauthentic. Her vote to authorize the Iraq War also struck many liberals as an opportunistic betrayal. In contrast, the forty-seven-year-old Illinois senator Barack

Obama, who burst on the scene with an uplifting keynote speech at the 2004 convention, seemed to offer exceptional candor and thoughtfulness. His confessional memoir, *Dreams From My Father*, written before he had serious presidential ambitions, disclosed romantic encounters, youthful drug use, and deep personal feelings of a sort rarely discussed by national politicians. Recalling Adlai Stevenson—and captivating reporters and intellectuals with a similar appeal—Obama positioned himself above politics, lamenting how the world of spin forced politicians to stifle their spontaneity and trim their candor. His main campaign promise, which had little to do with public policy, was to change the dysfunctional culture of Washington.

This was spin, too—the spin of no spin—and Obama fostered his image with help from a crack media operation. He hired a top Democratic pollster, Joel Benenson, and after a 2006 book tour launched a national "Obamamania" craze, he began conducting secret polls and focus groups in Iowa. He made creative use of the Internet, mainly for fund-raising and organizing, but also to reach younger voters who didn't watch TV news. He posted messages on influential niche blogs like *Daily Kos*, and early in 2008 his celebrity-filled YouTube music video, "Yes, We Can," went viral, enhancing the excitement and sense of insurgency around his campaign.[5]

More than new media, Obama's rhetoric built his following. A fluent and at times inspiring speaker, he promised to reconcile hostile camps and forge a new harmony. In his 2004 convention keynote address, he sketched out the commonalities between residents of "red" (conservative) and "blue" (liberal) states. In a March 2008 speech addressing inflammatory racial remarks by his Chicago pastor, he sympathized with both black and white perspectives—"to show that he is our ultimate figure of mediation," as Harvard professor Henry Louis Gates, Jr., said, "standing tall above quarrels that most of us assume to be irreconcilable." Under fire, Obama shrewdly turned his own candidacy into a referendum on voters' racism, subtly equating his election as an African-American president with the culmination of the civil rights movement. As a vote for Kennedy in 1960 could show the world that America was no longer bigoted against Catholics, supporting Obama would allow voters to proclaim themselves tolerant and enlightened when it came to race.[6]

Obama's feel-good message, though, also contained a strong, if submerged, negative component—an attack on Hillary Clinton as phony and untrustworthy. Trailing her in the polls in 2007, Obama and his media advisers decided they had to avoid a debate over experience and turn her

White House years into a liability. Joel Benenson, campaign strategist David Axelrod, and Obama's other spin doctors drafted a 12-page memo that recommended delicately impugning Clinton's character so that she no longer seemed like an agent of change. In October, the campaign wheeled out the slogan "Change We Can Believe In"—a dig at Clinton, implying that voters couldn't believe in her or her promises. Later, as the primary campaign intensified, some of Obama's supporters imputed racism to stray remarks made by Clinton or her surrogates. One memo, from the campaign's press secretary in the South Carolina primary, ticked off remarks by Bill and Hillary Clinton and their supporters that could be portrayed as anti-black. When Clinton responded by going negative herself, Obama—having seized the high ground—was able to deflect her sallies as desperate, nasty, or proof of a win-at-any-cost mentality. "Their reputation in the press was that they were ... *nice*," a Clinton staffer fumed. "We had the reputation of 'the War Room,' the tough guys." This time, that image didn't go over well.[7]

Obama's spin was far from foolproof. Early in the campaign, when Clinton was besting him in a string of debates, pundits noted his shortcomings as a communicator—the diffidence, the lack of warmth, the occasional peevishness—and his speeches veered toward the vague and platitudinous. His sheen of authenticity, moreover, was skin-deep. At one point Clinton's press aide Howard Wolfson hyped the revelation that chunks of Obama's remarks had come directly from speeches by Massachusetts governor Deval Patrick, a client of David Axelrod's in 2006, and that other campaign lines had been similarly recycled. This borrowing hardly constituted "plagiarism," as some charged, and the incident turned out to be a blip in a fast-moving campaign. But it momentarily reminded voters that Obama, too, relied on consultants, speechwriters, and pollsters—that his image, too, was constructed and assiduously tended.

Once Obama secured the nomination, McCain began questioning his rival's authenticity more full-throatedly. Because Obama's campaign hadn't emphasized policies so much as the promise of the candidate himself, suspicions lingered whether he was, underneath it all, a creature of hype. In an August TV ad, "Celeb," McCain turned what Obama's supporters had long touted as his "rock star" status against him. Noting his thin record of professional achievement, it likened him to frivolous media figures like Paris Hilton and Britney Spears. When Obama announced plans to give his convention speech in a football stadium, with classical pillars encircling the stage, the McCain campaign seized on the stunt as more proof of the Democrat's grandiosity. What was once deemed "an inspired stroke of campaign image making," as the *New York Times* wrote, became a unflattering symbol of image making itself.[8]

But the financial collapse in September all but ensured Obama's victory. The free-falling economy hardened antipathy to Bush and the Republicans, while Obama's self-possessed performance in the worst days of the crisis—in contrast to McCain's erratic, showboating response—suggested that his hand would be the steadier one at the tiller. Starting on September 15, when the financial panic began, Obama started pulling ahead of McCain in the polls once more, never to trail again.[9]

*   *   *

As president, Obama found that the adulatory coverage he enjoyed on the campaign trail quickly gave way to the old adversarial dynamic between press and president. Given the magnitude of the challenges before him— righting a depressed economy, winding down the Iraq and Afghanistan wars, passing a national health care plan—the newfound combativeness came as a rude shock.[10]

Obama reacted by trying to go over the Washington press corps' heads. Instead of using radio, like FDR, or niche media, like Bill Clinton, he turned to the Internet and social media, which during the campaign had created so much buzz about his candidacy. As president, he appointed a thirty-year-old "new media director," introduced a Twitter feed, and hired a videographer whose segments were uploaded to YouTube and the White House website. By his second term, the White House had created its own news service, like those long-forgotten efforts of Wilson, Hoover, and Reagan; Obama's system used digital transmission to provide social media sites with a steady stream of photos, videos, blog posts, and interviews. But if these channels gave the president a pipeline to his loyal followers, they had scant effect on the wider discourse. Throughout his presidency, supporters lamented that the young enthusiasts who had thrown their energies into his election never rallied behind his policy initiatives. Ginning up excitement over Obama's historic candidacy proved far easier than mobilizing activity on behalf of an economic stimulus or health care initiative.[11]

Merely getting the public's attention turned out to be harder than ever. The multiplication of news outlets, each pursuing its own agenda, hindered the new president from commanding the attention of the populace at large. In the twenty-four-hour news cycle, reporters updated their stories and pundits sounded off all day long, forcing the White House to keep pace. At first, the White House redoubled its efforts to spotlight the president, sending him to countless news and entertainment programs, from late-night comedy broadcasts to the full slate of Sunday-morning shows. But this saturation strategy raised concerns about overexposure and in time the White House reversed course, cutting back on photo ops, question-and-answer sessions, and interviews. That shift in turn triggered charges that Obama was unduly stingy with information. By 2013 the website *Politico*—the latest embodiment of the new, faster-paced Beltway media—was describing him as "a master at limiting, shaping, and manipulating media coverage."[12]

Most confounding of all to the White House was the united front mounted by the Republicans—including Rush Limbaugh, Fox News, and other right-wing media outlets. Lacking the temperament of a brawler or the skills of a Washington wheeler-dealer, Obama had in the past built support for his campaigns with stirring rhetoric. Some of his campaign staff imagined that those oratorical talents would help him as president to deliver the transformative change he promised. "I don't think there's been a president since Kennedy whose ability to move issues and people through a speech has been comparable," David Axelrod said. But in the face of truculent Republican opposition, the lofty words were unavailing. By the first summer of Obama's presidency, with the public frustrated by persistent unemployment and a bleak economic outlook, conservative activists and pundits were frequently driving the news.[13]

The toughest battles surrounded Obama's health care plan, which ran aground after facing ferocious Republican opposition, especially at congressional representatives' local town hall meetings. Although Obama's plan had its origins in a Republican blueprint from the conservative Heritage Foundation, the president's opponents conjured an image of a menacing, socialistic Big Brother that would set up "death panels" (a phrase popularized by Alaska governor Sarah Palin) deciding who would live and die. Caught off guard, the White House countered with its spin of no spin: It created a "reality check" website stocked with videos and fact sheets, modeled on a site that had debunked scurrilous rumors about Obama's birthplace and religion during the campaign. Axelrod announced the new website in August 2009 with an e-mail blast, enjoining Obama supporters "to spread the truth among your family, friends and other social networks." Journalists, too, pointedly dispelled falsehoods about the health care bill, including the "death panels" myth (an absurd distortion of the plan's technocratic mechanisms for assessing the costs of end-of-life care). But with different communities believing in different news sources, misunderstandings festered. Eventually the Democrats passed a bill that provided near-universal coverage—fulfilling a key campaign promise—but, lacking broad support, it remained a bone of contention into Obama's second term.[14]

As Obama's poll numbers slumped in 2009 and 2010, many observers remarked that the president had, in the reigning cliché of the day, "lost control of the narrative." Pundits urged him to adopt any number of media strategies or lines of argument to reclaim the upper hand. Supporters who had once admired his professed contempt for Washington spin now wished he were more fluent in it. "Leadership isn't just legislation. It's a matter of persuading people," Obama said on *60 Minutes* after the Democrats lost control of the House in the 2010 midterm elections. "We haven't always been successful at that." Though Obama's policies helped to create enough economic growth—and optimism—to win him a second term, he never recaptured the magic of 2008. Bent on denying him victories, Republicans blocked most of his proposals, and his job approval ratings remained relatively low. His ability to unify warring factions, the leitmotif of his public career, didn't work against a determined Republican opposition in the climate of twenty-first-century Washington. Pundits now limned a picture of what *Politico* called a "not-so-great communicator."[15]

But Obama's difficulties were not attributable, in the main, to failures of communication, persuasion, or spin. Nor had the silver-tongued, persuasive rhetorician of 2008 suddenly been replaced by a ham-handed, professorial bumbler. Like Hoover, Johnson, and Carter, Obama did not suddenly misplace the gifts about which so many had once rhapsodized. Rather, facing dismal economic conditions and rough political waters, he discovered that the talents that helped him win the presidency were no substitute for a different set of abilities—hardheaded negotiation, innovative policy making, creativity with executive power—that might soften or surmount the opposition's obstructionism. At moments, Obama conceded as much. "This country doesn't just agree with the *New York Times* editorial page," Obama said in his *60 Minutes* interview. "And, you know, I can make some really good arguments defending the Democratic position and there are going to be some people who just don't agree with me." Obama had not lost his ability to make really good arguments. But the challenges of the times called for something more.[16]

* * *

Beyond Republican intransigence and his own limitations, Obama's troubles did owe something to the media environment in which he served. The incessant messaging, the deluge of punditry, and the fragmentation of the media landscape had introduced new obstacles to putting a presidential message across. To many it seemed that America in the twenty-first century had become a "post-truth society" in which it was impossible to expect that the public could ever figure out the truth—or to hope that any consensus on what the truth was could even be established.

An intellectual vogue for neuropsychology and behavioral economics—seen in books like Westen's *Political Brain* and psychologist Jonathan Haidt's *Righteous Mind*—reinforced fears that many Americans had come to inhabit impermeable ideological bubbles. Echoing the work of midcentury social scientists like Paul Lazarsfeld and Hadley Cantril, who showed how people filter information through preexisting worldviews, twenty-first-century journalists and authors popularized cognitive concepts such as *selective exposure*, or the tendency to seek out agreeable news; *selective perception*, or placing trust in agreeable information; and the *hostile media phenomenon*, or believing news outlets to be biased against one's own position. The rise of ideologically based news gave Americans ammunition to reinforce their existing assumptions, and they talked past one another with frustrating frequency.

Yet despite the fears, this disputatiousness didn't mean an end to fact or to truth. Americans may have learned that politicians' claims to truth were invariably infused with bias or skewed by partiality, but that hardly rendered the political arena a zone of unbounded relativism. (Decades earlier, in emphasizing the limits of spin, Hannah Arendt had quoted the judgment of French premier Georges Clemenceau on the question of how history would assign responsibility for World War I. "This I don't know," he had supposedly said. "But I know for certain that they will not say Belgium invaded Germany.") Nor did the warring versions of events that dominate media discourse mean an end to the possibility of forging the kind of broadly supported compromises on which political action often depends. If Obama had been naive in 2008 about the Republicans' intransigence, he was correct that talk of red and blue states obscured underlying commonalities. Throughout the twentieth century, Americans had waged their political arguments loudly and out in the open, but had always at some point yielded to leadership that was in tune with public opinion. In the twenty-first century, the arguments may have seemed even louder and more intractable, but they were not fundamentally different in character.[17]

What changed, at least for the time being, the discourse about spin itself. From the Progressive Era through the debate about the invasion of Iraq, spin's detractors feared that the power of the mass media would give presidents too much power to persuade the public. Under Obama, the fear took a different form: not that the president could persuade the public of whatever he wished, but that no one would be able to persuade anyone of anything.[18]

Thus, as Americans were acknowledging the limits of presidential persuasion, they nonetheless remained anxious about spin. Was the public too credulous to resist the power of well-wrought words and images from the White House? Or were we all too tightly locked in our own private realities to be open to persuasion by anyone? Either way, Americans located the source of their political problems in the all-consuming culture of spin. Whether it worked too well or didn't work well enough, spin remained a source of unease—a focus for free-floating concerns about the nature and future of American democracy.

That spin was so often the answer, no matter what the question, suggested that spin itself wasn't the cause of our troubles so much as a site of intellectual struggle. Ever since Theodore Roosevelt first developed the public presidency, debates over spin—publicity or propaganda, news management or image making—had served as a proxy for debates over deeper questions about democracy and the leadership of public opinion: about the capacity of the public to make sound decisions; about the role of leaders and the press in shaping opinion; about the opportunities and dangers afforded by technology and by the rise of professionals trained in the traffic in words, images, and symbols.

The sheer pervasiveness of spin inevitably leaves an unpleasant aftertaste. The heavy investment in crafted talk and burnished images can make our political rhetoric and theater feel empty and even meretricious. Because it's ubiquitous and unremitting, and because it stands in opposition to the straight-up truthtelling that we idealize, spin is always going to strike us as a vexatious or lamentable feature of modern politics. Paradoxically, though, our persistent worry about spin, while at times debilitating, keeps us vigilant about its abuse. And ultimately democracy has to make room for dueling perspectives; politics always demands a give-and-take. As long as the public remains sovereign and public opinion reigns supreme, the debates will go on, the disputes will rage, the media will yammer and thrum, the people will make their arguments and form their judgments, and spin—much as we might crave relief from its relentlessness—will endure as an essential part of our political world.

Perhaps most important, if spin is used for misleading, it's also used for leading. As Arendt noted, bringing about political change requires offering the public an image of reality at odds with the way things are; all expressions of political vision rely on some gesture of negation or even deception. And as Lippmann knew, leadership requires the use of symbols to forge agreement. Throughout history, presidents, using the machinery of spin, have contributed to wartime hysteria and baleful complacency, resentment and fear. But they have also given us the golden flares of inspiration that moved the public, in their own times and for decades after: Theodore Roosevelt's bully fights against the trusts, Wilson's dreams of "pastures of quietness and peace," FDR's anchoring reassurances during the Depression, Eisenhower's summons to tame the atom, Kennedy and Johnson's resounding calls for civil rights, Reagan's challenge to tear down the wall of Soviet oppression, Obama's promise of an America where differences of race and region and party can finally be overcome.

The highlights of our political history, the greatest moments of American presidential leadership, have often been consciously forged not by men of impeccable virtue and purity of heart but by the careful and caring labors of speechwriters, pollsters, image crafters, and other professional spinners. To survey the scene today makes it hard not to wax Platonic and lament that all is phony. But to study spin's history, to see its long and deep connection to our politics, also makes it hard not to heed the wisdom of Aristotle: to see that it isn't really spin itself we fear but rather its use by the wrong leaders, at the wrong moment, for the wrong ends.

ACKNOWLEDGMENTS

EVERY BOOK is a collaboration, and I have many people to thank for their help in bringing this one to fruition. My agent, Peter Matson, the best in the business, took me on when I was just starting out and has over these many years offered sage advice and needed encouragement, especially during the rough patches. I also thank his assistants and others at Sterling Lord Literistic who helped along the way, including Holly Hilliard, Julia Kardon, and Rebecca Friedman.

At Norton, I again had the pleasure of working with Starling Lawrence, who helped ensure that *Republic of Spin* would be a book for both scholars and general readers, and for readers of both history and contemporary politics. Ryan Harrington meticulously managed the editing and production of the book; his clarity of thought, cooperativeness, and diligence are a model of professionalism. Rachel Salzman was once again conscientious and creative in overseeing the publicity. Laura Goldin provided invaluable commentary. I also thank the many others at Norton who helped bring the book to fruition.

If you think this book is long, you should have seen it before Susan Chumsky assiduously edited it. An extraordinary editor, Susan did a superb job of paring down the manuscript and improving it in countless ways with suggestions of both prose and content. I'm also grateful once again (after *The Agenda* and *Nixon's Shadow*) for the superb copyediting of Ann Adelman, who gave the manuscript greater consistency, clarity, and grace. Several friends, colleagues, and relatives also read chapters, offering important suggestions and saving me from errors. Special thanks to Suzanne Nossel, Robert Greenberg, Matt Dallek, Michael Kazin, Eric Rauchway, Jeff Shesol, Bradley Bloch, and especially Warren Bass and David Grann, who read and commented on the whole thing. For her amazing work in procuring the photographs for this book, my deep thanks go to Jill Cowan.

At Rutgers University, where I teach in both the History and Journalism and Media Studies departments, department chairs and deans have approved sabbaticals and fellowship leaves, provided research funding, and assisted me in various other ways; and many colleagues have helped me in small ways and large. I extend thanks to all my Rutgers colleagues but would be remiss if I failed to mention Rudy Bell, Jack Bratich, John Chambers, Paul Clemens, Ann Fabian, David Foglesong, Doug Greenberg, Susan Keith, Bob Kubey, Jackson Lears, Jim Masschaele, Claire McInerney, Harmut Mokras, Karen Novick, John Pavlik, Jorge Schement, Jimmy Swenson, and Mark Wasserman. Thanks also to the administrative and information technology staffs of the History Department and the School of Communication and Information; to the unfailingly helpful library staff; and to the Aresty Program and the Office of Research and Sponsored Programs, which have provided me with valuable research assistance.

One key year of writing this book was spent as a fellow at the Woodrow Wilson International Center for Scholars in Washington. My thanks there, again, extend to everyone who made the year so productive and enjoyable, especially Krishna Aniel, Arlyn Charles, Louisa Clark-Roussey, Kim Conner, Lucy Jilka, Sonya Michel, Aaron David Miller, and Mike Van Dusen. The interns were exceptionally bright and able, and I thank Esther Im, David Nelson, Laurel Sallack-Macupa. I also spent a semester as a visiting professor at Columbia University and extend my gratitude to the staff and my colleagues there, too, for their generosity and support.

There are many good friends, professional colleagues, and intellectual comrades from whose discussions and concrete suggestions I've profited. Others have commented on papers I gave, read the proposal or introduction, shared material with me, answered my queries, made helpful suggestions, or otherwise helped me in large ways and small. So thanks to Danielle Allen, Jonathan Alter, Eric Alterman, Brian Balogh, Roger Berkowitz, Karen Lehrman Bloch, Mark Brilliant, Alan Brinkley, Katie Brownell, Chris Capozzola, Jonathan Chait, John Milton Cooper, Matthew Dunne, Gareth Davies, Frank Foer, Samuel Freedman, Amy Fried, Judge Glock, Jeff Greenfield, Lara Heimert, Jeffrey Herf, Linda Hirshman, Andy Jewett, Richard John, David Karol, Ira Katznelson, Michael Kimmage, Roger Kriegel, Martha Joynt Kumar, Sam Lebovic, Jim Ledbetter, Mordecai Lee, Mel Leffler, Nick Lemann, Fred Logevall, Ruth Mandel, David Margolick, Dylan Matthews, Mike McCurry, Darrin McMahon, Tony Michels, Sharon Musher, Jonathan Nashel, Mark Nevin, Chris Nichols, Brendan Nyhan, Ken Osgood, Leo Ribuffo, Donald Ritchie, Amber Roessner, Randall Rothenberg, Brandon Rottinghaus, Michael Schudson, Jack Shafer, Bob Shapiro, Adam Sheingate, Rick Shenkman, Sheldon Stern, John Summers, Jeremi Suri, Elliot Thomson, Elsa Walsh, Steve Weisman, and Bob Woodward.

Various undergraduate and graduate students tracked down articles, scoped out archives, and assisted with other forms of research. They include Marsha Barrett, Michael Blaakman, Julia Bowes, Stephen Budinsky, Jonathan Bullinger, Tal Grebel, Christopher Hayes, Melissa Jannuzzi, Kevin Lerner, Simon Miles, Shira Roza, Bryan Sacks, Andrew Salvati, Kris Shields, and Maxine Wagenhoffer. I am very grateful as well to the many librarians and archivists who helped me and these research assistants with our labors. At home, Ariana Ali kept everything running smoothly.

I'm lucky to belong to an exceptionally close family, and although they may not realize how much their support has meant to me, my deepest gratitude is to Mom and Dad; Judith, Ira, Claire, and Sasha; Jonathan, Megan, Hank, and Maggie; and above all Suzanne, Leo, and Liza.

NOTES

A Note on Style

Constraints of space have forced a concision of citation style. All through the Notes, sources labeled as "key sources" for a given section or subject matter should be understood as having provided material *throughout* the relevant section or chapter, or, when noted, throughout the entire book, even when no additional citation indicates as much. In a handful of cases, I have repeated the "key source" citation for ease of reference. Archival and primary periodical source material is always provided, relying on the abbreviations below.

A bibliography can be found, as of January 2016, at www.republicofspin.com.

ABBREVIATIONS USED IN NOTES

Archives

ORAL HISTORY PROJECT, COLUMBIA UNIVERSITY, NEW YORK, NY

AWP-OH	Arthur W. Page Oral History
ES-OH	Eric Sevareid Oral History
GWB-OH	George W. Ball Oral History
JCH-OH	James C. Hagerty Oral History
JW-OH	James Wechsler Oral History
LRG-OH	L. Richard Guylay Oral History
ME-OH	Milton Eisenhower Oral History
SL-OH	Sigurd Larmon Oral History

DWIGHT D. EISENHOWER PRESIDENTIAL LIBRARY, ABILENE, KS

DDE-PPF	President's Personal Files
DDE-WHCF	White House Central Files
WERP	William E. Robinson Papers

LYNDON B. JOHNSON PRESIDENTIAL LIBRARY, AUSTIN, TX

LBJ-NSF	National Security Files
LBJ-OF-FP	Office Files of Fred Panzer
LBJ-OF-GC	Office Files of George Christian
LBJ-VRF	Vietnam Reference File
LBJ-WHCF	White House Central Files
WCWP	William C. Westmoreland Papers

JOHN F. KENNEDY PRESIDENTIAL LIBRARY, BOSTON, MA

FS-OH	Frank Stanton Oral History
JFK-PPP	John F. Kennedy, Pre-Presidential Papers
PEGS-OH	Pierre E. G. Salinger Oral History
PEGSP-WHSF	Pierre E. G. Salinger Papers, White House Staff Files
RFKP-PF	Robert F. Kennedy Papers, Political Files

LIBRARY OF CONGRESS, WASHINGTON, DC

AMP-LC	Archibald MacLeish Papers
CCP	Calvin Coolidge Papers
DJBP	Daniel J. Boorstin Papers
ELBP	Edward L. Bernays Papers
ETCP	Edward T. Clark Papers
GBCP	George B. Cortelyou Papers
GCP	George Creel Papers
GHGP	George H. Gallup Papers
HAP	Hannah Arendt Papers
JAFP	James A. Farley Papers
JSAP	Joseph Alsop and Stewart Alsop Papers
MBRS	Motion Picture, Broadcasting, and Recorded Sound Division
RCP	Raymond Clapper Papers
RWP	Robert Woolley Papers
TRP	Theodore Roosevelt Papers

NEW YORK PUBLIC LIBRARY, NEW YORK, NY

IPA	Institute for Propaganda Analysis Papers

RICHARD M. NIXON PRESIDENTIAL LIBRARY, YORBA LINDA, CA

RNPPS	Richard Nixon Pre-Presidential Series

MUDD MANUSCRIPT LIBRARY, PRINCETON UNIVERSITY, PRINCETON, NJ

AESP	Adlai E. Stevenson Papers
AKP	Arthur Krock Papers
ILLP	Ivy Ledbetter Lee Papers
RSBP	Ray Stannard Baker Papers

FRANKLIN DELANO ROOSEVELT PRESIDENTIAL LIBRARY, HYDE PARK, NY

AMP-FDR	Archibald MacLeish Papers
EHP	Emil Hurja Papers
FDR-OF	FDR-Official Files
FDR-PPF	FDR-President's Personal Files
HHP	Harry Hopkins Papers
SIRP	Samuel I. Rosenman Papers

HARRY S. TRUMAN PRESIDENTIAL LIBRARY, INDEPENDENCE, MO

JLR-OH	J. Leonard Reinsch Oral History

STATE HISTORICAL SOCIETY OF WISCONSIN, MADISON, WI

BBP	Bruce Barton Papers
RRP	Rosser Reeves Papers

STERLING LIBRARY, YALE UNIVERSITY, NEW HAVEN, CT

HLP	Harold Lasswell Papers
WLP	Walter Lippmann Papers

Periodicals

AC	*Atlanta Constitution* (or *Atlanta Journal & Constitution*)
AMer	*American Mercury*
Atlantic	*Atlantic* (or *Atlantic Monthly*)
BG	*Boston Globe*
CSM	*Christian Science Monitor*
CT	*Chicago (Daily) Tribune*
E&P	*Editor and Publisher*
Harper's	*Harper's Weekly* (or *Harper's Monthly*)
LAT	*Los Angeles Times*
NYHT	*New York Herald Tribune*
NYP	*New York Post*
NYT	*New York Times*
NYTM	*New York Times Magazine*
NYTr	*New York Tribune*
NYW	*New York World*
PR	*Partisan Review*
SEP	*Saturday Evening Post*
SR	*Saturday Review*
TNR	*The New Republic*
TNY	*The New Yorker*
USNWR	*U.S. News & World Report*
WP	*Washington Post*
WSJ	*Wall Street Journal*

Introduction: A World of Spin

1 Barack Obama, *The Audacity of Hope: Thoughts on Reclaiming the American Dream* (New York: Random House, 2006), 8, 123; Katie Rooney, "Obama: Country Needs 'Less Spin' and 'More Straight Talk,'" *Time.com*, 3/20/2008.

2 On Obama's campaign spin, see David Plouffe, *The Audacity to Win: The Inside Story and Lessons of Barack Obama's Historic Victory* (New York: Viking, 2009); Ryan Lizza, "Battle Plans: How Obama Won," *TNY*, 11/17/2008, 46–56. On his White House spin innovations, see *NYT*, 11/11/2010, A21; Arun Chaudhary, *First Cameraman: Documenting the Obama Presidency in Real Time* (New York: Times Books, 2012); Paul Boutin, "President Obama's New Twitter Feed," *NYTimes.com*, 5/1/2009; Saul Hansell, "Obama Renovates WhiteHouse.gov," *NYTimes.com*, 1/20/2009.

3 Peter Baker, "What Does He Do Now?" *NYTM*, 10/12/2010, 42.

4 Jeffrey Alexander, *The Performance of Politics: Obama's Victory and the Democratic Struggle for Power* (New York: Oxford University Press, 2010), 91; Ezra Klein, "The Unpersuaded," *TNY*, 3/19/2012, 38.

5 Plato, *Gorgias*, trans. with an intro. and notes by Robin Waterfield (New York: Oxford University Press, 1998); Everett Lee Hunt, "Plato and Aristotle on Rhetoric and Rhetoricians," in *Studies in Rhetoric and Public Speaking in Honor of James Albert Winans* (New York: Century Company, 1925), 3–60; George Kennedy, *The Art of Persuasion in Greece* (Princeton: Princeton University Press, 1963).

6 Aristotle, *Rhetoric*, trans. W. Rhys Roberts (Mineola, NY: Dover Publications, 2004); Bryan Garsten, *Saving Persuasion: A Defense of Rhetoric and Judgment* (Cambridge, MA: Harvard University Press, 2006); Danielle Allen, *Talking to Strangers: Anxieties of Citizenship Since Brown v. Board of Education* (Chicago: University of Chicago Press, 2004).

7 Joe McGinniss, *Selling of the President, 1968* (New York: Trident Press, 1969); Joe Klein, *Politics Lost: How American Democracy Was Trivialized by People Who Think You're Stupid* (New York: Doubleday, 2006).

8 See, e.g., Garth Jowett and Victoria O'Donnell, *Propaganda and Persuasion* (Newbury Park, CA: Sage Publications, 1986), 38–62.

9 David Zarefsky, "Public Sentiment Is Everything: Lincoln's View of Political Persuasion," *Journal of the Abraham Lincoln Association*, 15:2 (Summer 1994), 23–40; Erik McKinley Eriksson, "President Jackson's Propaganda Agencies," *Pacific Historical Review*, 6:1 (January 1937), 47–57.

10 Woodrow Wilson, *Congressional Government: A Study in American Politics* (Mineola, NY: Dover Publications, 2006 [1885]), 170 (this edition reprints Wilson's 15th, rev. with a new intro. in 1900).

11 On the "public," "rhetorical," or "modern" presidency dating to the Progressive Era, see George Edwards III, *The Public Presidency: The Pursuit of Popular Support* (New York: St. Martin's Press, 1983); Samuel Kernell, *Going Public: New Strategies of Presidential Leadership* (Washington, DC: CQ Press, 1986); Jeffrey Tulis, *The Rhetorical Presidency* (Princeton: Princeton University Press, 1987); and Lewis Gould, *The Modern American Presidency* (Lawrence: University Press of Kansas, 2003).

12 Key sources on the press and the presidency used throughout this book include James Pollard, *The Presidents and the Press* (New York: Macmillan, 1947); Elmer Cornwell, Jr., *Presidential Leadership of Public Opinion* (Bloomington: Indiana University Press, 1965); Robert Hilderbrand, *Power and the People: Executive Management of Public Opinion in Foreign Affairs, 1897–1921* (Chapel Hill, NC: University of North Carolina Press, 1981); George Juergens, *News from the White House: The Presidential-Press Relationship in the Progressive Era* (Chicago: University of Chicago Press, 1981); John

Tebbel and Sarah Miles Watts, *The Press and the Presidency: From George Washington to Ronald Reagan* (New York: Oxford University Press, 1985); W. Dale Nelson, *Who Speaks for the President? The White House Press Secretary from Cleveland to Clinton* (Syracuse, NY: Syracuse University Press, 1998); Stephen Ponder, *Managing the Press: Origins of the Media Presidency, 1897–1933* (New York: St. Martin's Press, 1999); and David Ryfe, *Presidents in Culture: The Meaning of Presidential Communication* (New York: Peter Lang, 2005).

13 Erwin Fellows, "Propaganda: History of a Word," *American Speech*, 34:3 (October 1959), 182–89; Harold Lasswell, *Propaganda Techniques in the World War* (New York: Knopf, 1927), 2.

14 Lawrence Jacobs and Robert Shapiro, *Politicians Don't Pander: Political Manipulation and the Loss of Democratic Responsiveness* (Chicago: University of Chicago Press, 2000), xiii–xv; Harry Frankfurt, *On Bullshit* (Princeton: Princeton University Press, 2005).

15 "Spin, n.1," OED Online, Oxford University Press; William Safire, *Safire's Political Dictionary*, 3rd ed., rev. (New York: Oxford University Press, 2008), 688–89; Randall Rothenberg, "The Age of Spin," *Esquire* (November 1996), 72.

16 *NYT*, 12/10/1982, A32; Lisa Stone, "Spin Alley: A Microcosm of Journalism's Struggles," *Nieman Reports* (Summer 2005), 20–23. "Spin" soon began appearing in book titles. See John Anthony Maltese, *Spin Control: The White House Office of Communications and the Management of Presidential News* (Chapel Hill: University of North Carolina Press, 1992); Larry Tye, *The Father of Spin: Edward Bernays and the Birth of Public Relations* (New York: Crown Publishers, 1998); Howard Kurtz, *Spin Cycle: Inside the Clinton Propaganda Machine* (New York: Free Press, 1998).

17 *NYT*, 10/21/1984, E22; *CT*, 11/11/1984, D3; *NYT*, 10/26/1986, 202; *BG*, 10/14/1988, 20; Associated Press, 10/6/1988; *CSM*, 11/1/1988, 11; Charles Kaiser, "A Great Leak Forward," *Spy* (May 1990), 94–95.

18 Michael Kinsley, "The Great Spin Machine," *Time*, 12/25/2000, 100–01.

19 Samuel Popkin, *The Reasoning Voter: Communication and Persuasion in Presidential Campaigns*, 2nd ed. (Chicago: University of Chicago Press, 1994 [1991]), 236. The demise of the nineteenth century's "spectacular politics," which engaged a wide swath of the electorate, depressed voter turnout and engagement. See Michael McGerr, *The Decline of Popular Politics: The American North, 1865–1928* (New York: Oxford University Press, 1986).

20 Research showing the "limited effects" of media messages flourished in the 1940s and 1950s. See, e.g., Paul Lazarsfeld, Bernard Berelson, and Hazel Gaudet, *The People's Choice: How the Voter Makes Up His Mind in a Presidential Campaign* (New York: Duell, Sloan & Pearce, 1944); Robert Merton, *Mass Persuasion: The Social Psychology of a War Bond Drive* (New York: Harper, 1946); and Joseph Klapper, *The Effects of Mass Communication* (Glencoe, IL: Free Press, 1960). Recent research affirming limited effects can be found in Henry Brady and Richard Johnston, *Capturing Campaign Effects* (Ann Arbor: University of Michigan Press, 2006), and George Edwards, *On Deaf Ears: The Limits of the Bully Pulpit* (New Haven: Yale University Press, 2003).

21 Walter Lippmann, "The Job of the Washington Correspondent," *Atlantic* (January 1960), 48. On tolerating deception in politics, see Martin Jay, *The Virtues of Mendacity: On Lying in Politics* (Charlottesville: University of Virginia Press, 2010).

PART I: THE AGE OF PUBLICITY

CHAPTER 1: Theodore Roosevelt and the Public Presidency

1 Key sources on Theodore Roosevelt include Theodore Roosevelt, *An Autobiography* (New York: Macmillan, 1913); Henry Pringle, *Theodore Roosevelt: A Biography* (New York: Cornwall Press, 1931); William Harbaugh, *Power and Responsibility: The Life and Times of Theodore Roosevelt* (New York: Farrar, Straus & Cudahy, 1961); Edmund Morris, *The Rise of Theodore Roosevelt* (New York: Coward, McCann & Geoghegan, 1979); Edmund Morris, *Theodore Rex* (New York: Random House, 2001); and Aida Donald, *Lion in the White House* (New York: Basic Books, 2007).

2 TR to Benjamin Harrison Diblee, 2/16/1898, in *The Letters of Theodore Roosevelt,* vol. 1, ed. Elting Morison (Cambridge, MA: Harvard University Press, 1951), 774–75, hereafter cited as Morison, *Letters*; Richard Hamilton, "McKinley's Backbone," *Presidential Studies Quarterly,* 36:3 (September 2006), 482–92.

3 TR to Brooks Brothers, 5/2/1898, in Morison, *Letters*, vol. 2, 822. Contrary to mythology, the yellow press wasn't responsible for starting the war. This fable took root only after World War I bred disillusionment with war. Lewis Gould, *The Presidency of William McKinley* (Lawrence: University Press of Kansas, 1980), 62–63; George Herring, "William McKinley, the War of 1898, and the New Empire," in *Selling War in a Media Age: The Presidency and Public Opinion in the American Century,* ed. Kenneth Osgood and Andrew Frank (Gainesville: University Press of Florida, 2010), 26–28; Mark Matthew Welter, "Minnesota Newspapers and the Cuban Crisis, 1895–1898: Minnesota as a Test Case for the 'Yellow Journalism' Theory," PhD diss., University of Minnesota, 1970.

4 Key sources on Theodore Roosevelt and the press include George Juergens, "Theodore Roosevelt and the Press," *Daedalus*, 114:1 (Fall 1982), 113–33; Thaddeus Seymour, Jr., "A Progressive Partnership: Theodore Roosevelt and the Reform Press—Riis, Steffens, Baker, and White," PhD diss., University of Wisconsin, 1985; and Doris Kearns Goodwin, *The Bully Pulpit: Theodore Roosevelt, William Howard Taft, and the Golden Age of Journalism* (New York: Simon & Schuster, 2013). On presidential campaigns, key sources used throughout the book are Gil Troy, *See How They Ran: The Changing Role of the Presidential Candidate* (New York: Free Press, 1991), and McGerr, *The Decline of Popular Politics*.

5 A key source on the San Juan Hill affair is Peggy and Harold Samuels, *Teddy Roosevelt at San Juan* (College Station: Texas A&M University Press, 1997).

6 Albert Smith, *Two Reels and a Crank* (Garden City, NY: Doubleday & Co., 1952), 57. Historians question whether Smith, the cameraman, actually went to Cuba. See Charles Musser, "The American Vitagraph, 1897–1901: Survival and Success in a Competitive Industry," in *Film Before Griffith,* ed. John Fell (Berkeley: University of California Press, 1983), 22–66.

7 Daniel Headrick, *The Invisible Weapon: Telecommunications and International Politics, 1851–1945* (New York: Oxford University Press, 1991), 82; Charles Brown, *The Correspondents' War* (New York: Scribner's, 1967); 312–24, 350–64; Richard Harding Davis, "The Rough Riders' Fight at Guasimas," *Scribner's* (September 1898), 259–73; Richard Harding Davis, "The Battle of San Juan," *Scribner's* (October 1898), 387–403; Edward Marshall, "A Wounded Correspondent's Recollections of Guasimas," *Scribner's* (September 1898), 273–76; *WP*, 4/13/1902, 15; *AC*, 5/28/1904, 6; Joseph Baylen and Jane Weyant, "Vasili Vereshchagin in the United States," *Russian Review*, 30:1 (July 1971), 258.

8 Smith, *Two Reels*, 62–63; J[ames] Tillapaugh, "Theodore Roosevelt and the Rough Riders," in *Hollywood's White House: The American Presidency in Film and History,*

ed. Peter Rollins and John O'Connor (Lexington: University Press of Kentucky, 2003), 98–99; *NYW*, 8/28/1898, 3.

9 John Dewey, "Theodore Roosevelt," *The Dial*, 2/8/1919, 115–16; Bruce Miroff, *Icons of Democracy: American Leaders as Heroes, Aristocrats, Dissenters & Democrats* (New York: Basic Books, 1993), 159; H. L. Mencken, "Meditation in E Minor," *TNR*, 9/8/1920, 38; Henry Stoddard, *As I Knew Them: Presidents and Politics from Grant to Coolidge* (New York: Harper & Bros., 1927), 311.

10 Theodore Roosevelt, *History as Literature and Other Essays* (New York: Charles Scribner's Sons, 1913), 143; Theodore Roosevelt, *The New Nationalism* (New York: Outlook Company, 1910), 195.

11 Mark Sullivan, *The Education of an American* (Garden City, NY: Doubleday, Doran & Co., 1938), 274; William Allen White, "One Year of Roosevelt," *SEP*, 10/4/1902, 4.

12 Owen Wister, *Roosevelt—The Story of a Friendship, 1880–1919* (New York: Macmillan, 1930), 15.

13 Jacob Riis, *The Making of an American* (New York: Macmillan, 1902), 381–82; Ray Stannard Baker, "Theodore Roosevelt," *McClure's* (November 1898), 23–32.

14 Dunn, *From Harrison to Harding*, 328; *E&P*, 8/1/1903, 1, 3; *E&P*, 8/27/1904, 1, 3; *E&P*, 7/22/1905, 2; *E&P*, 9/9/1905, 3; *E&P*, 9/30/1905, 1, 3.

15 William Allen White, *Masks in a Pageant* (New York: Macmillan, 1928), 309; Isaac Marcosson, *Adventures in Interviewing* (New York: John Lane Co., 1920), 85; Stoddard, *As I Knew Them*, 310; *E&P*, 11/11/1919, 20–22; Rodger Streitmatter, "Theodore Roosevelt: Public Relations Pioneer," *American Journalism*, 7:2 (Spring 1990), 103; *NYT*, 8/26/1905, 1; *NYT*, 4/16/1905, 1; *CSM*, 1/14/1909, 2.

16 Louis Brandeis, *Other People's Money: And How the Bankers Use It* (New York: F. A. Stokes, 1914), 92; *NYW*, 5/22/1895, 1–2; *NYT*, 12/4/1901, 6. On "publicity," see Kevin Stoker and Brad Rawlins, "The 'Light' of Publicity in the Progressive Era: From Searchlight to Flashlight," *Journalism History*, 30:4 (Winter 2005), 177–88; Adam Sheingate, "Publicity and the Progressive-Era Origins of Modern Politics," *Critical Review*, 19:2 (April 2007), 461–80.

17 Roosevelt, *Autobiography*, 357.

18 Safire, *Political Dictionary*, 695; Herbert Croly, *The Promise of American Life* (New York: Macmillan, 1909), 168.

19 Roosevelt, *Autobiography*, 357.

20 William Allen White, *The Old Order Changeth: A View of American Democracy* (New York: Macmillan, 1910), 39.

21 Robert Muccigrosso, "The City Reform Club: A Study in Late Nineteenth-Century Reform," *New-York Historical Society Quarterly*, 52:3 (July 1968), 239; *CT*, 3/16/1907, 5. On candidate-centered politics, see Martin Wattenberg, *The Rise of Candidate-Centered Politics: Presidential Elections of the 1980s* (Cambridge, MA: Harvard University Press, 1991), and Martin Wattenberg, *The Decline of American Political Parties, 1952–1980* (Cambridge, MA: Harvard University Press, 1984).

22 Dewey, "Theodore Roosevelt," 115; William Garrott Brown, "The Personality of Theodore Roosevelt," *Independent*, 7/2/1903, 1574.

23 Miroff, *Icons*, 180; TR to George Trevelyan, 6/19/1908, in Morison, *Letters*, vol. 6, 1088.

CHAPTER 2: William McKinley and the Passing of the Old Order

1 Thomas Wolfe, *The Complete Short Stories of Thomas Wolfe*, ed. Francis Skipp (New York: Simon & Schuster, 1987), 110; Richard Carwardine, "Abraham Lincoln and the Fourth Estate: The White House and the Press During the American Civil War," *American Nineteenth Century History*, 7:1 (March 2006), 8; Roosevelt, *Autobiography*, 362.

2   William Allen White, *Masks in a Pageant* (New York: Macmillan, 1928), 187.

3   Key sources on the 1896 election include Stanley Jones, *The Presidential Election of 1896* (Madison: University of Wisconsin Press, 1964), and R. Hal Williams, *Realigning America: McKinley, Bryan, and the Remarkable Election of 1896* (Lawrence: University Press of Kansas, 2010).

4   Roger Fischer, *Tippecanoe and Trinkets Too: The Material Culture of American Presidential Campaigns, 1828–1984* (Urbana: University of Illinois Press, 1988), 143–44; Thomas Beer, *Hanna* (New York: Knopf, 1929), 165.

5   Stephen Burge Johnson, *The Roof Gardens of Broadway Theatres, 1883–1942* (Ann Arbor: UMI Research Press, 1985), 57–61. Hammerstein was the grandfather of his namesake the Broadway composer.

6   George Parker, *Recollections of Grover Cleveland* (New York: Century Company, 1909), 174; David Barry, "News-Getting at the Capital," *Chattauquan* (December 1897), 283, 284; *Atchison Daily Globe*, 4/6/1897, 2; *NYTr*, 3/24/1897, 6; *NYT*, 3/28/1897, 4. Key sources on McKinley and the news include Stephen Ponder, "The President Makes News: William McKinley and the First Presidential Press Corps, 1897–1901," *Presidential Studies Quarterly*, 24:4 (January 1994), 813–36, and Martha Joynt Kumar, "The White House Beat at the Century Mark," *International Journal of Press/Politics*, 2:3 (June 1997), 10–30.

7   Key sources on the history of the press throughout the book include Michael Schudson, *Discovering the News: A Social History of American Newspapers* (New York: Basic Books, 1978), and Donald Ritchie, *Press Gallery: Congress and the Washington Correspondents* (Cambridge, MA: Harvard University Press, 1991).

8   Wilson, *Congressional Government*, 22.

9   Marcosson, *Adventures*, 18.

10 Barry, "News-Getting at the Capital," 282–86; [Ida Tarbell], "President McKinley in War Time," *McClure's* (July 1898), 214.

11 Key sources on Cortelyou include Benjamin Ford, "A Duty to Serve: The Governmental Career of George Bruce Cortelyou," PhD diss., Columbia University, 1963, and Michael Medved, *The Shadow Presidents: The Secret History of Chief Executives and Their Top Aides* (New York: Times Books, 1979), 96–106.

12 "The New Department and Its Chief," *Public Opinion*, 2/26/1903, 260.

13 O. O. Stealey, *130 Pen Pictures of Live Men* (New York: Publishers Printing Co., 1910), 113; W. W. Price, "Secretaries to the Presidents," *Cosmopolitan* (March 1901), 492.

14 Ira R. T. Smith, *"Dear Mr. President . . .": The Story of Fifty Years in the White House Mail Room* (New York: J. Messner, 1949), 41.

15 James Creelman, "Mr. Cortelyou Explains President McKinley," *Pearson's Magazine* (June 1908), 570; Tarbell, "McKinley in War Time," 213.

16 Richard Loomis, "The White House Telephone and Crisis Management," *Proceedings of the United States Naval Institute*, 95:12 (December 1969), 64; Gould, *Presidency of William McKinley*, 91–93.

17 W. W. Price, "How the Work of Gathering White House News Has Changed," *Washington Evening Star*, 12/16/1902, 32; *NYT*, 4/23/1899, 13.

18 Otis Goodall, "George B. Cortelyou," *Phonographic Magazine* (March 1901), 50.

19 Edward Lowry, *Washington Close-Up: Intimate Views of Some Public Figures* (Boston: Houghton Mifflin, 1921), 128.

20 Margaret Leech, *In the Days of McKinley* (New York: Harper & Bros., 1959), 586–603.

21 *NYTr*, 5/29/1904, B2; David Barry, *Forty Years in Washington* (Boston: Little, Brown, 1924), 280.

CHAPTER 3: The Rise of Public Opinion

1   William Wolff Smith, "Roosevelt and His Press Policy," *San Jose Mercury News*, 7/16/1905, 2.

2   James Bryce, *The American Commonwealth*, 2nd ed. (New York: Macmillan, 1891), 260. On the term *public opinion*, see W. Phillips Davison, "Public Opinion," in *International Encyclopedia of the Social Sciences*, ed. David Sills (New York: Macmillan, 1968), 188–97, and John Lukacs, *A New Republic* (New Haven: Yale University Press, 2004 [1984]), 263.

3   Key sources on Ross include Edward Ross, *Seventy Years of It: An Autobiography* (New York: D. Appleton-Century Co., 1937); John Lewis Gillin, "The Personality of Edward Alsworth Ross," *American Journal of Sociology*, 42:4 (January 1937), 534–35; Julius Weinberg, *Edward Alsworth Ross and the Sociology of Progressivism* (Madison: State Historical Society of Wisconsin, 1972); and Andrew Jewett, *Science, Democracy, and the American University: From the Civil War to the Cold War* (Cambridge: Cambridge University Press, 2012), 119–27.

4   Theodore Roosevelt, "A Letter," in Edward Ross, *Sin and Society: An Analysis of Latter-Day Iniquity* (Boston: Houghton Mifflin, 1907), ix–xi; *WSJ*, 11/12/1907, 8. In Ross's work, quotations in the ensuing paragraphs come from Edward Ross, *Social Control: A Survey of the Foundations of Order* (New York: Macmillan, 1901), and Edward Ross, *Social Psychology: An Outline and Source Book* (New York: Macmillan, 1915).

5   Ross claimed that he developed these terms "long before" he knew about Tonnies's German terms *Gemeinschaft* (community) and *Gesellschaft* (society) which, coined in 1887, would become canonical in sociology.

6   In Ross's day, "social control" didn't have any sinister overtones. Olivier Zunz, *Why the American Century?* (Chicago: University of Chicago Press, 1998), 50–51.

7   Edward Ross, "The Suppression of Important News," *Atlantic* (March 1910), 303–10; Ross, *Social Psychology*, 309, 313, 351.

8   See, e.g., Robert Park, *The Crowd and the Public and Other Essays*, ed. Henry Elsner, Jr., trans. Charlotte Elsner (Chicago: University of Chicago Press, 1972 [1904]).

9   Roosevelt, "A Letter," ix–xi.

10 Ross, *Seventy Years*, 245; *NYT*, 10/26/1902, 6.

11 Theodore Roosevelt, *The Roosevelt Policy* (New York: Current Literature Publishing Co., 1919), I:254, I:264; William Allen White, "One Year of Roosevelt," *SEP*, 10/4/1902, 4.

12 Throughout, key sources on the importance of rhetoric to the presidency, beginning in the early twentieth century, include Tulis, *The Rhetorical Presidency*; Richard Ellis, ed., *Speaking to the People: The Rhetorical Presidency in Historical Perspective* (Amherst: University of Massachusetts Press, 1998); and Martin Medhurst, ed., *Beyond the Rhetorical Presidency* (College Station: Texas A&M University Press, 1996).

13 William Kittle, "The Making of Public Opinion," *Arena* (July 1909), 449. Key sources on Roosevelt's speech include Richard Murphy, "Theodore Roosevelt," in *A History and Criticism of American Public Address*, vol. 3, ed. Marie Kathryn Hochmuth (New York: Longman's, Green & Co., 1955), 313–64; Harold Zyskind, "A Case Study in Philosophic Rhetoric: Theodore Roosevelt," *Philosophy & Rhetoric*, 1:4 (Fall 1968), 228–54; Kenneth Cmiel, *Democratic Eloquence: The Fight Over Popular Speech in Nineteenth-Century America* (New York: William Morrow, 1990); and Leroy Dorsey, "Preaching Morality in Modern America: Theodore Roosevelt's Rhetorical Progressivism," in *Rhetoric and Reform in the Progressive Era*, ed. J. Michael Hogan (East Lansing: Michigan State University Press, 2003), 49–83.

14 Croly, *Promise*, 174.

15 Charles Ponce de Leon, *Self-Exposure: Human Interest Journalism and the Emergence*

of Celebrity in America (Chapel Hill: University of North Carolina Press, 2002), 180; William Allen White, "Roosevelt: A Force for Righteousness," *McClure's* (February 1907), 389.

16 Richard Ellis, *Presidential Travel: The Journey from George Washington to George W. Bush* (Lawrence: University Press of Kansas, 2008), 207–11.

17 Oscar King Davis, *Released for Publication: Some Inside Political History of Theodore Roosevelt and His Times, 1898–1918* (Boston: Houghton Mifflin, 1925), 213.

18 Upton Sinclair, *The Autobiography of Upton Sinclair* (New York: Harcourt, Brace & World, 1962), 119.

19 Charles Willis Thompson, *Presidents I've Known and Two Near Misses* (Indianapolis: Bobbs-Merrill, 1929), 186.

20 Key sources on the Hepburn Act include John Morton Blum, *The Republican Roosevelt* (New York: Atheneum Press, 1962 [1954]), 87–105, and Juergens, *News*, 55–62.

21 TR to Baker, 9/13/1905; TR to Baker, 11/28/1906; TR to Baker, 11/22/1905, RSBP, Box 2. Juergens, *News*, 58.

22 *WP*, 1/4/1905, 6; *NYT*, 1/31/1905, 1; *BG*, 10/20/1905, 11; *AC*, 10/19/1905, 1; *NYT*, 10/20/1905, 9; *WP*, 10/20/1905, 6; Theodore Roosevelt, "Fifth Annual Message [to Congress]," 12/5/1905, http://www.presidency.ucsb.edu/ws/index.php?pid=29546.

23 TR to William Allison, 5/14/1906, TRP, Series 3; Ray Stannard Baker, "Railroads on Trial V: How Railroads Make Public Opinion," *McClure's* (March 1906), 535, 537; Scott Cutlip, "The Nation's First Public Relations Firm," *Journalism Quarterly*, 43:3 (Summer 1966), 269–80.

24 Stoddard, *As I Knew Them*, 311.

CHAPTER 4: "The Fair-Haired"

1 J. J. Dickinson, "Theodore Roosevelt, Press-Agent," *Harper's*, 9/28/1907, 1410.

2 Barry, *Forty Years*, 266–70.

3 Marcosson, *Adventures*, 86. On personal notes, see, e.g., TR to William Allen White, 8/11/1906, TRP, Series 3; TR to Baker, 10/21/1903, RSBP, Box 2.

4 Ray Stannard Baker, *American Chronicle: The Autobiography of Ray Stannard Baker* (New York: Scribner's, 1945), 197; Norman Hapgood, *The Changing Years* (New York: Farrar & Rinehart, 1930), 216.

5 Will Irwin, *The Making of a Reporter* (New York: G. P. Putnam's Sons, 1942), 157; William Allen White, *Autobiography*, 2nd ed., rev. and abridged, ed. Sally Foreman Griffith (Lawrence: University Press of Kansas, 1990 [1946]) 156; William Roscoe Thayer, *The Life and Letters of John Hay*, vol. 2. (Boston: Houghton Mifflin, 1915), 333; Louis Brownlow, *A Passion for Politics: The Autobiography of Louis Brownlow*, vol. 1 (Chicago: University of Chicago Press, 1955), 352; Davis, *Released for Publication*, 128.

6 Willis Abbot, *Watching the World Go By* (Boston: Little, Brown, 1934), 244; Rodger Streitmatter, "The Rise and Triumph of the White House Photo Opportunity," *Journalism Quarterly*, 65:4 (Winter 1988), 981.

7 Thompson, *Presidents I've Known*, 143; *E&P*, 11/11/1919, 20–22; J. Frederick Essary, *Covering Washington: Government Reflected to the Public Press* (Boston: Houghton Mifflin, 1927), 88.

8 Brownlow, *A Passion for Politics*, 399; Baker, *American Chronicle*, 191; Davis, *Released for Publication*, 135; Steffens, *Autobiography*, 509–15.

9 Thompson, *Presidents I've Known*, 118–19.

10 Essary, *Covering Washington*, 93–94.

11 Herman Henry Kohlsaat, *From McKinley to Harding* (New York: Scribner's, 1923), 150.

12 On the enduring dynamics of presidential press relations, see Douglass Cater, *The Fourth Branch of Government* (New York: Vintage Books, 1965 [1959]), and Michael Baruch Grossman and Martha Joynt Kumar, *Portraying the President: The White House and the News Media* (Baltimore: Johns Hopkins University Press, 1981).

13 *Kansas City Star*, 3/9/1902, 5; *BG*, 3/10/1902, 6; *Omaha World Herald*, 3/12/1902, 4.

14 Loeb to Cortelyou, 10/17/1905, GBCP, Box 62.

15 Barry, *Forty Years*, 271.

CHAPTER 5: Muckraking and Its Critics

1 Key sources on the muckrakers include Louis Filler, *Crusaders for American Liberalism* (New York: Harcourt, Brace & Co., 1939), reprinted as *The Muckrakers* (Stanford: Stanford University Press, 1976 [1968]); David Graham Phillips, *The Treason of the Senate*, intro. by George Mowry and Judson Grenier (Chicago: Quadrangle Books, 1964); John Semonche, "Theodore Roosevelt's Muck-Rake Speech: A Reassessment," *Mid-America*, 46:2 (April 1964), 114–25; Stephen Lucas, "The Man with the Muck Rake: A Reinterpretation," *Quarterly Journal of Speech*, 59:4 (December 1973), 452–62; Thomas Leonard, *The Power of the Press: The Birth of American Political Reporting* (New York: Oxford University Press, 1986); Doris Kearns Goodwin, *The Bully Pulpit* (2013); and Mark Neuzil, "Hearst, Roosevelt, and the Muckrake Speech of 1906: A New Perspective," *Journalism and Mass Communication Quarterly*, 73:1 (Spring 1996), 29–39.

2 Will Irwin, *The American Newspaper* (Ames: Iowa State University Press, 1969), 18; Mark Sullivan, *Our Times. Vol. 3: Pre-War America* (New York: Charles Scribner's Sons, 1930), 84.

3 George Alger, "The Literature of Exposure," *Atlantic* (August 1905), 210–13; Ida Tarbell, *All in the Day's Work: An Autobiography* (New York: Macmillan, 1939), 202, 242; Baker, *American Chronicle*, 158, 226.

4 Richard Hofstadter, *The Age of Reform* (New York: Knopf, 1955), 186.

5 Baker, *American Chronicle*, 94, 99–100, 170; Sullivan, *Our Times*. Vol. 3, 85; Hapgood, *Changing Years*, 63; Ellen Fitzpatrick, ed., *Muckraking: Three Landmark Articles* (New York: Bedford/St. Martin's Press, 1994).

6 Walter Lippmann, *Drift and Mastery: An Attempt to Diagnose the Current Unrest*, with revised intro. and notes by William Leuchtenburg (Madison: University of Wisconsin Press, 1985 [1914]), 25; David Barry, "The Loyalty of the Senate," *New England Magazine* (October 1906), 137–48 and (November 1906), 265–76.

7 Louis Brandeis and Samuel Warren, "The Right to Privacy," *Harvard Law Review*, 4:5 (December 1890), 193–220; Rochelle Gurstein, *The Repeal of Reticence: A History of America's Cultural and Legal Struggles Over Free Speech, Obscenity, Sexual Liberation, and Modern Art* (New York: Hill & Wang, 1996), 62.

8 Under Helen Gurley Brown in the 1960s, *Cosmopolitan* would become a leading women's magazine.

9 *WP*, 12/3/1906, 3; Barry, "Loyalty."

10 TR to Alfred Henry Lewis, 2/17/1906, in Morison, *Letters*, vol. 5, 156–57; Upton Sinclair, *American Outpost: A Book of Reminiscences* (New York: Farrar & Rinehart, 1931), 168.

11 Tarbell, *Day's Work*, 242; TR to Wister, 7/20/1901, in Morison, *Letters*, vol. 3, 127; TR to Steffens, 6/24/1905, in Morison, *Letters*, vol. 4, 1254–55.

12 *WSJ*, 2/16/1906, 1.

13 TR to Baker, 4/9/1906, RSBP, Box 2.

14 Baker, *American Chronicle*, 203; TR to Riis, 4/18/1906, in Morison, *Letters*, vol. 5, 212; TR to Lyman Abbott, 4/23/1906, in ibid., 218.

15 Samuel Moffett, "The Man with the Muckrake: Some Aspects of a Recent Presidential Sermon," *Collier's*, 4/28/1906, 19; Tarbell, *Day's Work*, 256–60.

16 Sinclair, *American Outpost*, 168; Baker to TR, 4/7/1906, RSBP; Steffens, *Autobiography*, 581–82.

CHAPTER 6: The Passion of Upton Sinclair

1 Roosevelt, "Fifth Annual Message [to Congress]," 12/5/1905, http://www.presidency .ucsb.edu/ws/index.php?pid=29546. Roosevelt fought for both a pure food and drugs bill and a meat inspection bill (technically an amendment to other legislation). Key sources on the meat inspection legislation battle include John Braeman, "The Square Deal in Action," in *Change and Continuity in Twentieth-Century America*, ed. John Braeman, Robert Bremner, and Everett Walters (Columbus: Ohio State University Press, 1964), 35–80; Eileen Finger Kantor, "Upton Sinclair and the Pure Food and Drugs Act of 1906," *American Journal of Public Health*, 66:12 (December 1976), 1202–05; William Parmenter, "*The Jungle* and Its Effects," *Journalism History*, 10:1–2 (Spring–Summer 1983), 14–34; Ilyse Barkan, "Industry Invites Regulation: The Passage of the Pure Food and Drug Act of 1906," *American Journal of Public Health*, 75:1 (January 1985), 18–26; James Harvey Young, "The Pig That Fell into the Privy: Upton Sinclair's *The Jungle* and the Meat Inspection Amendments of 1906," *Bulletin of the History of Medicine*, 59:4 (Winter 1985), 467–80; and James Harvey Young, "Two Hoosiers and Two Food Laws of 1906," *Indiana Magazine of History*, 88:4 (December 1992), 303–19.

2 Key sources on Sinclair throughout the book include Anthony Arthur, *Radical Innocent: Upton Sinclair* (New York: Random House, 2006); Kevin Mattson, *Upton Sinclair and the Other American Century* (Hoboken, NJ: John Wiley & Sons, 2006); and Sinclair's two very similar (in places verbatim) autobiographies, *Autobiography* (1962) and *American Outpost* (1931).

3 Upton Sinclair, *The Jungle: An Authoritative Text*, ed. Claire Virginia Eby (New York: W. W. Norton, 2003 [1906]); Upton Sinclair, "What Life Means to Me," *Cosmopolitan* (October 1906), 594.

4 Jack London, "What Jack London Says of *The Jungle*," *Chicago Socialist*, 11/25/1905, 2, reprinted in Sinclair, *The Jungle: An Authoritative Text*, 483–84.

5 Upton Sinclair, "Is 'The Jungle' True?" *Independent* (May 1906), 1129.

6 Upton Sinclair, "Stockyard Secrets," *Collier's*, 3/24/1906, 24; Marcosson, *Adventures*, 286.

7 TR to Sinclair, 3/15/1906, in Morison, *Letters*, vol. 5, 178; Marcosson, *Adventures*, 283.

8 TR to James Wilson, 3/12/1906, in Morison, *Letters*, vol. 5, 176; TR to Wilson, 3/22/1906, in ibid., 190.

9 Upton Sinclair, "The Condemned Meat Industry: A Reply to Mr. J. Ogden Armour," *Everybody's* (May 1906), 608–16; *CT*, 4/10/1906, 1, 4.

10 TR to Sinclair, 4/11/1906 in Morison, *Letters*, vol. 5, 208–09.

11 Sinclair, "Is 'The Jungle' True?", 1129–33.

12 TR to James Wadsworth, 5/26/1906, in Morison, *Letters*, vol. 5, 282.

13 TR to Sinclair, 5/29/1906, in ibid., 287; *NYT*, 5/28/1906, 2; Upton Sinclair, *The Brass Check: A Study of American Journalism* (Pasadena, CA: [self-published], 1919), 42–43.

14 Mark Sullivan, *Our Times*. Vol. 2: *America Finding Herself* (New York: Charles Scribner's Sons, 1926), 541.

15 *NYT*, 7/1/1906, 2.

16 *BG*, 2/18/1906, 39; *NYT*, 6/5/1906, 2.

17 Kittle, "The Making of Public Opinion," 433–52.

CHAPTER 7: The Dawn of Public Relations

1   Frances Butler Simkins, *Pitchfork Ben Tillman: South Carolinian* (Baton Rouge: Louisiana State University Press, 1944), 2–3; *NYT*, 1/18/1906, 1; *WP*, 1/18/1906, 1; James Creelman, "A Defender of the Senate," *Pearson's Magazine* (June 1906), 622–29.

2   Key sources on the rise of executive publicity agents throughout the book are James McCamy, *Government Publicity: Its Practice in Federal Administration* (Chicago: University of Chicago Press, 1939); J. A. R. Pimlott, *Public Relations and American Democracy* (Princeton: Princeton University Press, 1951); and Mordecai Lee, *Congress vs. the Bureaucracy: Muzzling Agency Public Relations* (Norman: University of Oklahoma Press, 2011). On TR's experience, see Stephen Ponder, "Executive Publicity and Congressional Resistance, 1905–1913: Congress and the Roosevelt Administration's PR Men," *Congress & the Presidency*, 13:2 (Autumn 1986), 177–86.

3   *NYT*, 11/7/1905, 8; *WP*, 12/14/1905, 1.

4   J. J. Dickinson, "Theodore Roosevelt Press-Agent," 1410; *NYT*, 12/14/1918; *NYT*, 1/18/1919, 4; Roswell Benedict, *Malefactor of Great Wealth* (New York: American Business Bureau, 1907), 397–401.

5   Mark Sullivan, *Our Times. Vol. 4: War Begins, 1909–1914* (New York: Charles Scribner's Sons, 1932), 118–19. Key sources on public relations and propaganda throughout this book include Barry Alan Marks, "The Idea of Propaganda in America," PhD diss., University of Minnesota, 1957; Lee William Huebner, "The Discovery of Propaganda: Changing Attitudes Toward Public Communication in America, 1900–1930," PhD diss., Harvard University, 1968; Scott Cutlip, *The Unseen Power: Public Relations, a History* (Hillsdale, NJ: Lawrence Erlbaum, 1994); Stuart Ewen, *PR!: A Social History of Spin* (New York: Basic Books, 1996); and J. Michael Sproule, *Propaganda and Democracy: The American Experience of Media and Mass Persuasion* (New York: Cambridge University Press, 1997).

6   Dewey, "Theodore Roosevelt," 116.

7   Ross, *Social Psychology*, 349–51.

8   Historians of public relations generally place its origins in the early twentieth century. Some, however, define *public relations* to include mass advocacy of any sort, tracing its origins to the earliest civilizations. See, e.g., Robert Brown, "St. Paul as a Public Relations Practitioner: A Meta-Theoretical Speculation on Messianic Communication and Symmetry," *Public Relations Review*, 29:1 (March 2003), 1–12, and "The Myth of Symmetry: Public Relations as Cultural Styles," *Public Relations Review*, 32:3 (September 2006), 206–12. Those who study the long history of mass persuasion have usually preferred the term *propaganda*. See Jowett and O'Donnell, *Propaganda and Persuasion*, and Oliver Thomson, *Mass Persuasion in History: An Historical Analysis of the Development of Propaganda Techniques* (Edinburgh: Paul Harris, 1977). See also Scott Cutlip, *Public Relations History: From the 17th to the 20th Century. The Antecedents* (Hillsdale, NJ: Lawrence Erlebaum, 1995).

9   See Alfred McClung Lee, *The Daily Newspaper in America: The Evolution of a Social Instrument* (New York: Macmillan, 1937), 434; Scott Cutlip, "Public Relations and the American Revolution," *Public Relations Review*, 2:4 (Winter 1976), 11–24; John Miller, *Sam Adams: Pioneer in Propaganda* (Boston: Little, Brown, 1936); M. J. Heale, *The Presidential Quest: Candidates and Images in American Political Culture, 1787–1852* (New York: Longman, 1982), 157–60.

10   Henry Pringle, "His Masters' Voice," *AMer* (October 1926), 145.

11   *WP*, 6/15/1912, 2; *WP*, 6/21/1912, 14. Journalistic exposés of public relations in these years include [Mark Sullivan], "Tainted News," *Collier's*, 2/23/1907, 5/4/1907, 6/29/1907, and 8/3/1907; Kittle, "The Making of Public Opinion," 433–52; and Will Irwin, "The Press Agent, His Rise and Decline," *Collier's*, 12/2/1911, 24–25, 39–41. No

byline appears on the *Collier's* series, but Ivy Lee recalled Sullivan as the author. Lee to W. H. Powell, 1/12/1923, ILLP, Box 3.

12 *AC*, 12/22/1907, B4. The key source on Lee is Ray Eldon Hiebert, *Courtier to the Crowd: The Story of Ivy Lee and the Development of Public Relations* (Ames: Iowa State University Press, 1966).

13 Karen Miller Russell and Carl Bishop, "Understanding Ivy Lee's Declaration of Principles: U.S. Newspaper and Magazine Coverage of Publicity and Press Agentry, 1865–1904," *Public Relations Review*, 35:2 (June 2009), 91–101.

14 Gordon Moon II, "George F. Parker: A 'Near Miss' as First White House Press Chief," *Journalism & Mass Communication Quarterly*, 41:2 (June 1964), 190.

15 On the Ludlow episode, additional key sources are Ron Chernow, *Titan: The Life of John D. Rockefeller, Sr.* (New York: Vintage Books, 2004 [1998]), 573–90; and Kirk Hallahan, "Ivy Lee and the Rockefellers' Response to the 1913–1914 Colorado Coal Strike," *Journal of Public Relations Research*, 14:4 (October 2002), 265–315.

16 *BG*, 12/9/1914, 9.

17 George Creel, "Poisoners of Public Opinion," *Harper's*, 11/7/1914, 436–38, and 11/14/1914, 465–66.

18 Sinclair, *Brass Check*, 311–13; Silas Bent, "Ivy Lee: Minnesinger to Millionaires," *TNR*, 11/20/1929, 369–72; David Sanders, "The Art of Fiction 44: Interview with Dos Passos," *Paris Review*, 12:46 (Spring 1969), 157–58.

19 Baker, "Railroads on Trial V: How Railroads Make Public Opinion," 547.

20 Irwin, "The Press Agent," 24–25, 39–41.

21 Government publicity aides were of course hired but given titles such as Director of Information and Editor-in-Chief. *NYT*, 8/20/1913, 8.

22 Robert Hilderbrand, *The Complete Press Conferences, 1913–1919*, vol. 50 of *The Papers of Woodrow Wilson*, ed. Arthur Link (Princeton: Princeton University Press, 1985), 260–61.

CHAPTER 8: Wilson Speaks

1 Ida Tarbell, "A Talk with the President of the United States," *Collier's*, 10/28/1916, 5–6, 37, 40–41. Key sources on Wilson throughout the book include Joseph Tumulty, *Woodrow Wilson As I Know Him* (Garden City, NY: Doubleday, Page & Co., 1921); David Lawrence, *The True Story of Woodrow Wilson* (New York: George H. Doran, 1924); Ray Stannard Baker, *Woodrow Wilson, Life and Letters*, 8 vols. (Garden City, NY: Doubleday, Doran & Co., 1927–39); Arthur Link, *Wilson*, 5 vols. (Princeton: Princeton University Press, 1947–65); John Morton Blum, *Woodrow Wilson and the Politics of Morality* (Boston: Little, Brown, 1956); and John Milton Cooper, *Woodrow Wilson: A Biography* (New York: Knopf, 2009).

2 Key sources on Wilson and rhetoric include Dayton David McKean, "Woodrow Wilson," in *History and Criticism of American Public Address*, ed. William Norwood Brigance, vol. 2 (New York: Russell & Russell, 1960 [1943]), 968–92; Hardin Craig, "Woodrow Wilson as an Orator," *Quarterly Journal of Speech*, 38:2 (April 1952), 145–48; Daniel Stid, "Rhetorical Leadership and Common Counsel in the Presidency of Woodrow Wilson," in *Speaking to the People: The Rhetorical Presidency in Historical Perspective*, ed. Richard Ellis (Amherst: University of Massachusetts Press, 1998), 162–81; Robert Alexander Kraig, *Woodrow Wilson and the Lost World of Oratorical Statesmanship* (College Station: Texas A&M University Press, 2004); and J. Michael Hogan, *Woodrow Wilson's Western Tour: Rhetoric, Public Opinion and the League of Nations* (College Station: Texas A&M University Press, 2006).

3 As Tillman had charged TR with deluding the public through his rhetoric, so TR charged Wilson: "He has covered his fear of standing for the right behind a veil of

rhetorical phrases. . . . He has kept the eyes of the people dazzled so that they know not what is real and what is false, so that they turn bewildered, unable to discern the difference between the glitter that veneers evil and the stark realities of courage and honesty, of truth and strength."—Theodore Roosevelt, *Americanism and Prepared-ness: Speeches of Theodore Roosevelt, July to November 1916* (New York: Mail and Express Job Print, 1917), 140.

4   J. A. Hendrix, "Presidential Address to Congress: Woodrow Wilson and the Jefferso-nian Tradition," *Southern Speech Journal*, 31:4 (Summer 1966), 285–94.

5   Woodrow Wilson, *The State: Elements of Historical and Practical Politics* (Boston: D. C. Heath & Co., 1894 [1889]), 566; Woodrow Wilson, *Constitutional Government in the United States* (New York: Columbia University Press, 1961 [1908]), 74.

6   Safire, *Political Dictionary*, 542–43; Woodrow Wilson, *The New Freedom*, ed. William Leuchtenburg (Englewood Cliffs, NJ: Prentice-Hall, 1961 [1913]), 75–86.

7   *NYT,* 4/8/1913, 1.

8   Stoddard, *As I Knew Them*, 485.

9   *NYTr,* 4/9/1913, 1; *WP,* 4/9/1913, 1.

10 Woodrow Wilson, "Address to a Joint Session of Congress on Tariff Reform," 4/8/1913, http://www.presidency.ucsb.edu/ws/?pid=65368.

11 *NYT,* 4/9/1913, 8; Brownlow, *A Passion for Politics*, 586.

12 TR to Wilson, 3/13/1900, in Morison, *Letters*, vol. 2, 1221; *NYT,* 9/28/1902, 1; *WP,* 11/29/1905, 9; *WP,* 12/3/1905, 3. On the two men generally, see John Milton Cooper, *The Warrior and the Priest: Woodrow Wilson and Theodore Roosevelt* (Cambridge, MA: Harvard University Press, 1983).

13 "Wilson and Roosevelt," *TNR,* 11/4/1916, 3–4.

14 Wilson, *Constitutional Government*, 22, 68, 73, 110, 170.

15 Douglas Bloomfield, "Joe Tumulty and the Press," *Journalism Quarterly*, 42:3 (Summer 1965), 415, 417.

16 Newton Baker, "Why We Went to War," *Foreign Affairs* (October 1936), 18.

17 Miroff, *Icons*, 174.

18 Terri Bimes and Stephen Skowronek, "Wilson's Critique of Popular Leadership," in *Speaking to the People: The Rhetorical Presidency in Historical Perspective*, ed. Richard Ellis (Amherst: University of Massachusetts Press, 1998), 147–48, 250n; Thompson, *Presidents I've Known*, 168–69, 288–89.

19 James Startt, *Woodrow Wilson and the Press: Prelude to the Presidency* (New York: Palgrave Macmillan, 2004), 203.

20 "The Spoken Message," *TNR,* 12/5/1914, 11–12.

CHAPTER 9: Pitiless Publicity

1   George Creel, *Rebel at Large: Recollections of Fifty Crowded Years* (New York: G. P. Putnam's Sons, 1947), 232. Key sources on Wilson and the press include Elmer Cornwell, Jr., "The Press Conferences of Woodrow Wilson," *Journalism & Mass Com-munication Quarterly*, 39:3 (September 1962), 292–300; David Michael Ryfe, "Betwixt and Between: Woodrow Wilson's Press Conferences and the Transition Toward the Modern Rhetorical Presidency," *Political Communication,* 16:1 (January–March 1999), 77–93; and Startt, *Wilson and the Press*.

2   John Milton Cooper, *Walter Hines Page: The Southerner as American, 1855–1918* (Chapel Hill: University of North Carolina Press, 1977), 238; Josephus Daniels, *The Wilson Era: Years of Peace* (Chapel Hill: University of North Carolina Press, 1944), 71.

3   Fielding, *American Newsreel*, 45, 69–72; Startt, *Wilson and the Press*, 202–04; Veronica

Gillespie, "Theodore Roosevelt on Film," http://memory.loc.gov/ammem/collections /troosevelt_film/trffilm.html.

4 Larry Wayne Ward, *The Motion Picture Goes to War: The U.S. Government Film Effort During World War I* (Ann Arbor: UMI Research Press, 1985), 13–17; Ernest Dench, "The President as a Movie Fan," *Motion Picture Classic* (July 1917), 64; David Mould, *American Newsfilm, 1914–1919: The Underexposed War* (New York: Garland Publishing, 1983), 263.

5 Thompson, *Presidents I've Known*, 274.

6 *E&P*, 3/27/1909, 1; Martha Joynt Kumar, "Source Material: Presidential Press Conferences: The Importance and Evolution of an Enduring Form," *Presidential Studies Quarterly*, 35:1 (March 2005), 168, n4.

7 *WP*, 3/16/1913, 4; *Hartford Courant*, 3/17/1913, 15; Lowry, *Washington Close-Ups*, 19.

8 Ames Brown, "President Wilson and Publicity," *Harper's*, 11/1/1913, 19–21.

9 *NYTr*, 3/15/1914, D6; Oswald Garrison Villard, "The Press and the President: Should the President Be Quoted Directly or Indirectly?" *Century* (December 1925), 197; Hugh Baillie, *High Tension: The Recollections of Hugh Baillie* (New York: Harper & Bros., 1959), 46–47.

10 Woodrow Wilson, "Remarks to the National Press Club," 3/20/1914, in Link, *Papers*, vol. 29, 362.

11 Creel, *Rebel*, 234; Henry Turner, "Woodrow Wilson and Public Opinion," *Public Opinion Quarterly*, 21:4 (Winter 1957–58), 515.

12 Wilson to Tarbell, 9/14/1916, in Link, *Papers*, vol. 38, 170–71.

13 Lippmann, "Washington Correspondent," 47–48; Barry, *Forty Years*, 309.

14 Woodrow Wilson, "The Modern Democratic State," 12/1/1885, in Link, *Papers*, vol. 69, 82–84, 89.

15 Woodrow Wilson, "Address to the South Carolina Press Association," 6/2/1911, in Link, *Papers*, vol. 23, 117.

16 Baker, *American Chronicle*, 386–87.

17 Thompson, *Presidents I've Known*, 297.

18 *NYTr*, 3/15/1914, D6; David Lawrence, "The President and the Press," *SEP*, 8/27/1927, 27; William Shepherd, "The White House Says," *Collier's*, 2/2/1929, 19; Creel, *Rebel*, 234.

CHAPTER 10: The Press Agents' War

1 The key source on Viereck throughout the book is Niel Johnson, *George Sylvester Viereck, German-American Propagandist* (Urbana: University of Illinois Press, 1972).

2 William McAdoo, *Crowded Years: The Reminiscences of William G. McAdoo* (Port Washington, NY: Kennikat Press, 1931), 324–30. On the Albert affair, see also Arthur Link, *Wilson: The Struggle for Neutrality* (Princeton: Princeton University Press, 1960), 554–56.

3 Key sources on Wilson and World War I before American entry include Mark Sullivan, *Our Times*. Vol. 5: *Over Here, 1914–1918* (New York: Charles Scribner's Sons, 1933); Link, *Wilson*; Cooper, *Woodrow Wilson*; and Justus Doenecke, *Nothing Less Than War: A New History of America's Entry into World War I* (Lexington: University Press of Kentucky, 2011).

4 McAdoo, *Crowded Years*, 328; House to Wilson, 8/10/1915, in Link, *Papers*, vol. 34, 158.

5 *NYW*, 8/15/1915, 1, and subsequent stories through 8/23. On German sabotage and espionage, see Henry Landau, *The Enemy Within: The Inside Story of German Sabotage in America* (New York: G. P. Putnam's Sons, 1937); Jules Witcover, *Sabotage at Black*

Tom: *Imperial Germany's Secret War in America, 1914–1917* (New York: Algonquin Books, 1989); and Tracie Provost, "The Great Game: Imperial German Sabotage and Espionage Against the United States, 1914–1917," Ph.D. diss., University of Toledo, 2003.

6   *Fatherland*, 8/25/1915, 48; *NYT*, 8/17/1915, 2; *NYT*, 8/17/1915, 2.

7   *NYT*, 9/9/1914, 8.

8   Fellows, "Propaganda: History of a Word," 182–89.

9   Paul Starr, *The Creation of the Media: Political Origins of Modern Communication* (New York: Basic Books, 2005), 223–24; Gilbert Parker, "The United States and the War," *Harper's* (December 1917), 522.

10 James Morgan Read, *Atrocity Propaganda, 1914–1919* (New Haven: Yale University Press, 1941), 201–04; Larry Zuckerman, *The Rape of Belgium: The Untold Story of World War I* (New York: NYU Press, 2004), 132–36.

11 Key sources on cinematic propaganda in World War I include Terry Ramsaye, *A Million and One Nights* (New York: Simon & Schuster, 1926), 726–27, 757–58, 777–88; Timothy Lyons, "Hollywood and World War I, 1914–1918," *Journal of Popular Film*, 1:1 (Winter 1972), 15–30; Kevin Brownlow, *The War, the West and the Wilderness* (New York: Knopf, 1979) 107–82; Ward, *Motion Picture Goes to War*; and Leslie Midkiff DeBauche, *Reel Patriotism: The Movies and World War I* (Madison: University of Wisconsin Press, 1997).

12 Wilson to Bryan, 6/7/1915, in Link, *Papers*, vol. 33, 349.

13 Link, *Papers*, vol. 35, 501.

14 *WP*, 1/23/1916, 3; *BG*, 1/30/1916, 25.

15 *NYT*, 2/2/1916, 1; *WP*, 2/1/1916, 2; "Editorial Notes," *TNR*, 2/5/1916, 1; Herbert Croly, "Unregenerate Democracy," *TNR*, 2/5/1916, 18.

16 *NYT*, 6/16/1916, 1.

17 Woolley to Creel, undated, RWP, Box 4; Woolley to Edward House, 9/6/1916, RWP, Box 7; McGerr, *Decline of Popular Politics*, 163–66; Sheingate, "Publicity and Modern Politics," 473.

18 Creel, *Rebel*, 155–56; Arthur Link and William Leary, Jr., "Election of 1916," in Schlesinger and Israel, *Elections*, vol. 6 (New York: Chelsea House, 1971), 2266.

19 McGerr, *Decline*, 167–68; *NYT*, 7/23/1916, 14; *NYTr*, 7/23/1916, 5; Stephen Fox, *The Mirror Makers: A History of American Advertising and Its Creators* (New York: William Morrow, 1984), 307.

20 Woodrow Wilson, "Address to the Senate of the United States: 'A World League for Peace,'" 1/22/1917, http://www.presidency.ucsb.edu/ws/?pid=65396.

21 David Kennedy, *Over Here: The First World War and American Society* (New York: Oxford University Press, 1980), 52–53; Randolph Bourne, "The State," in *The Radical Will: Selected Writings, 1911–1918*, preface by Christopher Lasch, selection and introductions by Olaf Hansen (New York: Urizen Books, 1977), 360–61; and "Twilight of Idols," in ibid., 339.

22 Woodrow Wilson, "An Address to a Joint Session of Congress Requesting a Declaration of War Against Germany," 4/2/1917, http://www.presidency.ucsb.edu/ws/?pid=65366.

23 Ibid.

CHAPTER 11: The Journey of George Creel

1   Lansing, Baker, and Daniels to Wilson, 4/13/1917, in Link, *Papers*, vol. 42, 55. Key sources on the Committee on Public Information include United States Committee on Public Information, *The Creel Report: The Complete Report of the Chairman of the Committee on Public Information—1917:1918:1919* (Washington, DC: Government

Printing Office, 1920); George Creel, *How We Advertised America: The First Telling of the Amazing Story of the Committee on Public Information That Carried the Gospel of Americanism to Every Corner of the Globe* (New York: Harper & Bros., 1920); James Mock and Cedric Larson, *Words That Won the War: The Story of the Committee on Public Information, 1917–1919* (Princeton: Princeton University Press, 1939); Walton Bean, "George Creel and His Critics: A Study of the Attacks on the Committee on Public Information, 1917–1919," PhD diss., University of California, 1941; Creel, *Rebel*; and Stephen Vaughn, *Holding Fast the Inner Lines: Democracy, Nationalism and the Committee on Public Information* (Chapel Hill: University of North Carolina Press, 1980).

2   Press release, 4/14/1917, in Link, *Papers*, vol. 42, 59; Wilson to Benedict Crowell, in Link, *Papers*, vol. 49, 449; *NYT*, 4/15/1917, 1; *BG*, 4/15/1917, 2. The government also used other agencies to publicize war aims. See Jackson Lears, *Fables of Abundance: A Cultural History of Advertising in America* (New York: Basic Books, 1994), 218–23.

3   Lippmann to Charles Merz, 4/11/1917, WLP, Series I, Reels 19, 20; "From the Diary of Josephus Daniels," 4/9/1917, and Wilson to Daniels, 4/12/1917, in Link, *Papers*, vol. 42, 23, 43; Peter Clark Macfarlane, "The Fortunes of Citizen Creel," *Collier's*, 7/19/1913, 5.

4   *WP*, 11/29/1912, 2; *CT*, 11/29/1912, 1; *CT*, 8/8/1916, 1; *NYT*, 4/15/1917, 1; George Creel, "The Next Four Years: An Interview with the President," *Everybody's* (February 1917), 129–39.

5   Robert Lansing, *War Memoirs of Robert Lansing* (Westport, CT: Greenwood Press, 1935), 322; Wilson to Tumulty, 7/11/1917, in Link, *Papers*, vol. 43, 146; Elmer Cornwell, "Wilson, Creel, and the Presidency," *Public Opinion Quarterly*, 23:2 (Summer 1959), 197–98.

6   Ponder, *Managing the Press*, 88; Lippmann to Wilson, 1/31/1917; Lippmann to Wilson, 2/6/1917; Lippmann to Wilson, 3/11/1917; Wilson to Lippmann, 4/7/1917; WLP, Series I, Reel 33. Ronald Steel, *Walter Lippmann and the American Century* (Boston: Little, Brown, 1980), xv; Arthur Bullard, *Mobilising America* (New York: Macmillan, 1917), 24–25.

7   A clause in the bill stated that "nothing in this section shall be construed to limit or restrict any discussion, comment, or criticism of the acts or policies of the Government." Nonetheless, the press and many elected officials found it intolerable. Two other restrictive provisions on speech—one on use of the mails, one on speech intended to cause "disaffection" from the nation—were narrowed. Geoffrey Stone, *Perilous Times: Free Speech in Wartime from the Sedition Act of 1798 to the War on Terrorism* (New York: W. W. Norton, 2004), 147–53.

8   Lee Simonson, "Mobilizing the Billboards," *TNR*, 11/10/1917, 41–43.

9   Walter Lippmann, "Blame and Praise from Mr. Creel," review of *How We Advertised America*, [name of publication not clear], 48–49, GCP, Box OV2.

10 Walter Lippmann, *Public Opinion* (New York: Free Press, 1997 [1922]), 31.

11 Robert Emery, "The Official Bulletin, 1917–1919: A Proto-Federal Register," *Law Library Journal*, 102:3 (Summer 2010), 441–48.

12 "Government Asks Artists to Make War Posters," *NYTM*, 5/20/1917, SM8; *NYT*, 1/20/1918, 63; *NYT*, 2/22/1918; Emery, "The Official Bulletin, 1917–1919," 444. In the Pro Quest Historical Newspapers Database, which I have used, articles from the *New York Times Magazine* are usually paginated with an "SM" (for *Sunday Magazine*) preceding the numeral. When "SM" appears in these notes, it indicates that the magazine article was retrieved via Pro Quest. However, Pro Quest is inconsistent in applying this system, and does not always use "SM" in citing *New York Times Magazine* articles.

13 DeBauche, *Reel Patriotism*, 80.

14 "The New Paternalism," *TNR*, 12/21/1918, 217; Christopher Capozzola, *Uncle Sam*

Wants You: World War I and the Making of the Modern American Citizen (New York: Oxford University Press, 2008).

15 Ward, *Motion Picture Goes to War*, 95, 117–18; DeBauche, *Reel Patriotism*, 36–38.

16 Woodrow Wilson, "Preliminary Statement to the Press regarding the Committee on Public Information," n.d., GCP, Series "Woodrow Wilson and the Committee on Public Information, 1917–1931, vol. I," Box 1; Kennedy, *Over Here*, 75, 84–86, 89.

17 *WP*, 10/7/1917, SM5; "Creel: An Announcement," *Everybody's* (January 1919), 25; Will Irwin, *The Making of a Reporter* (New York: G. P. Putnam's Sons, 1942), 352.

18 GCP, Box 8, Box OV7; *WP*, 7/10/1917, 2; *NYT*, 7/11/1917, 3; *WP*, 7/23/1917, 2; *WP*, 7/25/1917, 2; Melville Stone, *Fifty Years a Journalist* (Garden City, NY: Doubleday, Page & Co., 1921), 326–28; George Creel, "The 'Lash' of Public Opinion," *Collier's*, 11/22/1924, 8–9, 46.

19 *CT*, 4/5/1918, 4; *WP*, 4/10/1918, 3; *WP*, 5/15/1918, 5; *NYT*, 5/18/1918, 8; *NYT*, 6/14/1918, 8. Other sources quote Cannon slightly differently.

20 "Josephus Daniels to Wilson, with Enclosure" and "A Memorandum by George Creel," 4/11/1917, in Link, *Papers*, vol. 42, 39–41; "Committee on Public Information Preliminary Statement to the Press," in ibid., 304–13; Wilson to Webb, 5/22/1917, in ibid., 369–70; *BG*, 10/10/1917, 1; Executive Order 2729-A, 10/12/1917, http://www.presidency.ucsb.edu/ws/index.php?pid=75446. On wartime censorship generally, see Stone, *Perilous Times*, 147–53.

21 Lippmann, "Blame and Praise from Mr. Creel"; Walter Lippmann, "For a Department of State," *TNR*, 9/17/1919, 196.

22 C. H. Hamlin, *The War Myth in United States History* (New York: Vanguard Press, 1927), 92; George Sylvester Viereck, *Spreading Germs of Hate*, intro. by Edward House (New York: Horace Liveright, 1931), 168, 184, 210–11.

CHAPTER 12: Disillusionment

1 Key sources on Lasker include John Gunther, *Taken at the Flood: The Story of Albert D. Lasker* (New York: Popular Library, 1961 [1960]); Albert Lasker, *The Lasker Story: As He Told It* (Chicago: Advertising Publications, 1963); John Morello, *Selling the President, 1920: Albert D. Lasker, Advertising, and the Election of Warren G. Harding* (Westport, CT: Praeger Press, 2001); and Jeffrey Cruikshank and Arthur Schultz, *The Man Who Sold America: The Amazing But True Story of Albert D. Lasker and the Creation of the Advertising Century* (Boston: Harvard Business Review Press, 2010).

2 Key sources on advertising throughout the book include Fox, *Mirror Makers*; Lears, *Fables*; and Roland Marchand, *Advertising the American Dream: Making Way for Modernity* (Berkeley: University of California Press, 1985).

3 Gunther, *Taken at the Flood*, 92; *NYT*, 10/28/1918, 1.

4 Key sources on Baker include Robert Bannister, *Ray Stannard Baker: The Mind and Thought of a Progressive* (New Haven: Yale University Press, 1966), and Baker, *American Chronicle*.

5 Erik Barnouw, *A History of Broadcasting in the United States*. Vol. 1: *A Tower of Babel: To 1933* (New York: Oxford University Press, 1966), 51–52, 55–56; White, *Masks*, 374.

6 Key sources on Bernays throughout the book include Edward Bernays, *Biography of an Idea: Memoirs of Public Relations Counsel Edward Bernays* (New York: Simon & Schuster, 1965); Sidney Blumenthal, *The Permanent Campaign* (New York: Simon & Schuster, 1982 [1980]); and Larry Tye, *The Father of Spin: Edward Bernays and the Birth of Public Relations* (New York: Crown Publishers, 1998).

7 Wilson to Edward House, 12/17/1918, RSBP, Box 2.

8 Essary, *Covering Washington*, 149–50.

9   "The A.B.C. of Alliances," *TNR*, 5/24/1919, 108.

10 Henry Campbell Black, *The Relation of the Executive Power to Legislation* (Princeton: Princeton University Press, 1919), 183.

11 Link, *Papers*, vol. 63, 513; John Morton Blum, *Joe Tumulty and the Wilson Era* (Boston: Houghton Mifflin, 1951), 213.

12 Ray Tucker, "Part-Time Statesmen," *Collier's*, 10/28/1933, 26, 38.

PART II: THE AGE OF BALLYHOO
CHAPTER 13: Return to Normalcy

1   On Harding, key sources include Francis Russell, *The Shadow of Blooming Grove: Warren G. Harding in His Times* (New York: McGraw-Hill, 1968); Robert Murray, *The Harding Era: Warren G. Harding and His Administration* (Minneapolis: University of Minnesota Press, 1969); and Wayne Richard Whitaker, "Warren G. Harding and the Press," PhD diss., Ohio University, 1972.

2   Michael Schudson, *The Good Citizen: A History of American Civic Life* (New York: Free Press, 1998), 144–87; Richard Jensen, "Armies, Admen, and Crusaders: Types of Presidential Election Campaigns," *History Teacher,* 2:2 (January 1969), 33–50; Robert Westbrook, "Politics as Consumption: Managing the Modern American Election," in *The Culture of Consumption: Critical Essays in American History, 1880–1980,* ed. Richard Wightman Fox and T. J. Jackson Lears (New York: Pantheon Books, 1983), 145–73.

3   Oscar King Davis, "The Game and Cost of Making a President," *NYTM*, 8/9/1908, SM2; George Kibbe Turner, "Manufacturing Public Opinion: The New Art of Making Presidents by Press Bureaus," *McClure's* (July 1912), 316–27; *NYT*, 7/23/1916, 14; *NYTr*, 7/23/1916, 5.

4   Bruce Barton, "Here Is the Lever, Archimedes," BBP, Box 144.

5   Frank Cobb, "The Press and Public Opinion," *TNR*, 12/31/1919, 144.

6   Lippmann, *Public Opinion*, 61.

7   *NYT*, 9/3/1920, 3.

8   H. L. Mencken, "Gamalielese," and "Gamalielese Again," in *On Politics: A Carnival of Buncombe*, ed. Malcolm Moos (Baltimore: Johns Hopkins University Press, 1996), 41–42, 46–50; McAdoo, *Crowded Years,* 388–89.

9   *CT*, 11/2/1920, 5.

10 *NYT*, 9/4/1920, 8; *WP*, 8/22/1920, 26; Richard Boeckel, "The Man with the Best Story Wins," *Independent*, 5/22/1920, 244.

11 *NYT*, 9/5/1920, XX3. Where roman numerals are given, pagination is as rendered by the Pro Quest Historical Newspapers Database.

12 Judson Welliver, "Harding, Man and President," *American Review of Reviews* (September 1923), 272; Edward Lowry, "Mr. Harding Digging In," *TNR*, 5/18/1921, 341–42; *NYT*, 4/26/1921, 1.

13 *NYT*, 3/11/1923, XX1; Clinton Gilbert, *Behind the Mirrors: The Psychology of Disintegration at Washington* (New York: G. P. Putnam's Sons, 1922), 61; Stephen Ponder, "That Delightful Relationship: Presidents and White House Correspondents in the 1920s," *American Journalism,* 14:2 (Spring 1997), 179.

14 Key sources on White House speechwriting throughout the book include Robert Schlesinger, *White House Ghosts: Presidents and Their Speechwriters from FDR to George W. Bush* (New York: Simon & Schuster, 2008), and Carol Gelderman, *All the President's Words* (New York: Walker & Co., 1997).

15 "Writers and Their Work," *Hampton's Magazine*, 11/1/1909, 23, 5; *WP*, 3/18/1918, 9; Essary, *Covering Washington*, 97–98.

16 "The Washington Observer," *CSM*, 3/15/1922, 10.

17 Mencken, "Cal as Literatus," in *On Politics*, 132–33.

18 Safire, *Political Dictionary*, 260.

CHAPTER 14: Walter Lippmann and the Problem of the Majority

1 Key sources on Lippmann throughout the book include Steel, *Lippmann*, and Marquis Childs and James Reston, eds., *Walter Lippmann and His Times* (New York: Harcourt, Brace, 1959).

2 Lippmann to Reed, 2/21/1916, WLP, Series I, Reel 28.

3 Lippmann to Charles Merz, 4/11/1917, WLP, Series I, Reel 20; "Paul Kellogg Muckraked," *TNR*, 2/20/1915, 60–61; "George Creel Replies," *TNR*, 3/27/1915, 209–10; Heber Blankenhorn, "The War of Morale," *Harper's* (September 1919), 510–24.

4 Walter Lippmann and Charles Merz, "A Test of the News," *TNR*, 8/4/1920, 3. Quotations in the ensuing paragraphs are from Walter Lippmann, *Liberty and the News* (New York: Harcourt, Brace & Howe, 1920), and Walter Lippmann, *Public Opinion* (New York: Free Press, 1997 [1922]).

5 *NYT*, 3/21/1920, X1.

6 Herbert Croly to Lippmann, 1/4/1922, Lippmann to Croly, 1/5/1922, Croly to Lippmann, 1/18/1922, WLP, Series I, Reel 7; Walter Lippmann, "The World Outside and the Pictures in Our Heads" and "The Pseudo-Environment," *TNR*, 3/1 and 3/8/1922, 10–14, 44–48; John Dewey, "Public Opinion," *TNR*, 5/3/1922, 286.

7 James Bryce, *Modern Democracies*, vol. 1 (New York: Macmillan, 1921), 158–59.

8 Charles Merriam, review of Lippmann's *Public Opinion*, *International Journal of Ethics*, 33:2 (January 1923), 210–12; Robert Park, review of *Public Opinion*, *American Journal of Sociology*, 28:2 (September 1922), 232–34; Irwin Edman, "Our Foremost Philosopher at Seventy," *NYTM*, 10/13/1929, SM2.

9 Quotations in the ensuing paragraphs are from John Dewey, *The Public and Its Problems* (Denver: Swallow Books, 1954 [1927]).

10 John Dewey, review of Lippmann's *Public Opinion*, *TNR*, 5/3/22, 286–88. The idea of a "Lippmann-Dewey debate" is questioned in Michael Schudson, "The 'Lippmann-Dewey Debate' and the Invention of Walter Lippmann as an Anti-Democrat, 1986–1996," *International Journal of Communication*, 2:1 (2008), 1031–42; Sue Curry Jansen, "Phantom Conflict: Lippmann, Dewey, and the Public in Modern Society," *Communication and Critical/Cultural Studies*, 6:3 (September 2009), 221–45; and David Greenberg, "Lippmann vs. Mencken: Debating Democracy," *Raritan*, 32:2 (Fall 2012), 117–40.

11 Dewey, review of *Public Opinion*, 288.

CHAPTER 15: The Likes and Dislikes of H. L. Mencken

1 Ernest Hemingway, *The Sun Also Rises* (New York: Scribner's, 2006 [1926]), 49. Key sources on Mencken are Fred Hobson, *Mencken: A Life* (New York: Random House, 1994), and Marion Elizabeth Rodgers, *Mencken: The American Iconoclast* (New York: Oxford University Press, 2005).

2 See correspondence, WLP, Series I, Reel 19.

3 Lippmann to Mencken, 9/21/1926, Mencken to Lippmann, 9/22/1926, WLP, Series I, Reel 19.

4 *LAT*, 8/26/1923, III, 50; Mencken to Bernays, 1/26/1948, ELB, Box I:18. Quotations here and in this section are from H. L. Mencken, *Notes on Democracy, a new edition*, intro. and notes by Marion Elizabeth Rodgers (New York: Dissident Books, 2009 [1926]).

5   Mencken to unknown correspondent, 4/14/1922, forwarded to Lippmann, WLP Series
    I, Reel 19; H. L. Mencken, "Vox Populi," review of *Public Opinion* in *H. L. Mencken's
    Smart Set Criticism*, ed. William Nolte (Washington, DC: Regnery Gateway, 2001),
    121–30.
6   Mencken, "Vox Populi," 121–30.
7   Walter Lippmann, "The Near Machiavelli," *TNR*, 5/31/1922, 13–15.
8   H. L. Mencken, *My Life as an Author and Editor* (New York: Knopf, 1993), 376; H. L.
    Mencken, "Katzenjammer," review of Lippmann's *The Phantom Public*, *AMer* (Janu-
    ary 1926), 125–26.
9   Edmund Wilson, "Mencken's Democratic Man," *TNR*, 12/15/1926, 110.
10 Walter Lippmann, "H. L. Mencken," review of *Notes on Democracy* in *Men of Destiny*,
    with new intro. by Richard Lowitt (Seattle: University of Washington Press, 1970
    [1927]), 61–62.
11 Lippmann, "H. L. Mencken," in *Men of Destiny*, 63–67.
12 Quotations from Mencken's reportage are from H. L. Mencken, *A Religious Orgy in
    Tennessee: A Reporter's Account of the Scopes Monkey Trial*, intro. by Art Winslow
    (Hoboken, NJ: Melville House, 2006).
13 Walter Lippmann, "Why Should the Majority Rule?" *Harper's* (March 1926), 399–405.

CHAPTER 16: Bruce Barton and the Soul of the 1920s

1   Silas Bent, *Ballyhoo: The Voice of the Press* (New York: Boni & Liveright, 1927).
2   John Dewey, *Individualism Old and New* (Amherst, NY: Prometheus Books, 1999
    [1930]), 22.
3   Richard Warner, "Profiles: It Pays to Preach," *TNY*, 11/1/1930, 24. Key sources on
    Barton throughout the book include Richard Fried, *The Man Everybody Knew: Bruce
    Barton and the Making of Modern America* (Chicago: Ivan R. Dee, 2005); Leo Ribuffo,
    "Jesus Christ as Business Statesman: Bruce Barton and the Selling of Corporate Capi-
    talism," *American Quarterly*, 33:2 (Summer 1981), 206–21; and T. J. Jackson Lears,
    "From Salvation to Self-Realization: Advertising and the Therapeutic Roots of Con-
    sumer Culture, 1880–1930," in Fox and Lears, eds., *Culture of Consumption*, 1–38.
4   "The Press: With Hustle and Hope," *Time*, 10/24/1949, 81.
5   Bruce Barton, *The Man Nobody Knows: A Discovery of the Real Jesus* (Indianapolis:
    Bobbs-Merrill, 1925), 69–70, 107, 148, 159.
6   *NYT*, 5/10/1925, BR11.
7   Key sources on Coolidge and Barton include Robert Bishop, "Bruce Barton—Presi-
    dential Stage Manager," *Journalism Quarterly*, 43:1 (March 1966), 85–89, and Kerry
    Buckley, "A President for the 'Great Silent Majority': Bruce Barton's Construction of
    Calvin Coolidge," *New England Quarterly*, 76:4 (December 2003), 593–626.
8   "Concerning Calvin Coolidge," *Collier's*, 11/22/1919, 8ff.; "The Silent Man on Beacon
    Hill," *Woman's Home Companion* (March 1920), 15, 30, 88; "A Governor Who Stays
    on the Job," *Outlook*, 4/28/1920, 756–57; "Calvin Coolidge As Seen Through the Eyes
    of His Friends," *American Review of Reviews* (September 1923), 273–78.
9   Key sources on Coolidge include Calvin Coolidge, *Autobiography* (New York: Cosmo-
    politan Book Corp., 1929); Elmer Cornwell, "Coolidge and Presidential Leadership,"
    Public Opinion Quarterly, 21:2 (Summer 1957); Claude Fuess, *Calvin Coolidge: The
    Man from Vermont* (Boston: Little, Brown, 1940); Donald McCoy, *Calvin Coolidge:
    The Quiet President* (New York: Macmillan, 1967); and David Greenberg, *Calvin
    Coolidge* (New York: Times Books, 2006).
10 Edmund Starling, *Starling of the White House* (New York: Simon & Schuster, 1946),
    211, 243; Arthur Fleser, *A Rhetorical Study of the Speaking of Calvin Coolidge* (Lew-

iston, NY: E. Mellen Press, 1990), 68; H. L. Mencken, Editorial, *AMer*, 3/3/1929, 279; Lippmann, *Men of Destiny*, 17.

11 "The Danger of Too Much Coolidge," *TNR*, 12/26/1923, 109; C. Bascom Slemp, *The Mind of the President: As Revealed by Himself in His Own Words* (Garden City, NY: Doubleday, Page & Co., 1926), 10.

12 Barton to Edward Clark, 12/12/1923, ETCP, Box 1; Barton to Frank Stearns, 12/31/1923, ETCP, Box 1; Barton, "As Seen Through the Eyes," 273–78; Charles Merz, "The Campaign Opens," *Century* (July 1924), 309.

13 Hadley Cantril, *The Invasion from Mars: A Study in the Psychology of Panic* (Princeton: Princeton University Press, 1940). Key sources on the 1924 campaign include Terry Hynes, "Media Manipulation and Political Campaigns: Bruce Barton and the Presidential Elections of the Jazz Age," *Journalism History*, 4:3 (Autumn 1977), 93–98; Lewis Weeks, "The Radio Election of 1924," *Journal of Broadcasting*, 8:3 (Summer 1964), 233–43; and Dave Berkman, "Politics and Radio in the 1924 Campaign," *Journalism Quarterly*, 64:2–3 (Summer–Fall 1987), 422–28.

14 *NYT*, 6/25/1923, 2; *NYT*, 3/8/1925, XX15; *NYT*, 2/23/1927, 1. Key sources on Coolidge and radio include Douglas Craig, *Fireside Politics: Radio and Political Culture in the United States, 1920–1940* (Baltimore: Johns Hopkins University Press, 2000); Arthur Fleser, "Coolidge's Delivery: Everybody Liked It," *Southern Speech Journal*, 32:2 (Winter 1966), 98–105.

15 Will Irwin, *Propaganda and the News, or What Makes You Think So?* (New York: Whittlesey House, 1936), 249.

16 *NYT*, 7/18/1924, 3.

17 Daniel Leab, "Coolidge, Hays, and 1920s Movies: Some Aspects of Image and Reality," in *Calvin Coolidge and the Coolidge Era: Essays on the History of the 1920s*, ed. John Earl Haynes (Washington, DC: Library of Congress, 1998), 102; Bruce Bliven, "The Great Coolidge Mystery," *Harper's* (December 1925), 50.

18 *NYT*, 8/20/1924; "Coolidge," *Nation*, 6/18/1924, 696; Bliven, "The Great Coolidge Mystery," 45.

19 Barton to Coolidge, n.d., ETCP, Box 1; Clark to Barton, 10/2/1926, ETCP, Box 1; Coolidge to Clark, 10/28/1932, ETCP, Box 2; *NYT*, 9/23/1926, 4.

20 *BG*, 9/22/1926, A32; T.R.B., "Washington Notes," *TNR*, 10/13/1926, 216; *LAT*, 12/12/1926, 18; *NYT*, 9/28/1926, 27.

21 Calvin Coolidge, "Address Before the American Association of Advertising Agencies, Washington, D.C.," 10/27/1926, http://www.presidency.ucsb.edu/ws/?pid=412.

CHAPTER 17: "Silent Cal"

1 Essary, *Covering Washington*, 91; *NYT*, 8/15/1923, 3. A key source on Coolidge and the press is John Blair, "Coolidge the Image-Maker: The President and the Press, 1923–1929," *New England Quarterly*, 46:4 (December 1973), 499–522.

2 CCP, Reel 39, Case 36; *NYT*, 8/7/1927, XX11.

3 T.R.B., "Washington Notes," *TNR*, 1/20/1926, 239; Willis Sharp, "President and Press," *Atlantic* (August 1927), 244. See also Frank Kent, "Mr. Coolidge," *AMer* (August 1924), 385–90; Frank Kent, "Assailing the President," *Forum* (January 1927), 14.

4 "Government by Publicity," *TNR*, 9/22/1926, 111.

5 *NYT*, 9/5/1920, XX3; Stanley Walker, "Playing the Deep Bassoons," *Harper's* (February 1932), 365–75; "The Confessions of a Shirt-Stuffer," *TNR*, 3/3/1926, 35–38; Silas Bent, "The Art of Ballyhoo," *Harper's* (September 1927), 485–94.

6 Charles Merriam, "Government and Society," in President's Research Committee on Social Trends, *Recent Social Trends in the United States, Report of the President's*

Research Committee on Social Trends (New York: McGraw-Hill, 1933), 1513–14; J. Frederick Essary, "Uncle Sam's Ballyhoo Men," *AMer* (August 1931), 427.

7 *E&P*, 11/27/1919, 8.

8 Creel, "Lash of Public Opinion," 46.

9 "Coolidge," *Nation*, 6/18/1924, 696.

10 Samuel McCoy, "Trials of the White House Spokesman," *Independent*, 9/19/1925, 317–19; Oswald Garrison Villard, "The Press and the President," *Century* (December 1925), 193–200; Lindsay Rogers, "The White House 'Spokesman,'" *Virginia Quarterly Review* (July 1926), 350–66; Lawrence, "The President and the Press," 27, 117–18; Shepherd, "The White House Says," 47–49.

11 CCP, Reel 173, Case 3041; CCP, Reel 54, Case 72; "Visitin' 'Round at Coolidge Corners," FEB 8580, AFI/Harold Casselton/Ted Larson Collection, MBRS; *NYT*, 4/22/1925, 8; *NYT*, 8/7/1927, XX11; *NYT*, 5/28/1928, 74.

CHAPTER 18: The Overt Acts of Edward Bernays

1 *NYT*, 1/4/1931, XX7; Silas Bent, "Is Propaganda a Constructive Force in American Life Today? Negative," in *WOR Forum Book*, ed. S. Theodore Granik (New York: Falcon Press, 1933), 100–04; Bent, "Ivy Lee," 369–72.

2 Edward Bernays, "Is Propaganda a Constructive Force in American Life Today? Positive," in Granik, *WOR Forum Book*, 93–100.

3 Calvin Coolidge, "Address to the American Society of Newspaper Editors, Washington, D.C.," 1/17/1925, http://www.presidency.ucsb.edu/ws/?pid=24180; Ivy Lee, *Publicity: Some of the Things It Is and Is Not* (New York: Industries Publishing, 1925), 18–21, 38. This idea, hardly original to Lee, was gaining currency in the 1920s. See, e.g., Lippmann, *Public Opinion*, 217–23.

4 Bernays to Lee, 11/26/1927, ELBP, Box I:5. Lasswell, *Propaganda Techniques*, 4; Harold Lasswell, "Propaganda," in *Encyclopedia of the Social Sciences*, ed. Edwin R.A. Seligman (New York: Macmillan, 1933), 12:521–27.

5 Bruce Bliven, "Let's Have More Propaganda," *The World Tomorrow* (December 1926), 254–55.

6 John Dos Passos, "A Communication: Wanted: An Ivy Lee for Liberals," *TNR*, 8/13/1930, 371–72; Gilbert Gall, "Heber Blankenhorn: The Publicist as Reformer," *Historian*, 45:4 (August 1983), 513–28; Don Kirschner, "Publicity Properly Applied: The Selling of Expertise in America, 1900–1928," *American Studies*, 19:1 (Spring 1978), 65–78.

7 Walter Lippmann, "Blazing Publicity," *Vanity Fair* (September 1927), 47, 110; Lippmann, *Public Opinion*, 217–18.

8 Mencken to Bernays, 1/26/1948, ELBP, Box I:18; *WP*, 11/23/1991, B1.

9 Henry Pringle, "Mass Psychologist," *AMer* (February 1930), 155–62; John Flynn, "Edward Bernays: The Science of Ballyhoo," *Atlantic* (May 1932), 562–71.

10 Creel to Ernest Poole, 6/7/1918, ELBP, III:6; Bernays to Scott Cutlip, 3/10/1959, ELBP, I:40.

11 "Breakfast with Coolidge," 2/8/1962, ELBP, Box I:457; Clippings, ELBP, Box I:701; Edward Bernays, "Manipulating Public Opinion: The Why and The How," *American Journal of Sociology*, 33:6 (May 1928), 967; *NYT*, 10/18/1924, 1.

12 Edward Bernays, *Crystallizing Public Opinion* (New York: Boni & Liveright, 1923); Edward Bernays, *Propaganda*, intro. by Mark Crispin Miller (Brooklyn, NY: Ig Publishing, 2005 [1928]); ELBP, Box I:457. Frank Zeo, Ginger Esty, and Diane Cotman to Daniel Boorstin, n.d., DJBP, Box 86.

13 Bernays, *Crystallizing*, 59; Mencken implied that Bernays had only recited "all the tricks practiced by mob-masters since the day of Jeremiah," but called Bernays

"shrewd and well-informed." H. L. Mencken, review of Bernays's *Crystallizing Public Opinion*, *AMer* (May 1924), 123–24.

14 Bernays, *Propaganda*, 37–38.

15 Edward Bernays, "Putting Politics on the Market," *Independent*, 5/19/1928, 470–72.

CHAPTER 19: Master of Emergencies

1 Walter Lippmann, "The Peculiar Weakness of Mr. Hoover," *Harper's* (June 1930), 1; Paul Martin Lester, *On Floods and Photo-Ops: How Herbert Hoover and George W. Bush Exploited Catastrophes* (Jackson: University Press of Mississippi, 2010), 48.

2 William Leuchtenburg, *Herbert Hoover* (New York: Times Books, 2009), 32.

3 Lowry, *Washington Close-Up*, 204. Key sources on Hoover and the media include Craig Lloyd, *Aggressive Introvert: A Study of Herbert Hoover and Public Relations Management, 1912–1932* (Columbus: Ohio State University Press, 1972); Fauneil Rinn, "President Hoover's Bad Press," *San Jose Studies*, 1:1 (February 1975), 32–44; Louis Liebovich, *Bylines in Despair: Herbert Hoover, the Great Depression and the U.S. News Media* (Westport, CT: Praeger Publishers, 1994); and Brian Balogh, "Mirrors of Desires: Interest Groups, Elections, and the Targeted Style in Twentieth-Century America," in *The Democratic Experiment: New Directions in American Political History*, ed. Meg Jacobs, William Novak, and Julian Zelizer (Princeton: Princeton University Press, 2003), 222–49.

4 "Again Hoover Does an Emergency Job," *NYTM*, 5/15/1927, SM6; "A Washington Correspondent" [Robert Allen], "The Secretariat," *AMer* (December 1929), 385–95; John Barry, *Rising Tide: The Great Mississippi Flood of 1927* (New York: Simon & Schuster, 1997), 287.

5 Will Irwin, "If You See It in the Paper, It's—," *Collier's*, 8/18/1923, 27; "You Have a Sixth Sense for Truth," *Collier's*, 8/25/1923, 13–14, 27–28. Key sources on Irwin include Robert Hudson, *The Writing Game: A Biography of Will Irwin* (Ames: Iowa State University Press, 1982), and Will Irwin, *The Making of a Reporter* (New York: G. P. Putnam's Sons, 1942).

6 Will Irwin, "Can We Tame the Mississippi?" *World's Work* (August 1927), 407.

7 Will Irwin, *Herbert Hoover: A Reminiscent Biography* (New York: Century Company, 1928).

8 *LAT*, 9/18/1928, 4; *NYT*, 10/3/1928, 6; Joanne Morreale, *The Presidential Campaign Film: A Critical History* (Westport, CT: Praeger Publishers, 1993), 34; *Master of Emergencies*, uploaded to YouTube by the Herbert Hoover Presidential Library, www .youtube.com/watch?v=d12XBYFmGWE.

9 T.R.B., "Washington Notes," *TNR*, 12/5/1928, 67; [Robert Allen], "The Secretariat," 395; Harold Brayman, "Hooverizing the Press," *Outlook and Independent*, 9/24/1930, 123–25, 155–56. The title of press secretary was first applied to Steve Early under Franklin Roosevelt.

10 *NYT*, 1/3/1931, 3.

11 Paul Anderson, "Hoover and the Press," *Nation*, 10/14/1931, 383–84.

12 Abbot, *Watching the World Go By*, 345; Lippmann, "Peculiar Weakness," 6.

13 Essary, "Ballyhoo Men," 419–28; Mordecai Lee, "Government Public Relations During Herbert Hoover's Presidency," *Public Relations Review*, 36:1 (March 2010), 56–58.

14 *WP*, 10/14/1930, 1; *NYT*, 10/19/1930, 29.

15 Frank Parker Stockbridge, "President Hoover Describes His Contacts with the Press," *American Press*, 4/1930, 1, 7; Brandon Rottinghaus, "Limited to Follow: The Early Public Opinion Apparatus of the Herbert Hoover White House," *American Politics Research*, 31:2 (March 2003), 540–56.

16 Bernays to Arthur Woods, 11/28/1930, ELBP, I:397; *WSJ*, 10/25/1930, 2.

17 "Suggested Types of Publicity for Committee's Program"; "Minutes of the First Meeting of the Advisory Committee on Public Relations of the President's Emergency Committee for Employment," 12/2/1930, ELBP, I:396; Will Hays to Arthur Woods, 11/20/1930, ELBP, I:397; William Paley to Woods, 10/25/1930, ELBP, I:8; Radio address, ELBP, I:397.

18 "Relief by Publicity," *Nation*, 11/12/1930, 515; Bliven to Bernays, 2/16/1931, ELBP, I:397.

19 Irwin, *Propaganda*, 290–300, 312; *NYT*, 1/26/1936, BR6.

20 Key sources on Michelson include Charles Michelson, *The Ghost Talks* (New York: G. P. Putnam's Sons, 1944); "Michelson: Rise of a Cynic," *News-Week*, 8/7/1937, 16–17; Frank Kent, "Charley Michelson," *Scribner's* (September 1930), 290–96; Alva Johnston, "Hundred-Tongued Charley, the Great Silent Orator," *SEP*, 5/30/1936, 5–7, 32, 37.

21 Oliver McKee, Jr., "Publicity Chiefs," *North American Review* (October 1930), 411–18; Thomas Barclay, "The Bureau of Publicity of the Democratic National Committee, 1930–1932," *American Political Science Review*, 27:1 (February 1933), 63–65; Irwin, *Propaganda*, 291.

22 Frank Kent, *Political Behavior: The Heretofore Unwritten Laws, Customs and Principles of Politics as Practiced in the United States* (New York: William Morrow, 1928), 261–65; *NYT*, 8/25/1930, 2; *WP*, 8/27/1930, 1, 3.

23 An online search of newspapers found the term *Hooverville* to have originated with the inhabitants of shantytowns in Chicago and St. Louis. Not until the late 1940s did Michelson start getting credit for the coinage. *LAT*, 11/16/1930, A7; *NYT*, 9/27/1931, E5.

PART III: THE AGE OF COMMUNICATION

CHAPTER 20: Tuned to Roosevelt

1 "Address of President Roosevelt by radio," 3/12/1933, FDR-PPF, Box 14. Key sources on the Fireside Chats include Franklin D. Roosevelt, *FDR's Fireside Chats,* ed. Russell Buhite and David Levy (Norman: University of Oklahoma Press, 1992); Lawrence Levine and Cornelia Levine, *The People and the President: America's Conversation with FDR* (Boston: Beacon Press, 2002); and Amos Kiewe, *FDR's First Fireside Chat: Public Confidence and the Banking Crisis* (College Station: Texas A&M University Press, 2007).

2 Joseph Lash, *Dealers and Dreamers: A New Look at the New Deal* (New York: Doubleday, 1988), 277; Grace Tully, *F.D.R., My Boss* (New York: Charles Scribner's Sons, 1949), 100. The first Fireside Chat was given from the Oval Office. *NYT*, 3/19/1933, X8.

3 *WP*, 7/26/1933, 7; Frances Perkins, *The Roosevelt I Knew* (New York: Viking Press, 1946), 72; Samuel Rosenman, *Working with Roosevelt* (New York: Harper, 1952), 93.

4 Daniel Boorstin, "Selling the President to the Public," *Commentary* (November 1955), 425; Creel, *Rebel*, 290.

5 Michelson, *Ghost*, 56–57; Arthur Schlesinger, Jr., *The Age of Roosevelt*. Vol. 2: *The Coming of the New Deal* (Boston: Houghton Mifflin, 1959), 12.

6 *NYT*, 3/19/1933, X8.

7 *LAT*, 3/14/1933, 1; Steel, *Lippmann*, 301.

8 Bruce Barton, "This Magic Called Radio; What Will It Mean in Your Home in the Next Ten Years?" *American Magazine* (June 1922), 72.

9 Robert West, *The Rape of Radio* (New York: Rodin Publ., 1941), 427.

10 Key sources on FDR and the media include Graham White, *FDR and the Press* (Chicago: University of Chicago Press, 1979); Richard Steele, *Propaganda in an Open Society: The Roosevelt Administration and the Media, 1933–1941* (Westport, CT:

Greenwood Press, 1985); and Betty Houchin Winfield, *FDR and the News Media* (Urbana: University of Illinois Press, 1990).

11 Lawrence Sullivan, "Government by Mimeograph," *Atlantic* (March 1938), 306–15; Arthur Krock, "Press vs. Government: A Warning," *Public Opinion Quarterly*, 1:2 (April 1937), 45–49; Gordon Carroll, "Dr. Roosevelt's Propaganda Trust," *AMer* (September 1937), 1–31; Elisha Hanson, "Official Propaganda and the New Deal," *Annals of the American Academy of Political and Social Science*, 179 (May 1935), 176–86; Max Freedman, ed., *Roosevelt and Frankfurter: Their Correspondence, 1928–1945* (Boston: Little, Brown 1967), 214; *WP*, 6/21/1942, B4.

12 Rexford Guy Tugwell, *The Democratic Roosevelt: A Biography of Franklin D. Roosevelt* (Garden City, NY: Doubleday, 1957), 351; Helen Bullitt Lowry, "Political Revolution by Radio," *NYTM*, 7/20/1924, SM1, 14.

13 Saul Bellow, "In the Days of Mr. Roosevelt," in *It All Adds Up: From the Dim Past to the Uncertain Future* (New York: Viking, 1994), 28–29.

14 *WP*, 7/26/1933, 7; "The President Broadcasts," *Broadcasting,* 8/1/1933, 8; Erik Barnouw, *A History of Broadcasting in the United States*. Vol. 2: *The Golden Web: 1933–1953* (New York: Oxford University Press, 1966), 8.

15 Joseph Lash, *Franklin and Eleanor* (New York: Signet Classic, 1973 [1971]), 304; "Campaign: The Squire of Hyde Park," *Time*, 2/1/1932. The myth that the public was oblivious to Roosevelt's disability gained currency with Hugh Gallagher, *FDR's Splendid Deception: The Moving Story of Roosevelt's Massive Disability—And the Intense Efforts to Conceal It from the Public* (New York: Dodd, Mead, 1985). It is debunked in Anne Norton, *Republic of Signs: Liberal Theory and American Popular Culture* (Chicago: University of Chicago Press, 1993) 102–10, and Christopher Clausen, "The President and the Wheelchair," *Wilson Quarterly* (Summer 2005), 24–29.

16 Schlesinger, *Coming of the New Deal*, 559. Key sources on radio throughout the book include Erik Barnouw, *A History of Broadcasting in the United States*, 3 vols. (New York: Oxford University Press, 1966–70); Craig, *Fireside Politics*; David Goodman, *Radio's Civic Ambition: American Broadcasting and Democracy in the 1930s* (New York: Oxford University Press, 2011), 181–215; and Bruce Lenthall, *Radio's America: The Great Depression and the Rise of Modern Mass Culture* (Chicago: University of Chicago Press, 2007), 83–144.

17 Roosevelt, "Fireside Chats," 98–99.

18 Daniel Czitrom, *Media and the American Mind: From Morse to McLuhan* (Chapel Hill: University of North Carolina Press, 1982), 92–121; Jean Quandt, *From the Small Town to the Great Community: The Social Thought of Progressive Intellectuals* (New Brunswick, NJ: Rutgers University Press, 1970), 51–66.

19 *NYT*, 10/28/1928, 139; "Radio—the New Social Force," *Outlook*, 3/19/1924, 465; Eunice Fuller Barnard, "Radio Politics," *TNR*, 3/19/1924, 91; Mildred Adams, "'We the People' Speak," *NYTM*, 6/30/1935, SM9.

20 John Dewey, "The University of the Air," *School and Society*, 12/15/1934, 805.

21 MacLeish to FDR, 4/8/1942, AMP-LC, Box 19; Archibald MacLeish, *The Fall of the City: A Verse Play for Radio* (New York: Farrar & Rinehart, 1937), ix–xiii. Key sources on MacLeish throughout the book include Nancy Benco, "Archibald MacLeish: The Poet Librarian," *Quarterly Journal of the Library of Congress*, 33:3 (July 1976), 233–49; Signi Lenea Falk, *Archibald MacLeish* (New York: Twayne Publishers, 1965); Archibald MacLeish, *Archibald MacLeish: Reflections*, ed. Bernard Drabeck and Helen Ellis (Amherst: University of Massachusetts Press, 1986); Scott Donaldson, *Archibald MacLeish: An American Life* (Boston: Houghton Mifflin, 1992); and John Morton Blum, "Archibald MacLeish: Art for Action," in *Liberty, Justice, Order: Essays on Past Politics* (New York: W. W. Norton, 1993), 227–60.

22 Hadley Cantril and Gordon Allport, *The Psychology of Radio* (New York: Harper & Bros., 1935), 19–22, 31.

CHAPTER 21: Nazism and Propaganda

1 Derrick Sington and Arthur Weidenfeld, *The Goebbels Experiment: A Study of the Nazi Propaganda Machine* (New Haven: Yale University Press, 1943); Ralf Georg Reuth, *Goebbels* (New York: Harcourt, Brace, 1993 [1990]); Toby Thacker, *Joseph Goebbels: Life and Death* (New York: Palgrave Macmillan, 2010).
2 *NYW*, 4/8/1933, in ELBP, I:704; *NYHT*, 2/26/1932, in ELBP, I:703; Miriam Beard, "The Tune Hitlerism Beats for Germany," *NYTM*, 6/7/1931, SM4; *NYT*, 3/19/1933, E1.
3 Adolf Hitler, *Mein Kampf* (New York: Reynal & Hitchcock, 1939 [1925–27]), 230–34.
4 Ibid., 312–13; Hans Herma, "Goebbels' Conception of Propaganda," *Social Research,* 10:1 (Summer 1943), 200–18; Jeffrey Herf, "The 'Jewish War': Goebbels and the Anti-Semitic Campaigns of the Nazi Propaganda Ministry," *Holocaust and Genocide Studies,* 19:1 (Spring 2005), 51–80.
5 David Welch, "Nazi Propaganda and the *Volksgemeinschaft*: Constructing a People's Community," *Journal of Contemporary History,* 39:2 (April 2004), 213; Robert Gellately, *Backing Hitler: Consent and Coercion in Nazi Germany, 1933–1945* (New York: Oxford University Press, 2001).
6 Jeffrey Scott Demsky, "Going Public in Support: American Discursive Opposition to Nazi Anti-Semitism, 1933–1944," PhD diss., University of Florida, 2007; Clayton Laurie, *The Propaganda Warriors: America's Crusade Against Nazi Germany* (Lawrence: University Press of Kansas, 1996).
7 *NYT*, 10/10/1933, 1; Walter Goodman, *The Committee: The Extraordinary Career of the House Committee on Un-American Activities* (New York: Farrar, Straus & Giroux, 1968), 3–23.
8 Special Committee on Un-American Activities, *Investigation of Nazi Propaganda and Investigation of Certain Other Propaganda Activities,* 73rd Cong., 2nd Sess., 11–12/1934 (Washington, DC: Government Printing Office, 1935); Arthur Schlesinger, Jr., *The Age of Roosevelt.* Vol. 3: *The Politics of Upheaval* (Boston: Houghton Mifflin, 1960), 82–84; Philip Jenkins, *Hoods and Shirts: The Extreme Right in Pennsylvania, 1925–1950* (Chapel Hill: University of North Carolina Press, 1997), 114.
9 Ludwig Lore, "Nazi Politics in America," *Nation,* 11/29/1933, 615–17.
10 NYT, 5/18/1934, 1, 3; *NYT,* 7/11/1934, 11.
11 *WP,* 7/15/1934, B4.
12 Quotations in the ensuing paragraphs are from Edward Bernays, *Speak Up for Democracy* (New York: Viking Press, 1940).

CHAPTER 22: The Dark Side of Radio

1 W. H Auden, "September 1, 1939," in *The English Auden: Poems, Essays and Dramatic Writings, 1927–1939,* ed. Edward Mendelson (London: Faber & Faber, 1977), 39.
2 The key source on Long and Coughlin is Alan Brinkley, *Voices of Protest: Huey Long, Father Coughlin, and the Great Depression* (New York: Knopf, 1982).
3 *LAT,* 2/19/1936, 1; Ernest Bormann, "Huey Long: Analysis of a Demagogue," *Today's Speech,* 2:3 (September 1954), 16–20.
4 *NYT,* 5/12/1935, X11; Irwin, *Propaganda,* 249–50; Sigmund Neumann, "The Rule of the Demagogue," *American Sociological Review,* 3:4 (August 1938), 487–98.
5 *LAT,* 4/28/1938, 3.
6 *WP,* 11/13/1938, M8; Cantril, *Invasion,* 58–59.

7   *NYHT*, 11/2/1938, 21.

8   "A Clinical Study of Social Crisis," IPAP, Box 2; Katherine Pandora, "'Mapping the New Mental World Created by Radio': Media Messages, Cultural Politics, and Cantril and Allport's *The Psychology of Radio*," *Journal of Social Issues*, 54:1 (Spring 1998), 22.

9   Filene died shortly before the institute was launched. Key sources on the institute include William Stott, *Documentary Expression and Thirties America* (Chicago: University of Chicago Press, 1973), 22–25; Sproule, *Propaganda and Democracy*, 129–77; and Goodman, *Civic Ambition*, 247–53.

10 "Minutes of the First Meeting of the Board of Trustees of the Institute for Propaganda Analysis, Inc.," 2/10/1940; "Speakers Bureau, Institute for Propaganda Analysis," IPAP, Box 1; Cantril to Miller, 2/1/1938, Miller to Cantril, 2/2/1938, IPAP, Box 2; "The Public Relations Counsel and Propaganda," *Propaganda Analysis*, 1:11 (August 1938), 62; "Education: Propaganda Battle," *Time*, 1/24/1938, 28.

11 "Announcement," *Propaganda Analysis*, 1:1 (October 1937), 1–2.

12 "How to Detect Propaganda," *Propaganda Analysis*, 1:2 (November 1937), 1–4.

13 "The Attack on Democracy," *Propaganda Analysis*, 2:4 (January 1939), 1–16; "Father Coughlin: Priest and Politician," *Propaganda Analysis*, 2:9 (June 1939), 1–12.

14 "Communist Propaganda, U.S.A., 1939 Model," *Propaganda Analysis*, 2:6 (March 1939), 1–11; Cantril to Miller, 2/2/1939, IPAP, Box 2; Paul Douglas to Miller, 11/30/1938, IPAP, Box 2; *NYT*, 2/22/1941, 1.

15 Edgar Dale to Miller, 1/24/1938, and Edgar Dale, article draft, IPAP, Box 2; "The Movies and Propaganda," *Propaganda Analysis*, 1:6 (March 1938), 1–4; Bernard DeVoto, "The Fallacy of Excess Interpretation," *Harper's* (June 1938), 109–12; Miller to DeVoto, 5/27/1938, IPAP, Box 1.

16 *NYT*, 2/21/1941, 1; Max Lerner, "Propaganda in Our Time," review of Harold Lavine and James Wechsler's *War Propaganda and the United States*, TNR, 8/26/1940, 281–82.

17 Allan Nevins, "Propaganda: An Explosive Word Analyzed," *NYTM*, 10/29/1939, SM2; Kenneth Cmiel, "On Cynicism, Evil, and the Discovery of Communication in the 1940s," *Journal of Communication*, 46:3 (Summer 1996), 91–92; Lewis Mumford, *Values for Survival* (New York: Harcourt, Brace & Co., 1946), 39n.

18 Lerner, "Propaganda in Our Time," 282.

19 Eisinger, *Evolution*, 42; Paul Douglas to Miller, 5/7/1941, IPAP, Box 1; *NYT*, 5/31/1941, 13; Cantril to Lee, 5/30/1941, IPAP, Box 2; "We Say Au Revoir," *Propaganda Analysis*, 4:13 (January 1942), 1–6.

CHAPTER 23: Campaigns, Inc.

1   Key sources on Whitaker and Baxter include Carey McWilliams, "Government by Whitaker and Baxter," *Nation*, 4/14, 4/21, and 5/5/1951; Stanley Kelley, *Professional Public Relations and Political Power* (Baltimore: Johns Hopkins University Press, 1956); Robert Pitchell, "The Influence of Professional Campaign Management Firms in Partisan Elections in California," *Western Political Quarterly*, 11:2 (June 1958), 278–300; Irwin Ross, "Whitaker and Baxter: The Supersalesmen of California Politics," *Harper's* (July 1959), 55–61; and Irwin Ross, *The Image Merchants: The Fabulous World of Public Relations* (Garden City, NY: Doubleday, 1959), 65–83.

2   Key sources on the 1934 race include Creel, *Rebel*; Upton Sinclair, *I, Candidate for Governor: And How I Got Licked,* intro. by James Gregory (Berkeley: University of California Press, 1994 [1935]); Charles Larsen, "The Epic Campaign of 1934," *Pacific Historical Review*, 27:2 (May 1958), 127–31; Greg Mitchell, *The Campaign of the Century: Upton Sinclair's Race for Governor of California and the Birth of Media Politics* (New York: Random House, 1992); and Arthur, *Radical Innocent*.

3   George Creel, "What Roosevelt Intends to Do," *Collier's*, 3/11/1933, 7–9, 34–36.
4   *LAT*, 8/24/1934, A4; *WP*, 8/30/1934, 1.
5   Steel, *Lippmann*, 313; Schlesinger, *Upheaval*, 116; *LAT*, 9/24/1934, A1; *LAT*, 10/25/1934, 1; *NYT*, 10/27/1934, 1.
6   Cruikshank and Schultz, *The Man Who Sold America*, 299–301.
7   *CT*, 8/30/1934, 1.
8   *WP*, 6/6/1949, 7; *NYT*, 11/12/1949, 13.
9   Clem Whitaker, "The Public Relations of Election Campaigns," *Public Relations Journal*, 2:7 (July 1946), 7–8; William Lee Miller, "Can Government Be 'Merchandised'?" *Reporter*, 10/27/1953, 12; Leone Baxter, "Public Relations Precocious Baby," *Public Relations Journal*, 6:1 (January 1950), 7–8.

CHAPTER 24: The Wizard of Washington

1   Schlesinger, *Upheaval*, 242–47; Brinkley, *Voices*, 207–09, 284–86. Key sources on Emil Hurja include "Roosevelt, Farley & Co.," *Time*, 3/2/1936, 16–17; Thomas Sugrue, "Emil Hurja: Farley's Guess Man," *American Magazine* (May 1936), 22–23, 87–91; Alva Johnston, "Prof. Hurja, the New Deal's Political Doctor," *SEP*, 6/13/1936, 8–9; and Melvin Holli, *The Wizard of Washington: Emil Hurja, Franklin Roosevelt, and the Birth of Public Opinion Polling* (New York: Palgrave, 2002).
2   James Farley memo, 6/18/1935, Reel 1, Box 38, JAFP.
3   Franklin D. Roosevelt: "Message to Congress on Tax Revision," 6/19/1935, http://www.presidency.ucsb.edu/ws/?pid=15088; James Farley, *Jim Farley's Story: The Roosevelt Years* (New York: Whittlesey House, 1948), 51; *AC*, 5/3/1935, 21; *LAT*, 5/19/1935, A5; William Leuchtenburg, *Franklin D. Roosevelt and the New Deal, 1932–1940* (New York: Harper & Row, 1963), 152–54.
4   Lela Stiles, *The Man Behind Roosevelt: The Story of Louis McHenry Howe* (Cleveland: World Publishing, 1954), 197.
5   Leila Sussmann, *Dear FDR: A Study of Political Letter-Writing* (Totowa, NJ: Bedminster Press, 1963), 9–10, 61–64; Smith, *Dear Mr. President*, 213–15; Delbert Clark, "The President's Listening-In Machine," *NYTM*, 9/1/1935, SM3.
6   Hurja to FDR, 5/27/1936, PPF 2099; Memorandum, 4/17/1937, PPF 2099.
7   Untitled memorandum, Box 121, EHP.
8   Tom Smith, "The First Straw? A Study of the Origins of Election Polls," *Public Opinion Quarterly*, 54:1 (Spring 1990), 21–36; Richard Jensen, "Democracy by the Numbers," *Public Opinion*, 3:1a (February–March 1980), 54, 58.
9   "Gains in Montana . . . ," 9/12/1932, Box 69, EHP; "New England States . . . ," 10/12/1932, Box 69, EHP; E. Edward Hurja, "Analysis and Conclusions of 1932 Election Statistics," 11/3/1932, Box 77, EHP.
10 Press release, 11/4/1932, Box 69, EHP.
11 James Farley memo, 3/17/1934, JAFP, Reel 1, Box 37; *AC*, 8/2/1934, 2.
12 *WP*, 11/8/1934, 2; "Roosevelt, Farley & Co.," *Time*, 3/2/1936, 16–17.
13 *NYT*, 10/25/1936, E3.
14 Black leatherette binder, Box 73, EHP; Memorandum regarding black leatherette binder, FDR-PPF 2099.
15 *NYT*, 3/14/1937, E2.

CHAPTER 25: The Road to War

1   Richard Steele, "The Great Debate: Roosevelt, the Media, and the Coming of the War, 1940–1941," *Journal of American History*, 71:1 (June 1984), 69–92. Key sources on

FDR's decision to go to war are Robert Dallek, *Franklin D. Roosevelt and American Foreign Policy, 1932–1945* (New York: Oxford University Press, 1979), and Steven Casey, *Cautious Crusade: Franklin D. Roosevelt, American Public Opinion, and the War Against Nazi Germany* (New York: Oxford University Press, 2001).

2 Key sources on polling throughout the book include Jean Converse, *Survey Research in the United States: Roots and Emergence, 1890–1960* (Berkeley: University of California Press, 1987); David Moore, *The Superpollsters: How They Measure and Manipulate Public Opinion in America* (New York: Four Walls Eight Windows, 1995 [1992]); and Robert Eisinger, *The Evolution of Presidential Polling* (New York: Cambridge University Press, 2003).

3 Elmo Roper, *You and Your Leaders, Their Actions and Your Reactions, 1936–1956* (New York: William Morrow, 1957), 71; Richard Steele, "The Pulse of the People: Franklin D. Roosevelt and the Gauging of American Public Opinion," *Journal of Contemporary History*, 9:4 (October 1974), 206–07.

4 On FDR's third term decision, see Richard Moe, *Roosevelt's Second Act: The Election of 1940 and the Politics of War* (New York: Oxford University Press, 2013), 170–97.

5 Hadley Cantril, "The Bombardment of Ballots," *NYTM*, 6/14/1936, SM6. Key sources on Cantril include Gerard Lambert, *All Out of Step: A Personal Chronicle* (New York: Doubleday, 1956); Hadley Cantril, *The Human Dimension: Experiences in Policy Research* (New Brunswick, NJ: Rutgers University Press, 1967); Robert Eisinger and Jeremy Brown, "Polling as a Means Toward Presidential Autonomy: Emil Hurja, Hadley Cantril and the Roosevelt Administration," *International Journal of Public Opinion Research*, 10:3 (Autumn 1998), 237–56; and Albert Cantril, "Hadley Cantril: Perception, Polling, and Policy Research," *Society*, 44:3 (March–April 2007), 67–68.

6 Hadley Cantril, "America Faces the War: A Study in Public Opinion," *Public Opinion Quarterly*, 4:3 (September 1940), 387–88, 405.

7 Steel, *Lippmann*, 387–88.

8 Robert Burke, "Election of 1940," in Schlesinger and Israel, *Elections*, vol. 7, 2944.

9 Franklin Roosevelt, Press Conference, 12/17/1940, http://www.presidency.ucsb.edu/ws/index.php?pid=15913.

10 Robert Sherwood, *Roosevelt and Hopkins: An Intimate History* (New York: Harper, 1950), 226; James MacGregor Burns, *Roosevelt: The Soldier of Freedom* (New York: Harcourt Brace Jovanovich, 1970), 26–27.

11 David Niles to Grace Tully, 11/11/1942, FDR-PPF, Box 8229; Rosenman to Tully, 10/28/1943, SIRP, Box 14.

12 Hadley Cantril to Samuel Rosenman, 11/16/1943, SIRP, Box 14.

13 Franklin Roosevelt, "Statement on General MacArthur's Departure from the Philippines," 3/17/1942, at http://www.presidency.ucsb.edu/ws/index.php?pid=16237; FDR to Cantril, 11/12/1942; "Memorandum for the President," 12/15/1942, FDRL-PPF, Box 8229.

14 Hadley Cantril and Gerald Lambert, "Some Results from a Public Opinion Survey, Completed March 16, 1944"; Cantril to Rosenman, 9/15/1944; and other correspondence, SIRP, Box 14; Cantril to Frank Walker, 5/8/1944, PPF 8229; Harry Hopkins, "We Can Win in 1945," *American Magazine* (October 1943), 22–23, 99–100.

15 Cantril to Rosenman, 3/18/1944, Rosenman to Cantril, 3/20/1944, SIRP, Box 14; *NYT*, 3/5/1944, 19.

CHAPTER 26: The Facts and Figures of Archibald MacLeish

1 "Draft of a Speech to Be Delivered by Archibald MacLeish at Freedom House, Thursday, March 19, 1942," FDR-OF 4619.

2 In "Politics," a poem reminiscent of "Ars Poetica" in its resolute commitment to art, Yeats wrote: "And maybe what they say is true/Of war and war's alarms/But O that I were young again/And held her in my arms."

3 Frederick Stielow, "Librarian Warriors and Rapprochement: Carl Milam, Archibald MacLeish, and World War II," *Libraries and Culture,* 25:4 (Fall 1990), 520.

4 Archibald MacLeish, "The Irresponsibles," *Nation,* 5/18/1940, 618–23; Archibald MacLeish, "Post-War Writers and Pre-War Readers," *TNR,* 6/10/1940, 789–90.

5 Edmund Wilson, "Archibald MacLeish and 'the Word,'" *TNR,* 7/1/1940, 30–32; James T. Farrell, "On the Brooks-MacLeish Thesis," *PR* (January–February 1942), 38–47; Dwight Macdonald, "Kulturbolschewismus Is Here," *PR,* 11–12/1941, 442–51; Burton Rascoe, "The Tough-Muscle Boys of Literature," *AMer* (November 1940), 369–74; Malcolm Cowley, "Poets and Prophets," *TNR,* 5/5/1941, 639–40.

6 MacLeish to FDR, 9/29/1941, AMP-LC, Box 52; *NYT,* 10/8/1941, 1.

7 LaGuardia to FDR, 7/9/1941, AMP-LC, Box 52; FDR to LaGuardia, 7/14/1941, AMP-LC, Box 52; "The History of the Office of Facts and Figures," 9/23/1943, AMP-LC, Box 52; *NYT,* 12/16/1940, 1; newspaper clippings in ELBP, Box I:701.

8 *NYT,* 10/26/1941, 26; Executive Order 8922 Establishing the Office of Facts and Figures, at http://www.presidency.ucsb.edu/ws/index.php?pid=16024; MacLeish to FDR, 10/28/1941, AMP-LC, Box 19; *NYT,* 10/9/1941, 22. Key sources on the Office of Facts and Figures include Allan Winkler, *The Politics of Propaganda: The Office of War Information, 1942–1945* (New Haven: Yale University Press, 1978); John Morton Blum, *V Was for Victory: Politics and American Culture During World War II* (New York: Harcourt Brace Jovanovich, 1976); Clayton Koppes and Gregory Black, *Hollywood Goes to War: How Politics, Profits, and Propaganda Shaped World War II Movies* (New York: Free Press, 1989); and Gerd Horten, *Radio Goes to War: The Cultural Politics of Propaganda During World War II* (Berkeley: University of California Press, 2002).

9 *NYT,* 1/21/1941, 2.

10 "Sixth Draft: Inaugural Address, January 20, 1941," AMP-LC, Box 49; Frank Kluckhohn, "The Men Around the President," *NYTM,* 3/29/1942, SM9.

11 "Propaganda, Good and Bad: A Radio Discussion," 3/1/1942, AMP-LC, Box 43.

12 MacLeish, "The Strategy of Truth," 28.

CHAPTER 27: Propaganda and the "Good War"

1 "Office of Facts and Figures," 8/22/1941, AMP-LC, Box 52.

2 FDR to MacLeish, 12/2/1941, FDR-OF 4619; MacLeish to FDR, 1/14/1942, FDR-OF 4619; MacLeish to Grace Tully, 1/10/1942, FDR-OF 4619; "Victory Program, Book 5," HHP, Box 312; MacLeish to Harry Hopkins, 12/31/1941, HHP, Box 312.

3 FDR to Early, 12/30/1941, FDR-OF 4619; Early to MacLeish, 1/5/1942, FDR-OF 4619; MacLeish to FDR, 4/10/1942, AMP-LC, Box 19.

4 W. B. Lewis to MacLeish, 1/31/1942, AMP-LC, Box 43; FDR to MacLeish, 2/12/1942 AMP-LC, Box 19; MacLeish to FDR, 4/8/1942, AMP-LC, Box 19.

5 MacLeish to FDR, 1/2/1942, OF 4619; "American Propaganda Policy: Action, Analysis," AMP-LC, Box 52; Alan Barth, "The Bureau of Intelligence," *Public Opinion Quarterly,* 7:1 (Spring 1943), 66–76. The Office of Censorship, established after Pearl Harbor, censored military information and transmissions to and from foreign audiences; it did not censor domestic political opinion. See Michael Sweeney, *Secrets of Victory: The Office of Censorship and the American Press and Radio in World War II* (Chapel Hill: University of North Carolina Press, 2001).

6 *NYT,* 10/9/1941, 22; *CT,* 1/22/1942, 10.

7 "Address To Be Given by Archibald MacLeish Before Luncheon of American Soci-

ety of Newspaper Editors in New York City, 4/17/1942," AMP-LC, Box 46; *NYT*, 4/18/1942, 13.

8   *NYT*, 1/16/1942, 15; *CT*, 10/9/1941, 17.

9   "The History of the Office of Facts and Figures," 9/23/1943, AMP-LC, Box 52; MacLeish to FDR, 4/11/1942, Box 19, AMP-LC; *NYT*, 1/12/1942, 10.

10   MacLeish to FDR, 9/29/1941, AMP-LC, Box 52.

11   *CT*, 10/9/1941, 17; Cmiel, "On Cynicism," 91–95.

12   FDR to MacLeish, 2/12/1942, AMP-LC, Box 19; MacLeish to FDR, 2/25/1942, AMP-LC, Box 52; MacLeish to Harold Smith, 2/20/1942, AMP-LC, Box 52; *NYT*, 2/20/1942, 9.

13   *NYT*, 6/14/1942, 31; *NYT*, 6/14/1942, 1.

14   Press release, AMP-LC, Box 18; Malcolm Cowley, "The Sorrows of Elmer Davis," *TNR*, 5/3/1943, 591–93; Winkler, *Politics of Propaganda*, 39; Sydney Weinberg, "What to Tell America: The Writers' Quarrel in the Office of War Information," *Journal of American History*, 55:1 (June 1968), 73–89.

15   *WP*, 6/21/1942, B4.

PART IV: THE AGE OF NEWS MANAGEMENT

CHAPTER 28: The Underestimation of Harry Truman

1   Key sources on Truman include Herbert Lee Williams, *The Newspaperman's President: Harry S. Truman* (Chicago: Nelson-Hall, 1984); David McCullough, *Truman* (New York: Simon & Schuster, 1992); Franklin Mitchell, *Harry S. Truman and the News Media: Contentious Relations, Belated Respect* (Columbia: University of Missouri Press, 1998); and Zachary Karabell, *The Last Campaign: How Harry Truman Won the 1948 Election* (New York: Knopf, 2000).

2   Paul Boyer, *By the Bomb's Early Light: American Thought and Culture at the Dawn of the Atomic Age* (Chapel Hill: University of North Carolina Press, 1994 [1985]), 4. The key source on Page is Noel Griese, *Arthur W. Page: Publisher, Public Relations Pioneer, Patriot* (Atlanta: Anvil Publ., 2001).

3   AWP-OH, 58–59.

4   Harry S. Truman, "Statement by the President Announcing the Use of the A-Bomb at Hiroshima," 8/6/1945, http://www.presidency.ucsb.edu/ws/?pid=12169.

5   Alonzo Hamby, *Liberalism and Its Challengers* (New York: Oxford University Press, 1992 [1985]), 53; Clifton Truman Daniel, "Adventures with Grandpa Truman," *Prologue*, 41:1 (Spring 2009).

6   "How U.S. Tries to Influence You," *USNWR*, 6/15/1951, 18–19.

7   "Mr. Truman's White House," *Fortune* (February 1952), 78; *WP*, 1/17/1953, 8.

8   Elmer Cornwell, "The Presidential Press Conference: A Study in Institutionalization," *Midwest Journal of Political* Science, 4:4 (November 1960), 380; *NYT*, 2/12/1955, 8; *NYT*, 2/13/1955, 213.

9   JLR-OH, 8–15; J. Leonard Reinsch, *Getting Elected: From Radio and Roosevelt to Television and Reagan* (New York: Hippocrene Books, 1988), 13, 17.

10   *WP*, 5/4/1947, S5; *NYT*, 7/13/1947, 26; Reinsch, *Getting Elected*, 38.

11   Rick Shenkman, "Television, Democracy and Presidential Politics," in *The Columbia History of Post-World War II America*, ed. Mark Carnes (New York: Columbia University Press, 2007), 262–63; Philip Hamburger, "Television: Back to Chicago," *TNY*, 8/2/1952, 38–40; Amy Loveman, "Town Meeting by Oscillation," *SR*, 8/9/1952, 20.

12   Raymond Carroll, "The 1948 Truman Campaign: The Threshold of the Modern Era," *Journal of Broadcasting*, 24:2 (Spring 1980), 178; Mike Conway, "Before the Blog-

gers: The Upstart News Technology of Television at the 1948 Political Conventions," *American Journalism*, 24:1 (Winter 2007), 35, 38, 47.

13 *NYT*, 7/18/1948, X7; Reinsch, *Getting Elected*, 33.

CHAPTER 29: George Gallup's Democracy

1 "The Black and White Beans," *Time*, 5/3/1948, 21–23; *CSM*, 9/2/1947, 5; Paul Sheatsley, "The Founding of AAPOR," in *A Meeting Place: The History of the American Association for Public Opinion Research*, ed. Paul Sheatsley and Warren Mitofsky (Ann Arbor, MI: American Association for Public Opinion Research, 1992), 41–62.

2 *NYT*, 7/19/1936, 21; Williston Rich, "The Human Yardstick," *SEP*, 1/1/1939, 66.

3 George Gallup, "Polls and Prophets," *Current History and Forum*, 11/7/1940, 12–14. Gallup's theory about the *Digest*'s errors was endorsed by public opinion scholar Rensis Likert, and later widely popularized, but is now considered doubtful. See Rensis Likert, "Public Opinion Polls," *Scientific American* (December 1948), 7–11; Darrell Huff, *How to Lie with Statistics* (New York: W. W. Norton, 1954); Maurice Bryson, "The Literary Digest Poll: Making of a Statistical Myth," *American Statistician*, 30:4 (November 1976), 184–85; and Peverill Squire, "Why the 1936 Literary Digest Poll Failed," *Public Opinion Quarterly*, 52:1 (Spring 1988), 125–33.

4 Quotations in the ensuing paragraph come from George Gallup and Saul Forbes Rae, *The Pulse of Democracy: The Public-Opinion Poll and How It Works* (New York: Simon & Schuster, 1940).

5 Rae left polling to become a diplomat—Daniel Robinson, *The Measure of Democracy: Polling, Market Research, and Public Life, 1930–1945* (Toronto: University of Toronto Press, 1999), 3.

6 George Gallup, "The Changing Climate for Public Opinion Research," *Public Opinion Quarterly*, 21:1 (Spring 1957), 26.

7 Harry Truman, *Memoirs. Vol. 2: Years of Trial and Hope* (Garden City, NY: Doubleday, 1956), 177, 196; Truman, *Off the Record*, 310.

8 Brandon Rottinghaus, "Reassessing Public Opinion Polling in the Truman Administration," *Presidential Studies Quarterly*, 33:2 (June 2003), 330–31.

9 Raymond Carroll, "Harry S. Truman's 1948 Election: The Inadvertent Broadcast Campaign," *Journal of Broadcasting & Electronic Media*, 31:2 (Spring 1987), 121, 125–27; Harrison Summers, "Radio in the 1948 Campaign," *Quarterly Journal of Speech*, 34:4 (December 1948), 433. Dewey had media advisers too, including Gallup, Barton, and adman Rosser Reeves, but Truman turned this against Dewey, denouncing the "expensive Republican propaganda" as hokum to be ignored.

10 "The *Fortune* Survey," *Fortune* (October 1948), 29–32; Susan Herbst, *Numbered Voices: How Opinion Polling Has Shaped American Politics* (Chicago: University of Chicago Press, 1993), 110. Given magazines' lead time before publication, Roper had taken his last soundings before Truman began his tour—Robert Cobb Myers, "Opinion Polls and Public Policy," *Commentary* (November 1948), 475.

11 T.R.B., "Washington Wire," *TNR*, 11/15/1948, 3–4.

12 Rensis Likert, "The Polls: Straw Votes or Scientific Instruments," *American Psychologist*, 3:12 (December 1948), 556–57; Rensis Likert, "Why Opinion Polls Were So Wrong," *USNWR*, 11/12/1948, 24–25; *NYT*, 11/4/1948, 8; Samuel Lubell, "Who *Really* Elected Truman?" *SEP*, 1/22/1949, 15–17, 54–64.

13 On this debate, see Jerome Spingarn, "These Public-Opinion Polls," *Harper's* (December 1938), 97–104; Albert Blankenship, "Public Opinion Polls: A Symposium," *Journal of Marketing*, 5:2 (October 1940), 110–13; "Polls, Propaganda, and Democracy," *Propaganda Analysis*, 11/11/1940, 1–5; John Ranney, "Do the Polls Serve Democracy?"

Public Opinion Quarterly, 10:3 (Autumn 1946), 349–60; and Robert Cobb Myers, "Opinion Polls and Public Policy," *Commentary* (November 1948), 475–82.

14 Edward Bernays, "Attitude Polls—Servants or Masters?" *Public Opinion Quarterly,* 9:3 (Autumn 1945), 264–68. On congressional action against pollsters, see Walter Pierce, "Climbing on the Bandwagon," *Public Opinion Quarterly,* 4:2 (June 1940), 241–42; George Lewis, Jr., "The Congressmen Look at Polls," *Public Opinion Quarterly,* 4:2 (June 1940), 230; *WP,* 12/1/1944, 5; *WP,* 12/15/1944, 5; Benjamin Ginzburg, "Dr. Gallup on the Mat," *Nation,* 12/16/1944, 737–39; *WP,* 12/24/1944, B4; Martin Kriesberg, "What Congressmen and Administrators Think of the Polls," *Public Opinion Quarterly,* 9:3 (Autumn 1945), 333–37; and J. K. Javits, "How I Used a Poll in Campaigning for Congress," *Public Opinion Quarterly,* 11:2 (Summer 1947), 222–26.

15 Lindsay Rogers, "Do the Gallup Polls Measure Opinion?" *Harper's* (November 1941), 623–32; *NYT,* 11/28/1970, 29; Amy Fried, "The Forgotten Lindsay Rogers and the Development of American Political Science," *American Political Science Review,* 100:4 (November 2006), 555; Amy Fried, "Creator of *The Pollsters*: Lindsay Rogers and the Democratic Implications of Polling and Deliberation." Paper delivered at the 2005 Annual Meeting of the American Political Science Association, Sept. 1–4, Washington, DC. In the author's possession.

16 George Gallup, "A Reply to 'The Pollsters,'" *Public Opinion Quarterly,* 13:1 (Spring 1949), 179–80. Quotations in the ensuing paragraphs come from Lindsay Rogers, *The Pollsters: Public Opinion, Politics and Democratic Leadership* (New York: Knopf, 1949).

17 Other flaws would come to light years later. My father, born in 1934, tells of how as a child he was asked by his mother to invent answers to questionnaires she had to complete for the dairy industry. She would pose the questions over and over and he would give different answers according to his whim. On the unreliability of these poorly paid, non-professional workers, see Sarah Igo, "A Gold Mine and a Tool for Democracy: George Gallup, Elmo Roper, and the Business of Scientific Polling, 1935–1955," *Journal of the History of the Behavioral Sciences,* 42: 2 (Spring 2006), 109–34.

18 Walter Lippmann, *Essays in the Public Philosophy* (Boston: Little, Brown, 1955), 42–43.

19 Fried, "Forgotten Lindsay Rogers," 555–61; Eric Goldman, "Poll on the Polls," *Public Opinion Quarterly,* 8:4 (Winter 1944–45), 461–67.

20 Jensen, "Democracy by the Numbers," 59. On continuing doubts about polling, see, e.g., Christopher Hitchens, "Voting in the Passive Voice," *Harper's* (April 1992), 45–52.

CHAPTER 30: Psychological Warfare

1 Harry Truman, "Address on Foreign Policy at a Luncheon of the American Society of Newspaper Editors," 4/20/1950, http://www.presidency.ucsb.edu/ws/index.php?pid=13768; Sidney Hyman, *The Lives of William Benton* (Chicago: University of Chicago Press, 1969), 306–08. Key sources on psychological warfare include Walter Hixson, *Parting the Curtain: Propaganda, Culture and the Cold War, 1945–1961* (Houndmills, UK: Macmillan, 1997); Kenneth Osgood, *Total Cold War: Eisenhower's Secret Propaganda Battle at Home and Abroad* (Lawrence: University Press of Kansas, 2006); and Nicholas Cull, *The Cold War and the United States Information Agency: American Propaganda and Public Diplomacy, 1945–1989* (New York: Cambridge University Press, 2008).

2 Steel, *Lippmann,* 423. On the Voice of America, see Holly Cowan Shulman, *The Voice of America: Propaganda and Democracy, 1941–1945* (Madison: University of Wisconsin Press, 1990), and David Krugler, *The Voice of America and the Domestic Propaganda Battles, 1945–1953* (Columbia: University of Missouri Press, 2000).

3   John Henderson, *The United States Information Agency* (New York: Praeger Publishers, 1969), 40.

4   Hyman, *Benton*, 382–83.

5   Nancy Bernhard, *U.S. Television News and Cold War Propaganda, 1947–1960* (New York: Cambridge University Press, 1999), 86, 117, 140–41. The Smith-Mundt Act's prohibition on domestic propaganda remained on the books until 2013—John Hudson, "U.S. Repeals Propaganda Ban, Spreads Government-Made News to Americans," *Foreign Policy.com*, 7/14/2013.

6   Key sources on C. D. Jackson include Blanche Wiesen Cook, "First Comes the Lie: C. D. Jackson and Political Warfare," *Radical History Review,* 31 (December 1984), 42–70; H. W. Brands, "C. D. Jackson: Psychological Warriors Never Die," in *Cold Warriors: Eisenhower's Generation and American Foreign Policy* (New York: Columbia University Press, 1988), 117–37; and Ned O'Gorman, "The One Word the Kremlin Fears: C. D. Jackson, Cold War 'Liberation,' and American Political-Economic Adventurism," *Rhetoric & Public Affairs,* 12:3 (Fall 2009), 389–427.

7   Arthur Schlesinger, Jr., "Psychological Warfare: Can It Sell Freedom?" *Reporter*, 3/31/1953, 9–12.

8   Shawn Parry-Giles, *The Rhetorical Presidency, Propaganda, and the Cold War, 1945–1953* (Westport, CT: Praeger Publishers, 2002), 53.

9   Griese, *Arthur W. Page*, 360–65. On the Crusade for Freedom, see also Stacey Cone, "Presuming a Right to Deceive: Radio Free Europe, Radio Liberty, the CIA and the News Media," *Journalism History*, 24:4 (Winter 1998–99), 148–55.

10 C. D. Jackson, "Psychological Warfare," *Vital Speeches*, 11/15/1951, 71–73.

11 George Gallup, "What We Don't Know *Can* Hurt Us," *NYTM*, 11/4/1951, SM12, 50.

12 George Gallup, "Why We Are Doing So Badly in the Ideological War," *Vital Speeches*, 6/1/1952, 501–04; George Gallup, "The Battle We Are Losing," *Look*, 12/2/1952, 101; *WP*, 4/2/1953, 6; J. Michael Hogan, "The Science of Cold War Strategy: Propaganda and Public Opinion in the Eisenhower Administration's 'War of Words,'" in *Critical Reflections on the Cold War: Linking Rhetoric and History*, ed. Martin Medhurst and H. W. Brands (College Station: Texas A&M Press, 2000), 134–35.

13 Emmet John Hughes, *The Ordeal of Power: A Political Memoir of the Eisenhower Years* (New York: Dell, 1963 [1962]), 21; Dwight Eisenhower, *Mandate for Change, 1953–1956: The White House Years* (Garden City, NY: Doubleday, 1963), 72–73.

CHAPTER 31: Eisenhower Answers America

1   Key sources on Eisenhower include Hughes, *Ordeal of Power*; Eisenhower, *Mandate for Change*; Herbert Parmet, *Eisenhower and the American Crusades* (New York: Macmillan, 1972); and Jean Edward Smith, *Eisenhower in War and Peace* (New York: Random House, 2012).

2   LRG-OH, 63–64; Bruce Bliven, "Politics and TV," *Harper's* (November 1952), 27. Key sources on Eisenhower and the media are Sig Mickelson, *The Electric Mirror: Politics in an Age of Television* (New York: Dodd, Mead, 1972), and Craig Allen, *Eisenhower and the Mass Media: Peace, Prosperity, & Prime-Time TV* (Chapel Hill: University of North Carolina Press, 1993). An additional key source on postwar presidential press relations throughout the book is James Deakin, *Straight Stuff: The Reporters, the White House, and the Truth* (New York: William Morrow, 1984).

3   SL-OH, 26–27; Henry Cabot Lodge, *The Storm Has Many Eyes: A Personal Narrative* (New York: W. W. Norton, 1973), 109; Kathryn Cramer Brownell, "Showbiz Politics: Hollywood in American Politics," PhD diss., Boston University, 2011, 201.

4 Larmon to Eisenhower, 7/18/1952, WERP, Box 9. Key sources on TV and the 1952 race are Noel Griese, "Rosser Reeves and the 1952 Eisenhower TV Spot Blitz," *Journal of Advertising*, 4:4 (Autumn 1975), 34–38; John Hollitz, "Eisenhower and the Admen: The Television 'Spot' Campaign of 1952," *Wisconsin Magazine of History*, 66:1 (Autumn 1982), 25–39; Steve Barkin, "Eisenhower's Secret Strategy: Television Planning in the 1952 Campaign," *Journal of Advertising History*, 9:1 (December 1986), 18–28; Stephen Wood, "Television's First Political Spot Ad Campaign: Eisenhower Answers America," *Presidential Studies Quarterly*, 20:2 (Spring 1990), 265–83; and David Halberstam, *The Fifties* (New York: Villard Books, 1993).

5 Barton to Carle Conway, 6/9/1952, BBP, Box 13; SL-OH, 27–29; *NYT*, 6/15/1952, 1, 50; *NYT*, 6/16/1952, 16.

6 SL-OH, 27. By September, wrote Emmet Hughes, the speechwriting shop in the east corridor of the ninth floor of the Hotel Commodore buzzed with "draftsmen, researchers, stenographers, mimeographers, teletypists, who would help piece together all of the candidate's appeal to his listening electorate"—Hughes, *Ordeal*, 20–21.

7 Lodge, *The Storm*, 87, 99; Charles Kelly, *Tex McCrary: Wars, Women, Politics; An Adventurous Life Across the American Century* (Lanham, MD: Hamilton Books, 2009), 134–35; *WP*, 2/8/1952, C15; *NYT*, 2/11/1952, 31.

8 *NYT*, 9/23/1952, 14; Kelley, *Professional Public Relations*, 150. Additional key sources on campaign advertising throughout the postwar era include Edwin Diamond and Stephen Bates, *The Spot: The Rise of Political Advertising on Television*, rev. ed. (Cambridge: MIT Press, 1988 [1984]), and Kathleen Hall Jamieson, *Packaging the Presidency: A History and Criticism of Presidential Campaign Advertising*, 3rd ed. (New York: Oxford University Press, 1996).

9 *NYT*, 1/25/1984, A18.

10 Martin Mayer, *Madison Avenue, U.S.A.* (New York: Harper & Bros., 1958), 294.

11 Michael Levin, "How to Insure an Eisenhower Victory in November," 8/18/1952, "Program to Guarantee an Eisenhower Victory," RRP, Box 19; Kelley, *Professional Public Relations*, 189.

12 William Lee Miller, "Can Government Be 'Merchandised'?" *Reporter*, 10/27/1953, 14.

13 Michael Levin, "How to Insure an Eisenhower Victory in November," 8/18/1952, "Program to Guarantee an Eisenhower Victory," RRP, Box 19. The full list of spots appears in Wood, "Eisenhower Answers America," 275–79. Television spots from the 1952 campaign and others are at http://www.livingroomcandidate.org/.

14 Mayer, *Madison Avenue*, 297; Gordon Cotler, "That Plague of Spots from Madison Avenue," *Reporter*, 11/25/1952, 7–8. According to Wood, Reeves later denied that Eisenhower wrote any ads—Wood, "Eisenhower Answers America," 271.

15 Alman Taranton to Walter Thayer, 10/3/1952, RRP, Box 19; Miss Erickson, Mrs. Omrod, and Mrs. Somerville to Alman Taranton, 10/2/1952, RRP, Box 19.

16 Theodore H. White, *The Making of the President, 1960* (New York: Harper Perennial, 2009 [1961]), 47.

17 Alden Whitman, *Portrait—Adlai E. Stevenson: Politician, Diplomat, Friend* (New York: Harper & Row, 1965), 3; Irving Howe, "Stevenson and the Intellectuals," *Dissent* (Winter 1954), 13.

18 Kelley, *Professional Public Relations*, 205.

19 "Master Plan, Volunteers-for-Stevenson," n.d., 16 pp., ELBP, Box I:25. In 1956, Edward R. Murrow was also brought in to coach Stevenson, GWB-OH, 28.

20 Thomas Doherty, *Cold War, Cool Medium: Television, McCarthyism, and American Culture* (New York: Columbia University Press, 2003), 96; David Halberstam, *The Powers That Be* (New York: Knopf, 1979), 237.

21 *NYT,* 9/23/1952, 42.

22 *NYT,* 10/2/1952, 22; *NYT,* 10/6/1952, 13; *NYT,* 10/10/1952, 15; Wood, "Eisenhower Answers America," 272–73.

23 Alman Taranton to Walter Thayer, 10/16/1952, RRP, Box 19; Wood, "Eisenhower Answers America," 275.

24 LRG-OH, 86; GWB-OH, 25; Robert Bendiner, "How Much Has TV Changed Campaigning?" *NYTM,* 11/2/1952, SM13; *NYT,* 9/21/1952, E5; Joseph Seibert, *The Influence of Television on the Election of 1952* (Oxford, OH: Oxford Research Associates, 1954), 71; Edward Chester, *Radio, Television, and American Politics* (New York: Sheed & Ward, 1969), 88.

25 GWB-OH 24, 28; *NYT,* 11/9/1952, X13.

26 TV had little impact on the 1952 election outcome. See Kurt and Gladys Lang, "The Mass Media and Voting," in *American Voting Behavior,* ed. Eugene Burdick and Arthur Brodbeck (Glencoe, IL: Free Press, 1959), 217–35.

27 Reeves to Herbert Craig, 8/17/1953, RRP, Box 2.

28 Doherty, *Cold War, Cool Medium,* 81–82.

CHAPTER 32: Salesmanship and Secrecy

1 Key sources on Nixon throughout the book include Roger Morris, *Richard Milhous Nixon: The Rise of an American Politician* (New York: Holt, 1990), and David Greenberg, *Nixon's Shadow: The History of an Image* (New York: W. W. Norton, 2003).

2 D. B. Hardeman and Donald Bacon, *Rayburn: A Biography* (Austin: Texas Monthly Press, 1987), 382; Merle Miller, *Plain Speaking: An Oral Biography of Harry S. Truman* (New York: Putnam, 1974), 135.

3 Richard Nixon, *Six Crises* (Garden City, NY: Doubleday, 1962), 118. Assorted letters, RNPPS9.

4 Barton to Ben Duffy, 9/23/1952, BBP, Box 19; Earl Mazo, *Richard Nixon: A Political and Personal Portrait* (New York: Harper, 1959), 132.

5 *NYP,* 9/24/1952, 44; *NYP,* 9/25/1952, 26.

6 Steel, *Lippmann,* 483.

7 *WP,* 10/19/1952, 5B; *NYP,* 9/26/1952, 41.

8 Lester Seligman, "The President Is Many Men," *Antioch Review,* 16:3 (Autumn 1956), 314.

9 *WSJ,* 8/19/1953, 1, 6; Miller, "Can Government Be 'Merchandised'?" 15; Kelley, *Professional Public Relations,* 2; "The President & the Press," *Time,* 10/26/1953, 63–64.

10 LRG-OH, 52–55; L. Richard Guylay, "Public Relations," in James Cannon, *Politics U.S.A.: A Practical Guide to the Winning of Public Office* (Garden City, NY: Doubleday, 1960), 265; Griese, *Arthur W. Page,* 369; Bernays, *Biography,* 792; Fried, *The Man Everybody Knew,* 219; Eisinger, *Evolution,* 113–17; "The President & the Press," *Time,* 10/26/1953, 63–64.

11 Joseph Kraft, "The Dangerous Precedent of James Hagerty," *Esquire* (June 1959), 91; Robert Rutland, "President Eisenhower and His Press Secretary," *Journalism Quarterly,* 34:4 (December 1957), 452; "Authentic Voice," *Time,* 1/27/1958, 18.

12 Milton Mackaye, "Ike's Man Friday," *SEP,* 5/1960, 35, 54; "Authentic Voice," *Time,* 1/27/1958, 18; Rutland, "Eisenhower," 453.

13 "Direct from the President," *Time,* 12/28/1953, 47.

14 Kraft, "Dangerous Precedent," 91–94.

15 David Wise, *The Politics of Lying: Government Deception, Secrecy, and Power* (New York: Random House, 1973), 35; Hanson Baldwin, "Managed News: Our Peacetime Censorship," *Atlantic* (April 1963), 54.

16 "The President & the Press," *Time*, 10/26/1953, 63–64. The notion that Eisenhower deliberately spoke in bad prose is a myth rooted in a single statement he made to Hagerty before a press conference: "Don't worry, Jim; if that question comes up I'll just confuse them." In fact, the comment showed not that Ike misspoke on purpose but that, aware of his inarticulateness, he could joke about its unintended benefits. Normally he was more thin-skinned. He told Arthur Krock, "What the hell if I leave out verbs, hitch singular nouns to plural verbs and all that? They know what I mean, and that's what's important"—Arthur Krock, "Private Memorandum," 7/7/1960, AKP, Box 31.

17 Kraft, "Dangerous Precedent," 94; Schudson, *Discovering the News*, 170.

CHAPTER 33: The TV President

1 *NYT*, 6/4/1953, 25; "Half Hour in the Living Room," *Time*, 6/15/1953, 24; Samuel Becker, "Presidential Power: The Influence of Broadcasting," *Quarterly Journal of Speech*, 47:1 (February 1961), 17. A key source on television and the presidency throughout the postwar era is Robert Donovan and Ray Scherer, *Unsilent Revolution: Television News and American Public Life, 1948–1991* (New York: Cambridge University Press, 1992).

2 Craig Allen, "News Conferences on TV: Ike-Age Politics Revisited," *Journalism Quarterly*, 70:1 (March 1993), 18; Kumar, "Source Material," 185.

3 *CT*, 9/20/1953, N-D9; *NYT*, 5/24/1956, 16. On later attempts to use Fireside Chats, see William Leuchtenburg, *In the Shadow of FDR: From Harry Truman to Bill Clinton*, 2nd ed. rev. (Ithaca, NY: Cornell University Press, 1993 [1983]), 113, 189.

4 LRG-OH, 65–67; "The President & the Press," *Time*, 10/26/1953, 63–64; "The Peacemaker," *Time*, 8/13/1951; *WP*, 5/18/1955, 1, 13; Roger Kennedy, "Television," *TNR*, 5/30/1955, 22; *NYT*, 5/18/1955, 10; *NYT*, 12/24/1957, 22; Stephen Whitfield, *The Culture of the Cold War*, 2nd ed. (Baltimore: Johns Hopkins University Press, 1996 [1991]), 156–57; Robert Montgomery, *Open Letter from a Television Viewer* (New York: J. H. Heineman, 1968), 65–69.

5 JCH-OH, 79.

6 Cabell Phillips, "Q. and A. on the Press Conference," *NYTM*, 2/13/1955, 213; *NYT*, 1/20/1955, 1, 13; "New Channel," *Time*, 1/31/1955, 15.

7 *NYT*, 1/23/1953, 26; *NYT*, 2/28/1954, X11; *NYT*, 1/20/1955, 39.

8 Kumar, "Presidential Press Conferences," 183; T.R.B., "Washington Wire," *TNR*, 2/14/1955, 2; *NYT*, 5/24/1956, 16; ABC and DuMont did continue to run the press conferences. DuMont folded in 1955.

9 Montgomery, *Open Letter*, 64.

10 Jack Gould, "TV Techniques on the Political Stage," *NYTM*, 4/25/1954, SM12; Sam Boal, "Robert Montgomery Presents," *Coronet* (September 1954), 87.

11 SL-OH, 85–86; Richard Gehman, "He 'Produces' the President," *Good Housekeeping* (November 1955), 66; *WP*, 4/4/1954, ST11; *NYT*, 1/10/1954, E5; Craig Allen, "Robert Montgomery Presents: Hollywood Debut in the Eisenhower White House," *Journal of Broadcasting and Electronic Media*, 35:4 (Fall 1991), 435.

12 *CT*, 1/7/1954, 5; *NYT*, 1/10/1954, E5; "White House Assist," *Newsweek*, 1/18/1954, 51; *CT*, 3/13/1954, B1; *LAT*, 3/22/1954, 15; "The President Gestured," *Newsweek*, 4/19/1954, 54; Boal, "Robert Montgomery Presents," 89; *WP*, 4/7/1954, 51; "People of the Week," *USNWR*, 9/3/1954, 14.

13 T.R.B., "Washington Wire," *TNR*, 11/4/1957, 2; Allen, "Robert Montgomery Presents," 444.

14 Doherty, *Cold War, Cool Medium*, 101; Merriman Smith, "Evolution of Eisenhower

as Speaker," *NYTM*, 8/7/1955, SM18; "The President Gestured," *Newsweek*, 4/19/1954, 54; *CT*, 3/18/1954, N9; *WP*, 4/13/1954, 12.

15 Gould, "TV Techniques," SM44.

16 *WP*, 3/8/1958, A9; *LAT*, 3/22/1954, 15; *WP*, 8/20/1956, 6; Montgomery, *Open Letter*, 62.

17 Murphy to Hagerty, 9/14/1955; Hagerty to Murphy, 9/29/1955; Eisenhower to Don DeFore, 11/29/1955. DDE-WHCF, PPF, Box 343, PPF1-Q 1955; Steven Ross, *Hollywood, Left and Right: How Movie Stars Shaped American Politics* (New York: Oxford University Press, 2011), 134.

CHAPTER 34: "Atoms for Peace"

1 "The Report of the President's Committee on International Information Activities" [Jackson Committee Report], 6/30/1953, in U.S. Department of State, *Foreign Relations of the United States, 1952–1954*, vol. 2 (Washington, DC: U.S. Department of State, 1984), 1795–1899; Parry-Giles, *Rhetorical Presidency*, 136.

2 Schlesinger, "Psychological Warfare," 9–12.

3 Key sources on "Atoms for Peace" include John Lear, "Ike and the Peaceful Atom," *Reporter*, 1/12/1956, 11–21; Martin Medhurst, "Eisenhower's 'Atoms for Peace' Speech: A Case Study in the Strategic Use of Language," in *Cold War Rhetoric*, ed. Martin Medhurst, Robert Ivie, Philip Wander, and Robert Scott (Westport, CT: Greenwood Press, 1990), 29–50; Hogan, "Science of Cold War Strategy," 134–68; and Ira Chernus, *Eisenhower's Atoms for Peace* (College Station: Texas A&M University Press, 2002).

4 "Report by the Panel of Consultants of the State Department to the Secretary of the State," January 1953, in U.S. Department of State, *Foreign Relations of the United States, 1952–1954*, vol. 2 (Washington, DC: U.S. Department of State, 1984), 1056–91.

5 Hogan, "Science of Cold War Strategy," 153–57.

6 *NYT*, 8/14/1953, 1.

7 *WP*, 9/9/1953, 13; *WP*, 9/18/1953, 23; *WP*, 9/28/1953, 8.

8 Eisenhower never jettisoned the scare tactics behind Operation Candor. That same month he gave a speech to a group of church women warning that the hydrogen bombs could bring "sudden and mass destruction, erasure of cities, the possible doom of every nation and society"—*NYT*, 10/7/1953, 3.

9 JCH-OH, 203–05.

10 "Progress Report of Working Group on Implementation of the President's UN Speech, 12/9/1953 to 3/10/1954," in U.S. Department of State, *Foreign Relations of the United States, 1952–1954*, vol. 2, 1403–12.

11 *CSM*, 12/10/1953, 1.

CHAPTER 35: Vance Packard and the Anxiety of Persuasion

1 Vance Packard, "Moving In with the Eisenhowers," *American Magazine* (January 1953), 24–25, 93–97; Michael Nelson, "What's Wrong with Sociology?" *Washington Monthly* (June 1978), 44.

2 A key source on Packard is Daniel Horowitz, *Vance Packard and American Social Criticism* (Chapel Hill: University of North Carolina Press, 1994).

3 Robert Graham, "Adman's Nightmare: Is the Prune a Witch?" *Reporter*, 10/13/1953, 27–31.

4 David Seed, *Brainwashing: The Fictions of Mind Control; A Study of Novels and Films Since World War II* (Kent, OH: Kent State University Press, 2004), 48; Matthew Dunne, *A Cold War State of Mind: Brainwashing and Postwar American Society* (Amherst: University of Massachusetts Press, 2013); Edward Hunter, *Brainwashing: The Story of*

Men Who Defied It (New York: Farrar, Straus & Cudahy, 1956); Joost Meerloo, *Rape of the Mind: The Psychology of Thought Control, Menticide, and Brainwashing* (Cleveland: World Publishing, 1956); William Sargant, *Battle for the Mind: A Physiology of Conversion and Brain-Washing* (Garden City, NY: Doubleday, 1957); Richard Condon, *The Manchurian Candidate* (New York: McGraw-Hill, 1959).

5   Mayer, *Madison Avenue*, 305; Aldous Huxley, *Brave New World Revisited* (New York: Harper, 1958), 56.

6   Tony Tanner, *City of Words: American Fiction, 1950–1970* (New York: Harper & Row, 1971), 15; Eugene Burdick, *The Ninth Wave* (Boston: Houghton Mifflin, 1956); John Schneider, *The Golden Kazoo* (New York: Rinehart, 1956).

7   Albert Hastorf and Hadley Cantril, "They Saw a Game: A Case Study," *Journal of Abnormal and Social Psychology*, 49:1 (January 1954), 129–34; Eric Hoffer, *The True Believer: Thoughts on the Nature of Mass Movements* (New York: Harper, 1951), 103.

8   Quotations from the ensuing paragraphs come from Vance Packard, *Hidden Persuaders*, intro. by Mark Crispin Miller (Brooklyn: Ig Publishing, 2007 [1957]). See also Vance Packard, "Resurvey of 'Hidden Persuaders,'" *NYTM*, 5/11/1958, SM10.

9   *NYT*, 4/28/1957, BR2.

10 Loren Baritz, "Of Time and the Ostrich," *Nation*, 1/28/1961, 82–83.

11 *CSM*, 10/29/1957, 12; *CSM*, 1/7/1958, 3; Fox, *Mirror Makers*, 186.

12 Michael Schudson, "Criticizing the Critics of Advertising," *Media, Culture & Society*, 3:1 (January 1981), 5; "Is Vance Packard Necessary?" *Trans-Action* 2:1 (January–February 1965), 13. For a dissenting view, see Michelle Nelson, "*The Hidden Persuaders*: Then and Now," *Journal of Advertising*, 37:1 (Spring 2008), 113–26.

13 Lloyd Barenblatt, review of Packard's *The Hidden Persuaders*, *Public Opinion Quarterly*, 22:4 (Winter 1958–59), 579–80; Irving Kristol, "I Dreamed I Stopped Traffic . . . ," review of *The Hidden Persuaders*, *Encounter* (December 1957), 72–74.

14 Ian Brailsford, "'Madison Avenue Puts on Its Best Hair Shirt': U.S. Advertising and Its Social Critics," *International Journal of Advertising*, 17:3 (August 1998), 368–69; Raymond Bauer, "Limits of Persuasion: The Hidden Persuaders Are Made of Straw," *Harvard Business Review*, 36:5 (September–October 1958), 107; David Ogilvy, *Confessions of an Advertising Man* (London: Southbank Publ., 2004 [1963]), 145; Rosser Reeves, *Reality in Advertising* (New York: Knopf, 1961), 71–76.

15 Bauer, "Limits of Persuasion," 110.

PART V: THE AGE OF IMAGE MAKING

CHAPTER 36: The Unmaking of Presidential Mystique

1   Key sources on White include Theodore H. White, *In Search of History: A Personal Adventure* (New York: Harper & Row, 1978); Joyce Hoffmann, *Theodore H. White and Journalism as an Illusion* (Columbia: University of Missouri Press, 1995); and Thomas Griffith, *Harry and Teddy: The Turbulent Friendship of Press Lord Henry R. Luce and His Favorite Reporter, Theodore H. White* (New York: Random House, 1995).

2   Timothy Crouse, *Boys on the Bus* (New York: Ballantine Books, 1973 [1972]), 34.

3   April Koral, "Teddy White Says He's Not a Politician," *Writer's Digest*, 55:7 (July 1975), 22.

4   Riesman, *Lonely Crowd*, 163–87.

5   Stewart Alsop, "The Mystery of Richard Nixon," *SEP*, 7/12/1958, 29.

6   Norman Mailer, "Superman Comes to the Supermart," *Esquire* (November 1960), 119–27.

7   Koral, "Teddy White," 22.

8   Theodore Sorensen, *Kennedy* (New York: Harper & Row, 1965), 311; White, *Making, 1960*, 338.

9   Jonathan Yardley, "Sharp Pencils: How Three Pioneering Reporters Reshaped the Way the Press Covers Elections—and Politics Itself," *Smithsonian* (November 2006), 100–08; Crouse, *Boys on the Bus*, 36.

10   Crouse, *Boys on the Bus*, 37.

CHAPTER 37: The Great Debates

1   Key sources on the debates include White, *Making, 1960*; Sidney Kraus, ed., *The Great Debates: Kennedy vs. Nixon, 1960* (Bloomington: Indiana University Press, 1977 [1962]), and Alan Schroeder, *Presidential Debates: Fifty Years of High-Risk TV*, 2nd ed. (New York: Columbia University Press, 2008).

2   FS-OH, 4; PEGS-OH, 89; Reinsch, *Getting Elected*, 141.

3   David Greenberg, "I Paid for This Microphone," *Slate*, 9/13/2000, at http://www.slate .com/articles/news_and_politics/history_lesson/2000/09/i_paid_for_this_microphone .html. The West Virginia debate was carried nationally by NBC, MBS, and the Westinghouse network. See http://archive.today/qfKf.

4   Douglass Cater, "Who Is Nixon, What Is He?" *Reporter*, 11/27/1958, 13.

5   John F. Kennedy, "A Force That Has Changed the Political Scene," *TV Guide*, 11/14/1959.

6   Reinsch, *Getting Elected*, 141; *NYT*, 8/25/1988, 22.

7   FS-OH, 20; Don Hewitt, *Tell Me a Story: Fifty Years and 60 Minutes in Television* (New York: Public Affairs, 2001), 72; Reinsch recalls applying the makeup himself— Reinsch, *Getting Elected*, 141.

8   *NYT*, 9/27/1960, 1; Ben Bradlee, *A Good Life: Newspapering and Other Adventures* (New York: Simon & Schuster, 1995), 211; Allen, *Eisenhower and the Mass Media*, 174, n10; Fawn Brodie, *Richard Nixon: The Shaping of His Character* (New York: W. W. Norton, 1981), 427.

9   Louis Harris, Memorandum, RFKP-PF, Box 45; PEGS-OH, 90.

10   Horowitz, *Packard and Social Criticism*, 138; Nixon, *Six Crises*, 340; PEGS-OH, 91.

11   Diamond and Bates, *The Spot*, 112.

12   Arthur Krock, *The Consent of the Governed, and Other Deceits* (Boston: Little, Brown, 1971), 66.

13   *Toronto Globe and Mail*, 10/15/1960, 6.

14   Marshall McLuhan, *Understanding Media: The Extensions of Man* (New York: Signet Books, 1964), 261, 287.

15   David Vancil and Sue Pendell, "The Myth of Viewer-Listener Disagreement in the First Kennedy-Nixon Debate," *Central States Speech Journal*, 38:1 (Spring 1987), 16–27; Michael Schudson, "Trout or Hamburger: Politics and Telemythology," in *The Power of News* (Cambridge, MA: Harvard University Press, 1995), 113–23; David Greenberg, "Rewinding the Kennedy-Nixon Debates," *Slate*, 9/24/2010. http://www.slate.com /articles/news_and_politics/history_lesson/2010/09/rewinding_the_kennedynixon _debates.html.

CHAPTER 38: The Politics of Image

1   Frank Stanton, "A CBS View," in Kraus, *The Great Debates*, 65–72; Sig Mickelson, "The Use of Television," in Cannon, *Politics U.S.A.*, 285–301.

2   *NYT*, 9/27/1960, 75; *NYT*, 10/2/1960, X17; *WP*, 9/29/1960, A23; *WP*, 10/18/1960, A15; Steel, *Lippmann*, 516–17.

3   Max Ascoli, "Intermezzo," *Reporter,* 11/10/1960, 18; Henry Steele Commager, "Washington Would Have Lost a TV Debate," *NYTM,* 10/30/1960, SM13, 79, 80; Norman Cousins, "Presidents Don't Have to Be Quiz Champions," *SR,* 11/5/1960, 34.

4   *NYT,* 2/29/2004, 36; Peter Novick, *That Noble Dream: The "Objectivity Question" and the American Historical Profession* (New York: Cambridge University Press, 1988), 328–29, 333–34.

5   Daniel Boorstin, "Selling the President to the People," *Commentary* (November 1955), 421–27.

6   Boorstin to Bernays, 11/10/1955; Boorstin to Bernays, 8/15/1956; Bernays to Boorstin, 4/5/1957; Boorstin to Bernays, 1/22/1959; Boorstin to Bernays, 2/2/1959; all in DJBP, Box 14.

7   Clippings, DJBP, Box 352; Daniel Boorstin, "Democracy and Culture," unpublished talk for the Ohio State University Conference on "Popular/Mass Culture: American Perspectives," 10/28/1960, and "Mass Culture: Subject of the Third Conference on Humanities," publication not given, 12/1960, 5, DJBP, Box 196; "Talk to Wayfarers Club," Chicago, 10/18/1960, DJBP, Box 351; "Talk to Anshe Emet Ladies' Book Group," Chicago, IL, 10/24/1960, DJBP, Box 351; Daniel Boorstin, "The American Image," DJBP, Box 196.

8   Quotations in the ensuing paragraphs come from Daniel Boorstin, *The Image: A Guide to Pseudo-Events in America* (New York: Vintage Books, 1992 [1961]). The subtitle of the book was changed when the paperback was published.

9   Bruce Bliven, review of Boorstin's *The Image,* *National Observer,* 9/3/1962, in DJBP, Box 353; H. M. McLuhan, review of *The Image,* *Canadian Forum* (July 1962), 90–91; Kenneth Lynn, "On American Society," *Yale Review* (Summer 1962), 649–52; Stephen Whitfield, "The Image: The Lost World of Daniel Boorstin," *Reviews in American History,* 19:2 (June 1991), 308.

CHAPTER 39: The Kennedy Moment

1   Pierre Salinger, *With Kennedy* (Garden City, NY: Doubleday, 1966), 52–56.

2   *The Kennedy Presidential Press Conferences* (New York: E. Coleman Enterprises, 1978), 559.

3   Meeting summary, 12/27/1960, PEGSP, Box 6; Salinger, *With Kennedy,* 57.

4   Transcript of Press Briefing with Pierre Salinger, 6:00 p.m., 12/27/1960, PEGSP, Box 6; T.R.B., "Protected President," *TNR,* 12/12/1960, 2.

5   David Davies, *The Postwar Decline of American Newspapers, 1945–1965* (Westport, CT: Praeger Publishers, 2006), 97; Krock, *Consent of the Governed,* 66; PEGS-OH, 41–46.

6   Key sources on JFK and the press include Earl Hutchison, "Kennedy and the Press: The First Six Months," *Journalism & Mass Communication Quarterly,* 38:4 (December 1961), 441–52; Halberstam, *Powers That Be,* 363–90; and James Graham, "Kennedy, Cuba, and the Press," *Journalism History,* 24:2 (Summer 1998), 60–71.

7   Salinger to Mary Salisbury, 1/10/1960, PEGSP, Box 5; Salinger to Wilson, 1/14/1961, PEGSP, Box 11; "President's Press Conference Lectern," PEGSP, Box 11; Janet Travell to Salinger, 1/31/1961, PEGSP, Box 14; Hugh Sidey, *John F. Kennedy, President* (New York: Atheneum, 1963), 49; "Historic Conference," *Newsweek,* 2/6/1961, 56.

8   Douglass Cater, "How a President Helps Form Public Opinion: How a President Shapes Opinion," *NYTM,* 2/26/1961, SM38; Script for Kennedy News Conference television broadcast, Wednesday, 1/25/1961, PEGSP, Box 14.

9   Ryfe, *Presidents in Culture,* 111–12.

10   *NYT,* 1/26/1961, 12; Davies, *Postwar Decline,* 100–01; *E&P,* 1/7/1961, 9; *E&P,* 1/28/1961,

6; Roscoe Drummond, "Mr. Kennedy's Calculated Risk: The Presidential Press Conference Takes a Giant Step," *SR*, 2/11/1961, 82–84; *NYT*, 1/26/1961, 59; *NYT*, 11/2/1961, 36. See also Harry Sharp, Jr., "Live from Washington: The Telecasting of President Kennedy's News Conferences," *Journal of Broadcasting*, 13:1 (Winter 1968–69), 26.

11 *WP*, 4/21/1961, A8; Boorstin, *The Image*, 17; *WP*, 5/1 1961, 14B.

12 *WP*, 5/21/1961, E4; *NYT*, 3/16/1962, 15.

13 "JFK & the Conference," *Time*, 3/24/1961, 44.

14 Eisinger, *Evolution*, 119–20.

15 *NYT*, 4/7/1961, 1; *NYT*, 4/26/1961, 38; Chalmers Roberts, *The Washington Post: The First 100 Years* (Boston: Houghton Mifflin, 1977), 349–50. There is little evidence that Kennedy, as is sometimes alleged, called the *New York Times* to censor the story, although senior editors did, apparently on their own judgment, remove from Szulc's story a description of the invasion as "imminent" and a mention of the CIA. See W. Joseph Campbell, *Getting It Wrong: Ten of the Greatest Misreported Stories in American Journalism* (Berkeley: University of California Press, 2010), 68–84.

16 Arthur Schlesinger, Jr., *A Thousand Days: John F. Kennedy in the White House* (Boston: Houghton Mifflin, 1965), 287; John F. Kennedy, "Address Before the American Society of Newspaper Editors," 4/20/1961, http://www.presidency.ucsb.edu/ws/?pid=8076.

17 T.R.B., "The Worst and the Best," *TNR*, 5/1/1961, 2; *Kennedy Conferences*, 85; *NYT*, 4/22/1961, 1.

18 *Kennedy Conferences*, 90; *NYT*, 4/21/1961, 32; *NYT*, 4/22/1961, 1.

19 Gerald Johnson, "A Clean Break," *TNR*, 5/8/1961, 10.

20 Sorensen, *Kennedy*, 311; *WP*, 4/22/1961, A1; *NYHT*, 4/22/1961, 1, 3; Roberts, *The Washington Post*, 349–50; Arthur Krock, "Private Memorandum," 5/5/1961, AKP, Box 31.

21 *NYT*, 5/10/1963, 44.

22 Richard Reeves, *President Kennedy: Profile of Power* (New York: Simon & Schuster, 1993), 106; *NYT*, 5/12/1961, 28.

23 Robert Dallek, *An Unfinished Life: John F. Kennedy, 1917–1963* (Boston: Little, Brown, 2003), 371.

CHAPTER 40: News Management in Camelot

1 Fletcher Knebel, "Kennedy vs. the Press," *Look*, 8/28/1962, 17–21; Robert Manning, "The Man Who Comes to Dinner," *SR*, 3/11/1961, 88; Steel, *Lippmann*, 523–25; Robert Merry, *Taking on the World: Joseph and Stewart Alsop—Guardians of the American Century* (New York: Viking, 1996), xv–xxv, 357–59; Worth Bingham and Ward Just, "The President and the Press," *Reporter*, 4/12/1962, 18.

2 *WSJ*, 11/29/1961, 18; Tebbel and Watts, *Press and Presidency*, 482, 485.

3 Benjamin Bradlee, *Conversations with Kennedy* (New York: Pocket Books, 1976 [1975]), 28.

4 "The Kennedy 'Image'—How It's Built," *USNWR*, 4/9/1962, 56–59; Knebel, "Kennedy vs. the Press," 21.

5 Sorensen, *Kennedy*, 312; *Kennedy Conferences*, 283.

6 Sorensen, *Kennedy*, 311; Knebel, "Kennedy vs. the Press," 18–20; William Prochnau, *Once upon a Distant War: David Halberstam, Neil Sheehan, Peter Arnett—Young War Correspondents and Their Early Vietnam Battles* (New York: Random House, 1995), 402–44.

7 David Coleman, *The Fourteenth Day: JFK and the Aftermath of the Cuban Missile Crisis* (New York: W. W. Norton, 2012), 67–77; Hanson Baldwin, "Managed News: Our Peacetime Censorship," *Atlantic* (April 1963), 53–59.

8 Thomas Benson, *Writing JFK: Presidential Rhetoric and the Press in the Bay of Pigs*

Crisis (College Station: Texas A&M University Press, 2004), 57–60; John F. Kennedy, "Address 'The President and the Press' Before the American Society of Newspaper Publishers," http://www.presidency.ucsb.edu/ws/index.php?pid=8093.

9 *WP*, 5/7/1961, E1; Benson, *Writing JFK*, 67–70.

10 *NYT*, 4/30/1961, E11; "Information: News—and Responsibility," *Newsweek*, 5/8/1961, 24; *NYT*, 5/14/1961, E11; Benson, *Writing JFK*, 67.

11 *NYT*, 5/10/1961, 3; *WP*, 5/10/1961, A2; Clifton Daniel, "National Security and the Bay of Pigs Invasion," in *Killing the Messenger: 100 Years of Media Criticism*, ed. Tom Goldstein (New York: Columbia University Press, 1989), 107–18; Turner Catledge, *My Life and the Times* (New York: Harper & Row, 1971), 264.

12 Coleman, *Fourteenth Day*, 152; Daniel, "National Security," 117–18; Montague Kern, Patricia Levering, and Ralph Levering, *The Kennedy Crises: The Press the Presidency, and Foreign Policy* (Chapel Hill: University of North Carolina Press, 1983), 124–25; Graham, "Kennedy, Cuba, and the Press," 166–67.

13 When the article proved controversial, Salinger publicly denied that anyone had seen it before publication. Stewart Alsop and Charles Bartlett, "In Time of Crisis," *SEP*, 12/18/1962, 15–21; Merry, *Taking on the World*, 387–93. On the mythology of the Cuban Missile Crisis, see Sheldon Stern, *The Cuban Missile Crisis in American Memory: Myth Versus Reality* (Stanford, CA: Stanford University Press, 2012).

14 Arthur Krock to John F. Kennedy, [7/1960], AKP, Box 31; *NYT*, 10/23/1962, 35; Graham, "Kennedy, Cuba, and the Press," 64; *NYT*, 12/4/1962, 40.

15 Davies, *Postwar Decline*, 108; James Pollard, "The Kennedy Administration and the Press," *Journalism & Mass Communication Quarterly*, 41:1 (Winter 1964), 6, 13.

16 Coleman, *Fourteenth Day*, 150–59.

17 PEGS-OH, 150; *NYT*, 11/2/1962, 30; Lester Markel, "The 'Management' of News," *SR*, 2/9/1963, 50–51; Coleman, *Fourteenth Day*, 157.

18 Krock, "Press vs. Government," 45–49; Duncan Norton-Taylor to Krock, 2/19/1963, Krock to Andre Visson, 2/25/1963, AKP, Box 45; Arthur Krock, "Mr. Kennedy's Management of News," *Fortune* (March 1963), 82, 199, 201–02.

19 *WP*, 3/10/1963, E7.

20 *Kennedy Conferences*, 452.

CHAPTER 41: Crisis

1 Key sources on "Crisis" include Mary Ann Watson, "Adventures in Reporting: John Kennedy and the *Cinema Verité* Television Documentaries of Drew Associates," *Film & History*, 19:2 (May 1989), 26–43; Mary Ann Watson, *The Expanding Vista: American Television in the Kennedy Years* (New York: Oxford University Press, 1990); P. J. O'Connell, *Robert Drew and the Development of Cinema Verité in America* (Carbondale: Southern Illinois University Press, 1992), 168–95; and *Crisis: Behind a Presidential Commitment*, executive producer Robert Drew and producer Gregory Shuker, ABC Television Network, 10/21/1963 (New York: New Video Group, 2003, DVD).

2 Erik Barnouw, *Documentary: A History of the Non-Fiction Film* (New York: Oxford University Press, 1974), 236–38.

3 *WP*, 12/6/2003, C01.

4 John Cogley, "The Presidential Image," *TNR*, 4/10/1961, 30–31.

5 Gene Roberts and Hank Klibanoff, *The Race Beat: The Press, the Civil Rights Struggle, and the Awakening of a Nation* (New York: Knopf, 2006), 88–89; Sasha Torres, *Black, White, and in Color: Television and Black Civil Rights* (Princeton: Princeton University Press, 2003) 25, 28; David Garrow, *Bearing the Cross: Martin Luther King, Jr., and the Southern Christian Leadership Conference* (New York: William Morrow, 1986),

264; David Greenberg, "The Idea of 'The Liberal Media' and Its Roots in the Civil Rights Movement," *The Sixties: A Journal of History, Politics and Culture,* 1:2 (December 2008), 167–86.

6   Taylor Branch, *Parting the Waters: America in the King Years, 1954–1963* (New York: Simon & Schuster, 1988), 796–800.

7   Donovan and Scherer, *Unsilent Revolution,* 17.

8   Dallek, *Unfinished Life,* 602; Roberts and Klibanoff, *Race Beat,* 326–28.

9   Dan Carter, *The Politics of Rage: George Wallace, The Origins of the New Conservatism, and the Transformation of American Politics* (New York: Simon & Schuster, 1995), 143–44; Dan Carter, "Good Copy: George Wallace Understood That the Media Thrived on Confrontation," *Media Studies Journal,* 12:3 (Fall 1998), 40–47.

10 Branch, *Parting the Waters,* 822–23.

11 Carter, *Politics of Rage,* 144–47.

12 Diane McWhorter, *Carry Me Home: Birmingham, Alabama; The Climactic Battle of the Civil Rights Revolution* (New York: Simon & Schuster, 2001), 460–61.

13 Carter, *Politics of Rage,* 148–52; Reeves, *President Kennedy,* 521.

14 John F. Kennedy, "Radio and Television Report to the American People on Civil Rights," 6/11/1963, http://www.presidency.ucsb.edu/ws/?pid=9271.

15 Branch, *Parting the Waters,* 824; Roberts and Klibanoff, *Race Beat,* 332; *NYT,* 6/12/1963, 1; *WP,* 6/12/1963, 1.

16 *NYT,* 7/25/1963, 1; *NYT,* 7/27/1963, 16.

17 *NYHT,* 9/16/1963, 21.

18 *NYT,* 10/22/1963, 75; *NYT,* 10/27/1963, 125.

CHAPTER 42: "Let Us Continue"

1   Key sources on LBJ include Robert Dallek, *Flawed Giant: Lyndon Johnson and His Times, 1961–1973* (New York: Oxford University Press, 1998), and Robert Caro, *The Years of Lyndon Johnson.* Vol. 4: *The Passage of Power* (New York: Knopf, 2012).

2   Lyndon B. Johnson, *The Vantage Point: Perspectives of the Presidency, 1963–1969* (New York: Holt, Rinehart & Winston, 1971), 37; Lyndon B. Johnson, "Address Before a Joint Session of the Congress," 11/27/1963, http://www.presidency.ucsb.edu/ws/index.php?pid=25988&st=&st1=; *WP,* 11/28/1963, A10.

3   Lyndon B. Johnson, "The President's Thanksgiving Day Address to the Nation," 11/28/1963, online at http://www.presidency.ucsb.edu/ws/index.php?pid=25999&st=&st1=; *WP,* 3/17/1964, A17.

4   Doris Kearns Goodwin, *Lyndon Johnson and the American Dream* (New York: St. Martin's Press, 1991 [1976]), 53–55.

5   Russell Baker, *The Good Times* (New York: William Morrow, 1989), 281–82; Robert Caro, *The Years of Lyndon Johnson.* Vol. 3: *Master of the Senate* (New York: Knopf, 2002), 121.

6   Additional key sources on Johnson's 1964 campaign are Richard Goodwin, *Remembering America: A Voice from the Sixties* (Boston: Little, Brown, 1988); Jamieson, *Packaging*; and Robert Mann, *Daisy Petals and Mushroom Clouds: LBJ, Barry Goldwater, and the Ad That Changed American Politics* (Baton Rouge: Louisiana State University Press, 2011).

7   Paul Boyer, "From Activism to Apathy: The American People and Nuclear Weapons, 1963–1980," *Journal of American History,* 70:4 (March 1984), 821–44.

8   *NYT,* 10/27/1963, 152; Pete Hamill, "When the Client Is a Candidate," *NYTM,* 10/25/1964, SM30–31, 128–30.

9   Diamond and Bates, *The Spot,* 127; Blumenthal, *Permanent Campaign,* 136–37.

10 W. Terrence Gordon, *Marshall McLuhan: Escape into Understanding: A Biography* (New York: Basic Books, 1997), 231; Philip Marchand, *Marshall McLuhan: The Medium and the Messenger: A Biography* (Cambridge, MA: MIT Press, 1998), 208.

11 Tony Schwartz, *The Responsive Chord* (Garden City, NY: Anchor Press/Doubleday, 1973), 19, 25–26, 79, 82.

12 Most accounts refer to the flower as a daisy. Robert Mann says it was a dandelion. The Living Room Candidate website says it is a black-eyed Susan—http://www .livingroomcandidate.org/commercials/1964/peace-little-girl-daisy.

13 Schwartz, *Responsive Chord*, 93.

CHAPTER 43: The Credibility Gap

1 Safer's report can be found on YouTube, http://www.youtube.com/watch?v=hNYZZi25Ttg.

2 Key sources on the press and Vietnam include Halberstam, *Powers That Be*; Clarence Wyatt, *Paper Soldiers: The American Press and the Vietnam War* (New York: W. W. Norton, 1993); Prochnau, *Distant War*; and William Hammond, *Reporting Vietnam: Media and Military at War* (Lawrence: University Press of Kansas, 1998).

3 *NYT*, 2/15/1962, 1.

4 Marguerite Higgins, *Our Vietnam Nightmare* (New York: Harper & Row, 1965); *WP*, 9/23/1963, A17; "The View from Saigon," *Time*, 9/20/1963, 66–67.

5 *NYT*, 8/30/1964, 1.

6 Key sources on the Tonkin Gulf incident include Stanley Karnow, *Vietnam: A History* (New York: Penguin Books, 1983), 365–76; Edwin Moise, *Tonkin Gulf and the Escalation of the Vietnam War* (Chapel Hill: University of North Carolina Press, 1996); Fredrik Logevall, *Choosing War: The Lost Chance for Peace and the Escalation of War in Vietnam* (Berkeley: University of California Press, 1999), 193–221; Eric Alterman, *When Presidents Lie: A History of Official Deception and Its Consequences* (New York: Viking, 2004); and Dallek, *Flawed Giant*, 143–56.

7 Lyndon B. Johnson, "Radio and Television Report to the American People Following Renewed Aggression in the Gulf of Tonkin," 8/4/1964, http://www.presidency.ucsb .edu/ws/?pid=26418; Lyndon B. Johnson, "Remarks at Syracuse University on the Communist Challenge in Southeast Asia," 8/5/1964, http://www.presidency.ucsb.edu /ws/index.php?pid=26419; George Ball, *The Past Has Another Pattern: Memoirs* (New York: W. W. Norton, 1982), 379. The local weather conditions of the Tonkin Gulf give rise to a radar phenomenon known as "Tonkin Spook," which may have looked like torpedo attacks even to a trained observer.

8 Cater, *Fourth Branch*, 2–3, 13; *NYT*, 8/10/1988, A16.

9 Later, Thomas Ross, in classic Washington fashion, became a Pentagon spokesman under President Carter. Wise remained a lifelong student of government secrecy. *NYT*, 8/10/1988, A16; *NYT*, 10/28/2002, B9.

10 Eric Goldman, *The Tragedy of Lyndon Johnson* (New York: Knopf, 1969), 409–10; Wise, *Politics of Lying*, 22–23.

11 *WP*, 12/5/1965, A21; James Deakin, "LBJ's Credibility; or, What Happened to 'No Comment'?" *TNR*, 1/29/1966, 23–24.

12 *NYT*, 12/4/1966, E10; *NYT*, 7/1/1966, 34.

13 Joseph Califano, Jr., *The Triumph & Tragedy of Lyndon Johnson: The White House Years* (New York: Simon & Schuster, 1991), 10; Wise, *Politics of Lying*, 20–22.

14 Goodwin, *Johnson and the American Dream*, vii–ix; Ben Bagdikian, "Press Agent— But Still President," *Columbia Journalism Review*, 4:2 (Summer 1965), 10–13.

15 Steel, *Lippmann*, 550, 577–78, 582–85.

16 Panzer to LBJ, 6/16/1967, LBJ-OF-FP, Box 398. Key sources on the Progress Cam-

paign are Chester Pach, "'We Need to Get a Better Story to the American People':
LBJ, the Progress Campaign, and the Vietnam War on Television," in *Selling War in a
Media Age: The Presidency and Public Opinion in the American Century*, ed. Kenneth
Osgood and Andrew Frank (Gainesville: University Press of Florida, 2010), 170–95,
and George Herring, *LBJ and Vietnam: A Different Kind of War* (Austin: University of
Texas Press, 1994), 121–50.

17 McGeorge Bundy to LBJ, 9/3/1965, LBJ-NSF, Country File Vietnam, Box 195; Press
release, 9/9/65, LBJ-NSF, Country File Vietnam, Box 195; Jonathan Moore to Chester
Cooper, William Jorden, and Richard Sneider, 11/27/1965, LBJ-NSF, Country File
Vietnam, Box 197; Maltese, *Spin Control*, 6–7; "Astroturf, n." OED Online. Oxford
University Press. The Astroturf comparison appeared as early as 1972, but the politi-
cal usage did not catch on until the 1990s; *WP*, 5/7/1972, B1.

18 Tom Johnson to George Christian, 8/15/1967, LBJ-WHCF Confidential Files, Box 83;
Walt Rostow to LBJ, 8/15/1967, LBJ-NSF Komer-Leonhart File, Box 16. Previously, the
administration had convened a Vietnam Public Affairs Policy Committee and then a
Vietnam Public Affairs Working Group. Neither had been terribly effective. See LBJ-
NSF Country File Vietnam, Box 197; Herring, *LBJ and Vietnam*, 136, 143.

19 Dick Moose to Bill Bundy, et al., 11/21/1967, LBJ-NSF Komer Leonhart Files, Box 16;
"General Westmoreland's History Notes," 8/6–18/1967, WCWP, Box 13.

20 "Notes on the President's Conversation with Six Commentators," 8/11/1967, LBJ-
WHCF Meeting Notes Files, Box 3.

21 Lyndon B. Johnson, "The President's Veterans Day Tour of Military Installations,"
11/10/1967, http://www.presidency.ucsb.edu/ws/index.php?pid=28544; *NYT*, 11/11/1967, 1.

22 Goodwin, *Johnson and the American Dream*, 303.

23 Lyndon B. Johnson, "The President's News Conference," 11/17/1967, http://www.presi-
dency.ucsb.edu/ws/index.php?pid=28555; *NYT*, 11/18/1967, 1; Donovan and Scherer,
Unsilent Revolution, 172–73.

24 McGinniss, *Selling*, 209; Kathleen J. Turner, *Lyndon Johnson's Dual War: Vietnam and
the Press* (Chicago: University of Chicago Press, 1985), 205; "The Presidency: The Look
of Leadership," *Time*, 11/24/1967, 7.

25 Jim Jones to Fred Panzer, 12/28/1967, LBJ-WHCF Confidential Files, Box 83; *NYT*,
12/3/1967, 259; *WP*, 11/26/1967, A10; David Halberstam, "Return to Vietnam," *Harper's* (December 1967), 47–58.

CHAPTER 44: The New Politics

1 Key sources on LBJ and polling include Bruce Altschuler, *LBJ and the Polls* (Gaines-
ville: University of Florida Press, 1990); Lawrence Jacobs and Robert Shapiro, "The
Rise of Presidential Polling: The Nixon White House in Historical Perspective,"
Public Opinion Quarterly, 59:2 (Summer 1995), 163–95; Lawrence Jacobs and Robert
Shapiro, "Lyndon Johnson, Vietnam, and Public Opinion: Rethinking Realist Theory
of Leadership," *Presidential Studies Quarterly*, 29:3 (September 1999), 592–616; and
Eisinger, *Evolution*.

2 Assorted memoranda, LBJ-OF-FP, Box 398; *WP*, 4/26/1965, A17; William Honan,
"Johnson May Not Have Poll Fever, But He Has a Good Case of the Poll Sniffles,"
NYTM, 8/21/1966, 34–35.

3 Stewart Alsop, "Uncle Lyndon," *SEP*, 10/24/1964, 16; Honan, "Poll Fever," 34; *NYT*,
4/16/1964, 42; Bagdikian, "Press Agent—But Still President," 11.

4 Harris had officially retired from political polling to be a public pollster and wished
to avoid perceived conflicts of interest. He asked White House aides not to reveal his
work for them.

5 Herring, *LBJ and Vietnam*, 136.

6   *WSJ*, 9/15/1966, 1; *NYT*, 12/11/1966, 82. On consulting, key sources include James Perry, *The New Politics: The Expanding Technology of Political Manipulation* (New York: Clarkson N. Potter, 1968); David Lee Rosenbloom, *The Election Men: Professional Campaign Managers and American Democracy* (New York: Quadrangle Books, 1973); Larry Sabato, *The Rise of Political Consultants: New Ways of Winning Elections* (New York: Basic Books, 1981); Melvyn Bloom, *Public Relations and Presidential Campaigns: A Crisis in Democracy* (New York: Crowell, 1973); and Ray Hiebert, et al., eds., *The Political Image Merchants: Strategies in the New Politics* (Washington, DC: Acropolis Books, 1971).

7   Blumenthal, *Permanent Campaign*, 152; *WSJ*, 9/15/1966, 1, 24; Perry, *New Politics*, 41–69.

8   Joseph Napolitan, *The Election Game and How to Win It* (Garden City, NY: Doubleday & Co., 1972), 30, 34.

9   Ibid., 26–27, 41; Diamond and Bates, *The Spot*, 173–75.

10 *Nixon on the Issues* (New York: Nixon-Agnew Campaign Committee, 1968), 79.

11 Theodore H. White, *Making of the President, 1968* (New York: Harper Perennial, 2010 [1969]), 154; Maltese, *Spin Control*, 16. Key sources on Nixon in 1968 include McGinniss, *Selling of the President, 1968*; Jamieson, *Packaging*; and Greenberg, *Nixon's Shadow*.

12 Halberstam, *Powers That Be*, 591–92, 595–96; Stanley Kutler, *The Wars of Watergate: The Last Crisis of Richard Nixon* (New York: W. W. Norton, 1990), 70–71; Stephen Ambrose, *Nixon. Vol. 2: The Triumph of a Politician, 1962–1972* (New York: Simon & Schuster, 1989), 138.

13 Steel, *Lippmann*, 589; *WP*, 9/17/1968, A17.

14 Leonard Garment, *Crazy Rhythm: My Journey from Brooklyn, Jazz, and Wall Street to Nixon's White House, Watergate, and Beyond* . . . (New York: Times Books, 1997), 136–39; Raymond Price, personal interview with the author; Diamond and Bates, *The Spot*, 162. McGinniss stated that he did tell the staff he was writing a book.

15 Kiku Adatto, *Picture Perfect: The Art and Artifice of Public Image Making* (New York: Basic Books, 1993), 43–44, 64.

16 Alistair Cooke, "An M.A. in Political Cosmetics," *WP Book World*, 10/5/1969, 1; "Understanding Nixon," *National Review*, 12/16/1969, 1287; Garment, *Crazy Rhythm*, 136–39.

17 Perry, *New Politics*, 6; Bloom, *Public Relations and Presidential Campaigns*, 275.

18 Napolitan, *Election Game*, 1, 5, 12.

19 Hannah Arendt, "Truth and Politics," Box 79, HAP. Quotations in the ensuing paragraphs are from ibid. in *The Portable Hannah Arendt*, ed. Peter Baehr (New York: Penguin Books, 2000), 545–75, originally published as "Reflections: Truth and Politics," *TNY*, 2/25/1967, 49–88. See also a related essay, Hannah Arendt, "Lying in Politics: Reflections on the Pentagon Papers," *New York Review of Books*, 11/18/1971, 30–39.

20 Elisabeth Young-Bruehl, *Hannah Arendt: For the Love of the World*, 2nd ed. (New Haven: Yale University Press, 2004 [1982]), 393.

21 Hannah Arendt to "Artists' Protest," 6/3/1965, HAP, Box 62; Young-Bruehl, *Hannah Arendt*, 397.

PART VI: THE AGE OF SPIN

CHAPTER 45: The Permanent Campaign Arrives

1   H. R. Haldeman with Joseph DiMona, *The Ends of Power* (New York: Times Books, 1978), 70; Peter Goldman, "The President's Palace Guard," *Newsweek*, 3/19/1973, 24–38; Richard Nixon, *RN: The Memoirs of Richard Nixon* (New York: Simon & Schus-

ter, 1990 [1978]), 354. Key sources on Nixon and the media include Wise, *Politics of Lying*; Joseph Spear, *Presidents and the Press: The Nixon Legacy* (Cambridge, MA: MIT Press, 1984); Greenberg, *Nixon's Shadow*, 126–79; Kutler, *Wars of Watergate*, 161–84; and Maltese, *Spin Control*, 13–116.

2   David Wise, "Are You Worried About Your Image, Mr. President?" *Esquire* (May 1973), 119; Ambrose, *Nixon*, vol. 2, 314; *LAT*, 1/5/1999, 16.

3   Melvin Small, *The Presidency of Richard Nixon* (Lawrence: University Press of Kansas, 1999), 226.

4   John Ehrlichman, *Witness to Power: The Nixon Years* (New York: Simon & Schuster, 1982), 275.

5   Herbert Klein, *Making It Perfectly Clear* (Garden City, NY: Doubleday, 1980), 21; Maltese, *Spin Control*, 28, 92–94; Evan Thomas, *Being Nixon: A Man Divided* (New York: Random House, 2015), 260. On the Five O'Clock Group, see, e.g., Richard Nixon to John Ehrlichman, 1/25/1969, and Richard Nixon to John Ehrlichman and Bob Haldeman, 4/14/1969, in Bruce Oudes, ed., *From: The President: Richard Nixon's Secret Files* (New York: Harper & Row, 1988), 12, 23. On the Planning Group, a seemingly different body, see William Safire, *Before the Fall: An Inside View of the Pre-Watergate White House* (New York: Da Capo Press, 1975) 361–63, and Maltese, *Spin Control*, 89. There were also at various times a "Plans Committee," a "PR Group," and the "Image Factory"—Spear, *Presidents and the Press*, 95.

6   Jacobs and Shapiro, "Rise of Presidential Polling," 165–67, 177–80; Lawrence Jacobs and Robert Shapiro, "Presidential Manipulation of Polls and Public Opinion: The Nixon Administration and the Pollsters," *Political Science Quarterly*, 110:4 (Winter 1995–96), 519–38.

7   Small, *Presidency*, 235; Henry Kissinger, *White House Years* (Boston: Little, Brown, 1979), 307.

8   Nixon had the fewest press conferences of any president from Hoover to Carter, and the most televised speeches of any president from Kennedy to Bush—Small, *Presidency*, 228.

9   On these developments in journalism, see Thomas Patterson, *Out of Order* (New York: Knopf, 1993), 11–12, 61–93; and Katherine Fink and Michael Schudson, "The Rise of Contextual Journalism, 1950s–2000s," *Journalism: Theory, Practice, Criticism*, 15:1 (January 2014), 3–20.

10 H. R. Haldeman, *The Haldeman Diaries* (New York: G. P. Putnam's Sons, 1994), 473; Nixon, *RN*, 773.

11 Stanley Kutler, *Abuse of Power: The New Nixon Tapes* (New York: Free Press, 1997), 47–62; Haldeman, *Haldeman Diaries*, 502.

12 Key sources on Cadell, Rafshoon, and Carter's self-presentation include Blumenthal, *Permanent Campaign*, 44–75; Spear, *Presidents and the Press*; Maltese, *Spin Control*; and Leo Ribuffo, "Jimmy Carter and the Selling of the President, 1976–1980," in *The Presidency and Domestic Policies of Jimmy Carter*, ed. Herbert Rosenbaum and Alexej Ugrinsky (Westport, CT: Greenwood Press, 1994), 143–82.

13 Joseph Lelyveld, "The Selling of a Candidate," *NYTM*, 3/28/1976, SM16, 17, 65–71; Steven Brill, "Jimmy Carter's Pathetic Lies," *Harper's* (March 1976), 77–88.

14 *NYT*, 11/12/1987, B8. On Caddell, see also Eisinger, *Evolution*, 156–61; Moore, *Superpollsters*, 128–65.

15 Klein, *Politics Lost*, 43.

16 Eisinger, *Evolution*, 161; Blumenthal, *Permanent Campaign*, 59; Spear, *Presidents and the Press*, 264; Richard Reeves, "Maestro of the Media: The Prime-Time President," *NYTM*, 5/15/1977, cover, 17–19; *NYT*, 3/6/1977, 144; *NYT*, 5/16/1977, 29.

17 *NYT*, 10/27/1977, 25, B13; *WP*, 1/30/1978, A1–2.

18 Edwards, *Public Presidency*, 70; *WSJ*, 7/7/1978, 10; *WP*, 8/27/1978, A6; *NYT*, 11/7/1978, 24; *NYT*, 11/27/1978, A1.

19 "President McLuhan," *Nation*, 2/11/1978, 132–33; Garry Trudeau, *Stalking the Perfect Tan* (New York: Holt, Rinehart & Winston, 1978); Garry Trudeau, "The Man Behind the Cardigan," *TNR*, 5/20/1978, 20–21.

CHAPTER 46: The Reagan Apotheosis

1 Elizabeth Drew, "Letter from Washington," *TNY*, 7/31/1989, 74–81. Key sources on Reagan and the media include Blumenthal, *Permanent Campaign*, 283–300; Spear, *Presidents and the Press*; Mark Hertsgaard, *On Bended Knee: The Press and the Reagan Presidency* (New York: Farrar, Straus & Giroux, 1988); and Maltese, *Spin Control*.

2 *President Ronald Reagan's Initial Actions Project*, intro. by Arthur Laffer (New York: Threshold Editions, 2009).

3 Haynes Johnson, *Sleepwalking Through History: America in the Reagan Years* (New York: W. W. Norton, 1991), 162; Sean Wilentz, *The Age of Reagan: A History, 1974–2008* (New York: HarperCollins, 2008), 142; *NYT*, 3/18/2011, A27.

4 Michael Schudson, with Elliot King, "The Illusion of Ronald Reagan's Popularity," in Schudson, *The Power of News* (Cambridge, MA: Harvard University Press, 1995), 124–41; Daniel Rodgers, *Age of Fracture* (Cambridge, MA: Harvard University Press, 2011), 33; Morton Kondracke, "Reagan's I.Q.," *TNR*, 3/24/1982, 9–12.

5 Ehrman, *The Eighties*, 51; Steven Weisman, "The President and the Press: The Art of Controlled Access," *NYTM*, 10/14/1984, 34–37, 71–74, 80–82.

6 Martin Schram, *The Great American Video Game: Presidential Politics in the Television Age* (New York: William Morrow, 1987), 16, 33; Donovan and Scherer, *Unsilent Revolution*, 181. Lesley Stahl of CBS News has recounted a segment she did exposing the Reagan team's image making, which to her surprise prompted an appreciative call from the White House. "We're in the middle of a campaign, and you gave us four and a half minutes of great pictures of Ronald Reagan," an aide said. "And that's all the American people see." This oft-cited anecdote may reflect what administration officials believed, but no one knows whether visuals reliably trump verbal or written analyses. Schram, *Video Game*, 24–27; Schudson, "Telemythology," 115–16.

7 David Gergen, *Eyewitness to Power: The Essence of Leadership Nixon to Clinton* (New York: Simon & Schuster, 2001), 225.

8 "Factoid, n. and adj.," OED Online, Oxford University Press; *WP*, 1/21/1982, A1; *WP*, 2/20/1984, A3; "A Talk with Dave Gergen," *Washington Journalism Review* (April 1982), 41–45; Michael Dobbs, "The Rise of Political Fact-Checking: How Reagan Inspired a Journalistic Movement: A Reporter's Eye View" (Washington, DC: New America Foundation, 2012).

9 Lou Cannon, *President Reagan: The Role of a Lifetime* (New York: Simon & Schuster, 1992), 54; Herbers, "The President and the Press Corps," 45–46, 74–75, 96–98.

10 Steven Weisman, "Can the Magic Prevail?" *NYTM*, 4/29/1984, SM39.

11 Ronald Reagan: "Inaugural Address," 1/20/1981, http://www.presidency.ucsb.edu /ws/?pid=43130; *NYT*, 1/21/1981, A23; Rodgers, *Age of Fracture*, 31–32, 36; Ron Rosenbaum, "Who Puts the Words in the President's Mouth?" *Esquire* (December 1985), 250–51.

12 Cannon, *Role of a Lifetime*, 513; Schram, *Video Game*, 231.

13 Peter Goldman, "Making of a Landslide," *Newsweek* (December 1984), Election Extra, 88.

14 Cannon, *Role of a Lifetime*, 51; Neal Gabler, *Life: The Movie: How Entertainment Conquered Reality* (New York: Vintage Books, 2000), 108–15.

CHAPTER 47: Spinning Out of Control

1   Adatto, *Picture Perfect*, 88; Walter Shapiro, "It's the Year of the Handlers," *Time*, 10/3/1988, 18–25.
2   Joan Didion, "Insider Baseball," in *Political Fictions* (New York: Knopf, 2001), 34–37.
3   Diane Heith, "One for All: Using Focus Groups and Opinion Polls in the George H. W. Bush White House," *Congress and the Presidency*, 30:1 (Spring 2003), 83–86.
4   *WP*, 10/30/1988, A1; Kathleen Hall Jamieson, *Dirty Politics: Deception, Distraction, and Democracy* (New York: Oxford University Press, 1992), esp. 15–42; Donovan and Scherer, *Unsilent Revolution*, 246–48; Gabriel Sherman, *The Loudest Voice in the Room: How the Brilliant, Bombastic Roger Ailes Built Fox News—and Divided a Country* (New York: Random House, 2014), 125–28.
5   Fallows, *Breaking the News*, 61; Jamieson, *Dirty Politics*, 257. Kiku Adatto and Daniel Hallin each found that the length of sound bites between 1968 and 1988 shrank by more than 75 percent. This change showed a growing superficiality in campaign coverage but also a determination by reporters to contextualize their subjects' words by interspersing their own commentary—Adatto, *Picture Perfect*, 68; Daniel Hallin, "Soundbite News: Television Coverage of Elections, 1968–1988," in *We Keep America on Top of the World: Television Journalism and the Public Sphere* (New York: Routledge, 1993), 133–52; Fink and Schudson, "Contextual Journalism," 6.
6   Sidney Blumenthal, *Pledging Allegiance: The Last Campaign of the Cold War* (New York: HarperCollins, 1990), 304–05; Jamieson, *Dirty Politics*, 144–47, 283–88; Adatto, *Picture Perfect*, 73, 78–87, 144–45.
7   Jamieson, *Dirty Politics*, 283–88; Heith, "One for All," 86–88.
8   Bill Clinton, *My Life* (New York: Knopf, 2004), 425; George Stoney, "The War Room," *Cineaste* (April 1994), 57–58; Dee Dee Myers, "New Technology and the 1992 Clinton Presidential Campaign," *American Behavioral Scientist*, 37:2 (November 1993), 182.
9   Chris Hegedus, "Using the Drama of Cinéma Vérité to Tell Real Stories," *Nieman Reports* (Fall 2001), 61–63; Stephen Pizzello, "Waging a Film in the War Room," *American Cinematographer* (January 1994), 60; *NYT*, 1/31/1993, H15–16.
10 Hegedus, "Using the Drama," 62; *NYT*, 1/31/1993, H15–16; Pizzello, "Waging a Film," 64.
11 *NYT*, 10/13/1993, C15; *(Montreal) Gazette*, 1/26/1994, E10; *NYT*, 1/31/1993, H15–16; Shawn and Trevor Parry-Giles, "Meta-Imaging, *The War Room* and the Hyperreality of U.S. Politics," *Journal of Communication*, 49:1 (Winter 1999), 33–34.
12 Key sources on Clinton's media operation include Maltese, *Spin Control*, 215–39; Martha Joynt Kumar, *Managing the President's Message: The White House Communications Operation* (Baltimore: Johns Hopkins University Press, 2007); and Howard Kurtz, *Spin Control: Inside the Clinton Propaganda Machine* (New York: Free Press, 1998).
13 Fred Barnes, "Press Gang," *TNR*, 6/21/1993, 15–18.
14 On the pundits, see Eric Alterman, *Sound and Fury: The Making of the Punditocracy* (Ithaca, NY: Cornell University Press, 1999 [1992]). A few years later, a CNN pundit show appeared called *The Spin Room*—whose title implied, as the editor (and pundit) Michael Kinsley quipped, that "Twenty-first-century pols and pundits don't mind appearing on a show based on the official premise that whatever they say will be calculated and insincere"—Michael Kinsley, "The Great Spin Machine," *Time*, 12/25/2000. Kinsley, in launching the online magazine *Slate* in 1996, created a regular summary of the competing arguments about the week's issues called "The Week/The Spin."
15 Alterman, *Sound and Fury*, 10; Howard Kurtz, *Hot Air: All Talk, All the Time* (New York: Basic Books, 1997 [1996]), 102. On the degeneration of the Sunday shows, see James Fallows, *Breaking the News: How the American Media Undermine Democracy* (New York: Pantheon Books, 1996), 16–20.

16 *WP*, 6/9/1992, E7; Kurtz, *Hot Air*, 233; Sherman, *Loudest Voice*, 136.

17 Sherman, *Loudest Voice*, 196–99, 223–43.

18 Bill Kovach and Tom Rosenstiel, *Warp Speed: America in the Age of Mixed Media* (New York: Century Foundation Press, 1999), 19.

19 David Halberstam, Preface, in Kovach and Rosenstiel, *Warp Speed*, ix; Steven Brill, "Pressgate," *Brill's Content* (August 1998), 122–51, http://www.brillscontent.com/pressgate_index.shtml. Key sources on the Lewinsky saga include Ken Gormley, *The Death of American Virtue: Clinton vs. Starr* (New York: Crown Publishing, 2011), and Jeffrey Toobin, *A Vast Conspiracy: The Real Story of the Sex Scandal That Nearly Brought Down a President* (New York: Random House, 1999).

20 Kovach and Rosenstiel, *Warp Speed*, 17–18; Sherman, *Loudest Voice*, 232–33; Alterman, *Sound and Fury*, 267; Frank Rich, "The Age of the Mediathon," *NYTM*, 10/29/2000, *SM*58.

21 Sidney Blumenthal, "The Syndicated Presidency," *TNY*, 4/5/1993, 42–47; Kumar, *Managing the President's Message*, 39–42; Morris, *Behind the Oval Office*, 139–44.

22 John Zaller, "Monica Lewinsky's Contribution to Political Science," *PS: Political Science and Politics*, 31:2 (June 1998), 182–89; Regina Lawrence and W. Lance Bennett, "Rethinking Media Politics and Public Opinion: Reactions to the Clinton-Lewinsky Scandal," *Political Science Quarterly*, 116:3 (Fall 2001), 429–32; and Alterman, *Sound and Fury*, 275–76.

23 William Clinton, "Address to the Nation on Testimony Before the Independent Counsel's Grand Jury," 8/17/1998, http://www.presidency.ucsb.edu/ws/?pid=54794; *LAT*, 8/25/1998, 10; Eric Alterman, *What Liberal Media?: The Truth About Bias and the News* (New York: Basic Books, 2008), 144–46; Richard Lacayo, "Where the Right Went Wrong," *Time*, 12/21/1998, 107–08; William Bennett, *The Death of Outrage: Bill Clinton and the Assault on American Ideals* (New York: Free Press, 1998).

24 *NYT*, 11/10/1998, A29.

CHAPTER 48: George W. Bush and the "Truthiness" Problem

1 http://thecolbertreport.cc.com/videos/63ite2/the-word—truthiness.

2 Marc Peyser, "The Truthiness Teller," *Newsweek*, 2/13/2006; *NYT*, 1/22/2006, C16.

3 *NYT*, 11/19/2000, 37. Key sources on Florida include Jeffrey Toobin, *Too Close to Call: The Thirty-Six Day Battle to Decide the 2000 Election* (New York: Random House, 2001), and the Political Staff of the *Washington Post*, *Deadlock: The Inside Story of America's Closest Election* (New York: Public Affairs, 2001).

4 Ron Rosenbaum, "Derrida, Dame Edna, and George W., Postmodernist," *New York Observer*, 12/18/2000; Alan Wolfe, "Hobbled from the Start," *Salon.com*, 12/15/2000.

5 Joshua Micah Marshall, "The Post-Modern President," *Washington Monthly* (September 2003), 22–26; Ron Suskind, "Without a Doubt," *NYTM*, 10/17/2004, 44–51, 64, 102, 106. Key sources on Bush and the media include Kumar, *Managing the President's Message*; Ken Auletta, "Fortress Bush: How the White House Keeps the Press Under Control," *TNY*, 1/19/2004, 53–65; Frank Rich, *The Greatest Story Ever Sold: The Decline and Fall of Truth from 9/11 to Katrina* (New York: Penguin Press, 2006); and Michael Isikoff and David Corn, *Hubris: The Inside Story of Spin, Scandal and the Selling of the Iraq War* (New York: Three Rivers Press, 2007 [2006]).

6 *NYT*, 11/1/2001, A29; *NYT*, 8/5/2005, A15; Sidney Blumenthal, *The Rise of the Counter-Establishment: From Conservative Ideology to Political Power* (New York: Harper & Row, 1986); David Greenberg, "The Republican Flight from Reality," *Raritan*, 29:3 (Winter 2010), 45–74.

7 Chris Mooney, *The Republican War on Science* (New York: Basic Books, 2005); Frank-

lin Foer, "Closing of the Presidential Mind," *TNR*, 7/5 and 12/2004, 17–21; *NYT*, 2/8/2006, A13; *NYT*, 7/11/2007, A1.

8 Joshua Green, "The Other War Room," *Washington Monthly* (April 2002), 11–16.

9 Paul O'Neill suggested that Bush considered deposing Saddam as soon as he became president, and Bob Woodward reported that Bush had Gen. Tommy Franks draw up war plans in late 2001. By the summer of 2002, Bush's mind seems to have been made up—Ron Suskind, *The Price of Loyalty: George W. Bush, The White House, and the Education of Paul O'Neill* (New York: Simon & Schuster, 2004), 73–76; Bob Woodward, *Plan of Attack* (New York: Simon & Schuster, 2003), 9.

10 Bob Woodward, *Bush at War* (New York: Simon & Schuster, 2002), 99; Ron Suskind, *The One-Percent Doctrine: Deep Inside America's Pursuit of Its Enemies Since 9/11* (New York: Simon & Schuster, 2007 [2006]), 62.

11 Jacob Weisberg, *The Bush Tragedy* (New York: Random House, 2008), 196. These recent, politically charged events are more difficult than distant historical ones to discuss with detachment. Many people still believe that Bush administration officials deliberately lied about the intelligence that was used to support an invasion. Considerably more evidence supports the conclusion that they convinced themselves that this intelligence was far more conclusive than it actually was, and that they then made their case to the public with rhetoric that was often exaggerated or misleading. Either way, the debate over the run-up to the Iraq War raised anew questions about the power of presidential spin in American democracy.

12 Ben Fritz, Bryan Keefer, and Brendan Nyhan, *All the President's Spin: George W. Bush, the Media, and the Truth* (New York: Touchstone Books, 2004), 22; George W. Bush, "Address Before a Joint Session of the Congress on the State of the Union," 1/29/2002, http://www.presidency.ucsb.edu/ws/?pid=29644.

13 Kumar, *Managing the President's Message*, 85; *NYT*, 9/7/2002, A1.

14 *NYT*, 5/16/2003, A1; George W. Bush, "Address to the Nation From Ellis Island, New York, on the Anniversary of the Terrorist Attacks of September 11," 9/11/2002, http://www.presidency.ucsb.edu/ws/?pid=62948; George W. Bush, "Address to the United Nations General Assembly in New York City," 9/12/2002, http://www.presidency.ucsb.edu/ws/?pid=64069.

15 For the litany of dubious claims endorsed by Bush administration officials in convincing themselves of the wisdom of war, see Corn and Isikoff, *Hubris*, 209.

16 *NYT*, 9/8/2002, 25; *WP*, 9/19/2002, A18; *NYT*, 10/24/2002, A1; *NYT*, 10/21/2002, A9; *WP*, 2/7/2003, A21; *WP*, 8/10/2003, A01.

17 Karen Hughes, *Ten Minutes From Normal* (New York: Viking Press, 2004), 189; *NYT*, 5/16/2003, A1.

18 Weisberg, *Bush Tragedy*, 207–08; Todd Purdum and the Staff of the *New York Times*, *A Time of Our Choosing: America's War in Iraq* (New York: Times Books, 2003), 239–41.

19 Michael Elliott, et al., "So, What Went Wrong?" *Time*, 10/6/2003, 30–37.

CHAPTER 49: Barack Obama and the Spin of No Spin

1 On Lakoff and the search for a Democratic answer, key sources include Matt Bai, *The Argument: Billionaires, Bloggers, and the Battle to Remake Democratic Politics* (New York: Penguin Books, 2007), and Noam Scheiber, "Wooden Frame," *TNR*, 5/23/2005, 14–20.

2 George Lakoff, *Moral Politics: How Liberals and Conservatives Think* (Chicago: University of Chicago Press, 1996).

3 Matt Bai, "The Framing Wars," *NYTM*, 7/17/2005; George Lakoff, *Don't Think of an Elephant!* (White River Junction, VT: Chelsea Green, 2004).

4 Michael Lewis, "The Subversive," *NYTM*, 5/25/1997, 32–37, 48, 52, 58, 62; David Foster Wallace, "Up Simba," in *Consider the Lobster: And Other Essays* (New York: Little, Brown, 2006), 156–234.

5 John Heilemann and Mark Halperin, *Game Change: Obama and the Clintons, McCain and Palin, and the Race of a Lifetime* (New York: HarperCollins, 2010), 65.

6 David Remnick, *The Bridge: The Life and Rise of Barack Obama* (New York: Knopf, 2010), 435, 525.

7 Ryan Lizza, "Battle Plans: How Obama Won," *TNY*, 11/17/2008, 46–55; Halperin and Heilemann, *Game Change*, 118–20; Sean Wilentz, "Race Man," *TNR*, 2/27/2008; Sam Stein, "Obama Camp's Memo on Clintons' Politicizing Race," *Huffington Post*, 3/28/2008, http://www.huffingtonpost.com/2008/01/12/obama-camps-memo-on-clint_n_81205.html; Remnick, *The Bridge*, 514.

8 Alexander, *Performance*, 97–98, 185–86; *NYT*, 7/31/2008, A1; *NYT*, 8/28/2008, A22.

9 Daniel Gross, "Sept. 24, 2008: The Day John McCain Lost the Election," *Slate.com*, 11/4/2008; Alexander, *Performance*, 265.

10 On Obama and the press, see Ken Auletta, "Non-Stop News," *TNY*, 1/25/2010, 38–47, and Reid Cherlin, "The Presidency and the Press," *Rolling Stone* (August 2014).

11 Jim VandeHei and Mike Allen, "Obama, the Puppet Master," *Politico.com*, 2/18/2013; *NYT*, 1/26/2009, A1; *NYT*, 11/12/2010, A21; *NYT*, 1/25/2011, A12.

12 James Poniewozik, "Obamathon!" *Time*, 4/6/2009, 20; Jennifer Senior, "The Message Is the Message," *New York*, 8/10/2009, 22–27, 94; *NYT*, 9/18/2009, A21.

13 Paul Starr, "Governing in the Age of Fox News," *Atlantic* (January 2010), 95–98; Ken Auletta, "Non-Stop News," *TNY*, 1/25/2010, 38–47.

14 "White House Fires Back at Health Care 'Fictions,'" Agence France Presse, 8/10/2009; *WP*, 8/24/2009, C01.

15 *CT*, 9/15/2010, 23; Neal Gabler, "The President's Movie," *The American Prospect*, 12/6/2010, http://prospect.org/cs/articles?article=the_presidents_movie; *NYT*, 8/6/2011, SR1; Glenn Thrush, "The Not-So-Great Communicator," *Politico*, 9/6/2012; *60 Minutes* transcript, CBS News Transcripts, 11/7/2010, available through Lexis/Nexis.

16 *60 Minutes* transcript, 11/7/2010.

17 Arendt, "Truth and Politics," 52. On red and blue states, see Morris Fiorma, with Samuel Abrams and Jeremy Pope, *Culture War? The Myth of a Polarized America* (New York: Pearson Longman, 2005).

18 On this literature, see Farhad Manjoo, *True Enough: Learning to Live in a Post-Fact Society* (Hoboken, NJ: John Wiley & Sons, 2008). Other fashionable social science buzzwords included *confirmation bias* (akin to selective exposures) and *motivated reasoning* (akin to selective perception).

1. Theodore Roosevelt (Library of Congress)
2. George B. Cortelyou (Library of Congress)
3. Upton Sinclair (Library of Congress)
4. Ivy Ledbetter Lee (© Bettmann/Corbis)
5. George Creel (Library of Congress)
6. George Creel's Committee on Public Information Poster (Library of Congress)
7. Woodrow Wilson (Library of Congress)
8. Warren Harding and Albert Lasker (Library of Congress)
9. Photographers in the 1920s (Library of Congress)
10. Walter Lippmann (Library of Congress)
11. H. L. Mencken with beer (© Bettmann/Corbis)
12. Calvin Coolidge in Indian headdress (Library of Congress)
13. Bruce Barton (Library of Congress)
14. Edward Bernays (Library of Congress)
15. Charles Michelson (Library of Congress)
16. *Hoovervilles* (Hoover Library/National Archives)
17. Emil Hurja (Library of Congress)
18. Franklin Roosevelt, "Fireside Chat" (Library of Congress)
19. Clem Whitaker and Leone Baxter (Getty Images)
20. Archibald MacLeish with Franklin Roosevelt (Courtesy of the Franklin D. Roosevelt Library and Museum, Hyde Park, New York)
21. Nazi Propaganda in Madison Square Garden (© Corbis)
22. George Gallup (Getty Images)
23. Harry Truman campaigning (Harry S. Truman Library and Museum/Abbie Rowe, NPS)
24. Rosser Reeves ad script (Wisconsin Historical Society, WHS-116076)
25. Rosser Reeves (Wisconsin Historical Society, WHS-83073)

26. Dwight Eisenhower, James Hagerty, and Robert Montgomery (Courtesy of the Eisenhower Presidential Library and Museum)
27. Vance Packard (Portrait vertical files, 1855–present, PSUA 1212, Penn State University Archives, reproduced with the permission of Rare Books and Manuscripts, Special Collections Library, the Pennsylvania State Libraries)
28. Theodore H. White (© Bettmann/Corbis)
29. Marshall McLuhan (Photofest)
30. John F. Kennedy Press Conference (Abbie Rowe, White House Photographs. John F. Kennedy Presidential Library and Museum, Boston)
31. Pierre Salinger press pack (Abbie Rowe, White House Photographs. John F. Kennedy Presidential Library and Museum, Boston)
32. Lyndon Johnson's "Daisy" ad (Lyndon B. Johnson Library/Democratic National Committee)
33. Lyndon Johnson and Bill Moyers (Lyndon B. Johnson Library)
34. Still from Robert Redford's *The Candidate*, 1972 (© Sunset Boulevard/Corbis)
35. Richard Nixon and Roger Ailes (Courtesy of the Richard Nixon Library and Museum)
36. Pat Caddell and Jimmy Carter (Jimmy Carter Library/National Archives)
37. Michael Deaver (Ronald Reagan Library)
38. Ronald Reagan in Normandy (Ronald Reagan Library)
39. Bill Clinton, Hillary Clinton, and George Stephanopoulos (Courtesy of the William J. Clinton Presidential Library)
40. George W. Bush on flight deck of USS *Abraham Lincoln* (U.S. Navy photo by Photographer's Mate 3rd Class Lewis Hunsaker)
41. Barack Obama and David Axelrod (Official White House Photo by Pete Souza)

INDEX